SHAKESPEARE: THE CRITICAL HERITAGE

VOLUME 6 1774–1801

THE CRITICAL HERITAGE SERIES

GENERAL EDITOR: B. C. SOUTHAM, M.A., B.LITT. (OXON.)

Formerly Department of English, Westfield College, University of London

For a list of books in the series see the back end paper

SHAKESPEARE

THE CRITICAL HERITAGE

VOLUME 6 1774–1801

Edited by
BRIAN VICKERS

Professor of English and Renaissance Literature,
ETH, Zürich

ROUTLEDGE & KEGAN PAUL: LONDON, BOSTON AND HENLEY

First published in 1981
by Routledge & Kegan Paul Ltd
39 Store Street,
London WC1E 7DD,
9 Park Street,
Boston, Mass. 02108, USA, and
Broadway House,
Newtown Road,
Henley-on-Thames,
Oxon RG9 1EN
Photosetting by Thomson Press (India) Limited, New Delhi.
and printed in Great Britain by
Redwood Burn Ltd
Trowbridge and Esher

British Library Cataloguing in Publication Data

Shakespeare, the critical heritage.

Vol.6: 1774 – 1801
1. Shakespeare, William—Criticism
and interpretation—Addresses, essays, lectures
I. Vickers, Brian, b.1937
II. Series
822.3'3   PR2975   79-40169

ISBN 0-7100-0629-2

General Editor's Preface

The reception given to a writer by his contemporaries and near-contemporaries is evidence of considerable value to the student of literature. On one side we learn a great deal about the state of criticism at large and in particular about the development of critical attitudes towards a single writer; at the same time, through private comments in letters, journals or marginalia, we gain an insight upon the tastes and literary thought of individual readers of the period. Evidence of this kind helps us to understand the writer's historical situation, the nature of his immediate reading-public, and his response to these pressures.

The separate volumes in the *Critical Heritage Series* present a record of this early criticism. Clearly, for many of the highly productive and lengthily reviewed nineteenth- and twentieth-century writers, there exists an enormous body of material; and in these cases the volume editors have made a selection of the most important views, significant for their intrinsic critical worth or for their representative quality—perhaps even registering incomprehension!

For earlier writers, notably pre-eighteenth century, the materials are much scarcer and the historical period has been extended, sometimes far beyond the writer's lifetime, in order to show the inception and growth of critical views which were initially slow to appear.

Shakespeare is, in every sense, a special case, and Professor Vickers has presented the course of his reception and reputation extensively, over a span of three centuries, in a sequence of six volumes, each of which has documented a specific period.

In each volume the documents are headed by an Introduction, discussing the material assembled and relating the early stages of the author's reception to what we have come to identify as the critical tradition. The volumes will make available much material which would otherwise be difficult of access and it is hoped that the modern reader will be thereby helped towards an informed understanding of the ways in which literature has been read and judged.

B. C. S.

v

FOR
MORGAN DAVIES,
ALBERT FREILING,
AND
MICHAEL WALL

Contents

CONTENTS

Preface

This, the last of the projected number of volumes for Shakespeare in this series, brings the story up to the beginning of the nineteenth century. Those who have followed it through the six volumes will note many continuities of attitude and critical method, but also their gradual transformation, under the impact of debate and disagreement. What this volume shows especially clearly is the emergence of Romantic, and some modern, conceptions of Shakespeare directly out of the Neo-classic system, partly by extension (on the question of characterization, for instance), and partly by a re-formulation of the analytical model, in order to counter the negative criticisms of Shakespeare that the Neo-classic model had produced. In order to grant Shakespeare his true status, proclaimed on every side, it was necessary to reform the critical system, and the process can be traced here in the commentary of Capell, and in the analyses of Hamlet's character produced by Mackenzie, Richardson, and Robertson. As we read their work of the 1780s we see that we are within a stone's throw of Hazlitt and Coleridge.

Not all aspects of Shakespeare's reception and understanding reveal such a metamorphosis. In editing and textual criticism scholarship develops unevenly, with backward as well as forward movement. As I recorded in Vol. 2, when we turn from Pope's edition to Theobald's, we move from a brilliant poet but dilettante critic, tinkering with the text to make it conform to his own taste in language and morals, arbitrarily rejecting as spurious whatever did not please him, to the first modern scholar-critic, who established many of the methods by which Shakespeare's text was corrected and properly understood. I still maintain my high estimate of Theobald, although increased acquaintance with the work of Edward Capell has given me even greater respect for his combination of intelligence, good sense, enormous range of learning, minute accuracy, scrupulousness of detail, and the ability to visualize a text in theatrical terms, a grasp of its totality which is rare in any age and was unique in his own. Yet to make such an estimate of Capell demands much time and labour. Due to the unfortunate decision he made to issue the text alone in 1768, the first instalment of notes in 1774, and the remainder only after his death in 1781, Capell's edition never existed as a unity, and his immediate rivals, Steevens and Malone, were able to abuse him, publicly ignore and privately plagiarize him, with more or less impunity. (The full story of their treatment of him, depending as it does on many unpublished documents, has yet to be told.) Even today the difficulty of collating Capell's edition and notes (both recently reprinted)[1] means that it takes months to work through them. Yet, frustrated though one is by his system of reference, I never emerge from a day reading Capell without being refreshed and stimulated; and it is worth noting that in the collations to the Riverside edition, as G. B. Evans informs me, his name appears more frequently than that of any other textual critic. The editions of Steevens and Malone, by contrast, although of great value for their illustration of contemporary idioms and usage, and their knowledge of the Elizabethan theatre, are a disappointment as textual criticism, and the increasing arbitrariness of Steevens is, in the most damaging sense, a regression to the methods of Pope.

In the theatre the balance is even more negative. The Neo-classic adaptations hold the stage, even though their absurdities, and the awkward side-effects of their plot-adjustments, are all too visible. As yet no demand exists to replace them, indeed the first efforts by Kemble, the outstanding actor and impresario of the turn of the century, take the form of a return to Dryden and D'Avenant's *Tempest*, Tate's *Lear* and Cibber's *Richard III*. The conditions of production, also, in the ever-more gigantic London theatres, were inimical to the appreciation of Shakespeare, or indeed, one is tempted to say, of anything other than grand spectacle. In the realm of theatre reviewing, after the death of Garrick there seems to be a falling-off of interest or stimulus: no one had his magnetic personality, and it was some time before Mrs Siddons reached her maturity. Perhaps my sense of a decline in the quality of theatre-criticism is mistaken (there is no decline in quantity), and some future tillers of the soil may disprove it. I have included less material of this kind here, and do so with fewer misgivings since the excellent study by C. H. Gray[2]—after nearly fifty years, and despite the vast boom in research output and in the availability of scholarly resources, still the only serious study of this topic—gives a thorough account for this period, with more quotation than in the earlier chapters. His identifications of the reviewing work of William Woodfall, Charles Este, John Taylor, James Boaden, and George Steevens are important, and deserve to be followed up.

For the rest, literary criticism and commentary, the sheer bulk of material in this period has often seemed daunting. I have attempted comprehensive coverage of printed books, including all the editions of Shakespeare, with all their footnotes. There being as yet no cumulative edition, which would print each note in the original form in which it occurred, the only way of proceeding is to compare, page by page, the 1773 Johnson–Steevens edition with the 1778; the 1778 with Malone's 1780 *Supplement*; 1778 and 1780 with the 1785 edition by Steevens and Reed; 1780 and 1785 with Malone's edition of 1790; 1785 and Malone's 1790 with Steevens, 1793; and so on, recording each alteration and innovation as it occurs. This takes a great deal of time, and demands continual alertness, and an efficient cross-referencing system, if one is not to attribute to a later edition a note that appeared in an earlier one. For any such errors that may be discovered, I apologize now, and wish I could urge other students to this task with any enthusiasm. But it has proved one of the more deadening chores associated with this project. Yet, if the whole may be more than the sum of its parts, and if we can now achieve a better understanding of how Shakespeare was and is read, performed, understood, and why, then the effort will have been worth while.

In preparing this volume I have been privileged to use a number of great libraries, and wish to thank the staff of the British Library, the Cambridge University Library (especially Mrs J. E. Waller and the staff of the Rare Book Room), the Bodleian Library, Oxford (and especially Mr William Hodges and the staff of the Upper Reading Room); the Zentralbibliothek, Zürich; the Folger Shakespeare Library, Washington, D. C.; the Houghton and Widener Libraries of Harvard University; and the Henry E. Huntington Library, San Marino. For permission to reprint an excerpt from his edition of Walpole's *Book of Materials* I am grateful to the late W. S. Lewis; for various pieces of news about late eighteenth-century writings on taste I thank Mr Tadhg Foley of Merton College, Oxford; for help in tracing some especially elusive Latin quotations I thank Dr P. Flury, Generalredaktor,

Thesaurus Linguae Latinae, München; and for their help with the typescript and proof-reading I am especially grateful to Barbara Hoffman-Häberli, Susanne Müller, Bridget Kendall, and Ilse Fannenböck. For generous financial assistance I thank the Schweizerischer Nationalfonds zur Förderung der wissentschaftlichen Forschung.

To end on a personal note: when this edition was projected, I imagined that six volumes would be enough to take the story down to 1832, including Hazlitt, Coleridge, and the other main Romantic critics; the posthumous editions of Steevens and Malone; and the *History of the English Stage* by John Genest, which is, *inter alia*, the first modern history of the Shakespeare adaptations. In the event, the quantity and interest of the material I have found in the eighteenth century has not allowed me to progress beyond 1801. I should like to declare an interest in pursuing it farther, if demand existed and the publisher consented; yet, after so many years spent on this task, I must leave it for a while to complete other projects which have been long postponed. My position, then, might be said to resemble that of two eighteenth-century Shakespearians when they had ended their labours. On the one hand is William Dodd, completing his influential anthology, *The Beauties of Shakespeare*, in 1752, with the words

For my own part, better and more important things hence forth demand my attention, and I here, with no small pleasure, take leave of *Shakespeare* and the critics. (Vol. 3, pp. 470–1)

And on the other is Richard Farmer, closing his *Essay on the Learning of Shakespeare* in 1767 by promising that

when I am fairly rid of the Dust of topographical Antiquity, which hath continued much longer about me than I expected, you may very probably be troubled again with the ever fruitful subject of SHAKESPEARE and his COMMENTATORS. (Vol. 5, p. 279)

Which of the two I finally join with, time will tell.   B. W. V.

NOTES

1 Capell's edition (10 vols), and his *Notes and Various Readings* (3 vols), were reprinted by AMS Press Inc., New York (1973).
2 Charles Harold Gray, *Theatrical Criticism in London to 1795* (New York, 1931; reprinted 1964, 1971, by Benjamin Blom, Inc.). Chapters V and VI (pp. 191–311) cover the period 1770 to 1795.

Introduction

The last quarter of the eighteenth century saw an enormous consolidation of almost all the aspects of Shakespeare's reception presented in this series. His position as 'a Classic, and contemporary with all ages' (Mrs Griffith, No. 249) is firmly established; new editions and commentaries appear in 1778, 1780, 1783, 1785, 1790, and 1793; dozens of books of criticism or literary history have substantial discussions of his work, and incidental references abound in books, magazines, newspapers, lectures, novels, letters, theatre reviews, and poetry. His prestige is now so great that he is seen not only as England's greatest writer but as the world's greatest, an altogether exceptional human being. To Horace Walpole, writing in 1778, he is 'superior to all mankind'; in 1786 he finds him 'a predominant genius', compared with whom other writers may be held 'cheap enough', while 'to excel him—Oh! I have not words adequate to my contempt for those who can suppose such a possibility!'[1] The *Critical Review* began one of its many Shakespeare articles with a panegyric which typifies the general tone of admiration:

Every new enquiry into the dramatic works of Shakespeare renders the transcendency of his talents more conspicuous. While he possessed such an astonishing power of imagination in conceiving and describing characters as no other poet, either in ancient or modern times, ever displayed, he abounded also in sentiments and precepts of the greatest utility in the conduct of human life. With equal ease his unlimited genius pervaded philosophy and nature; and he informs the head, at the same time that he agitates the heart with irresistible emotions.[2]

The *Monthly Review*, the rival journal, did not fall behind in praise. Samuel Badcock, reviewing the 1778 edition of the Johnson–Steevens Shakespeare, welcomed it as a 'truly valuable edition of the Works of a poet who hath long been classed among the most astonishing phaenomena of human genius. Panegyric hath been exhausted in his praise; and the invention of a

Shakespeare only, could furnish fresh topics of encomium'. Another *Monthly* reviewer, Christopher Moody, answered the accusation—by 'men of cold and phlegmatic constitutions'—that 'the rage for Shakespeare has been carried to excess', by proclaiming that 'the genius of Shakespeare deserves all the homage that has been offered by a grateful posterity'.[3]

Posterity in England obliged: he was described as 'the great poet of nature, and the glory of the British nation'; 'the noblest genius', 'the greatest master of nature, and the most perfect characterizer of men and manners'; an 'immortal', 'this eagle genius'.[4] To William Belsham, Shakespeare is 'the most figurative writer . . . in our language', who surpasses all others in his skill in versification, in moving the passions, in 'fascinating and enchaining the attention', so that 'it is almost impossible to be guilty of excess in our applause' of him (a position which he disproves in the three pages of effusive praise that follow). To Robert Alves, Shakespeare was 'the greatest prodigy of Dramatic genius' the world ever produced, and he praised 'his vast invention, his sagacity and penetration of human nature, his native delineation of character, and strength and power of diction'; above all his genius, which 'shot wild and free', and attained 'the highest degree' man is capable of. 'Comprehensive and vast, he takes hold of nature in all her varieties of human character'; Richard Hole praised 'the wonder-working power' of his pen.[5] Almost all the writers represented in this volume pay their tributes, but three in particular stand out: Martin Sherlock (No. 286), who exceeds everyone ('He is a just, a due enthusiast to Shakespeare', Horace Walpole said of him),[6] Maurice Morgann (No. 254), whose 'Rhapsody' was often reprinted in journals as a separate item,[7] and the anonymous author of *A Farrago* (No. 302).

The poets did not fail to add their contribution. It goes without saying that all the poems to Shakespeare in this period (and most of those in others) are poems in praise. The author of *An Epistle from Shakespeare to his Countrymen* (1777) uses the plot whereby the bard is conjured up in some appropriate time and place, and then speaks words of encouragement to his admirers (usually David Garrick), and occasionally criticizes false taste. Here the poet, asleep at 4 a.m., sees a 'happy vision, and illusion sweet':

> I saw descending from a smiling sky
> A form of more than mortal dignity;

All that is pleasing, great, or good, was there,
All that we love, and all that we revere. (pp. 7–8)

In October 1785 the *Universal Magazine* printed 'A Tribute to the Memory of Shakespeare' by Louisa, who writes from Adelphi, with feeling:

Ah, my Sweet Shakespeare; oh, had I your art,
Or thy soft magnet to subdue the heart,
Then would I tell what joy I have receiv'd,
How oft I've smiled, how oft with you I've griev'd. (p. 215)

Her praises are temperate compared with those of *The Genius of Shakespeare. A Summer Dream* (1793), in which the poet falls asleep and records a vision of the bard's speech, and nature's awe-struck response:

He spake, and high,
As the blue sky
His awful head uprear'd;
The clouds around,
Dark when he frown'd,
In thunder shook the spheres;
And at his threats they trembled with pale fears;
But when he seem'd to weep, they all dissolv'd in tears.

Our confidence in the taste of the age may be restored by checking the reviewers' amused and incredulous response to this poem.[8] They were kinder to Alexander Thomson's *The Paradise of Taste* (1796), which the *Monthly* described as 'a visionary journey through a series of allegorical regions or compartments, in which are placed the most celebrated of antient and modern poets'. The seventh and last canto is called 'The Island of Fancy', where the poet meets Ovid, Ariosto, and Spenser; Aeschylus, Dante, Lee(!) and Collins(!); and, finally, Shakespeare alone. As the reviewer (John Aikin) put it, 'that the climax of poetical powers should finish with Shakespeare, will gratify every true Englishman'.[9] Here on a 'mass of rock', on 'the topmost height',

the regal throne
Of this romantic realm, stood Avon's bard alone.
Alone stood he—for there was none but he
On such a fearful precipice could stand;
Careless he stood, from fear and danger free,
And wav'd with ease that more than magic wand.

3

Thomson's comparison, resulting in Shakespeare excelling all other poets, was made frequently in this period. An earlier generation was content to make Shakespeare the equal of Homer, and that bracketing can be found here in the judgments of Hugh Blair and James Beattie.[10] But increasingly Shakespeare is seen as superior to Homer, whether in general terms—thus Anna Seward,[11] Martin Sherlock (No. 286), Henry Mackenzie (No. 287)—or in specific details, such as Twining's preference for the night-scene in *Henry V* over that in the *Iliad* (No. 297). As for the Greek tragedians, William Belsham puts Shakespeare above all of them,[12] as do Mrs Griffith (No. 249) and Hugh Blair (No. 272); Twining ranks Shakespeare with Euripides (No. 297), but Thomas Davies puts him above Euripides (No. 277), while the *Critical Review* (n.s. 2, 1791, 370f.) puts him above Aeschylus, as does Richard Cumberland (No. 288).

The chorus of praise was so insistent that some protested against the dangers of idolatry. The *Monthly Review* said of Belsham's book and its claim for Shakespeare's genius being 'supernatural' ('preternatural' was also heard, as in No. 282), that 'though our veneration for Shakespeare rises almost to idolatry, we cannot help thinking [it] extravagant'. The *Town and Country Magazine* said of *An Epistle from Shakespeare to his Countrymen* that it contained 'some touches of the panegyric that rather border upon the fulsome', and the *Critical* said of a similar production, Harrison's poem *The Infant vision of Shakespeare; with an Apostrophe to the immortal Bard* (1794), that

Could Shakespeare see these praises of himself, he certainly would accuse the panegyrist of having overstept the modesty of nature. Neither Shakespeare, nor any other writer, can deserve to have it said of him that, without his writings, the world would be benighted and miserable. . . . Such hyperbole is worse than a want of poetry: it is a want of sense.

Elsewhere in the *Critical Review* we find warnings that Shakespeare is loved so much that 'the step is easy from an eager fondness to indiscriminate idolatry'. Commenting on Malone's edition the reviewer attacked 'those infected with the *Shakespeareomania*', urging that 'as no author has higher beauties than Shakespeare, so none has greater absurdities, or, occasionally, pages of more vapid nonsense'.[13] Of the authors reprinted here, Francis Gentleman (No. 243, note 85) attacks the bardolatry of the Shakespeare

Jubilee and the myth of the mulberry-tree (although Malone lent his authority to this tradition: No. 299, note 1), while both William Shaw (No. 280) and Samuel Johnson (No. 301) attack indiscriminate praise.

Yet these caveats had no effects, least of all on one of the new developments in this period, prophetic of the tone of much nineteenth-century criticism, the tendency to write a sentimental biography of Shakespeare, imputing to him—on the evidence of the plays, or poems, or just from hearsay—admirable qualities in his personality or private life. Francis Gentleman, in the notes he added to Bell's edition of Shakespeare, finds in Isabella's plea for Claudio evidence of Shakespeare's own 'humane disposition, and love of mercy', and refers later to 'Shakespeare's darling principle of humanity' and his 'usual favourite subject, mercy, of which he seems to have had a very just and forceable feeling'. Mrs Griffith, similarly, alludes to 'Shakespeare's usual stile . . . on the great article of mercy'. Thomas Davies believed that only Shakespeare could have conceived of the generosity of Kent, and that in his drama 'humanity triumphs over selfishness'.[14] The belief in Shakespeare's superiority extended itself to his physical appearance: Samuel Badcock preferred the Droeshout engraving in the First Folio 'as it carries stronger marks of dignity and elevation of mind' than other portraits, 'and seems best to suit the genius of the man', while Samuel Felton said that 'We are well assured that every muse adorned his mind; and from what is handed down to us . . . we have some reasons to think that (like what is said of Rafaelle) every grace adorned his body'.[15]

The most influential of these sentimental biographers was Edmond Malone, at first in the *Supplement* (1780) which he published as an extension of the 1778 Johnson–Steevens edition. In his commentary there on the *Sonnets* Malone took phrases from the poems—'Like a deceived husband' in Sonnet 93, for instance—as texts for speculations about Shakespeare's private life, his jealousy, his will, and the evidence they supposedly give for his attitudes to his wife (No. 265, note 14). In reply Steevens—understanding, for polemical purposes, yet making a valid point—urged that

all that is known with any degree of certainty concerning Shakespeare, is—that he was born at Stratford upon Avon,—married and had children there,—went to London, where he commenced actor, and wrote poems and plays,—returned to Stratford, made his will, died, and was buried.

Steevens objected to Malone's reliance on 'unwarrantable conjecture', but Malone continued it in his edition of 1790. He perpetuated the mulberry-tree myth, and predicted the growth of Stratford as a centre which would be visited with 'a similar enthusiasm' to that which seeks Virgil's tomb (No. 299, note 1). He sees the infant Shakespeare being safe from a plague epidemic at Stratford, lying 'secure and fearless in the midst of contagion and death, protected by the Muses to whom his future life was to be devoted' (note 2); or writing about the death of Arthur in *King John* to express his own grief at the death of his son Hamnet (note 5). Malone praised Shakespeare's 'gentleness, modesty, and humility' (note 7), while accepting Aubrey's testimony to 'the beauty of our poet's person' (note 8). Steevens said of John Aubrey that he was an 'absurd gossip . . . a dupe to every wag who chose to practise on his credulity', but his collaborator in the 1793 edition, Joseph Ritson, scholar and controversialist extraordinary, rejected Warburton's theory that Shakespeare alluded to Mary, Queen of Scots, in *A Midsummer Night's Dream* with the concluding argument that 'nor was the "gentle Shakespeare" of a character or disposition to have insulted the memory of a murdered princess by so infamous a charge'.[16] To modern readers it comes as a relief to find James Anderson commenting on the dispute whether or not Shakespeare was a Catholic by making the fundamental objection:

Is it not absurd to think of judging of the private opinions of a dramatic writer by those he puts into the mouth of his characters; for these must speak as they would themselves have done, without any regard to the writer's own opinions. A Jew must speak as a Jew, a Christian as a Christian, and a Turk as a faithless Mussulman.[17]

That is a simple enough point, yet all too many critics in this period ignored it.

II

That brief account of the idolizing of Shakespeare in this period must be taken as an ever-present background during the following discussion of the major concepts at work in the literary criticism. For one of the paradoxes which this collection has established is that effusive praise of Shakespeare during the eighteenth century went side by side with the most devastating criticism of him. The opposed reactions are seen most clearly in a critical tradition which still flourished, the designation of his beauties and faults. In much of the criticism represented here both terms occur together, in some balanced relationship: such is the case with Pilon (No. 255), Steevens (No. 257, note 14), Walpole (No. 261), Mackenzie (No. 264), Jackson (No. 273), Richardson (No. 276), and Johnson (No. 301). In others the beauties are said to exceed the faults, as with Martin Sherlock,[18] Pinkerton (No. 281), a writer in the *Westminster Magazine* for 1785 (No. 282), and one in the *Bee* for 1791 (No. 300). Some argue, indeed, with William Belsham, that Shakespeare's faults 'afford the most decisive proof of his excellence', since, as John Stedman put it, his 'improprieties . . . are a certain proof of the natural powers' of Shakespeare, for that he could please without knowing the rules 'is a proof of his merit'.[19] Yet, against these apologies must be set such comments as that of the *Critical Review* on the 'pages of vapid nonsense' in Shakespeare; or Johnson's claim that he never wrote six lines together without fault;[20] or the similar judgments by Hugh Blair in 1783 (No. 272), or Nathan Drake in 1798 (No. 308), or the brief but savage listing of Shakespeare's faults by William Shaw (No. 280).

Idolized though he was for his excellence under some of the Neo-classic categories for drama (mastery over the passions; creating characters from nature; appropriateness of language), Shakespeare had violated too many of the other criteria of that system to escape without whipping. There are many complaints about his general offences against decorum—that is, at one level, standards of polite or reasonable behaviour, which would exclude coarseness, obscenity, violence, or the mixture of social ranks. Many of Francis Gentleman's notes on Shakespeare reflect perfectly typical eighteenth-century feelings of outrage, against the 'indecent' behaviour of Claudius in *Measure for Measure*; against the 'infamously licentious' language of Mistress Quickly, or the 'profane, and highly improper' satire in *Timon*; against the bawdy and nauseating language of Thersites; and the 'indecency' and 'fulsome ideas' in *Antony and Cleopatra*, rightly cut in performance.

7

Even in *A Midsummer Night's Dream* (the scene with Lysander and Hermia: 'Lie further off') he finds that some passages 'should be omitted, for though sounded in delicacy, they may raise warm ideas'.[21] If he is so solicitous for the audience's morality, it is no wonder that Gentleman should reject the rebels in *2 Henry VI*, or the indecorum of *King John*, or the violence of *Titus Andronicus* (No. 243, notes 68, 69, 17, 19, 70), or that Davies should find the blinding of Gloucester and the deaths at the end of *King Lear* insupportable (No. 277). George Steevens gave a historical palliation for the blinding, in that other Elizabethan plays were more violent (No. 257, note 16), and he also added notes to this 1778 edition to rebut the charge made by Dr Johnson in 1751[22] that 'dun' and 'blanket' in *Macbeth* were offences against decorum (No. 257, notes 7, 8). Yet he was outside the taste of his age in so doing: Capell, otherwise a sensitive and un-bigoted critic of Shakespeare's language, objected to this 'poor metaphor' of the 'blanket of the dark' (No. 263, notes 35, 36), while as late as 1794 the *Critical Review* could still protest against the 'vulgarity' created by these 'degrading words', 'blanket' and 'knife' (n.s. xii, p. 57).

Decorum was also understood in more literary terms, as in the injunctions to keep characters from different social groups separate, to have kings behaving like kings, and not to blend tragedy and comedy. Gentleman complains that the *dramatis personae* in *2 Henry VI* is 'the most strange assemblage of jumbled characters we know of', and objects to the Queen giving the Duchess a box on the ear: 'However termagant the queen might be, this violent breach of dignity and decorum is censurable and very unbecoming.' He finds too much 'ungentleman-like railing' between noblemen in this play, and finds the scene between Peter and his master 'a burlesque combat, a most farcical intrusion upon tragic dignity'.[23] Thomas Warton has a rhetorically expansive paragraph, in the manner of Dennis or Johnson, on Shakespeare's transitions 'from dukes to buffoons' (No. 266), while the grave-diggers' scene in *Hamlet* continued to be a test-case for Neo-classic theorists. John Penn pronounced it a fault, but found it more valuable than other writers' correctness; Frederick Pilon regretted it being 'stained with low ribaldry', and Edward Taylor used it as an example of Shakespeare mingling the sublime and the ridiculous.[24] Taylor protested at characters of higher social standing in Shakespeare being guilty of bawdry, drunkenness, and playing the fool; an anonymous essayist in 1789 said that in Shakespeare 'pathos is intermingled with buffoonery'; Henry James Pye, commentator on Aristotle, writing in 1792, concluded that 'the mixing the serious and the comic in one piece tends to destroy the efficacy of both, and is therefore a fault'. Pye can forgive Shakespeare mingling the tragic and comic, since 'he often introduces a stroke of humour in a grave, though never I believe in a pathetic scene', yet he fundamentally objects to 'that monster of the drama, the regular tragi-comedy', which juxtaposes distress and ridicule in a mixture that is simply 'absurd'.[25] Archibald Alison, in 1790, had also rejected tragi-comedy as 'utterly indefensible' in its mixture of ludicrous and serious, and wished that Shakespeare's 'taste' had been equal to his 'genius', or that 'his knowledge of the laws of Drama corresponded to his knowledge of the human heart', and John Penn attacked the genre in 1797.[26] Of the writers represented here Cooke dismisses tragi-comedy as 'egregiously unnatural' (No. 250), while Steevens speaks with some displeasure of Shakespeare's 'struggles to introduce comick ideas into tragick situations' (No. 265, note 19), and both Blair (No. 272) and Richardson (No. 276) disapprove of the mixture. To this extent, then, did Neo-classic criteria for the unity of drama persist.

Alison's confident invocation of 'the laws of Drama' is representative of critics in this period of all shades, from men of the theatre such as Francis Gentleman and Thomas Davies to more obviously academic critics such as Cooke or Taylor. Neo-classic terminology persists: Mrs Griffith speaks in such terms of 'the Fable' and 'the Moral' (No. 249), as does Dr Johnson (No. 301); Walwyn in his *Essay on Comedy* (1782: No. 271) uses five categories (plot, characters, manners, incidents, unities), as does Edward Taylor (No. 247). Many writers use such terms as 'catastrophe' (there are hardly many alternatives in English), but only a real dyed-in-the-wool Neo-classic like John Penn would defend not only the unities but the use of a chorus, urging William Mason's *Elfrida* as a model.[27] However, many theorists of criticism argued that evaluation could only be made if one started from fixed principles. A writer in a theatrical journal in 1793–4 began a series of essays entitled 'Strictures on the Drama: (1) The Elucidation of the Design' by announcing that he would test drama by rules and principles, since 'there is implanted in Man an universal love of order'.[28] Edward Taylor argued that critics must have an explicitly formulated standard (No. 247), while James Harris resolutely defended the necessity of the rules (in, it must be admitted, a rather circular argument: whatever pleases must have been written according to rules, even though none were known by the writer), and denied the traditional concept of genius and the rules as being incompatible (No. 267).

As far as Shakespeare is concerned, in addition to the 'faults' already touched on, criticism by the rules meant a discussion of the unities, and the concept of poetic justice. Those who believe histories of literature according to which the unities had been swept away by Dr Johnson's attack in his 1765 edition (Vol. 5, No. 205) will be surprised to see that the issue was by no means dead. Two men of the theatre, at the beginning and end of our period, show the persistence of this idea: Francis Gentleman criticizes *Cymbeline* for its 'monstrous breaches of dramatic unity', complains that the plot of *Hamlet* is 'irregularly carried on', that in *Richard III* the unities are 'grossly yet imperceptibly broken', and of the scene between Eros and Enobarbus in Act III of *Antony and Cleopatra* he says that it 'seems calculated merely to give Octavia some time for her journey; but the breaches of unity are so frequent and so violent in this piece, that such a point is of little consideration'.[29] In the excerpts reprinted here are more such criticisms. Writing in 1801 Arthur Murphy still considers it a noteworthy mark of Shakespeare's manner to describe his 'neglect of all regular design in the construction of his fable, without any regard to the unity of action, without order, and often without connection, crowding together a multiplicity of incidents, and a number of episodical characters'. Given this general position it is not surprising that Murphy should describe *The Winter's Tale* as

the most irregular production of that great but eccentric poet. The rules of time and place are totally violated; the former includes more than sixteen years. The action begins before *Perdita* is born, and extends to her wedding day .... The business is so complicated, and heterogeneous, that the strictest attention can not find a clue to guide us through this maze.[30]

Murphy notes that the unities of time and place are broken in *Macbeth* (No. 309), Walwyn makes the same observation about *The Merchant of Venice* (No. 271), and Steevens is glad to be able to demonstrate how the unity of time is 'rigidly observed' in *The Tempest* (No. 257, note 6). Consistently, Steevens dismisses *Richard III* for its 'improbabilities', deriving from Shakespeare's cramming the events of fourteen years into one play (No. 303, note 28).

It was generally agreed, throughout this period and among all schools of critics, that Shakespeare had often 'grossly violated' the unities of time and place, which were still held to be essential to drama. We find Shakespeare attacked for these failings by critics and theorists such as Edward Taylor (No. 247), John Stedman (No. 270), Hugh Blair (No. 272), William Richardson (No. 276), Archibald Alison, William Hodson, Henry James Pye, and John Penn;[31] we also find this point throughout the journals and reviews.[32] For those critics who accepted the Neo-classical conception of the unities a case could be made in defence of Shakespeare. It was widely held that preserving unity of character was one of Shakespeare's excellences, and as for the unity of action, that could be shown to have been preserved if one defined the play's subject correctly. So the anonymous author of one of the best essays on *Othello* in this period (No. 300), described the play as having for its subject 'the destruction of Desdemona', which Shakespeare never loses sight of; and a few years later Wolstenholme Parr, in another outstanding essay on *Othello*, said that in it 'the unity of action, which indeed ought never to be violated, is complete' (No. 305). But in general the discussion of the unities in this period is rather narrow: one of the few writers to return to the issue of dramatic illusion, which had been raised by Johnson's preface and the reactions to it, was Edward Taylor (No. 247), who—surprisingly perhaps, given the violence of his theoretical rejection of Shakespeare—writes on it perceptively.

Johnson's dismissal of Shakespeare's ethical attitudes—'he sacrifices virtue to convenience . . . seems to write without any moral purpose'—is quoted approvingly by Malone, a conservative critic, ever loyal to Johnson (No. 299, note 37), and his fellow-editor Steevens refers to what he calls Shakespeare's 'notorious neglect of poetic justice' (No. 303, note 50), while both Malone (note 19) and Davies (No. 277, note 8) blame Shakespeare for representing the betrayal of the rebels in *2 Henry IV* without any explicit condemnation. But otherwise the Neo-classic demand for the moral function of drama was held in this period (in marked

11

contrast to earlier ones) to have been satisfied by Shakespeare. Mrs Griffith devoted a whole book to this topic (No. 249), which was not only well reviewed but serialized in two journals between 1774 and 1778.[33] The Reverend Cutts Barton rejected Johnson's attack, stating that 'every page' of Shakespeare 'breathes morality supported by example'; an anonymous writer gave Shakespeare an even more exalted position: 'we everywhere find him striving to maintain the supremacy of heaven, and striking at human folly and arrogance'.[34] Similar general approval of Shakespeare's moral purpose can be found here in the excerpts from Taylor (No. 247), 'Reflector' in the *Westminster Magazine* (No. 282), Kemble (No. 285), and Richardson in several essays.

The principle of poetic justice was reaffirmed: William Taylor, one of the most prolific reviewers of this period (some 1,800 articles are ascribed to him), in an important review of Pye's commentary on the *Poetics*, took exception to Aristotle's rule that the fall of a bad man was not tragic. *Richard III* and *Macbeth* were exceptions, and in any case, if this rule were observed, it

would tend to banish retribution from the theatre, to preserve the tyrant whose villainy has molested us with habitual anxiety, and, by prohibiting poetical justice, to abolish that solution of the plot which has apparently the merit of being the most instructive.[35]

Some plays by Shakespeare were held to be particularly efficacious: *Macbeth* is 'the most instructive tragedy in the world', according to James Beattie (No. 251); it is 'one of the most *moral* pieces existing', according to James Harris, since 'It teaches us the danger of venturing, tho' but for *once*, upon a capital offence'; no greater 'dissuasive or dehortation from that dreadful crime' of murder can be found, Thomas Davies wrote, and he believed that Shakespeare had punished Polonius, Rosencrantz, and Guildenstern for meddling in other people's affairs.[36] Steevens believed that poetic justice was administered in *Pericles* (No. 265, note 16), Richardson found it in *Richard III* (No. 276), and in the rejection of Falstaff (No. 294), as did—with regrets, although the coherence of the system left them no real ground for complaint—Morgann (No. 254) and Cumberland (No. 288).

The more detailed the interpretation of crimes and punishment, however, the greater the danger of reducing the play to a banal moral. We may agree with the essayist that 'we have the satisfaction to see [Iago] dragged to deserved punishment' (No. 300), but it is difficult to agree with Johnson that 'in the first place' we learn from *Othello* 'this very useful moral, not to make an unequal match; in the second place, we learn not to yield too readily to suspicion' (No. 301). Still less can we agree with the actor James Fennell that in *Romeo and Juliet* Shakespeare applies poetic justice since 'Romeo deserts Rosalind for Juliet; and is therefore punished for his inconstancy to a prior attachment' (No. 298). Johnson had suggested that Shakespeare may have 'meant to punish' Juliet's 'hypocrisy' since she 'plays most of her pranks under the appearances of religion' (Vol. 5, p. 154), and Joseph Ritson indignantly rejected this indictment (No. 274). We may or may not agree with Ritson that Hamlet's death 'is not to be looked upon as a punishment; the most innocent, as Shakespeare well knew, are frequently confounded with the most guilty' (*ibid.*), yet that seems preferable to William Richardson's last thoughts on this character, the 'instruction' being that 'persons formed like Hamlet should retire, or keep aloof from situations of difficulty and contention', or else acquire 'such vigour and determination of spirit' as is needed to overcome them (No. 307).

III

The theoretical tenets of Neo-classicism (I may add that I use this term in a historically descriptive, not a pejorative sense) permitted the continuing judging of Shakespeare according to its criteria. Yet in this period, as in earlier ones, those criteria were often rejected. Predisposed as many modern readers are to welcome the rejection of critical systems, we must nevertheless record that not all of these rejections were intelligent, or constituted fresh thinking about literature, or life. I find it disappointing, for instance, that in the debate over tragi-comedy Shakespeare's use of comic scenes in tragedy was sometimes defended on the ground that the audience needed some light relief. This is the argument used by Beattie (No. 251), Steevens (No. 259), Davies (No. 277, note 10), James Fennell, and Sir Joshua Reynolds.[37] More critically respectable is the argument that the mingling of genres derived from Shakespeare's allegiance to a higher principle, nature, or truth to life: this is claimed by Mrs Griffith, Horace Walpole

(No. 261), and the author of a well-argued series of essays on *Julius Caesar* (No. 295).

Only occasionally do we find a head-on rebuttal of the supposed impropriety of tragi-comedy, indeed I find this only in the work of two critics, William Taylor, and Reynolds. In his long review of Pye's book for the *Monthly* Taylor challenged the author's censure of tragi-comedy:

This is surely a rash anathema. *The Tempest* so nearly realizes the perfect union of a solemn and a ludicrous fable into one inseparable whole, that a tragi-comedy cannot but seem practicable, in which all should delight yet nothing could be spared. In *Henry the Fourth*, would Mr. Pye wish for the absence of the *tragic* or of the *comic* portion of the fable?

Reviewing another Neo-classical treatise, Penn's *Letters on the Drama*, Taylor reiterated his position, and described how each plot in tragi-comedy affects the other. Reynolds contributed a note to Malone's 1790 edition defending tragi-comedy from critics who had formed their objections from theories, not from the 'experience of what pleases or displeases, which ought to be the foundation of all rules'. Reynolds buttressed this pragmatic point with the argument that the 'ideal excellence of uniformity' rests on an over-exalted conception of the human mind. In an essay on Shakespeare largely devoted to tragi-comedy, but not published until 1952, Reynolds used the 'genius drawing from nature' argument, but also the psychological one, that it is in the nature of the mind to attend to two things simultaneously.[38] The discussion is inconclusive, but reveals a readiness to reject critical tradition.

This rejection of orthodoxy was made with much more vigour in relation to the rules of drama, and especially the unities. In rejecting the rules critics used two well-established arguments, first that genius is above the rules and, second, that there is a higher appeal from truth to nature. 'Writers of transcendent genius overleap all rules', wrote George Colman; Hannah More was convinced that 'genius is antecedent to rules, and independent on criticism'; an essayist described Shakespeare's 'strong, fertile, and creative genius, irregular in conduct'; and another complained of 'the hardships our Dramatic Poets are subject to by the strictness of Aristotelian rules'.[39] Maurice Morgann wrote a splendidly vivid account of how Aristotle would have worshipped Shakespeare and rebuked Rymer (No. 254), an idea copied by Davies (No. 277).

14

Davies elsewhere stated that Shakespeare's 'superior judgement' transcended the rules; a Dublin undergraduate praised his 'intuitive perception', and Malone praised his rich endowment of natural genius.[40] The second of these traditional arguments, that Shakespeare's failure to observe the rules derives from his allegiance to 'truth and nature', is made by George Colman (*Monthly Review*, lviii (1775), p. 433), Horace Walpole (No. 261), and Henry Mackenzie (No. 264), among others.

The newer arguments included the straightforward assertion that if the rules did not adequately account for works of literature which gave pleasure, they should be abandoned. So Alexander Gerard argued that 'When a thing is contrary to rule, and yet actually pleases, we conclude with reason that the rule is false', and Reynolds, perhaps echoing him, wrote that

When a great genius has continued for ages to please, and to please by means contrary to the established art of pleasing, it is then high time to overhaul the rules of art, that they pass a new examination, that they be ·made more agreeable to the nature of man.[41]

More important than this argument was the rejection of the rules on the grounds that they were 'arbitrary', deriving from the specific situation of Greek literary criticism, a point made with vigour by Berkenhout (No. 252), and with more learning by Twining (No. 297), and Pye, who attacked the 'artificial rule of never altering the supposed spot of representation, because the Greek theatre never changed its scenes, which is about as reasonable as it would be not to wear shirts because the ancients had no linen'.[42] Twining, followed by Pye, was the first to introduce into English the case against Neo-classicism (Dacier is the critic most frequently attacked, but the system of course derives from Castelvetro and other sixteenth-century Italian theorists), which had been made by Metastasio and Lessing. These scholars pointed out that the concept of the unities is simply not found in Aristotle, that it is a modern construct with no authority.[43]

The commentators on the *Poetics* wrote, perhaps, for a too specialized audience, and do not seem to have attracted much attention. Elsewhere the case against the unities rested partly on the argument from example. Horace Walpole simply accepts Shakespeare's violation of the unities, but other writers urged that Shakespeare had shown, by his own practice, that the unities were

15

not essential: this is the position of Gerard,[44] Thomas Whately (No. 284), and Martin Sherlock (No. 286). A similarly pragmatic argument, developed more fully in this period, is that when the unities are observed in drama the results are displeasing: as John Berkenhout put it, 'I never saw or read a tragedy, or comedy, fettered by these unities, which did not seem improbable, unnatural, and tedious' (No. 252). The paradox was not lost on critics that this system was designed to ensure probability in the drama, but, as William Hodson said, if observed it 'lessens interest' (a word which still has the sense of involvement, emotional participation), and actually 'destroys probability'. The author of an essay in the *Bee* on *Othello* declared that strict attention to the unities was impossible and pointless,[45] while a writer for the *Westminster Magazine* (No. 282) delivered a witty account of the actual consequences for contemporary drama when the unities are observed. We might conclude that Neo-classical critical theory, setting out to remove what it saw as an absurdity or anomaly in literary practice, merely introduced others.

IV

Throughout this series I have presented the history of the critical and theatrical interpretation of Shakespeare as I have traced it in contemporary documents. Rather than tidy schemes, according to which one critical trend neatly replaces another, I have found the existence, side by side, of critical systems which are supposed to have annihilated or displaced earlier ones, but which did not. No major change in the way we think about literature, or anything else, is effected quickly. The end of the eighteenth century has been regarded as the time when an interest in Shakespeare's plays gave way to an interest in his characters. From the last two sections, and from the following one, it will be clear that an interest in the plays as whole aesthetic objects never disappeared. It is true that a greater interest in character does emerge now, and at times takes the form of justifying itself by arguing against the preoccupation with form. A convenient programmatic statement of this attitude is provided by Thomas Whately, at the beginning of his excellent essay on Shakespeare's characters (No. 284): 'The writers upon dramatic composition have, for the most part, confined their observations to the fable; and the maxims received amongst them for the conduct of it are emphatically called *The Rules of the Drama*.' According to Whately there is a more important subject for criticism: 'I mean the distinction and preservation of *character*, without which the piece is at best a tale, not an action. . . . '

But although Whately's practice of character-analysis does mark a change of emphasis, much of his criticism, and much of contemporary work on character, is traditional, in two main areas. First, the concept of 'the distinction and preservation of character' is a fundamental element of Neo-classical theory, its most familiar expression being the injunction of Horace, in the *Ars Poetica*:

> si quid inexpertum scaenae committis et audes
> personam formare novam, servetur ad imum,
> qualis ab incepto processerit, et sibi constet. (125–7)

('If it is an untried theme you entrust to the stage, and if you boldly fashion a fresh character, have it kept to the end even as it came forth at the first, and have it self-consistent'; tr. H.R. Fairclough, Loeb Library.) Many critics in previous volumes in this series apply this criterion to Shakespeare, as do many here, with both positive and negative results. Francis Gentleman balances both poles, observing that 'Though *Shakespeare* is peculiarly commendable for a general preservation of character, we find him sometimes slipping his noble characters into vulgarisms'. He can praise the character of King Henry VI as being 'most nicely preserved' throughout the three parts, approve of Aaron as being 'drawn most consistently . . . wicked', and of Bottom for being a consistent burlesque; yet he can also find the song 'The ouzel cock' to be 'too good for *Bottom*'; the language of the gardeners in *Richard II* has an 'exquisite style and fancy' but is too 'superior to persons in such low stations', as is the sea-captain's language in *2 Henry VI*.[46] The precision of Gentleman's judgments, whether or not we agree with them, shows how closely critics of this period were attuned to the decorum of character and language.

In general, Shakespeare is celebrated for his consistency in 'preserving' or 'supporting' character. William Belsham praised 'Shakespeare's skill in discriminating, and his attention to the preservation of his characters'; Richard Cumberland believed that Shakespeare 'considered preservation of character' vital to drama, a judgment shared by a Dublin undergraduate, a correspondent in

Walker's Hibernian Magazine for 1791, Henry James Pye, and Richard Hole.[47] Many of the authors represented here would agree.[48] Occasionally the conception of character-consistency leads to a challenge of the critical or textual tradition: that the accusations of other characters that Coriolanus is a boaster are not borne out by the text, where he frequently expresses a loathing for adulation, is a point made by Mrs Griffith (No. 249, note 12), Monck Mason (No. 283), and Malone (No. 299, note 25). The textual-critical tradition whereby Miranda is made to pun on the word 'maid' in her first meeting with Ferdinand is rejected by 'Charles Dirrill' on the grounds that this 'equivoque might serve for the character of a shrewd female flirt; but certainly not for that simplicity of nature which Shakespeare has bestowed upon Miranda throughout the play', a judgment arrived at independently by Thomas Pearne.[49]

Yet, as on virtually every other aspect of Shakespeare in the eighteenth century, no sooner do we note a positive appreciation of him than we must record its opposite. A regular writer for the *Critical*, reviewing Richardson's *Essays on Shakespeare's Dramatic Characters*, disputed whether 'fictitious personages' can really provide insight into the workings of the human mind, and held that in any case Shakespeare was less suited to this purpose

than many other authors; for his characters, except in his more finished plays, are by no means uniformly supported; and he sometimes seems to forget in the fifth act what he had intended in the first. We think both Hamlet and Polonius striking examples of this inconsistency.[50]

The case of Hamlet is a special one, which we must come back to, but it may be observed here that a whole class of Shakespeare criticism in this period consists of the attack, or defence, of individual characters. Steevens complained of Marina in *Pericles* that she, as one 'designed for a character of juvenile innocence, appears much too knowing in the impurities of a brothel' (No. 303, note 38). More substantial was the observation first made by Malone, and expanded by other writers, on the 'want of consistency' in the character of Emilia, who loves Desdemona yet does not seek to calm her distress at the loss of the handkerchief.[51]

The second traditional approach to character which continued to flourish in this period was the moral one. Not surprisingly, in view of the persistent expectation that drama should display a moral design and enforce justice, characters were regarded either as being essentially exempla of that design, or were directly criticized for their good or bad behaviour, often with no consideration of Shakespeare's overriding intent. In general, writers were willing to praise Shakespeare for his moral attitude to his creations, as we can see from the almost unanimously favourable reviews that William Richardson's series of moral essays on Shakespeare's characters received over a period of nearly thirty years. Richardson announces in his first book that he will analyse 'some of [Shakespeare's] remarkable characters', with the intention 'to make poetry subservient to philosophy, and to employ it in tracing the principles of human conduct' (No. 246). Similarly the young Kemble announces that his essay will 'more effectually serve ethicks' by analysing Macbeth's character in comparison with Richard III's (No. 285). Such explicitly didactic announcements can be found in many of the journal articles.

Mrs Griffith, after Richardson the next most highly regarded critic in this period, besides illustrating Shakespeare's morality at great length, indulges in a vigorous disapproval of the evil characters, such as Proteus, Richard III, or Lear's daughters (No. 249, notes 1, 2, 6), and gives generous praise of the good ones, Lear, Old Hamlet, and Desdemona (*ibid.*, notes 7, 16, 19). Francis Gentleman finds more to blame than to praise, disposing of Hamlet, Claudius, and Laertes (No. 243, notes 7 and 8), finding Leontes a monster of inhumanity (note 35), passing a divided judgment on Coriolanus (notes 40–3), but becoming increasingly confident that Antony is intended to be no more than an exemplum of decadence (notes 54, 56–9). Thomas Davies, by contrast, found Antony 'a great and generous soul', and praised the 'greatness of soul' in Cleopatra's last scenes—both unusual responses to this play in this period (No. 277, notes 21–3). For Davies, Cordelia is 'an example of filial piety', and in the work of Richardson the exemplary tradition finds its most persistent exponent: Lear is an instance of 'impetuous impulse'; in Timon Shakespeare 'illustrates the consequences of. . . inconsiderate profusion' (No. 276). If the critical approach via character always risks losing sight of plays as dramatic experiences, with Richardson both plays and characters are reduced to moral demonstrations, at times absurdly. Faced with Richard III's successful wooing of Lady Anne, Richardson's only deduction is that she must be intended as having 'a mind altogether frivolous, the prey of vanity, her prevailing, over-ruling passion'; Richard legitimately did not try to convince her understanding, 'for she had no understanding worth the pains of convincing' (No. 260). Like so many of the moralizing comments throughout eighteenth-century Shakespeare criticism, and indeed in other periods, this shows no sense for the design of the play as a whole. More intelligent are Stack's answer to Morgann (No. 292), and Kemble's to Whately (No. 285), both of which show the damaging effect that a misconception of character can have on our total experience of the play.

I have stressed the continuity of the moralizing approach, and of the demand for consistency, since they are fundamental to all the criticism of Shakespeare's characters in this period. The newer element is a tendency to analyse characters as if they were real human beings. This approach justifies itself by the almost universal praise for Shakespeare's knowledge of human nature. Hannah More said that he showed 'every varied position of the human mind, every shade of discrimination in the human character'; the Reverend Cutts Barton wrote that 'all the virtues, follies, vices, abilities and defects incident to human nature' were represented by Shakespeare.[52] Francis Gentleman found Shakespeare 'minutely correct in mental operations' (No. 243, note 47); he has left us 'the soul anatomized', according to the author of *Shakespeare. Containing the Traits of his Characters* (No. 248); Steevens celebrated Shakespeare's 'intimate acquaintance with every passion that sooths or ravages, exalts or debases the human mind' (No. 265, note 7); Malone agreed (*ibid.*, note 8).[53] Occasionally some advocates of the new approach justify an interest in character as against plot: George Colman, for instance, having stated that 'the nice discrimination of the various shades of the human mind, the pourtraying of character, was Shakespeare's great excellence', went on to argue that 'his fable is often comparatively defective. What is the conduct of the story of *Hamlet* viewed with the person of Hamlet and the Ghost?' A writer in the *English Review* said that 'in Shakespeare we forget the poet, and think only of the character',[54] while both Thomas Robertson (No. 293) and James Fennell (No. 298) argued that in *Hamlet* Shakespeare had wanted 'truth of character' and was ready to sacrifice plot to obtain it.

A further justification for giving more attention to individual characters was the general admiration for Shakespeare's psychological realism, according to which examining his characters is exactly the same as analysing real people. Reviewing Richardson's second book of *Essays on Shakespeare's Dramatic Characters*, one writer affirmed that

It is an attribute peculiar to Shakespeare only of all dramatic writers, that of his characters we may discourse, reason, and infer actions from principles with the same ease and certainty as of our most intimate friends, so deeply did he penetrate . . . that strange, mysterious, and almost inscrutable labyrinth, the human heart.

In the *English Review* the same sentiments were to be heard:

The intuitive mind of Shakespeare penetrated into the inmost recesses of the human breast. His mimic world contains such a variety of characters, so correctly and accurately delineated . . . that, reasoning on the character and conduct of his *ideal* beings, we shall find our conclusions will apply, in every respect, to the *realities* which pass continually before us.

Similarly, Christopher Moody in the *Monthly* wrote that 'by properly analysing the characters . . . considerable light may be thrown on the philosophy of the human mind'. [55]

The characters who most attracted this psychological approach in this period were Hamlet and Falstaff, with subsidiary attention being given to Macbeth and Richard III. But the psychological analysis is the last stage of an inquiry which uses the categories of consistency of character and morality, and which begins as either attack or defence. The character of Falstaff had been frequently accused of moral failings, especially cowardice, [56] so Maurice Morgann (No. 254) set out to defend him, a rather difficult task, which he conducted with much ingenuity. Unfortunately, his advocacy took some rather dubious courses: he did not begin at the beginning of *1 Henry IV*, with the sequence of impressions which Shakespeare so carefully built up; he tried to discredit all those to whom Shakespeare gave comments on Falstaff's cowardice, resulting in a remarkably negative account of Poins; he passed over some scenes that did not fit his account, and he misinterpreted others. He took all 'positive' references to Falstaff's fighting at face value, including Doll Tearsheet's and that of Colevile (missing the irony of a scene which shows how bluff and reputation can succeed); he made much of the good opinion of Falstaff held by such minor characters as Shallow, without considering that Shakespeare shows them deceived by Falstaff into

21

accepting his public estimate of himself, while in the soliloquies (whose function Morgann nowhere discussed) we are given an insight into his true make-up; Morgann took Falstaff's lies and evasions for truth (he *really* used 'the utmost speed in his power' to catch up with the army: 'he arrives almost literally *within the extremest inch of possibility*'). Falstaff's wounding of the dead Percy he described as '*indecent* but not cowardly', and his claim to have killed Percy is 'not meant or calculated for *imposition*', since it is spoken to the Prince, who could not be imposed on. Thus Morgann ignored both Hal's reaction:

> For my part, if a lie may do thee grace,
> I'll gild it with the happiest terms I have

and the fact that Falstaff wins general credit for his 'exploit'. Throughout Morgann considered Falstaff as a static character, seen at his most winning in Part I: the increasingly negative picture in Part II he ignored, apart from one belated paragraph towards the end. Morgann, like other critics of this school, did not consider dramatic structure, nor dramatic function. For him Falstaff was simply a character to be rehabilitated. Some contemporaries were impressed by his argument, but most rejected it as a paradoxical *jeu d'esprit*, and several pointed out what injury it would do to the play as a whole, and to our estimate of Shakespeare's ability as a dramatist.[57]

Morgann is an important critic, but rather on account of the observations which he makes in passing: the acute description of the 'latent' element in dramatic character, for instance, or his designation of 'choric' characters, or his defence of Shakespeare's puns. For too much of the time he indulges himself in re-creating an imaginary past for Falstaff, and granting him birth, fashion, learning, courage, and the tone, 'deportment and . . . manners of a gentleman'. We may reject this excessively partisan evaluation, but gain other valuable insights. Morgann's belief that 'those characters in *Shakespeare* which are seen only in part are yet capable of being unfolded and understood in the whole, every part being in fact relative, and inferring all the rest', is a position that, while a product of the age in which it was conceived, is also of continuing validity. The method may have been mis-used, but Morgann remains a writer of rare intelligence.

Morgann's essay on Falstaff, although involving subtle psychological speculation, was in essence a moral defence of the character. Some of his critics took exception to the hyper-subtlety, the best of these, Richard Stack, affirming that 'dramatic characters are not drawn for speculative ingenious men in their closets, but for mankind at large' (No. 292). Stack also showed how Morgann had distorted the shape and purpose of the play. But most of the subsequent discussion aimed at restoring the negative moral judgment on Falstaff, or at proving his cowardice to be consistent with the rest of his character. Walwyn, in his *Essay on Comedy*, said that 'Every trait' of his personality 'is consistent with each other. Had Shakespeare given him courage, he would have made him inconsistent with himself; the sordid and selfish may be desperate, but never courageous' (No. 271). More censorious are the author of an undated essay, who finds in Falstaff 'the traits of an artful, ambitious, vain, voluptuous, avaricious, cowardly, satirical, pleasant-witted knave', whom Shakespeare makes charming without losing sight of his villainy (No. 248), and William Richardson (No. 294), whose essay displays the twin goals of eighteenth-century criticism of Shakespeare's characters: to assess their consistency and pass judgment on their morality.

Morgann's essay did not convince the major critics and reviewers, but it had a fruitful effect in stimulating discussion of Falstaff, and in the essays by Stack and Richardson several new and important points emerged out of the challenge of answering him. The history of the criticism of Hamlet is just such a process of indictment and exculpation, with the need to answer a hostile verdict pushing critics on into new interpretations. The psychological analysis is, once more, the end-stage of a movement which begins in the traditional areas: Hamlet's character was criticized as being immoral and inconsistent. His cruelty to Ophelia is both at variance with his professed love for her and is inexcusably bad behaviour; his failing to kill Claudius while at prayer is inconsistent with his vow of revenge, while his professed reasons for not doing so, namely to send Claudius's soul to hell, are shocking; he shows no remorse for having killed Polonius, and none for Rosencrantz and Guildenstern; he claims to have donned the disguise of madness to evade Claudius's suspicion, but after his quarrel with Laertes he claims to be truly mad, or mentally unbalanced.

These and other 'faults' in his character (taking the word in both senses, an imperfection in the texture and a censurable error) had been denounced by earlier critics,[58] and continued to be attacked. A reviewer in the *Critical* said of his reason for not killing Claudius that this would be 'diabolical revenge' and 'infernal malice'; Malone described it as a 'horrid thought', Reed as a 'horrid sentiment'.[59] Davies described it as a 'horrid soliloquy . . . more reprehensible, perhaps, than any of Shakespeare's works' (No. 277, note 28), which was rightly rejected by Garrick. Francis Gentleman, predictably enough, approved its being cut since it tends 'to vitiate and degrade' Hamlet's character (No. 243, note 7), but Frederick Pilon noted the bad effect this theatre-cut has on our impression of Hamlet: 'This principal link being omitted in the representation, and no other cause substituted for Hamlet's continuing to procrastinate, he appears weak and inconsistent during the last two acts' (No. 255). James Harris was shocked at Hamlet's lack of remorse on killing Polonius (No. 267), while James Fennell attacked his indifference to the deaths of Rosencrantz and Guildenstern (No. 298). Fennell and another writer complain that Hamlet neglects his duty of revenge.[60]

Defenders of Hamlet, of whom there were many, sometimes rebutted these charges directly. Malone denied that he was to blame for the deaths of Rosencrantz and Guildenstern, since Shakespeare followed the source in Saxo Grammaticus 'pretty closely', and 'probably meant to describe [them] as equally guilty' as their counterparts there (No. 265, note 6); Thomas Davies agreed that they were Claudius's 'accomplices and instruments', 'willing spies' (No. 277, note 34). Richardson defended Hamlet from the charge of rudeness to Ophelia, claiming that this was the error of actors (No. 307). As for Hamlet wanting to send Claudius's soul to hell, a writer in the *Westminster Magazine* objected, it

may be unworthy of his character, but where is the man under similar provocations who would not have done the like, or at least into whose mind such a thought would not have intruded? Shakespeare does not intend Hamlet for a perfect character; he has given him the frailties that flesh is heir to.[61]

That objection would call in question the Neo-classic demand that characters be 'good' not only in the sense of being 'good in their kind', but good absolutely. Joseph Ritson took an equally straightforward line: had Hamlet failed to kill Claudius he would have betrayed his father's memory (No. 274, note 10).

Such refutations settle the immediate point, at any rate to the refuter's satisfaction, but raise no wider issues. Many of the defences of Hamlet, however, instead of refuting an accusation implicitly accept it, and seek to account for it by an explanation of his personality. Once again objections to inconsistency or immorality produce psychological analyses, undertaken as a process of exculpation. This procedure is not without its dangers. As in all forms of controversy, the refuter who accepts the accuser's diagnosis runs the risk of having his categories, and thus the shape of his whole discussion, determined by his opponent's formulation of them.

Earlier critics had complained that Hamlet's character was a mixture of contradictory elements, the implication being that Shakespeare had failed to unify them according to the Horatian canon (*servetur ad imum/qualis ab incepto processerit*): this is the burden of Aaron Hill's analysis in 1735 (Vol. 3, pp. 35f.), Francis Gentleman's in 1770 (Vol. 5, p. 383), and George Steevens's in 1772–3 (Vol. 5, pp. 488–9). All three writers sum up Hamlet's character in a series of self-contradicting antitheses, and the practice continued. A writer in the *London Magazine* criticized Voltaire for taking no notice of Hamlet's desire of revenge, and 'his struggles between this desire and his thorough want of conviction'.[62] The defenders could have denied the relevance of the criterion of character-consistency, thus strictly applied, but they did not. Henry Mackenzie, in 1780, even extended the series of antitheses: 'With the strongest purposes of revenge, he is irresolute and active; amidst the gloom of the deepest melancholy, he is gay and jocular . . .' (No. 264). But Mackenzie's reply was to deny that these oppositions are the sign of bad dramaturgy:

That *Hamlet*'s character, thus formed by Nature, and thus modelled by situation, is often variable and uncertain, I am not disposed to deny. I will content myself with the supposition that this is the very character which Shakespeare meant to allot him.

Whereas earlier critics had attacked the inconsistencies as the accidental result of Shakespeare's failure to integrate the play, apologists of this generation take them as deliberate. Mackenzie, attempting to reduce Hamlet's character to a 'fixed or settled principle', defined it as marked by extreme sensitivity, tending towards weakness or inaction. Similar analyses were made by William Richardson (Nos 246, 307), and Thomas Robertson (No. 293), who took the argument further, claiming that Shakespeare had arranged Hamlet's contradictory qualities in such a way as to cancel each other out, rendering him unable to act. The Romantic conception of Hamlet, from Coleridge to Bradley and beyond, is born here.

But if the defenders of Hamlet produced a viable model of the whole character, they were less happy in accounting for specific features. On Hamlet's given reasons for not killing Claudius at prayer, for instance, some went back to the tradition of William Dodd (Vol. 3, p. 474) and Thomas Sheridan (Vol. 4, p. 8), that the reasons are a mere 'excuse', and that really he is a coward, or has too much 'timidity'. Robertson, having defined gentleness as Hamlet's dominant trait, argued that in this speech Hamlet was really *imposing* upon himself; devising an excuse for his aversion to bloodshed, for his cowardice. Robertson's account is a psychological one, Richardson's, typically enough, is moral. He finds nothing else in Hamlet's character consistent with these violent sentiments, and argues that his given reasons are a lie designed to save his face, an excuse more 'suited to the opinions of the multitude'. This desperate defence leaves the character in a worse condition than the original accusation had done.

A similar process of action and reaction, an earlier critical position more or less determining a later reply, can be seen in the question of Hamlet's madness, especially in connection with the Ophelia scenes and with his self-justification to Laertes in the last act. While many writers continued to believe that the madness was assumed in order to outwit Claudius, some held that Hamlet was really mad. That quixotic figure William Kenrick, lecturing in a London tavern, claimed that Hamlet's 'madness was *real*, at least *essentially* so; and gave, as a plausible reason, that it was produced by Ophelia's inconstancy', and his mother's remarriage (No. 245). The reporter in the *Monthly Miscellany* listed some of the objections against this theory, but it was repeated by other more respected men. In the 1778 edition Steevens, while retaining all his notes criticizing Hamlet, added the palliation (which he attributes to Akenside) that the conduct of Hamlet was 'indefensible, unless he were to be regarded' as in some degree mad (No. 257, note 18). Madness would excuse Hamlet from much blame: his defenders naturally leapt at this argument, although hesitating to make their hero totally insane. Mackenzie believed that the madness is feigned, but that at the grave of Ophelia 'it exhibits some temporary marks of a real disorder' (No. 264). The anonymous author of a 1782 essay in which Hamlet defends himself from the charge of 'cruel and inconsistent conduct' has the hero uncertain whether 'much of my flighty extravagance was not owing to an imagination really disordered' (No. 269). Richardson, in 1783, presents Hamlet's reason as 'trembling on the brink of madness', although 'not amounting to actual madness' (No. 276). Richardson's quotation, and defence of the truth of the 'sore distraction' speech, led the way for many defenders of Shakespeare, who pronounced Hamlet subject to temporary fits of madness.[63]

One feeling unites these critics, giving an unusual coherence to their work, the wish to present Hamlet as an admirable character. The result was rather cloying, although it no doubt helped contribute to the dominance Hamlet was to have over all other Shakespeare characters during the nineteenth century. Both Ritson (No. 274) and Malone (No. 299, note 35) answer Steevens's charges point by point, finding Hamlet innocent of any fault. Mackenzie finds Hamlet 'naturally of the most virtuous and most amiable dispositions' (No. 264), and Richardson writes three long essays which he explicitly describes as being 'intended to justify his moral conduct'. Thomas Robertson, working within the two main contemporary approaches to character, defends Hamlet from the accusations of 'incongruity' and 'immorality', 'altogether exculpating him' from the charges of Steevens and others. He does so by finding consistency in Hamlet's divided spirit, his melancholy, and his position in Claudius's court. But he also adds even more panegyric to the tradition. While the attacks on Hamlet's vices were often crude, the defences leave us with an equally one-sided paean to his virtues.

A similar sequence of attack and defence can be seen with the third major character discussed in this period, Macbeth. The stimulus to debate was given by the posthumous publication of Thomas Whately's *Remarks on Some of the Characters of Shakespeare* (No. 284), one of the most intelligent essays of the period. Whately develops a long, contrasting analysis of two characters placed in similar situations, Richard III and Macbeth, which has some obvious faults (at times he exaggerates the contrast; he lapses into synopsis; and he neglects the design of the play and the dramatist's purpose), but is none the less full of penetrating criticism. The contrast between Macbeth's humane, social, family instincts and Richard's cold egoism; their different attitudes towards killing; Macbeth's desire for power since it will bring regard, Richard's merely out of a wish to dominate: these and other insights emerge fruitfully from Whately's antithetical model. Whately aroused controversy, however, by his description of Macbeth as 'a man not naturally very bold', deducing from his apprehensions before Duncan's murder evidence of Macbeth's physical cowardice. That Macbeth 'commits subsequent murders with less agitation than that of Duncan' was, Whately argued, 'no inconsistency in his character' but 'confirms the principles upon which it is formed', for 'he gets rid of fear by guilt, which, to a mind so constituted, may be the less uneasy sensation of the two'. As for Macbeth's reaction to Banquo, this is 'quite consistent with' his 'timidity', since he fears Banquo's 'superior courage'. That Macbeth is able to suppress his 'natural timidity' is evidence that 'he has an acquired, though not a constitutional courage'.

In reply, John Philip Kemble's *Macbeth re-considered* (No. 285) corrected the imbalance of Whately's analysis, pointing to Shakespeare's stress, in the opening scenes, on Macbeth's great physical courage, and showing that the motive for the murder of Banquo is ambition, not fear. More important, Kemble analyses the relationship between Macbeth's attitude to his own deeds and our attitude to him. If his unease before the murder of Duncan were to be explained in Whately's terms,

we must forego our virtuous satisfaction in his repugnance to guilt, for it arises from mere cowardice; and can gain no instruction from his remorse, for it is only the effect of imbecility. We despise him; we cannot feel for him . . . .

Whately's interpretation, then, would destroy the moral significance of the play: as a writer in the *English Review* put it, Kemble proves that 'the intrepidity of Macbeth cannot be called in question; and likewise judiciously remarks that the moral effect of the play depends greatly on the intrepidity of his character'; other writers noted the importance of our moral involvement with Macbeth's self-disgust.[64] In his series of essays on *Macbeth* (No. 288) Richard Cumberland began from Neo-classic premises, noting 'a remarkable preservation of character in Macbeth', and making a sharp definition of the ruling principle in the two main personae: 'Macbeth's principle is honour; cruelty is natural to his wife; ambition is common to both'. His approach is moralistic, too, showing that Macbeth, with his gradual fall into cruelty, has 'a moral advantage' over Richard III, to whom it comes naturally. Cumberland has a number of intelligent comments on dramatic structure, showing that an interest in character need not necessarily exclude a sense of literary form.

V

While the interest in character attracted newer writers on Shakespeare—the essays by Richardson, Mackenzie, Robertson, Whately, and Kemble were all first publications on Shakespeare—much traditional criticism continued to be produced deriving from aesthetic or formalist concerns: comments on dramatic form, the interrelation between character and drama, Shakespeare's language, wordplay, versification, imagery, and non-dramatic poetry. If the previous section has seemed to offer a more enlightened, less system-bound approach, then here we must record the familar eighteenth-century balance of praise and blame (which further inquiry may prove to have been more healthy than the indiscriminate adulation which Shakespeare attracted in the following century). Much of the criticism of dramatic structure is negative, but before dismissing it we should realize that the objections made by critics of this period tell us much about their norm or ideal conception of drama. Every age in defining Shakespeare defines itself.

One of the major criticisms was that scenes or characters in Shakespeare were not properly 'connected' to the plot, were not integral to the design. Johnson had complained of the scene with the Welsh captain in *Richard II* that it was 'unartfully and irregularly thrust in' (Vol. 5, p. 116). This is typical of the expectations of readers in this period, who could perceive linear connection, the syntagmatic linking of event to event, action to consequence, but could not perceive counterpointing, the paradigmatic use of scenes for commentary or thematic reflection. Morgann, in his definition of choric characters, is virtually the only exception. Otherwise critics impatiently reject what they cannot co-ordinate. Representative in this as in other attitudes was Francis Gentleman, who could not see the connection between Alcibiades and the main plot in *Timon*, dismissing his scenes as 'episodical. . . rather an excrescence than an ornament'; the scene between Mamillus and the ladies in *The Winter's Tale* (Act II, scene 1) is one of Shakespeare's 'many trifling excrescences'; the gardeners' scene in *Richard II* is 'totally unessential to the fable, however poetically beautiful'; the scene with Talbot in *1 Henry VI* is 'of no manner of use to the story'.[65] Similarly Davies rejected the scene between Polonius and Reynaldo as 'by no means essential to the play' (No. 277, note 24). Steevens found the clown's song at the end of *Twelfth Night* ('When that I was and a little tiny boy') 'utterly unconnected' with the play (No. 303, note 4), an opinion surprisingly shared by Capell (No. 263, note 77). Steevens elicits more agreement when he says that the characters in *Pericles* appear and disappear bewilderingly, the deficiency of 'liaison among the personages' being a mark of this play (No. 265, note 17). Both Monck Mason and an anonymous writer object to the dumb-show in *Hamlet* as superfluous, since Claudius's conscience would have been caught by it before he sat through the play.[66] Several critics invoke the canon of simplicity to protest against Shakespeare's overloading his plot with episodes and constantly introducing new characters and 'fresh matter'.[67] Here we can see an eighteenth-century norm for drama, as the working-out of a given and limited set of characters and issues. Solicitude for the coherence of plot led Andrew Eccles to issue quasi-variorum editions of *King Lear* and *Cymbeline* in which the scenes were re-arranged to improve 'the progression of the fable' and make the parts depend upon each other, to form a consistent whole in respect to time and place. Reviewers did not thank him for his pains.[68]

Objections to Shakespeare's dramatic structure were especially levelled against the endings, much in the spirit of Johnson's disparaging comments (Vol. 5, pp. 65f., 123). Thomas Twining said that in general Shakespeare neglected the endings of his plays; Pye objected to the 'premature catastrophe' in *The Merchant of Venice*: he considered the plot to be complete with the outcome of the trial, and regarded the scenes at Belmont as superfluous, an opinion shared by Walwyn and by William Taylor, who made the same accusation against *Henry VIII*, arguing that since Wolsey and Catherine are the chief characters the play ends with their departure, the last act being superfluous.[69] Another popular topic was to point to discrepancies or 'loose ends' in the plot, and pronounce that Shakespeare occasionally forgot himself. Malone, who had in general a rather low opinion of Shakespeare's artistry, frequently states that Shakespeare did not give himself the trouble to compare the several parts of his play (e.g. No. 275, note 4; No. 299, notes 23 and 30). He finds a loose end in the plot of *The Winter's Tale*, and his collaborators Steevens and Blackstone make the same observation on *A Midsummer Night's Dream* and *Othello*.[70]

Yet not all the comments on Shakespeare's handling of plot were negative. Francis Gentleman expresses a warm appreciation for the increasing tension in *Othello* (No. 243, note 1), and *Richard III* (notes 3, 4, 6). He even praises the last Act of *Antony and Cleopatra* as being truly tragic, despite Antony's absence (note 62), and celebrates both the exposition and conclusion of *The Comedy of Errors* (notes 72, 74), while Steevens praises the denouement of *Cymbeline* for being intricate but natural (No. 257, note 15). Richard Cumberland makes several intelligent observations on *Macbeth*, and William Taylor has a sensitive account of how less important characters, such as Duncan and Julius Caesar, are rightly less than fully defined and distinguished.[71] Stack shows how Shakespeare builds up judgments and impressions from the first scene (No. 292: a sequence fractured by Morgann), and stresses the important point that 'the poet's designs as to the character . . . have a powerful influence on the plot'. W.N. draws attention to the remarkable feature of *Othello*, that Shakespeare must have had a clear idea from the beginning of what Iago was going to do, yet presents so much from Iago's point of view as an improvisation with no definite goal (No. 300). These are all observations which a modern critic might be proud of having made.

The interplay between character and plot is also seen, as in Maurice Morgann's intelligent note on the interaction of reason and fancy in *King Lear*, 'in the real madness of *Lear*, in the assumed wildness of *Edgar*, and in the Professional *Fantasque* of the *Fool*, all operating to contrast and heighten each other' (No. 254), a point quickly picked up by Steevens (No. 259) and Mackenzie (No. 264). Whereas Steevens could complain that Shakespeare's presentation of Julius Caesar is unflattering, Davies suggests that 'Caesar was to be lessened in order to aggrandize Brutus'.[72] Richardson, whose character-portraits are usually static, nevertheless shows that the catastrophe in *2 Henry IV* is produced organically out of the interaction of Hal and Falstaff, in the former's 'self-deceit' and the latter's 'discernment', the collision between which produces a natural sequence of events: 'none of them are foreign or external, but grow, as it were, out of the characters' (No. 294). W.N.'s essay on *Othello* discusses the reaction of the characters to the denouement (No. 300), if in rather formal terms; more sensitive is Wolstenholme Parr, who makes a psychological analysis of Othello, since 'so much of the conduct of men depends on the habits of early life', and traces the implications of such an upbringing on such a character (No. 305).

As to the sense of the plays as theatre-experience, very few critics in this period have much to contribute, not even the drama reviewers. All the more impressive, then, are the notes of Edward Capell (No. 263), who added to his excellence as an editor and scholar the rare ability to visualize action and representation in terms of the theatre. Capell urges the need to attend to Shakespeare's 'ideas . . . in the disposing of his action, and in the place of his scene' in order to obtain 'a thorough conception of him' (note 10). He means not just the theatrical representation but the locality of action as Shakespeare imagines it, such as his note on Act II of *Macbeth*. He explains how a scene must be 'conceiv'd by a reader', such as the murder of Caesar,[73] or the precise sequence of entries in the masking scene in *Much Ado* (note 47)—a sequence which several modern editors still mistake. All the evidence is in the text, but it needs care and imagination to synthesize it properly: this Capell shows in his note on the scene where Lear awakes, where he has Lear on stage, and the music playing softly, from the beginning of the scene (note 29), as an integral part of Lear's cure, an adjustment that is also faithful to Renaissance ideas on the curative power of harmony. Elsewhere Capell reconstructs the placing and movement of characters during the banquet scene in *Macbeth*, and inserts the necessary stage-directions for the appearance of the ghosts in *Richard III*, explaining Shakespeare's failure to do so as proof that he 'thought it (wrongly) within a

manager's province'.[74] His comment on Oswald's posting between
Goneril and Regan (note 27) shows that he is one of the few critics
in this period to respond to more complex dramatic situations as
they unfold. He also sees the potential meaning of gesture in the
denouement of a tragedy, *King Lear* (note 30), or a comedy, *The
Two Gentlemen of Verona* (note 79). He is unique in this period in
seeing that Shakespeare's theatre was fundamentally verbal, not
visual, lacking modern resources for verisimilitude, yet with a
resulting gain in artistic freedom: 'his imposing was not by eyes
but by ears: the former his stage deny'd him, and therefore left him
at liberty to fix upon any action that lik'd him, and that suited his
plot' (note 58). The implications of that position have only begun
to be pursued in our time.

VI

Turning from dramatic structure to language we are struck, once
again, by the affront which Shakespearian invention, and
Elizabethan English, gave to eighteenth-century ideas of correctness. Although earlier critics, such as Upton (Vol. 3, No. 114) and
Hurd (Vol. 4, No. 162), had urged a descriptive approach to
Shakespeare, to establish his own system of grammatical usage
rather than merely belabour him for not meeting present-day
standards of correctness, such injunctions had been forgotten. As
will by now be abundantly clear, of all the traditions in
Shakespeare criticism in the eighteenth century, that to do with
language and style was the most tenuous and short-lived. There are
some purely descriptive observations, such as Ritson's on the
(over fifty) instances of a singular verb agreeing with a plural noun,
and Mason's that Shakespeare uses personal and impersonal
pronouns 'indiscriminately', or 'frequently confounds the active
and passive participles', and the definite and indefinite article.
Mason also noted specifically Shakespearian usages, such as
'pretend' meaning 'intend', and 'exorcise' meaning not to lay
spirits but to raise them.[75] Malone has some neutral observations,
as on Shakespeare's use of nouns as verbs (No. 265, note 2), and
gives a list of unusual words used in *Othello*, but he and Steevens
more often draw attention to Shakespeare's 'offences against
grammar', his 'harsh' or 'incorrect' language, his 'licentious
phraseology'; or they claim that the ends of his sentences do not

correspond to the beginnings.[76] Yet, in his preface to the 1790 edition, Malone can award Shakespeare the highest Augustan honour, that of being 'the great refiner and polisher of our language' (No. 299, Preface, *ad fin.*).

As for Shakespeare's use of metaphor, judgments were also mostly negative. Malone seems to hark back to Warburton when he complains that 'Shakespeare seldom attends to the integrity of his metaphors', or that he 'as usual'—or 'with his usual laxity'—'forgets to make his simile answer on both sides'. Malone puts this down to Shakespeare starting an idea, then leaving it with 'very slight connection' to pursue another, and this conception of a hasty, inspired writer not given to correcting his work is shared by Steevens, Davies, and Gerard.[77] Malone also holds the Neo-classic belief that characters under stress do not naturally use similes (we recall Johnson's criticism of *Lycidas*), pointing accusingly to Romeo and Othello doing so (No. 265, note 4). William Belsham also objected to Othello's 'Pontick sea' simile, as had many critics before him, while Cooke complained that figurative language was 'too light and airy' for a mother with two murdered sons (in *Richard III*), and Richardson thought that Hamlet's 'Frailty, thy name is woman' was an expression 'too refined and artificial for a mind strongly agitated'. Davies held that language from the heart needs no ornament, Beattie pronounced that an agitated mind does not run into allegories or long-winded similes, Hodson believed that images were 'ambitious ornaments' in tragedy, therefore dangerous, and both Colman and Mason objected to Shakespeare's use of 'frigid conceits'. Occasionally we find a critic explicating one of Shakespeare's longer analogies, without attacking it: Malone so treats Constance's famous simile on grief in *King John*, and Henley explicates Richard II's conceit of the dial and the clock.[78] Yet Priestley could condemn Constance's analogy as being 'too much the comment of a cool observer', and criticize Shakespeare for mixing his metaphors (No. 253), a schoolmasterly reproof also made by Blair (No. 272), and Steevens (1778 edition: X, p. 483).

Great displeasure was aroused by Shakespeare's frequent use of one of the most common figures of rhetoric, *ploche*, the repetition of a word. Monck Mason wrote that 'Nothing can be more in the style of Shakespeare than the repetition in the second line of the same words that he used in the first', but he still disapproved of Iago's echoing use of 'trash . . . trash' (*Othello*, 2.1.303). Although Malone found the repetition in Macbeth's 'Cleanse the stuffed bosom of that perilous stuff' (5.3.44) 'certainly unpleasing', he would not emend because 'Shakespeare was extremely fond of such repetitions'.[79] Steevens shared the dislike, while admitting the authenticity of the style: 'the repetition of the word *trash* is much in Shakespeare's manner, though in his worst'. The animus is evidently sign of a collision between eighteenth-century ideas of poetic diction and Elizabethan ones, but Steevens unfortunately allowed his animus to affect his judgment as an editor, emending in the 1778 edition what he called the 'nauseous iteration' of Macbeth's 'stuff' so as to read 'foul bosom', and both Mason and Ritson objected to this illicit change.[80] Steevens restored the original in 1785, but without acknowledgment.

The rhetorical figure which attracted most displeasure was, as ever, the pun. Some writers merely note, or gloss, Shakespeare's wordplay, or describe it as the taste of the age in which he wrote,[81] but most attack it mercilessly. Malone complains of a 'wretched quibble', and often finds that 'the sense is almost lost in the jingle of words'. Steevens apologizes for Shakespeare: 'I am afraid our bard is at his quibbles again'. He finds most jingles 'disgusting', yet is prepared to use the presence or absence of puns as a test of the authenticity of a play.[82] Francis Gentleman constantly complains about 'low quibbling comedy', 'paltry punning', comic scenes being 'incumbered with quibble and obscurity', and his displeasure is shared by Mrs Griffith, Francis Douce, Alexander Gerard, and another ten writers represented here.[83] Occasionally we find a critic refusing to believe that Shakespeare would pun. Reviewing Malone's 1790 edition, Thomas Pearne denied that a quibble is intended in Macbeth's 'And make the green, one red', or in Othello's 'Put out the light', and claimed that the 'whole corps' of *Monthly* reviewers, 'which is pretty numerous, are ready to hold up their hands' in his support. Another reviewer, dealing with Steevens's 1793 edition, said of Lady Macbeth's 'gild/guilt' (2.2.56f.: 'Could *Shakespeare* possibly mean to play upon the similitude of *gild* and *guilt*?' Johnson had asked, perhaps in disbelief: Vol. 5, p. 143) that Shakespeare may have punned,

but fond as he was of quibbles, to suspect him of designing it in this animated passage is almost to deny him common sense: he could hardly have intended it without betraying as great a want of feeling as of taste.

Loyal as this reviewer was, other critics could complain, with Davies, that Portia 'saves the life of the Merchant by the help of a quibble',[84] or regret that Shakespeare should have 'supported, with uniform propriety, one of the most difficult characters' ever attempted, Othello, but 'at last fall off, and put a trifling conceit in the mouth of a dying man' (No. 300).

The overwhelming verdict was against Shakespeare's wordplay; but there were some exceptions. William Cooke, following Kames (Vol. 4, pp. 480f.), showed how Shakespeare used puns to characterize Faulconbridge (No. 250), and Ritson referred puns to their dramatic situation, as did Capell, who perceptively notes that the punning-combat in *Romeo and Juliet* (Act II, scene 4) shows Romeo 'in a new light', now more than a match for Mercutio after his declaration of love to Juliet (No. 263, note 55). Of the punning dialogue between Antonio and Sebastian in *The Tempest*, mocking Gonzalo, Capell says that it 'opens to us their characters', their 'levities' showing their lack of gratitude or concern for the king, contrasting with 'the love, loyalty, and sobriety' of Gonzalo.[85] Besides these remarks on dramatic function there are signs of an increased understanding of the nature of wordplay: Beattie rejects the idea that it derives its force from 'an opposition of meanness and dignity', rather from 'a mixture of sameness and diversity—sameness in the sound, and diversity in the signification'. Thomas Pearne, denying that Miranda would pun on the word 'maid', defined the characters and situation in which wordplay usually is found:

> the equivoque either proceeds from some ignorant illiterate character. . . or else it is made in some playful, ironical, sarcastic, or other sportive mood . . . . These things, likewise, when of the latter kind, are always expressed in such a way that the speakers perceive that there is a change of meaning, and shew clearly to the reader that they do so.

Since Ferdinand does not react, no pun was intended.[86] But the best of all the defences of Shakespeare's wordplay is the brief but pregnant note by Morgann (p. 175 below), another proof of his critical intelligence.

If readers of Shakespeare in this period did not like figures of wordplay or the repetition of similar sounds, they certainly disapproved of Shakespeare's use of rhyme; indeed, this is an almost unanimous reaction. If we take the main editors and critics, they are all agreed that Shakespeare 'knowingly sacrificed grammar to rhyme . . . when he found it convenient': this is frequently stated by Mason and Malone,[87] while even Capell, who has so many sensitive observations on Shakespeare's poetry, regards rhyme as one of 'the time's vices' (No. 263, note 44). Davies censures D'Avenant's adaptation of *Macbeth* for pleasing a Restoration audience by introducing 'the jingle of rhyme', while, conversely, Fennell praises Garrick's version of *Romeo and Juliet* for cutting 'the perpetual jingling of rhymes that Shakespeare was so very fond of'. A third man of the theatre, Francis Gentleman, delivers the most outspoken attacks on what he dismisses as 'rhiming excrescences',[88] protesting at 'alternate rhimes'—the most 'strange and unnatural' type (No. 243, note 73). He finds the rhymed speech that ends *Antony and Cleopatra* 'contemptible' (note 29), and reserves most scorn for the octosyllabic rhymes of the Duke in *Measure for Measure*: 'namby-pamby versification', he calls it, and 'abominable' (notes 15, 16). Gentleman is uninhibited, but his negative judgments on rhyme are typical of this whole period, in which it is regarded as an inexplicable and unnecessary feature of Shakespeare's art, the only saving grace being that he abandoned it as he got older.

The question of chronology was also raised in the comments on Shakespeare's versification. Here two contradictory models were applied: according to the first, of which Steevens is the leading exponent, Shakespeare's early verse is rough and irregular, maturity bringing him smoothness and polish. According to the second—which would be the view of modern scholars, and which is represented here by Capell—the early verse is regular and relatively inexpressive, while the mature style is more varied, more powerful, and more irregular. Steevens writes of *The Tempest*, for instance, that 'it was evidently one of the last works of Shakespeare; and it is therefore natural to suppose the metre of it must have been exact and regular'. Elsewhere he writes that modern ears have been 'tuned to verse harmony by Pope', which may explain, although it does not justify, the extraordinary steps he took to regularize Shakespeare's metre in the 1793 edition.[89] Contrary evidence, of greater metrical freedom in the late plays, had been available since 1758 with Richard Roderick's pioneer essay on the verse of *Henry VIII* (Vol. 4, pp. 338ff.), but this was brusquely rejected by Malone and Steevens.[90] Capell, by contrast, can point to the early plays and describe their general characteristic as a metrical 'tameness', lacking the variety which Shakespeare was soon to develop (No. 263, notes 68, 78).

In addition to many incidental comments on the beauty, expressiveness, and metrical freedom of Shakespeare's verse, only some of which I have been able to include here, Capell wrote a long and remarkable essay on Shakespeare's verse, unique in its own time, and indeed since, this being notoriously one of the most difficult and least-studied topics in Shakespeare.[91] Capell's *'brief Essay'* begins from first principles, defining the constituent parts of verse, voice, pronunciation, time, and metre, using stress rather than quantity as the determining factor. He classifies and illustrates Shakespeare's normal practice in iambic and trochaic, and lays great stress on his use of the pause, and other extra-normal features such as 'the redundant syllable', all of which are explained as licences taken by Shakespeare in order to give 'sufficient variety to verse design'd for the stage'. Capell attempts a descriptive prosody, drawing attention to the activities of Pope and Hanmer in hacking the text about to achieve a Procrustean pentameter: other contemporaries, such as Francis Gentleman, would tolerate no irregularity in verse.[92] Capell's analysis is at times dense, and his use of such terms as 'Semi-breve Trochee' and 'Semi-breve Iambus' shows the great difficulty of accounting for monosyllables and short feet, but the whole essay is a remarkable scholarly and critical achievement, illuminated by a keen ear and a good sense of dramatic function. While the clique around Malone, Farmer, and Steevens ignored, slighted, plagiarized, and abused Capell, one person at least gave him full credit. The *English Review* said that the essay 'is in our opinion the chef d'oeuvre of this writer', containing 'much closeness of thought and ingenuity of discovery', and granting the poet his true freedom. Capell 'has ascribed to Shakespeare a versification full of eccentricities, and full of a rich and inexhaustible variety'. The reviewer said that no subject had been 'less accurately investigated than that of English prosody', and thanked Capell for breaking the ground for others to follow:[93] some two hundred years later I offer readers this virtually unknown landmark in Shakespeare studies as an illuminating essay in its own right, and an incitement to further work.

Most of the commentary on Shakespeare's language and poetry so far discussed has been critical and negative, and that is an accurate reflection of contemporary taste. Yet at some point, however harsh they had been, nearly all of these writers found something to praise. Francis Gentleman could become warmly appreciative of some favourite passages, while there are general appreciations by Blair (No. 272), by Samuel Badcock—'The grand characteristic of Shakespeare's language is energy—an energy which astonishes the imagination!'—and by such writers as Belsham and Alves.[94] Johnson, playing the *enfant terrible*, criticizes Edgar's 'Dover cliff' speech, and Macbeth's description of night ('the beetle and the bat detract from the general idea of darkness,—inspissated gloom': No. 301). In sharp contrast is Capell's response: 'the scene is in the highest degree beautiful, both for passion and poetry' (No. 263, note 42). Equally warm, and unhackneyed, is his response to 'a most exalted conception' and sign of Shakespeare's 'Genius' in *Timon of Athens* (notes 66, 67), and his defence of Juliet's epithet 'fiery-footed steeds', criticized by Heath for 'impropriety': 'it is well cover'd by a beauty which its usage produces—an exulting and triumphing air in the verse's flow'.[95]

Capell stands out in this period for his understanding of the expressive functions of poetry, in characterization and in specific dramatic contexts. His many notes on the suitability of language to character mark him as a rare critic of Shakespeare's style, while he is the only commentator to wrestle with the difficulties of language in *Troilus and Cressida*. Comments by other critics are, in comparison, rather disappointing and conventional: Cumberland notes the frequency of Macbeth's imagery as a sign of his response to gloom; Mason defends the 'Dover cliff' speech, since Edgar is describing only 'an imaginary precipice'; Beattie praises Shakespeare's simplicity; Richardson shows Falstaff's liking for 'the ridiculous comparison'.[96] Otherwise we find little perceptive criticism.

Steevens has few comments on Shakespeare's poetry, but on one issue he expressed himself forcibly, and influentially; Shakespeare's sonnets and poems. These had not been included in Johnson's edition of 1765, nor in Steevens's revisions of it in 1773 and 1778, but when Malone came to issue his two-volume *Supplement* in 1780 he printed the *Sonnets*, *Venus and Adonis*, *The Rape of Lucrece*, *The Passionate Pilgrim*, and *A Lover's Complaint*. Steevens had reprinted the *Sonnets* in 1766, but without com-

mentary: now Malone added a commentary, as he had for the
plays, and invited Steevens to supply notes. The result was a
running controversy, as Steevens expressed a violent dislike of
Venus and Adonis (No. 265, note 7) and the *Sonnets* (notes 9–12).
He rejects the narrative poem for the odd reason that Adonis is not
more responsive to Venus, and has a perverse liking for hunting;
and for the less personal reason that the story is spun out too long,
and lacks drama. Malone defends the narrative poems
—somewhat uneasily—(No. 265, note 8; 1790 edition, No. 299,
notes 37, 38) since they were extremely popular in their day, must
have appealed to Elizabethan taste, and the poets of that period were
given to writing at great length. Steevens's case against the sonnets
is partly moral (on sonnet 20 he finds it 'impossible to read this
fulsome panegyrick, addressed to a male object, without an equal
mixture of disgust and indignation') and partly literary, since he
finds 'laboured perplexities of language' and 'studied deformities
of style' throughout, and dismisses their artificiality: 'But what has
truth or nature to do with Sonnets?' Malone tries to defend them
from the implicit charge of homosexuality by showing that
expressions of affection between men were common in the
Elizabethan age (No. 299, notes 42, 43). Malone, never much at
ease in aesthetic matters, expresses his own difficulty in understanding the sonnets (No. 265, note 11), offers one hesitant defence of
them as poetry (No. 299, note 40), and seems more at home in
using them for biographical speculation (No. 265, note 14;
No. 299, notes 42, 43).

The objections made by Steevens were expressed with all his
polemical energy, but they were generally shared, not some
personal idiosyncrasy. Francis Gentleman, giving a perfunctory
preface to Bell's shoddy reprint of the poems, said that 'many of his
subjects are trifling, his versification mostly laboured and quibbling, with too great a degree of licentiousness'. Yet to have
censured the offending passages, he believed, would be an 'over-
strained . . . piece of prudery' (No. 243, note 86). By the time of
his 1793 edition Steevens was ready to take that step, announcing
in the preface that he has not reprinted 'the Sonnets,
&c . . . . because the strongest act of Parliament that could be
framed would fail to compel readers into their service'(No. 303).
His objections were directed not only against Shakespeare's
practice but against the sonnet as a form, which he expresses with

wit and parody (No. 265, note 15). Malone, loyal to Shakespeare, defends the genre, and for once in his life finds himself virtually alone among Shakespeare critics. The dominant attitude to the sonnet in the eighteenth century was dislike. Monck Mason found Shakespeare's collection 'very miserable', blaming this 'quaint and languid kind of poem of Italian origin', unsuitable to the English language. Ritson regretted the valuable time that Shakespeare

sacrificed to the false taste of his age, in the composition of above 150 sonnets (the most difficult and insipid metrical structure ever invented), which, though from the pen of this immortal bard, we can scarcely endure to read!

In the *Monthly Review* Ogle wrote that 'to be confined within the limits of fourteen lines . . . and those lines crampt by an ill-contrived recurrence of rhimes, is a situation not to be voluntarily sought by poets'. A later reviewer, Thomas Pearne, agreed with Steevens's 'condemnation' of the poems, 'which . . . are in general very paltry', and both the *British Critic* and the *Critical Review* accepted his 'suppression' of them. At the end of this period Nathan Drake endorses Steevens for 'forbearing to obtrude such crude efforts upon the public eye'. Of all the many ways in which eighteenth-century attitudes to Shakespeare differ from our own, this wholesale rejection of the sonnets is the most striking. The solitary exception was Capell.[97]

VII

In studying the reception of Shakespeare, or of any other major writer, over a long historical period the modern reader is involved in a constant series of adjustments and comparisons. We work with a triangle, consisting of Shakespeare in his age, the eighteenth-century critics in theirs, and ourselves in our own: which, no less than the others, has a critical and aesthetic system that is inherited, consciously or not, and shaped by many influences. We can juxtapose our understanding of Shakespeare with the eighteenth century's understanding of him, and with our understanding of them. This triple process of comparative interpretation ought to make us see that our position is also time-bound, and culture-bound, ought to prevent us from feeling any easy sense of superiority. Another age will arise that may look at our Shakespeare criticism with reactions ranging from indulgent apology to disbelief and contempt. One aim of studying the critical judgments of the past is to make us aware of the relationship, in their work as in our own, between judgment and interpretation, and the critical assumptions or methodology that—often unconsciously—produce those judgments. We will not be led into a complacent sense of progress.

Yet in one area it is legitimate to speak of progress, since indeed it can be clearly traced through this sequence of texts, and that is in Shakespeare scholarship. Sustained study, the searching of archives, parish registers, manuscript collections in the British Museum, those of Oxford and Cambridge colleges—these and other resources led in this period, thanks to the work of Capell, Ritson, Malone, Steevens, Reed, Douce, and many more, to a striking improvement in the state of knowledge about Shakespeare's language and sources, the chronology of his plays, Elizabethan printing and publishing, and above all the Elizabethan and Jacobean theatres. Yet, then as now, scholarship is controlled by taste or critical assumptions that are often unquestioned. To the people of the eighteenth century, with their model of history as a progress of ever-greater refinement which had placed them in the highest degree of culture yet known, it was perhaps inevitable that Shakespeare's age should continue to be regarded, as it had been by Dr Johnson and Mrs Montagu, as one of barbarity. Before Shakespeare, we are often told, even by Samuel Badcock, 'the drama was little cultivated, or understood. Not one play that was published before 1592 will bear a second reading'. *Enfin Shakespeare vint*: that is the message of critics who confine the period before him to some Gothic darkness. In Malone's words, 'At length (about the year 1591) the great luminary of the dramatic world blazed out. . . . '[98]

It must have been a satisfying feeling to write such a sentence, with its dramatic moment of change. Yet, like much else, it shows Malone's allegiance to older attitudes, for in this period we find the gradual recognition that Shakespeare had learned much from the great flowering of English Renaissance humanism. John Berkenhout, in his 'Biographical History of Literature' (No. 252), rejoices to find himself reaching 'the daylight of the sixteenth century', when 'we are dazzled with a multiplicity of authors in various branches of literature', including 'Kings, queens, and many of our nobility'. Horace Walpole, in his *Anecdotes of Painting in England* (1762), had shown the high state of culture in the court of Henry VIII,[99] and John Andrews, in *An Inquiry into the Manners, Taste, and Amusements of the Two Last Centuries in England* (1782), vigorously attacked the Augustans' image of Tudor barbarism by describing the 'flourishing condition of literature and the polite arts' in the age of Queen Elizabeth: 'they were held in the highest estimation, and cultivated by all ranks' (p. 72). Andrews writes to 'obviate the absurd notions of some' contemporaries, who ascribe to the Elizabethans 'an asperity of manners' due to their 'want of polite improvements in their ways of living' (pp. 74f.). The most important of these more enlightened accounts of Elizabethan culture was Thomas Warton's *History of English Poetry* (Vol. I: 1774; II: 1778; III: 1781). Warton has not entirely freed himself from giving an exaggerated place to Shakespeare, for he writes of Marlowe that

His tragedies manifest traces of a just dramatic conception, but they abound with tedious and uninteresting scenes, or with such extravagancies as proceeded from a want of judgment, and those barbarous ideas of the times, over which it was the peculiar gift of Shakespeare's genius alone to triumph and to predominate. (III, p. 455)

Yet, drawing on some sound scholarship of the age, Warton gives a sensible account of Elizabethan literary history, ending indeed by describing it as 'the golden age of English poetry' (No. 266). In the rediscovery of the past the commentaries on, and editions of, Shakespeare had played no little role, by the vast amount of documentation they contained. A reviewer of the 1785 edition in the *Critical* noted the cumulative effect of these annotations: 'they point out the state of society, of science, and the more polished amusements of that time', while Philip Neve found that the quantity of research expended on Shakespeare made the editions of great educational value: 'So large and valuable a body of criticism is this commentary now become that perhaps there is no work, or series of works, that could so far contribute to form and establish a taste for antient English literature, as the notes that are at present subjoined to his Plays'.[100]

One particular topic within the knowledge of 'antient English literature' that concerns us is the extent of Shakespeare's education. A number of writers had pointed to similarities between Shakespeare and classical authors, and deduced that he had had a good education in Latin, and perhaps knew some Greek. Richard Farmer set out to refute these charges in his *Essay on Shakespeare's Learning* (1767), and succeeded in showing that many more translations of the classics were available to Shakespeare than had previously been supposed, and that the poet certainly drew on North's Plutarch, and Golding's Ovid. Yet still, as Capell, Colman, and Guthrie proved,[101] there was substantial evidence of Shakespeare's knowledge of Latin. The dispute continued into this period. Farmer went on collecting materials for a third edition of his book (all these notes are in the Folger Shakespeare Library), and in notes contributed to later editions and in many as yet unpublished letters reaffirmed his case, which was solidly backed by the other two of the triumvirate, Steevens and Malone, who lost few opportunities of reiterating that Shakespeare knew no Latin. Yet at the same time they, other contributors to the editions they put out, and many writers in the journals, were constantly finding more parallels between Shakespeare and the classics. Their position was contradictory. The only writers to affirm Shakespeare's knowledge of Latin are Capell, who shows convincingly how his Latin quotations are integrated into the dramatic context, and are reshaped by him, or even invented, in perfectly correct metre (No. 263, notes 6, 9, 14), and Colman, reviewing Capell and reiterating his own arguments.[102]

The question of Shakespeare's knowledge of languages, or of books, is important for the determination of his indebtedness. It had long been known that Shakespeare had had specific sources for most of his plays, and a typical, but unusually virulent, Neo-classic critic, Mrs Charlotte Lennox (Vol. 4, No. 141), claimed that when Shakespeare deviated from his sources it was invariably for the worse. The first full scholarly and critical discussion was that of Capell in 1768 (Vol. 5, pp. 321ff.), showing that Shakespeare's invention and reshaping of his materials was considerable. In many comments in the *Notes and Various Readings* (printed 1779–80) he compared plays with their sources, both in the whole and in specific episodes, to demonstrate Shakespeare's free rehandling of narrative and character, his re-moulding, improving on his sources, falsifying facts where he intends to re-dispose emphasis (making Antony less unpleasant than he was in reality),[103] and showing how he departed from the ground-work of *The Winter's Tale* 'in many particulars that are to the play's advantage' (No. 263, note 81). George Colman took a similar view, commenting on the old play of *King Leir*: 'Such were the sparks, such the fuel, that served to light up and feed the genius of Shakespeare'. Comparison of the dramatist with his sources, Colman wrote, 'will rather serve to raise than depreciate his genius in the estimation of the reader',[104] an opinion shared by Beattie (No. 251) and Samuel Badcock (No. 262).

Yet, on the other side, there is the figure of Malone, pronouncing that Shakespeare intended to follow the source for *Hamlet* just as it exists in Saxo Grammaticus. In 1780 Malone claimed that 'the poet intended to tell his story as it had been told before' (No. 265, note 5), deducing from that supposition Shakespeare's attitude to the guilt of Rosencrantz and Guildenstern (note 6), and asserting that the author of *Pericles* 'pursued the story exactly as he found it', a practice 'which Shakespeare is known to have followed in many plays, and to which most of the faults that have been urged against his drama may be imputed' (note 18). In the 1790 edition Malone noted that there was a play *'within a play'* in Kyd's *Spanish Tragedy*, and added: 'if the old play of *Hamlet* should ever be recovered, a similar interlude, I make no doubt, would be found there' (I, part 1, p. 306). This is to move from stating that Shakespeare had models to denying him any invention. Later in that edition he said of the betrayal of the rebels in *2 Henry IV* that 'Shakespeare here, as in many other places, has merely followed the historians' (No. 299, note 19), and explained the irregular mythology of *Venus and Adonis* with the suggestion that Shakespeare 'merely, . . . in the present instance, as in many others, followed the story as he found it already treated by preceding English writers' (*ibid.*, note 37). This is to reduce Shakespeare to a mere passive copier from the easiest available source, and although Steevens subsequently protested that Shakespeare was to be interpreted from the plays themselves, not from their sources (No. 303, note 50), Malone's prestige influenced Warton and others,[105] his low view of Shakespeare's art standing in sharp contrast to Capell's.

One cannot write the history of Shakespeare scholarship or criticism in the eighteenth century, unfortunately, without descending to personalities. Groups were formed with coherent opinions, the Malone–Steevens–Farmer triumvirate opposing Capell, Colman, and the rest—until Malone and Steevens split up and opposed each other. The same grouping of parties can be seen in the controversies over the authenticity of half a dozen disputed plays. In 1768 Capell had argued for the genuineness of the three parts of *Henry VI*, *Titus Andronicus*, *Love's Labour's Lost*, and *The Taming of the Shrew* (Vol. 5, pp. 306ff.). On *Titus Andronicus* Capell subsequently added a note on the integrity of its style, and its Latinisms, within Shakespeare's development (No. 263, note 68). Malone quoted the earlier note in the 1778 edition merely to mock Capell, and at that point denied Shakespeare's authorship. In the 1785 edition Malone speculated that *Titus*, *Locrine*, and the play in *Hamlet* were all written by Marlowe.[106] In 1790, however, he printed *Titus* in Volume X with the title 'A Tragedy Erroneously Ascribed to Shakespeare', described it as 'a spurious piece', and thought that Heminge and Condell included it in the First Folio only because Shakespeare 'wrote a few lines in it' (X, pp. 375–7; No. 299, note 44). Quite missing from Malone's account is any consideration of the testimony of Shakespeare's editors, or of the similarities with the other plays. But a later passage in Volume I, written after the discovery of the Dulwich College papers, grants at least one scene to Shakespeare, and in the 1793 edition Steevens and Malone add many parallels to other Shakespeare plays (e.g. XIII, pp. 291f., 306, 316–18, etc.). It seems as if Malone's scholarship had been affected by his distaste for the piece, one shared by Steevens (cf. No. 257, notes 12, 13). On this issue we must prefer Capell, or Mrs Griffith (No. 249, note 9), or Ritson (No. 274).[107]

Malone and Steevens presented a united front here, but on *Pericles* they differed at some length in 1780, attacking each other's interpretation (No. 265, notes 15, 16). Malone argued that it was authentic, Steevens that Shakespeare had merely corrected it, and although he disputed the point then, by 1790 Malone had come round to Steevens's point of view (No. 299, note 11), which indeed was ably expressed, and used a number of criteria for determining authorship. On the *Henry VI* trilogy Malone also changed his mind, first pronouncing it authentic (1780 *Supplement*, 1.205), but then writing a long dissertation in 1787 to argue for part-authorship (1790: VI, pp. 377–429: excerpt in No. 299, note 23). Unfortunately, Malone's case that the plays are revisions is based on a misunderstanding of the relationship between the Folio, which gives the authentic text, and the Quartos. Malone thought that these were old plays, which Shakespeare had revised, whereas in fact they are 'Bad' Quartos, versions reconstructed from actors' memories. Malone cannot be blamed for not knowing this, but the point I make is the uncertainty of many of the scholarly criteria then employed. At least Malone was cautious, and careful, unlike Ritson, who—aided and abetted by Steevens—began a phase of 'disintegration' of Shakespeare's text in the 1793 edition. On the whim of the moment, it often seems, and with no evidence to support their intuitions, they decided that *The Comedy of Errors* was 'not originally' Shakespeare's, but the work of 'some inferior playwright' who had enough Latin to read Plautus' *Menaechmi* in the original (once again Farmer's argument for Shakespeare's lack of learning proved to have damaging consequences). Steevens, who had never liked Shakespeare's early plays, agreed (No. 303, note 11), while Ritson went on to stigmatize *The Two Gentlemen of Verona*, *Love's Labour's Lost*, and *Richard II* as not wholly Shakespearian (note 10). Ritson claimed that the 'alternately rhyming parts' of *Love's Labour's Lost* were 'apparently by an inferior hand', the remains of the old play (1793: V, p. 379), and on similar reasons of taste alone, unsupported by any evidence, Ritson and Steevens dismissed the masque in *Cymbeline* as an interpolation (No. 303, note 36), truly a harking-back to the attitudes and methods of Pope. Steevens believed that the Fool's part in *Lear* included actors' gags (note 40), and they jointly agreed that *Troilus and Cressida* was in many places not Shakespearian (notes 29–31). This disturbing piecemeal rejection of passages or scenes merely because they did not suit a critic's taste would be enough to make us question any easy idea of the automatic progress of scholarship. Knowledge does advance, but it also stands still, or reverts to earlier states, unless it keeps a grasp on basic principles and can justify its deductions by reference to a valid methodology. Steevens and Ritson seem to have forgotten everything, and might have undone the work of decades.

Turning to the treatment of Shakespeare's text by his editors and commentators, in one area there was a steady advance of knowledge, and that was the glossing of the text from contemporary literature and social history to establish norms of linguistic usage or explain difficult allusions. Thomas Pearne, reviewing Malone, described the commentator on Shakespeare as 'a dealer in obscurity and a haberdasher of difficulties' (*Monthly Review*, n.s. xii, 1793, p. 56). One commentator spent forty years of his life collecting materials to elucidate Shakespeare, and anyone who has the stamina to work through the 1,800 double-column pages of Edward Capell's *Notes and Various Readings* will learn a great deal about the meaning of the text and its contemporary context, as in the vast collection of illustrative quotation, the third volume, called *The School of Shakespeare*. I have not included much of this material here, since it has been absorbed into our general knowledge about Shakespeare and his age, but some of the notes explaining the allusions of Poor Tom (No. 263, notes 22, 24, 25), and Lear in his madness (note 28), or Leontes in his (note 80), are still valuable. Capell well sums up the principle at stake in his comment after explaining the meaning of 'Banbury cheese': 'This remark may appear trivial, and even ridiculous, to a multitude of readers; but may not be so look'd upon by foreigners, and times long distant' (note 45).

The great repository for such notes was the Johnson–Steevens edition. Steevens had sole responsibility for the enlarged versions that appeared in 1773 and 1778 (No. 257) but for 1785 (No. 279) he shared the task with Isaac Reed, announcing that he had ceased to edit Shakespeare, although that edition includes many new notes by Steevens and his collaborators, indeed it gives credit to over fifty commentators. Malone had contributed to the 1778 edition, and in 1780 issued a substantial two-volume supplement to it (No. 265), containing more notes, allusions, appendices, errata, and further notes, a bewildering amount of material to which he added a second appendix in 1783 (No. 275). Malone issued a duodecimo edition in 1786, and in 1790 produced the ten (in fact eleven) volume edition (No. 299) for which he became famous. Steevens, galled by Malone's rather disparaging treatment of him, decided to emerge from retirement, and by extraordinarily intense work produced in eighteen months a fifteen-volume edition (No. 303). Of course, none of these editions began from scratch, either for the text or for the notes; each used its predecessors, notes being regarded as public property: since they were signed they became familiar in their various reappearances, as contemporary comments show.[108]

Anyone looking at these notes today is bound to be impressed by the quantity, and range, of learning that they display, digested and addressed to the specific textual difficulties. Already in 1778 Steevens made a vast addition of illustrative quotations, providing

48

a fund of learning about sixteenth- and seventeenth-century literature and social customs. Information abounds about swords, fans, brothels, rare words such as 'pict-hatch' or 'baccare' (for which Steevens manages to find three quotations); rare texts are ransacked, for one word ('Mome' meaning 'Mum') Steevens citing Heywood's *Rape of Lucrece*, Ingeland's *The Disobedient Child*, Robert Wilson's *Cobler's Prophecy*, *Tom Tyler and his Wife*, and *Albion's England*. He draws on manuscripts, such as the Chester collection of *Whitsun Mysteries*, Middleton's *The Witch*, and the play of the Werewolf, from a manuscript in King's College, Cambridge.[109] Publication of such an edition marked a great contribution to learning, and it stimulated further research: the reviewers at the time commonly discussed particular passages, adding their own suggestions, while the journals for years to come would carry small or large corrections and additions. Introducing the 1785 edition Isaac Reed said that 'the zeal for elucidating Shakespeare' had not abated, the same 'laborious search into the literature, the manners, and the customs of the times' was producing ever-more information (I, pp. i f.). Reed himself made many valuable additions, as did Steevens and Malone, Henley, Holt White, and (in the 1793 edition) Francis Douce. But in the 1780s and 1790s we find increasing complaints that the notes had become too voluminous. Porson, writing his first review for the *Monthly* in 1788, allowed that 'The present age may justly boast of the great improvements which it has made in the art of note-writing', but added caustically that the illustration of the author is 'only an incidental object; the first grand purpose of the critic is to display his own wit and learning', adding irrelevancies if need be.[110] For his 1790 edition Malone made substantial cuts in the number and length of the notes he had printed, but Steevens—who had compiled some of the longest notes, as on the potato as an aphrodisiac, on stewed prunes, or on a phrase such as 'cry aim' (for which there are two pages of quotation)—called Malone's 'a very succinct edition', and in his own of 1793 returned to the expansive tradition, producing the biggest edition of Shakespeare. Well might Lord Hailes complain that the text was now so swollen as to become 'the burden of many camels'.[111]

Yet while impressed as we must be with the amount of knowledge brought for elucidation, the work of these editors on the text of Shakespeare was less satisfactory. An experienced and intelligent reader of any text in any period can guess at a necessary correction, and his suggestions can have the force of virtual certainty, and indeed be confirmed by more systematic inquiry. Such was the contribution made in this period by John Monck Mason (No. 283), who disarmingly explained that he had relied on others to collate the texts, but was nevertheless able, by sheer good sense, to correct many of Steevens's errors, and to suggest many useful alterations; such piecemeal improvement was made by other writers included here (Nos 281, 289). But any textual criticism that wishes to make a more coherent contribution must establish the authentic texts, group them according to provenance and authority, collate them for variant readings, and select from alternatives according to some coherent and rational system. These principles, although become vastly more complex in our own age, were well enough understood in the eighteenth century, which had of course some distinguished models in the editing of classical texts. The need for collation, for instance, had been stated by Tyrwhitt (Vol. 5, No. 210) and put into practice by Capell in 1768 (Vol. 5, No. 220), and by Jennens in a series of editions from 1770 on (e.g., Vol. 5, No. 225).

Collation is an extremely time-consuming business, and one which is difficult to do fully accurately. Yet it is essential, and that they acknowledged it to be essential can be deduced from the fact that Johnson, Malone, and Steevens all claimed, at one time or another, to have carefully collated the early texts of Shakespeare. A mere glance at their notes, and a comparison of them with the notes of Jennens, or the quantities of 'various readings' published by Capell, will at once arouse scepticism, while anyone who sits down to compare their work with the originals will soon find how little they did. One reader who did this with vehement and acrimonious accuracy was Joseph Ritson, whose *Remarks, Critical and Illustrative, on the Text and Notes of the Last Edition of Shakespeare* (1783) keeps up the high standard of that genre invented by Theobald in *Shakespeare Restored* (1726), the criticism of a Shakespeare edition. I have selected a few of Ritson's notes which include literary criticism, notably his defence of Hamlet (No. 274), but much of his book consists of precise indications of the errors and inaccuracies caused by the failure to collate the early editions. Ritson finds dozens of instances where Johnson and Steevens are simply wrong in their statements about which reading is in which edition, showing over and over again that they did not even consult the Folio. Johnson had said that *Hamlet* was more correctly printed there than other plays, and Ritson comments that such an

assertion could only proceed from his never having looked into it. If any one play is in that edition more incorrect than all the rest it is *Hamlet*. Even the accuracy of Mr. Steevens has suffered some hundreds of its various readings to escape him. (p. 190 note)

Ritson subsequently performed the same office for Malone, in his *Cursory Criticisms on the Edition of Shakespeare published by Edmond Malone* (1792), which exposed his failure to collate properly, and criticized the editor's 'total want of *ear* and *judgment*' (pp. vi–ix). Malone took great offence at these criticisms, filling his own copy of the book with abuse, and defending himself with equal acrimony, the quarrel between them declining to a sad level.[112] Yet Malone did not learn from it: in the 1790 edition his collations are just as piecemeal and random. Steevens, who was also attacked by Ritson, subsequently joined forces with him—perhaps to spite Malone, with whom he had fallen out—but despite their collaboration on the 1793 edition Steevens was not moved to change his practice on collation, either. Indeed, he developed in exactly the opposite direction, making many scornful references to pedants who would shackle an editor by scrutinizing every word in every text.[113] We must not let Steevens's wit and polemical brilliance blind us to the fact that, like Malone, he was seriously deficient in one of the fundamental duties of an editor. The only correct example in this period was provided by Capell, and, as in all other aspects, his work never achieved recognition, partly due to the abuse heaped on it by Malone, Steevens, and co.,[114] and partly due to the unfortunate way his life-work reached the public, in instalments over a period of fifteen years.

Malone and Steevens, having helped to ensure that Capell would not be taken seriously, enjoyed much prestige in their own day, and still do. Much of it they deserved, but if we move from collation to their general conception of Shakespeare's texts, we meet another disappointment. The question at issue is the status, and provenance, of the First Folio (1623) compared with the various Quartos of the plays. In his edition of 1725 (Vol. 2, No. 71) Pope had undermined the authority of the Folio as being the work of ignorant 'player editors', a travesty which was exposed by Theobald (No. 74) and by the actor John Roberts (No. 77), both of whom defended the Folio and gave a sensible account of its relation with the Quartos. Johnson was rather vague in his edition, claiming that the First Folio was the only text of authority, although in practice he followed Pope in occasionally referring to the Quartos. The first proper discussion of the relationship between Folios and Quartos was made by Capell in the introduction to his edition of 1768 (Vol. 5, pp. 304–7, 311f.), distinguishing the authentic Quartos from the 'surreptitious' ones, and pointing out that the Bad Quartos often preserve a good text, while the Good Quartos abound in all manner of faults (pp. 305f.). He was the first to show that the Folio editors, despite claiming to be issuing fresh and correct texts, in fact set their text from the Quartos in print, and that both Quartos and Folios, in their subsequent re-editions, are merely printed from the preceding one (pp. 306f.). He also judged each text on its merits, and selected the most authentic as his copy-text, enlarging and correcting it by reference to the others (pp. 311f.). This is a sound evaluation of the situation, and a still valid mode of proceeding.

Knowing Capell's discussion, then, it is with some surprise that we find Malone in 1790 announcing that 'the true state of the ancient copies of this poet's writings has never been laid before the publick' (No. 299), a hit not only against Capell but against Steevens, who had discussed the question several times (Vol. 5, Nos 211, 212, 240), in the last of which he freely plagiarized Capell's account. What Malone offers as the first 'true' discussion derives much from Capell, with of course no acknowledgment: that the Folio was printed from the Quartos, and that only the first edition of a play has any authority. Malone makes one new point about the Quartos, but a bad one: where Capell had distinguished thirteen 'Good' Quartos and four 'Bad' ones (that is, 'imperfect and stolen copies': *Henry V, The Merry Wives of Windsor, King John,* and *The Taming of the Shrew:* Vol. 5, pp. 304f.), Malone accepted the first two of this latter group as being 'mutilated and imperfect' but said of the remaining fifteen that 'they were all surreptitious, that is, stolen from the playhouse and printed without the consent of the authour or the proprietors'. This is to destroy a fundamental distinction, and lay all the Quartos under suspicion. Malone dismissed this issue rather briefly, and devoted the greater part of his introduction to the Second Folio, not an issue of equal importance in establishing Shakespeare's text. Johnson had said that the First Folio was the only one of authority, but Steevens had argued that the Second Folio was important for, although incorrectly printed, in places it had 'various readings' which were the proof of deliberate editing, perhaps by a person who had access to Shakespeare's original manuscripts, or knew of the continuing acting tradition. Malone attacked this case at great length, arguing that the 'editor' of the Second Folio (if such a person ever existed) was ignorant both of Shakespeare's phraseology, and of his metre, dismissing him and Pope as 'the two great corrupters of our poet's text'.[115]

While Steevens (No. 303, preface) undoubtedly overstated the degree to which the Second Folio was edited, as we would now understand that process, Malone just as obviously understated the value of its corrections, which were at least made by a printer whose English was much nearer Shakespeare's than any subsequent editor's. Both Steevens and Ritson showed that in many places the Second Folio turned unintelligibility into sense, so that Malone's *a priori* rejection of it could only be denying himself a fruitful aid. But, more damaging still to Malone's professions, they were able to show that in many cases (Steevens computed 186) Malone had actually chosen the Second Folio reading, only acknowledging the fact in a few of these.[116] On this as on other issues, a modern reader will feel, Malone lacked both common sense and flexibility. He was prone to taking a stand and clinging to it in the face of all evidence to the contrary. Steevens and Ritson provide the best account of Malone's *idée fixe* about the Second Folio, but they also expose a much more serious limitation in his work as an editor, his treatment of Shakespeare's verse.

For reasons that are not entirely clear, Malone set out to prove that the Second Folio was ignorant of Shakespeare's metre, and did so by arguing that it had got the quantity of many words wrong. Unfortunately, Malone's proposed corrections turn out to be eccentric, and frequently impossible: we may concede that on occasions 'fires, hire, hour' are disyllabic, but can we make two syllables out of 'Charles', 'arms', 'pours', 'ropes', 'our', or 'burn'? Can 'neither' and 'rather' be monosyllabic, or 'Rouen'? Can any of the following be trisyllabic: 'English; Henry;

dazzled; country; tickled'? And can 'contrary' be quadrisyllabic? Very often the reader of Malone's edition will find a note suggesting that he give a new or unnatural stress to a word. Usually Malone does so because he finds the text (often the First Folio) defective in the length of the pentameter line, often a syllable or so too long or too short. So a line in *The Winter's Tale*:

> The pretty dimples of his chin, and cheek, his smiles (2.3.102)

can only be scanned, he claims, by pronouncing both 'dimples' and 'of his' as monosyllables: Ritson pounced on that impossibility,[117] and Steevens devoted much time, and wit, to listing the resulting absurdities.[118] The problem is that while Malone may solve an immediate problem by syllabificatory manipulations he raises others in the process. As Thomas Pearne said,

> Mr. Malone does not seem to be aware that, by drawing out the pronunciation of some of the poet's words, and by compressing that of others; by reading monosyllables as if they were dissyllables, and *vice versa*, he loses more than he gains. The process does indeed reduce lines which are redundant, or deficient, to the due number of syllables: but at the same time it often so displaces the accents of the remaining words as totally to change their pronunciation and to ruin the reading of the whole.[119]

It is puzzling that a man who had spent as much of his life reading Shakespeare as Malone had should think that Shakespeare's verse was regular. But Malone clung to his convictions rigidly, producing rigid and unnatural verse, a method and a text at the opposite extreme from Capell's granting Shakespeare a versification 'full of eccentricities, and full of a rich and inexhaustible variety'.

Malone's former collaborator, later his most severe critic, George Steevens, was gifted at discovering the motes in other men's eyes, and it must be said that in general he had a far better sense of Shakespeare's language than Malone did, and excelled him in reasoning power and common sense.[120] However, on the question of Shakespeare's metre—of which every editor reveals his conception implicitly in treating every line of every play, and which in practical terms involves the consideration of several thousand 'irregular' or disputed lines—Steevens reveals himself to be no more enlightened than Malone. Where Steevens had shown, in the four earlier editions on which he collaborated, an awareness of Shakespeare's metrical irregularity, in the 1793 edition he adopted the view that Shakespeare's verse was always regular when it left the poet's pen. (Perhaps he was implicitly opposing Capell; or perhaps he was agreeing with Malone but demonstrating his differing treatment of the issue.) According to Steevens, then, any irregularity in the verse was due to the inaccuracy of the transcribers of the plays in manuscript, or to the printers. He therefore makes many unauthorized changes 'for the sake of metre', attacking the 'ignorant play-house editors' and just as ignorant actors, and he evolves a theory to justify his alterations—mostly by omission—to the text.

The tone and the cumulative effect of these changes take us back to the worst textual traditions of Pope, Hanmer, and Warburton. By constantly impugning the accuracy of the 'play-house' editors, Heminge and Condell, Steevens would undermine all confidence in the authority of the First Folio, and give himself a free hand for alteration. In the Preface (No. 303) he says that Shakespeare's text has reached us through various soils, and 'stagnated at last in the muddy reservoir of the first folio', pouring scorn on the actors as textual authorities when compared to 'a Warburton, a Johnson, a Farmer, or a Tyrwhitt'. Steevens has re-grouped the clique around him, omitting Malone, in what is a painfully crude attempt to discredit the major authentic edition. 'But little respect is due to the anomalies of the play-house editors', he writes, and he certainly showed none.[121] In particular, he argues, the players did not understand ellipsis (a rhetorical figure which, he had claimed earlier, was seldom used by Shakespeare: No. 265, note 17). The reasoning behind Steevens's new claim may be stated as follows: many lines exceed the regular pentameter by one or two syllables; they can be normalized by cutting one, or occasionally two, words; this cut will leave a gap in the sense; but that gap can be explained as a deliberate ellipsis on Shakespeare's part; the actors did not understand ellipsis, and therefore inserted the one or two words here deleted. Steevens states his theory in the preface, claims to have the benediction of Farmer, repeats it formally in the notes (No. 303, notes 3, 19) and in dozens of cases proceeds to emend the text.[122]

There is, needless to say, no evidence for any such process of interpolation, and all of these changes can be dismissed as arbitrary and capricious. The principle involved is not only a scholarly one, however, but derives from taste and critical theory. Steevens asks, if 'we find the smoothest series of lines among our earliest dramatic writers (who could fairly boast of no other requisites for poetry) are we to expect less polished versification from Shakespeare?' (note 3). That is, this period's general conception of Shakespeare as the luminary who suddenly burst forth out of the dark ages encourages Steevens to think that he must have excelled in all aspects of drama. So he formally recants: 'Though I once expressed a different opinion, I am now well convinced' that Shakespeare's metre was originally regular (*ibid.*). Yet the conception has unfortunate consequences for his critical perceptions. Whereas in 1778 he had said of the uncompleted conclusion of Macbeth's 'If it were done' soliloquy—

> And falls on the other—

that the incompleteness strongly marks the state of Macbeth's mind (No. 257, note 9), in 1793 he recants again:

I, also, who once attempted to justify the omission of this word ['side', added by Hanmer], ought to have understood that Shakespeare could never mean to describe the agitation of Macbeth's mind by the assistance of a halting verse.

It seems as if his theory must be held just as rigidly as Malone's, not even admitting that common stylistic rhetorical theory whereby dislocations of language represented mental disturbances. However, Steevens will not accept Hanmer's suggestion, 'side', since the word has been used in the plural only two lines before. Arguing that the 'general image, though confusedly expressed, relates to a horse who, overleaping himself, falls, and his rider under him', he reads 'And falls *up*on the other', explicating the resulting exceedingly awkward image and ending with one of his caustic dismissals of the issue: 'Such hazardous things are long-drawn metaphors in the hands of careless writers' (No. 303, note 14). It is disturbing to find Steevens vilifying both Shakespeare and his editors in order to promote his own theories about the desirable regularity of blank verse. Some contemporaries noted this development with regret: but it was not a development but a retrogression.

Malone and Steevens were not entirely irresponsible as

Shakespeare editors, but if we are to evaluate their contribution to textual studies, then it must be said that they did not add on to a developing tradition, but spent time which might have been profitably used in collating early texts to pursue their own personal idiosyncrasies. Their theoretical discussions of Shakespeare's text were designed merely to justify their own obsessions, and their editorial practice demonstrated them at length. One can find more fruitful observations not controlled by their critical systems, the significance of which, indeed, neither they nor anyone else at this time realized. Such were their identification of variant issues of the same Quarto, or Malone's discovery that the First Folio was proof-corrected during printing:[123] these are discoveries whose full meaning was not perceived until modern times, in the work of W. W. Greg and Charlton Hinman, for instance.

Yet, if our final evaluation of Malone and Steevens as textual critics must be negative, it would be unjust not to restate their positive contributions as editors of Shakespeare. First and foremost, they brought an enormous amount of information to bear on elucidating the meaning of the text, both in terms of Elizabethan usage and as concerns recondite allusions. Perhaps their greatest contribution in this period was the rediscovery of information about the Elizabethan theatre. Steevens claimed to have read almost every drama antecedent to Shakespeare (1778: III, p. 310) and he draws on remarkably wide knowledge, both of printed books and manuscripts. Malone contributed his first attempt at a chronology to the 1778 edition (I, 269–346), with accompanying documentation, but it was in his 1780 *Supplement* to that edition, in the long essay on the Elizabethan theatre (I, 1–160), that Malone first showed his abilities in this area. He discussed such topics as the cost of admission, theatre design, the balcony over the stage, the strewing of rushes on the floor, actors' wages, and extant documents, giving the first transcript of *The Platt of the Secound Parte of the Seven Deadlie Sins*, that unique record of Elizabethan production plans. In a later section Malone added further notes, and reprinted more documents (I, 382–96), thus making the first coherent attempt to collect and evaluate this information. Malone is not entirely original (Capell was the first to make use of the Stationer's Register, and his account of the essential bareness of the Elizabethan stage predates Malone's very similar statement), nor is he free from unsupported assumptions (he thought that the Elizabethan stage had a front curtain).[124] But his sifting of the relevant sources, which by the time of the 1790 edition fills a whole volume (Volume I, part 2, pp. 1–284), was a great achievement, especially if compared with the state of knowledge before him. In the 'Emendations and Additions' placed at the end of that volume (pp. 288–331)—a constant feature of all Malone's work on Shakespeare, as he lived through a process of unceasing correcting and amplifying—he printed the Henslowe papers from Dulwich College, those crucial documents for a knowledge of the Elizabethan theatre, which Steevens also reprinted in 1793.[125] Malone also vastly increased his notes to Rowe's *Life of Shakespeare*, assembling many of the materials towards a biography (in the 1785 edition it occupies 28 pages, in 1790 it needs 67): it is not too much to say that in this area the work of such modern scholars as E. K. Chambers and W. W. Greg is handsomely anticipated. Here, at least, their editions deserved to be welcomed as the best that had yet appeared.

VIII

Throughout the period of their editorial labours Malone and Steevens (especially) frequently attended the London theatres, where Shakespeare continued to be one of the staples of the repertory. Yet the major Neo-classic adaptations—Dryden and D'Avenant's *Tempest*, Cibber's *Richard III*, Tate's *Lear*, Garrick's *Romeo and Juliet*—held the stage still, and critical opinion about them was as divided as it had been for the previous forty years. The adapters' work was welcomed by those connected with the theatre, who knew that the alterations had been made to suit public taste, which seems to have been remarkably constant between the 1680s and the 1830s. Francis Gentleman praised the Dryden–D'Avenant *Tempest*, Garrick's *Cymbeline*, *Winter's Tale*, and even applauded his cuts in Act I of *Hamlet*; Thomas Davies approved of Garrick's *Taming of the Shrew* adaptation, and Cibber's *Richard III* (as did George Steevens), and said that *King Lear* had been unpopular until Tate adapted it: with its happy ending it was now deservedly popular.[126] The ending of *King Lear* was an issue that could unite the most diverse groups: we find it praised here by the moralist, that apostle of family harmony, Mrs Griffith (No. 249), as well as by that scything Neo-classic theorist Edward Taylor (No. 247), who is virtually alone in this period in approving Garrick's omission of the 'puerilities' of the gravediggers in *Hamlet* (see Vol. 5, No. 236 and following). Davies criticized Garrick's *Hamlet* sharply, and recorded with satisfaction how the spectators 'would not part with their old friends, the Gravediggers' (No. 277). For once Garrick found that his audience's taste was not the same as his own.

The continuing success of the adaptations in the theatre did not, however, silence criticism of them. The best-informed and most sharply written attack on them came from the pen of George Steevens (No. 259), an essay which is particularly perceptive on the side-effects of the alterations on the whole dramatic structure, their distortions of character and motive. The most unpopular adaptation was Garrick's *Hamlet*, which was attacked not only by Davies but by Colman, Murphy, Walpole, Mackenzie, Steevens, and a writer in the *Critical Review* for 1801.[127] Tate's *Lear* received some scathing attacks from Steevens, who commented on Johnson's remark that 'the public has decided' the issue in favour of Tate: 'Dr. Johnson should rather have said that the managers of the theatres-royal have decided, and the public has been obliged to acquiesce in their decision. The altered play has the upper gallery on its side. . . .' In 1778 the *Morning Chronicle* carried a letter from 'J.R.' hoping that the English would not continue to

anger our immortal Shakespeare's shade by laughing at his *Lear*—a propos, it is inconceivable to me what could induce the manager, or the town, to suffer that wretched jumble of impropriety and childish rhapsody. . . exhibited under the appellation of *King Lear*; when our divine bard has, in his *King Lear*, so nobly and inimitably shewn the utmost power of the Tragic Muse.

I am not at all singular in thinking the curtailing and the alterations in general, of Shakespeare's plays are a very great disgrace to our taste and understanding.

Other critical comments on Tate's version came from Colman, James Harris, and James Boaden.[128]

It would be easy to claim that taste had finally shifted against 'the contemptible alterations', as Malone called them (No. 299), and if we look at the reactions to D'Avenant's *Macbeth* or Cibber's *King*

John the position seems clear.[129] Yet when the young John Philip Kemble mounted *The Tempest* in the winter of 1789 he restored much of the Dryden–D'Avenant text, with further alterations by himself, many of them operatic, which he subsequently published: at least critics were unanimous in disliking the resulting concoction. Kemble's *Coriolanus* of that year was a severely cut version of Shakespeare's text, eked out with passages from James Thomson's 1749 adaptation (see Vol. 3, No. 144).[130] These half-hearted gestures typify a period in which the new adaptations which appeared were small-scale tidyings-up, such as Thomas Hull's *Timon of Athens* or *The Comedy of Errors*, or new centos of the history plays, in Cibber's style, such as those by James Valpy. A curiosity in any period would be the *Antony and Cleopatra* by Henry Brooke (No. 256), printed but never performed, and dismissed by Garrick in the *Monthly*. The power of the managers, or the power of the audience: these were the determining factors. Thomas Davies recorded how Garrick had wanted to restore the Fool in *Lear*, the part to be played by Woodward, 'who promised to be very chaste in his colouring, and not to counteract the agonies of Lear; but the manager would not hazard so bold an attempt'.[131]

Garrick himself was still acting at the beginning of the period represented here, and in 1775 the *London Chronicle* found his Lear still very effective, and in that year Lichtenberg wrote his famous account of Garrick as Hamlet. But the evidence of his declining abilities was all too great: the *London Magazine* visited his last season, 1776, to take leave of an actor who had overcome 'so many native imperfections' by his strong conception, discrimination, 'and the most expressive countenance and propriety of action that ever united in one man.' In May the critic reported on his Richard III, and although he did not approve of the way Garrick 'threw an air of ridicule on some of the most serious passages of the play, and by so doing, commanded plaudits from the galleries', yet he found that 'his faults were *few*, his merits were *many*'. When he revisited the production in June, however, a performance attended by George III[132] 'and his amiable consort', he had to report 'a most incredible *falling off* in the course of a very few days, in his abilities, or in his inclination to exert them'. A defect in Garrick's voice, which he had noted earlier, 'was very perceptible', but he spared it as much as possible, and instead 'was lavish of his looks and constrained attitudes: and in some of the deepest and most affecting scenes, like one of Shakespeare's clowns, set the galleries in a roar'. In the last two acts he finally put forth all the powers he had been husbanding. As Lear he was even more 'apparently deficient': 'In some of the most violent and passionate scenes in the three first acts, he was as tame as a dove; and what his greatest admirers were astonished at, he declined being *half mad enough*'.[133] The holding back of energies is obviously a sign of age and fatigue, for Garrick was after all aged fifty-nine at the time. He retired that season, and died on 20 January 1779.

Reaching a fair estimate of Garrick's contribution to the knowledge and appreciation of Shakespeare remains difficult. His lifelong friend and critic, Samuel Johnson, was disposed to deny him any achievement: 'BOSWELL: But has he not brought Shakespeare into notice? JOHNSON: Sir, to allow that would be to lampoon the age' (No. 301). Walpole was consistent in his dislike of Garrick as a writer and adapter, and Steevens accused him of influencing the taste of the age by pursuing his own interests: 'a strict Attention to his own Emolument, and a careful Estimate of his own Abilities'.[134] But apart from these critical voices Garrick was warmly celebrated, many examples of what we might call the 'Shakespeare–Garrick Poem' appearing in the journals. In one, Shakespeare's ghost appears, in order to approve of his *Hamlet* alteration and to give him *carte blanche* for any further ventures.

> Freely correct my Page:
> I wrote to please a rude unpolish'd age;
> Thou, happy man, art fated to display
> Thy dazling talents in a brighter day;
> Let me partake this night's applause with thee,
> And thou shalt share immortal fame with me.

In another, Shakespeare's ghost breathes patriotic sentiments, and praises '*my Garrick*':

> To him, great leader of the scenic train,
> His Shakespeare's genius never spoke in vain.
> His the applause, the secret powers were mine;
> He was but man, I made him half divine.

And in a prose dialogue the bard's ghost appears to 'applaud . . . a soul so like my own', and to beg Garrick not to retire. This 'Shakespeare' criticizes the bardolatry of the Stratford Jubilee, reproves Garrick for overacting in Cibber's *Richard III*, and admits his own faults, especially punning, the vice of the times. His 'favourite son' magnanimously agrees to soldier on 'a year or two longer'.[135] All these tributes reveal the continuance of the myth of Garrick having been largely responsible for the revival of Shakespeare, which modern scholarship has shown to be false. Yet there was no doubt that the death of Garrick left a gap in the theatre for attracting audiences to Shakespeare, which the talents of such actors as Henderson, Mrs Siddons, and Kemble took many years to supply.[136]

Other features of the London theatres in these years were inimical to the intelligent presentation of Shakespeare. The crudeness of the acting, with its degrading of many scenes into coarse humour, was the subject of many complaints, and by all accounts the witches' scenes in *Macbeth* seem to have been treated as comic. Complaints about actors' ranting, or greediness, are also heard—Thomas Sheridan, when acting Romeo, used to appropriate Mercutio's Queen Mab speech to himself.[137] Audience taste was another factor: the *London Magazine* said of Garrick's comic treatment of Richard III, which had the galleries in 'convulsions of laughter', that 'the absurd effect of his manner of playing this part of the character was not all to be attributed to the actor; to speak impartially, it might be fairly *divided* between him and his auditors in the upper regions'. Thomas Davies records how Garrick tried to restore the rebels' council-scene in *1 Henry IV*, traditionally cut, but that 'after the first or second night's acting, finding that it produced no effect, he consented to omit it'. The audience was the arbiter of taste, and its taste was conservative. Davies also records that the experiment was made of restoring the fainting of Lady Macbeth in performance:

but, however characteristical such behaviour might be, persons of a certain class were so merry upon the occasion that it was not thought proper to venture the Lady's appearance any more. Mr. Garrick thought that even so favourite an actress as Mrs. Pritchard would not, in that situation, escape derision from the gentlemen in the upper regions.

The audience could only have been induced 'to endure the hypocrisy of Lady Macbeth' by some outstanding performance: otherwise, actors and managers had to bow to the wishes of the gallery. It is recorded as one of the triumphs of Mrs Siddons, when she first acted Lady Macbeth, to put down the candle she carried during the sleep-walking scene, in order to perform properly the business of washing her hands. This was a great departure from tradition, and the manager tried to persuade her not to do it, but she persisted, and established this eminently sensible action.[138]

The theatre audience, cramped together in over-heated and exceedingly uncomfortable conditions during excessively long performances, displayed only moderate powers of concentration, keeping up a flow of talk throughout the performance. There are many complaints about their inattentiveness, the fact that they went to the theatre not for the play but for the actors, and their proneness to excessively emotional reactions.[139] The theatre-managers were also held responsible for the unadventurous choice of repertoire and for making major cuts in the text: Arthur Murphy (No. 309) reminded them of their responsibility to improve public taste. Since the managers had a monopoly over serious drama in the two London theatres (excluding oratorios, and lower forms of drama), it was in their interest to maximize profit, and one way of ensuring this was to enlarge the theatres. Garrick enlarged Drury Lane in 1775, and an account of 1780 estimated that both it and Covent Garden could hold about 2,300 spectators. After the reconstruction of Covent Garden in 1782 it could seat 2,500, but after rebuilding in 1792 it could hold 3,013; Drury Lane, after its remodelling in 1794, could seat just over 3,600. H. J. Pye said that the acoustic of Drury Lane had been ruined by the alteration, and hoped that the further expansion of 1792 would improve it. The results, though, were disastrous for the audience's participation in the play, or even its ability to see and hear it. William Taylor protested against

the excessive size of our theatres (a natural consequence of the monopoly which restricts us to two in the season), which renders it impossible for the dialogue to be heard by distant spectators, and compels the managers to provide song and show for their gratification. Opera-houses are fit only for operas.

As a result, Taylor said, the dramas of Shakespeare 'are giving place to musical pageants', and indeed the evidence from the theatre seems to suggest a decline in the number of Shakespeare performances, and a move towards greater, and cruder, spectacle.[140] The situation in the theatre stands in odd contradiction to the universal idolatry of Shakespeare so evident elsewhere. 'Tis good an old age is out'?

IX

As readers will have by now realized, the sheer volume of material devoted to Shakespeare in this period is enough to tax any historian's stamina, or patience. Nearly all of it, whatever judgments we make of its merit, is the product of serious study and a sincere devotion to the task of understanding and appreciating his plays. Yet in addition some works were published which can only be described as bizarre or eccentric. There was a curious attempt by James Hurdis to rewrite the chronology of Shakespeare according to mere whim, and the equally uninformed attempt by 'Charles Dirrill' to controvert Malone's dating of *The Tempest*.[141] Another work which flaunted all canons of scholarship was James Plumptre's *Observation on Hamlet* (1796), 'an Attempt to prove that [Shakespeare] designed it as an indirect censure on Mary Queen of Scots'. As the *Monthly Review* put it, the author, on reflection, 'may think it rather unlikely that he should have found out an intention in Shakespeare which no other person ever suspected'; yet Plumptre issued an *Appendix* the following year. In his own copy, now in the Folger Shakespeare Library, Plumptre inserted the unanimously hostile reviews he had received, and among several humiliating anecdotes cheered himself with the observation that 'there are some people whose bad word is better than their good one. Mr. Steevens said of this book, together with the Appendix, that it was not only the worst book that had ever been, but that ever would be written'.[142] A challenger for that title as regards editions of Shakespeare must be the *Macbeth* put out in 1799 by Harry Rowe, 'Trumpet-Major to the High-Sherriffs of Yorkshire; and Master of a Puppet-Show', which indulged in senseless emendations (such as 'When the hurly-burly's *over*'), and which moved one critic to suggest that 'some anonymous wag has made free with his name'.[143]

One anonymous wag who made free with Shakespeare's name, in one of the most remarkable episodes in a century which had seen other forgeries (Macpherson's Ossian, Chatterton's Rowley papers), was the young William Henry Ireland, who, between 1794 and 1796, forged signatures, letters, legal documents, and even two plays (*Vortigern* and *Henry II*), purporting to be by Shakespeare. These forgeries, done on old parchment and in a superficially convincing Elizabethan hand, deceived not only Ireland's father, Samuel Ireland—whose last years were clouded by shame and disgrace once the forgeries had been exposed—but a number of scholars and antiquaries. The son did the forgeries, and the unwitting father published them, in *Miscellaneous Papers and Legal Instruments under the Hand and Seal of William Shakespeare. . .* (1796). A first refutation was published in January 1796 by James Boaden, as a *Letter to George Steevens Esq.*, but the thorough exposure was made by Malone's *Inquiry into the Authenticity of Certain Miscellaneous Papers*, published in March of that year. Malone showed that Ireland's eccentric spelling (Lear's 'Unfriended, new adopted' as 'Unnefreynnededde newe adoppetedde') was completely un-historical, that the handwriting supposed to be Queen Elizabeth's was not authentic, and was the work of a 'drunkard or a madman', that the vocabulary was modern, the contemporary references wrong, and so on. The balloon of public sensation—which had even led to *Vortigern* being performed at Drury Lane—was burst once and for all. Although his father, and a loyal friend, George Chalmers, both attacked Malone's scholarship, Samuel Ireland owned up, first in a brief pamphlet, *An Authentic Account of the Shakespearian Manuscripts*, in December 1796, then in the voluminous but confused *Confessions* of 1803. Ireland seems to have been a compulsive liar eager for notoriety, but the real puzzle is how he managed to deceive so many people for so long. Otherwise the episode has no significance for the history of the interpretation of Shakespeare.[144]

More significant is Boydell's Shakespeare Gallery, a venture that seemed to some commentators to be cashing in on the vogue for Shakespeare but which claimed to have a serious intent, namely the revival of English historical painting. John Boydell, an engraver and print-seller, commissioned paintings of Shakespearian subjects which he exhibited at the Shakespeare Gallery in Pall Mall, and subsequently issued as prints and as illustrations to an edition of Shakespeare. The artists involved included Fuseli, Romney, Reynolds, Angelica Kauffmann, and Barry, and the enterprise was a commercial success but ended in a sudden collapse. As the excerpts reprinted here will show (No. 296), comment ranged from enthusiastic acceptance[145] to informed criticism both of the conception and execution. The appeal to the newer sensibility, with its enthusiasm for terror and horror, is clear from the response of Samuel Felton (No. 291), and the limitations of this sensibility are shown up by the reviewer in *Walker's Hibernian* (No. 296c) who, however, describes 'the excesses of horror, extravagance, vulgarity, and absurdity' as being 'the characteristic defects of the author whose works were their model'. The writer criticizes the 'taste of the nation' for idolizing Shakespeare's errors along with his beauties, yet expresses his happiness 'that the work has taken place before the bigotry of Shakespeare is too far diminished among us to be able to support it'. If the story contained in these volumes were to be continued, it would be seen how long that day was in coming.

NOTES

1 *Horace Walpole's Correspondence*, ed. W. S. Lewis *et al.* (New Haven and London, 1937–), XXIV, p. 415 (Vol. VIII of the letters to Sir Horace Mann); XXXIII, p. 543 (Vol. II of the letters to the Countess of Upper Ossory); XXXI, p. 331 (to Hannah More, 4 November 1789).

2 *Critical Review* (hereafter abbreviated as *CR*), xxxix (1775), p. 203.

3 Badcock: *Monthly Review* (hereafter *MR*), lxii (1780), p. 12; Moody: *ibid.*, lxxix (1788), p. 155. Identification of authors in this journal derives from the editor, Ralph Griffiths, whose marked file is now in the Bodleian, meticulously edited by B. C. Nangle: *The Monthly Review. First Series, 1749–1789. Indexes of Contributors and Articles* (Oxford, 1934), and *Second Series, 1790–1815* (Oxford, 1955).

4 *Sentimental Magazine*, ii (September 1774), p. 425; Hester Chapone, *Letters on the Improvement of the Mind . . . addressed to a young lady* (1772), pp. 172–3; *European Magazine*, xiii (April 1788), p. 254.

5 Belsham, *Essays, Philosophical, Historical and Literary* (1789: pp. 16–32, Essay II, 'On SHAKESPEARE'), pp. 18, 19, 25, 27, 28–30; Alves, *Sketches of a History of Literature* (Edinburgh, 1794), pp. 115f., 187ff. Hole, *Essays, by a Society of Gentlemen at Exeter* (Exeter, 1796), pp. 250, 270.

6 Walpole, *Correspondence*, II, p. 302 (15 February 1782; to William Cole).

7 See, for example, the *Universal Magazine*, July 1777; *Walker's*

Hibernian Magazine, viii (April 1779), pp. 221–2; *New London Magazine*, v (October 1789), pp. 487–9.

8 See *MR*, n.s. xiv (1794), pp. 345–6 (dreams 'should be at least intelligible'); *CR*, n.s. vii (1795), p. 355 (must have been written in a dream, too: 'Can we conceive that a man in his senses and *broad awake*, would write in such a rambling incoherent manner?'); *British Critic*, iv (1794), pp. 302–3 ('he must have mistaken the delirium of a fever for the visions of sleep'; 'strong marks of derangement'); *English Review*, xxiii (1794), pp. 307–8 ('what better could be expected when the genius sets out with telling us that *judgment was asleep?*').

9 *MR*, n.s. xxi (1796), pp. 274–80. The section on Shakespeare was reprinted in the *Universal Magazine*, ci (December 1797), p. 430, and in the *Edinburgh Magazine or Literary Miscellany*, xi (January 1798), p. 64.

10 Blair, *Lectures on Rhetoric and Belles Lettres* (1783 edition, 3 vols), I, p. 54; Beattie, *Elements of Moral Science*, II (1793), p. 609.

11 Seward, 'On Shakespeare's Monument at Stratford-upon-Avon', in Dodsley's *Collection of Poems by Several Hands* (1782), II, p. 315.

12 Belsham, *Essays* (1789), p. 17.

13 *MR*, n.s. ii (1790), pp. 6f.; *Town and Country Magazine*, May 1777; *CR*, n.s. xii (1794), pp. 66–7; lxii (1786), p. 321; n.s. iii (1791), p. 363.

14 Gentleman: notes in Bell's edition (the plays are sometimes paginated separately), III: *Measure for Measure*, pp. 14, 29; VIII: *Titus Andronicus*, p. 14; Griffith, *The Morality of Shakespeare's Drama Illustrated* (1775), p. 404. See also Gentleman's life of Shakespeare, No. 243, note 85. Davies: *Dramatic Miscellanies*, 3 vols (1784), II, pp. 288f., 299f.

15 Badcock: *MR*, lxii (1780), p. 14; Felton: No. 291.

16 Malone: 1790 edition, I, p. 321; Steevens: 1793 edition, I, p. iii; Ritson: *ibid.*, V, p. 175.

17 Anderson, *Bee*, ii (March 1791), p. 199.

18 Sherlock, *Letters from an English Traveller* (1780), p. 58.

19 Belsham, *Essays* (1789), pp. 16f.; Stedman: No. 270.

20 Johnson: Boswell, *Life of Johnson*, ed. G. B. Hill (Oxford, 1934), II, p. 96; Mrs Piozzi, in *Johnsonian Miscellanies*, ed. G. B. Hill (Oxford, 1897), I, p. 185; Johnson, *Lives of the Poets*, ed. G. B. Hill (3 vols, Oxford, 1905), I, p. 464 note.

21 Gentleman: in Bell's edition, III: *Measure for Measure*, p. 21; IV: *2 Henry IV*, pp. 15, 33; V: *Timon of Athens*, pp. 124f., 128; VI: *Troilus and Cressida*, p. 239; VI: *Antony and Cleopatra*, pp. 269, 271, 278; VIII: *Midsummer Night's Dream*, p. 159.

22 *Shakespeare: The Critical Heritage*, Vol. 3, pp. 436ff.

23 Bell's edition, VII, pp. 178, 193, 200, 203, 210.

24 John Penn, *Letters on the Drama* (1797), p. 54; Pilon: No. 255; Taylor: No. 247.

25 *Lounger's Miscellany*, no. 17 (14 February 1789), p. 99; Pye, *A Commentary illustrating the Poetic of Aristotle* (1792), pp. 126f.

26 Alison, *Essays on the Nature and Principles of Taste* (1790), pp. 108f.; Penn, *Letters* (1797), pp. 53ff.

27 Penn, *Letters* (1797), pp. 7f., 23ff. On Mason's *Elfrida* see Vol. 3, Nos 131–3.

28 *Thespian Magazine and Literary Repository*, nos 1–2, p. 134.

29 Gentleman: in Bell's edition, II: *Cymbeline*, p. 233; III: *Hamlet*, p. 1; III: *Richard III*, p. 3; VI: *Antony and Cleopatra*, p. 312.

30 Murphy, *The Life of David Garrick, Esq.* (1801), I, pp. 176, 284, and p. 154 on *Much Ado about Nothing*: 'The plot is crowded with . . . a great deal of episodical business, which by a multiplicity of incidents destroys the unity of action.'

31 Alison, *Essays on the Nature and Principles of Taste* (1790), pp. 105ff.; for Taylor, in addition to the excerpts in No. 247, see *Cursory Remarks on Tragedy* (1774), pp. 95f., 99; William Hodson, *Observations on Tragedy* (1780: sometimes appended to his *Zoraida*), p. 74 (unity of action essential); Pye, *A Commentary* (1792), p. 133 (on the storm in *King Lear* continuing over the division between Acts II and III, a fixed time in stage-representation, but during which Shakespeare also asks us to imagine that the French army has been mustered and shipped to England); John Penn, *Letters* (1797), pp. 7f., 25f., 46ff.

32 Complaints about Shakespeare's neglect of the unities can be found, for example, in the *English Review*, iii (1784), p. 169; *CR*, n.s. v (1792), p. 208; *CR*, xxxviii (1774), pp. 114–9: a favourable review of Taylor's book; *MR*, lvii (1777), pp. 194f.; *Edinburgh Magazine*, ii (1785), p. 219; *European Magazine*, xv (1789), pp. 14f. ('For surely no poet more frequently or more grossly violated the unity of action, which is in all cases indispensable, than Shakespeare').

33 The *Universal Magazine* ran it from vol. LV (December 1774) until January 1777, at least; the *Westminster Magazine* ran it from vol. IV (March 1776) to November 1778, rearranging it under alphabetical topics ('Advice, Affection'), which was precisely how she did not want to present her material, as she explains in the preface.

34 Barton, *Modern Characters by Shakespeare* (1788), p. iii; *Thespian Magazine and Literary Repository*, nos 1–2, p. 187.

35 *MR*, n.s. xviii (1795), pp. 121–33, and p. 129; on Taylor see Nangle, *The Monthly Review, Second Series*, pp. 66f. Compare also this typical statement, from a low-level compilation (*The Playhouse Pocket-Companion, or Theatrical Vade-Mecum*, 1779), on the two

provinces of drama, tragedy and comedy: 'In them virtue is either rendered amiable and rewarded, or vice punished, and held up to detestation, scorn, and ridicule' (p. 13).

36 Harris, *Philosophical Arrangements* (1775), pp. 228f.; Davies, *Dramatic Miscellanies* (1784), II, pp. 147–8; III, p. 138.

37 Fennell, *Prompter*, iii (27 October 1789), pp. 14f.; Reynolds: F. W. Hilles (ed.), *Portraits by Sir Joshua Reynolds* (1952), pp. 118ff.

38 *MR*, n.s. xviii (1795), p. 123; *ibid.*, n.s. xxii (1797), pp. 231f. (including a discussion of dramatic illusion); Reynolds: Malone's 1790 edition, I, part 1, pp. 143–4, and *Portraits*, ed. Hilles, pp. 107–22.

39 Colman, *MR*, lviii (1778), p. 108; Hannah More, prefatory letter to *Poems on Several Occasions* by 'Ann Yearsley, a Milkwoman of Bristol': cit. from excerpt in the *Universal Magazine*, lxxvii (1785), p. 33; 'Essay on Comedy', *ibid.*, lxxxix (1791), p. 5; *Lounger's Miscellany*, xvii (14 February 1789), 97ff.

40 Davies, *Dramatic Miscellanies* (1784), I, p. 108; 'Observations on the First Act of Shakespeare's *Tempest*' by 'a young Gentleman, an undergraduate in the University of Dublin', *Transactions of the Royal Irish Academy*, ii (1788), pp. 39–53, at p. 40; Malone, 1790 edition, I, part 1, p. 141 note.

41 Gerard, *An Essay on Taste*, 3rd edition (1780), p. 258 (this passage added only in this edition); Reynolds, *Portraits*, ed. Hilles, p. 117.

42 Pye, *A Commentary* (1792), p. 134.

43 Twining, *Aristotle's Treatise on Poetry, translated* (1789), pp. 226–30; Pye, *A Commentary* (1792), pp. xf., 130–7, 183.

44 Walpole: *Correspondence*, XXV (= Vol. IX of the letters to Sir Horace Mann), p. 68, letter of 6 July 1780 ('but is not my letter like one of Shakespeare's historic plays, insurrections, a marriage, trials, a court-pageant'); and XXXIII (= Vol. II of the letters to the Countess of Upper Ossory), p. 553; Gerard, *An Essay on Taste*, p. 258.

45 Hodson, *Observations on Tragedy* (1780), p. 75; *Bee* (January 1791), p. 61.

46 Gentleman: in Bell's edition, VII: *3 Henry VI*, p. 315; VII: *2 Henry VI*, p. 220; VIII: *Titus Andronicus*, p. 78; VIII: *A Midsummer Night's Dream*, pp. 147, 166; VII: *Richard II*, p. 58; VII: *2 Henry VI*, p. 238.

47 Belsham, *Essays* (1789), p. 19; Cumberland, *Observer*, ii, p. 247 (see also the excerpts reprinted as No. 288 in the text); Anon., 'Observations on . . . *The Tempest*', *Transactions of the Royal Irish Academy* (1788), pp. 49–51; *Walker's Hibernian Magazine* (February 1791), pp. 118ff.; Pye, *A Commentary* (1792), p. 126; Hole, *Essays, by a Society of Gentlemen at Exeter* (1796), p. 252.

48 For praise of Shakespeare's 'preservation of character' see here Gerard (No. 244), Mrs Griffith (No. 247), Morgann (No. 254), Capell (No. 263), Mackenzie (Nos 264, 287), Harris (No. 267), Anonymous in 1782 (No. 269), Walwyn (No. 271), Richardson (Nos 276, 294, 307), Davies (No. 277), Anonymous in 1785 (No. 278), Pinkerton (No. 281), Whately (No. 284), Kemble (No. 285), Cumberland (No. 288), Steevens (Nos 290, 299, 303), Stack (No. 292), Robertson (No. 293), Anonymous in 1789 (No. 295), Malone (No. 299, note 12: 'It is one of Shakespeare's unrivalled excellencies, that his characters are always consistent'), Anonymous in 1791 (No. 300), and Parr (No. 305).

49 Dirrill [a pseudonym for Richard Sill], *Remarks on Shakespeare's Tempest* (1797), p. 68; Pearne: reviewing Malone's 1790 edition, *MR*, n.s. xiii (1794), p. 244.

50 *CR*, lvii (1784), p. 101, and lviii (1785), p. 59; see also Blackstone's accusation that Shakespeare had forgotten himself with respect to Hamlet's age: Malone's *Supplement* (1780), I, pp. 360f., a point contested by Ritson in *Remarks, Critical and Illustrative* (1783), p. 238: 'men may study, or reside at the university, to *any age*'.

51 Malone: in the 1783 *Second Appendix* (No. 275, note 4), reprinted in the 1785 edition (X, p. 655); W.N. in the *Bee* (1791) (No. 300); both writers had been anticipated by an anonymous correspondent to *Walker's Hibernian Magazine* (February 1780), p. 72.

52 More: *Universal Magazine*, lxxvii (1785), p. 31; Barton, *Modern Characters by Shakespeare* (1788), pp. i f. See also *CR*, n.s. xviii (1796), p. 71; Hole, *Essays* (1796), p. 251; Blair, *Lectures on Rhetoric and Belles Lettres* (1783 edition), III, p. 373.

53 Similar praise of Shakespeare's knowledge of psychology can be found in Morgann (No. 254), Mackenzie (No. 264), Stedman (No. 270), Davies (No. 277), and two anonymous writers (Nos 282, 295).

54 Colman, *MR*, lxii (1780), pp. 186f.; *English Review*, iii (1784), p. 170.

55 *European Magazine*, xiv (1788), pp. 422, 424; *English Review*, xiv (1789), p. 96; *MR*, lxxxi (1789), p. 54.

56 On Falstaff's cowardice see, in this series, Margaret Cavendish (Vol. 1, p. 43), Dryden (Vol. 1, pp. 139, 258), Rowe (Vol. 2, p. 195), Gildon (Vol. 2, p. 239), Corbyn Morris (Vol. 3, p. 124), Arthur Murphy (Vol. 4, p. 275), Johnson (Vol. 5, p. 124), Mrs Montagu Vol. 5, p. 332), Paul Hiffernan (Vol. 5, p. 413), and No. 248 above; see also D. Fineman's meticulous edition, *Maurice Morgann, Shakespearian Criticism* (Oxford, 1972), p. 362. For an account of the deficiencies of this edition, caused by a too-enthusiastic identifi-

cation with Morgann, see my review in *Yearbook of English Studies*, 2 (1974), pp. 276–9).

57 Morgann was praised in the *Critical Review*, xliii (1777), p. 397—who used him, however, as another stick with which to beat Capell (perhaps Steevens was responsible); by Kenrick in the *London Review*, v (1777), p. 372; and by the *European Magazine*, xiv (1788), pp. 423f., preferring Morgann's generous picture of Falstaff to Richardson's critical one. Yet the reviewer doubted the ascription of courage, since Hal 'tells him gravely and expressly to his face that he is "*a natural coward without instinct*" ', an opinion which is 'hard to be refuted'. Morgann was criticized by Colman in the *Monthly*, lvii (1777), pp. 79f. ('his taste seems rather vitiated by singularity and caprice; and his ingenuity betrays him into false refinement . . . . We are not pleased to forego the judicious investigations of acute critics for the sake of the *special pleadings of literary counsel*'); by Ralph Griffiths, *MR*, n.s. vii (1792), p. 62; by Moody, *MR*, lxxxi (1789), p. 54; by *CR* in February 1791 (n.s. ii), pp. 552f. (Morgann's work 'always appeared to us as a *jeu d'esprit*, designed to show how much might be said on a desperate subject; how far what seemed incredible might be rendered probable'. This reviewer also praises Stack's exposure of 'how much' Morgann 'conceals, what he refines, and in what manner he eludes or changes different circumstances to render his position probable'); and by the *British Critic*, ix (1797), p. 363. Dr Johnson predicted that Morgann would emerge again in defence of Iago; Malone described the *Essay* as a 'fanciful and absurd' piece of work, and jotted down in his copy another Johnsonian comment: 'When this pamphlet first appeared, Dr. Johnson being asked his opinion of it, replied "all he should say, was, that if Falstaff was not a coward, Shakespeare knew nothing of his art" ' (Bodleian, Malone 140 (1)). Further criticism of Morgann can be found in the text below from Davies (No. 277), an anonymous writer (No. 278, note 6), Mackenzie (No. 287), and Richardson (No. 294). For the later reception of Morgann see Fineman's account, *op. cit.* (see note 56), pp. 11–36, which is not, however, neutral.

58 See especially George Stubbes (Vol. 3, No. 87), an unsigned essay (Vol. 3, No. 134), Mrs Lennox (Vol. 4, No. 141), Francis Gentleman (Vol. 5, No. 227), and, most prolific and most vociferous, George Steevens (Vol. 5, Nos 234, 235, 237, 238, 240).

59 *CR*, lxiii (1787), p. 23; Malone and Reed: 1785 edition, X, p. 418.

60 Fennell: No. 298; 'J.H.' in the *Westminster Magazine*, vii, supplement (1779), p. 665, in 'Stanzas occasioned by a late visit to the Poets'-Corner, in Westminster Abbey':

In Hamlet find we much to praise and blame,
   As we in diff'rent lights his actions view;
His filial duty is a noble flame,
   But does he *nobly* his *revenge* pursue?

Prepar'd th' incestuous Murd'rer to destroy,
   Does he not, *mentally*, commit a crime,
When he thus leaves him in his *best employ*,
   'Up, sword, and know thou a more horrid time'?

61 'Philo-Dramatis', 'False Criticisms on Shakespeare', *Westminster Magazine*, x (1782), pp. 82–3.

62 *London Magazine*, xlv (1776), p. 183.

63 See also Ritson (No. 274)—a critic not usually given to agreeing with others, but closing ranks on this issue; Robertson (No. 293); and the *Critical Review* for 1801 (n.s. xxxii, pp. 189–95), arguing that Hamlet is presented by Shakespeare as 'really agitated into an inconsistent wildness' from the moment of the Ghost's departure, although his plan is only adopted at the end of that scene; Hamlet's 'irresolute inconsistency' is attributed to his reason being unhinged (pp. 191f.). An earlier writer in that journal, in 1787, noted that it was usual to say that Hamlet's behaviour to Ophelia is 'inconsistent with his general character', and is so brutish that 'to avoid the contradiction Shakespeare has been supposed to represent Hamlet as actually mad, or at least so much agitated as at times to approach towards lunacy'. Reference to the source, however, shows that the character corresponding to Ophelia was sent as a lure to catch Hamlet, so the reviewer deduces that in Shakespeare also the madness is feigned for politic reasons: *CR,* lxiii (1787), p. 22.

64 *English Review*, ix (1787), p. 71; on our involvement with Macbeth's virtuous qualities see also Beattie (No. 251) and Davies (No. 277). Steevens shows his ability to pick up what others had thought, and rephrase it more pithily, in his essay deriving from Whately: Macbeth's 'genuine intrepidity had forsaken him when he ceased to be a virtuous character' (No. 290).

65 Gentleman: Bell's edition, V: *Timon of Athens*, pp. 115, 118; V: *The Winter's Tale*, p. 164; VII: *Richard II*, p. 56; VII: *1 Henry VI*, p. 153. Similar objections can be found, in the selection printed here, to *Hamlet* (No. 243, notes 8, 11), *King John* (note 19), *Timon of Athens* (note 32: one is bound to agree with him), *The Winter's Tale* (notes 33, 36), *Twelfth Night* (note 45), *Troilus and Cressida* (notes 50, 53), and *Antony and Cleopatra* (note 54).

66 See No. 278, note 14, and Mason, *Additional Comments on the Plays of Shakespeare, Extended to the Late Editions of Malone and Steevens*

([1798]: notes appended to Mason's comments on Beaumont and Fletcher), pp. 62f.

67 Of *Antony and Cleopatra* Thomas Davies objected that 'the minutiae of events described lessen the grandeur of the whole', and that the 'crowd of events' necessarily destroys 'the simplicity of the fable': *Dramatic Miscellanies* (1784), II, pp. 335–6, 368; James Fennell complained of *Hamlet* that the 'continual intervention of new agents and fresh matter . . . wholly destroys the idea of a Drama' (No. 298); and Arthur Murphy criticized *Much Ado* since 'the plot is crowded with . . . a great deal of episodical business, which by a multiplicity of incidents destroys the unity of action': *The Life of David Garrick, Esq.* (1801), I, p. 154. All three writers, be it noted, were connected with the theatre, as actors or authors or life-long associates of the companies. Neo-classical criteria were not the prerogative of academic critics.

68 Eccles, *The Plays of Lear and Cymbeline* (1794), reviewed in *CR*, n.s. xi (1794), pp. 387–90; *British Critic*, vi (1795), pp. 299–301. The latter preferred to read Shakespeare as he was, 'with all his imperfections, as well as with his merits'.

69 Twining, *Aristotle's Treatise on Poetry* (1789), pp. 101, 261; Pye, *A Commentary* (1792), p. 174; Walwyn: No. 271; Taylor, *MR*, n.s. xviii (1795), pp. 127, 126. Pye (pp. 174f.) and Taylor (p. 127) agreed that a defect in *As You Like It* was that Adam and Jaques are not sufficiently involved in the catastrophe.

70 Malone, *Supplement to the Edition of Shakespeare's Plays, Published in 1778* (1780), I, p. 144; Blackstone, *ibid.*, I, pp. 115 (on *A Midsummer Night's Dream*) and 364 (on *Othello*); Steevens, 1778 edition, *Othello*, X, pp. 446, 520. Monck Mason, in his *Comments on the Last Edition of Shakespeare's Plays* (1785), notes that 'Shakespeare seems to have forgotten himself' concerning the drowning of Ophelia, since there is no circumstance that suggests she did so intentionally (p. 395). Similar objections to an inaccuracy or 'oversight' in *Macbeth* were made by Steevens (No. 303, note 20) and the *CR*, lviii (1784), p. 57, while a reviewer in the latter journal twice claimed that Shakespeare had forgotten his own designs in *Hamlet*: *CR*, lvii (1784), p. 102, and lviii (1784), p. 59.

71 Cumberland, *Observer*, ii (1786), pp. 237, 242f., and No. 288. Taylor, *MR*, n.s. xviii (1795), p. 127.

72 Steevens: 1785 edition, VIII, p. 49; Davies: No. 277, note 14.

73 Capell, *Notes and Various Readings* (1780), II, part i, p. 10 (*Macbeth*); I, part ii, pp. 105–6 (*Julius Caesar*).

74 Capell, *ibid*: II, part i, p. 177 (*Julius Caesar*); p. 18 (*Macbeth*); p. 191 (*Richard III*).

75 Ritson: *Remarks, Critical and Illustrative, on the Text and Notes of the*

Last Edition of Shakespeare (1783), p. 54; Mason, *Comments* (1785), pp. 225, 400, 411, 214, 216.

76 Malone: 1790 edition, IX, p. 483; 1778 edition, II, p. 288 (also Steevens); VIII, p. 441; IX, p. 220 (Steevens); 1785 edition: II, pp. 108–9 ('an expression equally hardy and licentious . . . an absolute catachresis'); 1790 edition: III, pp. 356, 411, 466; IV, pp. 156, 551; V, p. 112; VII, p. 564; IX, pp. 239, 467, 487. See also the selections from 1790 reprinted here: No. 299, notes 10, 26, 29.

77 Malone: *Supplement* (1780), I, p. 167; 1785 edition: I, pp. 265f.; 1790 edition: II, p. 169; IV, p. 56; V, p. 170. Steevens: 1785 edition: II, p. 203; III, p. 37; Davies: *Dramatic Miscellanies* (1784), II, pp. 16, 343; Gerard: No. 244. The concept of correctness of metaphor, as used by Johnson to emend Macbeth's 'way of life' to 'May of life' (see Vol. 3, p. 181) was challenged both by Capell (*Notes*, II, part i, pp. 28–9: is such a 'strict accordance of metaphor' beautiful, or proper?) and Pinkerton (No. 281, note 5).

78 Belsham: *Essays* (1789), p. 22; Cooke: No. 250; Richardson: No. 246; Davies: *Dramatic Miscellanies* (1784), I, pp. 315f.; Beattie: No. 251; Hodson: *Zoraida*, p. 98; Colman: Preface to Beaumont and Fletcher, in his *Prose on Various Occasions* (1778), II, p. 156; Mason: *Comments* (1785), p. 167; Malone: No. 299, note 17; Henley: 1785 edition: V, p. 257.

79 Mason, *Comments* (1785), pp. 117, 410; Malone: *Supplement*, I, pp. 165, 160.

80 Steevens: 1778 edition: X, p. 496; 1793 edition: VI, p. 144; X, p. 355; VII, p. 562; Mason, *Comments*, p. 150 (the emendation was made 'without authority, merely for the sake of the ear; a very improper liberty, for which he would have censured any other editor with some asperity'); Ritson: *Remarks*, p. 79; also B. H. Bronson, *Joseph Ritson. Scholar-at-Arms* (Berkeley, Calif., 1938), p. 412.

81 Malone, 1790 edition: X, p. 547; *Supplement*, II, p. 578; Francis Gentleman, No. 243, note 85 (Shakespeare excelled everyone at it); Beattie, No. 251.

82 Malone, 1793 edition: XI, p. 284; *Supplement*, I, p. 423; Steevens, 1778 edition: III, p. 345; *Supplement*, I, p. 492; 1793 edition: XIV, pp. 559, 561, and No. 303, note 45. Steevens's use of the presence of puns as a sign of authenticity: No. 257, note 13 (on *Titus Andronicus*), and No. 265, note 19 (on *A Yorkshire Tragedy*). Similarly the *CR* reviewer finds *1 Henry VI* only partly authentic, but claims Talbot's speech, 'full of rich and poetic imagery, and tinctured with the true Shakespearean blot—a pun at the most serious moment': *CR* n.s. iii (1791), p. 366.

83 Gentleman: No. 243, notes 26, 79, 85; also in Bell's edition, V: *Timon of Athens*, p. 99; VI: *Two Gentlemen*, p. 8 ('this scene of

egregious quibble'); VII: *Richard II*, pp. 26 (incredulous that a healthy man 'would so quibble on a word', let alone one like Gaunt, 'supposing himself near death'), 65 (the buckets; later lines are 'pregnant with the most ludicrous quibble'); VIII: *The Comedy of Errors*, pp. 96, 101; VIII: *Love's Labour's Lost*, p. 233. Griffith: *The Morality of Shakespeare's Drama Illustrated* (1775), p. 63; Douce: 1793 edition: IX, p. 154; Gerard: No. 244; also Taylor (No. 247); Anonymous (No. 248); Cooke (No. 250); Priestley (No. 253); Steevens (No. 257, note 22); Capell (*Notes* (1780), II, part i, pp. 38, 46–7); Blair (No. 272); Davies (No. 277); Anonymous (No. 300); and Drake (No. 308). See also Blackstone, *Supplement*, I, p. 79 (fewer puns in the later plays); *CR*, lxii (1786), p. 326 (punning for Shakespeare is 'the shadow for which he often loses the substance'); Felton, *Imperfect Hints*, part 2 (1788), p. 56 note (we forgive his 'fond habit', 'a luxury which he could not resist').

84 *MR*, n.s. xiii (1794), pp. 260ff.: see pp. 262ff. for an acute analysis of 'green', meaning 'the sea's *greenness*, or *green colour*'; *British Critic*, i (1793) pp. 137f.; Davies, *Dramatic Miscellanies* (1784), II, p. 394.

85 Ritson, *Remarks* (1783), p. 29; Capell, *Notes* (1780), II, part i, p. 38; I, part ii, p. 53; II, part ii, p. 62.

86 Beattie, *Essays. On Poetry and Music, as They Affect the Mind* (1776), pp. 341f.; Pearne, *MR*, n.s. xiii (1794), p. 244.

87 Mason: *Comments* (1785), pp. 143, 325, 413; Malone: *Supplement*, I, p. 746; 1790 edition: VIII, p. 243; IX, p. 612; X, p. 565. Malone also used frequency of rhyme as a criterion to settle the plays' chronology, observing that in his later work Shakespeare 'grew weary of the bondage of rhyme' (No. 257, note 2): the critical attitude behind that seemingly scholarly observation is all too evident.

88 Davies: *Dramatic Miscellanies* (1784), II, pp. 116f.; Fennell: No. 298; Gentleman: in Bell's edition, III: *Hamlet*, p. 47; V: *Julius Caesar*, p. 61; VI: *Troilus and Cressida*, p. 202; VII: *Richard II*, pp. 7 ('Patience suffers many shocks from the unnecessary rhimes which frequently occur in this play'), 10; VII: *1 Henry VI*, p. 153 ('a continued jingle . . . which is very exceptionable'); VIII: *A Midsummer Night's Dream*, p. 182 (an Act end-rhyme would be better if 'set to musick'); VIII: *Love's Labour's Lost*, p. 208 ('We have already complained of unnecessary jingles, and are sorry to meet with it so offensively multiplied in this play').

89 Steevens: 1793 edition: III, p. 113; XIV, p. 154.

90 Malone and Steevens: 1778 edition: I, pp. 316–7; Malone: 1790 edition: I, part 1, pp. 341f.

91 See my review of D. Sipe, *Shakespeare's Metrics*, in *Yearbook of English Studies*, 1 (1971), 241–3. Reference to the standard bibliographies

by Ebisch and Schücking, G. R. Smith, J. G. McManaway and J. A. Roberts (1975), and David Bevington (1977) will show how little has been done. Some valuable models exist: the work of Paul Fussell, for instance, in *Theory of Prosody in Eighteenth-Century England* (New Haven, Conn., 1954) and *Poetic Meter and Poetic Form* (New York, 1965).

92 Gentleman: in Bell's edition, VII: *1 Henry VI*, pp. 127 (protesting that 'pronunciation is varied and adulterated again, by placing, in flow of versification, a stress upon the second, instead of the first syllable': the line begins '*In contráry parts*', as Gentleman marks it), 170 ('Contráct': 'another trespass on pronunciation'); VIII: *Love's Labour's Lost*, p. 222 ('To give this line an easy flow in utterance, we must accent the second syllable of *importunes*, though the stress properly falls on the last. The *licencia poetica* should never lay traps for false pronunciation, if possible').

93 *English Review*, iii (March–May 1784), pp. 168–79, 272–8, 342–51: passages quoted from pp. 344–6. See also the review by Colman, *MR*, lxix (1783), pp. 483–8, and lxx (1784), pp. 15–23.

94 Badcock: *MR*, lxii (1780), pp. 421f.; Belsham, in *Essays* (1789), praises 'the beauty and energy' of Shakespeare's diction (pp. 22f.), finds him 'the most figurative writer, Ossian perhaps excepted, in our language', celebrates the 'variety and richness of his imagery' (p. 25) and 'the unrivalled skill or rather felicity of his versification' (p. 27). See also Mason (No. 283, note 3), Pinkerton (No. 281, note 4), Davies (No. 277, note 15), and Steevens (No. 303, note 23).

95 Capell, *Notes* (1780), II, part ii, p. 14. For other comments on dramatic function see No. 263, notes 7, 13, 17, 18, 40, 59, 70, 72, 75.

96 Cumberland: *Observer*, ii (1786), pp. 250f.; Mason: No. 283; Beattie: No. 251; Richardson: No. 294.

97 Mason: No. 283, note 7; Ritson, *A Select Collection of English Songs* (1783), I, p. lviii: cit. in Bronson, *Joseph Ritson. Scholar-at-Arms*, p. 85; Bronson notes (p. 187) that Ritson's *English Anthology* (1793–4), a kind of Golden Treasury, includes only one Shakespeare sonnet; *MR*, lxxxi (1789), p. 366; *MR*, n.s. xiii (1794), p. 267; *British Critic*, i (1793), p. 55; *CR*, n.s. xii (1794), p. 391; Drake: No. 308. Capell left notes for an edition of the Poems (Trinity College, Cambridge, MS 5), in which he suggested, on stylistic grounds, that the *Sonnets* 'must have been compos'd at different periods', judged them superior to other Elizabethan collections, and found them unique in that 'a single thought, vary'd and put in language poetical, is the subject of each sonnet; a thing essential to these compositions. . . .' He noted the beauty yet obscurity of *The Phoenix and the Turtle*, and praised the narrative poems for 'a style flowing and copious, natural and lively images, a rich vein of

fancy. . . .' H. Hart (see head-note to No. 263) reprints the preface, pp. 215–18.

98 Badcock: *MR*, lxiii (1780), 249; Malone: 1790 edition, I, part 2, p. 32. For similar verdicts see *Thespian Magazine and Literary Repository*, i–ii (1793–4), p. 136; William Jackson, *Thirty Letters*, 3rd edition (1793), pp. 72ff.; Nathan Drake, No. 308.

99 See L. Lipking, *The Ordering of the Arts in Eighteenth-Century England* (Princeton, N.J., 1970), p. 135.

100 *CR*, lxiii (1787), p. 21; Neve, *Cursory Remarks on some of the ancient English Poets, particularly Milton* (1789), p. 29.

101 For earlier discussions of Shakespeare's knowledge of the classics see Whalley (Vol. 3, No. 113), Upton (Vol. 3, No. 114), Guthrie (Vol. 3, No. 107), Hurd (Vol. 3, No. 128; Vol. 4, No. 162), and Smart (Vol. 4, No. 149). Farmer's attack can be found in Vol. 5, No. 214, and the contrary case by Capell, No. 220, Colman, No. 217, and Guthrie, No. 215.

102 Colman praised Capell's discussion of Shakespeare's learning when he reviewed *Notes and Various Readings* in *MR*, lxix (1783), p. 484. In the 'Postscript' to the Appendix to the second edition of his translation of Terence, added to his *Prose on Several Occasions* (1787), II, pp. 179–88, he has his last word on the topic, showing once more how Farmer has misquoted and misrepresented his opponents. The whole discussion could have been much more fruitful if the triumvirate had been willing to concede Shakespeare any Latin.

103 See Capell, *Notes* (1780), I, part ii, pp. 61, 84, 98, 108–9, 110, 111, 112, 113f., 120f.; II, part iii, p. 154; part iv, pp. 45, 48, 51f., 95, 166f., 171. For similar comments see No. 295, an anonymous essay, well-informed and highly discriminating.

104 Colman, *MR*, lxi (1779), pp. 296, 299.

105 See Warton, No. 266, notes 2, 3, 4; and Fennell, No. 298.

106 Malone: 1778 edition: VIII, pp. 560–62; 1785 edition: X, p. 360.

107 Capell's arguments for the authenticity of *Titus* were approved by Colman, *MR*, lxx (1784), pp. 16f. The play was rejected by Badcock: *MR*, lxii (1780), pp. 16 note, 22; by the *British Critic*, i (1793), p. 135, and iii (1794), p. 645 note; by Mason (No. 283: 'this abominable tragedy') and Pinkerton (No. 281: 'stupid play').

108 So the *Monthly*, dealing with the 1785 edition, gave a list of the best notes, with their authors' names: *MR*, lxxv (1786), pp. 76f.; the *Critical* commented of the same edition that 'the various notes are pretty well known': *CR*, lxii (1786), p. 323. Arthur Sherbo has recently corrected a misconception that Steevens was not involved with the 1785 edition, showing that it included over 400 additions or corrections to his 1778 notes: see Sherbo, 'George Steevens's

1785 Variorum *Shakespeare*', *Studies in Bibliography*, 32 (1979), pp. 241–6.

109 1778 edition: I, pp. 270, 272f., 274f.; II, p. 195; III, p. 125.

110 Porson: *MR*, lxxviii (1788), pp. 197f.; similar complaints were made by the *Westminster Magazine*: 'The Holy Scriptures have scarcely had more commentators than Shakespeare, making allowances for the short time his Works have been in the hands of the world': x (1782), p. 82. The *English Review* criticized the whole concept of a variorum edition, with its farrago of notes, each disagreeing with its predecessor(s) at the foot of the page, 'so that a reader at all inquisitive can scarcely keep his eyes from them, and is frequently drawn into the whirlpool, in spite of all his efforts': iii (1784), p. 179; the *Critical Review* asked whether there were to be no bounds: 'Must we search from whence he copied every line? Must we ascertain with anxiety every trifling word? . . . We have little hesitation in saying that these minute particulars *have* been carried too far': n.s. iii (1791), p. 362. The *Critical* repeated its complaint a few years later: 'so many editions of Shakespeare, with vast commentaries, have recently appeared, that it is no wonder the public begins to be satiated with the subject': n.s. xi (1794), p. 387. The *British Critic* commented: 'it is now a very general opinion, that poor Shakespeare is already almost killed with kindness, overwhelmed and oppressed with notes till his delightful pages become absolutely terrific': vi (1795), p. 300, and later welcomed the plain text edition by Joseph Rann, since the publisher had not been 'wandering in the endless labyrinth of controversial criticism, nor crowding his pages with everlasting commentaries': iii (1794), p. 645. A witty account of the irrelevancies, and obscenities, of Steevens's notes was given by T. J. Mathias in *The Pursuits of Literature* (1794), as in the 14th edition, with full notes (1808), pp. 81–6.

111 Steevens on 'cry aim': 1778 edition: I, pp. 293f. At times in the 1793 edition Steevens expresses his own sense of the excess of notes, joking that the reader will at one point cry '*No more*' (XI, p. 154; also XV, p. 79). Lord Hailes: 'Critical Remarks on the late Editions of Shakespeare's Plays', *Edinburgh Magazine*, IV (1786), p. 355. Arthur Sherbo has pointed out to me that Hailes's authorship of this article is attested by the 1815 edition, in a note on *Two Gentlemen*, 5.2.29.

112 Malone's copy of Ritson's *Cursory Criticisms* is in the Bodleian, Malone 150 (4). Malone replied in *A Letter to the Rev. Richard Farmer . . . Relative to the Edition of Shakespeare published in MDCCXC., and some Late Criticisms on that Work* (1792): see Bronson, *Joseph Ritson. Scholar-at-Arms*, on this controversy.

Contemporary reviewers told Malone that he ought not to have replied: Pearne, *MR*, n.s. xii (1793), pp. 111f.; *CR*, n.s. v (1792), p. 113.

113 For Steevens's mocking remarks on collation and too great accuracy in editing see the preface to the 1793 edition (excerpts in No. 303), and that edition, VIII, p. 113; also *CR*, lvi (1783), pp. 81ff., a review ascribed to Steevens with some certainty by Bronson, *Joseph Ritson. Scholar-at-Arms*, pp. 468f. A reviewer of his 1793 edition in the *Critical* drew attention to his specious attacks on collation: n.s. xii (1794), pp. 395f.

114 Some attacks on Capell were published, such as Malone's mockery of his views on *Titus Andronicus* (1778: VIII, pp. 561f.), or his claim that Capell was guilty of hundreds of errors and unjustified emendations (first made in 1783: No. 275, note 1, expanded in 1790: VII, p. 392 and reprinted in 1793: XII, pp. 361f.), or his dismissal of the *Notes and Various Readings*: 'two ponderous volumes in quarto, written in a style manifestly formed on that of the clown' in *Measure for Measure*: No. 299, note 6. Malone's copy of Capell's edition, now in the British Library (Press-mark c 60 g 10–) is full of virulent abuse, matched only by his copy of the *Notes*, now in the Folger Shakespeare Library (Press-mark 5.b.112). Steevens claimed in his private correspondence that Capell was too insignificant to be worth his attention, yet he continued both to abuse and plagiarize him.

115 Malone's attack on the Second Folio (which claims that all its deviations from the First Folio are 'arbitrary' or 'capricious' and derive from the 'ignorance' of the editors) began in the 1785 edition: see, for example, I, p. 381; II, pp. 63, 291, 478f.; III, p. 518; IV, pp. 66, 88, 163, 236, 386, 467, 508f.; in the 1790 edition see, for example, II, p. 63; VII, p. 203 ('which has been the source of at least one half of the corruptions that have been introduced in our author's works'), 341; IX, p. 149; etc.

116 For Ritson on Malone's attitude to the Second Folio see *Cursory Criticisms* (1792), pp. 1–9, which shows that Malone's readings often pervert metre and sense, where F_2 gives a perfectly good text; pp. 9–26, where Ritson gives a list of 192 places where F_2 corrects F_1, and shows that Malone has in fact adopted eighty-eight of them; see also Bronson, *Joseph Ritson. Scholar-at-Arms*, p. 508. As Bronson notes earlier, Malone's 1790 edition derives in at least fifty places from Ritson's *Remarks* 1783), but Ritson's work 'has been minimized in every way which Malone could reconcile to his own conscience' (p. 495). For Steevens's comments on Malone's attack on the Second Folio see, for example, his 1793 edition, III, pp. 33, 124 (Malone scorns F_2 but uses it frequently), 283, 450; IV, pp. 81

(claiming that the F_2 editors had access to play-house manuscripts), 141, 161, 240, 379 ('the value of the second folio, it seems, must on all occasions be disputed'), etc.

117 Ritson, *Cursory Criticisms* (1792), pp. 58f., 'it must be confessed will make one of the prettyest namby pamby lines that we can anywhere meet with:

The pretty *dimp's of's* chin, and cheek, his smiles.'

Ritson lists more of 'these little Malonian beauties', calling him 'our metrical Procrustes', 'our infallible metre-master'. Malone defended his practice of polysyllabilization in *A Letter* (1792), pp. 30ff. See Bronson, *Joseph Ritson. Scholar-at-Arms*, pp. 508–12, on Ritson's exposure of Malone's 'deficiency of ear', with the conclusion that no one who studies the controversy will dispute: Ritson 'proves his point against Malone's ear'.

118 For some of Steevens's notes on Malone's syllabification see his 1793 edition, III, pp. 38, 87f.; IV, pp. 113, 297 ('our' as a disyllable); V, pp. 87 ('lover' monosyllabic), 135 ('sure' disyllabic at the end of a line); VI, pp. 41, 279; VII, p. 72 ('How is the word—*dimples*, to be monosyllabically pronounced?'), etc.

119 *MR*, n.s. xii (1793), p. 112; the *British Critic*, i (1793), p. 58, stated that 'the protraction of such words as burn, sworn, arms, charms, &c. into two syllables is what, we apprehend, would not have been tolerated by English ears at any period of our language', and suggested that Malone may have been misled by Irish pronunciation. It noted that Malone was evidently working on the principle that 'the lines of Shakespeare were all intended to be perfect, which probably was not the case', and observed that even when altered the lines often do not look like regular verses.

120 For especially clear examples of Steevens's superiority over Malone in understanding Shakespeare's language see, for example, the 1793 edition, V, pp. 306, 309, 339, 481; VI, p. 136; IX, p. 47; XII, p. 94; XIV, p. 238 (Malone noted that Lear's mad speech 'Ay, every inch a king' was printed in 'the old copies' as prose, and added 'I doubt much whether any part of it was intended for metre'). For instances of Steevens's superior reasoning power, which finds natural solutions where Malone's are awkward and wrong-headed, see, for example, VII, pp. 337, 532; IX, pp. 171, 284, 554; XII, p. 140; XIII, p. 284; XIV, p. 423; XV, pp. 533f.

121 1793 edition, VI, p. 9; see also VII, p. 181 ('I suppose this incorrect phraseology to be the mere jargon of the old players'); VIII, p. 500 ('the badness of the playhouse copies, or the carelessness of printers'); XII, p. 42 ('the gibberish of a theatre, or the blunders of a transcriber'); etc. The *Critical Review* attacked Steevens for claiming the right to alter F_1 whenever 'common sense and the laws of metre'

required it, and said of his 'silly ridicule' of the actors that he should produce evidence that they spoiled the text, or else his wit would be judged absurd and censurable: *CR*, n.s. xii (1794), pp. 393f.

122 Instances of Steevens emending' 'for the sake of metre': 1793 edition, III, pp. 35, 100 (Hanmer had cut off a foot to make a verse regular: 'By means as innocent the versification of Shakespeare has, I hope, in many instances been restored. The temerity of some critics had too long imposed severe restraints on their successors': a justification for casting off all restraint); IV, pp. 9, 11; V, p. 62; VI, p. 553; VII, pp. 327, 344, 460, 479; etc.

123 On *King Lear*, for instance, in the 1778 edition Steevens disputed a reading given by Jennens ('attaskt') since it was in neither of the Quartos he knew (it comes from the corrected state of Q_1). He subsequently stated that there were two Quartos which 'differ from each other, though printed in the same year, and for the same printer' (IX, pp. 403, 452), only to retract this opinion later (p. 564). But by 1793, in response to Malone's statement that both Quartos read '*We*, and that of which the first signature is B, reads—*We* that too late *repent's*', Steevens can reply that 'My copy of the quarto, of which the first signature is A_1, reads:—"*We* that too late *repent's us*"', (XIV, p. 69). In the 1790 edition Malone had reported that the First Folio must have been proof-corrected during printing, since he had discovered copies in varying states (I, part 2, p. 157), and now Steevens applies the discovery to *King Lear*: 'some of the quartos (like the Folio 1623) must have been partially corrected while at press' (XIV, p. 76). Having recorded more variants, he postulates the existence of a third Quarto (pp. 87f.), and goes on to make the suggestion that Quarto and Folio present discordant texts, not both designed to be preserved (p. 113). All these discoveries were only properly understood in modern times, and the last suggestion by Steevens anticipates a controversy which has just begun. See M. J. Warren, 'Quarto and Folio *King Lear* and the Interpretation of Albany and Edgar', in D. Bevington and J. L. Halio (eds), *Shakespeare, Pattern of Excelling Nature* (Newark, Del., and London, 1978), pp. 95–107.

124 On Capell's pioneering use of the Stationer's Register see Colman's review of *Notes and Various Readings* in *MR*, lxx (1784), p. 22: in his notes on the chronology Capell 'has given copies of the Stationer's books, obtained by the friendship of Mr. Draper, as they were afterwards procured by Mr. Steevens, through the kindness of Mr. Longman'. Steevens, of course, gives credit neither to Capell nor to Draper, but to Mr Lockyer Davies. For Capell's description of the bareness of the Elizabethan stage see *Notes and Various Readings*, part i, (1774), *Antony and Cleopatra*, p. 52. Where Capell writes that the

spectator had nothing to aid his imagination from the production resources, Malone has written in the margin of his copy, 'This was not so, blockhead!'. Yet compare Malone's own account in 1780: No. 265, note 1. Malone's belief in a front curtain can be seen from his note on the word 'blanket' in *Macbeth*: this is perhaps a reference to 'the coarse *woollen* curtain of his own theatre, through which probably, while the house was yet but half-lighted [*sic*], he had himself often *peeped*' (1793: VII, p. 377).

125 1793:. II, pp. *495ff.: it seems as if the discovery had been Steevens's: in 1790 Malone merely said that the manuscripts had been 'obligingly transmitted to me': I, part 2, p. 288.

126 For Gentleman see, in Bell's edition, II: *Cymbeline*, pp. 233, 235; III: *Hamlet*, p. 25 ('judiciously shortened'); III: *The Tempest*, pp. 3, 5, 6 ('a better acting play'); IV: *2 Henry IV*, p. 5 (approving the theatre-cut of Act I, scenes 1–3); and on *The Winter's Tale*: No. 243, note 33. For Davies see *Memoirs of the Life of Garrick* (1781), I, pp. 275ff. (against his *Winter's Tale*, but for his *Shrew*), and *Dramatic Miscellanies* (1784), I, p. 3 (*Richard III*) and No. 277, notes 16, 17 (on *Lear*). The *Critical Review* preferred Tate's *Lear*: lviii (1784), pp. 58f. ('we still prefer the happy conclusion: reason opposes it, while the tortured feelings at once decide the contest'), and Steevens preferred Cibber's *Richard III*: No. 303, note 28.

127 For Colman on Garrick's *Hamlet* see *MR*, lxx (1784), p. 459; Walpole: No. 261 (the gravedigger's scene, 'the finest piece of moral pathos that can be imagined, was sillily omitted by Garrick'); Mackenzie: No. 264; Davies: No. 277; Steevens: No. 303, note 46; Murphy: No. 309; *CR*, n.s. xxxii (1801), p. 194.

128 Steevens: 1778 edition: IX, p. 566; *Morning Chronicle and London Advertiser*, no. 2925 (5 October 1778); Colman, in *MR* lxx (1784), p. 459, is astonished that Thomas Davies should 'approve of the ridiculous *loves* between Edgar and Cordelia, first insinuated into the play by Tate, and so religiously and injudiciously retained by the actors . . . so wretched an alteration, weakening the main interest, and tending to degrade the filial tenderness of Cordelia'. Colman thinks Garrick was 'of all men, most equal to exhibit' Lear, but doubts whether, in the last scene, he would have been strong enough to carry Cordelia. James Harris: No. 267; and for James Boaden's attack on Tate's 'puny addition', in Bell's *Oracle*, 24 November 1789, see C. H. Gray, *Theatrical Criticism in London to 1795* (New York, 1931, 1971), p. 290.

129 On D'Avenant's *Macbeth* see Davies, *Dramatic Miscellanies* (1784), II, pp. 116–8; Murphy, No. 309; and Colman, *MR*, lxx (1784), p. 458. On Cibber's *King John* see Gentleman, No. 243, note 9; Thomas Davies, *Dramatic Miscellanies* (1784) I, pp. 4, 35, 52.

130 See the criticisms by James Fennell: No. 298 and *CR*, n.s. ii (1791), p. 105: 'The simplicity and beauty of Shakespeare's plot were destroyed, we think, by Dryden's alterations. These, however, Mr. Kemble has most injudiciously adopted; and we cannot too severely reprehend his retaining the most ridiculous scene, where the power of sympathy eases the wound when rubbed on the sword that inflicted it.' On his *Coriolanus* see G.C.D. Odell, *Shakespeare from Betterton to Irving* (New York, 1920, 1966), II, pp. 56ff., and II, pp. 58ff. on *The Tempest*.

131 Hull's *Timon of Athens* (Covent Garden, 13 May 1786) is 'merely a revival of Shadwell's ill-starred venture, and brings back to the stage the impossible Evandra-Melissa stuff': Odell, *Shakespeare from Betterton to Irving*, II, p. 49. Hull's *Comedy of Errors* was a more original venture, with sentimental comedy introduced: *ibid.*, II, pp. 45–8; the *Critical Review* liked it: n.s. xii (1794), p. 465. Kemble retained Hull's version for many years, and in 1809 restored almost all of Tate's *King Lear* (*ibid.*, II, p. 55), while in 1811 he revived Cibber's *Richard* III (*ibid.*). On Valpy's *The Roses* (1795), a compilation from the histories, see *CR*, n.s. xvi (1796), p. 359. For Garrick's review of Brooke see *MR* lix (1778), p. 361 ('The spirit of Shakespeare is wholly evaporated in this alteration'). On Garrick's wish to restore the Fool see Davies, *Dramatic Miscellanies* (1784), II, pp. 266f.

132 Since George III was the patron of the London theatres, it would be an oversight not to record one famous account of his views on Shakespeare, as Fanny Burney recorded in her Diary for 19 December 1785: ' "Was there ever", cried he, "such stuff as great part of Shakespeare? Only one must not say so! But what think you? what? Is there not sad stuff?—what?—what?" ' *The Diary and Letters of Madame d'Arblay*, ed. Austin Dobson (6 vols, 1904–5), II, p. 344.

133 *London Chronicle*, 21–3 May 1775, p. 493 ('He never appeared so great in the character before. The curse at the close of the first act, his phrenetic appeal to heaven at the end of the second on Regan's ingratitude, were two such enthusiastic scenes of human exertion, that they caused a momentary petrefaction thro' the house, which he soon dissolved as universally into tears'); Georg Lichtenberg, *Letters from England*, ed. M. L. Mare and W. H. Quarrell (Oxford, 1938), pp. 6–11, 13–17, 30–2; excerpts in A. M. Nagler, *A Source Book in Theatrical History* (New York, 1952, 1959), pp. 364–9; *London Magazine* (May–June 1776), pp. 230f., 286f. For appreciations of Garrick's acting see T. Davies, *Memoirs of the Life of David Garrick* (1780, 1784) and *Dramatic Miscellanies* (1784): excerpts in No. 277; Arthur Murphy, *The Life of David Garrick, Esq.* (1801):

excerpts in No. 309; and in this volume Taylor (No. 247), Felton (No. 291), and an anonymous writer (No. 302). An unusual account of Garrick's speaking of 'To be or not to be' can be found in Joshua Steele, *An Essay Towards Establishing the Melody and Measure of Speech*. . . (1785; 2nd edition as *Prosodia Rationalis*), pp. 39–48.

134 Steevens: No. 259; Walpole, letter to Lady Ossory, 1 February 1779, on 'the pomp of Garrick's funeral', finding it 'perfectly ridiculous' that an actor should enjoy an accolade exceeding anything Shakespeare received. He acknowledges Garrick's 'real genius', which was unequalled in tragedy or comedy, yet 'What stuff was his Jubilee Ode, and how paltry his prologues and epilogues!': *Correspondence*, XXXIII (= to the Countess of Upper Ossory, Vol. II), pp. 86–8.

135 'Shakespeare *and* Garrick, *a New* Dialogue, *occasioned by the* Alterations *lately made in the Tragedy* of Hamlet, *as acted at the Theatre Royal in* Drury-lane', *Universal Magazine* February 1776), pp. 101f. Anon., *An Epistle from Shakespeare to his Countrymen* (1777), pp. 11ff.; 'Dialogue betwixt Shakespeare and Mr. Garrick', *Weekly Magazine or Edinburgh Amusement*, xlv (August 1779), pp. 200–2. The *Monthly Review* commented on the poems appearing after Garrick's death that they were all rather uninspired: lx (1779), pp. 162 ('The Muses have not strewed the flowers of Parnassus over Garrick's bier in such profusion as might have been expected'), 232, 315f.

136 That Garrick deserved the credit for the Shakespeare revival is stated in this collection by Francis Gentleman, No. 243, note 85; Malone, No. 299; and Murphy, No. 309. Modern evidence against it has been listed in earlier volumes of this series: Vol. 3, pp. 11–14; Vol. 4, pp. 24–9; Vol. 5, pp. 12–16. See also P. Sawyer, 'John Rich's Contribution to the Eighteenth-Century London Stage', in K. Richards and P. Thomson (eds), *Essays on the Eighteenth-Century English Stage* (London, 1972), pp. 97–104, at 97f.

137 On actors coarsening the plays see Francis Gentleman in Bell's edition, II: *King Lear*, pp. 29, 65 (the Steward's fall never fails to create laughter); V: *Julius Caesar*, pp. 45, 47; and No. 243, notes 21, 23, 28. On the witches' scenes as comic see the *Edinburgh Magazine and Review* (1774), pp. 626–7; William Hodson, *Observations on Tragedy* (1780), p. 87 note; Davies, No. 277, note 10; *CR*, n.s. x (1794), pp. 146f., and n.s. xii (1794), p. 63: this reviewer offers practical suggestions to convert this 'ridiculous mummery', this 'raree-show fit only for children', into a serious and tragic experience. On actor's rant see the *Prompter* (1789), p. 17; for Sheridan's theft of the Queen Mab speech see Steevens, No. 259 and 1793 edition: V, p. 365.

138 *London Magazine* (May 1776), p. 231; Davies, *Dramatic Miscellanies*

(1784), I, p. 255; II, p. 152. Francis Gentleman records that Iago's kneeling to swear his vow of loyalty to Othello, that masterstroke of hypocrisy, drew laughter and excration from the audience (Bell's edition, I: *Othello*, p. 204). Their response, vociferous enough, seems to have been at bottom a moral one. On Mrs Siddons's Lady Macbeth see, for example, C. B. Hogan, Introduction to *The London Stage, 1660–1800. Part 5: 1776–1800*, 3 vols (Carbondale, Ill., 1968), I, xcvii. On the persistence of traditional stage business see also Steevens, 1793 edition: XV, p. 226.

139 See No. 282, and No. 298 (the author, James Fennell, a minor actor, speaks for average audience taste in his complaints that Shakespeare goes on too long), and Hogan, *The London Stage, 1776–1800*, I, pp. cxcvif. This great theatre historian's account of the audience in this period, although presented with many apologies, amounts to a devastating indictment of a group whose attendance at the theatre was largely for the spectacle, or songs or dances, or divertissement, or social assignations. They were noisy (pp. cciff.), inattentive, talking throughout the performance (pp. cvii, clxxix, ccvf.), they were violent (pp. ccf.), could destroy performances and close the theatres by rioting (pp. ccivf.), were bullying, asserting their 'rights and privileges' as Mr Hogan calls them, making actors and managers obey their wills, the most obstreperous section being the gallery (pp. lii, lxxvi, clii, cxcv–cci). Reading Mr Hogan's account makes one glad not to have had to be a member of that audience.

140 On the enlargement of the theatres see the *London Chronicle*, 23–6 September 1775; *MR*, lxiii (1780), p. 253; Pye, *A Commentary* (1792), p. 156 note; Taylor in *MR*, n.s. xviii (1795), pp. 127f.; Hogan, *The London Stage, 1776–1800*, I, pp. xliiiff., and p. xcvi on the decline of acting standards that resulted, and p. clxxxiv on the increase in takings. On the decline in Shakespeare performances see Odell, *Shakespeare from Betterton to Irving*, II, 19f; and Hogan, *op cit.*, p. cxli. Mr Hogan does not follow the practice of earlier editors of these invaluable volumes in computing the percentage of performances of Shakespeare compared with all other drama, but his list of the most frequently performed plays (pp. clxxiff.) tells its own story: the most popular was *Hamlet* (164 performances) but coming only fifth in the overall list; *Macbeth* is seventh (150 times), *The Merchant of Venice* and *Romeo and Juliet* ninth equal (119 times). In a period where comedies outnumbered tragedies by five to one (p. clxviii), it is not surprising that in the lists of the most popular plays only four serious ones are to be found, all by Shakespeare. Most of the serious drama performed was imported from Germany (p. clxxvi, and many complaints in the journals during the 1790s), and the deadness of English drama during this period can be seen from Mr Hogan's

conclusion, that 'of all the more than seven hundred new pieces written between 1776 and 1800 only two remain alive, Sheridan's *School for Scandal* and his *Critic*' (p. clxxiv).

141 Hurdis, *Cursory Remarks upon the Arrangement of the Plays of Shakespeare* (1792); 'Dirrill', *Remarks on Shakespeare's Tempest* (1797). The *Monthly* said of Dirrill's book that it was 'of little importance': n.s. xxiii (1797), pp. 355–6.

142 *MR*, n.s. xx (1796), p. 101; Plumptre's copy is Folger Library, S.a. 150, 151.

143 *British Critic*, xvi (1800), p. 438; *MR*, n.s. xxx (1799), pp. 255–7.

144 *The Great Shakespeare Forgery* (New York, 1965) by Bernard Grebanier, claims to have corrected all previous versions yet gives no documentation. S. Schoenbaum, *Shakespeare's Lives* (Oxford, 1970) is detailed and scholarly.

145 Favourable notices in the journals (one suspects 'puffing') included *CR*, lxiii (1787), p. 17; the *General Magazine and Impartial Review* (April 1788), pp. 209f.; *MR*, n.s. i (1790), pp. 427–9. Edward Jerningham's poem, *The Shakespeare Gallery* (1791), was well received by the *English Review*, xvii (1791), pp. 230f., and *CR*, n.s. ii (1790), pp. 201–3. Horace Walpole, commenting on Boydell's edition, exclaimed: 'mercy on us! *Our* painters to design for *Shakespeare*! His commentators have not been more adequate'. Bartolozzi, a slender miniaturist, is supposed to do *Macbeth*: 'Salvator Rosa might, and Piranesi might dash out Duncan's castle—but Lord help Alderman Boydell and the Royal Academy!' (Walpole, *Correspondence*, XXXIII, p. 547: 15 December 1786, to Lady Ossory). Later, having visited the exhibition, Walpole reported that 'The Shakespeare Gallery is truly most inadequate to its prototypes—but how should it be worthy of them? could we recall the brightest luminaries of painting, could they do justice to Shakespeare? was Raphael himself as great a genius in his art as the authour of *Macbeth*? and who could draw Falstaff, but the writer of Falstaff?' (*Correspondence*, XV, p. 206: 21 September 1790, to Sir David Dalrymple). Relevant modern studies include W. M. Merchant, *Shakespeare and the Artist* (Oxford, 1959); T.S.R. Boase, 'Illustrations of Shakespeare's Plays in the Seventeenth and Eighteenth Centuries', *Journal of the Warburg and Courtauld Institutes*, x (1947), pp. 193–207; Horst Oppel, *Die Shakespeare-Illustration als Interpretation der Dichtung* (Wiesbaden, 1965: Akademie der Wissenschaften und der Literatur in Mainz, Abhandlungen der Geistes- und Sozial-wissenschaftlichen Klasse, Jahrgang 1965, Nr. 2); and Winifred H. Friedman, *Boydell's Shakespeare Gallery* (New York, 1976), a full study, including nearly three hundred illustrations of the paintings and engravings concerned.

Note on the Text

The texts in this collection are taken from the first printed edition, unless otherwise stated. The date under which a piece is filed is that of the first edition, with two exceptions: plays, for which, usually, the first performance is used (for such information I have relied on *The London Stage* for the period 1660 to 1800); and those works for which the author gives a date of composition substantially earlier than its first printing. The place of publication is London, unless otherwise indicated.

Spelling and punctuation are those of the original editions except where they seemed likely to create ambiguities for the modern reader. Spelling has, however, been standardized for writers' names (Jonson not Johnson, Rymer not Rhimer), for play titles, and for Shakespearian characters.

Omissions in the text are indicated by three dots: [. . .].

Footnotes intended by the original authors are distinguished with an asterisk, dagger, and so on; those added by the editor are numbered. Editorial notes within the text are placed within square brackets.

Act-, scene-, and line-numbers have been supplied in all quotations from Shakespeare, in the form 2.1.85 (Act II, scene 1, line 85). The text used for this purpose was *The Riverside Shakespeare*, ed. G. B. Evans (Boston: Houghton Mifflin, 1974).

Classical quotations have been identified, and translations added, usually those in the Loeb Library.

243. Francis Gentleman, commentary on Shakespeare

1774

From *Bell's Edition of Shakespeare's Plays, As they are now performed at the Theatres Royal in London; Regulated from the Prompt Books of each House, by Permission; with Notes Critical and Illustrative; By the Authors of the Dramatic Censor* (9 vols, 1773–4). First issued in 1773, this edition was reprinted in 1774 with numerous small alterations to the notes and introductions; vol. IX, 'Shakespeare's Poems', is dated 1 September 1774.

On Gentleman see the head-note to Vol. 5, No. 227; on Bell and his edition see Stanley Morrison, *John Bell, 1745–1831* (Cambridge, 1930), and M. St C. Byrne, 'Bell's Shakespeare', *Times Literary Supplement* (31 January 1948), p. 65.

[1] [End-note to *Othello*]
At the end of the Third Act a reader or spectator is induced to think his feelings cannot be touched more sensibly, but there is such a well conceived succession of events, such variation of circumstances, such preservation of characters, such a noble melifluence of writing, and such a melting climax of catastrophe, that sensation is played upon, with increasing force, to the very last speech. (I, 232)

[2] [On *King Lear*, 2.4.104: 'Tell the hot duke that—No, but not yet . . . ']
Here falls in a fine turn of recollection for the actor who performs *Lear*. It is one of the noblest breaks we recollect: indeed the whole speech is inimitable. This is a melting address; the numerous transitions are most masterly. *Lear*'s struggles against his powerful injuries, and his own strong feelings, are exquisite; the daughters working him severally up to madness, and his at length falling into

it, are an irresistible combination that none but *Shakespeare* could frame or express. (II, 32)

[3] [On *Richard III*, Act III]
It is a very peculiar merit in this play that each act rises above the other, and that the whole piece is alive, with increasing spirit, to the end. (III, 42)

[4] [*Ibid.*, Act IV]
There is a remarkable, quick, and animating succession of incidents through the whole fourth Act, which concludes with inexpressible spirit. (III, 56)
Richard's full revelation of character, with the remarkable bustle of business which the fourth Act contains, invigorates it very much, and places an audience on the topmost bent of expectation. (III, 57)

[5] [*Ibid.*, 5.5: Cibber's version of the fight between Richard III and Richmond; see Vol. 1, pp. 127–8]
There cannot be a stronger proof of a very singular impression upon an audience than that general murmur which the meeting of *Richmond* and *Richard* always occasions, followed by the eager applause that attends the tyrant's fall; and we may without fear of censure say that this play, as acted, shows that the alterations have been produced from a very extensive and settled knowledge of stage effect: we have been studious to find error, but could not materially. (III, 68)

[6] [End-note to *Richard III*]
The fifth Act of this piece is more replete with interesting business and spirit, than any other we know. (III, 70)

[7] [On *Hamlet*, 3.3.73ff.: 'Now might I do it, now 'a is a-praying']
A long speech of *Hamlet*'s is here commendably thrown aside, first, as being unnecessary, and next, as tending to vitiate and degrade his character, much.[1] (III, 53)

[8] [*Ibid.*, 4.4; Hamlet's meeting Fortinbras' army, and the soliloquy 'How all occasions do inform against me']
The author has here introduced a very unessential scene, unworthy

[1] Cf. Gentleman's comments in 1770: Vol. 5, pp. 378f.

the closet and stage, therefore properly consigned to oblivion; though *Hamlet*'s soliloquy, in Mr. *Garrick*'s alteration, is preserved, not censurably. In the original state of the play the whole is quite superfluous; besides, the Prince seems to take a violent resolution, yet is no more heard of till we find he has been shipwrecked. (III, 61)

[9] [*Ibid.*, 4.7.140ff.: 'I'll anoint my sword']
This treacherous plot upon the life of *Hamlet* is truly villainous on the part of the King, and pitifully mean in *Laertes*, though he has lost a father; for no revenge can be just that is not open and manlike. It is a bad feeling of the human heart, in its best shape; what must it be, in the worst?[1] But no censure should fall on *Shakespeare* for this —he drew character, not perfection. (III, 67)

[10] [*Ibid.*, 5.1: the gravediggers' scene]
These characters, and their quibbling humour,[2] may be exceptionable to over-nice critics; yet even to them, methinks, the moral reflections occasioned by the grave, &c. make ample amends; and though their dialogue is often stigmatized as mere gallery stuff, yet we think that sensible[3] boxes may be pleased and instructed by it. For which reason it is cause of concern to think Mr. *Garrick* has too politely frenchified his alteration of this piece, by endeavouring to annihilate what, though Mr. *Voltaire* could not like it, has indubitable merit. (III, 69)

[11] [*Ibid.*, end-note; added in second edition]
The fifth Act of this play is by no means so good as the three first; yet it engages attention in public by having a good deal of bustle, and, what *English* audiences are fond of, many deaths. (III, 82)

[12] [On *The Tempest*, 1.2: Prospero's magic]
Being professed foes to all sentiments and characters which inculcate ideas of enchantment, conjuration, or supernatural appearances, we necessarily declare ourselves against the very foundation of this play; however, as what *Prospero* utters in point of sentiment is all through both nervous and sensible, he requires a

---

[1] The last two sentences were added in the second edition.
[2] The first edition reads 'These gentry . . . certainly trespass upon decorum. . . .' (III, 71).
[3] In the sense 'having more acute power of sensation; sensitive' (*OED*, II.2).

performer of oratorical ability to support him: venerable appearance is likewise requisite. (III, 7)

[13] [*Ibid.*, 3.1: Ferdinand and Miranda]
We know not a prettier or more delicate pattern of love than this scene exhibits; it is not quite so warm as that in the second Act of *Romeo and Juliet*; but, considering *Miranda*'s sequestered education, has equal merit. (III, 36)

[14] [*Ibid.*, 4.1.152ff.: 'The cloud-capp'd tow'rs . . .']
Of this passage, so universally known and so justly admired, we may say that it possesses eastern magnificence of idea, cloathed with the chastest elegance; no author ever soared beyond, and *Shakespeare* himself but rarely comes up to it. (III, 48)

[15] [*Ibid.*, Epilogue]
This address to the audience is sensible, and the lines happily avoid namby-pamby jingle by running agreeably into each other; the last distich we object to, as alluding too closely to the Lord's-prayer. (III, 62)

[16] [On *Measure for Measure*, 3.2.261ff.: 'He who the sword of heaven will bear/Should be as holy as severe']
The sentiments of this soliloquy are just and instructive; but the namby-pamby versification in which they are conveyed to our apprehension is abominable. (III, 41)

[17] [On *King John*, 2.1: the dispute between King Philip and King John. The first edition reads:]
This encounter of the King's is not unlike that of Prettyman and Volscius, in *The Rehearsal*; with this difference, that the burlesque Princes are rather more polite than the real Monarchs; and the Bastard, regardless of all decorum, appears a Billingsgate bravo. The scene, as here offered to view, is considerably, and we think very justifiably, curtailed. (IV, 16)
[The second edition reads:]
The scene, as here offered to view, is considerably, and we think very justifiably, curtailed for representation; the behaviour of the Bastard is sometimes too licentious in the presence of monarchs; but it is probable some of his speeches were meant to be spoken

aside; the others should be somewhat corrected by a nicety of manner in the deliverance. (IV, 16)

[18] [*Ibid.*, 5.2.8ff.]
Though this scene is undoubtedly too long in the original, yet we could wish *Salisbury*'s speech stood thus:

> *To be a widow maker—oh, and there,*
> *Where honourable rescue and defence,*
> *Cries out upon the name of Salisbury:*
> *But such is the infection of the time,*
> *That for the health and physic of our right,*
> *We cannot deal, but with the very hand*
> *Of stern injustice, and confused wrong:*
> *And is't not pity—oh, my grieved friends—*
> *That we, the sons and children of this Isle,*
> *Should live to see so sad an hour as this;*
> *Wherein we step after a stranger march*
> *Upon her gentle bosom, and fill up*
> *Her enemies rank? I must withdraw and weep, &c.*

And we think the Dauphin's reply should stand as follows:

> *—an earthquake of nobility.*
> *Oh, what a noble combat hast thou fought,*
> *Between compulsion and brave respect;*
> *Let me wipe off this honourable dew*
> *That silverly doth progress on thy cheeks.* (IV, 56)

[19] [End-note to *King John*]
Much the greater part of this Tragedy is unworthy its author; a rumble-jumble of martial incidents, improbably and confusedly introduced; the character of *Constance* intire, four scenes, and several speeches of *Faulconbridge*'s, are truly *Shakespearean*. *Colley Cibber* altered this piece, but as we think for the worse; it is more regular, but more phlegmatic than the original. (IV, 64)

[20] [On *1 Henry IV*, 5.4.77: Hal's defeat of Hotspur]
Though *Henry*'s gallant behaviour must give pleasure, yet we think every generous mind must feel for *Percy*'s fall; as, though a rebel, he seems to act upon just principles and very aggravated provocation. It is a very nice, and almost unparalleled point, to bring two characters in mortal conflict on the stage where, as in the

present case, we must rejoice at the success of one and grieve for the fate of the other. (IV, 71)

[21] [*Ibid.*, 5.4.129: 'Embowelled?']
The supposed dead man's rising is a most risible incident, and his soliloquy keeps pace with it; however, we conceive the son of sack's rolling and tumbling about the stage to get *Hotspur* on his back, is too much in the stile of pantomime mummery; it may, and certainly does, create laughter for the time; but such ludicrous attacks upon reason are beneath *Shakespeare* and the stage. (IV, 72)

[22] [On *2 Henry IV*, 2.1.85ff.: Mistress Quickly's accusation of Falstaff]
It is impossible to write any thing more characteristically for an ignorant, froward, talkative woman, than this jumbled piece of ridiculous circumlocution. (IV, 17)

[23] [*Ibid.*, 2.4.110ff.]
The character of *Pistol* is violently outré, and though it might be intelligibly satirical when written, yet at present it is triflingly obscure, and depends more upon oddity of figure and extravagance of deportment than what he says. To confess the truth, we cannot much relish the humour of this scene till the Prince and *Poins* enter; and even then *Falstaff*'s detection seems languid compared to his laughable dilemma's in the first part. (IV, 27)

[24] [*Ibid.*, 5.5.47ff.: Hal's rejection of Falstaff]
A truly majestic rebuff to the licentious companion of his dissipated hours; mingled with a humane attention for one whom, though he can no longer sport with, he may justly pity. (IV, 76)

[25] [End-note to *2 Henry IV*]
This dramatic Olio, for such *Henry* the Fourth's second part is, contains some very insipid ingredients, with several richly seasoned for critical taste. The author has been complimented for his support of *Falstaff*'s character; but though it may be a better second part than any other author could have drawn, yet we are bold to pronounce all the comedy of this piece, out of comparison, inferior to that of the first part: more low, much more indecent, consequently less deserving of approbation. Several passages in

the tragic scenes are inimitably fine; but, on the whole, we cannot think it either a good acting or reading composition; however, it is much better for both in this edition than as it was originally written.

There are several judicious transpositions in the last act, which, however, is still laboured and heavy. (IV, 78)

[26] [Head-note to *Henry V*]
Our Fifth *Henry*, notwithstanding his unpardonable levity and dissipation while a prince, shone with such resplendant lustre and dignity when a monarch that *Shakespeare*, who had shewn his foibles, was under a kind of necessity to produce him in an improved state, and if we judge by the outset of his prologue, he summoned all his powers to do the hero justice. Nor has he failed: the character is faithfully and ably drawn; it is furnished with language and sentiments suitable; being placed also in the most advantageous point of view. 'Tis true, the plot is irregular, and tainted with some low quibbling comedy which, as we think, contrary to some idolators of *Shakespeare*, greatly disgrace the serious part. However, upon the whole we may safely and cordially admit that there are several passages in this piece equal to any other the author ever wrote; it would be exceedingly painful to find fault, but that we have many more agreeable opportunities to praise. (IV, 3)
[The second edition concludes:]
'Tis true, the plot is irregular; but its very wildness is an additional beauty. The comic scenes, wherewith this piece is interspersed, are admirably written. An over-nice critic might perhaps dispense with them; but they are very entertaining in the performance; and the author undoubtedly felt the necessity of relieving his sublimer passages, which, till the fifth act, shine with one uniform martial fire. —On the whole this piece, we presume, must be allowed to be a very capital performance. (IV, 209)

[27] [On *Julius Caesar*, 3.1.230ff.]
The real patriot is finely distinguished here from the pretended one; *Brutus*,conscious that he struck for liberty alone, suspects no ill consequences from *Antony*'s having the rostrum; while *Cassius*, who acted from malevolence and ambition, justly forebodes the real event. (V, 43)

[28] [*Ibid.*, 4.3.308ff.: the performing texts added a concluding passage to Act IV]

> *Both.* It shall be done, my lord.　　　[*Exeunt.*
> *Bru.* Sure they have rais'd some devil to their aid;
> And think to frighten *Brutus* with a shade;
> But ere the night closes this fatal day
> I'll send more ghosts, this visit to repay.

As these four uncharacteristic, bouncing lines are used in representation by way of sending the actor off with a flourish, we insert them; though very disgraceful to *Brutus* and *Shakespeare*. We have seen the ghost introduced a second time; but such an addition is insufferable ignorance. (V, 66)

[29] [*Ibid.*, 5.5.68ff.]
This elogium of *Antony*'s upon a dead foe is elegant, comprehensive, and generous. The piece should conclude with it, unless something better was supplied; for *Octavius*'s jingles are contemptible, and seem as if *Shakespeare* had suddenly tired, and patched a conclusion any way. (V, 75)

[30] [On *Timon of Athens*, 4.1.1ff.: Timon's curse of Athens]
However highly provoked, there is in this speech of general execration something unworthy a generous mind; but it is not unnatural, as the heart which undistinguishingly dispenses favours may, turned to the opposite way, be easily supposed as unlimitedly vindictive. Should this be allowed the author is yet culpable for mingling indecency, as he has done, with temporary madness. (V, 121)

[31] [*Ibid.*, 5.1.223: Timon's exit]
This languid departure of the principal character must leave an audience unsatisfied; and all that follows is so detached from the main plot, except *Timon*'s epitaph, that cutting every line out would rather serve than maim the piece. It is merely patching up a conclusion with ingredients totally void of critical relish. (V, 146)

[32] [End-note to *Timon of Athens*]
The last act of this play has neither much to praise, nor much to condemn; of the conclusion we may speak in *Shakespeare*'s own words, that it is most lame and impotent. (V, 148)

[33] [Head-note to *The Winter's Tale*]
That *Shakespeare* was particularly right in his choice of a title for this piece, very imperfect criticism must allow, for it has all the improbabilities and jumble of incidents, some merry and some sad, that constitute *Christmas* stories. There are many beauties even in wildness; it is a parterre of poetical flowers sadly choked with weeds. Mr. *Garrick* has furnished a very good alteration, which we had no right to offer as *Shakespeare's* . . . .[1] (V, 151)

[34] [*Ibid.*, 1.2.108ff.: Leontes' jealousy]
The origin and progress of jealousy are mostly unaccountable, but we never met with so strange a picture as this exhibited by *Leontes*, who, from what he himself has desired, picks out suspicion; indeed some passages which follow this speech in the original show his majesty to be little better than a bedlamite; but to the credit of our author they are properly omitted. (V, 156–7)
[The second edition reads:]
The origin and progress of jealousy, conceived of sudden and unjust surmise in the sufferer's own brain (not planted there by the malice and misrepresentations of another, as instanced in *Othello*) and the severe anguish and self-reproach in consequence of being undeceived, are truly and pathetically painted in this character of *Leontes*. Some over-rash and almost frantic expressions are justly omitted in this alteration. The scene is thereby rendered not only less exceptionable but warmer and more affecting in representation. (V, 146)

[35] [Ibid., 1.2.316ff.]
The proposing of and assenting to *Polixenes*'s death by treacherous means, upon such slight vaporous surmises, shows *Leontes* a monster of inhumanity as well as of folly. (V, 160)
[The second edition reads:]
. . . surmises, can only be palliated by the state of a jealous mind, which is a temporary frenzy and will run into any extremes to gratify its resentment. (V, 151)

[36] [*Ibid.*, 1.2.462: Polixenes' departure]
This obscure and precipitate retreat of a monarch, tho' in danger, abates dignity much. It might have been rendered better by putting

[1] See Vol. 4, No. 150.

some spirited objections into the mouth of *Polixenes*, which *Camillo* might have over-ruled; at present shameful pusillanimity appears.

The first act, resting almost on the childish irregular feelings of *Leontes*, can give little pleasure, less instruction. (V, 164)

[37] [*Ibid.*, 4.4: the sheep-shearing scene]
There is a vein of poetical pastoral beauty runs through the whole scene where *Florizel* and *Perdita* are concerned, not to be surpassed. Their figures should be delicately fine, and their expression, to do the charming picturesque sentiments they have furnished justice, should be meltingly harmonious. Their ideas would thaw the breast of frozen age; and their style, without a tincture of inflation, suits their high birth. (V, 193)

[38] [*Ibid.*, 5.1.186: 'I now came from him']
Both the characters and time in this piece travel with very astonishing speed. (V, 216)

[39] [Head-note to *Coriolanus*]
We must very much applaud *Shakespeare* for his frequent choice of historical subjects, and his strict adherence to those he selected; however, we think here he got upon rather a barren spot. Genius could not mount on free wing; for heroism, and that rather of a savage kind, without any additional concerns that might engage attention or touch the heart is too limited an idea for five acts. Wherefore we find that our author was under the tiresome necessity of employing near three acts of the five in tedious repetitions of fulsome panegyrics on his hero. What the theme would allow he has struck out, and we readily allow *Coriolanus, Menenius*, and *Volumnia* to be well supported; but the piece, altogether, can never be much a public or private favourite. (V, 229)

[40] [*Ibid.*, 3.3.67ff.: 'How? traitor?']
This vehement burst of passion upon the aggravation of so opprobrious a term as traitor is much in character. Though *Coriolanus*'s behaviour is in several points romantic, and not defensible, yet this animated acceptance of and reproach to the popular sentence displays great magnanimity of resolution; it raises our pity for a great man so situated, though greatly his own seeking. The important share he has in this act renders it better,

and more an object of attention and concern than either of those
before it. (V, 277)

[41] [*Ibid.*, 5.3.182: Coriolanus' capitulation to his mother]
We consider *Coriolanus* as very languid in his mode of yielding to so
material a sacrifice of his honour, and the trust reposed in him; his
struggles should have been of a more feeling nature. The scene also
ends most flatly. (V, 304)

[42] [*Ibid.*, 5.6.39ff.: Aufidius' grievances against Coriolanus]
If any justification can be offered for conspiracy against the life of a
man, *Aufidius* seems here to offer a very good one; for certain it is
from the face of affairs that *Coriolanus* behaved like a traitor abroad,
intirely like a brute, and partly like a fool at home. (V, 308)

[43] [*Ibid.*, 5.6.130: the murder of Coriolanus]
The treacherous barbarity of *Aufidius* and his ruffian crew must
raise great indignation; yet the fall of *Coriolanus* works no effect
similar to that of other great *Romans* presented in the drama, *Brutus*,
Cato, &c. Their deaths touch feelingly the human heart; they sink
under a virtuous necessity by committing what in their time was
deemed the noblest instance of resolution, acts of suicide. But the
hero of this piece is such an enthusiast to sanguinary actions, so
brutally rough, so peculiarly proud, so improperly vindictive, and
at last so shamefully weak, that it must be a very susceptible bosom
indeed which yearns for his fate. (V, 310–11)

[44] [*Ibid.*, 5.6.146: Aufidius:]
My rage is gone,—time it was we think—how long would this assassin
have had it remain after the object of his envy was dead? The
crocodile concern he affects deserves only to be laughed at.
    The fifth act rises very considerably above the fourth; the
intercession scene is important and pathetic; but what comes after
falls off, and we are not interested by the catastrophe. (V, 311)

[45] [Head-note to *Twelfth Night*]
This play, which might very properly borrow a title from another
of our Author's pieces—the COMEDY OF ERRORS—is in its plot very
complicate, irregular, and in some places incredible. The grave
scenes are graceful and familiar: the comic ones full charged with

humour; but rather of the obsolete kind.—*Malvolio*'s ridiculous self-sufficiency is displayed in a most masterly manner. *Sir Toby* and *Sir Andrew* keep pace with him; and *Viola*, though romantic in her love, is delicately sustained. Very few pieces have more spirit than *Twelfth Night*, or more pleasingly unravel in their catastrophe, an intanglement of characters and circumstances. Action must render it more pleasing than perusal. (V, 315)

[46] [*Ibid.*, 2.4.110ff.: 'she never told her love']
The matchless picturesque beauty of this speech is so obviously striking that to enlarge upon it would seem an insult to the reader's conception. Suffice it then to say, *Shakespeare* himself never surpassed it. (V, 342)

[47] [On *The Two Gentlemen of Verona*, 1.2.50ff.: Julia's soliloquy on Proteus' letter]
This ticklish wavering of a young, a delicate mind, upon being first seriously addressed, is very natural; indeed, upon all occasions our author appears minutely correct in mental operations, both philosophically and practically. (VI, 11)

[48] [On *The Taming of the Shrew*, 'Induction', 1.79: 'Enter Players']
Shakespeare missed no opportunity of realizing some characters, by introducing others as fictitious,[1] and his regard for the stage is properly manifested by taking care that exalted characters should ever treat the actors with respect. (VI, 76)

[49] [*Ibid.*, 5.2.160ff.: Katherina's speech on women's duty 'to serve, love, and obey']
This speech must ever stamp credit on its author. There is a fine display of relative knowledge, thrown out in a nervous, yet very intelligible manner; and we wish that not only every unmarried, but also married lady were perfect in the words and practice; however, it is too long for stage utterance. (VI, 150)

[50] [Head-note to *Troilus and Cressida*]
The great end of every drama is, or should be, instruction relished

---

[1] Gentleman makes similar comments on the play-scene in *Hamlet*, and on Brutus' and Cassius' references to future ages acting their parts (*Julius Caesar*, 3.1.111ff.).

by amusement; so far as any production fails of this, it fails in value. Judging similarly of *Troilus and Cressida*, it is a very censurable effusion of dramatic fancy; for except some very fine sentiments scattered up and down, it is void of the essential requisites; besides, characters are so oddly blended, the scenes are so multiplied, and the plot so very strangely wound up, that we think it stands but a poor chance of giving either public or private satisfaction. (VI, 155)

[51] [*Ibid.*, 1.2.230ff.]
There is no doubt but *Shakespeare* meant *Pandarus* as a character of humour, but it is in a very peculiar stile, and requires very extraordinary talents to personate him exact to the author's intention. (VI, 169)

[52] [*Ibid.*, 1.3.197ff.: Ulysses' account of Achilles' criticism of the Greek leaders]
There is a very commendable idea broached here against those who prefer immediate action to prescient calculation; but with deference to our author, we think he makes *Ulysses* deliver himself in terms too complicate and cramp. (VI, 176)

[53] [End-note to *Troilus and Cressida*]
This play has a very weak unworthy conclusion. In some parts fine fancy and great poetry is to be found; but on the whole the fable is too incompleat, the scenes too short, and too quickly huddled on each other to give much chance for success in action. (VI, 258)

[54] [Head-note to *Antony and Cleopatra*]
Whether this play, tho' excellently wrote, has any chance for long existence on the stage, is very doubtful. Twenty years since[1] that very able and successful Dramatic Modeller, Mr. *Garrick*, produced it under the most probable state of reformation; yet, tho' elegantly decorated and finely performed, it too soon languished. *Antony* and *Cleopatra* are the chief marked characters in it: he is a flighty infatuated slave to an excess of love and luxury; she a tinsel pattern of vanity and female cunning, which work the downfal of both. A double moral may be inferred, namely, That indolence and dissipation may undo the greatest of men; and that beauty, under

---

[1] In 1759, assisted by Capell: see Vol. 4, No. 178.

the direction of vanity, will not only ruin the possessor, but admirer also. (VI, 261)

When we meet two such celebrated names, and consider our author's great abilities, we are naturally led to expect a very capital piece. Those characters are accordingly very greatly supported; but the whole piece, as it stands here, seems rather too incorrect and confused for action. (VI, 263)

[55] [*Ibid.*, 2.2.177ff.: 'The barge she sat in . . . ']
The luxury of *Antony* is well pointed out by *Enobarbus*, and the description he gives shortly after of her meeting *Antony* is admirably poetical. *Dryden*, in *All for Love*,[1] has boldly ventured a comparison upon the identical circumstance; but, though capital, we think him inferior to *Shakespeare*, though he has disposed the description better by putting it in *Antony*'s mouth. (VI, 288)

[56] [*Ibid.*, 3.11]
Antony, through this scene, manifests an irresistible attachment, though he feels strongly its disgraceful ruinous effects. (VI, 323)

[57] [*Ibid.*, 3.13.182ff.: 'Let's have one other gaudy night']
Antony, though like a lion in the toils, and sensible from whence his dilemma proceeds, perseveres like all weak men in the gratification of a delusive injurious appetite. (VI, 330)

[58] [*Ibid.*, 4.8]
In every speech almost our author has shown *Antony*'s reigning foibles, love, luxury, boasting, and ostentation. This short scene is most spiritedly supported. (VI, 340)

[59] [*Ibid.*, 4.14.50: 'Eros!—I come, my queen! . . . ']
Here the portrait of a man over-powered with amorous credulity is most faithfully described. *Antony* is by no means a valuable, yet he is occasionally a pitiable character; upon the same principle that we admire heroism, we commiserate, under particular circumstances, folly. (VI, 345)

[60] [*Ibid.*, 5.2.49ff.: 'Sir, I will eat no meat . . . ']
Cleopatra in this speech displays great and becoming magnanimity

[1] See Vol. 1, pp. 175–6.

of spirit, finely opposed to the equivocal treacherous behaviour of *Octavius*. (VI, 356)

[61] [*Ibid.*, 5.2.82ff.: 'His legs bestrid the ocean . . . ']
This panegyric upon fallen *Antony* is liberal and affectionate; the fancy and imagery are exquisite, nor does the expression fall short of them. (VI, 357)

[62] [End-note to *Antony and Cleopatra*]
Notwithstanding the fifth Act wants the assistance of *Antony*, who, as a main pillar, should not have been cast down so soon, yet it is rather the most regular and affecting of the whole. *Cleopatra* in it is very consistent; and supported by an actress possessing grace, power, and feeling, must work very tragic effects. (VI, 366)

[63] [On *Richard II*, 3.2.6ff.: 'Dear earth, I do salute thee . . . ']
Richard's address to the earth is pathetic and fanciful, but rather romantic and ill adapted to the serious important situation of his affairs: the author appears sensible of this by calling it a senseless conjuration. (VII, 44)

[64] [*Ibid.*, 3.2.209ff.: Richard's acceptance of defeat by Bolingbroke]
Richard here discovers his true character, a most wretched shameful pusillanimity, a cowardice and despondency that would stigmatize a private man, much more a monarch, who from birth, education, and station, ought to think with more magnanimity and act with more resolution. (VII, 50)

[65] [*Ibid.*, 4.1.207ff.: 'With mine own tears I wash away my balm']
Richard, in his mode of resignation, shows some degree of insanity, for which his distressful situation may, as he all through shows a feeble mind, apologize. (VII, 66)

[66] [*Ibid.*, 5.5.1ff.: Richard's prison soliloquy]
The thirty-nine indented lines would, for recitation particularly, be better omitted than retained, as they tend more to puzzle conception, than to inform judgment. The author seems to have indulged his own fancy, without consulting either the stage or closet. (VII, 82)

[67] [On *2 Henry VI*, 3.3: the death of Cardinal Beauford]
The many instances *Shakespeare* has, in other pieces, given of his conception of madness and perturbation of mind, leaves us nothing to say of this speech but that it is better than any other author could have written on such a subject; the appeals to imagination are extremely forceable, and the whole scene horridly fine. (VII, 237)

[68] [*Ibid.*, 4.2: the Jack Cade scenes]
We more cordially wish the whole of this crew suppressed than any characters or passages we have met in our author; for though *Jack Cade* and his associates are essential to history, and might have created a real tragedy, they are miserable members to compose parts of one for representation. (VII, 242)

[69] [On *3 Henry VI*, 1.1.16ff.: the by-play with the decapitated head of Somerset]
This scene in description, though not a positive action, may be stiled a slaughter house one. Shewing and kicking about heads is totally inconsistent with stage representation; and it is almost impossible to conceive how our author, so frequently delicate, elegant, and humane, could suffer such spectacles to disgrace the labours, or rather spontaneous effusions of his matchless pen. (VII, 278)

[70] [Head-note to *Titus Andronicus*]
Without some evident use to society in general no literary production, however fanciful or plausible, can claim estimation. Upon this principle, though in different parts *Titus Andronicus* bears strong, nay evident, marks of *Shakespeare*'s pen yet he has fixed upon such characters and incidents as are totally offensive. Human nature is shewn in a most partial and deplorable state; depraved as we sometimes find it, it is scarce to be imagined that such an infernal groupe as is huddled together in this piece could meet in so small a compass. Hence this play must be horrid in representation, and is disgustful in perusal. Indeed it is matter of great wonder how *Shakespeare*'s humane heart could endure the contemplation of such inhuman actions and events, through the course of five acts. (VIII, 3)

[71] [*Ibid.*, 1.3.10ff.: Tamora: 'The birds chaunt melody on every bush . . .']
This *Gothic* queen is not only very indecent here, but strangely romantic; yet her speech is both fanciful and poetical. (VIII, 25)

[72] [On *The Comedy of Errors*, 1.1]
Few authors, except *Shakespeare*, could have told *Egeon*'s long story in so easy a flow of natural expression as we find it here; notwithstanding one hundred and three lines of narration are assigned to him in three speeches, even decently recited they must please. (VIII, 86)

[73] [*Ibid.*, 3.2]
Of all Dramatic colloquial versification, alternate rhimes are most strange and unnatural; certainly *Shakespeare* meant by such variations of stile to relieve his genius, or to please some reigning caprice in his day. (VIII, 106)

[74] [End-note to *The Comedy of Errors*]
The eclaircissement of plot in this play flows very naturally from the circumstances, and must please intelligent auditors and readers, as must in our idea the whole of this Act. (VIII, 134)

[75] [Head-note to *A Midsummer Night's Dream*]
In the piece before us *Shakespeare* had evidently two great and very material points in view; Novelty and Originality, the sure road, if attained, to permanency and fame. To these favourite objects he paid such attention as sometimes to forget probability, though he always preserved character. The following piece has great poetical and dramatic merit, considered in general; but a puerile plot, an odd mixture of incidents, and a forced connexion of various stiles throw a kind of shade over that blaze of merit many passages would otherwise have possessed. There is no character strongly marked, yet the whole shews a very great master dallying with his own genius and imagination in a wonderful and delightful manner. (VIII, 137)

[76] [*Ibid.*, 1.1. 171ff.]
There could not be a prettier or more fervent set of oaths coined in the amorous stile than those uttered by *Hermia* with so much

affectionate delicacy; but we wish the Author had not here, nor on any other occasion, changed pleasing emphatic blank verse for unpleasing unnatural rhimes. (VIII, 144)

[77] [*Ibid.*, 3.2.378ff.]
The Fairy descriptions all through this play are abundantly rich, but *Puck* here surpasses all the rest, being awfully charming; though all departed bodies have wormed beds, yet giving them to the wicked peculiarly is finely conceived. (VIII, 179)

[78] [Head-note to *Love's Labour's Lost*]
Shakespeare never sported more with his desultory muse than in tacking together the scenes of this piece; he certainly wrote more to please himself than to divert or inform his readers and auditors. The characters are by no means masterly, the language is cramp; the scenes possess a wearisome sameness, and the sentiments, except a few, appear at this day much laboured, though we believe they flowed spontaneously from our Author's creative imagination. It must certainly be accounted one of *Shakespeare*'s weakest compositions, and does no great credit to his muse. (VIII, 205)

[79] [*Ibid.*, 1.2: Armado's catechism of Moth]
Whenever we meet with a scene of paltry punning, miserable word catching, and fritters of wit, which is too often the case in this undertaking; we most cordially lament that our author lived in an age when such trash was palatable. (VIII, 217)

[80] [*Ibid.*, 4.1.60ff.: Armado's letter to Jaquenetta]
Shakespeare has made his Don an epistolary enthusiast, and has furnished him with a train of ideas, and a peculiarity of stile no author but himself could have produced. (VIII, 237)

[81] [*Ibid.*, 4.3.324–42: Berowne's panegyric to love]
This and the following eighteen lines are inexpressibly beautiful and pregnant with fancy; they feelingly speak their great Author. (VIII, 255)

[82] [*Ibid.*, 5.1: the word-battle between Armado and Holofernes]
That *Shakespeare* was not only possessed of a very poetical but a very patient genius, many of his pieces verify, but this in

particular; for sure no man besides himself ever pursued ideas through such labyrinths of expression, nor ever cloathed them more enigmatically. (VIII, 239)

[83] [*Ibid.*, 5.2.760ff.: Berowne on love]
It is amazing to conceive the superabundant descriptions of love in its various shapes and influences which *Shakespeare* draws, and all just though very different; this is not one of the least pleasing and poetical. (VIII, 282)

[84] [End-note to *Love's Labour's Lost*]
We are now come to the end of this whimsical piece; if barely leaving off dialogue and dropping the curtain can be called a conclusion: we rather think it a simple escape from readers and an audience. The fifth Act is much longer and heavier than any of the others; we have pointed out the most obvious omissions, but many more might be made without impropriety. (VIII, 287)

[85] [From *The Life of Shakespeare*]
. . . As an Author, no man has been more complimented, no man more abused; in the latter respect, we mean by multiplied and unworthy editions of his works, most of which were mere jobs. We shall not point out at large the commentators who, in our idea, come within this view; but we may safely assert that some of the most celebrated writers within the last fifty years have been mutilators of *Shakespeare*. He has been almost as much traded upon, and as vilely interpreted as the Bible.

Theobald, in our opinion, is the only ingenious liberal Critic. He evidently wished to do the Author justice; and though he often went conjecturally too far, yet in the main he illustrated *Shakespeare* better than any other commentator, neither the laborious Bishop of *Gloster*, nor the tremendous Dr. *Johnson* excepted; both of whom evidently served themselves much more than they did the subject of their prodigious productions. . . . (IX, 5)

From all we can trace, his life, from the commencement of manhood was a calm, uniform scene of existence; not perturbed with violent passions, nor marked with uncommon events; not clouded with adversity, nor tempted by the delusive glare of dangerous prosperity; for prosperity may undoubtedly be termed dangerous when it shines on us with meridian beams.

As to his character, it must be fished out of his writings; from whence, though abundant outlines offer, it is very critical to ascertain a strict likeness.* Some years before his death (which happened in the year 1616, and the 53d year of his age) he spent in comfortable retirement amidst respectable select acquaintance, who admired his talents, and acknowledged his amiable qualifications as a companion. (IX, 8)

[On Pope's claim that Shakespeare was more original than Homer: cf. Vol. 2, p. 403]

By the by, our *British Homer* has trespassed on the *Grecian* by positive assertion, without offering proof; we admire *Shakespeare* as much as he could do, but would not urge a partial and prejudicial comparison against the capital merits of antiquity. *Shakespeare* was not without *some* learning: all the subjects of his dramas are taken from history or romance, and his knowledge of character evidently arose from observation of mankind; therefore his merit, like *Homer*'s, must come from some tincture of the learning or some cast of the models before him.

That he has given strong marks of originality to his supernatural beings, is true: but this does not entitle him to the preference here contended against. (IX, 10)

The power of this incomparable dramatist over the passions has been, and is, both felt and acknowledged by all persons of even common sensation who have heard his pieces well performed, or even read them attentively. He never attempts rage, grief, love, jealousy, patriotism, terror, or pleasantry but he works the master strings of sympathetic feeling in each degree. But did *Shakespeare*'s power stop here? By no means; he is equally great in calm, philosophical, argumentative reflection; in allusions and descriptions; in choice of materials for his great purposes; and, in general, working them up to the greatest advantage. (IX, 11–12)

Mr. *Pope*, whom we chiefly trace, says, 'That as he has written better, so he has written worse than any other.' The latter point we contend against, for however he trifled to indulge a quibbling and pedantic taste, which prevailed in and disgraced his time; yet we make no scruple to declare that though he may be below himself in those frivolous excursions of fancy, he is far above any

* A man who knows when he has enough, and with that competence prudently retires from bustling life, proves himself a real philosopher, and in his retreat gives us pleasing ideas of a temporal elysium.

other author even in that way; as to flattering such a despicable taste, he was doubly obliged to it both as author and actor. We judge him more blameable in another point than this, which has been rarely, if ever before, noticed; that is, indulging the redundancy of his own imagination so far that frequently, when a favourite thought struck him, he spun it out and dwelt upon it not only beyond the limits of dramatic dialogue but beyond the much more extended bounds of epic poetry.* (IX, 13–14)

We mentioned a poem by *Ben Jonson*, which, to vindicate his character from the charge of envy and malevolence, we transcribe, with occasional remarks. [Prints Jonson's poem 'To the memory of my beloved, The Author Mr. William Shakespeare', from the First Folio: see Vol. 1, No. 1.]

[On Jonson's line 'He was not of an age, but for all time']

Could there be conceived a more comprehensive or more delicate panegyric than this? He who writes temporally, however striking, useful and entertaining, is but a subordinate genius; he who writes for futurity, and upon universal principles, is capital. In this light, *Jonson* justly draws *Shakespeare*; what more *Dryden*[1] would have had we cannot say, unless such gross daubing as he bestowed in many of his adulatory dedications upon miserable characters; and this would have been disgraceful to the critic and friend. (IX, 23)

[On the lines 'Yet must I not give nature *all*; thy art,/My gentle *Shakespeare*, must enjoy a part']

Ben, not satisfied with allowing his friend all natural powers, gives him here the advantages of art; hence it appears he would not have willingly withheld any due point of praise. (IX, 24)

[On the conclusion]

We know not nor can conceive a warmer compliment than this, wherein *Jonson* throws himself and all other authors aside, to make *Shakespeare* not only the main but the sole pillar of the stage. (IX, 25)

... From the remarks we have offered, and we hope not unjustly, it may be inferred that the preceding lines have more of friendship than fancy in them, much more of labour than of genius; they

* For many proofs of this, consult his historical plays particularly.
[1] For Dryden's comment see Vol. 1, p. 23 ('An Insolent, Sparing, and Invidious Panegyric').

contain strength of thought, but want ease of expression; *Ben*'s constant fault.

From a review of our Author, it is beyond a doubt that Nature never favoured a son of *Parnassus* more; and we may add, that as Nature formed him to delineate so she formed Mr. *Garrick* to express. At all times persons of taste and judgment must have admired *Shakespeare*; but it is certain that he never reached the zenith of his glory till the inimitable Actor had studied and illustrated him. There is an amazing similarity between the writing of one and the acting of the other; they both appear regardless of rules and mechanism. The beautiful wildnesses of nature seem to have attracted both, and in different stiles they appear to have pursued the same track; though Mr. *Garrick* is never so entirely luxuriant, nor so trifling, yet it is certain that he feels and manifests a very uncommon glow of looks, action, and utterance, equal to his favourite Author's boldest flights of fancy. (IX, 25–6)

[On the Stratford Jubilee and nascent bardolatry]

We are willing to allow an author of *Shakespeare*'s merit every *secular homage*, but what we have now mentioned is beyond doubt a degree of *profane idolatry*, which is even carried to popish extragavance by searching after, and most curiously preserving, in different shapes, pieces of a mulberry tree planted by his own hand. Enthusiastic admirers may depend on it that his works will last much longer than any remnants of the tree, and need no such perishable proofs of their fame.

Mr. *Garrick* has not only been serviceable by his masterly performance, but essentially so by some most judicious alterations and reformations, which have restored some pieces to the stage which otherwise must have lain in oblivion. Pruning and altering this Author has been censured by some of his over-sanguine admirers; however, there is no reason to doubt his ready acquiescence, had he lived at this day, to almost every step of that kind which has been taken, both by Mr. *Garrick*, and some other judicious critics before his time, *Tate, Dryden*, &c.

As he wrote so profusely in both species of the drama it may not be improper to suggest, according to our opinion, in which he claims the preference; and this we are ready to pronounce without hesitation in favour of Tragedy. His comic scenes have great vivacity, but are in general much incumbered with quibble and obscurity; *Falstaff* excepted, who may be stiled the eldest born son of humour. But his *Macbeth, King Lear, Othello,* and *Julius Cæsar* (exclusive of other pieces in the serious cast) overballance a whole library of laughter produced by the most sterling wit or most genuine pleasantry. The strength and magnificence of his solemn ideas, the sinewy, yet smooth flow of his expression, the elevated propriety of his imagery, his happy introduction and fanciful support of similies, with an unparalleled judicious and just selection of characters, place him above all panegyrick, except the cordial and unlimited applause of admiring audiences.

As to the religious principles of this great man, we are not positively ascertained; but from the liberality of sentiment and universal benevolence which breathe through his works we are led to believe him of the established church; though some strokes of Popery appear in his *Hamlet*.

In regard to his political tenets, they seem inextricable, and we are sorry to pronounce him rather a time-server; for though upon *Roman* subjects he has promulged the noblest ideas of general and particular liberty, yet in his plays founded on *English* history he has advanced laborious deceptive arguments in favour of divine right, non-resistance, passive obedience, &c. But this being chiefly done under the reign of a *Stuart*, though to be lamented, need not be wondered at.

As a private man, we have all imaginable reason to suppose him a humane, mild, affable member of society, who had prudence without avarice, and philosophy to be satisfied with a competence; but one who moved through life as a shining and benign planet, calculated to shed pleasure and advantage. We could dwell much longer, with great satisfaction to ourselves, on the agreeable subject of paying grateful tribute, faint as it may be, to so valuable a memory; but few who read this will want animation or further information on the subject. Therefore we shall, as a just and concise climax of praise, conclude with an observation from his own works which seems prophetically suggested for himself:

> ————Take him for all in all,
> We shall not look upon his like again.   [*Hamlet*, 1.2.187–8]
> (IX, 27–9)

[86] [From the Introduction to the *Poems*]

... After elucidations of *Shakespeare*'s Plays it would be superfluous to urge anything here respecting his merit as a Dramatist, more than to say that as he never has been, so probably he never will be, equalled in that view. But as it is common for authors to excel in one case and fall very short in others, so the Swan of *Avon*, in our idea, falls as far short of himself in his Poems as he rises above others in his Plays. (IX, 34)

If *Shakespeare*'s merit, as a poet, a philosopher, or a man, was to be estimated from his Poems, though they possess many instances of powerful genius he would, in every point of view, sink beneath himself in these characters. Many of his subjects are trifling, his versification mostly laboured and quibbling, with too great a degree of licentiousness. After this last assertion it may be reasonably urged why pieces confessedly censurable should be republished? To which challenge we have only to plead that a desire of gratifying the admirers of our Author with an *entire* edition of his works has induced us to suffer some passages to remain, which we are ourselves as far from approving as the most scrupulous of our Readers. But upon consulting the critics we were told that to have expunged them might appear as over-strained a piece of prudery in Literature, as the Regent Duke of *Orleans*'s action was in the Arts; who, toward the latter part of his life, had castigated to *imperfection* certain pieces in his fine collection of statues and painting, in order to render them more decent objects of inspection. (IX, 36)

244. Alexander Gerard, on Shakespeare's genius

1774

From *An Essay on Genius* (1774).

On Gerard see the head-note to Vol. 4, No. 171.

It will be generally allowed that Shakespeare is, in point of genius, superior to Milton. The preference arises from the superiority of his invention. In the lower accomplishments of a poet he is often defective. But the richness of his descriptions, the multiplicity and justness of his characters, the variety, the compass, and the propriety of his sentiments bear the deepest marks of their being original; and at the same time that the internal excellences of his works display a luxuriance of invention, we know that his education gave him but slender opportunities of being acquainted with those ancient masters from whom he could have borrowed any of his beauties, or by whose example he could have even improved his natural powers. (13)

Shakespeare's judgment was not enough improved to enable him always to avoid improper subjects, unnatural and improbable incidents, forced and quibbling expressions, or to perceive the regularity and simplicity which best suits the nature of the drama; but in supporting the propriety of character, in marking the fit expressions and the natural effects of the several passions, and in many other particulars he displays such an uncommon accuracy of judgment as leads us to impute his blemishes rather to the bad taste of those for whom he wrote, than to any defect in his own understanding. (74)

A fertile imagination is apt to overload a work with a superfluity of ideas: an accurate judgment rejects all that are unnecessary. Shakespeare was not always able to keep the richness of his fancy from displaying itself in cases where judgment would have directed him to control it. That very exuberance of imagination which commands our admiration is sometimes indulged so far as necessarily to incur our censure. We need not be at a loss for an example. In the *Midsummer Night's Dream* Helena, upbraiding Hermia, describes the closeness of their early friendship in the most natural manner, by expressive circumstances suited to the state of childhood. [Quotes 3.3.198ff.] But here the Poet's own imagination takes fire, and he goes on:

> So we grew together
> Like to a double cherry, seeming parted,
> But yet an union in partition,
> Two lovely berries moulded on one stem;
> Or with two seeming bodies, but one heart,
> Two of the first, like coats in heraldry,
> Due but to one, and crowned with one crest.   [208ff.]

And his imagination has crouded together more images than would have been proper though he had been describing infant friendship in his own person, not to mention that some of them are frigid and far-fetched. But the redundance is the more faulty as the description is put into the mouth of Helena, who was too little at ease, too much distracted with vexation, to be at leisure to search for a multitude of similitudes. (78–80)

Sometimes again it happens that tho' each of the ideas is subservient to the end in view, yet they are so incongruous that they cannot be all adopted with propriety. Shakespeare describes the terrors of death by a variety of very striking and poetical images: 'Ay, but to die, and go we know not where'. [Quotes *Measure for Measure*, 3.1.119ff.]. All the ideas here introduced are conducive to the poet's design, and might have been suggested by the correctest fancy. It is only judgment that can disapprove the uniting of them in the same description, as being heterogeneous, derived partly from Christian manners, and partly from pagan notions. (83–4)

245. William Kenrick, lectures on Shakespeare

1774

From reviews of Kenrick's lectures in the *Monthly Miscellany*, February-April 1774. Kenrick also published some of these lectures as *Introduction to the School of Shakespeare Held, on Wednesday Evenings, In the Apollo, at the Devil Tavern, Temple Bar. To which Is Added A Retort Courteous On the Criticks, As delivered at the Second and Third Lectures* (1774).

On Kenrick see the head-note to Vol. 5, No. 207.

SCHOOL OF SHAKESPEARE

On Wednesday, Feb. 2 the Doctor resumed his task, and chose the tragedy of *Hamlet* for that evening's entertainment.—Previous to the lecture, he again replied to others of the Critics who still continued to attack him in the public papers, and then began his evening's exhibition.

The Doctor took up a general view of the Play, which he premised was one of the most moral and sententious of any of the Poet's productions. After this (in opposition to general opinion) he urged that the character of Hamlet was much more moral and consistent than his commentators usually allow him; that his madness was *real*, at least *essentially* so; and gave it as a plausible reason that it was produced by Ophelia's inconstancy, and the defeat of his ambition by his mother's second marriage with his uncle; as well as the unnaturalness of that union.

Though the arguments the Doctor urged for these opinions were some of them scholar-like and entertaining, we must differ from him on many accounts. In the first place, Hamlet himself tells us, after seeing the Ghost, that he means to *assume* a *feigned* madness, and enjoins Horatius and Marcellus in consequence to secrecy; now when a man could in *cold blood* lay so settled a plan of conduct it can scarcely come under the denomination of real madness.——The charge against Ophelia's inconstancy we must also dissent from, as she acted with *reserve* to Hamlet *only* with a view to *please* her father Polonius, who desires her to return the Prince all his presents; yet when she comes to do this the very manner of the act, with her comment on it, shews the deed to bear no correspondence with her heart, as will appear from the following passage:

> *Ophelia.*—My Lord, I have remembrance of yours,
> That I have long'd long to re-deliver;
> I pray you now receive them.
> *Hamlet.*—No, I never gave you aught.
> *Oph.*—My honoured Lord, you know right well you did;
> And with them words of so sweet breath composed,
> As made the things more rich.   [3.1.92ff.]

The Ghost was another character in this play which the Doctor thought *differently* of from most commentators, by speaking *indifferently* of it, and in which he departed from the opinion of Mr. Addison[1] and some of the ablest of the English and French critics.

Such are the outlines of this lecture on *Hamlet*, which we think much inferior to the Doctor's other two lectures, both in point of *judgment* and *recitation*. (80)

[16 Feb.] In his remarks on the Tragedy of *Othello* we cannot but think him superlatively great; and he also gave his audience sufficient proof of the soundness of his judgment. For, though none of Shakespeare's Commentators ever doubted but that Othello was of a real *black* complexion, and though every performer of that character has followed the same opinion and put on an *absolute negro face*, yet the Doctor asserted that he was *not* a *black*, and at worst only of a *tawny* colour. This assertion he supported by the following arguments:

First, That a young Lady of Desdemona's delicacy of sentiment could never have fallen in love with a Negro; and more particularly, if we suppose him 'ill-favoured and old,' as Shakespeare calls him, we must conceive a greater idea of Desdemona's indelicacy; whereas, supposing him *tawny* there is nothing very unnatural in it.

Secondly, It could not be imagined that the Venetians would

---

[1] See *Spectator*, no. 44: Vol. 2, pp. 275f.

depute the chief command of their forces to a Negro; whereas, that a Moor should occupy this important trust was nothing extraordinary, in a country where an intercourse with the Moorish race had been long established.

A third presumptive proof was deduced from Othello's religion. He was a Christian; for he recounts the taking a circumcised enemy to the state by the throat. The Moors, the Lecturer observed, were strongly inclined at one time to Christianity, though that mode of faith hath since been extirpated from almost every country inhabited by Moors. And what corroborated his opinion, was a passage which seemed to indicate that he was descended from the Moorish Kings of Old Spain.

From these considerations, we cannot but think the Doctor's hypothesis to be the true one; nor can we conceive the propriety of Shakespeare's calling Othello the *Moor of Venice* unless he meant that specific tribe of Moors between whom and the inhabitants of Old Spain a frequent intercourse had been carried on by wars and treaties; and his describing Othello as one of *those Moors* unquestionably ascertained his colour. (134–5)

On March 16, the Critique of the Evening was opened, as usual, by descanting on the blunders of other Commentators. A few readings which had puzzled the Critics were mentioned, but the whole force of the Lecturer's ability in logic were reserved to combat the generally received opinion of Macbeth's character as drawn by Shakespeare. He contended that Macbeth exceeded his wife in moral turpitude and total depravity of principle; an assertion to which we can by no means subscribe.

The Doctor thus maintained the argument: 'That Macbeth was not so much seduced by the persuasions of his wife as by his own alacrity, to do evil; for tho' the murder of Duncan might be imputed to female influence yet, as Macbeth plans and determines upon other murders, to the designs of which his wife not being privy, the mind from whence they originated must be depraved in the extreme.' In one word, he affirmed 'the character of Macbeth to be an object of AVERSION; his fears betrayed cowardice; his religious dread superstition; his bloody resolves paltry ambition. Lady Macbeth was an object of PITY rather than hatred, because influenced by no principle, social, religious, or moral.'

In reply to this we only beg leave to observe that nothing but a love of paradoxical singularity could have seduced any man to maintain a proposition so fantastic; a proposition which will eternally militate against the feelings of every reader of *Macbeth*; a proposition founded on a very confined knowledge of human nature, and maintainable only upon principles totally repugnant to the workings of the human heart. (192)

246. William Richardson, on the morality of Macbeth and Hamlet

1774

From *A Philosophical Analysis and Illustration of some of Shakespeare's remarkable Characters* (1774). The two remaining chapters are 'On the Character of the Melancholy Jaques', and on Imogen. The book was reprinted in 1780, with small corrections.

William Richardson (1743–1814), professor of humanity at Glasgow University, was a much respected teacher and citizen, and a leading member of the literary society. His subsequent volumes of Shakespeare essays were all well received, and besides contributing to numerous Scottish journals he published poems and plays. See R. W. Babcock, 'William Richardson's Criticism of Shakespeare', *Journal of English and Germanic Philology*, 28 (1929), pp. 117–36.

[From the Introduction]

No writer has hitherto appeared who possesses in a more eminent degree than Shakespeare the power of imitating the passions. All of them seem familiar to him, the boisterous no less than the gentle, the benign no less than the malignant. . . .

. . . The genius of Shakespeare is unlimited. Possessing extreme sensibility, and uncommonly susceptible, he is the Proteus of the drama; he changes himself into every character, and enters easily into every condition of human nature. . . .

Many dramatic writers of different ages are capable, occasionally, of breaking out with great fervour of genius in the natural language of strong emotion. No writer of antiquity is more distinguished for abilities of this kind than Euripides. His whole heart and soul seem torn and agitated by the force of the passion he imitates. He ceases to be Euripides; he is Medea; he is Orestes. Shakespeare, however, is most eminently distinguished not only by these occasional sallies but by imitating the passion in all its aspects, by pursuing it through all its windings and labyrinths, by moderating or accelerating its impetuosity according to the influence of other principles and of external events, and finally by combining it in a judicious manner with other passions and propensities, or by setting it aptly in opposition. He thus unites the two essential powers of dramatic invention, that of forming characters and that of imitating, in their natural expressions, the passions and affections of which they are composed. It is, therefore, my intention to examine some of his remarkable characters, and to analyze their component parts: an exercise no less adapted to improve the heart, than to inform the understanding. (39–42)

. . . My intention is to make poetry subservient to philosophy, and to employ it in tracing the principles of human conduct. The design surely is laudable: of the execution, I have no right to determine. (43)

[From ch. 1, 'On the Character of Macbeth']

In the character of Macbeth we have an instance of a very extraordinary change. In the following passages we discover the complexion and bias of his mind in its natural and unperverted state. [Quotes 'Brave Macbeth', 1.2.16ff.]

The particular features of his character are more accurately delineated by Lady Macbeth. [Quotes 'Yet I fear thy nature', 1.5.15ff.]

He is exhibited to us valiant, dutiful to his Sovereign, mild, gentle, and ambitious: but ambitious without guilt. Soon after we find him false, perfidious, barbarous, and vindictive. All the principles in his constitution seem to have undergone a violent and total change. Some appear to be altogether reduced or extirpated:

others monstrously overgrown. Ferocity is substituted instead of mildness, treasonable intentions instead of a sense of duty. His ambition, however, has suffered no diminution. On the contrary, by having become exceedingly powerful, and by rising to undue pretensions, it seems to have vanquished and suppressed every amiable and virtuous principle. (46–7)

Every variation of character and passion is accompanied with corresponding changes in the sentiments of the spectator. Macbeth, engaged in the defence of his country, and pursuing the objects of a laudable ambition, is justly honoured and esteemed. But the distraction which ensues from the conflict between vitious and virtuous principles render him the object of compassion mixed with disapprobation.

The chief obstacle in the way of our selfish desires proceeds from the opposition of our moral faculties. . . . Accordingly, when the notion of seizing the crown is suggested to Macbeth, he appears shocked and astonished. Justice and humanity shudder at the design. He regards his own heart with amazement: and recoils with horror from the guilty thought. [Quotes 'This supernatural soliciting', 1.3.130ff.]

Though virtuous principles appear in this instance to predominate, his ambition is not repulsed. The means of gratifying it seem shocking and impracticable, and he abandons the enterprize, without renouncing the passion. The passion continues vehement: it perseveres with obstinacy: it harasses and importunes him. He still desires: but, deterred by his moral feelings he is unable to proceed directly, and indulges romantic wishes: 'If chance will have me king, why chance may crown me/Without my stir.' [1.3.143f.] Inward contention of mind naturally provokes soliloquy. The reason of this appearance is obvious. In the beginning of life, feeble and unable to assist ourselves, we depend entirely upon others; we are constantly in society; and, of course, if we are affected by any violent emotions we are accustomed to utter them. Consequently, by force of association and habit, when they return excessive on any future occasion, impatient of restraint, they will not be arrested by reflection but vent themselves as they were wont. We may observe, in confirmation of this remark, that children are often prone to soliloquy: and so are men of lively passions. When the contending principles are of equal energy our emotions are uttered in broken and incoherent sentences, and the disordered state of our mind is expressed by interrupted gestures, absence of attention, and an agitated demeanour.

> *Banquo.* Look how our partner's rapt. [1.3.142]

> *La. Macb.* Your face, my thane, is as a book where men
> May read strange matters: [1.5.62f.]

But when the inward disorder proceeds from the violence of passion, unopposed by internal feelings and thwarted only by external circumstances, our soliloquies, if we are disposed to them, are more coherent. Macbeth, reasoning anxiously concerning the consequences of his design, reflecting on the opinions of mankind, on the hatred and infamy he must incur and on the resentment he must encounter, overcome by fear, relinquishes his undertaking.

> If it were *done* when 'tis done, then 'twere well
> 'Twere done quickly: [Quotes 1.7.1–25, 31–5.]

Thus the irregular passion is again repulsed: yet symptoms of the decay of virtue are manifest. (62–7)

Thus, by considering the rise and progress of a ruling passion, and the fatal consequences of its indulgence, we have shown how a beneficent mind may become inhuman, and how those who are naturally of an amiable temper, if they suffer themselves to be corrupted will become more ferocious and more unhappy than men of a constitution originally hard and unfeeling. The formation of our characters depends considerably upon ourselves; for we may improve, or vitiate, every principle we receive from nature. (84–8)

[From ch. 2, 'On the Character of Hamlet']
. . . Such is the condition of Hamlet. Exquisitely sensible of moral beauty and deformity, he discerns turpitude in a parent. Surprize, on a discovery so painful and unexpected, adds bitterness to his sorrow; and, led by the same moral principle to admire and glory in the high desert of his father, even this admiration contributes to his uneasiness. Aversion to his uncle, arising from the same origin, has a similar tendency and augments his anguish. All these feelings and emotions uniting together, are rendered still more violent, exasperated by his recent interview with the Queen, struggling for utterance, but restrained.

[Quotes the 'too too solid flesh' soliloquy (1.2.129ff.): Hamlet's indignation] is not entirely effaced; and he expresses it by a general reflection: 'Frailty, thy name is woman!' This expression is too refined and artificial for a mind strongly agitated, yet it agrees entirely with just such a degree of emotion and pensiveness as disposes us to moralize. Considered as the language of a man violently affected, it is improper; considered in relation to what goes before and follows after, it appears perfectly natural. (106–7)

The condition of Hamlet's mind becomes still more curious and interesting. His suspicions are confirmed, and beget resentment. Conceiving designs of punishment, conscious of very violent perturbation, perceiving himself already suspected by the King, afraid lest his aspect, gesture, or demeanour should betray him, and knowing that his projects must be conducted with secrecy, he resolves to conceal himself under the disguise of madness. [Quotes the 'antic disposition' speech, 1.5.170–9.]

. . . Accordingly, Hamlet, the more easily to deceive the King and his creatures, and to furnish them with an explication of his uncommon deportment, practises his artifice on Ophelia. [Quotes Ophelia's account of how Hamlet came to her, 'with his doublet all unbrac'd . . . ': 2.1.74ff.]

There is no change in his attachment, unless in so far as other passions of a violent and unpleasing character have assumed a temporary influence. His affection is permanent. Nor ought the pretended rudeness and seeming inconsistency of his behaviour to be at all attributed to inconstancy or an intention to insult. Engaged in a dangerous enterprise, agitated by impetuous emotions, desirous of concealing them, and for that reason feigning his understanding disordered; to confirm and publish this report, seemingly so hurtful to his reputation, he would act in direct opposition to his former conduct and inconsistently with the genuine sentiments and affections of his soul. He would seem frivolous when the occasion required him to be sedate; and, celebrated for the wisdom and propriety of his conduct, he would assume appearances of impropriety. Full of honour and affection, he would seem inconsistent; of elegant and agreeable manners, and possessing a complacent temper, he would put on the semblance of rudeness. To Ophelia he would shew dislike and indifference, because a change of this nature would be, of all others, the most remarkable, and because his affection for her was passionate and sincere. Of the sincerity and ardour of his regard he gives undoubted evidence.

> I lov'd Ophelia: forty thousand brothers
> Could not, with all their quantity of love,
> Make up my sum.   [5.1.269ff.]
>   (125–30)

[Richardson summarizes the closet-scene, and concludes:] All the business of the tragedy, in regard to the display of character, is here concluded.[1] Hamlet, having detected the perfidy and inhumanity of his uncle, and having restored the Queen to a sense of her depravity, ought immediately to have triumphed in the utter ruin of his enemies, or to have fallen a victim to their deceit. The succeeding circumstances of the play are unnecessary; they are not essential to the catastrophe; and, excepting the madness of Ophelia and the scene of the grave-diggers, they exhibit nothing new in the characters. On the contrary, the delay cools our impatience; it diminishes our sollicitude for the fate of Hamlet, and almost lessens him in our esteem. Let him perish immediately, since the poet dooms him to perish; yet poetical justice would have decided otherwise.

On reviewing this analysis a sense of virtue—if I may use the language of an eminent philosopher without professing myself of his sect—seems to be the ruling principle. In other men it may appear with the ensigns of high authority; in Hamlet it possesses absolute power. United with amiable affections, with every graceful accomplishment, and every agreeable quality, it embellishes and exalts them. It rivets his attachment to his friends, when he finds them deserving; it is a source of sorrow, if they appear corrupted. It even sharpens his penetration; and if unexpectedly he discerns turpitude or impropriety in any character, it inclines him to think more deeply of their transgression than if his sentiments were less refined . . . . Men of other dispositions would think of gratifying their friends by contributing to their affluence, to their amusement, or external honour; but the acquisitions that Hamlet values, and the happiness he would confer, are a conscience void of offence, the peace and the honour of virtue. Yet with all this purity of moral

---

[1] Compare Steevens, Vol. 5, pp. 448, 452, 456, etc. Richardson retained this paragraph in the second 'corrected' edition of 1780, but removed it when he collected his essays into one volume: cf. the fifth edition, 1798, p. 117

sentiment, with eminent abilities, exceedingly cultivated and improved, with manners the most elegant and becoming, with the utmost rectitude of intention, and the most active zeal in the exercise of every duty, he is hated, persecuted, and destroyed. (148–52)

247. Edward Taylor, Shakespeare's faulty tragedies

1774

From *Cursory Remarks on Tragedy, on Shakespeare, and on certain French and Italian Poets, Principally Tragedians* (1774).

According to an article in the *Gentleman's Magazine* for December 1797, this essay was written by Edward Taylor (*c*. 1741–97), who was educated at Eton and Trinity College, Cambridge (however, his name appears in none of the biographical dictionaries for those institutions). Subsequently, it seems, he attended the University of Göttingen, where he studied law, which he never practised. Having travelled widely, and mastered seven languages, 'at the age of 30 he retired to the country; and the last 26 years of his life were spent in retirement, in the pursuits of elegant literature, and in the practice of every virtue that can adorn and dignify human nature' (lxvii, pt 2, p. 1076). He also published *Werter to Charlotte, a poem* (1784; based on Goethe's *Die Leiden des jungen Werther's*), a translation of Musaeus' *Hero and Leander* (1783), and of the *Memoirs of Guy Joli, private secretary to Cardinal de Retz* (1775). D. Nichol Smith described *Cursory Remarks* as 'the last direct descendant of Rymer's *Short View of Tragedy* . . . . But it is a degenerate descendant. If it has learned good manners, it is unoriginal and dull': *Eighteenth Century Essays on Shakespeare*, second edition (Oxford, 1963), p. xxii.

[From the Preface]

Yet, oh unpardonable temerity! the author has presumed to be severe in his strictures on Shakespeare, the idol of his countrymen; in whose praises so many productions have lately appeared, and written, too, with great ingenuity and plausibility. . . .

By the situation of our country we are divided from the rest of the world, and hence perhaps the reason why we are in general contented with our own writers, and seem to think that perfection in modern literature is confined within the narrow limits of Great Britain. . . . Some few of our wits indeed, for reasons which need not be here assigned but which truth and impartiality can never approve, have treated with uncommon acrimony the writers of other countries, with whom at the same time they seem to have had but a very slender acquaintance. The author wishes to be able to refute their calumnies, and to be himself candid and impartial. (v–vii)

[From the Introduction]

The end of tragedy is to please and instruct; the means by which that end is to be obtained are terror and pity; these only are productive of the true pathetic, these only can inspire that sympathetic distress, that delicate melancholy which we feel for the misfortunes of others, more pleasing to a sensible mind than the noisier and more transient joys of mirth. . . . To awaken this tender passion the tragedian must place before us the representation of actions that have, or that might have happened.

. . . It is the duty therefore of the tragic poet to adhere strictly to verisimilitude, not only in the subject of the drama but in the conduct of it. . . . The action should be one, and such as may be presumed to have happened, if not in the time of the representation at least in the space of twenty four hours, that it may have some resemblance to truth. . . . The unity of place is to be observed, for the tragic poet and the magician are different.

But from this opinion a certain critic will be found to dissent, for he affirms that the unities are not essentially necessary. [Quotes Johnson's Preface, Vol. 5, pp. 70f.]. But the question is not about the reality but the seeming possibility of the action represented. . . . It is possible for me to conceive that a person might appear at this instant with an army on his march to Poland; but it is not possible for me to conceive that he should return victorious from that country in the space of an hour and a half. . . [for] neither the dragons of Medea nor the Hippogriff of Astolfo could have transported him thither and back again in so short a time. If Hannibal and Augustus were to be introduced upon the stage together it would be contradictory to all history, and an extension of time with a vengeance; yet it would not be so absurd, under certain restrictions at least, as Fortinbras and his victory in Poland. For they might be brought together on the stage without any mention of the events that happened between the periods of their several existence, whereas the duration of the action in the tragedy of *Hamlet* fixes with precision the time that elapses between the first appearance of Fortinbras and his return from a far distant country.

[Quotes Johnson, Vol. 5, p. 70, 'The objection' to 'Cleopatra'.] But the objection is not only to the impossibility, but to the impropriety of changing the place; for the spectator does not imagine that he is at Alexandria, he knows he is in a theatre; and whilst he is there, if he knows he is not at Alexandria he must know à fortiori that he cannot be at Alexandria and at Rome too. . . . The objection to removing the scene of action from one place to another arises from the disgust we feel at being presented with one palpable impossibility upon another. (1–7)

. . . But were we to see a landscape in which the Pantheon at Rome, the Mansion House at London, the story of Apollo and Daphne, and the Israelites passing the Red Sea were to be represented; if, I say, we were to behold such an extravagant medley on one piece of canvas, altho' every part of it were finished in the most masterly manner, the whole painting must necessarily appear monstrous, and could not fail to displease and disgust. A play is an imitation of nature; to resemble nature it must resemble truth, or the probability of truth. . . . (12)

[Quotes Johnson's argument that the spectators rather 'lament the possibility than suppose the presence of misery' on stage (Vol. 5, p. 71). Taylor argues that our reaction to Garrick as Lear in the storm-scene does not depend on our consideration whether or not we might one day be in the same situation as Lear: 13–16.]

When I hear Mr. Garrick speak the preceding lines with a sensibility and propriety unknown to others, I feel a mixture of pity and indignation; pity for the miseries of the old father, indignation at the treatment shewn him by his inhuman daughters. I feel, because he seems to feel; and that I do involuntarily and instantaneously. I feel instantaneously, because the indignant sigh escapes me long before I can assimilate and weigh consequences in my mind, and by a chain of com₁ˡex ideas and comparative modes find out that possibly in a course of years I too may experience

> How sharper than a serpent's tooth it is
> To have a thankless child.   [1.4.287ff.]

I feel involuntarily, because the imitation of anguish and distress is so vivid and exact that I think, nay I am sure, that for a moment it seems real, at least to me it does. An object of seeming misery, painted in all the fascinating colours of countenance and gesture, and expressing its agonizing feelings in all the powerful eloquence of words is before our eyes; we see, we hear, we pity. The tear stands trembling in the eye, a chill runs through the whole frame, and the heart beats with convulsive throbs, before we can ask ourselves whether the grief represented in so lively a manner be real, or fictitious. (16–18)

Whoever in the midst of a scene in which Mr. Garrick calls forth all his wonderful powers to paint distress in himself and excite pity in his audience; I say, whoever at such a critical instant can turn aside to view any other object, or not forget his own situation and be wholly wrapt up in that of the inimitable performer, is to be pitied, not envied, for his composure and sang froid. In fact at all theatrical exhibitions which deeply interest and affect we rather perceive than think. When we behold Lear's countenance, the very picture of distress, and hear him speak the very language of woe, the mind is rather passive than active; it perceives, and cannot avoid perceiving, as Mr. Locke justly observes, whilst the eyes and ears are open. . . .

It appears therefore that there is a certain degree of delusion, transient and momentary though it be; for as soon as we begin to reflect, our pity subsides, our judgment informs us we have been deceived, and we are happy to find that it was but a deception.

[When Garrick as Lear divides his kingdom 'with calmness and composure', then 'our mind remains unagitated'.] But when he seems racked by the contending passions of sorrow and resentment we are then no longer calm and indifferent; our passions, like his, are actuated, and it is then that by a sympathy congenial to our natures we feel for his unhappy situation; and he strikes us as an old and wretched father, more sinned against than sinning. If he did not appear to us in this light we should remain uninterested, unaffected spectators; and in fact are so, as soon as we reflect and become conscious that he is Mr. Garrick, and not Lear; that his misery is fictitious, and not real. (19–23)

ON SHAKESPEARE

It has been the prevailing fashion for some years past to launch out into the most extravagant praises of our countryman Shakespeare, and to allot him beyond all competition the first place as a tragic writer. Compared with him Corneille, Racine, and Voltaire are fantastic composers, void of historical truth, imitation of character, or representation of manners; mere declaimers, without energy or fire of action, and absurdly introducing upon all occasions tedious, insipid, uninteresting love-scenes. But, prejudice apart, is he so transcendently their superior. . .? Shall I venture to proceed further, and ask if he be in general even a good tragic writer? We have seen in the preceeding pages what are some of the most material rules for dramatic compositions, as prescribed by Aristotle and other eminent masters in the art of criticism. . . . But these were either totally unknown to Shakespeare, or wilfully neglected by him. Instead of confining the action to a limited time he takes in the space of days, months, and even years; instead of adhering to the unity of place, by a preposterous magic he transports the spectator in the shifting of a scene from Italy to Britain, from Venice to Cyprus, from the court of England to that of France: and shall I not be permitted to exclaim, 'Quodcunque ostendis mihi sic incredulus odi'?[1] But Shakespeare can say with the musician in Homer,[2] ['I am taught by myself, but the god has inspired in me the song-ways of every kind.'].

[1] Horace, *Ars Poetica*, 188: 'Whatever you thus show me, I discredit and abhor.'
[2] *Odyssey*, 22.346ff.; tr. Richmond Lattimore.

His genius therefore is not to be restrained by the shackles of critic laws; his audacious fancy, his enthusiastic fire are not to submit to the tame institutions of an Aristotle or a Quintilian. So then he is to be indulged in transgressing the bounds of nature, in neglecting to give to fiction the air of truth, and in imposing the most palpable incongruities and most striking impossibilities on the audience, because he dares. . . .

In most countries, England excepted, certain positions and rules have been holden sacred and inviolable, in the literary as well as in the political world. These did the antient Greek tragedians observe and cultivate, and to these have the most eminent amongst the modern Italians and French scrupulously adhered. But our excentric English tragedian has presumed to quit the beaten track, and has boldly ventured to turn aside into the regions of the most wild, most fantastic imagination. With an unprecedented, with an unpardonable audacity, has he overleaped the pale of credibility, a boundary too confined for his romantic genius. Presented by him with impossibilities instead of the appearance of truth, we remain undeluded spectators. . . . And although we may be affected by particular passages in any one of his plays, yet the whole of the representation cannot be very interesting on account of its extravagance. Let us not therefore approve, let us not even extenuate those faults in Shakespeare that justice, that common sense would lead us to condemn in others. But with an impartiality that becomes every man who dares to think for himself, let us allow him great merit as a comic writer, greater still as a poet, but little, very little, as a tragedian. . . .

Perhaps it will be said that Shakespeare wrote when learning, taste, and manners were pedantic, unrefined, and illiberal; that none but such motley pieces as his are could please the greater part of his audience, the illiterate, low-liv'd mechanics; that some of his characters were necessitated to speak their language, and that their bursts of applause were to be purchased even at the expence of decency and common sense. When we consider his situation and circumstances, that . . . he was exposed to all the miseries of poverty and want; that to live he was constrained to write, and to adapt himself to the humour of others; it must be acknowledged that he deserves our pity rather than our censure. But when we come to consider him as a tragic writer and to weigh his merit as such, a standard must be established by which our judgments are to be determined. Where then are we to look for this nice criterion of merit but in those works that have been the delight of past ages, and are the admiration of the present?

Let it not be advanced as a merit, let it not be urged even as an excuse, that Shakespeare followed nature in the busy walks of men; that he presented her as he found her, naked and unadorned: for there are parts of nature that require concealment. . . . The scene of the grave-diggers in *Hamlet* is certainly real life, or as it is vulgarly termed highly natural, yet how misplaced, how unworthy the tragedian! . . .

To the credit of the present times indeed these puerilities are now omitted; let us hope they will not be the only ones, nor let us be afraid to reject what our ancestors, in conformity to the grosser notions then prevalent, beheld with pleasure and applause. (31–41)

It must be acknowledged that Shakespeare abounds in the true sublime; but it must be allowed that he abounds likewise in the low and vulgar. And who is there, that after soaring on eagle wings to unknown regions and empyreal heights, is not most sensibly mortified to be compelled the next moment to grovel in dirt and ordure? In the first case (and if he mounts with Shakespeare it will frequently happen) he may chance to be dazzled with the excessive glare, even till his 'eye-balls crack.'. . . What a contrast there is between the sublime and the bathos! yet how closely are they united in Shakespeare! Fired with the exalted sentiments of his heroes, from whose mouths virtue herself seems to dictate to mankind, we feel our hearts dilate, the current of our blood flow swifter in every vein, and our whole frame wound up to a pitch of dignity unfelt, unknown before. Although we could not expect that our enthusiasm should remain in its full energy and force, yet of itself it would subside by degrees into a benign complacency and universal philanthropy. How cruel is it then to hurry us from heroes and philosophers into a crew of plebeians, grave-diggers, and buffoons; from the bold tropes and figures of nervous and manly eloquence, from sage lessons of morality such as a Minerva might have inspired or a Socrates have taught, to the obscure jest or low quibble, that base counterfeit of wit. . . .

Shakespeare's preternatural beings seem to need little or no justification; they are such as were sanctified by tradition and vulgar credulity. He has supported them with dignity and solemnity, has made them greatly instrumental in the catastrophe of his pieces. . . . The ghost in *Hamlet* is neither useless nor introduced improperly; it comes to reveal unknown, unexpiated crimes: here is the *dignus vindice nodus*.[1] (42–5)

The morals of Shakespeare's plays are in general extremely natural and just; yet why must innocence unnecessarily suffer? why must the hoary, the venerable Lear be brought with sorrow to the grave? Why must Cordelia perish by an untimely fate? the amiable, the dutiful, the innocent Cordelia! She that had already felt the heart-rending anger of a much beloved but hasty mistaken father! She that could receive, protect, and cherish a poor, infirm, weak, and despised old man although he had showered down curses on her undeserving head! That such a melancholy catastrophe was by no means necessary is sufficiently evinced by the manner in which the same play is now performed. Ingratitude now meets with its proper punishment, and the audience now retire exulting in the mutual happiness of paternal affection and filial piety. Such, if practicable, should be the winding up of all dramatic representations, that mankind may have the most persuasive allurements to all good actions: for although virtue depressed may be amiable, virtue triumphant must be irresistable. . . .

It is not my design to condemn those tragedies in which innocence falls a victim to treachery or violence. We see but too many instances of it in real life; consequently it cannot be improper for the stage, which ought to represent living manners. I would be understood therefore not to reject other tragedies, but to give the preference to those in which death, punishment, or remorse await the guilty only. And as at all dramatic representations I am to see but an imitation of nature, let the delusion be on the side of virtue, that I may still flatter myself with the pleasing belief that to be good is to be happy. (45–9)

[Taylor now compares Shakespeare with Tintoretto, whose 'enthusiasm of genius' is marred by 'neglectful . . . finishing'.] The resemblance between the painter and the poet is striking. In our English bard what a glow of fancy, what a rapidity of imagination, what a sublimity in diction, what strength, what a distinction of characters, what a knowledge of the human heart! Yet how

---

[1] *Ars Poetica*, 191f.: 'And let no god intervene, unless a knot come worthy of such a deliverer.'

inattentive to propriety and order, how deficient in grouping, how fond of exposing disgusting as well as beautiful figures! (50)

And is then poor Shakespeare to be excluded from the number of good tragedians? He is; but let him be banished, like Homer from the republic of Plato, with marks of distinction and veneration; and may his forehead, like the Grecian bard's, be bound with an honourable wreath of ever-blooming flowers.

If, after what I have said, any passionate admirer of Shakespeare shall think that I hold cheap the idol of his heart, he is mistaken: I too can willingly offer incense at the same shrine; I too can feel with an equal degree of transport all his unrivaled strokes of nature, all his wonderful descriptive and creative powers; can love with Romeo, be jealous with Othello, can moralize with Hamlet, grow distracted with Lear. But I cannot talk bawdry with Mercutio, nor intoxicate myself with Cassio; I cannot play the fool with Polonius, nor the puppy with Oswald. In fine, whilst we consider thee, O divine Shakespeare, in any other light than that of a tragic poet,

> ——tibi maturos largimur honores,
> Nil oriturum alias, nil ortum tale fatentes.[1]   (51–2)

[Taylor finds Corneille's *Cinna*] less disgusting to a liberal mind than the vulgar dialogue of carpenters and coblers in the *Julius Cæsar* of Shakespeare, or the chopt hands, greasy night-caps, and stinking breaths so minutely discribed by Casca; indecorums for which the many brilliant and sublime passages in the same play by no means sufficiently atone. (69)

[On Metastasio, *La Clemenza di Tito*: quotes the soliloquy of Sestus.] We find here no studied expressions, no obscure allusions, no misplaced similies. Although figures of speech might suggest themselves on other occasions, in his situation they would be unnatural. A person in his circumstances can hardly be supposed to see daggers in the air, nor would the ideas of sleep, dreams, witchcraft, Hecate, wolves, the rape of Lucretia, and giants croud all at once upon his mind, too much occupied with the thoughts of what he is about to commit, to suffer him to attend to circumstances which, though not foreign to the purpose, are at most but

---

[1] Horace, *Epistles*, 2.1.16f.: 'Upon you we bestow honours betimes, . . . and confess that nought like you will hereafter arise or has arisen ere now.'

collaterally connected with it. The reader will perceive that I allude to a speech of Macbeth's in which he fancies he sees the dagger before him, and particularly to the following lines, which he speaks just before he enters Duncan's chamber to murder him. [Quotes *Macbeth*, 2.1. 49–56, reading 'giant' for 'ghost' in line 56.] These lines may to some appear beautifully descriptive, but in my opinion so much imagery carries with it the appearance of study, and to me therefore they seem but ill adapted to the situation of the speaker. On the other hand, in the soliloquy of Sestus we find no simile, no allusion to any story of antiquity, and even the metaphorical expression is of the simplest kind. (193–5)

248. Unsigned essay, on the cowardice of Falstaff

c. 1774

From *Shakespeare. Containing the Traits of his Characters* (n.d.). The British Library copy is dated 'about 1774', and since the writer does not refer to Morgann's book I incline to date it before 1777. The Falstaff essay was reprinted in *Walker's Hibernian Magazine* (February 1780), pp. 66–8.

INTRODUCTION

The knowledge of human nature has been, and still is universally allowed the most proper study of man. The philosophy of the passions gains us, by a thorough acquaintance with the beauties and defects of the soul, over it an entire empire. In a word, we know ourselves. . . .

Who shall teach us, it may be asked. But can such a question be asked when so great a master as SHAKESPEARE has left to the world, if I may so term it—the soul anatomized? In his works we trace the origin, destination, and end of not only, still to speak metaphorically, the Veins, Arteries, but even the least Fibre. By him we are taught the *true* health of the soul. He discovers the consequence of perverted passion; how it deluges the mind, and destroys society.

To develope his characters is an arduous task; though, being agreeable to me, I will endeavour it. If so fortunate as to succeed either in the entertainment or instruction of my Reader, I shall be amply satisfied. What I propose is, under the Patronage and Protection of the Public, Weekly to publish what I conceive to be the greatest beauty of SHAKESPEARE—THE TRAITS OF HIS CHARACTERS. . . . (3–4)

FALSTAFF

That reverend vice, that grey iniquity, that father ruffian, that vanity in years! [*1 Henry IV*, 2.4.453ff.]

In Falstaff are to be found the traits of an artful, ambitious, vain, voluptuous, avaricious, cowardly, satirical, pleasant-witted knave.

It may be matter for astonishment that so conspicuous a knave could render himself so agreeable to an audience as to afford more general entertainment than, I believe, any character has done that was ever exhibited on the stage. Consider the above motto, which perfectly agrees with his character, and if possible with-hold your astonishment that, instead of his being an object of entertainment, he is not an object of disgust and detestation. . . .

Falstaff made the pleasantness of his wit the ladder to his knavish designs, and dependence on Prince Henry. . . . His intimacy with the Prince he cherished for these reasons: it gratified his vanity, fed his expectations, was his shield from justice, and gained him credit and authority over his myrmidons.

He displays his knowledge how to win the heart by considering, that when a man herds with his inferiors it is most commonly for the purpose merely of enjoying that authority and complimentary homage which he could not among his equals. . . . (17–18)

The reason of his affording so much entertainment is the same that excuses Prince Henry's being so fond of his company. He flatters while he reproves, is always in a good temper, tho' apparently against his inclination. His knavery, vices, and follies he frankly confesses, which lessens that abhorrence we should otherwise have for him, and prepares us to be the more pleased with the pleasantry of his humour; this being much greater than his wit, which is in general but paltry puns, 'quips and quidities,' to use his own expression. I quote the following as an example of his admirable mixture of flattery with reproof, and frankness in confessing his viciousness: '—Before I knew thee, Hal, I knew nothing; and now am I, if a man should speak truly, little better than one of the wicked.' [1.2.93ff.]

Falstaff, like other villains, can excuse himself to himself at the same time he does to others. He says, 'Why, Hal, 'tis my vocation, Hal,'tis no sin for a man to labour in his vocation.' [1.2.104f.] (20–2)

It has been a much disputed point whether Falstaff were a coward or not. If an involuntary betray of fear in the moment of danger may be termed cowardice, how shall we otherwise construe his saying 'Zounds! will they not rob us?' [2.2.65]

His answer to the Prince accusing him of cowardice, 'Indeed I am not John of Gaunt, your grandfather; but yet no coward, Hal,' [2.2.67f.] should not be credited in his favour, further than to evince how a man may mistake his own disposition. The truly valiant are diffident of themselves, while the arrant coward flatters himself that he possesses what he could not bear the thought of wanting. The villain sooner knows himself than the coward. Falstaff confesses he is the one, but disowns the other.

When Prince Henry reproaches his running away, he replies, 'Ah! no more of that, Hal, if thou lov'st me.' [3.4.283] If he has any sensibility of feeling it is in not bearing the imputation of his want of valour.

Here follows another involuntary proof of his own cowardice. We are apt to imagine others feel as we suppose ourselves should in a like situation. Falstaff, after relating the forces raised against the king, and by such bold, resolute warriors, asks 'But tell me, Hal, art not thou horribly afeard?' [Quotes 2.4.365f.]

The effects we feel at what I next quote are sufficient to convince us how dangerous wit and humour are in the power of knaves. They take our hearts in despite of our senses. Although we know them to be all that is bad, yet we cannot withhold our affections. [Quotes the 'banish Falstaff' speech, 2.4.474ff.] (24–7)

His misapplying the money given him to raise recruits for the king's service ill requites his Hal's friendship. But we almost forget his villainy in his humorous description of it. [Quotes 'I have misused the King's press damnably': 4.2.12ff.]

Nothing convinces the coward he is so but the approach of danger. Falstaff, now approaching the place and day of battle, says

> The latter end of a fray, and beginning of a feast,
> Fits a dull fighter, and a keen guest.   [4.2.79f.]

His observations on honour, although they be natural to his character, I think should be suppressed in the representation; by reason as honour is the soul of society nothing should be so publicly expressed as to lessen our esteem for it.

Among all the villainous acts of Falstaff there is not one which disgusts us, except his wounding the vanquished Percy. In this he appears more than the coward—the cruel assassin. I should suppose Shakespeare made him guilty of it to prevent our being too fond of such a villain. . . . (28–32)

249. Elizabeth Griffith, Shakespeare and domestic morality

1775

From *The Morality of Shakespeare's Drama illustrated* (1775).

Mrs Elizabeth Griffith (1720?–93) was for a time an actress in Dublin and London, but achieved status as a writer with *A Series of Genuine Letters between Henry and Frances* (2 vols, 1757), a selection from her correspondence with her husband before their marriage; they published two companion epistolary novels. As a dramatist she enjoyed most success with *A Double Mistake* (1766), acted on twelve successive nights at Covent Garden, and with *The School for Rakes* (1769), a translation of Beaumarchais' *Eugénie*. She produced many translations and novels, her last book being *Essays to Young Married Women* (1782). Her book on Shakespeare is extensive (528 pages), and owes much to Dr Johnson and Mrs Montagu (No. 221 in Vol. 5).

PREFACE

Among the many writers of our nation who have by their talents contributed to entertain, inform, or improve our minds, no one has so happily or universally succeeded as he whom we may justly stile our first, our greatest Poet, Shakespeare. For more than a century and a half this Author has been the delight of the Ingenious, the text of the Moralist, and the study of the Philosopher. Even his cotemporary writers have ingenuously yielded their plaudit to his fame, as not presuming it could lessen theirs, set at so great a distance. Such superior excellence could never be brought into a comparative light; and jealousy is dumb when competition must be vain. For him, then, they chearfully twined the laurel-wreath, and unrepining placed it on his brow; where it will ever bloom, while sense, taste, and natural feelings of the heart shall remain amongst the characteristics of this, or any other nation that can be able to construe his language. He is a Classic, and cotemporary with all ages. (v)

This last-mentioned Editor [Johnson] is the only one who has considered Shakespeare's writings in a moral light; and therefore I confess myself of opinion that he has best understood them, by thus pointing to their highest merit and noblest excellence. And from several passages in the Doctor's Preface, particularly where he says that 'From his writings, indeed, a system of *social duties* may be selected; for he who thinks reasonably, must think *morally*' [Vol. 5, p. 65], as well as from frequent reflections of my own respecting the œconomical conduct of life and manners which have always arisen in my mind on the perusal of Shakespeare's works, I have ventured to assume the task of placing his Ethic merits in a more conspicuous point of view than they have ever hitherto been presented in to the Public.

My difficulty will not be *what to find* but *what to chuse*, amidst such a profusion of sweets and variety of colours; nay, sometimes, how to separate the moral from the matter in this Author's writings; which are often so contexted that, to continue Doctor Johnson's allegory above quoted, they may be compared to an intermixture of the physic with the kitchen garden, where both food and medicine may be culled from the same spot.

Shakespeare is not only my Poet but my Philosopher also. His anatomy of the human heart is delineated from *nature*, not from *metaphysics*; referring immediately to our intuitive sense, and not wandering with the school-men through the pathless wilds of theory. We not only *see* but *feel* his dissections just and scientific. (viii–ix)

There is a Moral sometimes couched in his Fable which, whenever I have been able to discover, I have pointed out to the Reader; and from those pieces where this excellence is deficient in the Argument, as particularly in his Historical Plays (where poetical justice cannot always obtain, human life not being the whole of our existence), I have given his moral and instruction in detail by quoting the passages as they happen to lie detached, or referring to the scope and tenor of the dialogue.

In these remarks and observations I have not restricted myself to morals purely ethic, but have extended my observations and reflections to whatever has reference to the general œconomy of life and manners, respecting prudence, polity, decency, and decorum; or relative to the tender affections and fond endearments of human nature; more especially regarding those moral duties which are the truest source of mortal bliss—domestic ties, offices, and obligations. (xii–xiii)

[1] [On *The Two Gentlemen of Verona* and its authenticity]

And indeed, were I to offer any doubt upon this point myself, it should not be so much from the objections adduced by the editors, as on account of the unnatural inconsistency of character in the person of Proteus; who in the first Act, and during above half the second, appears to stand in the most amiable and virtuous lights, both of morals and manhood, as a fond lover and a faithful friend; and yet suddenly belies his fair seemings by an infidelity towards the first object, and a treachery with regard to the second. 'Tis true indeed, that in the latter end he expresses a sort of contrition for his crimes; but yet this still seems to remain equivocal; as it does not appear to have arisen from any remorse of conscience, or abhorrence of his baseness, but rather from a disappointment in his pursuit, and an open detection of his villainy.

There are but few instances of this kind that I remember to have met with throughout the drama of Shakespeare; for however he may sport, as he often does, with the three *unities* of Aristotle, *time, place,* and *action*, he seldom sins against a fourth, which I am surprised the Critics have not added, as being worth them all—namely, that of *character*; the tenor of which is generally preserved from first to last in all his works. (25–6)

[The play lacks passages of moral comment.] And it is this circumstance which has induced the critics to suspect this Play not to have been originally one of Shakespeare's, but only revised and enriched with fragments by him; as it may be deemed to be not *a jewel*, but only *a lump of paste* set round *with sparks*. (27)

[2] [On *Measure for Measure*, 3.1.119ff.: 'Ay, but to die', where Claudius 'pleads for life, even on the most abject terms']

Isabella's indignation against her brother on this occasion, though it has no relation to the subjects we are upon, yet as it may have an effect in raising the same resentment against vice and meanness in the minds of my readers, I think it worthy to be inserted here. [Quotes 3.1.138ff.] (47)

[3] [On *1 Henry IV*]

There is likewise another character in this rich Play of a most peculiar distinction; as being not only *original* but *inimitable*, also. No copy of it has ever since appeared, either in life or description. Any one of the Dramatis Personæ in Congreve's Comedies, or indeed in most of the modern ones, might repeat the wit or humour of the separate parts with equal effect on the audience as the person to whose rôle they are appropriated; but there is a certain characteristic pecularity in all the humour of Falstaff that would sound flatly in the mouths of Bardolph, Poins, or Peto. In fine, the portrait of this extraordinary personage is delineated by so masterly a hand that we may venture to pronounce it to be the only one that ever afforded so high a degree of pleasure, without the least pretence to merit or virtue to support it.

I was obliged to pass by many of his strokes of humour, character, and description because they did not fall within the rule I had prescribed to myself in these notes; but I honestly confess that it was with regret whenever I did so; for were there as much moral, as there certainly is physical good in laughing, I might have transcribed every Scene of his, throughout this, the following Play, and the *Merry Wives of Windsor*, for the advantage of the health, as well as the entertainment of my readers. (228)

[4] [On Richard III's wooing of Lady Anne]
. . . I shall take the liberty of remarking on the very improbable conclusion of it.

Women are certainly most extremely ill used in the unnatural representation of female frailty here given. But it may, perhaps, be some palliation of his offence to observe that this strange fable was not any invention of the poet; though it must indeed be confessed that he yielded too easy a credence to a fictitious piece of history, which rested upon no better authority than the same that affirmed the deformity of Richard; which fact has lately, from a concurrence of cotemporary testimonies, been rendered problematical at least, by a learned and ingenious author.[1] (312–3)

[5] [On *King Lear* and Tate's adaptation]
The Critics are divided in their opinions between the original and the altered copy. Some prefer the first as a more general representation of human life, where fraud too often succeeds and innocence suffers: others prefer the latter, as a more moral description of what life should be.

But argument in this, as in many other cases, had better be left quite out of the question; for our feelings are often a surer guide than our reason; and by this criterion I may venture to pronounce that the reader or spectator will always be better pleased with the happy, than the unfortunate catastrophe of innocence and virtue.

Besides, if Dramatic exhibitions are designed, as they certainly should be, to recommend virtue and discourage vice, there cannot remain the least manner of dispute in our minds whether Shakespeare or Tate have fulfilled Horace's precept of *utile dulci* the best. However, if *pity* and *terror*, as the Critics say, are the principal objects of Tragedy, surely no Play that ever was written can possibly answer both these ends better than this performance, as it stands in the present text. (351)

---

[1] Horace Walpole, *Historic Doubts on Richard III* (1768).

[6] [On *King Lear*, 1.4.274ff.: 'Hear, Nature, hear']

The curses which the justly provoked father denounces here against his unnatural daughters are so very horrid and shocking to humanity that I shall not offend my Reader by quoting them; though Shakespeare, I am convinced, supplied them merely in order to raise an abhorrence in his audience against two of the greatest crimes in the black list of deadly sins, namely ingratitude and undutifulness; and to shew, as the injured parent most emphatically expresses it in the same passage,

> How sharper than a serpent's tooth it is
> To have a thankless child!   [288f.]
>   (358)

[7] [On *King Lear*, 2.4.99–110: 'Fiery? the fiery Duke? . . . . May be he is not well']

The surprize and resentment expressed in the first part of the above speech is just and natural; but the pause of recollection which afterwards abates his anger is extremely fine, both in the reasonableness of the reflection and the humanity of the sentiment.

This beautiful passage, with many others of the same tender kind which follow in the course of developing Lear's character, and which I shall occasionally refer back from to this note, render this unhappy man a real object both of commiseration and esteem, notwithstanding the weakness, passion, and injustice he has so fully exposed in the beginning of this Play.

No writer that ever lived was capable of drawing a mixed character equal to Shakespeare; for no one has ever seemed to have dived so deep into Nature. (359)

[8] [On *King Lear*, 4.1.37f.]

> *Gloucester*. As flies to wanton boys, are we to the Gods;
> They kill us, for their sport.

This is a most impious and unphilosophic reflection. Poor Gloucester seems, by this expression, to have been rather soured than softened by his misfortunes; which his attempted suicide afterwards proves still further. Such a sentiment must certainly surprize us, in Shakespeare, when uttered by a person of so good a character as Gloucester. It could not so offend in the mouth of Edmund, though better not spoken at all. (365)

[9] [On *Titus Andronicus* and its authenticity]

. . . I should suppose the intire Piece to be his, and for a very singular reason; because the whole of the fable, as well as the conduct of it is so very *barbarous*, in every sense of the word, that I think, however he might have been tempted to make use of the legend in some hurry or other for his own purpose, he could hardly have adopted it from any other person's composition. We are quick-sighted to the faults of others, though purblind to our own. Besides, he would never have strewed such sweet flowers upon a *caput mortuum* if some child of his had not lain entombed underneath. . . .

I should imagine, from the many shocking spectacles exhibited in this Play, that it could never have been represented on any theatre except the Lisbon scaffold, where the duke d'Aveiro, the Marquis of Tavora, *cum suis*, were so barbarously massacred for the supposed Jesuits' plot against the present king of Portugal. And yet Ben Jonson assures us that it was performed in his time *with great applause*; and we are also told that it was revived again, in the reign of Charles the Second, *with the same success*.[1] The different humours and tastes of times! It would be not only hissed but driven off the stage at present. (403–4)

[10] [On *Macbeth*, 2.2.1f.]

Lady Macbeth, speaking here of Duncan's grooms, says

> That which hath made them drunk, hath made me bold;
> What hath quenched them, hath given me fire.

Our sex is obliged to Shakespeare for this passage. He seems to think that a woman could not be rendered compleatly wicked without some degree of intoxication. It required two vices in her; one to intend and another to perpetrate the crime. He does not give *wine and wassail* to Macbeth; leaving him in his natural state, to be actuated by the temptation of ambition. (412–13)

[11] [On *Coriolanus*, 1.3.1–25: Volumnia on how she sent Coriolanus to the wars 'When yet he was but tender-bodied, and the only son of my womb']

This place affords us a description of the characteristic *Roman*

---

[1] For Jonson's testimony see Vol. 3, p. 307, Vol. 4, p. 560. For Ravenscroft's adaptation, see Vol. 1, No. 18, and Steevens's comment, Vol. 5, p. 533.

Matron of those times, set in contrast with the *Woman of Nature*. . . .

There appears to be a vast difference here between the sentiments of these two matrons; but this may well be accounted for from the difference of their situations and circumstances of life. Volumnia, having been left a widow in the infancy of her son, and taking upon herself the charge of his education, had, it may be supposed, soon silenced the tenderness of a mother in her breast and assumed the spirit of a father, to fulfil her trust; and by constantly endeavouring to inspire her pupil with the chief virtues of a Roman, magnanimity and love of his country, she may be said in a manner to have educated herself at the same time to bravery, fortitude, and contempt of death. (436)

[12] [On Coriolanus' character]

As I have quoted several descriptions of character before in the course of this work, for the reason already given in its proper place, as being within the prescription of moral; and besides that those were merely imaginary, though truly copied from real life, I think that this one of Coriolanus, being sufficiently vouched from authentic story,* ought therefore to be more particularly remarked upon in these notes.

In the first Scene of former Act, in a passage above quoted, one of the discontented citizens charges him with paying himself for his services *with being proud*; and his reproach was just. But yet here he seems to appear in a light the very reverse of such a character; for when the herald, in the voice of Rome, is proclaiming his merits, he stops him short by crying out

> No more of this; it does offend my heart.
> Pray now, no more.   [2.1.159f.]

He manifests the same modestly also in the Sixth Scene following. When he appears to be uneasy in his seat, upon the applause given him for his prowess, one of the senators says to him

> Sit, Coriolanus, never shame to hear
> What you have nobly done.

To which he replies

* Plutarch, Livy etc.

Your honour's pardon—
I'd rather have my wounds to heal again,
Than hear say how I got them. . . .   [2.2.65–79]

Again, when he is pressed to harangue the people in order to get himself elected Consul, he answers in the same stile and spirit of character,

I beseech you,
Let me o'er-leap that custom; for I cannot
Put on the gown, stand naked, and intreat them. . . .
                                        [2.2.134–48]

But these seeming contradictions form, in effect, but one character still. The over-valuing his merits, and the under-valuing the applause of them, are both equally founded in pride, fierceness, and impatience. Plutarch draws a comparison of Coriolanus with Alcibiades; but I think he more resembles Achilles, as described by Horace: 'Vigilant, irascible, inflexible, harsh, and above all laws; acknowledging no rights but those of conquest.'* (438–40)

[13] [On *Cymbeline*, 3.4.38ff.: Imogen's answer to Posthumus' accusation of infidelity]

False to his bed! What is it to be false?
To lie in watch there, and to think on him?
To weep 'twixt clock and clock? If sleep charge nature,
To break it with a fearful dream of him,
And cry myself awake? That's false to's bed! is't?

Nothing, in situation of circumstance, in thought, or expression can exceed the beauty or tender effect of the above passage. It catches such quick hold of our sympathy that we feel as if the scene was real, and are at once transported amidst the gloom and silence of the forest, in spite of all the glare of the Theatre and the loud applause of the audience. It is in such instances as these that Shakespeare has never yet been equalled, and can never be excelled. What a power of natural sentiment must a man have been possessed of who could so adequately express that kind of ingenuous surprize upon such a challenge, which none but a woman can possibly feel! Shakespeare could not only assume all characters, but even their sexes too. This whole Scene is beautiful,

* *Ars Poetica*, 121f.

but falls not within our rule to transcribe any more of it here. The Commentators are all dumb upon this fine passage—not silent in admiration, but frozen into scholastic apathy. (481)

[14] [On *Troilus and Cressida*, 1.2.278ff.]

Cressida's speech here, in reference to her wooer Troilus, contains very just reflections and prudent maxims for the conduct of women in the dangerous circumstance of love. What she says would become the utterance of the most virtuous matron, though her own character in this piece is unluckily a bad one. But our Author's genius teemed so fertile in document that he was unable to restrain its impulse and coolly wait for a fit opportunity of adapting the speaker to the speech. Shakespeare's faults arise from richness, not from poverty; they exceed, not fall short; his monsters never want a head, but have sometimes two.

> Yet hold I off. . . Women are angels wooing?
> Things won are done; joy's soul lies in the doing.

(487)

[15] [On *Romeo and Juliet*]

Were it my province to have selected the poetical beauties of our Author there are few of his Plays that would have furnished me more amply than this. The language abounds with tenderness and delicacy, and seems to breathe the soul of youthful fondness. But neither the fable nor the dialogue can afford much assistance toward my present purpose; as the first is founded on a vicious prejudice unknown to the liberal minds of Britons, that of entailing family feuds and resentments down from generation to generation; and the second, as far at least as the lovers are concerned, though poetical and refined, is dictated more by passion than by sentiment.

But as my young Readers might not forgive my passing over this Play unnoticed, I shall just observe that the catastrophe of the unhappy lovers seems intended as a kind of moral, as well as poetical justice, for their having ventured upon an unweighed engagement together without the concurrence and consent of their parents. (497)

[16] [On *Hamlet*, 1.5.84ff.: the Ghost's injunction to Hamlet not to harm Gertrude]

He repeats the same fond caution to him again, in Act III:

But, look! Amazement on thy mother sits;
O step between her and her fighting soul; . . .   [3.4.112f.]

No Eastern sentiment inspired by the first beams of the Sun, and refined by the sublimest morality of Confucius, ever rose to so high a pitch as the tenderness expressed in these two passages toward his wife—even after her crimes. Have either the Greek or Latin masters of the Epic afforded us so beautiful an instance of forgiveness, and of love subsisting even beyond the grave? They have both of them presented us with scenes after death; but compare the behaviour of *Dido* upon meeting *Æneas* in the Elysian fields with this, as being the most parallel passage I can recollect. He had not been any thing near so culpable towards her as this queen had been to her husband; and yet the utmost temper that the *heathen* Poet could bring his Ghost to upon that occasion, was merely to be silent, and not upbraid *in speech*; though he makes her sufficiently mark her resentment by her *looks and behaviour*. (508)

[17] [On *Othello*]
Shakespeare has written three pieces on the subject of jealousy; the *Winter's Tale, Cymbeline*, and this one, besides the character of Ford, in the *Merry Wives*. But such was the richness of his genius that he has not borrowed a single thought, image, or expression, from any one of them to assist him in any of the others. The subject seems rather to have grown progressively out of itself, to have inspired its own sentiments and have dictated its own language. This Play, in my opinion, is very justly considered as the last and greatest effort of our Author's genius, and may therefore be looked upon as the *chef d'œuvre* of dramatic composition. (519)

[18] [On *Othello*, 1.3.317–31]
I have before observed upon the exuberance of Shakespeare's document and moral. He so much abounds in maxim and reflection that he appears frequently at a loss to find proper characters, throughout even his own extensive drama, sufficient to parcel them out to; so that he is frequently obliged to make his fools talk sense, and set his knaves a-preaching. An instance of the latter impropriety may be seen in the following passage, which contains both sound philosophy and useful admonition. But that it may

have the better effect on my readers, I wish that whenever they remember the speech they could contrive to forget the speaker.

> *Iago.* Virtue? a fig. *'Tis in ourselves that we are thus, or thus.* [521]

[19] [On *Othello*, 3.4.141–51]

It has often surprized me to find the character of Desdemona so much mistaken and slighted as it too generally is. It is simple, indeed, but that is one of its merits: for the simplicity of it is that of *innocence* not of *folly.* In my opinion, she seems to be as perfect a model of a wife as either this author, or any other writer, could possibly have framed. She speaks little; but whatever she says is sensible, pure, and chaste. The remark she makes in this place, on the alteration of Othello's manners towards her, affords a very proper admonition to all women in her situation and circumstances.

> . . . *Nay, we must think men are not gods;*
> *Nor of them look for such observance always,*
> *As fits the bridal.*

She had said to himself before:

> Be't as your fancies teach you—
> *Whate'er you be, I am obedient.*

And afterwards, in confessing herself before Iago and Emilia:

> . . . Unkindness may do much,
> *And his unkindness may defeat my life,*
> *But never taint my love.*   [4.2.152–62]

And further on, where Emilia says to her of Othello, 'I wish you had never seen him!' she replies,

> So would not I. *My love doth so approve him,*
> *That ev'n his stubbornness, his checks and frowns,*
> *Have grace and favour in them.*

As the married state is both the dearest and most social connection of life, I think this a proper passage to conclude my observations with, on a work in which is comprehended the compleatest system of the œconomical and moral duties of human nature that perhaps was ever framed by the wisdom, philosophy, or experience of *uninspired* man. (523–4)

[20] A GENERAL POSTSCRIPT.

. . . So far from being insensible to the other excellencies of this Author, I have ever thought him by much the greatest poet of our nation for sublimity of idea and beauty of expression. Perhaps I may even think myself guilty of some injustice in limiting his fame within the narrow confines of these kingdoms; for, upon a comparison with the much venerated names of Antiquity, I am of opinion that we need not surrender the British Palm either to the Grecian Bay, or the Roman Laurel with regard to the principal parts of poetry; as thought, sentiment, or description. And though the dead languages are confessed to be superior to ours, yet even here, in the very article of diction, our Author shall measure his pen with any of the ancient *styles* in their most admired compound and decompound epithets, descriptive phrases, or figurative expressions. *The multitudinous sea, ear-piercing fife, big war, giddy mast, sky-aspiring, heaven-kissing hill, time-honoured name, cloud-capt towers, heavenly-harnessed team, rash gunpowder, polished perturbation, gracious silence, golden care, trumpet-tongued, thought-executing fires*; with a number of other words, both epic and comic, are instances of it. But with regard to the moral excellencies of our English *Confucius*, either for beauty or number, he undoubtedly challenges the wreath from the whole collective Host of Greek or Roman Writers, whether ethic, epic, dramatic, didactic or historic.

Mrs. Montagu says, very justly, that 'We are apt to consider Shakespeare only as a poet; but he is certainly one of the greatest moral philosophers that ever lived.' And this is true; because in his universal scheme of doctrine he comprehends manners, proprieties, and decorums; and whatever relates to these, to personal character, or national description falls equally within the great line of morals. Horace prefers Homer to all the philosophers

> Qui, quid sit pulchrum, quid turpe, quid utile, quid non,
> Pleniùs et meliùs Chrysippo et Crantore dicit.[1]

And surely Shakespeare *pleniùs et meliùs* excels him again as much as the living scene exceeds the dead letter, as action is preferable to didaction, or representation to declamation. (525–6)

---

[1] *Epistles*, 1.2.3: 'Who tells us what is fair, what is foul, what helpful, what not, more plainly and better than Chrysippus or Crantor.'

250. William Cooke, Shakespeare's language

1775

From *The Elements of Dramatic Criticism* (1775).

William Cooke, or Cook (d. 1824), born and educated in Ireland, having married at 19 and soon squandered his wife's fortune, came to London in 1766, entered the Middle Temple in 1770, and was called to the bar in 1775. He was a lifelong friend of Goldsmith, and a member of Johnson's club. Cooke adapted Beaumont's *The Capricious Lady* (1783), published *Memoirs of Charles Macklin* (1802, 1804), *Memoirs of Samuel Foote* (3 vols, 1805), and achieved some fame with *Conversation: a didactic poem* (1796), which included 'characters' of Johnson's club (he was afterwards known as 'Conversation Cooke'). Also ascribed to him are a life of Johnson and some satirical poetry. His *Elements* were translated into French and German.

... A person sometimes is agitated at once by different passions; and the mind, in that case, vibrating like a pendulum, vents itself in sentiments that partake of the same vibration, as in the three following instances: [Quotes *Henry VIII*, 3.1.143ff.; *Othello*, 4.1.240–57; 4.1.166–86.] (59–61)

As imagery and figurative expression are discordant in the highest degree with the agony of a mother who is deprived of two hopeful sons by a brutal murder; therefore the following passage is a specimen of diction too light and airy for so intense a passion. [Quotes *Richard III*, 4.4.9–14.] A thought that turns upon the expression instead of the subject, commonly called a *play of words*, is unworthy of that composition which pretends to any degree of elevation; yet Shakespeare has made this sacrifice to the age he lived in in many instances, particularly in the following: [Quotes

149

'Too much of water hast thou poor Ophelia', *Hamlet*, 4.7.185; and Antony's pun on 'hart'/'heart', *Julius Caesar*, 3.1.208ff.] But though Shakespeare has thus descended to a play of words, he has sometimes introduced it for the marking a peculiar character, as in the following passage.[1] [Quotes Faulconbridge in *King John*, 2.5.496ff.] (76–7)

Immoral sentiments exposed in their native colours, instead of being concealed or disguised: thus lady Macbeth, projecting the death of the king, has the following soliloquy. [Quotes 'Come all you spirits', *Macbeth*, 1.5.40ff.] This speech we cannot think natural; the most treacherous murder, we hope, was never perpetrated by the most hardened miscreant without compunction;[2] in that state of mind it is a never-failing artifice of self-deceit to draw the thickest veil over the most wicked action, and to extenuate it by all the circumstances which imagination can suggest; and if the mind even cannot bear disguise the next attempt is to thrust it out from its counsel altogether, and rush in upon action without thought; this last was her husband's method:

> Strange things I have in head, that will to hand,
> Which must be *acted*, ere they must be *scann'd*.

[3.5.138f.]

(66–7)

[On tragi-comedy]

One of the great requisites both of tragedy and comedy is *unity* of action; now in a tragi-comedy there are *two* distinct actions carrying on together, to the perplexity of the audience, who, before they are well engaged in the concernments of one part are diverted to another, and by those means espouse the interest of neither. From hence likewise arises another inconvenience equally as absurd, which is that one half of the characters of the play are not known to each other; they keep their distances like the *Montagues* and *Capulets*, and seldom begin an acquaintance till the last scene of the fifth act, when they all meet upon the stage to wind up their own stories.

In short, the very basis of this species of the drama is egregiously unnatural; for as Aristotle has justly laid down *compassion* to be one of the great springs of tragedy, how incompatible is *mirth*, or more

---

[1] This is plagiarized from Kames: Vol. 4, p. 480.
[2] This is another plagiarism from Kames: cf. Vol. 4, p. 476.

commonly *low humour*, with so refined and exalted a sensation? and is it not evident that the poet must destroy the former by mixing it with the latter? (119–20)

251. James Beattie, Shakespearian tragedy

1776

From *Essays. On Poetry and Music, as They Affect the Mind* (1776).

James Beattie (1735–1803), poet, essayist, and philosopher, held the chair of moral philosophy and logic in Marischal College, Aberdeen, for thirty years from 1760. He first made his reputation as a poet, especially with *The Minstrel* (1771, four editions by 1774, when the second book was added; second edition, 1777). A rather unoriginal philosopher, he published *An Essay on Truth* (1770), and to its second edition appended three essays: that represented here, 'On Laughter and Ludicrous Composition', and 'On the Utility of Classical Learning'. He also published *Dissertations moral and critical* (1783, 1786). He was awarded a pension of £200 by the king in 1773. He had many friends in London; Mrs Thrale once declared that 'if she had another husband she would have Beattie'.

[On crime and punishment in tragedy]

[Poetry] is an imitation of human action; and therefore poetical characters, though elevated, should still partake of the passions and frailties of humanity. If it were not for the vices of some principal personages the *Iliad* would not be either so interesting or so moral:—the most moving and most eventful parts of the

Æneid are those that describe the effects of unlawful passion;—the most instructive tragedy in the world, I mean *Macbeth*, is founded in crimes of dreadful enormity: ... (72–4)

[On 'bad or mixed characters' in drama, and the poet's task to blend faults and attractive qualities]

Who does not esteem and admire Macbeth for his courage and generosity? Who does not pity him when beset with all the terrors of a pregnant imagination, superstitious temper, and awakened conscience? Who does not abhor him as a monster of cruelty, treachery, and ingratitude? His good qualities, by drawing us near to him make us, as it were, eye-witnesses of his crime, and give us a fellow-feeling of his remorse; and therefore his example cannot fail to have a powerful effect in cherishing our love of virtue, and fortifying our minds against criminal impressions. Whereas, had he wanted those good qualities, we should have kept aloof from his concerns or viewed them with a superficial attention; in which case his example would have had little more weight than that of the robber, of whom we know nothing but that he was tried, condemned, and executed. (76–8)

[On comedy in tragedy: too much 'grief and horror' can damage us, and it is perverse 'to torment ourselves with imaginary misfortune'. The satyr plays in the Greek theatre, and the farces in the modern, may legitimately cheer a spectator up at the end of a tragedy]

...A man, especially if advanced in years, would not chuse to go home with that gloom upon his mind which an affecting tragedy is intended to diffuse: and if the play has conveyed any sound instruction, there is no risk of its being dissipated by a little innocent mirth.

Upon the same principle, I confess that I am not offended with those comic scenes wherewith our great Dramatic Poet has occasionally thought proper to diversify his tragedies. Such a licence will at least be allowed to be more pardonable in him than it would be in other Tragic poets. They must make their way to the heart as an army does to a strong fortification, by slow and regular approaches; because they cannot, like Shakespeare, take it at once and by storm. In their pieces therefore, a mixture of comedy might have as bad an effect as if besiegers were to retire from the outworks they had gained, and leave the enemy at leisure to fortify them a second time. But Shakespeare penetrates the heart by a single effort, and can make us as sad in the present scene as if we had not been merry in the former. With such powers as he possessed in the pathetic, if he had made his tragedies uniformly mournful or terrible from beginning to end no person of sensibility would have been able to support the representation.

As to the probability of these mixed compositions, it admits of no doubt. Nature every where presents a similar mixture of tragedy and comedy, of joy and sorrow, of laughter and solemnity in the common affairs of life. The servants of a court know little of what passes among princes and statesmen, and may therefore, like the porter in *Macbeth*, be very jocular when their superiors are in deep distress. The death of a favourite child is a great affliction to parents and friends; but the man who digs the grave may, like Goodman Delver in *Hamlet*, be very chearful while he is going about his work. . . . I grant that compositions like those I would now apologize for cannot properly be called either tragedies or comedies. But the name is of no consequence; let them be called *Plays*: and if in them nature is imitated in such a way as to give pleasure and instruction, they are as well entitled to the denomination of *Dramatic Poems* as any thing in Sophocles, Racine, or Voltaire. (202–4)

[On figurative language and the representation of feeling]

Tropes and Figures promote strength of expression, and are in poetry peculiarly requisite, because they are often more *natural* and more *imitative* than proper words. In fact, this is so much the case that it would be impossible to imitate the language of passion without them. It is true that when the mind is agitated one does not run out into allegories, or long-winded similitudes, or any of the figures that require much attention and many words, or that tend to withdraw the fancy from the object of the passion. Yet the language of many passions must be figurative, notwithstanding; because they rouse the fancy, and direct it to objects congenial to their own nature, which diversify the language of the speaker with a multitude of allusions. The fancy of a very angry man, for example, presents to his view a train of disagreeable ideas connected with the passion of anger, and tending to encourage it; and if he speak without restraint during the paroxysm of his rage, those ideas will force themselves upon him and compel him to give them utterance. 'Infernal monster! (he will say)—my blood boils at him; he has used me like a dog; never was man so injured as I have been by this barbarian. He has no more sense of propriety than a stone. His countenance is diabolical, and his soul as ugly as his countenance. His heart is cold and hard, and his resolutions dark and bloody,' &c. This speech is wholly figurative. It is made up of *metaphors* and *hyperboles*, which, with the *prosopopeia* and *apostrophe*, are the most passionate of all the figures.—Lear, driven out of doors by his unnatural daughters in the midst of darkness, thunder, and tempest, naturally breaks forth (for his indignation is just now raised to the very highest pitch) into the following violent exclamation against the crimes of mankind, in which almost every word is figurative. [Quotes 'Tremble thou wretch', 3.2.51ff.] The vehemence of maternal love, and sorrow from the apprehension of losing her child, make the Lady Constance utter a language that is strongly figurative, tho' quite suitable to the condition and character of the speaker. [Quotes *King John*, 3.4.93ff.] (265–6)

As the passions that agitate the soul and rouse the fancy are apt to vent themselves in tropes and figures, so those that depress the mind adopt for the most part a plain diction without any ornament. For to a dejected mind, wherein the imagination is generally inactive, it is not probable that any great variety of ideas will present themselves; and when these are few and familiar the words that express them must be simple. As no author equals Shakespeare in boldness or variety of figures, when he copies the style of those violent passions that stimulate the fancy; so, when he would exhibit the human mind in a dejected state no uninspired writer excels him in simplicity. The same Lear whose resentment had impaired his understanding while it broke out in the most boisterous language, when, after some medical applications he recovers his reason, his rage being now exhausted, his pride humbled, and his spirits totally depressed, speaks in a style than which nothing can be imagined more simple or more affecting: [Quotes 'Pray, do not mock me', 4.7.58ff.]

Desdemona, ever gentle, artless, and sincere, shocked at the unkindness of her husband and overcome with melancholy, speaks in a style so beautifully simple and so perfectly natural, that one knows not what to say in commendation of it: [Quotes 'My mother had a maid call'd Barbary', 4.3.26ff.]

154

[From 'On the Utility of Classical Learning']

It has been said that 'school-learning has a tendency to encumber the genius, and consequently to weaken rather than improve the mind.' Here opens another field for declamation. Who has not heard the learned formality of Ben Jonson opposed to Shakespeare's 'native wood-notes wild;' and inferences made from the comparison, very much to the discredit not of the learned poet only, but of learning itself? . . .

The present objection is founded on what every man of letters would call a mistake of fact. . . It would be difficult to prove, even by a single instance, that genius was ever hurt by learning. Ben Jonson's misfortune was not that he knew too much, but that he could not make a proper use of his knowledge; a misfortune which arose rather from a defect of genius or taste than from a superabundance of erudition. With the same genius, and less learning, he would probably have made a worse figure.— His play of *Catiline* is an ill-digested collection of facts and passages from Sallust. Was it his knowledge of Greek and Latin that prevented his making a better choice? To comprehend every thing the historian has recorded of that incendiary, it is not requisite that one should be a great scholar. By looking into Rose's translation any man who understands English may make himself master of the whole narrative in half a day. It was Jonson's want of taste that made him transfer from the history to the play some passages and facts that suit not the genius of dramatic writing; it was want of taste that made him dispose his materials according to the historical arrangement, which, however favourable to calm information, is not calculated for working those effects on the passions and fancy which it is the aim of tragedy to produce. It was the same want of taste that made him, out of a rigid attachment to historical truth, lengthen his piece with supernumerary events inconsistent with the unity of design, and not subservient to the catastrophe; and it was doubtless owing to want of invention that he confined himself so strictly to the letter of the story. Had he recollected the advice of Horace, . . . he must have avoided some of these faults. [Quotes *Ars Poetica*, 131ff., on not being a 'slavish translator'.] A little more learning, therefore, or rather a more seasonable application of what he had, would have been of great use to the author on this occasion.

Shakespeare's play of *Julius Caesar* is founded on Plutarch's life of Brutus. The poet has adopted many of the incidents and speeches recorded by the historian, whom he had read in Sir Thomas North's translation. But great judgement appears in the choice of passages. Those events and sentiments that either are affecting in themselves, or contribute to the display of human characters and passions, he has adopted; what seemed unsuitable to the drama is omitted. By reading Plutarch and Sophocles in the original, together with the *Poetics* of Aristotle and Horace's epistle to the Pisoes, Shakespeare might have made this tragedy better; but I cannot conceive how such a preparation, had the poet been capable of it, could have been the cause of his making it worse. It is very probable that the instance of Shakespeare may have induced some persons to think unfavourably of the influence of learning upon genius; but a conclusion so important should never be inferred from one instance, especially when that is allowed to be extraordinary and almost supernatural. From the phenomena of so transcendent a genius we must not judge of human nature in general; no more than we are to take the rules of British agriculture from what is practised in the Summer Islands. (525–9)

252. John Berkenhout, Shakespeare defended from Voltaire

1777

From *Biographia Literaria; or, a Biographical History of Literature: Containing the Lives of English, Scottish, and Irish Authors, from the Dawn of Letters in these Kingdoms, to the present Time, Chronologically and Classically arranged. Vol. 1. From the Beginning of the Fifth to the End of the Sixteenth Century* (1777).

John Berkenhout, M.D., (1730?–91) had been an officer in both the Prussian and English armies before he took up medicine. As well as several distinguished books on medicine, natural history, and this biographical history (of which only the first volume was published), he undertook an official mission to America, translated Count Tessin's letters to Gustavus III from the Swedish, spoke five other languages, and excelled in botany, chemistry, mathematics, music, and painting.

[From the Preface]

Like a traveller who began his journey whilst the sun was yet far beneath the horizon, I rejoice to find myself at last in the daylight of the sixteenth century. There is, I confess, some pleasure and perhaps some utility in tracing the stream of science to its source: it is nevertheless but a dreary journey, through a dubious country, and with only now and then the transient light of a Sirius, a Jupiter, a Venus, to guide us on our way. And indeed the most diligent enquirer will find among our English authors, previous to the invention of printing, very few books that will afford him either pleasure or instruction. In the sixteenth century we are dazzled with a multiplicity of authors in various branches of literature. Kings, queens, and many of our nobility honoured the press with their productions. Linacre, in 1519, founded the college of physicians. Colet, Grocyn, Latimer, and Lilly revived the learning of Greece and Rome. Spenser by his example taught our poets melody. But the reader probably now wishes to dismiss his guide. The writers of this century are too well known to require an officious index. I must however take the liberty to add a few words concerning Shakespeare, whose genius I shall ever contemplate with some degree of enthusiasm. I address myself particularly to the celebrated Monsieur de Voltaire, whose comprehensive abilities and repeated effusions of universal philanthropy I shall always honour and applaud. As the scourge of sanctified tyranny and the advocate of oppressed innocence, be his opinions what they will, he deserves the thanks of all mankind. Mr. de Voltaire has more than once, but particularly in a late publication,[1] endeavoured to ridicule our enthusiastic admiration of Shakespeare. His opinions are universally diffused, and deservedly regarded; it is therefore of importance to convince him of his

[1] *Lettre à l'Académie française* (1776): text with commentary in *Voltaire on Shakespeare*, ed. Theodore Besterman (Geneva, 1967), pp. 186–209.

error: and this I think may be done without attempting to vindicate any of the passages which he has quoted as ridiculous or absurd.

The first general objection to Shakespeare is his total disregard of the three unities of time, place, and action. I allow the charge, and am convinced that Shakespeare was perfectly right; because I never saw or read a tragedy or comedy, fettered by these unities, which did not seem improbable, unnatural, and tedious. Can any thing be more ridiculous than to imagine, because the Greeks thought fit to prescribe certain arbitrary rules for the composition of tragedy and comedy, that therefore every other nation to the end of time was bound to observe these rules, and precluded from inventing any other species of dramatic entertainment? Many of Shakespeare's best plays are neither tragedies nor comedies but *histories*, properly and designedly so called by the first editors of his works; a species of dramatic composition in which the least regard to these foolish unities would have been absurd. A dramatic history, or historical tragedy, is the exhibition of a succession of pictures representing certain interesting events in a regular series. Every scene is a separate picture, and the real interval of time between each is of no importance to the spectator. Hogarth's *Marriage à la mode* is an historical tragedy upon canvas, against which, I presume, no critic will urge the want of the three unities. If Hogarth had painted Shakespeare's history of *Hamlet* would he have omitted the obnoxious scene of the grave-diggers? Or did any man of real taste, fine feelings, and sound judgement ever wish, in reading *Hamlet*, that this scene had not been written? The more I consider these Greek unities the more I am convinced of their absurdity. It were infinitely better for the English stage if their chimerical existence in Nature had never been supposed. Who that should see a Slingsby dance in chains would doubt that he would have danced better without them? Was there ever a reader capable of enjoying Sterne's excentricity who wished that he had written by rule? Or, to come nearer to the point, was there ever a man of even common understanding who wished that Shakespeare's ghosts and witches had been sacrificed to any rules whatsoever? If these *unities* had existed in Nature, Shakespeare was so well acquainted with her that I trust he would have found them out: but Nature is so far from prescribing *the unities* to a dramatic writer that if he means to accomplish the principal design of the theatre, amusement, they must be carefully avoided. They were the invention of dullness, and are only leading-strings for puny poetasters. As to some particular scenes or speeches which have been ridiculed because they are too low or vulgar for modern delicacy, it is quite sufficient to observe that they were properly adapted to the taste and manners of at least a part of the audience for whom they were written. This is an argument of so much weight that it ought for ever to preclude all attempts to ridicule Shakespeare on that account. (xxix–xxxiv)

[From the Life of 'William Shakespeare, The Prince of Dramatic Poets, and the Glory of this Nation', pp. 397–401]

The learned editors of the works of this immortal bard have exerted their utmost power in praise of his extensive genius and universal knowledge of human nature. If indeed there ever existed an inspired writer (if by inspiration we mean originality), Shakespeare was indisputably inspired. 'His characters,' says Mr. Pope, 'are so much Nature's self, that it were injurious to call them by so distant a name as copies.'[1] It is astonishing, when we consider the infinite variety of his characters, that a poet who from his education had so little opportunity of acquiring a knowledge of mankind should, as it were by intuition, have delineated the whole world with such accuracy and truth! But to an English reader it is sufficient, independent of his judgement, to appeal to his feelings. Some foreigners have foolishly attempted to ridicule particular scenes, and to condemn his inattention to *their* rules of the drama; but such criticisms serve only to expose their total ignorance of his capacity, his design, his invention. He despised their rules as he would have despised their criticisms. Some of his plays are intentionally neither tragedies nor comedies but a natural mixture of both; others are professedly historical; but they are always just representations of human nature, call them by what name you will. They say Shakespeare was illiterate. The supposition implies more than Panegyric with a hundred tongues could have expressed. If he was unlearned he was the only instance of a human being to whom learning was unnecessary; the favorite child of Nature, produced and educated entirely by herself; but so educated that the pedant Art had nothing new to add. (401)

[1] Vol. 2, p. 404.

253. Joseph Priestley, lectures on Shakespeare

1777

From *A Course of Lectures on Oratory and Criticism* (1777).

Joseph Priestley (1733–1804) achieved distinction as a scientist with his work on the chemical properties of gases, as the 'discoverer of oxygen', and as author of a history of electricity (1767). In addition to many scientific works he published a great number of books on theological, religious, historical, educational, political, and social matters. His lectures on oratory derive from his time as tutor of languages and belles-lettres at the Dissenting Academy of Warrington (1761–7). They are rather conventional examples of the 'beauties and faults' school of criticism.

This connexion of vivid ideas and emotions with reality will easily furnish the mind with pretences for justifying the extravagance of such passions as love, gratitude, anger, revenge, and envy. If these passions be raised, though ever so unreasonably, they are often able by this means to adjust the object to their gratification. Besides, since, in consequence of almost constant joint impressions, all ideas are associated with other ideas similar to themselves, these passions, while the mind is under their influence and as it were wholly occupied by them, will excite in abundance all such ideas as conspire with themselves, and preclude all attention to objects and circumstances connected with, and which would tend to introduce, an opposite state of mind. . . .

An attention to these affections of our minds will show us the admirable propriety of innumerable fine touches of passion in our inimitable Shakespeare. How naturally doth he represent Cassius, full of envy at the greatness of Cæsar, whose equal he had been, dwelling upon every little circumstance which shows the natural weakness of him whom fortune had made his master. Speaking of their swimming together cross the Tiber, he says [Quotes 'Help me, Cassius', 1.2.111; and 'Give me some drink, Titinius', 1.2.127.] (92–3)

With equal regard to nature doth he represent Hamlet as shortening the time that intervened between the death of his father and the marriage of his mother with his uncle, because that circumstance heightened and gratified his indignation.[1] [Quotes *Hamlet*, 1.2.138ff.] (94)

It is a direct consequence of the association of ideas that when a person hath suffered greatly on any account he connects the idea of the same cause with any great distress. This shews with what propriety Shakespeare makes King Lear, whose sufferings were owing to his daughters, speak to Edgar, disguised like a lunatic, in the following manner: 'What, have his *daughters* brought him to this pass?' [3.4.63f.] And Macduff, 'He hath no children.' [4.3.216]

Writers not really feeling the passions they describe, and not being masters of the natural expression of them are apt, without their being aware of it, to make persons under the influence of a strong emotion or passion speak in a manner that is very unsuitable to it. Sometimes, for instance, they seem rather to be describing the *passion of another* than expressing their own. Sometimes the language of persons in interesting circumstances shows such an excursion of mind from the principal object as demonstrates that their minds were not sufficiently engrossed with it. . . . Even our Shakespeare himself, though no writer whatever hath succeeded so well in the language of the passions, is sometimes deserving of censure in this respect; as when Constance, in *King John*, says to the messenger that brought her a piece of disagreeable news

> Fellow, be gone, I cannot brook thy sight:
> This news hath made thee a most ugly man.   [3.1.36f.]

The sentiment and expression in the former line is perfectly natural, but that in the latter resembles too much the comment of a cool observer. Of the same kind, but much more extravagant, is the following passage, which is part of the speech of Constance giving her reasons why she indulged her grief for the loss of her son. [Quotes 'Grief fills the room up of my absent child', 3.4.93ff.]

Shakespeare's talent for wit and humour, and the genius of the times in which he wrote, have upon many occasions betrayed him

[1] Cf. Steele, *Tatler*, no. 106: Vol. 2, p. 210.

into the second impropriety, which is to make persons under strong emotions speak as if their minds were not sufficiently engrossed with the principal object of their concern. Would even a child, apprehensive of having his eyes instantly burned out, speak as he hath represented young Arthur to have spoken, in order to persuade his executioner to desist from his purpose?

> In good sooth the fire is dead with grief.
> Being create for comfort, to be used
> In undeserved extremes. See else yourself,
> There is no malice in this burning coal. . . . [4.1.105ff.]

More improbable still is it that King John, in the agonies of death, and with his stomach and bowels inflamed with intense heat, would pun and quibble in the manner that Shakespeare represents him to have done; and that when he was not able to procure any thing to cool his inward heat he should say, 'I beg *cold comfort*' [5.7.42].

If we censure those writers who represent persons as speaking in a manner unsuitable to their situation, with much more reason may we censure those who represent persons as thinking and speaking in a manner unsuitable to *any character*, or any circumstances whatever. Among these unnatural sentiments we may rank the avowing, or open undisguised proposal of wicked purposes: because human nature is so constituted that direct vice and wickedness is universally shocking. For this reason men seldom entertain the thought of it in their own minds, much less propose it to others, but either under the appearance of virtue or of some great advantage, and with some *salvo* for the immorality of it.

With admirable propriety doth King John hint to Hubert how much he would oblige him if he would remove prince Arthur out of his way. But the following soliloquy of the Bastard Falconbridge in the same play is certainly unnatural. [Quotes 'Gain be my lord', 2.1.593ff.]

In a much more unnatural and extravagant manner is Lady Macbeth represented talking to herself when she is projecting the death of the king. *Macbeth* [1.5.38ff.] (103–6)

The most important rule respecting the choice of metaphors, where they are proper, is that different metaphors should not be confounded together in the same sentence: because in this case the sense, if it be realized in the imagination, will appear to imply an *absurdity*. And since every new application of a word that hath the effect of a metaphor doth raise an idea of the object to which it was primarily affixed, for the same reason that every scene presented to the mind of the reader should be at least *possible* and consistent, these pieces of scenery, though ever so transient, should be so too; and when there is a manifest inconsistency in such little pictures a reader of taste is justly offended. Out of the numberless examples I might produce of this fault in writers, I shall select the following from Shakespeare, in which the marriage of King John with Constance is referred to.

> For by this knot thou shalt so surely tie
> Thy now unsured assurance to the crown,
> That yon green boy shall have no sun to ripe
> The bloom that promises a mighty fruit.   [2.1.470ff.]

Here it may justly be asked, how can the *tying a knot* prevent the sun's *ripening fruit*? The King's marriage with Constance is certainly very properly expressed by tying a knot; and as that event would cut off the reasonable hopes that Arthur might otherwise entertain of succeeding to the throne, this is likewise beautifully described by saying he would then have *no sun to ripen the bloom which promised a mighty fruit*. But though these metaphors when viewed asunder appear proper and beautiful, when they are joined the result is a manifest absurdity.

Not only should writers avoid the near union of different terms which are highly metaphorical, they should also favour the imagery which metaphors raise in the mind by intermixing no plain and natural expressions with them. Thus in the passage quoted above, the *boy* should have been kept out of sight, and the *tree* or *plant* have been substituted in its place for the *sun* to act upon. (189–90)

Shakespeare uses a low and degrading metaphor when he makes King John exhort the people of Angiers to *save unscratched their city's threatened cheeks*; meaning that they should save their walls from being battered. The allusion is merely verbal when, in the same play, Constance, lying on the ground, is made to say

> ——For my grief's so great,
> That no support but the huge firm earth
> Can bear it up.   [3.1.71ff.]

163

Figures of this sort are nothing more than *puns*; for the sense of the passage depends upon the double-meaning of the word. Grief is said to be supported in a figurative sense, but the earth supports things in a literal sense. (194)

The general rule for the use of the metonymy is plainly this; that in all cases, provided the sense be in no danger of being mistaken, a writer is at liberty to substitute, instead of a proper term, any word which, by its associations, can bring along with it ideas that can serve to heighten and improve the sentiment. But it follows from this observation that when the sense doth not require to be heightened and improved, as in the ordinary forms of expression in conversation, on which no emphasis is ever laid, the figure is impertinent and useless: as when Prospero, in the *Tempest* of Shakespeare, speaking to his sister [*sic*] Miranda, says

> The fringed curtains of thine eyes advance,
> And say what seest thou. [1.2.409f.]

To mention the *eye-lids* at all, much more to denominate them by such a figurative periphrasis, was quite superfluous. (238)

254. Maurice Morgann, on Falstaff

1777

From *An Essay on the Dramatic Character of Sir John Falstaff* (1777; reprinted 1820, 1825).

Maurice Morgann (*c*. 1725–1802) held various political posts (like Joseph Priestley he was a protégé of the Earl of Shelburne) and wrote several books on current social issues, especially concerning America and Canada. He was universally liked for his modesty and intellectual gifts. He directed his executors to destroy all his papers, but his amendments and revisions (*c*. 1789–90) of his Falstaff essay survive, and have been well edited by Daniel A. Fineman, *Maurice Morgann: Shakespearian Criticism* (Oxford, 1972).

This volume also includes Morgann's unpublished commentary on *The Tempest,* which he believed to be Shakespeare's first play, but revised at the end of his career.

The ideas which I have formed concerning the Courage and Military Character of the Dramatic Sir *John Falstaff* are so different from those which I find generally to prevail in the world, that I shall take the liberty of stating my sentiments on the subject; in hope that some person as unengaged as myself will either correct and reform my error in this respect; or, joining himself to my opinion, redeem me from what I may call the reproach of singularity.

I am to avow, then, that I do not clearly discern that Sir *John Falstaff* deserves to bear the character so generally given him of an absolute Coward; or, in other words, that I do not conceive *Shakespeare* ever meant to make Cowardice an essential part of his constitution. . . .

It must, in the first place, be admitted that the appearances in this case are singularly strong and striking; and so they had need be to become the ground of so general a censure. We see this extraordinary Character, almost in the first moment of our acquaintance with him, involved in circumstances of apparent dishonour; and we hear him familiarly called *Coward* by his most intimate companions. We see him, on occasion of the robbery at *Gads-Hill,* in the very act of running away from the Prince and *Poins*; and we behold him, on another of more honourable obligation, in open day light, in battle, and acting in his profession as a Soldier, escaping from *Douglas* even out of the world as it were; counterfeiting death, and deserting his very existence; and we find him, on the former occasion, betrayed into those *lies* and *braggadocioes* which are the usual concomitants of Cowardice in Military men and pretenders to valour. These are not only in themselves strong circumstances, but they are moreover thrust forward, prest upon our notice as the subject of our mirth, as the great business of the scene. No wonder, therefore, that the word should go forth that *Falstaff* is exhibited as a character of Cowardice and dishonour.

What there is to the contrary of this it is my business to discover. Much, I think, will presently appear; but it lies so dispersed, is so latent, and so purposely obscured that the reader must have some patience whilst I collect it into one body, and make it the object of a steady and regular contemplation.

But what have we to do, may my readers exclaim, with principles *so latent, so obscured*? In Dramatic composition the *Impression* is the *Fact*; and the Writer who, meaning to impress one thing, has impressed another is unworthy of observation.

It is a very unpleasant thing to have, in the first setting out, so many and so strong prejudices to contend with. All that one can do in such case is to pray the reader to have a little patience in the commencement; and to reserve his censure, if it must pass, for the conclusion. . . . (1–4)

It is not to the *Courage* only of *Falstaff* that we think these observations will apply: no part whatever of his character seems to be fully settled in our minds; at least there is something strangely incongruous in our discourse and affections concerning him. We all like *Old Jack*; yet, by some strange perverse fate, we all abuse him, and deny him the possession of any one single good or respectable quality. There is something extraordinary in this: it must be a strange art in *Shakespeare* which can draw our liking and good will towards so offensive an object. He has wit, it will be said; chearfulness and humour of the most characteristic and captivating sort. And is this enough? Is the humour and gaiety of vice so very captivating? Is the wit, characteristic of baseness and every ill quality, capable of attaching the heart and winning the affections? Or does not the apparency of such humour, and the flashes of such wit, by more strongly disclosing the deformity of character, but the more effectually excite our hatred and contempt of the man? And yet this is not our *feeling* of *Falstaff*'s character. When he has ceased to amuse us, we find no emotions of disgust; we can scarcely forgive the ingratitude of the Prince in the new-born virtue of the King, and we curse the severity of that poetic justice which consigns our old good-natured companion to the custody of the *warden*, and the dishonours of the *Fleet*. . . . (10–11)

In drawing out the parts of *Falstaff*'s character, with which I shall begin this Inquiry, I shall take the liberty of putting Constitutional bravery into his composition; but the reader will be pleased to consider what I shall say in that respect as spoken hypothetically for the present, to be retained, or discharged out of it as he shall finally determine.

To me then it appears that the leading quality in *Falstaff*'s character, and that from which all the rest take their colour, is a high degree of wit and humour, accompanied with great natural vigour and alacrity of mind. This quality, so accompanied, led him probably very early into life, and made him highly acceptable to society; so acceptable as to make it seem unnecessary for him to acquire any other virtue. Hence, perhaps, his continued debaucheries and dissipations of every kind.—He seems by nature to have had a mind free of malice or any evil principle; but he never took the trouble of acquiring any good one. He found himself esteemed and beloved with all his faults; nay *for* his faults, which were all connected with humour and for the most part grew out of it. As he had, possibly, no vices but such as he thought might be openly professed so he appeared more dissolute thro' ostentation. To the character of wit and humour, to which all his other qualities seem to have conformed themselves, he appears to have added a very necessary support, *that* of the profession of a *Soldier*. He had from nature, as I presume to say, a spirit of boldness and enterprise; which in a Military age, tho' employment was only occasional, kept him always above contempt, secured him an honourable reception among the Great, and suited best both with his particular mode of humour and of vice. Thus living continually in society, nay even in Taverns, and indulging himself, and being indulged by others, in every debauchery; drinking, whoring, gluttony, and ease; assuming a liberty of fiction, necessary perhaps to his wit, and often falling into falsity and lies, he seems to have set, by degrees, all sober reputation at defiance; and finding eternal resources in his wit, he borrows, shifts, defrauds, and even robs, without dishonour.—Laughter and approbation attend his greatest excesses; and being governed visibly by no settled bad principle or ill design, fun and humour account for and cover all. By degrees, however, and thro' indulgence, he acquires bad habits, becomes an humourist, grows enormously corpulent, and falls into the infirmities of age; yet never quits, all the time, one single levity or vice of youth, or loses any of that chearfulness of mind, which had enabled him to pass thro' this course with ease to himself and delight to others; and thus at last, mixing youth and age, enterprize and corpulency, wit and folly, poverty and expence, title and buffoonery, innocence as to purpose, and wickedness as to practice; neither incurring hatred by bad principle, or contempt by

Cowardice, yet involved in circumstances productive of imputation in both; a butt and a wit, a humourist and a man of humour, a touchstone and a laughing stock, a jester and a jest, has Sir *John Falstaff*, taken at that period of his life in which we see him, become the most perfect Comic character that perhaps ever was exhibited. . . . (17–20)

I cannot foresee the temper of the reader, nor whether he be content to go along with me in these kind of observations. Some of the incidents which I have drawn out of the Play may appear too minute, whilst yet they refer to principles which may seem too general. Many points require explanation; something should be said of the nature of *Shakespeare*'s Dramatic characters*, by what

* The reader must be sensible of something in the composition of *Shakespeare*'s characters which renders them essentially different from those drawn by other writers. The characters of every Drama must indeed be grouped; but in the groupes of other poets the parts which are not seen do not in fact exist. But there is a certain roundness and integrity in the forms of *Shakespeare* which give them an independence as well as a relation, insomuch that we often meet with passages which, tho' perfectly felt, cannot be sufficiently explained in words, without unfolding the whole character of the speaker; and this I may be obliged to do in respect to that of *Lancaster*, in order to account for some words spoken by him in censure of *Falstaff*.— Something which may be thought too heavy for the *text* I shall add *here*, as a conjecture concerning the composition of *Shakespeare*'s characters: not that they were the effect, I believe, so much of a minute and laborious attention as of a certain comprehensive energy of mind, involving within itself all the effects of system and of labour.

Bodies of all kinds, whether of metals, plants, or animals, are supposed to possess certain first principles of *being*, and to have an existence independent of the accidents which form their magnitude or growth. Those accidents are supposed to be drawn in from the surrounding elements, but not indiscriminately; each plant and each animal imbibes those things only which are proper to its own distinct nature, and which have besides such a secret relation to each other as to be capable of forming a perfect union and coalescence. But so variously are the surrounding elements mingled and disposed that each particular body, even of those under the same species, has yet some *peculiar* of its own. *Shakespeare* appears to have considered the being and growth of the human mind as analogous to this system. There are certain qualities and capacities which he seems to have considered as first principles; the chief of which are certain energies of courage and activity according to their degrees; together with different degrees and sorts of sensibilities, and a capacity, varying likewise in the *degree*, of discernment and intelligence. The rest of the composition is drawn in from an atmosphere of surrounding things; that is, from the various influences of the different laws, religions and governments in the world; and from those of the different ranks and inequalities in society; and from the different professions of men, encouraging or repressing passions of particular sorts, and inducing different modes of thinking and habits of life; and he seems to have known intuitively what those influences in particular were which this or that original constitution would most freely imbibe and which would most easily associate and coalesce. But all these things being, in different situations, very differently disposed, and those differences exactly discerned by him, he found no difficulty in marking every individual, even among characters of the same sort, with something peculiar and distinct.—Climate and complexion demand their influence; '*Be thus when thou art dead, and I will kill thee, and love thee after,*' is a sentiment characteristic of, and fit only to be uttered by a *Moor*. [*Othello*, 5.2.18f.]

arts they were formed, and wherein they differ from those of other writers; something likewise more professedly of *Shakespeare* himself, and of the peculiar character of his genius. After such a review we may not perhaps think any consideration arising out of the Play, or out of general nature, either as too minute or too extensive.

Shakespeare is, in truth, an author whose mimic creation agrees in general so perfectly with that of nature that it is not only wonderful in the great, but opens another scene of amazement to the discoveries of the microscope.

[Morgann attacks Voltaire, and the editors of Shakespeare: Pope, Warburton, Johnson.]

Yet whatever may be the neglect of some, or the censure of others, there are those who firmly believe that this wild, this uncultivated Barbarian has not yet obtained one half of his fame; and who trust that some new Stagyrite will arise, who instead of pecking at the surface of things will enter into the inward soul of his compositions, and expel, by the force of congenial feelings, those foreign impurities which have stained and disgraced his page. And as to those *spots* which will still remain, they may perhaps become invisible to those who shall seek them thro' the medium of his beauties, instead of looking for those beauties, as is too frequently done, thro' the smoke of some real or imputed

---

But it was not enough for *Shakespeare* to have formed his characters with the most perfect truth and coherence; it was further necessary that he should possess a wonderful facility of compressing, as it were, his own spirit into these images, and of giving alternate animation to the forms. This was not to be done *from without*; he must have *felt* every varied situation, and have spoken thro' the organ he had formed. Such an intuitive comprehension of things and such a facility must unite to produce a *Shakespeare*. The reader will not now be surprised if I affirm that those characters in *Shakespeare*, which are seen only in part, are yet capable of being unfolded and understood in the whole; every part being in fact relative, and inferring all the rest. It is true that the point of action or sentiment which we are most concerned in is always held out for our special notice. But who does not perceive that there is a peculiarity about it which conveys a relish of the whole? And very frequently, when no particular point presses, he boldly makes a character act and speak from those parts of the composition which are *inferred* only, and not distinctly shewn. This produces a wonderful effect; it seems to carry us beyond the poet to nature itself, and gives an integrity and truth to facts and character which they could not otherwise obtain. And this is in reality that art in *Shakespeare* which, being withdrawn from our notice, we more emphatically call *nature*. A felt propriety and truth from causes unseen, I take to be the highest point of Poetic composition. If the characters of *Shakespeare* are thus *whole*, and as it were original, while those of almost all other writers are mere imitation, it may be fit to consider them rather as Historic than Dramatic beings; and when occasion requires, to account for their conduct from the *whole* of character, from general principles, from latent motives, and from policies not avowed. (58–62, notes)

obscurity. When the hand of time shall have brushed off his present Editors and Commentators, and when the very name of *Voltaire*, and even the memory of the language in which he has written, shall be no more, the *Apalachian* mountains, the banks of the *Ohio*, and the plains of *Scioto* shall resound with the accents of this Barbarian. In his native tongue he shall roll the genuine passions of nature; nor shall the griefs of *Lear* be alleviated, or the charms and wit of *Rosalind* be abated by time. There is indeed nothing perishable about him, except that very learning which he is said so much to want. He had not, it is true, enough for the demands of the age in which he lived, but he had perhaps too much for the reach of his genius and the interest of his fame. *Milton* and he will carry the decayed remnants and fripperies of antient mythology into more distant ages than they are by their own force intitled to extend; and the *Metamorphoses* of *Ovid*, upheld by them, lay in a new claim to unmerited immortality.

Shakespeare is a name so interesting that it is excusable to stop a moment, nay it would be indecent to pass him without the tribute of some admiration. He differs essentially from all other writers: him we may profess rather to feel than to understand; and it is safer to say, on many occasions, that we are possessed by him than that we possess him. And no wonder;—he scatters the seeds of things, the principles of character and action, with so cunning a hand yet with so careless an air, and, master of our feelings, submits himself so little to our judgment that every thing seems superior. We discern not his course, we see no connection of cause and effect, we are rapt in ignorant admiration, and claim no kindred with his abilities. All the incidents, all the parts, look like chance, whilst we feel and are sensible that the whole is design. His Characters not only act and speak in strict conformity to nature but in strict relation to us; just so much is shewn as is requisite, just so much is impressed; he commands every passage to our heads and to our hearts, and moulds us as he pleases, and that with so much ease that he never betrays his own exertions. We see these Characters act from the mingled motives of passion, reason, interest, habit, and complection, in all their proportions, when they are supposed to know it not themselves; and we are made to acknowledge that their actions and sentiments are, from those motives, the necessary result. He at once blends and distinguishes every thing;—every thing is complicated, every thing is plain. I restrain the further expressions of my admiration lest they should not seem applicable to man; but it is really astonishing that a mere human being, a part of humanity only, should so perfectly comprehend the whole; and that he should possess such exquisite art that whilst every woman and every child shall feel the whole effect, his learned Editors and Commentators should yet so very frequently mistake or seem ignorant of the cause. A sceptre or a straw are in his hands of equal efficacy; he needs no selection; he converts every thing into excellence; nothing is too great, nothing is too base. Is a character efficient like *Richard* [*III*], it is every thing we can wish: is it otherwise, like *Hamlet*, it is productive of equal admiration. Action produces one mode of excellence, and inaction another. The Chronicle, the Novel, or the Ballad; the king, or the beggar, the hero, the madman, the sot, or the fool; it is all one;—nothing is worse, nothing is better: the same genius pervades and is equally admirable in all. Or, is a character to be shewn in progressive change, and the events of years comprized within the hour;—with what a Magic hand does he prepare and scatter his spells! The Understanding must, in the first place, be subdued; and lo! how the rooted prejudices of the child spring up to confound the man! The Weird sisters rise, and order is extinguished. The laws of nature give way, and leave nothing in our minds but wildness and horror. No pause is allowed us for reflection: horrid sentiment, furious guilt and compunction, air-drawn daggers, murders, ghosts, and inchantment, shake and *possess us wholly*. In the mean time the *process* is completed. *Macbeth* changes under our eye, *the milk of human kindness is converted to gall; he has supped full of horrors*, and his *May of life is fallen into the sear, the yellow leaf*; whilst we, the fools of amazement, are insensible to the shifting of place and the lapse of time, and, till the curtain drops, never once wake to the truth of things, or recognize the laws of existence.

On such an occasion, a fellow like *Rymer*, waking from his trance, shall lift up his Constable's staff and charge this great Magician, this daring *practicer of arts inhibited*, in the name of *Aristotle* to surrender; whilst *Aristotle* himself, disowning his wretched Officer, would fall prostrate at his feet and acknowledge his supremacy.—'O supreme of Dramatic excellence!' (*might he say*) 'not to me be imputed the insolence of fools. The bards of *Greece* were confined within the narrow circle of the Chorus, and hence they found themselves constrained to practice for the most part the precision, and copy the details of nature. I followed them, and knew not that a larger circle might be drawn, and the Drama extended to the whole reach of human genius. Convinced, I see that a more compendious *nature* may be obtained; a nature of *effects* only, to which neither the relations of place or continuity of time are always essential. Nature, condescending to the faculties and apprehensions of man, has drawn through human life a regular chain of visible causes and effects: but Poetry delights in surprise, conceals her steps, seizes at once upon the heart, and obtains the Sublime of things without betraying the rounds of her ascent. True Poesy is *magic*, not *nature*; an effect from causes hidden or unknown. To the Magician I prescribed no laws; his law and his power are one; his power is his law. Him, who neither imitates, nor is within the reach of imitation, no precedent can or ought to bind, no limits to contain. If his end is obtained, who shall question his course? Means, whether apparent or hidden, are justified in Poesy by success; but then most perfect and most admirable when most concealed.'*. . . (57–71)

---

* These observations have brought me so near to the regions of Poetic *magic* (using the word here in its strict and proper sense and not loosely as in the *text*), that, tho' they lie not directly in my course, I yet may be allowed in this place to point the reader that way. A felt propriety, or truth of art, from an unseen, tho' supposed adequate cause, we call *nature*. A like feeling of propriety and truth, supposed without a cause, or as seeming to be derived from causes inadequate, fantastic, and absurd,—such as wands, circles, incantations, and so forth,—we call by the general name *magic*, including all the train of superstition, witches, ghosts, fairies, and the rest.—*Reason* is confined to the line of visible existence; our *passions* and our *fancy* extend far beyond into the *obscure*; but however lawless their operations may seem, the images they so wildly form have yet a relation to truth, and are the shadows at least, however fantastic, of *reality*. . . . Extravagant as all this appears, it has its laws so precise that we are sensible both of a local and temporary and of an universal magic; the first derived from the general nature of the human mind, influenced by particular habits, institutions, and climate; and the latter from the same general nature abstracted from those considerations. Of the first sort the *machinery* in *Macbeth* is a very striking instance; a machinery which, however exquisite at the time, has already lost more than half its force; and the Gallery now laughs in some places where it ought to shudder.—But the magic of the *Tempest* is lasting and universal.

There is besides a species of writing for which we have no term of art, and which holds a middle place between nature and magic; I mean where fancy either alone, or mingled with reason, or reason assuming the appearance of fancy, governs some real existence. But the whole of this art is pourtrayed in a single Play: in the real madness of *Lear*, in the assumed wildness of *Edgar*, and in the Professional *Fantasque* of the *Fool*, all operating to contrast and heighten each other. There is yet another feat in this kind which *Shakespeare* has performed:—he has personified *malice* in his *Caliban*, a character kneaded up of three distinct natures, the diabolical, the human, and the brute. The rest of his preternatural beings are images of *effects* only, and cannot subsist but in a surrounding atmosphere of those passions from which they are derived. *Caliban* is the passion itself, or rather a compound of malice,

I have now gone through the examination of all the Persons of the Drama from whose mouths any thing can be drawn relative to the Courage of *Falstaff*, excepting the Prince and *Poins*, whose evidence I have begged leave to *reserve*, and excepting a very severe censure passed on him by Lord *John* of *Lancaster*, which I shall presently consider. But I must first observe that, setting aside the jests of the Prince and *Poins* and this censure of *Lancaster*, there is not one expression uttered by any character in the Drama that can be construed into any impeachment of *Falstaff*'s Courage;—an observation made before as respecting some of the Witnesses: it is now extended to all. And though this silence be a negative proof only, it cannot, in my opinion, under the circumstances of the case and whilst uncontradicted by facts, be too much relied on. If *Falstaff* had been intended for the character of a *Miles Gloriosus*, his behaviour ought and therefore would have been commented upon by others. *Shakespeare* seldom trusts to the apprehensions of his audience; his characters interpret for one another continually, and when we least suspect such artful and secret management. The conduct of *Shakespeare* in this respect is admirable, and I could point out a thousand passages which might put to shame the advocates of a formal Chorus, and prove that there is as little of necessity as grace in so mechanic a contrivance.* But I confine my

---

servility, and lust, *substantiated*; and therefore best shewn in contrast with the lightness of *Ariel* and the innocence of *Miranda*.—*Witches* are sometimes substantial existences, supposed to be possessed by or allyed to the unsubstantial: but the Witches in *Macbeth* are a gross sort of shadows, 'bubbles of the earth,' as they are finely called by *Banquo*.—*Ghosts* differ from other imaginary beings in this, that they belong to no element, have no specific nature or character, and are effects, however harsh the expression, supposed without a cause; the reason of which is that they are not the creation of the poet, but the servile copies or transcripts of popular imagination, connected with supposed reality and religion. Should the poet assign the true cause, and call them the mere painting or *coinage of the brain*, he would disappoint his own end, and destroy the being he had raised. Should he assign fictitious causes, and add a specific nature and a local habitation, it would not be endured; or the effect would be lost by the conversion of one being into another. The approach to reality in this case defeats all the arts and managements of fiction.—The whole play of the *Tempest* is of so high and superior a nature that *Dryden*,[1] who had attempted to imitate in vain, might well exclaim that

> *Shakespeare*'s *magic* could not copied be,
> Within that circle none durst walk but He.   (71–7, notes)

* Enobarbus, in *Antony and Cleopatra*, is in effect the Chorus of the Play; as Menenius Agrippa is of *Coriolanus*.

[1] Cf. Vol. 1, p. 79.

censure of the Chorus to its supposed use of comment and interpretation only.

Falstaff is, indeed, so far from appearing to my eye in the light of a *Miles Gloriosus* that, in the best of my taste and judgment, he does not discover, except in consequence of the robbery, the least *trait* of such a character. . . . (75–8)

But there is a formidable objection behind. *Falstaff* counterfeits basely on being attacked by *Douglas*; he assumes in a cowardly spirit the appearance of death to avoid the reality. But there was no equality of force; not the least chance for victory or life. And is it the duty then, *think we still*, of true Courage to meet, without benefit to society, *certain death?* Or is it only the phantasy of honour?—But such a fiction is highly disgraceful;—true, and a man of nice honour might perhaps have *grinned* for it. But we must remember that *Falstaff* had a double character, he was a *wit* as well as a *soldier*; and his Courage, however eminent, was but the *accessary*; his wit was the *principal*, and the part which, if they should come in competition, he had the greatest interest in maintaining. Vain indeed were the licentiousness of his principles if he should seek death like a bigot, yet without the meed of honour; when he might live by wit and encrease the reputation of that wit by living. But why do I labour this point? It has been already anticipated, and our improved acquaintance with *Falstaff* will now require no more than a short narrative of the fact.

Whilst in the battle of *Shrewsbury* he is exhorting and encouraging the Prince who is engaged with the *Spirit Percy*—'*Well said Hal, to him Hal,*'—he is himself attacked by the *Fiend Douglas*. There was no match; nothing remained but death or stratagem; grinning honour, or laughing life. But an expedient offers, a mirthful one:—take your choice *Falstaff*, a point of honour or a point of drollery.—It could not be a question: *Falstaff* falls, *Douglas* is cheated, and the world laughs. But does he fall like a Coward? No, like a buffoon only; the superior principle prevails, and *Falstaff* lives by a stratagem growing out of his character, to prove himself *no counterfeit*, to jest, to be employed, and to fight again. That *Falstaff* valued himself, and expected to be valued by others, upon this piece of saving wit is plain. It was a stratagem, it is true; it argued presence of mind; but it was moreover, what he most liked, a very laughable joke; and as such he considers it; for he continues to counterfeit after the danger is over, that he may also deceive the Prince and improve the event into more laughter. He might, for ought that appears, have concealed the transaction; the Prince was too earnestly engaged for observation; he might have formed a thousand excuses for his fall; but he lies still and listens to the pronouncing of his epitaph by the Prince with all the waggish glee and levity of his character. The circumstance of his wounding *Percy* in the thigh, and carrying the dead body on his back like luggage, is *indecent* but not cowardly. The declaring, though in jest, that he killed *Percy* seems to me *idle*, but it is not meant or calculated for *imposition*; it is spoken to the *Prince himself*, the man in the world who could not be, or be supposed to be, imposed on. But we must hear, whether to the purpose or not, what it is that *Harry* has to say over the remains of his old friend.

> *P. Hen.* What, old acquaintance! could not all this flesh
> Keep in a little life? Poor *Jack*, farewell!
> I could have better spared a better man.
> Oh! I shou'd have a heavy miss of thee,
> If I were much in love with vanity.
> Death hath not struck so fat a *deer* to-day,
> Tho' many a *dearer* in this bloody fray;
> Imbowelled will I see thee by and by;
> Till then, in blood by noble *Percy* lye.   [5.4.102ff.]

This is wonderfully proper for the occasion; it is affectionate, it is pathetic, yet it remembers his vanities, and, with a faint gleam of recollected mirth, even his plumpness and corpulency; but it is a pleasantry softned and rendered even vapid by tenderness, and it goes off in the sickly effort of a miserable pun.*. . . (101–5)

---

*The censure commonly passed on *Shakespeare's puns* is, I think, not well founded. I remember but very few, which are undoubtedly his, that may not be justifyed; and if *so*, a greater instance cannot be given of the art which he so peculiarly possessed of converting base things into excellence.

> For if the Jew do cut but deep enough,
> I'll pay [the forfeiture] *with all my heart.*
>   [*Merchant of Venice*, 4.1.280f.]

A play upon words is the most that can be expected from one who affects gaiety under the pressure of severe misfortunes; but so imperfect, so broken a gleam can only serve more plainly to disclose the gloom and darkness of the mind; it is an effort of fortitude which, failing in its operation, becomes the truest, because the most unaffected *pathos*; and a skilful actor, well managing his tone and action, might with this miserable pun steep a whole audience suddenly in tears.

Though the robbery at *Gads-Hill*, and the supposed Cowardice of *Falstaff* on that occasion are next to be considered, yet I must previously declare that I think the discussion of this matter to be *now* unessential to the reestablishment of *Falstaff's* reputation as a man of Courage. For suppose we should grant in form that *Falstaff* was surprized with fear in this single instance, that he was off his guard and even acted like a Coward; what will follow, but that *Falstaff*, like greater heroes, had his weak moment and was not exempted from panic and surprize? If a single exception can destroy a general character, *Hector* was a *Coward*, and *Antony* a *Poltroon*. But for these seeming contradictions of Character we shall seldom be at a loss to account, if we carefully refer to circumstance and situation.—In the present instance *Falstaff* had done an illegal act; the exertion was over; and he had unbent his mind in security. The spirit of enterprize, and the animating principle of hope, were withdrawn.—In this situation he is unexpectedly attacked; he has no time to recall his thoughts or bend his mind to action. He is not now acting in the Profession and in the Habits of a Soldier; he is associated with known Cowards; his assailants are vigorous, sudden, and bold; he is conscious of guilt; he has dangers to dread of every form, present and future; prisons and gibbets, as well as sword and fire; he is surrounded with darkness, and the Sheriff, the Hangman, and the whole *Posse Commitatus* may be at his heels.—Without a moment for reflection is it wonderful that, under these circumstances, '*he should run and roar, and carry his guts away with as much dexterity as possible*'?

But though I might well rest the question on this ground, yet as there remains many good topics of vindication, and as I think a more minute inquiry into this matter will only bring out more evidence in support of *Falstaff's* constitutional Courage, I will not decline the discussion. I beg permission therefore to state fully, as well as fairly, the whole of this obnoxious transaction, this unfortunate robbery at *Gads-Hill*. . . . (113–16)

[Morgann analyses this scene, claiming that it is not intended to 'expose the false pretences of a real Coward'. Then he comes to the scene (2.4) where Hal and Poins confront Falstaff.]

We now behold him, fluctuating with fiction, and labouring with dissembled passion and chagrin. Too full for utterance, *Poins* provokes him by a few simple words, containing a fine contrast of affected ease,—'*Welcome*, Jack, *where hast thou been?*' But when we hear him burst forth, '*A plague on all Cowards! Give me a cup of sack. Is there no virtue extant!*' [2.4.113ff.]—we are at once in possession of the whole man, and are ready to hug him, guts, lyes and all, as an inexhaustible fund of pleasantry and humour. *Cowardice*, I apprehend, is out of our thought; it does not, I think, mingle in our mirth. As to this point, I have presumed to say already, and I repeat it, that we are in my opinion the dupes of our own wisdom, of systematic reasoning, of second thought, and after reflection. The first spectators, I believe, thought of nothing but the laughable scrape which so singular a character was falling into, and were delighted to see a humourous and unprincipled wit so happily taken in his own inventions, precluded from all rational defence and driven to the necessity of crying out, after a few ludicrous evasions, '*No more of that*, Hal, *if thou lov'st me.*' [2.4.283]

I do not conceive myself obliged to enter into a consideration of *Falstaff*'s lyes concerning the transaction at *Gad's-Hill*. I have considered his conduct as independent of those lyes; I have examined the whole of it apart, and found it free of Cowardice or fear, except in one instance, which I have endeavoured to account for and excuse. I have therefore a right to infer that those lyes are to be derived not from Cowardice, but from some other part of his character, which it does not concern me to examine. . . . (131–3)

Tho' I have considered *Falstaff*'s character as relative only to one single quality, yet so much has been said that it cannot escape the reader's notice that he is a character made up by *Shakespeare* wholly of incongruities:—a man at once young and old, enterprizing and fat, a dupe and a wit, harmless and wicked, weak in principle and resolute by constitution, cowardly in appearance and brave in reality; a knave without malice, a lyar without deceit; and a knight, a gentleman, and a soldier, without either dignity, decency, or honour. This is a character which, though it may be decompounded, could not, I believe, have been formed, nor the ingredients of it duly mingled, upon any receipt whatever. It required the hand of *Shakespeare* himself to give to every particular part a relish of the whole, and of the whole to every particular part;—alike the same incongruous, identical *Falstaff*, whether to the grave Chief Justice he vainly talks of his youth, and offers to *caper for a thousand*; or cries to Mrs. *Doll*, '*I am old, I am old,*' [*2 Henry IV*, 2.4.271] though she is seated on his lap, and he is courting her for busses. How *Shakespeare* could furnish out sentiment of so

177

extraordinary a composition, and supply it with such appropriated and characteristic language, humour and wit, I cannot
tell. . . . (146–7)

But it may be well worth our curiosity to inquire into the
composition of *Falstaff*'s character. Every man we may observe
has two characters; that is, every man may be seen externally, and
from without;—or a section may be made of him, and he may be
illuminated from within.

Of the external character of *Falstaff* we can scarcely be said to
have any steady view. *Jack Falstaff* we are familiar with, but *Sir
John* was better known, it seems, *to the rest of Europe* than to his
intimate companions; yet we have so many glimpses of him, and he
is opened to us occasionally in such various points of view, that we
cannot be mistaken in describing him as a man of birth and fashion,
bred up in all the learning and accomplishments of the times;—of
ability and Courage equal to any situation, and capable by nature of
the highest affairs; trained to arms, and possessing the tone, the
deportment, and the manners of a gentleman;—but yet these
accomplishments and advantages seem to hang loose on him, and
to be worn with a slovenly carelessness and inattention. . . . (167–8)

Such a character as I have here described, strengthened with that
vigour, force, and alacrity of mind of which he is possessed, must
have spread terror and dismay thro' the ignorant, the timid, the
modest, and the weak. Yet is he however, when occasion requires,
capable of much accommodation and flattery;—and in order to
obtain the protection and patronage of the great, so convenient to
his vices and his poverty, he was put under the daily necessity of
practising and improving these arts; a baseness which he compensates to himself, like other unprincipled men, by an increase of
insolence towards his inferiors.—There is also a natural activity
about *Falstaff* which, for want of proper employment, shews itself
in a kind of swell or bustle which seems to correspond with his
bulk, as if his mind had inflated his body and demanded a
habitation of no less circumference. Thus conditioned he rolls (in
the language of *Ossian*) like a *Whale of Ocean*, scattering the smaller
fry; but affording, in his turn, noble contention to *Hal* and *Poins*;
who, to keep up the allusion, I may be allowed on this occasion to
compare to the Thresher and the Sword-fish.

To this part of *Falstaff*'s character many things which he does and says, and which appear unaccountably natural, are to be referred.

We are next to see him *from within*: and here we shall behold him most villainously unprincipled and debauched; possessing indeed the same Courage and ability, yet stained with numerous vices, unsuited not only to his primary qualities but to his age, corpulency, rank, and profession;—reduced by these vices to a state of dependence, yet resolutely bent to indulge them at any price. These vices have been already enumerated; they are many, and become still more intolerable by an excess of unfeeling insolence on one hand and of base accommodation on the other.

But what then, after all, is become of *old Jack?* Is this the jovial delightful companion—*Falstaff*, the favourite and the boast of the Stage?—by no means. But it is, I think however, the *Falstaff* of Nature; the very stuff out of which the *Stage Falstaff* is composed; nor was it possible, I believe, out of any other materials he could have been formed. From this disagreeable draught we shall be able, I trust, by a proper disposition of light and shade, and from the influence and compression of external things, to produce *plump Jack*, the life of humour, the spirit of pleasantry, and the soul of mirth. (170–2)

A character really possessing the qualities which are on the stage imputed to *Falstaff* would be best shewn by its own natural energy; the least compression would disorder it, and make us feel for it all the pain of sympathy. It is the artificial condition of *Falstaff* which is the source of our delight; we enjoy his distresses, we *gird at him* ourselves, and urge the sport without the least alloy of compassion; and we give him, when the laugh is over, undeserved credit for the pleasure we enjoyed. . . . (175)

Such, I think, is the true character of this extraordinary buffoon; and from hence we may discern for what special purposes *Shakespeare* has given him talents and qualities which were to be afterwards obscured, and perverted to ends opposite to their nature. It was clearly to furnish out a Stage buffoon of a peculiar sort; a kind of Game-bull which would stand the baiting thro' a hundred Plays, and produce equal sport, whether he is pinned down occasionally by *Hal* or *Poins*, or tosses such mongrils as *Bardolph* or the Justices sprawling in the air. There is in truth no such thing as totally demolishing *Falstaff*; he has so much of the invulnerable in his frame that no ridicule can destroy him; he is safe even in defeat, and seems to rise, like another *Antæus,* with recruited vigour from every fall; in this, as in every other respect, unlike *Parolles* or *Bobadil*: they fall by the first shaft of ridicule, but *Falstaff* is a butt on which we may empty the whole quiver whilst the substance of his character remains unimpaired. His ill habits, and the accidents of age and corpulence, are no part of his essential constitution; they come forward indeed on our eye, and solicit our notice, but they are second natures, not *first*; mere shadows, we pursue them in vain. *Falstaff* himself has a distinct and separate subsistence; he laughs at the chace, and when the sport is over gathers them with unruffled feather under his wing. And hence it is that he is made to undergo not one detection only, but a series of detections; that he is not formed for one Play only, but was intended originally at least for two; and the author, we are told, was doubtful if he should not extend him yet farther, and engage him in the wars with *France*. This he might well have done, for there is nothing perishable in the nature of *Falstaff*. He might have involved him, by the vicious part of his character, in new difficulties and unlucky situations, and have enabled him, by the better part, to have scrambled through, abiding and retorting the jests and laughter of every beholder. (176–8)

255. Frederick Pilon, on acting Hamlet

1777

From *An Essay on the Character of Hamlet As Performed by Mr. Henderson* (1777); second edition in the same year, both anonymous.

Frederick Pilon (1750–88) gave up the study of medicine to become an actor; he worked for Griffin the bookseller on the *Morning Post*, and after Griffin's death took to the drama, writing numerous farces and comic operas for Covent

Garden between 1778 and 1786. Colman, in the *Monthly*, said that 'this Essay is not ill-written; to say the truth, rather too well written—for the *style* evidently engrosses the attention of our theatrical critic'; yet it contained 'many judicious observations': lvii (1777) p. 320. John Henderson (1747–85) made his début as Hamlet, and gained fame in 1777 with his Shylock (for Colman, at the Haymarket).

The writings of Shakespeare have maintained the post of eminence so long that most people feign or possess some relish for them. His beauties have been acknowledged by every man of fine taste, and his obscurities elucidated by the most subtle, elaborate, and learned commentators this country has produced; to venture therefore upon the investigation of a subject apparently exhausted, might be as hazardous as it seems barren. But though it would be presumption in an artist to design the model of a temple or a palace after a master in architecture, it surely cannot arraign his discretion to fix on a single column, and catch some minute beauty in the architrave or frieze which may have escaped a mind expanded to embrace a vaster object.

The writer of this essay means to insulate the character of Hamlet from the other persons of the drama; and after having considered the philosophic Prince in regard to situation, temper, passions, and understanding, to examine with coolness and impartiality Mr. Henderson's representation of him; compare shade with shade, and tint with tint, then finally ascertain the degree of conception and execution that gentleman exhibited in his performance.

This species of criticism has at least novelty to recommend it; for though taste and learning dedicate every effort to establish the reputation and perpetuate the memory of the poet, the actor, to whom he is often indebted for more than one laurel, is rarely honored with a leaf to protect him from oblivion. The graces of action, the harmony of elocution, and the energy of soul which distinguishes the favourite of the sister muses purchase a transitory fame which perishes with the possessor, and had Garrick no personal interest with Apollo, the smiles of Thalia and the favor of Melpomene would have been a precarious tenure on immortality.

The character of Hamlet, though not the most finished, is certainly one of the most splendid efforts of Shakespeare's genius.

He has combined in it every circumstance which can affect the heart or interest the understanding. He represents a Prince in the bloom of life, plunged into a deep melancholy, at the death of a father whom he tenderly loved. The filial piety of a son is finely contrasted by the levity of a mother, who in defiance of censure, and the ties of consanguinity, marries her deceased husband's brother. [Quotes 'Ere yet the salt', 1.2.154f.]

Hamlet's understanding is sound, and his sensibility exquisite. He is moreover adorned with every liberal accomplishment which can distinguish the gentleman and the scholar; his reasonings are deep, and his passions ardent; and as both are excited by great and adequate motives, his character affords the most ample field for the display of theatrical abilities. . . . (1–3)

Mr. Henderson spoke the soliloquy previous to the entry of Horatio and Marcellus with great feeling and propriety, and preserved a beauty in this speech which is either lost or rendered ridiculous by the generality of performers. It is Hamlet's taking his tablets out, in order to set down 'That man may smile, and smile, and be a villain.' [1.5.108] This is an action strong emotion may dictate, but which nothing else can authorize. Therefore, if the actor be not animated it will pass unnoticed, or appear like the flight of a lunatic. Mr. Henderson felt, and nature sustained no injury. At the conclusion of the first act Hamlet becomes a new character; determined on avenging the murder of his father, and justly alarmed for his own safety, he assumes the mask of insanity, to conceal his intentions and lull the suspicions of the king his uncle. There is no part of acting more difficult to exhibit, than that of madness. It require great flexibility of voice and countenance to express the rapid succession of images that float across a distracted fancy. The eye should be wild, yet vacant, and the tones piercing. It is true, Hamlet's madness is feigned; but it is evident from the following lively description that the poet meant it should be counterfeited with great strength of imagination and masterly touches of nature. 'My Lord as I was sewing in my closet' [Quotes 2.1.74ff.] . . . (13–14)

From the king's confusion at the murder of Gonzago Hamlet is convinced of his guilt. His doubts therefore are removed respecting the veracity of the ghost, and he determines upon revenge the first opportunity. Upon finding the king at prayers he is about to put him to death; but recollecting that it was not in the moment of contrition he killed his father, that he took him full of bread, 'With all his crimes, broad blown, as flush as May.' [3.3.81] he resolves to defer his vengeance to the unprepared hour of pleasure and debauch. This principal link being omitted in the representation, and no other cause substituted for Hamlet's continuing to procrastinate, he appears weak and inconsistent during the last two acts. . . . (19)

One of the principal defects in this tragedy is the almost total exclusion of Hamlet from the fourth act; so long losing sight of the chief personage in the drama, our interest for him is diminished. As the piece was originally written Hamlet has three scenes in the fourth act, but two of which are retained, though the third contains a most beautiful soliloquy, in which Hamlet justifies himself for suspending the revenge he promised his father. In Mr. Garrick's alteration this speech is preserved. The opening of the fifth act is stained with low ribaldry, but so intimately connected with striking beauties that it would be impossible to expunge the one without losing the other. Hamlet's reflections upon the last humiliating state of human nature are awful and affecting, particularly those upon the skull of Yorick, when he beholds the sad disfigured remains of a man who was once dear to him mouldring into dust, hideous with deformity, the food and habitation of the worm; but the genius of Shakespeare penetrated all nature, and his voice is heard from the tomb. (21–2)

256. Henry Brooke, adaptation of
Antony and Cleopatra

1778

From *A Collection of the Pieces formerly published by Henry Brooke, Esq. . . . Plays and Poems Now First Printed* (4 vols, 1778).

Henry Brooke (1703?–83), was educated at Trinity College, Dublin, reputedly by Swift's friend Sheridan, and moved to London in the 1730s, where he was encouraged and praised by Lord Lyttelton and Pope, while his polemical writings against the Irish Catholics were praised by Garrick and led to him being given a government sinecure. Garrick thought highly of Brooke, and attempted to persuade him to write for the stage, offering a shilling a line if he would write exclusively for him; but Brooke rejected the proposal haughtily, and Garrick never forgave him. Brooke wrote poetry, plays, and several novels, of which *The Fool of Quality* (1766–70) had the greatest success: it was republished in an abbreviated edition by John Wesley in 1780, and again by Charles Kingsley in 1859, both editors praising its morality. His collected works (which include an adaptation of *Cymbeline*: Vol. III, pp. 169–256) were issued by friends in an attempt to raise money after he had collapsed following the deaths of his wife and children, but the collection was made hastily and did not succeed. Garrick reviewed it unfavourably in the *Monthly Review*, lix (1778), pp. 359–65. In this adaptation (which was never performed) Brooke gives his heroes two children called Alexander and Cleopatra.

[Act I, scene 2]

ANTONY, CLEOPATRA, and Attendants, are discovered in a splendid galley; soft flutes playing. They sail down to the front of the stage, and then go off through the side wings.

CLEO. Call in the messengers.—As I am Egypt's Queen,
Thou blushest, ANTONY; and that blood of thine
Is Cæsar's homager.—The messengers!
     ANT. No messengers, I say!
Let Rome in Tyber melt, and the wide arch
Of the rais'd empire fall!—Why live the gods,
But to enjoy?
A world of care had not been worth my winning;
Did it not give a CLEOPATRA to me,
I'd cast it to the kites for carrion.   (II, 335–6)

[Act II, scene 1]

AGRIP. All my appetite is in my eyes. I long to feast them on
your CLEOPATRA.

ENOB. Ay, AGRIPPA! she, indeed, is the dish of dishes—such
as never shall come to table again, till nature shall provide a new
service of women.

AGRIP. Where, pray you, did ANTONY first meet with her?

ENOB. In Cilicia. She had given aid to Cassius; and ANTONY
sent for her in high dudgeon, to answer many charges preferred
against her. If I were not unhappy at description, I would give you
the manner of it.

AGRIP. Any how.

NOBL. Any how.

AGRIP. Let us have it, we beseech you.

ENOB. Why, she came down the river Cydnus, in a galley,
whose poop and sides were inlaid with burnished gold, and
appeared to whiz and burn along the water. The oars were silver,
and kept stroke to the sound of flutes and hautboys. The sails were
of Tyrian purple, the tackle of silk; and the streamers, like flaming
meteors, seemed to kindle the very gales that came to cool
them.—But, as for herself, I shall say nothing; for, though I hate
her more heartily than ever I loved my mother, yet I would not do
her injustice.—She beggars description.

AGRIP. Nay, good now, ENOBARBUS!—as I am a Roman you
tell it rarely.

ALL. Rarely, rarely!

ENOB. Under a canopy of golden tissue, whose curtains were
thrown aloft, she lay, carelessly reclined, out-picturing the

goddess, whose picture is said to have out-copied nature. Her wenches, dressed like Nereids or the Graces of the Ocean, here steered the helm, here handled the cordage, and here shifted the silken sails : while boys, quivered and winged like dimpled Cupids, kept fanning off the air that kindled at her cheek. In her eye was glory, and in her smile fascination. The city threw forth all its people upon her, and left ANTONY alone on his tribunal in the market-place, whistling after the wind, that flew to meet CLEOPATRA.

AGRIP. Why your account is enough to empty Rome also, and bring Italy into Egypt!

NOBL. All to Egypt, all to Egypt!

AGRIP. But, is it certain that your emperor is married to this wonder?

ENOB. As sure as an Egyptian priest can fetter him.

AGRIP. An ANTONY, however, can never be bound to any thing, save his liking; and he, you know, is an inconstant, and a voluptuary.

ENOB. I tell thee, AGRIPPA, inconstancy itself must be a captive to CLEOPATRA. Age cannot wither, not custom make common her infinite perfections. (352–3)

[Act II, scene 2]

ANTONY enters, with young ALEXANDER and CLEOPATRA fondling on each side.

ANT. Away, ye little rogues, ye wanton varlets!
Away, I am not in the humour now,
To wrestle with your fondness—
To ride the may-rods, or to roll the slope,
Or play at marble pellets—Hence, ye roguelings!
I am not in the vein.

ALEX. Sister!
Do you take hold of one leg, while I take hold
Of t'other, and then I'll warrant you!

CLEO. Now, ALLY, now!—
I lay a good round wager we have him down!

ANT. There now, I am down already.   [Sits.

What would ye more?—How dare you use me thus?
Know ye not I'm an emperor?
  ALEX. Yes, yes—but, father,
What matters being an emperor?
  ANT. What matters, sirrah?—
Marry, and that's a pregnant question too!
What matters?—why, to wear a crown, as I do.
  CLEO. Don't believe him, brother.
I'll tell you what's to be an emperor—
It is to speak big words, and to be strong,
And to throw others down, as we throw him.
  ALEX. Then, PATTY, we are stronger than an emperor.
  ANT. Indeed, and that's true too.

   To them enters CLEOPATRA.

  CLEO. What, have my little teizers got about you? (354–5)

[Act V, scene 9]

Changes to the MONUMENT

  CLEO. No, IRAS, death is what I wish for—either
To fall into the nothing whence I rose,
Or take my future lot among immortals.—
Dying—'tis that I dread!—
I stand, I tremble, as upon the brink
Of some unfathom'd flood, and wish to plunge,
But dare not!—
  IRAS. Yet, take comfort, sweetest mistress!   (420)

[Act V, scene 11]

ANTONY enters, supported by Officers.

  ANT. Gently, my friends, or I am gone!
O—there!   [They let him down.
Adieu—take with you my eternal thanks
For this, your latest service—so—friends—leave me!
Would I had another world to part among you,
Better than that we have lost!   [Exeunt Officers.

CLEO. Woe, woe—alas!—the soldier's pole is fallen!
O—wither'd is the garland of the war!
And there is nothing left remarkable
Beneath the visiting moon!

ANT. True, thou sweet bird, whose song made all my
summer!—
The long, long winter's come; and we must moult,
Never to plume again!—O, pardon, love!—
Have I your pardon for my rash suspicions?
I weep for it in blood!

CLEO. I'll not survive you,
If swords, or knives, or drugs, or serpents, have
Edge, sting, or operation.

ANT. Loveliest, dearest,
Live, live, I charge you—think on our poor infants!
I am dying, Egypt, dying!—Tell me;
Wilt thou remember, ANTONY?—that hope
Is my last cheer—a light for steps that enter
On the dark journey!

CLEO. O—he is going—going!

ANT. I would fain stay longer with thee—
A little longer!—but—it will not be.
Shall we not meet—shall we not meet again?—
Perhaps—in happier climes!—
Now—now I feel what's death—'tis nature's wreck—
Torn from herself!—
It is—it is to part from CLEOPATRA—
Never to join again!—
Thine image, now, is all that's left me—O—
O, CLEOPATRA!—   [Dies.

CLEO. Gone!—
Is it possible—or did we only dream?

CHARM. Dream, madam?

CLEO. Yes.—
I dream'd there was an emperor ANTONY—...   (423–4)

257. George Steevens and others, edition of Shakespeare

1778

From *The Plays of William Shakespeare, in Ten Volumes, with the Corrections and Illustrations of various Commentators: to which are added Notes by Samuel Johnson and George Steevens. The Second Edition revised and augmented* (1778).

On Steevens see the head-note to Vol. 5, No. 211; for the earlier versions of 1765 and 1773 see Nos 205 and 240. This edition was favourably reviewed, by Samuel Badcock in the *Monthly Review*, lxii (1780), pp. 12–26, 257–70, and in the *Critical* (perhaps by Percival Stockdale), xlvii (1779), pp. 129–36, 172–83; but it was attacked by Joseph Ritson, No. 274.

[From the 'Prefatory Material']
[1] [From Edmond Malone, 'An Attempt to ascertain the Order in which the Plays attributed to Shakespeare were Written']
Every circumstance that relates to those persons whose writings we admire interests our curiosity. The time and place of their birth, their education and gradual attainments, the dates of their productions and the reception they severally met with, their habits of life, their private friendships, and even their external form are all points which, how little soever they may have been adverted to by their contemporaries, strongly engage the attention of posterity. Not satisfied with receiving the aggregated wisdom of ages as a free gift, we visit the mansions where our instructors are said to have resided, we contemplate with pleasure the trees under whose shade they once reposed, and wish to see and to converse with those sages whose labours have added strength to virtue, and efficacy to truth.

Shakespeare above all writers since the days of Homer, has excited this curiosity in the highest degree; as perhaps no poet of any nation was ever more idolized by his countrymen. An ardent desire to understand and explain his works has, to the honour of the present age, so much encreased within these last thirty years, that more has been done towards their elucidation during that period than perhaps in a century before. All the ancient copies of his plays hitherto discovered have been collated with the most scrupulous accuracy. The meanest books have been carefully examined only because they were of the age in which he lived, and might happily throw a light on some forgotten custom, or obsolete phraseology: and this object being still kept in view, the toil of wading through *all such reading as was never read* has been chearfully endured, because no labour was thought too great that might enable us to add one new laurel to the father of our drama. Almost every circumstance that tradition or history has preserved relative to him or his works has been investigated, and laid before the publick; and the avidity with which all communications of this kind have been received sufficiently proves that the time expended in the pursuit has not been wholly misemployed.

However, after the most diligent enquiries, very few particulars have been recovered respecting his private life or literary history: and while it has been the endeavour of all his editors and commentators to illustrate his obscurities and to regulate and correct his text, no attempt has been made to trace the progress and order of his plays.[1] Yet surely it is no incurious speculation to mark the gradations* by which he rose from mediocrity to the summit of excellence; from artless and uninteresting dialogues to those unparalleled compositions which have rendered him the delight and wonder of successive ages. (I, 269–71)

[Malone's chronology of composition; the titles in italics are those he considers unlikely to be Shakespeare's.]

1. *Titus Andronicus*,	1589.
2. LOVE'S LABOUR'S LOST,	1591.
3. FIRST PART OF KING HENRY VI.	1591.

[1] See Capell's introduction to his 1768 edition: Vol. 5, pp. 326f., and his chronology, first printed in 1780: below, pp. 251ff.

* It is not pretended that a regular scale of gradual improvement is here presented to the publick; or that if even Shakespeare himself had left us a chronological list of his dramas it would exhibit such a scale. All that is meant is, that, as his knowledge increased, and as he became more conversant with the stage and with life, his performances *in general* were written more happily and with greater art. . . .

4.	SECOND PART OF KING HENRY VI.	1592.
5.	THIRD PART OF KING HENRY VI.	1592.
6.	*Pericles,*	1592.
7.	*Locrine,*	1593.
8.	THE TWO GENTLEMEN OF VERONA,	1593.
9.	THE WINTER'S TALE,	1594.
10.	A MIDSUMMER NIGHT'S DREAM,	1595.
11.	ROMEO AND JULIET,	1595.
12.	THE COMEDY OF ERRORS,	1596.
13.	HAMLET,	1596.
14.	KING JOHN,	1596.
15.	KING RICHARD II.	1597.
16.	KING RICHARD III.	1597.
17.	FIRST PART OF KING HENRY IV.	1597.
18.	THE MERCHANT OF VENICE,	1598.
19.	ALL'S WELL THAT END'S WELL,	1598.
20.	*Sir John Oldcastle,*	1598.
21.	SECOND PART OF KING HENRY IV.	1598.
22.	KING HENRY V.	1599.
23.	*The Puritan,*	1600.
24.	MUCH ADO ABOUT NOTHING,	1600.
25.	AS YOU LIKE IT.	1600.
26.	MERRY WIVES OF WINDSOR,	1601.
27.	KING HENRY VIII.	1601.
28.	*Life and Death of Lord Cromwell,*	1602.
29.	TROILUS AND CRESSIDA,	1602.
30.	MEASURE FOR MEASURE,	1603.
31.	CYMBELINE,	1604.
32.	*The London Prodigal,*	1605.
33.	KING LEAR,	1605.
34.	MACBETH,	1606.
35.	THE TAMING OF THE SHREW,	1606.
36.	JULIUS CÆSAR,	1607.
37.	*A Yorkshire Tragedy,*	1608.
38.	ANTONY AND CLEOPATRA,	1608.
39.	CORIOLANUS,	1609.
40.	TIMON OF ATHENS,	1610.
41.	OTHELLO,	1611.
42.	THE TEMPEST,	1612.
43.	TWELFTH NIGHT,	1614.

(274–5)

[2] [On *Love's Labour's Lost*]

Shakespeare's natural disposition leading him, as Dr. Johnson has observed, to comedy it is highly probable that his first dramatick production was of the comick kind: and of his comedies none appears to me to bear stronger marks of a first essay than *Love's Labour's Lost*. The frequent rhymes with which it abounds,* of which in his early performances he seems to have been extremely fond, its imperfect versification, its artless and desultory dialogue, and the irregularity of the composition may be all urged in support of this conjecture. (280–1)

[3] [On *A Midsummer Night's Dream*]

The poetry of this piece, glowing with all the warmth of a youthful and lively imagination, the many scenes that it contains of almost continual rhyme, the poverty of the fable, and want of discrimination among the higher personages, dispose me to believe that it was one of our author's earliest attempts in comedy.

It seems to have been written while the ridiculous competitions prevalent among the histrionick tribe were strongly impressed by novelty on his mind. He would naturally copy those manners first with which he was first acquainted. The ambition of a theatrical candidate for applause he has happily ridiculed in *Bottom* the weaver. But among the more dignified persons of the drama we look in vain for any traits of character. The manners of Hippolita *the Amazon* are undistinguished from those of other females.

---

* As this circumstance is more than once mentioned in the course of these observations, it may not be improper to add a few words on the subject of our author's metre. A mixture of rhymes with blank verse in the same play, and sometimes in the same scene, is found in almost all his pieces, and is not peculiar to Shakespeare, being also found in the works of Jonson and almost all our ancient dramatick writers. It is not, therefore, merely the use of rhymes mingled with blank verse, but their *frequency*, that is here urged as a circumstance which seems to characterize and distinguish our poet's earliest performances. In the whole number of pieces which were written antecedent to the year 1600, and which for the sake of perspicuity, have been called his *early compositions*, more rhyming couplets are found than in all the plays composed subsequently to that year, which have been named his *late productions*. Whether in process of time Shakespeare grew weary of the bondage of rhyme, or whether he became convinced of its impropriety in a dramatick dialogue, his neglect of rhyming (for he never wholly disused it) seems to have been *gradual*. As, therefore, most of his early productions are characterized by the multitude of similar terminations which they exhibit, whenever of two early pieces it is doubtful which preceded the other I am disposed to believe (other proofs being wanting), that play in which the greater number of rhymes is found, to have been first composed. This, however, must be acknowledged to be but a fallible criterion; for the *Three Parts of K. Henry VI*, which appear to have been among our author's earliest compositions, do not abound in rhymes.[1] (280–1, notes)

[1] The 1790 edition adds: 'but this probably arose from their being *originally* constructed by preceding writers' (Vol. I, part 1, p. 294).

Theseus, the associate of Hercules, is not engaged in any adventure worthy of his rank or reputation, nor is he in reality an agent throughout the play. Like K. Henry VIII. he goes out a-Maying. He meets the lovers in perplexity, and makes no effort to promote their happiness; but when supernatural accidents have reconciled them he joins their company, and concludes his day's entertainment by uttering some miserable puns at an interlude represented by a troop of clowns. Over the fairy part of the drama he cannot be supposed to have any influence. This part of the fable, indeed (at least as much of it as relates to the quarrels of Oberon and Titania) was not of our author's invention.—Through the whole piece the more exalted characters are subservient to the interests of those beneath them. We laugh with Bottom and his fellows, but is a single passion agitated by the faint and childish sollicitudes of Hermia and Demetrius, of Helena and Lysander, those shadows of each other?—That a drama of which the principal personages are thus insignificant, and the fable thus meagre and uninteresting, was one of our author's earliest compositions, does not, therefore, seem a very improbable conjecture; nor are the beauties with which it is embellished inconsistent with this supposition; for the genius of Shakespeare, even in its minority, could embroider the coarsest materials with the brightest and most lasting colours. (285–7)

[4] [On *Julius Caesar*]

A tragedy on the subject, and with the title of *Julius Cæsar*, written by Mr. William Alexander, who was afterwards Earl of Sterline, was printed in the year 1607. This, I imagine, was prior to our author's performance. Shakespeare, we know, formed seven or eight plays on fables that had been unsuccessfully managed by other poets; but no contemporary writer was daring enough to enter the lists with him in his life-time, or to model into a drama a subject that had already employed his pen. . . . (332)

[5] ['Conclusion']

If the dates here assigned to our author's plays should not, in every instance, bring with them conviction of their propriety, let it be remembered that this is a subject on which conviction cannot at this day be obtained: and that the observations now submitted to the publick do not pretend to any higher title than that of 'AN

ATTEMPT to ascertain the chronology of the dramas of Shakespeare.'. . .

To some, he is not unapprized, this enquiry will appear a tedious and barren speculation. But there are many, it is hoped, who think nothing that relates to the brightest ornament of the English nation wholly uninteresting; who will be gratified by observing how the genius of our great poet gradually expanded itself till, like his own Ariel, *it flamed amazement* in every quarter, blazing forth with a lustre that has not hitherto been equalled, and perhaps will never be surpassed. (346)

[From the Notes]
[6] [On *The Tempest*, 5.1.136:]

——*who* three hours *since.*] The unity of time is most rigidly observed in this piece. The fable scarcely takes up a greater number of hours than are employed in the representation; and from the very particular care which our author takes to point out this circumstance in so many other passages, as well as here, it should seem as if it were not accidental, but purposely designed to shew the admirers of Ben Jonson's art, and the cavillers of the time, that he too could write a play within all the strictest laws of regularity, when he chose to load himself with the critick's fetters.

The *Boatswain* marks the progress of the day again—*which but three glasses since*, &c. and at the beginning of this act the duration of the time employed on the stage is particularly ascertained; and it refers to a passage in the first act, of the same tendency. The storm was raised *at least* two glasses after mid-day, and Ariel was promised that *the work should cease* at the *sixth hour.* STEEVENS. (I, 106)

[7] [On *Much Ado About Nothing*, 4.2.28:]
'*Fore God, they are both in a tale*:] This is an admirable stroke of humour. *Dogberry* says of the prisoners that they are false knaves, and from that denial of the charge, which one in his wits could not but be supposed to make, he infers a communion of counsels, and records it in the examination as an evidence of their guilt. SIR J. HAWKINS. (II, 345)

[8] [On *Macbeth*, 1.5.49: 'my keen knife']
The word *knife*, which at present has a familiar meaning, was

anciently used to express a *sword*. So in the old black letter romance of *Syr Eglamoure of Artoys*, no date:

> Through Goddes myght, and his *knyfe*,
> There the gyaunte lost his lyfe.

Again, in Spenser's *Faery Queen*, b.1.c.6: 'the red-cross knight was slain with paynim *knife*.' STEEVENS. (IV, 478)

[9] [*Ibid.*, 1.5.48ff.:]
 To cry, Hold, hold!——]
On this passage there is a long criticism in the *Rambler*. JOHNSON. [See Vol. 3, pp. 436–8.]
 In this criticism the epithet *dun* is objected to as a mean one. Milton, however, appears to have been of a different opinion, and has represented Satan as flying 'in the *dun* air sublime.' STEEVENS. (IV, 478)

[10] [*Ibid.*, 1.7.28]
Hanmer has on this occasion added a word which every reader cannot fail to add for himself. He would give:

> *And falls on the other* side.

But the state of Macbeth's mind is more strongly marked by this break in the speech than by any continuation of it which the most successful critic can supply. STEEVENS. (IV, 486)

[11] [On *Richard III*, 1.1.27:]
[*And* descant *on mine own deformity*] *Descant* is a term in music, signifying in general that kind of harmony wherein one part is broken and formed into a kind of paraphrase on the other. The propriety and elegance of the above figure, without such an idea of the nature of *descant*, could not be discerned. SIR J. HAWKINS. (VII, 6)

[12] [On *Coriolanus*, 2.1.166: 'My gracious silence, hail!']
 By *my gracious silence* I believe the poet meant *thou whose silent tears are more eloquent and grateful to me, than the clamorous applause of the rest!* So, Crashaw:

> *Sententious show'rs! O! let them fall!*
> *Their cadence is rhetorical.*

195

Again, in the *Martial Maid* of Beaumont and Fletcher:

> *A lady's tears are silent orators,*
> *Or should be so at least, to move beyond*
> *The honey-tongued rhetorician.*

Again, in Daniel's *Complaint of Rosamond*, 1599:

> *Ah beauty, syren, fair enchanting good!*
> *Sweet silent rhetorick of persuading eyes!*
> *Dumb eloquence, whose power doth move the blood,*
> *More than the words, or wisdom of the wise!*

Again, in *Every Man out of his Humour*: 'You shall see sweet *silent rhetorick,* and *dumb eloquence* speaking in her eye.' STEEVENS.

I believe the meaning of *my gracious silence* is only *thou whose silence is so* graceful *and becoming. Gracious* seems to have had the same meaning formerly that *graceful* has at this day. So, in the *Merchant of Venice*: 'But being season'd with a *gracious* voice.' MALONE (VIII, 377)

[13] [On *Titus Andronicus*]

Whatever were the motives of Heminge and Condell for admitting this tragedy among those of Shakespeare, all it has gained by their favour is to be delivered down to posterity with repeated remarks of contempt;—a Thersites babbling among heroes, and introduced only to be derided. STEEVENS (VIII, 463)

[14] [End-note on *Titus Andronicus*, added to the 1773 text (see Vol. 5, p. 533); after the quotation from Ravenscroft Steevens continues:]

It rarely happens that a dramatic piece is alter'd with the same spirit that it was written; but *Titus Andronicus* has undoubtedly fallen into the hands of one whose feelings were congenial with those of its original author.

In the course of the notes on this performance I have pointed out a passage or two which, in my opinion, sufficiently prove it to have been the work of one who was acquainted both with Greek and Roman literature. It is likewise deficient in such internal marks as distinguish the tragedies of Shakespeare from those of other writers; I mean, that it presents no struggles to introduce the vein of humour so constantly interwoven with the business of his serious dramas. It can neither boast of his striking excellencies nor his acknowledged defects; for it offers not a single interesting situation, a natural character, or a string of quibbles, from the first scene to the last. That Shakespeare should have written without commanding our attention, moving our passions, or sporting with words, appears to me as improbable as that he should have studiously avoided dissyllable and trissyllable terminations in this play and in no other. . . .

Could the use of particular terms employed in no other of his pieces be admitted as an argument that he was not its author, more than one of these might be found; among which is *palliament* for *robe*, a Latinism which I have not met with elsewhere in any English writer, whether ancient or modern; though it must have originated from the mint of a scholar. I may add that *Titus Andronicus* will be found on examination to contain a greater number of classical allusions &c. than are scattered over all the rest of the performances on which the seal of Shakespeare is un-dubitably fixed.—Not to write any more *about and about* this suspected *thing*, let me observe that the glitter of a few passages in it has perhaps misled the judgment of those who ought to have known that both sentiment and description are more easily produced than the interesting fabrick of a tragedy. Without these advantages many plays have succeeded; and many have failed, in which they have been dealt about with the most lavish profusion. It does not follow that he who can carve a frieze with minute-ness, elegance, and ease has a conception equal to the extent, propriety, and grandeur of a temple. STEEVENS. (VIII, 560–1)

[15] [On *Cymbeline*, 5.3.30ff., the masque; Steevens quotes Pope's dismissal of this scene (see Vol. 2, p. 418) as 'foisted in afterwards for meer show', not by Shakespeare.]

Every reader must be of the same opinion. The subsequent narratives of Posthumus, which render this masque, &c. un-necessary (or perhaps the scenical directions supplied by the poet himself), seem to have excited some manager of a theatre to disgrace the play by the present metrical interpolation. Shakespeare, who has conducted his fifth act with such matchless skill, could never have designed the vision to be twice described by Posthumus, had this contemptible nonsense been previously delivered on the stage. . . . (IX, 323)

[16] [*Ibid.*, 5.5]

Let those who talk so confidently about the skill of Shakespeare's contemporary, Jonson, point out the conclusion of any one of his plays which is wrought with more artifice, and yet a less degree of dramatic violence than this. In the scene before us all the surviving characters are assembled; and at the expence of whatever incongruity the former events may have been produced, perhaps little can be discovered on this occasion to offend the most scrupulous advocate for regularity: and, I think, as little is found wanting to satisfy the spectator by a catastrophe which is intricate without confusion, and not more rich in ornament than in nature. STEEVENS. (IX, 323)

[17] [On *King Lear*, 3.7.66ff.: the blinding of Gloucester]
In *Selimus, Emperor of the Turks*, one of the sons of *Bajazet* pulls out the eyes of an aga on the stage, and says,

> Yes thou shalt live, but never see that day,
> Wanting the tapers that should give thee light.
>
> [*Pulls out his eyes.*

Immediately after, his hands are cut off. I have introduced this passage to shew that Shakespeare's drama was not more sanguinary than that of his contemporaries. STEEVENS.

In Marston's *Antonio and Mellida*, pt. ii, 1602. Piero's tongue is torn out on the stage. MALONE. (IX, 491)

[18] [On *Hamlet*, 5.1.22ff.:]

crowner's quest-law.] I strongly suspect that this is a ridicule on the case of Dame Hales, reported by Plowden in his commentaries, as determined in 3 Eliz.

It seems her husband Sir James Hales had drowned himself in a river, and the question was whether by this act a forfeiture of a lease from the dean and chapter of Canterbury, which he was possessed of, did not accrue to the crown; an inquisition was found before the coroner, which found him *felo de se*. The legal and logical subtilties arising in the course of the argument of this case gave a very fair opportunity for a sneer at *crowner's quest-law*. The expression, a little before, that *an act hath three branches,* &c. is so pointed an allusion to the case I mention that I cannot doubt but that Shakespeare was acquainted with and meant to laugh at it.

It may be added that on this occasion a great deal of subtilty was used to ascertain whether Sir James was the *agent* or the *patient*; or, in other words, whether *he went to the water, or the water came to him*. This cause of Sir James's madness was the circumstance of his having been the judge who condemned *Lady Jane Grey*. Sir J. HAWKINS. (X, 372)

[19] [End-note to *Hamlet*: repeating the charge of the 'immoral tendency' of Hamlet's character from 1773 (see Vol. 5, pp. 540f.), Steevens adds:]

The late Dr. Akenside once observed to me that the conduct of Hamlet was every way unnatural and indefensible, unless he were to be regarded as a young man whose intellects were in some degree impaired by his own misfortunes; by the death of his father, the loss of expected sovereignty, and a sense of shame resulting from the hasty and incestuous marriage of his mother. (X, 412–13)

[20] [On Voltaire's critique of *Hamlet*: cf. Vol. 4, pp. 90f. and above, pp. 157ff.]

The first remark of Voltaire on this tragedy is that the former king had been poisoned by his brother and *his queen*. The guilt of the latter, however, is far from being ascertained. The Ghost forbears to accuse her as an accessary, and very forcibly recommends her to the mercy of her son. I may add, that her conscience appears undisturbed during the exhibition of the mock tragedy, which produces so visible a disorder in her husband who was really criminal. . . . STEEVENS (X, 422)

[21] [On *Othello*, 4.1.42:]

Noses, ears, and lips.] Othello is imaging to himself the familiarities which he supposes to have passed between Cassio and his wife. So, in the *Winter's Tale*:

> Cheek to cheek,—meeting *noses*—
> Kissing with inside *lip*, &c.—

If this be not the meaning, we must suppose he is meditating a cruel punishment for Desdemona and her suspected paramour:

> ——raptis
> *Auribus*, et truncas inhonesto vulnere *nares*.[1]
> STEEVENS. (X, 567)

[1] Virgil, *Aeneid*, 6.497ff. (the mutilated face of Deiphobus, killed in the Trojan war): 'his ears wrenched from despoiled brows, and his nostrils lopped by a shameful wound'.

[22] [*Ibid.*, 5.2.7: 'Put out the light']

This has been considered as a very difficult line. *Fielding* makes *Betterton* and *Booth* dispute about it with the *author himself* in the other world.[1] The punctuation recommended by Dr. Warburton gives a spirit to it which I fear was not intended. It seems to have been only a *play upon words*. *To put the light out* was a phrase for *to kill*. In the Maid's tragedy, Melantius says,

> ——'Tis a justice, and a noble one,
> *To put the light out* of such base offenders.
>
> FARMER.

Put out the light. This phrase is twice used in *Sidney's Arcadia* for killing a lady, p. 460 and 470. edit. 1633. STEEVENS. (X, 602)

[23] [*Ibid.*, 5.2.21f.: 'This sorrow's heavenly;/It strikes where it doth love'. Johnson commented: 'I wish these two lines could be honestly ejected. It is the fate of *Shakespeare* to counteract his own pathos': Vol. 5, p. 165.]

Perhaps the poet would not have retained both these images had he published the play himself, though in the hurry of composition he threw them both upon paper. The first seems adopted from the fabulous history of the crocodile, the second from a passage in the scripture. STEEVENS. (X, 603)

258. Unsigned article, in defence of Polonius

1779

From 'The Character of Polonius, in *Hamlet*, Critically Examined', in the *Westminster Magazine*, vii (January 1779, pp. 17–18; February, pp. 76–8; March, pp. 123–5), reprinted in *Walker's Hibernian Magazine* in February, March, and May. The essay is signed 'Elidurus'.

---

[1] Fielding, *A Journey from this World to the Next*, Bk 1, ch. 8: in *Miscellanies* (1743).

. . . POLONIUS is not a conceited, pragmatical old driveller—not a mere retailer of dull phrases and tedious advices, not the hackneyer of stale jests and tiresome see-saws—as he hath been painted by many men of learning, and represented by every Player. He is an able Statesman, a subtle Politician, and a facetious, witty Courtier; he is an old man, with some peculiarities—now and then veering on the garrulous, but having still the main object in pursuit prevalent. He is the adviser and executor of his King's commands; and in the last office he stoops, like a very Statesman, to any means that can attain his ends. He is pliant and conforming, suiting himself to the temper of the man he wishes to discover; in short, he is the sensible Man, and the intelligent Minister. . . .

Consider then, in the first place, *the situation of* POLONIUS: he is *Chamberlain, Minister*, and sole *Confidant* to a deep-settled *villain*, guilty of fratricide, usurpation, and incest. Illustrious knaves do not chuse *fools* to hold the reins of their Government.—Conscious of their own demerits, and jealous of their subjects;—continually in anxiety, and pressed with every doubt that wickedness creates;—they do not intrust their safety to the management of weak and unnerved hands. What tyrant King or usurping Villain had his first Minister of State an *ideot*?

In the second place, *the esteem he is held in* proves his sagacity, his financeering powers, if we may be allowed the expression, and the wisdom with which he conducted himself both in public and private life. What greater compliment could, by a Prince (and not a weak one), be paid to a subject, than the King does to POLONIUS, when he speaks to his son LAERTES? [Quotes 1.2.42–9.] By this it appears, beyond the idea of refutation, that he considered POLONIUS as the *prop*, the *strength*, the *support* of his Throne, the principal stay and bulwark of his kingdom, without whose Atlas-shoulder his State would totter and decay. He was the *defence*, the *guard*, the *hand*, the *blood* of Denmark. Could a Driveller be so?

Pol. Th' Ambassadors from Norway, my good Lord, are joyfully return'd.

King. Thou still hast been the father of good news.

[2.2.41f.]

Observe, the King is always on the tiptoe of courtesy to him. He never is the object of ridicule to the *King* which he is to the *Player*: the *King* considers him a *Man*; the *Player* represents him an *Ape*. Nay, he was esteemed a *man of wit* at Court: the Queen particularly

201

marks his talent in her answer, 'More matter with less *art*.' [2.2.95]

It hath been an established maxim, that the true *wit* dwells upon the subject of narration, to embellish it with those lively strokes of imagination which steal upon the heart, and please the livelier movements of the soul. If it is said, as probably the sour Critic may be inclined to say, that his wit consists in playful alliteration, and in spinning out, dwelling upon, and changing the meaning of a word; to this we can readily reply that it is the tone of SHAKESPEARE'S scene to copy Nature. At the time he lived and wrote, alliterations and quick transitions were held as the sallies and the starts of wit, and in his noblest characters he rejects not the public opinion, but yields to the ruling biass of the day. In the same scene, his description of HAMLET'S madness hath been highly relished for its progressive humour, and laughable propriety. . . . (17–18)

What man of the least penetration would esteem that man a *fool*, who speaks the following language: [Quotes the advice to Laertes, 1.3.59–80.]

Let us seriously consider how this speech would appear drest in the frippery of humour. How should we relish these noble sentiments, if cooked and presented to us covered with the garbage of *buffoonery*? What a code of sage maxims is contained in the above speech! What a vein of instruction! It is not a bundle of scholastic dogmas, produced from the fusty chronicles of former times, but a mine of precious sayings, pouring from a bosom of philosophy, acquainted with the ways of men, and whose knowledge was established by the deepest penetration, experience, and reflection. This is one of those scenes which the *comic* Player is obliged to leave in *shade*, for his impudence of brow dare not bring it to the *light* in the drapery of *laughter*.

In his scene with Ophelia, how sensible and just his reflections are! never bordering on the Fool; never expressive of the *Ape*. Drawn as they are from the source of observation, they teem with the sagest sentiments, and ought to be engraven upon every maiden heart. [Quotes 1.3.115–31.]

The first scene of the second Act would of itself establish *Polonius*'s reputation for wisdom, were there no other evidence to be found in the Play. It contains his instructions and advice to *Reynaldo* how to pry into the conduct of his Son, and proves him to have a consummate knowledge of the World. . . .

Having thus examined the character in its various respects of situation, esteem and conduct, I beg leave to submit to the consideration of your Readers the matter in dispute. The foregoing are the reasons why I conceive *Polonius* to be a skilful and an experienced Politician: the following are those suggested by the Critics and the Players to prove that he is a *Fool*. [Quotes 'Do you see yonder cloud?', 3.2.365–72.]

This passage, say they, proves that *Polonius* was very destitute of penetration, or he must have seen *Hamlet*'s evident intention of mockery.—How ridiculous is this remark!—The very passage itself is the plainest evidence of *Polonius*'s wisdom.—Considering *Hamlet* in a state of insanity, he is not foolish enough to contradict him in the phantasies of his seemingly disordered brain; but strives by every condescendance to ingratiate himself, that he may be able to serve the ends of the King his master.—They further quote the words of *Hamlet* on the death of *Polonius*.

Thou wretched, rash, intruding Fool, farewel! (3.4.31ff.)

May I not be permitted to say that the word *fool* does not so often signify *Idiotism*, as talents joined to a bad heart, misapplied, or in opposition to those who give the term?. . .

May we not conclude, after having considered in the present instance how widely different from the Author the Critics have judged of the character of *Polonius*, that the true mode of estimating the value of a character is to sum up the attributes conferred on it by the Author, and not to rest satisfied with the superficial garb in which it is represented by the Player? (123–5)

259. George Steevens, on the alterations of Shakespeare

1779

From 'Observations on the plays altered from Shakespeare', in the *St. James's Chronicle*, no. 2809 (13–16 March 1779). Steevens's authorship is recorded by Malone in his collection of Shakespeariana in the Bodleian Library.

> *Witmore.* Alterations, Sir!
> *Marplay.* Yes, Sir, Alterations.—I will maintain it, let a Play be never so good, without Alteration it will do nothing.
>
> Fielding's *Author's Farce.*

From a Catalogue annexed to the last Edition of Shakespeare it appears that only Six of his Plays have escaped the Ravages of critical Temerity, or theatrical Presumption. They have suffered equally under the Hands of the Learned and the Ignorant, the Academick and the Player*. Those who have succeeded best in their Attempts have omitted many Beauties which they could not torture to their own Designs.† Where the Drama has been contracted, the Catastrophe has been unnaturally hastened.‡ Where

---

* Mr. Hawkins has entirely banished the Queen and Iachimo from his altered *Cymbeline*,[1] and has almost annihilated the Character of Posthumus, who is not permitted to appear till the Middle of the-fourth Act.—Mr. Cibber, in his *King John*,[2] bestows the warlike Propositions of the Bastard on Lady Constance; and puts the flowery and descriptive Lines of a Chorus to *King Henry V*. into the Mouth of King Richard III, who is preparing with Anxiety for a Battle on which his Crown and Life depended.

† The whole Progress of Leontes' Jealousy is struck out of the *Winter's Tale*,[3] as it is at present altered and abridged. The original Romeo is said by his Confessor to have deserted Rosaline and engaged in a fresh Amour. As there was no Crime in quitting the Service of a hard-hearted Mistress, I am too dull to perceive the Necessity of this Variation from the original Play.

‡ Othello is not permitted on the Stage to be effectually wrought by the Scenes in which he listens to the Conversation of Iago with Cassio, and is witness to Iago's Attempt on his Lieutenant's Life: And yet at last is Othello represented as 'perplexed in the Extreme.'

[1] See Vol. 4, No. 175.   [2] See Vol. 3, No. 102.
[3] See Vol. 4, No. 150.

Deficiencies have been supplyed, they have been always such as refuse to coalesce with the Stile and Structure of the Original*; *non vultus non color unus.*[1] The Scenes have sometimes been abridged, to favour the Indolence of a Performer; and sometimes (to gratify his paltry Ambition of uttering the most splendid Lines in the Piece) the Sentiments and Imagery appropriated to one Character have been transferred to another.† He who should attend the Representation of Shakespeare's Tragedies as they were first written might perhaps complain of their Length; but when they are curtailed for Exhibition we are certain to discover that somewhat materially necessary to Display of Character, or Perspicuity of Fable, has been removed.‡ Shakespeare seems to have been regarded as an Author who might be safely amplified or abbreviated as Chance or Interest should direct; and because succeeding Writers have so confidently talked of the Dramatick Art of Ben Jonson, we have too precipitately allowed that a less Degree of it was to be found in his

* Thus has it fared with the different Additions made to *Timon,*[2] at the several Revivals of that Play. Lord Lansdowne, in his Reformation of the *Merchant of Venice,*[3] has introduced a ridiculous Scene of a Banquet, during which the Jew is placed at a separate Table, and drinks to his Money, as to his only Mistress.

† In the Performance of *As you Like it,* the celebrated Speech that describes the wounded Stag, and the Behaviour of the humourist Jaques, is taken from one of the Lords, its original Proprietor, and is given to Jaques himself.—In the new *Hamlet*[4] the dying Words of Laertes are transferred to the Prince of Denmark. An Alteration of *Romeo and Juliet,* as exhibited in Ireland, affords a yet more striking Example of the same Practice. The Manager[5] who played the Part of Romeo, contrived to possess himself of the celebrated Speech of Mercutio concerning the Freaks of Queen Mab. Like Bottom the Weaver, (to borrow Dr. Johnson's Words) those histrionical Reformers 'are for engrossing every Part, and excluding their Inferiors from all possibility of Distinction.' They are desirous to enact Pyramus, Thisbe, and the Lion, at the same time.

‡ In the *First Part of King Henry IV.* the Dispute between Hotspur and Owen Glendower (a Scene introduced by Shakespeare to develop and exalt the Character of the former) is always suppressed on the Stage.—In the *second Part* of the same Play, the beginning Scene is constantly omitted, being already worked up into Cibber's Alteration of *King Richard III.*[6] The Scene in which Colevile surrenders to Falstaff is likewise lost to the Audience.—In the last Alteration of *Cymbeline,* (I mean as acted, not as printed) the Physician who provides the supposed Poison for the Queen is entirely kept out of sight, so that the Spectators are by no Means prepared for the return of Imogen to life.

Other Alterations from our Authour would undoubtedly supply yet more apposite Instances of the same Absurdities; but human Patience has its Limits; and though the Hope of procuring a Reprieve for the Text of Shakespeare, as often as hasty Editors have condemned it, might give alacrity to a Commentator, and support him through much laborious Investigation; yet to peruse all these vamped and mutilated Dramas with Attention would be little less in effect than to attend the Poet's Execution.

1 *Aeneid,* 6.47: 'nor countenance nor colour the same'.
2 See Vol. 1, No. 17; Vol. 5, No. 232. 3 See Vol. 2, No. 43. 4 See Vol. 5, p. 465.
5 Malone notes: 'Mr. Sheridan'. 6 See Vol. 2, p. 106.

great Contemporary. But the Reverse is indisputably the Truth. Shakespeare, together with his Art, possessed the happy Power of disguising it. The Progress of his Events in general, so nearly approaches to the ordinary course of Nature that it should seem as if Contrivance had little Share in its Direction. In Shakespeare, as in Jonson, we enjoy all the brightness of the Lamp; but it is in the latter only that we are offended by its Exhalations.

It may be added, that the Taste of those who would separate the mingled Dramas of our Authour may be suspected of Caprice or Depravation, especially as some Portion of Comedy is expected by a modern Audience to diversify their serious Entertainment. Shakespeare thought, and justly thought, himself capable of attracting and detaining Hearers, without Assistance from the coarse Buffooneries of any meaner Playwright. His Stage supplyed all that Variety which different Propensities demand, and are at present reduced to look for in distinct and discordant Pieces, most shamelessly exhibited on the same Evenings and in the same Theatres with his own. His Comedy and Tragedy are by no means forced into Union, but are engrafted on each other, and so engrafted that they appear alternately as the natural Produce of one ample and luxuriant Story. His Characters and Situations owe much of their Power to judicious Contrast, and the Mirth of Lear's Fool (who is now ejected), so far from being unseasonable, is placed in significant Opposition to the frensy of his Master. The comick Efforts of Shakespeare cannot be said to counteract his Tragick Effusions; for it should be remembered that in every Piece which he has called a Tragedy the Sensations resulting from the Calamities of Love, the Punishment of Guilt, or the Fall of Ambition, are always forcibly impressed on the Audience in his concluding Scenes; nor is the Loquacity of the Nurse, the Impertinence of the Clown, or the Licentiousness of the Porter permitted to disturb the Emotions raised by the Tomb of Juliet, the detection of Iago, or the Despair of Macbeth.

Were any Parnassian Code of Statutes extant, by which the Rage of modernizing ancient Pieces could be repressed, all wanton and unnecessary Change in those of Shakespeare should be prohibited. A Society was once instituted to promote the Revival of his Plays; a second is almost needful to secure them from Adulteration. The pretended Reformers of Shakespeare, whether old or modern, Players or Pedants, may be compared to injudicious Picture-

Cleaners, who sometimes with their Varnish crack the Canvas of a Raphael, and sometimes daub it over with their own Colours.

A degree of insidious Caution, however, pervades the Alterations made by the Moderns in our Authour's Plays. These Gentlemen have usually taken care to print a larger Portion of their Originals than is ever suffered to be spoken on the Stage. They will risque any Violence to the Poet before a passive Audience, but are commendably afraid of the Tribunal of a discerning Reader.

Neither have these Changes been always effected for the generous Purpose of restoring the irregular Pieces of so great a Poet to the Publick; but because such Pieces, when revived and altered, would occupy a Place on the Stage to the Exclusion of fresh Productions, which carry half their Profits to their Authour. Small Encouragement can the Muse expect when they whose Interest it is to banish new Dramatick Writers have been permitted, without the Advantages of Learning or superiour Understanding, to exalt themselves into the sole Judges of Dramatick Merit. Is it not absolutely certain that both *Cato* and *Phædra and Hippolytus* would have been rejected had they been offered to a modern Manager? And yet, so lately as in the Days of Betterton and Booth these poetical and declamatory Dramas were received with Applause. But Managers at that Period had the Modesty to ask Advice from their Superiors. They were then kept in proper Subordination, nor as yet had learned to consider Authours as under-Agents to a Theatre. Add to this, that Betterton and Booth possessed all the Magick of commanding Status and Deportment, of plain and manly Elocution. To such Characters as Brutus, Melantius, and Cato, their Voice and Action imparted Strength and Dignity. But these Players and these Managers have been succeeded by others, who have discouraged every Mode of Dramatick Writing which afforded no Room for a Display of the mechanick Parts of their Profession, and their own peculiar Talents. To speak more plainly, the Taste of the present Times has been too much influenced by the Practice of *one*[1] who had been long and meritoriously our Stage's Leader; and his Practice was invariably founded on a strict Attention to his own Emolument, and a careful Estimate of his own Abilities, which, though great and various, were not consummate and universal.

---

[1] Malone notes: 'Mr. Garrick'.

260. William Richardson, on Richard III's wooing

1779

From the *Mirror*, no. 66 (25 December 1779). The editor, Henry Mackenzie, describes the piece as sent 'by a correspondent, from whom, if I mistake not, I have formerly received several ingenious communications'. Richardson claimed the authorship in his *Essays on some of Shakespeare's Dramatic Characters, To which is Added, An Essay on the Faults of Shakespeare* (1798), p. 218, in which this essay is reprinted (pp. 209–18).

On Richardson see the head-note to No. 246 above.

Few of Shakespeare's tragedies have obtained higher reputation than *The Life and Death of Richard the Third*. Yet, like every other performance of this wonderful poet, it contains several passages that can hardly admit of apology. Of this kind are the instances it affords us of vulgarity and even indecency of expression.

At the same time, in censuring Shakespeare we ought to proceed with peculiar caution; for on many occasions those passages which, on a cursory view, may be reckoned blemishes, on a closer examination will appear very different, and even lay claim to considerable excellence. In his imitations of Nature he is so very bold, and so different from other poets, that what is daring is often, in a moment of slight attention, deemed improbable; and what is extraordinary is too rashly pronounced absurd. Of this, in the work above mentioned the strange love-scene between *Richard* and *Lady Anne*, the widow of Prince *Edward Plantagenet*, affords a striking example. It seems, indeed, altogether unnatural that *Richard*, deformed and hideous as the poet represents him, should offer himself a suitor to the widow of an excellent young prince, whom he had murdered, at the very time she is attending the funeral of her father-in-law, whom he had also slain, and while she is expressing the most bitter hatred against the author of her misfortune. But in attending closely to the progress of the dialogue, the seeming extravagance of the picture will be softened or removed. We shall find ourselves more interested in the event, and more astonished at the bold ability of *Richard*, than moved with abhorrence of his shameless effrontery or offended with the improbability of the situation. When a poet like *Shakespeare* can carry us along by the power of amazement, by daring displays of Nature, and by the influence of feelings altogether unusual but full of resistless energy, his seeming departure from probability only contributes to our admiration; and the emotions excited by his extravagance, losing the effect which, from an inferior poet, they would have caused, add to the general feelings of pleasure which the scene produces.

In considering the scene before us it is necessary that we keep in view the character of *Lady Anne*. The outlines are given us in her own conversation: but we see it more completely finished and filled up, indirectly indeed but not less distinctly, in the conduct of *Richard*. She is represented of a mind altogether frivolous, the prey of vanity, her prevailing, over-ruling passion; susceptible, however, of every feeling and emotion and, while they last, sincere in their expression, but hardly capable of distinguishing the propriety of one more than another; or, if able to employ such discernment, totally unaccustomed and unable to obey her moral faculty as a principle of action; and thus exposed alike to the authority of good or bad impressions. There are such characters; persons of great sensibility, of great sincerity, but of no rational or steady virtue produced or strengthened by reflection, and consequently of no consistency of conduct.

Richard, in his management of *Lady Anne*, having in view the accomplishment of his own ambitious designs, addresses her with the most perfect knowledge of her disposition. He knows that her feelings are violent; that they have no foundation in steady determined principles of conduct; that violent feelings are soon exhausted; and that the undecided mind, without choice or active sense of propriety, is equally accessible to the next that occur. He knows, too, that those impressions will be most fondly cherished which are most a-kin to the ruling passion; and that in *Lady Anne* vanity bears absolute sway. All that he has to do, then, is to suffer the violence of one emotion to pass away, and then, as skilfully as possible, to bring another more suited to his designs and the complection of her character into its place. Thus he not only discovers much discernment of human nature, but also great command of temper, and great dexterity of conduct. [Quotes and discusses 1.2.33–121, ending 'Your beauty was the cause of that effect'.] In these lines, beside a confirmation of the foregoing remark, and an illustration of *Richard*'s persevering flattery, there are two circumstances that mark great delicacy and fineness of painting in *Shakespeare*'s execution of this excellent scene. The resentment of *Lady Anne* is so far exhausted that her conversation, instead of impetuous, continued invective, assuming the more patient and mitigated form of dialogue, is not so expressive of violent passion as it denotes the desire of victory in a smart dispute, and becomes merely 'a keen encounter of wits.' The other thing to be observed is that *Richard*, instead of specifying her husband and father-in-law in terms denoting these relations, falls in with the subsiding state of her affections towards them; and, using expressions of great indifference, speaks to her of 'those Plantagenets, *Henry* and *Edward*.'

Lady Anne having listened to the conversation of *Richard*, after the first transport of her wrath occasioned by the death of the *Plantagenets*, shewed that the real force of the passion had suffered abatement; and by listening to his exculpation it seems entirely subdued. In all this the art of the poet is eminent, and the skill he ascribes to *Richard* profound. Though the crafty seducer attempts to justify his conduct to *Lady Anne*, he does not seek to convince her understanding, for she had no understanding worth the pains of convincing, but to afford her some pretence and opportunity of giving vent to her emotion. When this effect is produced he proceeds to substitute some regard for himself in its place. As we have already observed, he has been taking measures for this purpose in every thing he has said; and, by soothing expressions of adulation during the course of her anger, he was gradually preparing her mind for the more pleasing, but not less powerful dominion of vanity. . . .

In the close of the dialogue we may trace distinctly the decline of her emotion. It follows the same course as the passion she expresses at the beginning of the scene. She is at first violent; becomes more violent; her passion subsides; yet some ideas of propriety wandering across her mind, she makes an effort to recall her resentment. The effort is feeble; it amounts to no more than to express contempt in her aspect; it is baffled by a new attitude of adulation; and, by a pretended indirect appeal to her compassion, she is totally vanquished.

Through the whole of this scene our abhorrence, our disgust and contempt, excited by cruelty, falsehood, meanness, and insignificance of mind are so counterbalanced by the feelings that arise on the view of ability, self-possession, knowledge of character, and the masterly display of human nature as that, instead of impairing, they rather contribute force to the general sensation of pleasure. The conduct of *Richard* towards a character of more determined virtue, or of more stubborn passions, would have been absurd: towards *Lady Anne* it was natural, and attended with that success which it was calculated to obtain. (261–4)

261. Horace Walpole, Shakespeare's natural genius

1779–80

From Walpole's *Book of Materials*, a notebook with entries dating from 1759 to 1786. This selection is from *Notes by Horace Walpole on Several Characters of Shakespeare*, ed. W. S. Lewis (Farmington, Conn., 1940), who dates this passage *c.* 1779–80. For a fully annotated edition see now Lars Troide (ed.), *Horace Walpole's Miscellany, 1786–95* (New Haven, Conn., 1977).

On Walpole as a Shakespeare critic see the head-notes to Nos 202 (Vol. 4, p. 546) and 237 j (Vol. 5, pp. 483f.).

Shakespeare, in that most beautiful scene between Northumberland and Lady Percy in the *Second part* of *Henry 4th* makes Lady Percy in her fond description of her husband Hotspur say,

> And speaking thick, which nature made *his* blemish,
> Became the accents of the valiant. [2.3.24f.]

Shakespeare, who looked into all nature, knew that what was graceful in a hero, tho' a defect, would be mimicked by the apes and coxcombs of the age. There is a pretty simplicity in the older bard; in our countryman that slight sketch is worked up by the hand of a master into a portrait of human nature. It is a picture that exhibits mankind, as well as the likeness of a single character. They are those strokes that raise Shakespeare above all authors who ever wrote. Many copyists have imitated his language—if they did aim at his intuition into nature, they miscarried so entirely that we cannot trace their attempts. The inimitable scene I have mentioned is never acted, because no principal actress will condescend to speak but two speeches; tho' it would be sufficient fame for any actress that ever existed to pronounce those two speeches with all the pathetic tenderness and enthusiasm with which they ought to be spoken.

The scene of the grave-diggers in *Hamlet*, the finest piece of moral pathos that can be imagined, was sillily omitted by Garrick, because it had been generally acted in a buffoon manner, and because French critics, who did not understand it, condemned it as low. I have seen old Johnson[1] play the first grave-digger in the very spirit in which Shakespeare wrote it. He jested slightly with his companion before Hamlet entered, marking the insensibility that habitude produces in men accustomed to sights that shock or impress with melancholy those not broken to them;—but when the Prince entered Johnson resumed his seriousness to a certain degree, yet not so much as to destroy the stronger emotions of Hamlet. It was natural to a grave-digger to recall the wantonness of a young merry courtier, and recount it as he felt it—but to the Prince it brought back reflection on the happy hours of his childhood, which he could not but compare with the dismal scenes that had ensued, and with his own present melancholy situation. In this just light the skull of his father's jester roused the indignation of Hamlet and egged him on to the justice he meditated on his uncle; and thus that rejected scene hastened on the catastrophe of

[1] Benjamin Johnson (1665?–1742), an actor, of the Drury Lane company.

the tragedy, and more naturally than the most pompous exhortation would have done from the mouth of Horatio. A spark falling on combustible matter may light up a conflagration. A great master produces important events from a trifle, naturally introduced. A piddling critic would waste his time in describing the torch with dignity that set fire to the combustion. Compare Ben Jonson's *Catiline* with *Hamlet*. The former is all pedantry and bombast. Are the royal dignities of the Ghost, of the Queen or of Hamlet lowered by the variety of familiar incidents taken from common life that are introduced into the tragedy? The rules of Aristotle, of Bossu, are ridiculous and senseless if they prohibit such conduct and operations of the passions. Is there an incident in all Racine, Corneille, Voltaire, Addison or Otway, so natural, so pathetic, so sublime, as Prince Arthur's reprimanding Hubert [for] his having bound a handkerchief wrought by a princess on the jailor's temples?[1] It is that contrast between royalty and the keeper of a prison that exalts both, and augments the compassion for Arthur. Dr Johnson has dared to say that when Shakespeare aimed at being sublime he was bombast; that is, Johnson had no idea of sublimity but in the pomp of diction, and he himself in his common conversation is always hyperbolic and pedantic. He talks like ancient Pistol, and is the very thing he condemns. Is there no sublimity in ennobling a vulgar image or expression? Voltaire did not know there is, any more than Johnson. The Frenchman condemns Hamlet's expression *of a bare bodkin*; every Englishman of taste feels the happy energy of the phrase.

I do not doubt but we lose many beauties in the ancients from not understanding the whole force of their language and allusions: but it would be the extremity of folly to sacrifice our glory, Shakespeare, to French critics, who undoubtedly cannot comprehend half his merit. Will Dr Johnson or Voltaire reject this passage:

> When your own Percy, when my heart—dear Harry,
> Threw many a northward look to see his Father
> Bring up his powers—but he did look in vain!
> Who then persuaded you to stay at home!
> There were two honours lost, yours and your son's.
>
> [*2 Henry IV*, 2.3.12ff.]

No words can be more trite, more vulgar, less laboured, less selected—*my heart—dear Harry* would suit the mouth of Mrs.

[1] See *King John*, 4.1.41ff.

Quickly—yet how tender when wrung from the lips of a wife, who felt the loss of her domestic happiness, and was not considering herself as the partner of a hero of a conspiracy!

> Who then persuaded you to stay at home!

Would not that line be ridiculously bad, and familiar, if not ennobled by distress and sentiment? Is not the cadence of the whole passage harmonious, tender, and accented by grief! In short, let Dr Johnson translate these five lines into his decompounds of Greek frenchified—aye, let him put them into any words but those simple ones employed by Shakespeare, and see if they will be improved. O Shakespeare, thou first of men, I am happy to possess that language in which thou didst write, that not one of thy excellencies are lost on me!

I purposely forbore to quote the lines that follow, because they rise to genuine poetry in proportion as the enthusiasm of the speaker rose. Shakespeare's exquisite taste knew how to distribute simple language to grief and argument, and exalted diction to enthusiastic love. Raise the expression in the first five lines, and you would destroy the musical energy of the succeeding. Pope's *Epistle of Eloisa* is one continued strain of poetic love, laboured and polished to the highest perfection—but is Eloisa as natural as Lady Percy? There is another merit in the latter, of which there is not the smallest trace in the former. The images of Eloisa might be those of any popish age, nay are too gorgeous for those in which she lived—whereas Lady Percy exhibits the image of the plain wives of our old barons in that savage age. She regrets the enjoyments of domestic life, recalls the honours paid to her husband, but does not drop a hint of any luxury she had tasted but in him. Constance in *King John* is precisely such a mother, as Lady Percy is a widow: they dwell on no ideas that are foreign to their grief.

But there would be no end to a comment on Shakespeare's beauties—he has faults enough to glut the critics, but let them not dare to meddle with his excellencies, which no other mortal ever could attain. How would Voltaire or the greatest genius of any nation have been puzzled if proposed to them to specify in tragedy that their hero stammered, or to call him by a nickname! Yet how beautiful is the description of Hotspur's speaking thick, and calling him my heart—dear *Harry!* (10–17)

262. Samuel Badcock, Shakespeare's originality

1780

From a review of the Johnson–Steevens edition of 1778 in the *Monthly Review*, lxii (January 1780), pp. 12–26.

Samuel Badcock (1747–88), a dissenting minister who finally conformed to the Church of England and was ordained in 1787, was a prolific reviewer, contributing over two hundred articles to the *Monthly Review*, and writing for half a dozen other journals. His contributions to the *Westminster Magazine* are listed in the *Gentleman's Magazine*, lviii, pt 2 (1788), p. 595; for his contributions to the *Monthly* see B. C. Nangle, *The Monthly Review. First Series, 1749–1789. Indexes of Contributors and Articles* (Oxford, 1934); also John Nichols, *Literary Anecdotes of the Eighteenth Century* (London 1812–15, 9 vols), V, pp. 217–42.

[Badcock quotes Steevens's discovery of the MS of Thomas Middleton's play *The Witch*, and Malone's deduction that 'the songs beginning *Come away*, &c. and *Black spirits*, &c. being found at full length in Middleton's play, while only the two first words of them are printed in *Macbeth*, favour the supposition that Middleton's piece preceded that of Shakespeare. . . ' .]

By the very numerous quotations from old plays, ballads, histories, and romances which Mr. Steevens hath produced to illustrate some obscure passages in Shakespeare, a hasty and superficial critic might be tempted to question his peculiar, and almost unrivalled claim to originality: or if he were not so presumptuous as to question what the united suffrages of the best judges have allowed him, yet at least to qualify it by a colder praise than hath been hitherto bestowed on him. It must, indeed, be acknowledged by the most enthusiastic admirer of this immortal poet that many of his plays, which owe their chief beauties to a

215

boldness of invention and a wildness of fancy, appear to have been in some degree indebted, either for plot, management, or machinery, to other writers. This remark receives confirmation from the discovery of Middleton's MS. play, above mentioned; in which somewhat of that imagery that hath equally astonished, charmed, and terrified us, in the closet and the theatre, in the tragedy of *Macbeth* may be traced out by a curious and discerning eye. How far Shakespeare was indebted to old English translations of the Greek and Latin classics—to Stow, Hall, Holinshed, and the translator of Hector Boethius's *History of Scotland*, hath been sufficiently noticed by preceding critics. It was, indeed, left to the indefatigable Mr. Steevens to turn over a thousand dull and insignificant entries at Stationers Hall in order to discover all the *minutiæ* of dates and titles which bore any reference to Shakespeare; and after a most laborious research, with an eye (as Dr. Johnson says of the *sagacious* Mr. B—'s) that looked *keenly on vacancy*, he made a discovery of several plays on similar subjects with many of Shakespeare's which were prior to his, and even before his first entrance on the stage. All this may be true: nay, we have not a doubt of the fact. But nothing that hath yet been produced of Shakespeare's plagiarism can deprive him of one tittle of his almost prescriptive right to all the honours of a great and unequalled original. The most captious critic, in the fulness of a desire to find fault, must allow that Shakespeare's borrowed ornaments sit on him with a more natural grace and elegance than on their original proprietors. They are so exquisitely disposed of—so nicely blended with what is unquestionably his own property, that we know not where the borrowed parts end nor where the original ones begin. The whole appears to be the production of the same master: *simplex duntaxat et unum*.[1] We may, perhaps, assert that in the general and more disgraceful sense of the word this great poet never appears to have borrowed at all. He had read indeed; and his capacious mind was stored with a vast treasure of knowledge and observation. He had reflected on the great acquisitions he had made; had arranged them in his mind with much care and exactness. By these means they became incorporated with his own natural, and in the truest sense of the term, *unborrowed* reflections. Hence it is obvious to suppose that when he addressed himself to composition, he drew indiscriminately from the immense store-

[1] Horace, *Ars Poetica*, 23: 'let it at least be simple and uniform'.

house of his mind whatever was fit for his purpose, whether of native or acquired knowledge—indifferent, and perhaps unconscious whose property any part of it might be. This is not an uncommon circumstance. The utmost circumspection cannot always prevent its occurrence: for it is difficult to distinguish the power of invention from that of reflection. Fancy may claim for its own what had been first only adopted by memory.

Shakespeare hath the admirable art not only of applying his borrowed parts with propriety, but of embellishing and improving them. He adds to them a grace and dignity which at least are his own. In the tragedy of *Macbeth* his spirits, though similar in name to those of Middleton (particularly the presiding Deity hath in each the Grecian name of Hecate), yet they differ from Middleton's in almost every essential attribute of conduct and character. Middleton's fairies are light, frisky beings, who wreak their malice on small culprits, and revenge little mischiefs. Shakespeare's are brought on the stage for purposes of higher account. They are to be the instruments of dire events—revolutions that were worthy the council of the Gods. This great object was of sufficient importance to excuse the interposition of supernatural beings. Hence, what Middleton invented to amuse, Shakespeare's more daring genius improved into an instrument of terror. This he hath accomplished with wonderful propriety: and we admire that skill and power which, on so slight a basis, could erect such a stupendous fabric.

Shakespeare's witches seem to be fully aware of the high importance of the subject of their incantations, by the number of the ingredients which they throw into the cauldron. Hecate is anxious for its success; and enquires into the particulars of the infernal mixture. They solemnly cast in their respective share of the composition: but instead of *the gristle of a man hang'd after sun set* (i.e. a murderer, according to Middleton's play) they throw in *the grease that's sweaten from a murderer's gibbet*; and instead of Middleton's *fat of an unbaptised child* they mix with the other ingredients of the cauldron *the finger of birth-strangled babe*. Perhaps it may be impossible to describe the precise difference in the energy of these expressions. It must be felt from their several effects on the imagination. Considered in that view, the difference is very great: at least it is felt to be such by us; and from a variety of circumstances of this kind we are persuaded that Shakespeare never sat down to write from another's copy. His language was the

217

natural expression of a mind fraught with the boldest conceptions, and the most lively ideas: and when the whole of Middleton's play is published, perhaps our convictions will be still farther corroborated of Shakespeare's having never considered it as a *model* for his scene of the witches in *Macbeth*, however he might have fallen on some particular modes of expression that were scarce avoidable on the same subject.

The scene of the witches with Macbeth, after their incantations at the cauldron, is inexpressibly solemn: and the expedient of shewing a future race of Kings wonderfully striking and sublime. Distance and obscurity assist and increase that terror which is one capital source of sublimity. But as if that were not sufficient, others are shewn in a glass as the descendents of Banquo, whose ruin he was contriving. To see them exalted to the height of power and authority was an object to strike ambition to madness.—We have made these remarks in order to evince how essentially different the gay witches of Middleton are from the awful *sisters* of *Macbeth*. (23–6)

263. Edward Capell, notes on Shakespeare

1780

From *Notes and Various Readings to Shakespeare* (3 vols, printed 1779–80, published 1783). This collection, totalling 1,823 pages, mostly double-column, the third volume of which comprises *The School of Shakespeare*, an anthology (in 655 pages) of contemporary texts illustrating the plays, finally completes (posthumously) the edition of Shakespeare which Capell had begun publishing in 1768 (Vol. 5, No. 220). As with the first instalment of Notes, which he had published separately in 1774 (Vol. 5, No. 242) but reprinted here, each of the four parts of the Notes consists of (i) notes on the text of the plays; (ii) errata in the text of his 1768 edition; (iii) 'Various Readings', or textual variants in the Quarto and

Folio editions of Shakespeare. The four sections, which take the plays in alphabetical order, nine plays in each, are paginated separately, two sections to each volume. Page-references here take the form: I.ii. 47, etc., meaning Vol. I, part ii, p. 47. At the end of the final section Capell adds a short note on the chronology of the plays, and a long essay on Shakespeare's metrics.

On Capell see the head-note to Vol. 5, No. 220, and H. H. Hart, 'Edward Capell: The First Modern Editor of Shakespeare' (Ph.D. dissertation, University of Illinois, 1967; University Microfilms order no. 68–8098).

---

[1] [On *Henry V*, 4.6.34ff.: the King's order to kill the prisoners]
The '*alarum*' spoke of in this line, the King's wrong surmize about it, and his consequent order, are chronicle facts, as will be found among the extracts from Holinshed; and in them too it will be seen that this seemingly cruel order had a nobler and more justifiable motive than is imputed to it by Gower in the end of his first speech; who is made to say so, 'tis probable, to shew the wrong judgment that inferiors not unfrequently make of the actions of kings. (I.ii. 20–1)

[2] [*Ibid.*, 4.8.40: 'Give me thy glove, soldier. Look, here is the fellow of it'.
This is one of those free kind of verses with which the Poet's good sense taught him to give ease and propriety to dramatick dialogue. The three last syllables of it are redundant, its fourth foot a trochee, and its first what is call'd an anapest, the thesis[1] of voice in that foot being on '*thy*'. The second of the moderns [Pope]—acknowledging no such verses as this, and who has done his best throughout Shakespeare to make a clear riddance of all he found of the sort, prints the whole speech as prose; and is follow'd by his successors here, as well as in much the greater part of other similar matters. (I.ii. 21)

[3] [On *1 Henry VI*, 1.2.133: Pucelle: 'Glory is like a circle in the water,/Which never ceaseth to enlarge itself . . . ']

---

[1] Thesis: the stressed syllable of a foot in verse: see. p. 254.

219

Methinks, at reading this simile and the application of it, we are transported (one knows not how) on the sudden out of some rough country into a fair garden; and as suddenly carry'd back again, when their reading is over. In short, the simile is a gem badly set; and so unfit for the speaker's wearing besides that, in all likelihood, it was not meant for her originally, but stuck upon her for the sake of preserving it. (I.ii. 26–7)

[4] [*Ibid.*, 1.4.69]
The measure of a line near to this must be made out by protracting '*enfeebled*' into a quadrisyllable, pronouncing—enfeebeled. Which protraction of the (*l.*) in this word, and of (*m, n, r, & s*) in some others, is founded upon the nature of those letters; four of which have the power of a syllable in many cases, even in prose. This is clearly distinguish'd in *prism, chasm, impregn* &c; in *mingl'd, handl'd, fish's*, and others innumerable; and as for (*r.*) the fifth of them, the protraction of that is most frequent in the poets of Shakespeare's time. In him we have *air, fire, hour, hair*, &c. dissyllables, and *desire* a trissyllable; many of which are vanish'd out of modern editions of him, whenever their compilers could find a convenient expletive to fill up the vacancy. (I.ii. 28)

[5] [*Ibid.*, 3.1.51: Winchester: 'Rome shall remedy this.'/Gloucester: 'Roam hither then.'
There is not in all Shakespeare a sentence more characteristic of the person to whom it is given than this is of Winchester; the position of the words that compose it, and the slow march of them, owing to the concurrence of two trochees, are peculiarly expressive of pride and surliness. But as expression of passions and characters do upon most occasions (we may nearly say all) give place to smooth versifying in the four latter moderns,[1] it was not to be expected that such beauties should be prefer'd to it here; and accordingly we find the sentence beginning with '*this*' in their copies:—*This Rome shall remedy*, which the nicest ear of this time can have no objection to.

After this instance of their fidelity as editors, and of their judgment in the language of passions and characters, we shall not

[1] The 'moderns' are the five modern editors of Shakespeare: (1) Rowe; (2) Pope; (3) Theobald; (4) Hanmer (the 'Oxford' edition); (5) Warburton. See Capell's comments on them, Vol. 5, pp. 308–10.

wonder to see two of them (the second and fourth) read in 1. 13:—*Go thither then.* (I.ii. 32)

[6] [On *2 Henry VI*, 2.1.51: '*Medice teipsum*', and 1.24: '*Tantanae animis caelestibus irae*' (*Aeneid*, 1.11)]
The elegant piece of Latin that follows (which the first modern has murder'd by putting in—*cura*), and that before it from Virgil, shew a continuance of the Poet's acquaintance with the learning that he had gather'd at school so late as the second draught[1] of these plays, for the first has them not. Both of them are of the utmost necessity in the places they severally occupy; for without them the thought that follows is lame, and wants introduction. (I.ii. 43)

[7] [*Ibid.*, 3.2.73ff.: Queen Margaret's speech to Henry VI]
The whole speech is cram'd full of false thoughts and *aukward* expressions, and that purposely; to shew that no word of it came indeed from the heart, but is all a strain'd affectation of a grief that is not felt. See how this same speaker bemoans herself when she is indeed touch'd, in the scene between her and Suffolk, and note the diversity. (I.ii.47f.)

[8] [*Ibid.*, 3.3: the death-scene of Cardinal Beauford]
A speech recorded by Hall of this Cardinal's suggested the awful scene we have here, and this thought in particular. The scene has never been equal'd on any theatre, never will be. (I.ii. 49)

[9] [*Ibid.*, 2.1.117: Suffolk's Latin speech, '*Pene gelidus timor occupat artus.*']
It is not known from whence the Latin of the page after this is taken. 'Tis suitable, and introduc'd with propriety; expressing the speaker's feelings, yet hiding from those who should not discover them. (I.ii. 51)

[10] [*Ibid.*, 5.1.109: 'Wouldst have me kneel?', and the importance of clear stage-directions, much neglected and confused in previous editions]
The ideas of this great Poet were as clear in the disposing his action and in the place of his scene as we see them in other matters; and he

---

[1] Capell takes the 'Bad' Quarto of this play, *The first part of the Contention betwixt the two famous Houses of Yorke and Lancaster* (1594), to be Shakespeare's first draught.

rarely fails to mark both of them properly by some expression or other in each scene. As they are both of great consequence to our obtaining a thorough conception of him, it has been a principal object with this editor to mark those expressions, and, when mark'd, to transplant into his directions of all sorts what they plainly suggested. (I.ii. 56)

[11] [On *3 Henry VI*, 2.5: King Henry's soliloquy on the battle-field]
In the working-up of this scene simplicity is push'd to the uttermost; and yet with such mastery in all the first part of it that we find ourselves strongly affected; in the latter part it degenerates, and we have there a conceit or two and some pastoral quaintnesses. (I.ii. 64)

[12] [*Ibid.*, 5.5.38: King Edward's stabbing of Prince Edward: 'Take that, the likeness of this railer here']
Taking it's latter words (as they should be) ironically, it is almost too horrid for Richard himself. Chroniclers report the fact diversly, as their extracts will shew; Shakespeare takes the way he thought fittest to give a striking image of that age's barbarity. (I.ii. 70–1)

[13] [On *Henry VIII*, 1.4.46ff.: a bawdy toast by Lord Sands, and Anne Bullen's equally bawdy reply]
These words are in character, and so is the health that follows: and in the Lady's reply to it (however we may condemn it as gross at this time of day) the Poet shews his great insight; for in this addiction to levities lay her character, or that which distinguish'd her, and she bled for them shortly. He gives us only this *trait* of it, his purpose leading him contrary; but 'tis a strong one, and may serve instead of a million. The King's portrait has always been acknowledg'd a finish'd one; and all who rise from the reading of it, rise with a full persuasion that they have seen the identical Henry lay'd on paper. One minute part of it, is a certain coarseness of diction, that has its dignity too; of this the concluding words of this act exhibit a specimen, and there is another before it in his reply to the Chamberlain. (I.ii. 81)

[14] [*Ibid.*, 3.1.41: Wolsey: '*Tanta est erga te mentis integritas, regina serenissima*']

The circumstance of addressing in Latin, the Poet had from his chronicle, but no Latin of any kind. That in the page before is his own; and, respecting only the flow of it, may vye with any rhetorical sentence in that language that can be produc'd. (I.ii. 86)

[15] [On *Julius Caesar*, 3.2.12ff.: Brutus' speech to the people] Every true admirer of Shakespeare has good cause for wishing that there had been some authority to question this speech's genuineness. But editions afford it not; and it has the sanction besides of many likenesses to other parts of his work, and of this in particular; in which we have already seen too great a number of things hardly defensible, and more are behind, some of which will be spoke to. The truth is, his genius sunk in some measure beneath the grandeur of Roman characters; at least in this play, which we may judge from thence to have been the first he attempted. His Cæsar is more inflated than great, and the oratory of this speech has no resemblance whatever to that which Brutus affected, which was a nervous and simple laconism. The last modern thinks the present harangue a design'd imitation of it; which can not be assented to, nor the Poet's knowledge of styles set so low. It is more likely that he either could not come up to it, or judg'd it improper, or else sacrific'd this and his other weaknesses to the bad taste of the people he writ for. For the dress he has put it in (that is, its prose), it may be conjectur'd, his motive was to distinguish it in that article likewise from the oration of Antony. All that follows is verse, or its portions; free verse. . . . (I.ii. 107–8)

[16] [*Ibid.*, 3.2.188: Antony: 'Even at the base of Pompey's statuë/(Which all the while ran blood)']
This verse's defect might proceed from intention, the event spoken of is impress'd by it stronger; which event has a place in all accounts of this action, and is much dwelt upon by those dealers in judgments the old recorders of it. Shakespeare, as a poet, improves on them; making it more a judgment than they do by representing this '*fall*' as quite contiguous, the '*statue*' sprinkl'd with '*blood*' and its '*base*' streaming with it, as altars with the blood of the sacrifice. But you will say, perhaps, that this was not a notion to be impress'd by this orator, and upon these hearers. True; nor was this his design, nor their conception of him. For the expressions have two faces: one, looking towards what has been mention'd, a sense

223

gather'd from history; the other, of meer pitifulness, excited by this description of one lying in wounds at the foot of his enemy, and that one a '*Cæsar*.' And to heighten this pitifulness, what is said of the *blood* is so express'd that its gross hearers would understand by it the blood of the insensible statue; weeping, as other statues had done in their opinion, at an act of such horror. (I.ii. 108–9)

[17] [On *King Lear*, 1.1.55ff.: Goneril: 'Sir, I love you more than words can wield the matter']
Not only the extravagance of these sisters' professions, but the words they are dress'd in paint their hearts to perfection. In Regan's we have '*Felicitate*,' an affected expression, and before it a line that's all affectation ['square of sense']; the governing phrase in it is borrow'd (as thinks the editor) from some fantastical position of the rosycrucians or cabalists, who use it . . . for—'the full complement of all the sense.' Goneril is nothing short of her sister in either particular, when her speech has it's due. (I.ii. 141)

[18] [*Ibid.*, 2.1.40ff.: Edmund pretending to Gloucester that Edgar had wanted him to join in the murder of their father]
His study'd delays, and his father's eagerness, are well painted; and when the son at last answers him [at 1.42], a wrong way should be pointed to . . . ; this, or words of this kind, is imply'd after '*made*,'—*Or how else it was, I know not, 'But suddenly he fled.'* Abruptions, and slips in construction, are the proper language of falsehood at first setting out; when it has gather'd breath and is settl'd its language is so too: and accordingly, Edmund proceeds roundly [at 11. 64ff.]. (I.ii. 154)

[19] [*Ibid.*, 2.3.10: Edgar: 'Blanket my loins, elf all my hair in knots']
What writer now would dare to coin two such verbs? Yet where find the words to express so well what is express'd in that line? (I.ii. 159)

[20] [*Ibid.*, 2.4.153: Lear: 'Do you but mark how this becomes the house!']
This is one of the lines that *mark* Shakespeare; and the disturbers of it, which have been many, have only shewn by their changes their small real acquaintance with him. '*The house*' is an expression

worthy his genius: fathers are not the heads only of a house or a family but its representatives; they are *the house*, what affects them affects the rest of its body. Regan therefore is call'd upon to observe an action in which she is concern'd and then say her opinion of it; and she does accordingly shew herself hurt by it, and declares it '*unsightly*,' unbecoming her and her father, *i.e. the house*. (I.ii. 160)

[21] [*Ibid.*, 3.2.68ff.: Lear: 'Come on, my boy. How dost, my boy?']
The king's tenderness for his fool (see his speech that comes next), and that fool's faithfulness and love of his master, are great height'nings both of the daughters' unnaturalness and (consequently) of this play's effect as a tragedy; the first shewing the king's affectionate nature, the other the just returns to such nature and the almost constant effects of it. To this love of his master should be attributed the satire that runs through all the fool's songs, his riming moralities, and almost his every speech that has fallen from him 'till now; being all seemingly calculated to awaken that master (under shew of diverting him) to a sense of his error, and to spur him on to some remedy. (I.ii. 164)

[22] [*Ibid.*, 3.4.9: the Folio reads 'suum, mun, nonny, Dolphin my Boy, Boy *Sesey*: let him trot by.']
That of the folio must have been the issue of the proper brain of those editors, or some one of their comrades who was wise enough to think that stuff without meaning might suit a madman; and he has accordingly fitted him with what is void of it absolutely, and this stuff the modern editors follow. But Shakespeare was of another opinion; his real nor his counterfeit madman throw out nothing that has not vestige of sense, nothing quite unintelligible: such a sense in this passage the quarto's, though corrupt, have preserv'd to us.

It now remains to acquaint you with what appears to this editor to be the general sense of the place they stand in. Edgar feigns himself one who is surveying his horses and marking their paces; that his '*boy*', whom he calls '*dolphin*' (or dauphin) is about to stop one of them, and cries out to that boy in wild language—'*Ha!* no, leave to do it; *let him trot by*.' If any one, upon the score of this *dolphin*, will say—he feigns himself Neptune, he shall not be oppos'd in it. Johnson sneers at this passage;[1] of which, possibly, he had as little conception as the player that alter'd it. (I.ii.167)

[23] [*Ibid.*, 3.4.129ff.: Edgar: 'Poor Tom, that eats the swimming frog, the toad . . . ']

What a picture does this speaker exhibit of the life and subsistence of such a wretch as he is then personating! What assemblage of all nature's abhorrences! (I.ii. 168)

[24] [*Ibid.*, 3.4.128ff.: Edgar:]

> Child *Rowland* to the dark tower came,
> His word was still, fie, fo, and fum,
> I smell the blood of a *British* man.

Such the words of this speech, and such the form of it in the folio's and all succeeding editions; nor has any interpretation been made of it more than of the words it begins with, which hardly wanted interpreting. For every observing reader of Spenser, and of the writers of his class, knows that '*child*' is a common appellative of the knight in romances, deriv'd from the first gross importers of them into our language from out the Spanish and French, in which he is call'd *enfant*, and *infante*; and all know that '*Rowland*' is only Roland pronounc'd rustically, and Roland a contraction of Orlando; so that *Child Rowland* is the knight sir Orlando. But what insight have we got by all this into the general sense of these lines, or their particular propriety? and yet the one and the other should be there, or Shakespeare is not the writer we take him for. Sense (certainly) they have none as they stand, for never any Orlando express'd himself as he is made to do there; and if sense be wanting propriety must be out of the question. The alteration of one word, and that made by authority of the quarto's, will assist in setting all things to rights. They have '*come*' instead of '*came*:' which *come* is put absolutely, as grammarians express it, and signifies being come; and is, moreover, a rime to '*fum.*' For what Edgar is made to say in this place is either really part of some ballad that is not yet discover'd, or else made to resemble one; is a stanza of such ballad,

---

[1] Johnson's note reads: 'Of this passage I can make nothing. I believe it corrupt: for wildness, not nonsense, is the effect of a disordered imagination. The quarto reads *hay no on ny, Dolphins, my boy, cease, let him trot by*. Of interpreting this there is not much hope or much need. But any thing may be tried.' (1765 edition, VI, p. 90; *Johnson on Shakespeare*, ed. A. Sherbo, New Haven, Conn., and London, 1968, p. 686).

and wants its second line. The purport of which line is not hard to guess at, and some critical readers who have attended to what has gone before will (perhaps) have anticipated the editor in what is to follow. In short, this lost line did certainly speak of some *Giant*, the inhabitant of that '*dark tower*,' and smeller-out of *Child Rowland* who comes to encounter him. It was thought too much presumption to perfect this stanza in the text; but the world may not be displeas'd to see it done in a note, and that in sense and rime too, as follows:

> Child *Rowland* to the dark tower come,
> The giant roar'd, and out he ran;
> His word was still,—*Fie, fo, and fum,*
> I *smell the blood of a* British *man.*

That the stanza has now a plain and just sense, it is suppos'd will be granted. But where (will some ask) is its propriety, its adaptation to persons and circumstances? This will be made as plain as the other by a brief recalling of facts, and observing the situation of Edgar.—Driven from his father by treachery, proclaim'd traitor by order of that father, and a price set upon his head; forc'd to assume the madman for safety, and take the shelter of a miserable hovel against the violence of a storm: when suddenly,—beyond his expectation, and enough to his terror no doubt,—he finds before the door of this hovel that very father whom he stands in such dread of; is spoke to by him, and bid to reenter it. Which as he is about to do this stanza drops into his mind; wild, and suitable to his character, and yet covertly expressive of his condition: for *Child Rowland* is he himself; the *dark tower* his hovel; and the *fie-fo-fum giant* his father Gloucester; who, he fears, might have the giant's sagacity, and accost him in no less dreadful a manner. (I.ii. 168–9)

[25] [*Ibid.*, 3.6.6f.: Edgar: 'Frateretto calls me . . . ']
This is spoken immediately upon Gloucester's exit, or rather while he is going, and not yet out of hearing. It all arises from him, and is a tacit memento to him, '*Nero*' being the image of his cruelty, and call'd '*angler in the lake of darkness*' only from being plung'd or immers'd in it. . . . Gloucester's parting expressions [l.3: 'I will not be long from you'] are strongly ominous, and (no doubt) were intended so. The next scene brings him to them indeed, but in a way that was not meant by him; making him partner in their

calamities, and fitting him for the society of him that was most wretched amongst them. (I.ii. 170)

[26] [*Ibid.*, 4.2.31ff.: Albany to Goneril: 'I fear your disposition;/That nature which contemns its origin/Cannot be bordered certain in itself']
The Poet's force of expression is the cause that many parts of these speeches want interpreting; and first, the part immediately following the words we have quoted.—The words of l.33. imply—that none have any *certain* assurance that such a *'nature'* as the former line speaks of will keep itself within such bounds as humanity and womanhood set to it, be *'border'd in itself;'* and are given as a reason, why the speaker fears his wife's *'disposition.'* The succeeding maxim is like it; but with this difference,—that it puts the lady on thinking what the end of such a nature will be: that as a branch sliver'd from the tree it sprang out of, and so parted from it's *'material* or radical *sap,'* withers, and comes to uses of fire; so she, who, by *contemning* her *origin*, tears herself from a father in the way that she and her sister had done, must expect the heaviest inflictions of providence in this world and the next. (I.ii. 174–5)

[27] [*Ibid.*, 4.5.4: Regan to Oswald: 'Lord Edmund spake not with your lord at home?']
This question, as it is now put, and as the folio's have given it, is of great consequence: the quarto's and the four latter moderns have made it an idle one, by reading *lady* for *'lord.'* For what imported it Regan to know if Goneril was spoke with *'at home?'* the matter that she dreaded might as well pass by the way, and in that she knew that *'Edmund'* accompany'd her. This question's answer, which (perhaps) she expected, encreases her jealousy; his abrupt sending-off without doing what he had in commission, (settling matters with Albany) has the appearance of hiding him, and of something private between him and the lady: which lady she is bent on anticipating, on being beforehand with her, and therefore speaks and acts openly; sending, as it should seem, by the Steward [at l.33] a ring to Edmund; with licence to tell all to his mistress, as well what she had done as what said. (I.ii. 177–8)

[28] [*Ibid.*, 4.6.183: Lear: 'This' a good block']
It has been ask'd, what is the meaning of *'block'* in this sentence,

and what connection it has with what is found in the sentence that follows it; for in such a writer as Shakespeare there is something like connection in the ideas even of a madman. In the speech before this the mode of Lear's madness is chang'd; it is calm, and shews some sparks of reason. He knows Gloucester, and his condition; tells him he must be patient; throws out one of the topicks of comfort, and says he will '*preach*' to him. Upon this he puts himself in posture of one who would preach, and pulls off his hat. Scarce has he utter'd a few words when some fumes of a wilder nature fly up; the *hat* catches his eye, and sets fire to another train of ideas. The words '*This a good block?*' are spoke looking upon the hat; and this is follow'd by a second conceit, which has its rise from the same circumstance, about '*felt*,' and the use it might be put to. (I.ii. 179–80)

[29] [*Ibid.*, 4.7: Capell points out confusion in the stage-directions in previous editions. Instead of having Lear carried on in a chair at line 23, he has him on-stage from the beginning of the scene, 'upon a Bed, asleep'. The Folios also omit line 24, given to the Doctor: 'Please you draw near.—Louder the music there!']
Their mode of bringing in Lear was a meer stage convenience; and for that conveniency too those folios sink the speech at l. 24, and (in that) a noble thought of the Poet's, in this editor's judgment. What he gathers from the words that conclude it, is this, that a soft '*musick*' should be heard at the scene's opening, and behind the bed, which is distant; that this musick had been Lear's composer, and (together with his composure) his cure; that it is now call'd-to by the Doctor for the purpose of waking him by such strains as were proper, rising gradually; which is not a noble thought only, but just, and of good effect on the scene. . . . (I.ii. 181)

[30] [*Ibid.*, 5.3.264ff.: Kent: 'Is this the promis'd end?' The two following speeches (Edgar: 'Or image of that horror?'; Albany: 'Fall and cease.') were omitted by Pope, Hanmer, Theobald, and Warburton, even though they are in both Quarto and Folio texts.]
What follows has the authority of both those impressions, and of strong and forcible reasons to boot, and yet is dismiss'd by them; namely the two speeches of Edgar and Albany following Kent's; speeches equally well adapted with his to the persons they come from, who are young and of quicker feeling than him, and yet are

made by four moderns (the four last) to stand by without any expression of it, and such a sight in their view. The impropriety of this could not but occur to these gentlemen: but the speeches that should cure it were difficult; and rather than be at pains to conceive them, rejection was chosen. And yet the pains requir'd were not great. The '*horror*' of which this sight was an image, according to Edgar, is the horror of the last day or day of judgment, call'd emphatically *that* horror. Albany's '*Fall, and cease!*' were made very intelligible by the action accompanying; the wide display of his hands and the lifting-up of his eye, both directed toward the heavens, would shew plain enough that it is they who are call'd upon to *fall*, and crush a world that is such a scene of calamity. The brevity of the expression in both speeches, which is the cause of their obscurity, is at the same time their greatest beauty. *Fall, and cease!* is—Fall, heaven! and let things cease! *Vide* this same play, [3.1.7: 'change or cease']. (I.ii. 188)

[31] [*Ibid.*, 5.3.284f.: Kent: 'Where is your servant Caius?' Lear: 'He's a good fellow, I can tell you that.']
Lear's speech at l.285 is much perfecter than alteration has made it. He knows '*Caius*' is living, and speaks of him as living at first. His speaking contrary afterwards is no other than a way of expressing his own perfect abandonment to all the outrage of fortune; who, he thinks, could never admit of that person's living who was either useful or dear to him. Hence he pronounces this person '*dead*', and long-since dead, to the great encrease of that speech's affection. Instantly upon this his mind breaks and is wand'ring, and he falls into a stupid and senseless apathy. Out of which he awakes in his last minutes, and gives vent to some other piercing exclaims; is suffocated almost by a rising of new grief, and, in the burst of it, dies. Of his apathy those expressions are evidence that come from him in two little speeches after that at l.285. Kent's reflection on one of them [l. 291] has great tenderness; his words have been misconceiv'd by some moderns, and therefore alter'd, their true force is as follows;—'Welcome, alas! here's no welcome for me or any one.' (I.ii. 189)

[32] [*Ibid.*, 5.3.305: Albany: 'O, see, see!']
The last words of his speech are occasion'd by seeing Lear exert himself to embrace the body he lay upon once more, and pour his

agonies over it. His expressions about the *'lips'* of that body might proceed from an imagination of motion in them; or else from some actual convulsive appearance, for such is said to have happen'd to bodies in that circumstance. Kent's finishing speech is a speech of despondency, of one who takes his leave of the world and all its concerns. And Albany, who, with due regard to his character, closes the dreadful scene of poor Lear's catastrophe, expresses his sense of it, and the impression it makes on him, by saying in his finishing sentence that his *life* would be shorten'd by it. (I.ii. 189)

[33] [On *Macbeth*, 1.3: the verse of the Witches' scene]
The measures us'd in this scene, their variety, and the peculiar aptness of some of them, are great height'ners of its numerous characteristical beauties; horror, and the wildness which opinion affixes to such characters, breathing as well in them as the images, which are selected with great happiness. The last page presents a very minute one at l.9, whose pertinency may not be perceiv'd, and yet explaining may be pay'd with derision. *Tails* are the rudders of water-animals, as the *'rat'* is occasionally; so that by the Witch's comparison is intimated in effect that she would find her port without rudder as well as sail in a sieve. (II.i. 2)

[34] [*Ibid.*, 1.5.1: Lady Macbeth (reading): *'They met me . . .'*]
Parcel only of a letter, as may now be seen by its form; so agreeable to the owner that she gives it another reading, and then descants upon it in the style of one that had given it consideration before. (II.i. 7)

[35] [*Ibid.*, 1.5.40: Lady Macbeth: 'Come, you spirits']
The *'spirits'* call'd upon next (1.40.), and by another name afterwards (1.48.), should be Dæmons; to whom ancient opinion imputed influence upon the *'thoughts,'* and all the *'mischiefs'* of nature or the creation. The visionary notions of witchcraft are mingl'd with this idea; and in the latter passage they are summon'd magnificently to suck encrease of malignity from the *'gall'* of her breasts. What pity that these and other sublimities utter'd in these addresses should have so poor a close as that metaphor gives them which concludes her last to the *'Night!'* ['the blanket of the dark'] (II.i. 7)

[36] [*Ibid.*, 1.5.44ff.: Lady Macbeth: 'nor keep peace between the effect and *it*': Folio reads '*hit*']
The substantive which the amended word stands for is—'*purpose:*' which *purpose* is represented as warring upon the '*effect*,' *i.e.* aiming to master it; and the evil powers above-mention'd are entreated to stop *remorse* and *compunction* from interfering in this war, *shaking* purpose, and *keeping peace* between that and the effect. This seems to have been the Poet's idea in his usage of this rather vulgar allusion—keeping peace, which is a second mole upon the beauty of his other conceptions in this speech. (II.i. 7–8)

[37] [*Ibid.*, 1.7.1ff.: Macbeth's soliloquy, 'If it were done . . . ']
'*Faculties*,' l.17, by which are meant commonly powers of body or mind, mean there the king's civil powers, his powers as a king. The exalted images following, of '*pity*' and the '*cherubin*,' are much injur'd in the three latter copies by changing '*couriers*' to *coursers*, which is '*horsing*' upon a *horse*. And the putting *side* in the text (as the fourth modern has done at [l.28]), instead of leaving it to the conception, destroys a capital beauty. The broken measure and broken sense of that line painting admirably the speaker's condition; appall'd (as he expresses it afterwards) even to starting, by the sound of his wife's tread. *v.* [2.2.55: 'How is't with me . . . '] (II.i. 9)

[38] [*Ibid.*, 2.2.34ff.: Macbeth's apostrophe to sleep]
In the middle parts of that speech *sleep* is characteriz'd as the *hurt mind's* balm, *labour's* bath, knitter-up or dissolver of *care's entanglements*, and death of '*life*.' The proper meaning of *life*, thus connected, is a life of woe and calamities; quieted for a while, at the conclusion of each day, by the short death of sleep; a longer sleep will be its final and true quieter. (II.i. 12)

[39] [*Ibid.*, 2.3: the Porter's scene: omitted by Pope and Hanmer]
This soliloquy of the Porter, and his subsequent discourse with Macduff, cannot be parted with at any rate; as it is by the second and fourth moderns, who begin their scene with Macduff's question at [l.42: 'Is thy master stirring?']: which question the asker answers himself, and Macbeth's entry succeeds it immediately, or co-incides with it rather, for he is seen entring. So that nothing (in effect) intervenes between his exit and entry, his

dress cannot be shifted, nor his *hands* wash'd, and he must come on as he can, full mark'd with these testimonies of his guilt. To give a rational space for discharge of these necessary actions, was this excluded scene thought of; which is masterly in its way, and open to no objections but such as lye against all comic mixture with things serious. (II.i. 12–13)

[40] [*Ibid.*, 2.3.112ff.: Macbeth: 'His silver skin lac'd with his golden blood'. Pope had emended to 'goary': cf. Johnson's comment, Vol. 3, p. 176]
The change is uncritical; *goary* is full as idle as '*golden.*' In truth, amendment of any sort (if it could be attain'd) there, and in other parts of that speech, would counteract the poet's intention. His ridiculous metaphors, strain'd thoughts, and unnatural expressions must have been design'd (as is observ'd by the last modern) as paintings of one that acted a part, and felt nothing of what he labour'd to set so tragically forth. From this source issu'd those much-contested expressions in l.116; '*breech'd with gore*' is bloody'd up to the hilt, up to its haft or dudgeon, as that visionary dagger is painted which presents itself to the speaker [at 2.1.33]; '*unmannerly*' is savagely, contrary to civil manners, and is predicated of the action of stabbing, justly censur'd for savageness, when daggers were plung'd up to their hilts. But the terms (as said before) are unnatural, perhaps more so than the intention can justify. (II.i. 14)

[41] [*Ibid.*, 3.2.16: Macbeth: 'But let the frame of things disjoint, both the worlds suffer'. Pope rewrote this line]
But in what a state is that thought transmitted to us by moderns! The second (who never willingly pardon'd any the Poet's noble redundancies, nor stuck at means of retrenching them) jumbles the words of l.16. in strange manner, and out of them rose the nonsense that follows;—*But let both worlds disjoint, and all things suffer*; and this his successors take from him and hand down without noting that 'tis a change. Shakespeare's line imports a will in the speaker that the frame of nature should perish, and even his own interests, here and in the world to come, suffer and be confounded. What their line means let others find if they can; in the editor it excites the idea of a couple of paste-board globes crush'd together. (II.i. 16–17)

[42] [*Ibid.*, 3.2.49: Macbeth: 'that great bond/Which keeps me pale']
The '*bond*' spoke of is the moral tye on the speaker to abstain from actions similar to that he was about and had then order'd. Of this bond '*Night*' is made the tearer and canceller, as under her veil would pass the action that did it. The scene is in the highest degree beautiful, both for passion and poetry; we see the '*bat*' and his cloister, the light thick'ning, and the '*crow*' upon wing, and even hear the '*beetle*' in the expressions that paint him. (II.i. 17)

[43] [On *Measure for Measure*, 2.2.117–34: Isabella's appeal to Angelo]
We may not admire the thought of this passage, but the poet must father it; nor greatly that of a passage after. . . . The thought there, and again in her next speech is not just, nor quite fit for the speaker; that they have Lucio's applause condemns their justness; but she only vents them as '*sayings*,' and as an artful introduction to the *argumentum ad hominem* which she urges soon after. (II.i. 39–40)

[44] [*Ibid.*, 3.2.261ff.: the Duke: 'He who the sword of heaven will bear/Should be as holy as severe']
Speeches, and parts of speeches, in rime, (some in measures properly lyrical, like the sententious one here) are found in all parts of Shakespeare; and should be look'd upon as the time's vices, sacrifices of judgment to profit, but not always unwilling ones; for such speeches are not of ill effect in all places, of which the present is instance. But his lovers have cause to wish, notwithstanding, that he had less consider'd his audiences and comply'd less with their taste; for it happens but too often that constraints of rime or of measure operate badly on his expression, causing breaches of grammar, strange and scarce allowable ellipsis's, and usage of terms improper. What, for instance, but the necessities spoken of shall excuse the expression of that couplet which follows this we have quoted?[1] which before we can have any conception of we must first supply a (*to*) before '*go*' to make it grammar; and that done, our conception may be as follows;—that he may *know* or find *in himself* a *pattern* of good walking, feel a *grace* enabling *to stand* in it, *and* a *virtue* of power *to go* or press forward. . . . The concluding lines of this speech owe their darkness to purpose. They are

---

[1] 'Pattern in himself to know,/Grace to stand, and virtue go'.

riddles, but not of any great difficulty; nor altogether so free of it that the following short comment should be look'd upon as an affront:—so the feigning Angelo shall, by means of me a feign'd friar, be punish'd with false Isabel for his false attempt on her, and made perform his old contract with Mariana.

In these lyrical speeches, as we may call them, there is almost always in Shakespeare an interchange of those iso-dunamous measures, the Iambic and the Trochaic: in this the intermixture is equal; eleven lines of each measure being the speech's whole complement, which is mention'd as a memento to the reciter. (II.i. 49–50)

[45] [On *The Merry Wives of Windsor*, 1.1.128: Bardolph to Slender: 'You Banbury cheese!']
Sarcasm upon Slender's thinness; which, the speaker would insinuate, was as outrageous as that of the cheeses of this denomination, the manufacture of a town in Oxfordshire. This remark may appear trivial, and even ridiculous, to a multitude of readers; but may not be so look'd upon by foreigners, and times long distant. (II.i. 77)

[46] [On *Much Ado About Nothing*, from the head-note]
What the player editors say in their preface of the mind and hand of this Poet's going together, and of his making no blots, if we can give it credit of any play it must be of this. Its fluency is prodigious; and the hasty current of it has (possibly) betray'd its writer at times into expressions we may condemn. (II.i. 119)

[47] [*Ibid.*, 2.1: the masking-scene. Whereas Rowe, and later editions, make Margaret and Ursula enter at line 1, Capell brings them on at line 86, so giving much better sense to the passage where Ursula penetrates Antonio's disguise (ll. 112–24); otherwise they have been on-stage together from the beginning, and would have known each other's identity]
Just conceptions of an action that is presenting are as necessary as a just conception of words; they are drawn indeed from the words, where directions are not assisting, but by a larger view of them than a reader is often willing to take. Of the busy action of this scene no view whatever can help us to such conception, reading it in the moderns. They set out with making Hero's two gentle-

women, Margaret and Ursula, enterers with their mistress; contrary to old editions and contrary to reason, such entry enhancing much the consistency of what passes between Antonio and Ursula. . . . [Capell reconstructs the sequence of entry and conversation.] Leonato (the house's master), his niece, daughter, and brother, enter before the rest, and they only are privy to each other's persons and dresses. They receive their visitors, masqu'd; and the Prince—having singl'd-out Hero by chance or otherways,—after a few speeches open, engages her in a conversation apart, his last words intimating its nature. While this is passing between them Benedick, who is in search after Beatrice, lights upon Margaret; a sharp one, her voice suiting her sharpness. This voice (which she raises at l.104) betrays her to Benedick, who quits her smartly and hastily, a manner resented slightly by Margaret, who expresses it in her prayer; for her *good dancer* means one that could move as nimbly as the one who had just left her. The remaining part of the action, down to the masquers' exit inclusive, is now perfectly clear'd (as we conceive) by the present words of that exit and of some preceding directions. (II.i. 121–2)

[48] [On *Othello*, 1.3.139: Othello: 'And portance in my travel's history']
The simple meaning of which is 'And how I bore myself in those travels of which I gave him the history'. But the dress it wears in this diction adapts it to character, and the dignity of tragedy. (II.i. 140)

[49] [*Ibid.*, 2.1.303f.: Iago: 'this poor trash of Venice, whom I trace for his quick hunting']
This passage's metaphor does not begin at '*trash*', as editors have fancy'd, but at '*trace;*' with which *trash* is combin'd for the only sake of allitterating. The word is us'd in great seriousness, and in the sense it bears always, the sense in which Bianca is treated with it by this same speaker, at [5.l.85]; but the metaphor part is all ironical. '*Quick hunting*' is hunting with quick scent: a leading hound of this sort is in most packs; and when he opens, the rest '*trace*' him, follow him in his track, without employing their own scents. Such a hound the speaker makes Roderigo sarcastically; adding, to make the sarcasm fuller, that if this quick-scented hound would but '*stand the putting-on*' upon scents that were found for

him, he the finder would do so and so. The particular scent intended at present is the scheme against Cassio just imparted. (II.i.143)

[50] [*Ibid.*, 4.1.1ff.: Iago: 'Will you think so?']
This is both a singular and a natural opening of this fourth act. It is plainly seen in this speech and the two following what artifice Iago had been upon before ent'ring, and how it had been receiv'd. In going on he grows more explicit; and on bringing the matter home to the point that was first intended, we see its dreadful effect in the 'Fit' produc'd by it. What he administers as comforts, under colour that they were customary liberties and might be innocent, are insinuations that Desdemona had us'd them; in his second there is allusion (undoubtedly) to the practices of some religious enthusiasts, ancient or modern. (II.i.151)

[51] [On *Richard II*, 5.1: editors make Act V begin with the scene where the Queen meets Richard on his way to the Tower]
The making Act the fifth begin here is absurd every way; and must have been the players' contrivance, who first broach'd it for some stage purpose of clearing away the pageantry that had been us'd in the last scene. The poor King's commitment closes properly the action of his deposing, and should not be disjoin'd from it. His death, and the circumstance by which it was forwarded (*viz*. the conspiracy), is as properly the subject of Act the fifth and the last, and admits no extraneous one. Add too, that in the division obtaining hitherto the fourth is but of one scene, and is disproportion'd in length; that that one closes, as it were, with the King's exit for the place of his commitment; and that reason requires his meeting the Queen on his way thither should have no such intervention as their division creates for it. (II.i. 170)

[52] [On *Richard III*, 1.2: 'Enter the corse of Henry the sixth'. Capell notes that the interment of the king took place on 29 May 1471, according to Stow, and that Richard married the lady he courts here soon afterwards, since their son was aged 10 when created Prince of Wales in July 1483]
The action then of this scene (that is, the enterrment) is in truth the play's first, according to history, upon which the poet is trespasser six year at least, in making the commitment of Clarence a prior

incident. But the step was necessary for the better knitting together this life's enormities, and disposing them into a play; which is done with great artifice, difficulties being consider'd. His bringing into't queen Margaret, is another trespass; but one that none will condemn in him after seeing the many beauties produc'd by it. (II.i. 174)

[53] [On *Romeo and Juliet*, from the head-note: Shakespeare's intention in using a chorus]

The chief service it was design'd for was taking-off the attention from overmuch marking a fault in his action's conduct; namely, an individual's quick appearance in one place who had just been seen in another; and for this it is render'd useless by their disposition,[1] an Act's interval (as in them) doing the thing as well. But how absurd is that interval! A lover of Romeo's stamp, newly struck, must return instantaneously, let scenery say what it will; the action was unavoidable, and what offence there is in it is well cover'd by the invention of that Chorus. [By his Act-division, Capell claims, the Acts are of more equal length, and also correspond to the structural divisions of the play.] The first is now strictly the thing it ought to be, a *protasis* of the action, without further engaging in it. In the second the inflammable Romeo catches fire at a new love; has an interview with her; is well heard, and a marriage agreed upon. The third settles the time of marriage, and perfects it; interposes a fatal chance between that and consummating; means at last are concerted for it, and the Act closes with laying seeds for what brings on the catastrophe. In the fourth the newly-united lovers take leave and seperate; a new marriage is press'd upon Juliet; a draught swallow'd by her to avoid it, and the destin'd bridegroom and parents find her seemingly dead. Within these three lyes what criticks consent to call the *epitasis*; and upon them ensues the drama's *catastrophe*, defining necessarily the fifth Act in the present copy and others. But the management of all before in those others is the strangest imaginable. Their several actions or businesses, which are each a sort of unities now, are all broke by them, and their times likewise; to the great dark'ning in our conceptions of the progress of the general action, and the

---

[1] Other editors make the second chorus ('Now old desire doth in his death-bed lie') mark the transition from Act I to Act II. Capell places it between his 2.2 and 2.3; 2.1 in most editions is his 2.3.

introducing of some absurdities: *v.* the latter scenes of their third act. [In which the parting of Romeo and Juliet at dawn follows immediately after the 'Good night' of Capulet (3.4.35); in Capell this scene begins Act IV, thus giving an interval between the two scenes.] (II.i.1–2)

[54] [*Ibid.*, 1.3: the scene between Lady Capulet and the Nurse] The better half of this scene has worn hitherto the habit of prose in all preceding editions, old and new. The freedom of Shakespeare's numbers, in comic characters, suited not the poetical modern who gave the *ton* to those after him in all affairs of this sort, and his edition disclaiming them, the others disclaim them too; though a greater stain on their Author can hardly be than to pass upon us as prose of his writing such apparent verse as are the speeches [From ll. 1 to 59]. (II.i. 4)

[55] [*Ibid.*, 2.4.46–100: the punning wordplay between Romeo and Mercutio, all of which was omitted by Pope and Warburton] The omitted part's wit is not greatly to be applauded; neither is it very much short of what we have from the same speaker, Mercutio, before and after. Romeo's share of it shews him in a new light, and one that he is no where else seen in, a match for the other's best in his own way; his cause of being so lying in his newly-rais'd spirits from what had happen'd. This last consideration alone should have repriev'd it: but when we add its authentickness (which appears on the face of it) and its great and open necessity for producing fit junction, we cannot but stand amaz'd at that criticism which has thought omission permissible. (II.ii. 10)

[56] [*Ibid.*, 4.3.38ff.: Juliet's soliloquy before drinking the potion] That elliptical mode of speaking at [4.2.31ff.] is common, and a beauty in free discourse. In [4.3.38ff.] we have beauties that are something related to it, but of a higher kind; for, but those elliptical breakings-off in that fine speech, nothing could have painted so well a mind so agitated. Two attempts are made by the speaker to say what would be her state if she *liv'd*; but the horrors of her condition intrude on her, and her thread is twice broke ere this point is concluded. (II.ii. 17)

[57] [On *The Taming of the Shrew*, 1.1.239ff.: Tranio: 'So could I, faith, boy, to have the next wish after,/That Lucentio indeed had Baptista's youngest daughter']

The whole of this speech is injur'd as well in moderns by them making it prose. The speech after it wears in all old editions its verse form, and the first modern keeps it; but that too loses it in the rest, and even the rime of these speeches was not sufficient to awaken a poetical editor to a discovery that so openly offers itself though rime had been. For prose has its numbers, and the ear feels them; but the numbers of these speeches are not those of any prose whatsoever. Their rime is of the whimsicalest, and next to none in one couplet. But we see this elsewhere, and both there and here in that whimsicalness lyes the places' chief humour: foreign and dead languages are made to bend and contribute to it, and English measures and rimes appear in those idioms; as in a page before this, where a sentence of Terence is molded into a riming six-foot heroick,[1] and a while after comes a riming Italian couplet in English dogrel.[2] (II.ii. 27–8)

[58] [On *The Tempest*, 1.1: 'A tempestuous noise of thunder and lightning heard']

No well-advis'd poet will think, at this time of day, of bringing into his piece an action like to that of this scene; as, under every advantage that stages now derive from their scenery, or can ever derive were mechanism even push'd to the utmost, such action will want the power of imposing in that degree that we ourselves have made necessary. But this touch'd not Shakespeare, his imposing was not by eyes but by ears; the former his stage deny'd him, (see a note upon *Antony and Cleopatra*[3]) and therefore left him at liberty to fix upon any action that lik'd him, and that suited his plot. The other mode of imposing he has been at pains to provide for, by drawing his sea-characters justly, and by putting into their mouths the proper terms of their calling. (II.ii. 54)

[59] [*Ibid.*, 1.2.66ff.: Prospero: 'My brother and thy uncle, call'd Antonio—/I pray thee mark me—that a brother should/Be so perfidious!—he whom. . .']

---

[1] 'If love have touch'd you, nought remains but so,/"*Redime te captum quam queas minimo*"' (1.1.161f.).

[2] '*Alla nostra casa bene venuto—/Molto honorato signior mio Petruchio*' (1.2.25f.)

[3] See *Notes and Various Readings*, part i (1774), pp. 51–3.

There is great perplexity in the construction of this speech, owing evidently to the number of circumstances parenthetically thrown into it; which mode of speaking is not us'd without design, but affected here and in other places, particularly of this scene, to mark a branch of Prospero's character, which is garrulity. [Subsequently] the speaker himself is lost in his own deviations; and reduc'd, in l.77, to the necessity of beginning his tale anew. (II.ii. 56)

[60] [*Ibid.*, 1.2.229: 'the still-vex'd Bermoothes'. Capell defends this spelling, being a 'defective attempt to give in English the Spanish sound of Bermudas', and indicates that Shakespeare could not have learned about them 'earlier than 1612, perhaps later'] These are the reasons: in 1609 sir George Sommers (of whom the islands are also call'd Sommer Islands), the first Englishman certainly, and for ought appears to the contrary the first European who set his foot on them, was cast upon them by shipwreck; stay'd a year on them; return'd to them again from Virginia, and then dy'd on them. That colony calls them within its limits; and the then managers of it sold them to some particulars, members of their society, who in April 1612 '*sent thither a ship with 60 persons, who arived and remayned there very safely.*' The furnisher of these particulars, and of the extract that follows them, speaking of the islands themselves, says further, they were '*of all Nations said and supposed to bee inchanted and inhabited with witches and devills, which grew by reason of accustomed monstrous Thunder, storme, and tempest neere unto them.*' Now as these particulars must, from the nature of them, have been the subject as well of writings as talk at the time they were passing, the presumption is, first, that the afore-mention'd epithet rose from them; and next, that they were also suggesters of Sycorax and her sorceries, of the preter-natural Being subjected to her, and of Prospero's magick; which if it be allow'd, then is this play prov'd by it a late composition, and weight added to the opinion that makes it the Poet's last; a circumstance that might determine the players to place it foremost in their publish'd collection. (II.ii. 58)

[61] [*Ibid.*, 2.1.9–107: the punning wit of the dialogue between Antonio, Sebastian, and Gonzalo. Pope declared this an in-

terpolation of the actors, and omitted it for its 'impertinence and impropriety']

... charges that lye against it most certainly, almost beyond palliating; but of its authenticity we have other-guess evidence; and in that very speech first which, according to this opinion, should follow the present speech. For what can be made without it (as is said by the next modern) of that wish which begins in his second line, by readers who, but in what intervenes, have heard nothing of any *'daughter'* he has, or where she's *'marry'd'* to? The condemn'd passage is not without other proofs of authentickness, but this one is sufficient. And in ease of what is objected to it, it may be observ'd that the levities of Sebastian and partner open to us their characters, and prepare us for what is coming; shewing them nothing touch'd with their own and their king's deliverance, and their common condition; and their behaviour on this occasion sets off and heightens the love, loyalty, and sobriety of the other parties attending, and chiefly Gonzalo's. (II.ii. 62)

[62] [*Ibid.*, 2.1.148ff.: Gonzalo's ideal commonwealth]
The speech that offers these changes, and one after it, prove the writer's acquaintance with one he has not been trac'd in by any annotator or editor; for thus old Montaigne, speaking of the Indian discovery and of the new people's manners: 'C'est une Nation, diray-je a Platon, en laquelle il n'y a *aucune esperance de trafiq, nulle cognoissonce de Lettres*, nulle science de nombres, *nul nom de Magistrat*, ny de superiorité politique, *nul usage de service, de richesse, ou de pauvreté, nuls contracts, nulles successions, nuls partages, nulles occupations qu' oysives*, nul respect de parenté que commun, nuls vestements, *nulle agriculture, nul metal, nul usage de vin ou de bled. Les paroles mesmes, qui signifient* le mensonge, *la trahison*, la dissimulation, l'avarice, l'envie, la detraction, le pardon, *inouyes*. Combien trouveroit il la Republique qu'il a imaginée, loin de cette perfection?' (*Essais de* Montaigne, 3. *Vol.* 12°. 1659. Bruxelles. *Vol. 1.* p. 270.) This person who shall compare this passage with the translations of it that were extant in Shakespeare's time will see reason to think he read it in French. (II.ii. 63)

[63] [*Ibid.*, 4.1.60ff.: the Masque]
Written in compliance with fashion, the time swarming with them (witness the works of Jonson, which in manner are sunk by them),

242

and against the grain seemingly, being weak throughout, faulty in rimes, and faulty in its mythology. Matters not within the province of Ceres, such as '*sheep*' and '*vines*,' are attributed to her both in the speech of Iris and the ill-riming song; and, were moderns follow'd in some of the speech's readings, *flowers* likewise, its '*pioned*' and '*tilled*' being in them *pionied* and *tulip'd*. The propriety of other matters that follow, as the '*broom-groves*' that yield a '*shadow*' for walking in, the '*pole-clipt vineyard*' (once imagin'd a hop-ground), and the '*sea-marge, steril and rocky-hard*,' for Ceres to '*air*' herself, is past the editor's fathoming, and must be left by him to heads of more reach. (II.ii. 68)

[64] [*Ibid*., the Epilogue]
The epiloguizing speech is in the magical character, the latter part strongly; for in that is found a happy allusion to the reputed '*ending*' of magicians and negromancers. The speech's numbers are various, passing from the Iambic to trochees, and then Iambicks again, as is this Poet's custom; and in two of his Iambicks we have the foot of one syllable, which has examples elsewhere; but the speech is eas'd of them in the four latter moderns by the thrusting-in of some expletives into its third and twelfth line. (II.ii. 73)

[65] [On *Timon of Athens*, from the head-note, on the corrupt nature of its text]
The multitude of its corruptions in old copies, and of those particularly of the sort that this speech suffers, distinguish the play before us from almost any in Shakespeare; and 'tis but very small part of them that have been discover'd and mended by later editors. It has both the same origin with the plays upon Roman subjects (namely, Plutarch), and carries with it the same marks in its verse; points that weigh with the editor to make him think them all four compositions of like date, and struck off together or as 'twere at one heat. If there be amongst them a play of another æra, it should be the *Julius Cæsar*, for the measures of that are what would now be call'd purer (something purer) than those of its three companions. (II.ii. 73)

[66] [*Ibid*., 4.3.68f.: Alcibiades: 'How came the noble Timon to this change?' Timon: 'As the moon does, by wanting light to give']

A most exalted conception, rising by just degrees, and in the end over-whelming us; for who can read the hemistich and not be lost in astonishment? another almost its equal begins at ll. 109ff.: 'Be as a planetary plague when Jove/Will o'er some high-vic'd city hang his poison/In the sick air.' (II.ii. 87)

[67] [*Ibid.*, 4.3.177ff.: Timon: 'Common mother, thou'—*digging the earth*]
[Here Shakespeare makes] display of that Genius which could rise at once and unaided to the grandeurs of ancient imag'ry. . . . (II.ii.90)

[68] [On *Titus Andronicus*: from the head-note. Capell thinks that Shakespeare's source was the ballad 'The Lamentable and Tragicall History of Titus Andronicus', but that he probably] had also the assistance of that which was the ballad's ground-work, some barbarous history, the produce of monkish ignorance, and an absolute forgery. However that be, he has shewn his own better reading in some of his play's dressings; in which are classic quotations and classical images, but of a low form, and that smell of the ferula. And such, no doubt, was his learning, which he carry'd through life, adding to it a knowledge of the Italian and French languages proportion'd to this of Latin; and the reasons we have it in greater quantity in this play, and in the rest that are touch'd upon in some pages of the '*Introduction*,' [see Vol. 5, pp. 319f.] are, first, that the times requir'd it, as those other plays testify that were his models for this; and next, that he was in better capacity to feed this strange humour, his school learning hanging about him fresh. Nor is he only an imitator in this business of interlarding these his first plays with scraps of Latin; but their numbers too, and those of this play especially, are the numbers of that time's play-wrights; too constrain'd and too regular, and wanting that rich variety which his ripen'd judgment and experience of what was proper for dialogue and for the ease of delivery, taught him to introduce by degrees into plays that came after them. (II.ii. 99)

[69] [*Ibid.*, 3.1.249ff.: Marcus: 'Alas, poor heart, that kiss is comfortless.']
'*To* Lavinia, *seeing her kiss the Heads of her Brothers*', had follow'd

these words as a direction, would the place have admitted it. The
behaviour of all these personages upon this dreadful occasion is
singularly proper, and the horrid '*laugh*' of the father has
something great in it, even for Shakespeare. (II.ii. 105)

[70] [On *Troilus and Cressida*, 1.1.48: Troilus: 'O Pandarus! I tell
thee, Pandarus,—']
This sweet character, model of faithful love and its purity, is too
enrapt in this place to speak connectedly, and his line has no suite;
the thread is broken, and drop'd, and another taken up; and that
too, towards its middle, is spun nearly too thin for holding. (II.ii.
115)

[71] [*Ibid.*, 1.2.196: Cressida to Pandarus: 'Will he give you the
nod?']
To '*give the nod*' was never any phrase, as has been asserted, for 'to
give one a mark of folly'; 'tis a meer extempore archness of that
speaker, and a laying-out for that proverbial expression which
follows in [l. 198], importing—being a *noddy* now, you shall be
more noddy then. The character of the lady is open'd with great art:
we have seen her libertine cast in some speeches gone by, [ll. 117,
129f.] and more follow; and her soliloquy upon quitting the scene
prepares us for what ensues, for in that is seen the jilt and the artful
one. (II.ii. 116f.)

[72] [*Ibid.*, 1.3: the Greek council scene]
The speeches we are now come to want the best of pointing, and
great care has been taken that they should be so furnish'd; but they
will want besides all a reader's attention, knowledge of
Shakespeare's manner, and some aids from the '*Glossary*,' ere that
veil will be penetrated which conciseness, oratory, figures highly
daring in most places, overmuch so in some, throw on those of this
scene and on some of a following, the third of act III; for of them,
though not of the play in general, that observation holds good [by
Pope, that the play is full 'of observations, both moral and
politick'.] (II.ii. 116)

[73] [*Ibid.*, 1.3.54–69: Ulysses' praise of the speeches of
Agamemnon and Nestor]
This specimen of his oratory shews the speaker a flatterer; which

was indeed a branch of his character, but 'tis carry'd too far. Some Homerican outlines appear too in those of the other personages, Trojan and Greek, but very imperfect; and no wonder, when the poet's aids in designing them were (probably) no other than what he gather'd from Chapman, or in conversation. (II.ii. 118)

[74] [*Ibid.*, 4.5.19–53: Cressida's being kissed by the Greeks 'in general'. Pope and Warburton omitted this sequence]
Reason there is none but dislike of it, for which perhaps there are grounds; but the misfortune is, it cannot be parted with; the sending Cressida off as they do is a first-rate absurdity, as a brother observes upon them, whose reasons are nothing hard to collect. The wipe[1] Patroclus receives from her at [ll.38f.: 'The kiss you take is better than you give'] is of like nature with some he finds from Thersites in places that we have seen and shall see. What Ulysses addresses to her [at ll. 54ff.] is a wipe on his part, and a rebuke for her forwardness; the words of his third speech [ll. 49f.] import a declining the kiss he is bid to '*beg*,' and his fourth [l. 52] does it openly; which gives occasion to Diomed, who sees his lady affronted, to call her off. The fine description that follows of her and others her like has terms truly Shakespearian, that ask a little explaining: '*motive*' is moving power; '*coasting welcome*' seems a metaphor taken from shipping, who salute in passing by putting out their colours; '*ere it comes*' is ere the tongue gives it; and '*spoils of opportunity*' is the spoil'd by opportunity, by well-tim'd advantages which the spoiler, man, takes of them. (II.ii. 133–4)

[75] [*Ibid.*, 5.2.142ff.: Troilus' speech after witnessing his betrayal by Cressida: 'O madness of discourse,/That cause sets up with and against itself']
Reflecting on something passing within him that contradicted his late assertions: they had hitherto gone on the side of '*This is not she;*' and now his exclamation's conclusion is, '*this is, and is not Cressid.*' This '*discourse*' of his reason, passing inwardly, and setting up arguments (*causes*) with and against itself, he calls '*madness*' and a '*bifold* (two-fold) *authority;*' and then proceeds to lay down (explain it is not) wherein this *bi-foldness* lay, in this strange manner: '*where reason can revolt/Without perdition, and loss assume all reason/Without revolt;*'—the decyphering of which the annotator who has pro-

[1] Wipe: insult, mockery.

ceeded thus far must leave to others, with this apology for himself:
Davus sum, non Oedipus.[1]

The *'inseperate thing'* in l.48, is the speaker's union with Cressida,
which he thought was inseperable, but finds now, by a fight
commenc'd in his soul, that there is *division* made in it which is at
once wide as sky is from earth and of such subtlety withal that
seperation is unperceiveable. This enigma he solves by calling for
instances; and finds one in his heart which tells him that Cressida is
still his, and so no seperation; another in his remembrance of
what had but just pass'd, that contradicts his heart and makes
division unmeasurable. Passion, labouring to express itself
strongly, is the cause of this intricacy, and withal of that beautiful pleonasm at the speech's conclusion, which sets Diomed's conquest in a light so disgustful ['fractions of her faith, orts of her
love,/The fragments, scraps, the bits and greasy relics/Of her o'er-
eaten faith, are given to Diomed']. Antiquity may be challeng'd to
shew in all its descriptions an apter, grander, stronger and juster-
worded comparison than Troilus fetches a while after to illustrate
his sword's violence: the impetus of a *spout*'s vortex creates a
corresponding one in the sea, which has some appearance of '*ear*;'
and its noise is such that this *ear of Neptune* may well be said to be
dizzy'd by it. (II.ii. 137f.)

[76] [On *Twelfth Night*, 1.5.51f.: the Clown to Maria: 'As there is
no true cuckold but calamity, so beauty's a flower.']
Apothegms in such a mouth as this speaker's are of themselves
laughable, and the Poet has made them doubly and trebly so by
giving him such as have no relation whatever one to other, and yet
putting them argument-wise; by corrupting one of them oddly,
'cuckold' for *school* or else (which is the Oxford text) *counsellor*; and
by both these methods obscuring their little pertinency to what is
in hand, and making shew as they had none. But this is not the case
absolutely; his first murder'd apothegm squints at his *'turning
away,'* and his latter is a memento to this lady. Much of this
gentleman's wit lyes in coining strange names, and putting words
out of joint, sometimes oddly enough; specimens of his manner in
this page, are *'Quinapalus,'* and *'dexteriously';* and at [2.3.22ff.]
comes a much stranger knot of them. (II.ii. 142)

---

[1] Terence, *Andria*, 194: 'I am Davus, not Oedipus'.

[77] [*Ibid.*, 5.1.389ff.: the Clown: 'When that I was . . . ']
Either this song was one then in vogue, which he who personated
the Clown (M^r. Kemp, perhaps) might be famous for singing; or
else the composition of him the said Clown, and so lug'd into the
play without rime or reason; or if indeed Shakespeare's
writing—of which it has small appearance—a thing idly drop'd
from him upon some other occasion, and recommended by the air
it was set to. For to the play it has no relation; not is it suitable to
the person 'tis given to, who is a wag, and no fool, and therefore
cannot with any propriety be made the retailer of so much
nonsense as is contain'd in this song. Whoso wishes to strike a few
sparks of reason from it must lay aside the grammarian and turn
decypherer; as thus: the pursuits of this speaker and his disappointments in some of them, in four stages of life, are severally
describ'd in as many stanza's. In the first, his Infancy; the follies of
which were consider'd as follies and not regarded, '*a foolish thing was
but a toy;*' his Youth inclin'd him something to knavery, and to be a
little light-finger'd, but in this he had but sorry success, for '*gainst
knaves and thieves men shut their gate.*' Nor had he much better luck in
his confirm'd Manhood; when, thinking to rule the wife he then
took by big-talking and '*swaggering,*' he *throve* ill in his project, and
found himself mistaken in that too. The fourth and last stage of
him, Age (wickedly express'd by '*when I came unto my beds*') drove
him to be companion with '*toss-pots,*' and endeavour to drown his
cares in good liquor. The concluding stanza is made to epilogize, is
intelligible, and something in character, for its connection with
those that preceed it is a meer badinage. But what connection there
is, or what propriety, in the burden of the stanzas afore-said, it will
be hard to discover; unless we shall be pleas'd to admit that the
sorrows of life, and the troubles which attend it throughout, are
alluded-to in the words of that burden. (II.ii. 153)

[78] [On *The Two Gentlemen of Verona*: from the head-note. Pope
had observed that the style of this play was less figurative and more
natural than most of Shakespeare, 'though suppos'd to be one of
the first he wrote']
—Why that is the cause: and this simpleness, or (more properly)
tameness, is the character of all his first plays, more or less; as
would appear on tracing-out their succession, a thing that may be
attempted. Within no long time he knew his audiences better, and

having felt their pulse, and his own powers, he fell into a diction more animated, and numbers of more variety. As those other pieces came on it is probable that this was lay'd by; and with it one its cotemporary and in many respects its brother, the *Comedy of Errors*, for a leading circumstance of that play, and one of the present, are pick'd out by him as materials for the play that was last commented [*Twelfth Night*], which follow'd these we are speaking of at the distance of some ten or twelve years at least. (II.ii. 154)

[79] [*Ibid.*, 5.4.83: Valentine to Proteus: 'All that was mine in Silvia I give thee']
That proceeding of Valentine's which brings on this re-union of Proteus with Julia, has an odd appearance undoubtedly; and can scarce be made rational but by conceiving it a tryal of his friend's declar'd penitence. Something in the action—a squeeze, a look—might make such his intention known to Sylvia, and so to an audience. However this be, it has the best effect possible upon the unwinding the play's under-plot, an effect too that comes on so immediately that any other which his declaration is calculated to have produc'd is superseded and quash'd by it; and his whole subsequent behaviour to Proteus and Thurio is a most strong argument that the proceeding is right accounted for here. (II.ii. 160)

[80] [On *The Winter's Tale*, 1.2.138ff.: Leontes: 'Affection! thy intention stabs the centre']
'*Affection*,' the thing apostrophiz'd, is told in it that when full bent is given it, full *intentiveness*, man often receives a stab in his center, *i.e.* his heart; meaning that he is in that case subject to jealousy. Thou (this full-bent affection) mak'st possible, says the speaker, things which others hold not so; hast fellowship with dreams, with what's unreal, nay even with nothing, art that nothing's co-agent in working out thy own torment. And having said this, suddenly, (by a wonderful but natural turn in so sick a mind as this speaker's), out of these reflections, which make the passion ridiculous and are of force to have cur'd it, matter is drawn by him to give his madness sanction, by saying that since nothings were a foundation for it, somethings might be, and were: '*Then, 'tis very credent,*| *Thou may'st co-join with something; and thou dost;*' subjoining to this assertion '*And that to the infection of my brains,*| *And hard'ning of my*

249

brows'—for this only should follow it; the other line between hooks[1] being, in the editor's judgment, a first draft of the Poet's, corrected by what comes after and meant by him for rejection. (II.ii. 163)

[81] [*Ibid.*, 3.1.1ff.: Shakespeare's deviation from his source]
. . . Delphos is foolishly made an *isle* in the book which was this play's ground-work. But as much its ground-work as 'twas, 'tis departed from in many particulars that are to the play's advantage; and should have been so in this, for the reasons that have been given. If that capital grossness of which the model is guilty, of making Bohemia maritime, appears also in Shakespeare, his inducement might be as follows; the name, which has harmony and is pleasing, stood connected so with Sicilia in the minds of his whole audience, that removing it had been removing foundations. The fault had been over-look'd in the story-book, which was popular and then a great favourite, and he was in no fear but it would be so in the play. His changing all the other names generally throughout the fable, arose partly from judgment and partly from his ear's goodness, which could not put up with Garinter, Franion, Pandosto, and such like, which have neither musick in themselves nor relation to the places the scene is lay'd in. (II.ii. 169)

[82] [*Ibid.*, 3.2: the character Antigonus]
On this character and his Wife, and of that excellent one the Clown (the Shepherd's son), Lodge[2] has no traces; and in him a boat—left to the waves' mercy, and open—conveys the Child into Sicily from Bohemia, which he makes the jealous king's country. Autolycus is another engrafted character; new as Shakespeare manages it, but suggested by Lodge's Capnio, a servant of the young prince's employ'd to carry his things aboard (the only action in which the story engages him), in doing which he lights upon the old Shepherd, and decoys him as in the play. These, and the under-characters generally, such as Mopsa, Dorcas, &c. are additions, and of the Poet's inventing; which may serve to shew the story-book's poverty, to the undispos'd to look further. (II.ii. 171–2)

[83] [*Ibid.*, 4.4.297ff.: the song 'Get you hence']

---

[1] Capell brackets as spurious l. 144: 'All that beyond commission, and I find it'.

[2] Capell seems to have confused Greene, the author of *Pandosto*, with Lodge.

A song of pure trochees, its third line excepted and the line that rimes to it; and there too are found a couple of trochees at the head of two of them, in each stanza one. It is of wonderful sweetness, and musical without musick, as are all the songs of this Poet in general; has been slovenly printed, and no division observ'd in it, that is, of stanza; its second ends with a line which would have more spirit if it proceeded from both women. (II.ii. 176)

[84] [From a note on the chronology]

The long task of explaining, and of accounting for emendations—borrow'd as well as new, and of all magnitudes—being thus brought to a conclusion, here the pen might be drop'd, and leave taken of (we hope) an indulgent reader. But as it may have happen'd that, from what is scatter'd up and down in these '*Notes*' upon two subjects, the *time* of writing the plays and the *measures* that they are writ in, a fuller knowledge of both may be the wish of some persons, it shall be endeavour'd to gratify it in the best manner that we are able. And first of the first, *The* ORDER *and* TIME *of writing*. Every note of time that the plays themselves have afforded, or but seem'd to afford, has been singl'd out and remark'd upon; and it has generally prov'd that the notices gather'd from thence have co-incided with other documents that carry conviction with them. These documents are, the play's earliest impressions; entries in a book of that time; and the witness of writers in it. Of one capital writer full mention is made in a note in the '*Introduction*,' and before it is one that speaks of the entries; their evidence is the compleatest we can have, and here follows its whole and perfect remainder.[1] (II.ii. 183)

[Capell then combines this evidence to give a chronology, of which he says:] It is offer'd with some confidence on the part of the drawer-up; and will (at least) be found sufficiently just for that critick to work by, whose object is weighing this Author's pieces, and adjusting the comparative merits of them. Three of those pieces (the *King John; Hamlet*; and *The Taming of the Shrew*) have each a double place in the List, and for this reason: two we know with full certainty to be pieces quite distinct from another two that bear a like title, and have grounds very sufficient for saying near as

---

[1] Capell refers to Francis Meres' list of Shakespeare's plays in his *Palladis Tamia* (1598), and to the books of the Stationers' Company, a source of evidence that he was the first to discover: cf. the 1768 edition, Introduction, I, pp. 5–8, notes.

much of the *Hamlet*; they must therefore have been wrought up anew, and at a new period, and this period we have ventur'd to guess at. The lights we had to proceed by, as well in these as the rest, (exclusive of what the Extract has yielded) appear in different Notes that must be resorted to severally by the dispos'd to examine them. . . . Further, the engager in this subject should take this along with him, that in all or most of these plays some evidence of their date rises from out the style and the numbers of them, and he will observe in a case or two that the opinion conceiv'd of it rests wholly on these particulars; which, if he has taste, he will not think should be set aside as incompetent.

SCHEME *of their Succession; drawn from what has preceded, and from Evidence touch'd upon in the 'Notes.'*

1591.	*King John*, 2 parts[1]
1591.	*Henry VI*, parts 2 and 3
1593.	*Hamlet*[2]
	The Taming of the Shrew[3]
1594.	*Titus Andronicus*
	Love's Labour's Lost
	All's Well that Ends Well
1595.	*King John*
	The Two Gentlemen of Verona
1596.	*Richard II*
	Richard III
	Comedy of Errors
1597.	*Romeo and Juliet*
	A Midsummer Night's Dream
	1 Henry IV
1598.	*2 Henry IV*
	Merchant of Venice
1599.	*Henry V*
	Much Ado About Nothing

[1] Capell refers to the anonymous two-part play, *The troublesome Reigne of Iohn King of England* (1591), which most scholars regard as Shakespeare's source; a few, however, consider it to be a 'Bad Quarto' based on Shakespeare's play.

[2] Capell's dating for this first, supposedly lost version of *Hamlet* derives from (i) the title page of the 'Good Quarto' of 1605, which describes it as 'Newly imprinted and enlarged to almost as much againe as it was, according to the true and perfect Coppie'; and (ii) an allusion in Thomas Lodge's *Wits Miserie* (1596) to a ghost crying 'Hamlet, revenge!' in some earlier play—not necessarily by Shakespeare, as scholars now think.

[3] This is the 'Bad Quarto' version, which seems to derive from a source common to Shakespeare's play.

1600.   *1 Henry VI*
1601.   *The Merry Wives of Windsor*
1602.   *Troilus and Cressida*
        Measure for Measure
1605.   *Hamlet*
        As You Like It
1606.   *Macbeth*
        The Taming of the Shrew[1]
1607.   *Twelfth Night*
        King Lear
1608.   *Coriolanus*
        Julius Caesar
        Antony and Cleopatra
        Timon of Athens
1611.   *Othello*
1612.   *Cymbeline*
1613.   *Henry VIII*
        The Winter's Tale
1614.   *The Tempest*

(II.ii. 185–6)

[85] *A brief* ESSAY *on* VERSE, *as of* SHAKESPEARE's *modeling; its Principles, and its Construction.*

Difference of duration runs through all the parts of which speech is compos'd, its *letters*, its *syllables*, and its *words*. Some vowels are shorter than other some, and vowels in general shorter than most consonants; and these too differ among themselves, the open being longer than the liquid, and the close longest of all. *Syllables*, which are constructed of letters, must have difference in them according as they are form'd; and from their infinitely-vary'd durations a vary'd melody rises that is the radical principle of what in speech is call'd harmony. But when syllables meet together in *words*, or in sentences where the word is a syllable, the ear finds itself struck by a duration distinct from the other, and overcoming that other in all instances. The agent in this duration is voice; which, if made to fall on one syllable is constrain'd to relieve itself in the next, and has it not in its power to lay an equal and several

---

[1] Capell takes Petruchio's line 'This is a way to kill a wife with kindness' (4.1.208) as a reference to Heywood's play *A Woman killed with Kindness*, published in 1607, 'the very year in which appear'd the *Taming of the Shrew*, then publish'd to take advantage of the alter'd play's run' (II.ii. 40). The reasoning here lacks support.

θεςις (for that is the term in use) upon even two contiguous syllables, though in different words; except a rest intervene, which if the sense makes not voice must. Of this *thesis* monosyllables have only a capability; and it falls on them, sometimes with intervention of one syllable, sometimes of two, or of even three in some cases, but those are rare. When one only intervenes, and no circumstance chances to encrease its duration, that thesis is weak. Dissyllables have one, and that strong; and the word of three syllables the same where its seat is the second; but if another has it then is that trissyllable provided of two of them, of which one only is strong. In words exceeding that measure, whether of four, five, six, or even more syllables, the thesis is mostly alternate, and may reach to four; but whatever the number of them one is always predominant, as was said of the other words, and for such as are of that nature the proper title is *Accent*. The weaker, and that upon monosyllables, are best distinguish'd by *Ictus*, which will be the term in what follows.

Thus by natural necessity a difference is establish'd in syllables, that is the true basis of a *Time* that is call'd *numeric*. Such of them as are acted on by the voice in either of the ways above-spoke of are render'd *long* by such acting (long potentially, for the verse-man makes free with them, as we shall see), and the relief that must follow it causes *shortness*, but in that too is licence. And this acting and suspension of acting meeting always in speech, and forming a sort of unison, a relief and its thesis are consider'd as one member, and call'd a *Foot*. If the relief preceeds, the foot is call'd an *Iambus*; if the thesis, a *Trochee*; and as these two, with certain licences proper to them, will be found adequate to the purpose of accounting for all the measures in use with us, lyrical and heroic, it will perhaps be admitted that they only have a right to the epithet *proper*, and that *improper* is fittest for some feet that will be spoke of hereafter.

Verse is measur'd by Feet, in a process call'd scansion; and five feet ordinarily, with addition now and then of a sixth, is the complement of the line that is call'd *heroic*. The feet are sometimes wholly Iambi, as thus—

> *The nights│are whole│some; then│no plan│ets strike,*
> *No fai│ry takes,│no witch│hath power│to charm,*
> *So hal│low'd and│so gra│cious is│the time.*   [*Hamlet*, 1.1.162ff.]

or sometimes admit the Trochee among them,—

But, look,|the morn,|in rus|set man|tle clad,
Walks o'er|the dew|of yon'|high east|ward hill:
Break we|our watch|up;   [*Ibid.*, 1.1.166ff.]

Which admission of the Trochee is subject to great constraint at this present, the foot rarely appearing in the Heroic of modern poets, but at a line's beginning or after some great pause. That of Shakespeare introduces it every where (its fifth foot excepted), and under all circumstances; as may be seen in this one couplet which ends a speech of Macbeth's:

The eye|wink at|the hand;|yet let|that be,
Which the|eye fears,|when it|is done,|to see.   [*Macbeth*, 1.4.52f.]

and he is at times so profuse of them that he has verses in which the Trochee outnumbers the Iambus; as witness these which are given to his Richard the third,—

1.   *We are|not safe,|Clarence,|we are|not safe.*   [1.1.70]
2.   *Let me|put in|your minds,|if you|forget,*   [1.3.130]

and this other which comes from Troilus, in [4.4.138] of that play,—

Lady,|give me|your hand;|and, as|we walk, &c.

The examples are very perfect and full, and want support from no others; but might have it, if necessary, from many hundreds. The reason of this admixture is the close relation the feet bear to each other, having no difference but in their syllables' order. And hence too it is that, in what we may call the lyrical parts of him—his speeches under five feet—we find him changing his measure, passing from the Iambic to the Trochaic, and *vice-versâ*, and not a single time only in one speech; a strong instance of which is that fine soliloquy which closes act the third of his *Measure for Measure*. These lyrical Iambics, and others elsewhere, consist of four entire feet, his Trochaics of only three and a semi-foot; and both the one and the other admit the same interchange, in different parts of them, that is practis'd in the Heroic, Trochees ent'ring the Iambic, and Iambi the other line; as into this, for example,—

Toad, that|under|the cold|stone,   [*Macbeth*, 4.1.6]

—presently upon which comes a signal diversity belonging to these measures, that will be spoke of hereafter.

More observable still—as being a perpetual accompaniment, which the Trochee is not—is that property of the Heroic which was barely mention'd of late, *videlicet* the *Pause.** This it owes to necessity, as the syllable does its relief, for no entire verse can be pronounc'd without a rest in some part of it or other, and that rest is the pause. It may be plac'd without harshness, and even with great advantage to general melody, in any one part of it; only, if very near the beginning or near the end, there is usually (perhaps, always) a second pause aiding it, as may be seen in the examples that follow.

1 & 2.

—*Stay,* | |*you imperfect speakers,* | *tell me more:* [Macbeth, 1.3.70]

—*Might be the be-all* \ *and the end-all* \ *here,*
  But here, | |*upon this bank* \ *and shoal of time,*   [1.7.5f.]

—*What, sir,* | |*not yet at rest?* | *The king's a-bed;*   [2.1.12]

3.

Art thou not, | |*fatal vision,* | *sensible*
To feeling, | |*as to sight?* | *or art thou but* &c.   [2.1.36f.]

4, 5, & 6.

That memory, | |*the warder of the brain,*
Shall be a fume, | *and the receit of reason*
A limbeck only; | |*When in swinish sleep*
Their drenched natures lye, | |*as in a death,* &c.   [1.7.65ff.]

7.

Rebellious head, | *rise never,* | |*'till the wood*
Of Birnam rise, | *and our high-plac'd Macbeth*
Shall live the lease of nature, | |*pay his breath*
To time, | *and mortal custom.* | |*Yet my heart* &c.   [4.1.97ff.]

---

* In marking, and (first) of the *Pauses*: the verse's chief pause is denoted by a double line following it. Of *Redundancies*: the single oblique stroke, if at the verse's end, signifies that the syllable or syllables *after* it are of that kind; if at its beginning, that *before* is cut off by it. The single or double stroke in its other parts marks redundancy there of a syllable or two syllables following. The *common* and the *semi-breve Trochee*, and the *semi-breve Iambus*, are denoted each by a difference in the type of that syllable that is the long in them; feet unmark'd are *Iambi*, of the sort that is titl'd *common*. (II.ii.231)

8 & 9.

Why should I play | the Roman fool, | | and die
On mine own sword? | whiles I see lives, | the gashes
Do better upon them: [5.8.1ff.]

If such a one | be fit to govern, | | speak:
I am | as I have spoken.   [4.3.101f.]

Thus, instead of three, to which the rimer confines himself now-a-days, these great Poets chose to employ the *Pause* in their verse in nine several places; and—besides variety, which is itself a great ornament—produc'd out of it some of the most striking beauties with which their poems are decorated.

But the Dramatist was not yet contented. Neither the free use of the Trochee, nor this of the Pause, seem'd to him to give sufficient variety to verse design'd for the stage. By reflecting therefore upon the nature of our language in general and of our verse in particular, and by aid of a most excellent ear, he invented, and threw into his verse, two varieties more. Some traces of them he might find in the poets that went before him, but his large use of them, the improvements they receiv'd from his hand, and their reduction to rule make them properly and truly inventions; and his verse stands distinguish'd by them from the verse of all other poets whatever, to this day.

One of these varieties is the *Redundant Syllable*; and the Pause being dispatch'd, it may now be made clear to us. The end of lines had been ornamented with it before Shakespeare; but whether doubly, and even trebly, as he has done, cannot be justly said upon memory, nor much matters it to enquire; 'tis familiar with the Italians, and might be gather'd from them. To the middle parts of verse he first introduc'd it, and his manner shews judgment and design. The Pause in a verse of five feet is a kind of division. When full, or approaching something to fulness, the member so cut off has the air of a smaller verse, of one (perhaps), two, three, or four feet, terminated by the pause; at any one of which pauses—as if the member it seperates were indeed a verse, and that the end of it—the Redundant Syllable is occasionally brought in by this Poet; being (as the name signifies) no part of the general heroic line, nor ent'ring into its scansion any more than the syllable or syllables so denominated which we often find at its end. Here follow examples of the final redundant syllable, single, double, and treble; and of the middle redundant syllable single, in two parts of the verse, as well the whole verse as that which is divided; all lying within a very small compass, in two passages only of *Cymbeline*.

1.　　　　　Imo.　*Nay,|be brief:*
I see|into|thy end,|and am|almost
A man|alread'y.|
　　　　　Pis.　*First, make|yourself|but like'one.*
Fore-think|ing this,|I have|alread|y fit,
('Tis in|my cloak-|bag) doub|let, hat,|hose, all
That an|swer to'them:|Would you|[but,]in|their ser'ving,
And with|what im|ita|tion you|can bor'row
From youth|of such|a sea'son,|'fore no|ble Lu'cius
Present|yourself,|desire|his ser|vice,**[1] doubt'less
With joy|he will|embrace|you; for|he's hon'ourable,
And, doub|ling that,|most ho'ly.|Your means|abroad
You have|me, rich;|and I|will nev|er fail
Begin|ning, nor|supply'ment.|
　　　　　Imo.　*Thou art all|the com'fort* &c.　　　　[3.4.165ff.]

2.　　　*Lucius|hath wrot|alread|y to|the em'peror*
How it|goes here.|It fits|us there|fore, &c.　　　[3.5.20f.]

Examples of all these redundancies might be multiply'd almost *in infinitum*, there being very few pages of Shakespeare in which some of them may not be met with, and a small search would furnish out all. These redundant syllables, therefore, are as much a part of his regular prosody as either the Trochee or the Pause. But some others that have been mention'd or hinted at—to wit, those which are found now and then after the first foot of a verse, or after the fourth, or after small or no pause—are more properly licenses; and to be us'd very sparingly, if at all, as the ear is not pleas'd with them. Here are three for the reader to judge of, the two first out of *Measure for Measure*, the other out of the last-quoted play:-

1.　　　————*See|that Clau'dio*
Be ex|ecu'ted|by nine|to-mor|row mor'ning:　　　[2.1.33.f]

2.　　　————*I for|a while*
Will leave'you;|but stir|not you,|'till you|have well
Deter|mined|upon|these slan|derers.　　　[5.1.257ff.]

3.　*If it|be so|to do|good ser|vice, nev'er*
Let me|be coun|ted ser|vicea'ble.|How look'I,

[1] Capell uses asterisks to signify a hypothetical lacuna in the text.

That I|should seem|to lack|human|ity,
So much|as this|fact comes|to?   [*Cymbeline*, 2.3.14ff.]

Another of these redundancies, which is hardly of greater frequency than the two we have just spoke of, should be put in their class; this is the middle redundant syllable, double. *Cymbeline* offers one;—

*Bu*t his|neat cook|¹ ¹ery!|He cut|our roots|in char¹acters;
And sauc'd|our broths,|as Ju|no had|been sick,
And he|her di|eter.   [4.2.49ff.]

Macbeth another;—

Than on|the tor|ture of|the mind|to lye
In rest|less ec¹¹stasy.|Duncan|is in|his grave; &c.   [3.2.21f.]

and more might be pick'd up; which to some will seem plainly what they are call'd, but others may think the verses they stand in six-foot verses. For greater ease of the reader, and for his fuller conviction in these latter particulars and some others that are behind, there will be found at this *Essay*'s conclusion a sortment of different examples, each under its head; and under that of Redundancies will come a line that is singular, having three middle syllables *extra* scansion.

There is yet a further particular in the verse of this Poet which has relation to these we are speaking of, and that is an *initial redundancy*; for though his Plays are diversify'd throughout with portions of verse of all sizes—one foot, one and half; two, two and half; and so on to the end—yet a half-foot, or syllable, should rather be reckon'd what we have call'd it, and what it wears the appearance of in the present edition. *King Lear* has three of them, all very remarkable, and of great effect in their place:—

1.   *Do;¹Kill thy|physici|an, and|the fee|bestow*
     Upon|thy foul|disease.   [1.1.163f.]

2.   *Sir,¹Will you,|with those|infir|mities|she owes,*
     Unfrien|ded, &c.   [1.1.202f.]

3.   *Corde|lia,|Corde|lia, stay|a lit¹tle.*
     Ha!¹What is't|thou say'st?&c.   [5.3.272f.]

Of which three little monosyllables¹ the last only has had the luck

¹ In the *Notes* Capell says that in these three passages the monosyllables 'have all the best effect possible in their severall places, denoting fervour, and earnestness . . .' (I.ii.143).

to keep his station in moderns: the others are vanish'd quite out of them, as are also most of the sort throughout Shakespeare, and much the greater part of his *middle redundancies*. And his lines of six feet too, call'd Alexandrines—another diversity in his measure, which he has with great judgment, and sometimes with no little happiness chose to make use of—have met a similar fate in the hands of these gentlemen. From whom the Poet has much the same treatment as had the guests of Procrustes, his lines being either cut short by the foot or the syllable, or else violently drawn out in length (for this too is the case in some places with what was meant for hemistichs), to fit them to the measure of their sorry bed, which is one of five feet, and that precisely, without want or exceeding. (II.ii. 187–94)

[Capell then discusses the abundance of monosyllables in the English language.]

But in all the language, throughout, no syllables dwell a shorter time upon the ear than the two concluding ones of some words of three syllables whose accent is on the anti-penultima, the frequent and almost general seat of it in words of that length. The multiplicity of these is so great, and their lightness so great withal, that ear of our Poet was struck with it; and a little reflection upon the nature of these words, and of the shorter ones mention'd before, led him to make a further distinction in the time of short syllables, from which his verse derives another variety, more us'd, and of more advantage to it, than his other great invention above, the Redundant Syllable, middle.

Monosyllables, however constructed, have no time in them-selves (as was said before in this '*Essay*'), but are determin'd this or that by the sense; which, in a verse consisting wholly of them or even chiefly, singles out the emphatical, or such as are so comparatively, and giving them that position which is necessary for the making-out its five times (whole times), distributed properly, leaves the rest without thesis, and in a state of admitting such times as suit the feet that compose it. These times the Poet under considering makes of two sorts, half-times and quarter-times, and gains two sorts of feet by it. To the feet which we must call for distinction sake the *common Iambus* and the *common Trochee*, belongs the common half-time; and of these two syllables are the components. But where two preceed or follow the whole time, which is often the case in him, those two are but of quarter-times each, and the feet they stand in bear exactly the same relation to those of two syllables which the Anapest and Dactyl do to the Spondee; and to these feet may be given with full propriety the names *Semi-breve Trochee*, and *Semi-breve Iambus*. In Heroics the quarter-times that belong to them are mostly lay'd on such syllables as are describ'd in the section preceding; or on others their like, as are the final unaccented syllables of all words of length. But this rule is departed from in the verse of another measure, that will be spoke of ere long.

Of these *semi-breve* feet examples are so continual and various that judgment knows not where to select them. All pages present them, both of Shakespeare and Milton; and the latter, whose proper province it was to accommodate sound to sense, and to draw poetical images of things that have motion, is indebted to this kind of foot for the most remarkable painting in all his works. It is in his description of the fifth day's creation, in which the air and the waters were peopl'd with their several inhabitants. Having mention'd the smaller-siz'd fishes, and some of the middle, he speaks then of the larger in these words:

> ————————————*part huge|of bulk,*
> *Wallowing|unwiel|dy, enor|mous in|their gait,*
> *Tempest|the o|cean:*   [*Paradise Lost*, VII.410ff.]

in which you have the quarter-time foot of both sorts; and with it a striking instance of its effect. Here follow some few out of Shakespeare: whose purpose in using them was different from that of Milton's in this place, intending only to make his numbers more various, and to give his metrical dialogue all the freedom of prose:—

> 1.   HER. *Nay, but|you will.|*
>   POL. *I may|not, ver|ily.|*
>   HER. *Ver'ily!*
>   *You put|me off|with lim|ber vows:|But I,*
>   *Though you|would seek|to unsphere|the stars|with oaths,*
>   *Would yet|say,—Sir,|no go|ing. Ver|ily,*
>   *You shall|not go;|a la|dy's ver|ily is*
>   *As po|tent as|a lord's.*   [*Winter's Tale*, 1.2.45ff.]

> 2.   *Fear you|his tyr|annous pas|sion more,|alas,*
>   *Than the|queen's life?|a gra|cious in|nocent soul;*
>   *More free,|than he|is jeal|ous.*   [*Ibid.*, 2.3.28ff.]

261

3.   ————————*Care not\for is\sue;*
The crown\will find\an heir:\Great Al\exan'der
Left his\to the wor\thiest; so\his suc\cessor
Was like\to be\the best.
      Leo. *Thou good\Pauli'na,—*
Who hast\the mem\ory of\Hermi\one,
I know,\in hon\our,—o,\that ev\er I
Had squar'd\me to\thy coun\sel!   [*Ibid.*, 5.1.46ff.]

4.   *Yet if\my lord\will mar\ry,—if\you will\, sir;*
No rem\edy, but\you will;\give me\the of\fice,
To choose\you a queen:\she shall\not &c.   [5.1.76ff.]

5.   ————————*Had\our prince*
(Jewel\of chil\dren) seen\this hour,\he had pair'd
Well with\this lord;\there was\not a\full month
Between\their births.
      Leo. *Pr'ythee, no\more; cease;\thou know'st,*
He dies\to me\again,\when talk'd\of: [5.1.115ff.]

6.   ————————*your gal\lery*
Have we\pass'd through,\not with\out much\content
In man\y sin\gular\ities; but\we saw\not
That which &c.————————   [5.3.10ff.]

7.   *Comes it\not some\thing near?*
      Leo. *Her nat\ural pos\ture!—*
*** ————————*But yet,\Pauli'na,*
Hermi\one was\not so\much wrin\kl'd; noth\ing
So a\ged, as\this seems.————————   [5.3.23ff.]

8.   *I am sor\ry, sir,\I have thus\far stir'd\you: but*
I could\afflict\you far\ther.————————   [5.3.74f.]

9.   Pol. *She embra\ces him.*
      Cam. *She hangs\about\his neck;*
If she\pertain\to life,\let her\speak too.   [5.3.111f.]

To prove the certain existence of this kind of foot the instances
given are very clear and sufficient. But the reader who would have
more satisfaction, may pick up multitudes of them in any one play;
though more in some than in others, and in none more than in his
Henry the Eighth, the singularity of whose numbers has been often
remark'd upon[1] but the cause of it never pointed out, which is,
chiefly, the great abundance of *semi-breve feet* scatter'd in it

[1] Especially by Richard Roderick: see Vol. 4, pp. 338ff.

throughout. They are introduc'd too in *Song*, to which they seem peculiarly fitted, at least to some sorts of it. Here is one that is almost wholly made up of them, taken out of the play from which we had the other examples:

> *Will you buy|any tape,*
> *or lace|for your cape,*
> *my dain|ty duck,|my dear-|a;*
> *any silk,|any thread,*
> *any toys|for your head,*
> *of the new'st,|and fin'st,|fin'st, wear-|a?*
> *come to the|ped'ler;*
> *money's a|med'ler,*
> *that doth |utter |all men's |ware-|a.*   [4.4.315ff.]

and one a little before presents a line that has three of these feet in it;—

> *for a quart |of ale |is a dish |for a king.*   [4.3.8]
>   (II.ii. 195–8)

. . . First, order requires a finishing of what further remains to say concerning the said Heroic.

And the first matter that offers is one which the writer fairly acknowledges he shall scarce be able to solve satisfactorily to make accord with that system which he himself has advanc'd, and many others before him, that makes accent the foundation of versifying. Those others (with greater wisdom perhaps, but not greater honesty) overpass it unnotic'd, and as they never were struck with it, which the multitude of lines that present it makes downright impossible. For, from one end of this Poet to the other are scatter'd here and there in his pages dissyllable words whose ultima, though an accent, is shorten'd, or (more properly) made to stand in short place, the word's other syllable making on such occasion the half-time of a Trochee, whose whole falls on some monosyllable and of the lightest complexion often, as are articles &c. But before we proceed to reasoning it will be right to establish the fact by examples that cannot be controverted.

> *The pangs|of des|pis'd love,|the law's|delay,*   [*Hamlet*, 3.1.71]
>
> *No, let|the can|dy'd tongue|lick ab|surd pomp;* [*Ibid.*, 3.2.60]
>
> *Observe|my un|cle: if|his oc|cult guilt*   [3.2.80]

263

O gen|tlemen,|see, see!|dead Hen|ry's wounds
Open|*their con|geal'd mouths,|and bleed|afresh!*

[*Richard III*, 1.2.55f.]

*He af|ter hon|our hunts,|**I** af|ter love.*   [*Two Gentlemen*, 1.1.63]
————————*your eye|in Scot land*
*Wo*u*ld cre|ate sol|diers, make|our wom|en fight,*

[*Macbeth*, 4.3.186f.]

And what now is to be said of such feet? Must we call them a licence, a wantonness of the poet's, which he indulges to give his numbers diversity? Or shall we not rather look about for some cause of them in the nature of voice itself? and some analogous usages of its direction in other cases? Accent we see displac'd by it frequently, in the verse of every poet before Shakespeare and since; and a large list of words, whose accents he himself has made free with, follow in place assign'd. (II.ii. 200–1)

. . . —But here the reader should be appris'd of a doctrine we forbore to state in its place, relating to all such Trochees as either follow the Iambus immediately, or follow one another without a mark'd pause between, mark'd by punctuation. Namely, that in every such case pause is made by the voice; and having in it a power that answers a half-time, that power is intervention sufficient to obviate an objection to what has gone before about times, arising from those examples where the Trochee follows the Iambus. And such pause, or a fainter, has good effect in the other case, a concurrence of Trochees; in which (without it) is languor, and a want of distinction. Two instances shall serve, for the present, in proof of either assertion; of the latter, this from the Poet's *Troilus*—

DIO. **I** *shall*—|*have it|again.*|CRE. *What, this?*|DIO. *Ay. that,* [5.2.76]

and of the former, this beautiful one from his *Love's Labour's Lost*:

Whip to|our tents,|as roes—|run o'er|the land.   [5.2.309]

Such another pause as the last (to wit, that between Trochee and Trochee) is requir'd too at every verse's end, however closely connected with the sense of the verse after; a point which some very great speakers have been known to fail in, something to the impeachment of their delivery.

This uncommon, and (as many will say of it) this unpleasing

assemblage of a Trochee and an Iambus so constituted as we have seen in the last section, should have been an invention; the verse of poets preceding not affording examples of it, so far as is known. Exclusive of what *is* urg'd in behalf of it, the necessities—first, of giving all possible variety to numbers us'd in the drama; and next, of expressing passions and characters by such as answer that end, as many do of this cast—will reach farther than to excuse of it with the truly-judicious reader who shall give it consideration.

Nor will such a one much approve a reduction (practis'd often by editors, and often injuriously) of a measure the Poet uses that is not his invention but a known branch of the Heroic, now the only remaining one that asks the writer's considering. This measure is the verse of six feet, a verse solely intitl'd to the appellation (Heroic) in the esteem of the present French, and of some in Shakespeare's day also; and certainly not improper, in any view, for that occasional use of it which we find him making in all his plays, as well the late as the early ones. To this French line he sometimes gives the middle French *cæsure* (improperly call'd so), witness:

> *What an | swer makes | your grace | to the reb | els' sup | plica'tion?*
> [*2 Henry VI*, 4.4.7]

which being utterly void, even by itself, of the ease that should be in dialogue, we find substituted for it in his line the true Latin *cæsura*; that is, the word that forms its third foot runs on, and has a syllable in it that makes the first of the foot after; the over-formal French *cæsure* standing for the more part condemn'd by him to either dogrel, or sonnet, or the mock heroics of Pistol and Thisbe. Here are some from the lady:—

> *Most ra | diant Pyr | amus, | most lil | ly-white | of hue,*
> *Of col | our like | the red— | rose on | trium | phant briar.*
> [*Midsummer Night's Dream*, 3.1.93f.]

and here another from Pistol—

> *The heavens | thee guard | and keep, | most roy | al imp | of fame!*
> [*2 Henry IV*, 5.5.42]

and a sonnet all in this measure, beginning,—

> *If love | make me | forsworn, | how shall | I swear | to love?*
> [*Love's Labour's Lost*, 4.2.105ff.]

Of dogrel there will be call to speak presently, and then will this measure shew itself as a member of one that goes by the other name. A re-instating of this formal division having taken place in all verse of this length that is us'd by poets since Shakespeare, 'tis probable that what he esteem'd properer may not be relish'd at present, and that harshness will be objected to it, for which there is some foundation. The subjoin'd specimens will shew too that he thought it equally capable of some of those differences which we have seen in his five-foot verse, to the great advantage of that:-

1.   *How proud,|how per|empto|ry, and|unlike|himself?*

                                   [*2 Henry VI*, 3.1.8]

2.   *They call|false cat|erpil|lars, and|intend|their death.*

                                   [*Ibid.*, 4.4.37]

3.   *Was not|your fa|ther, Rich|ard, earl|of Cam|bridge,**
    For trea|son ex|ecu|ted in|our late|king's days?

                                   [*1 Henry IV*, 2.4.90f.]

4.   *To deeds|dishon|oura|ble? You|have ta|ken up* &c.

                                   [*2 Henry IV*, 4.2.26]

5.   *Let us|be sac|rifi|cers, but|not butch|ers, Caius.*

                                   [*Julius Caesar*, 2.1.166]

6.   *Is not|so es|tima|ble, prof|ita|ble nei|ther,*

                                   [*Merchant of Venice*, 1.3.166]

7.   ——————————————*now|this mask*
    Was cry'd|incom|para|ble; and|the ensu|ing night
    Made it|a fool,|and beg|gar.

                                   [*Henry VIII*, 1.1.26f.]

8.   *The fire,|that mounts|the liq|uor' till|'t run o'er,**
    In see|ming to|augment|it, wasts|it? Be|advis'd:

                                     [*Ibid.*, 1.1.144f.]

9.   *His high|ness hav|ing liv'd|so long|with her,|and she*
    So good|a la|dy,   [2.3.2f.]

10.   *Come, come,|my lord,|you'd spare|your spoons,|you shall have**
    Two no|ble part|ners with|you;|the old|dutchess|of Nor|folk,
    And la|dy mar|quess Dor|set; Will|these please|you?*

                                     [5.2.201ff.]

11.   ——————————————Tim. *Commend|me to|them;*
    And tell|them, that,|to ease|them of|their griefs,*

Their fears | of hos | tile strokes, | their a | ches, los | ses,*
Their pangs | of love, | with oth | er in | cident throes*
That na | ture's frag | il ves | sel doth | sustain*
In life's | uncer | tain voy | age, | I will | some pleas | ure do | them,
I'll teach | them to prevent | wild Al | cibi | ades' wrath.

[*Timon of Athens*, 5.1.197ff.]

Into some or other of these six-foot verses enter (besides the Trochee, as common) the final and the middle redundancy, and the semi-breve Iambus; the pause too is vary'd, as in the ordinary measure. In the first seven quotations is exemplify'd the Latin *cæsura*; and what the French call such in the last line of the eleventh. Examples of this measure, and of the foot that was last observ'd upon, are multiply'd out of *Henry the eighth*, to lead readers into remarking that the strangeness of that play's measures does not lye in the introduction of the semi-breve foot only, to which they saw it attributed not long before. There is found in *Antony and Cleopatra*[1] an Heroic of seven feet, except we admit in '*monument*' (one of its words) a middle redundancy of two syllables; and these are all the diversities of the verse so denominated.

Something has pass'd already, where the Trochee was treated of, about the *Lyrical Measures* which Shakespeare brings into his dialogue. And, for such of them in which the matter is serious, that something may serve, with this only addition, that into three speeches (which we must also call serious) of the measure there spoken of a novelty is introduc'd which the Poet might catch from Holinshed, in this popular distich to which he has given place in his own *Henry the fifth*:

I*f that | you will | France | win,*
Then with | Scotland | first be | gin. [1.2.167f.]

where by meer power of voice, by dwelling a while upon it, '*France*' becomes a foot by itself: and the same happens to '*first*,' and to '*moon's*,' words of two other passages, where the feet are of good effect in their way, an image of the beings they come from lying mostly in them. These passages follow in the Collections, and after them, come a number of others; taken either from song, or from the mouth of light characters, whose humour they heighten not inconsiderably.

In *Song* the Poet ranges as others do, and lines of one foot, one &

[1] 'Lock'd in her monument: She had a prophesying fear' (4.14.120).

half, and so on, enter their composition in different parts of him. Nay, his dialogue wears the dress of them sometimes; as witness a speech of Puck's that closes act the third of his *Midsummer Night's Dream*. The most singular of his songs (if in truth it be song) is one with which the Clown makes his exit in *Twelfth Night* [4.2.102ff.];[1] which, upon the score of that oddity, shall follow the examples last spoke of, broken and mark'd as they are to point out the measure. Out of some of these songs—and one, chiefly, in *Much Ado About Nothing*, [5.3.12ff.: 'Pardon, goddess of the night'], and a second in the play lately-mention'd [quoted below]—will rise the greatest objections to what has gone before about the Dactyl, and its iso-dunamous brethren, the Spondee and Anapest. Both are call'd dactylic by writers who have spoke of these songs; and the inattentive will be apt to think he hears in the second that impossible Spondee, intermingl'd with what are certainly the common Iambus and the common Trochee. But the deception in either song is from matter; which being of the elegy cast, all the numbers move slowly, and some are form'd purposely out of syllables that can scarcely move otherwise, of which the first song is instance, whose feet (whatever they are) are pure without mixture. The other merits transcription on account of its various-ness as well of measure as feet; and the proper names of these latter, in the writer's opinion, will appear in his marking :-

I.

Come away,|come away,|death,
and in sad|cypress|let me be|lay'd;
fly away,|fly away,|breath;
I am|slain by a|fair cruel|maid:
my shrowd|of white,|stuck all|with yew,
o'prepare'it;
my part|of death|no one|so true
did share'it.

2.

Not a flower,|not a flower|sweet,
on my black|coffin|let there be|strown;
not a friend,|not a friend,|greet

[1] This is the song 'I am gone, sir . . . '; in the *Notes* Capell says that 'the speech's numbers are exquisite' (II.ii. 152).

my poor|corps, where my|bones shall be|thrown:
a thou|sand thou|sand sighs|to save,
　　　　lay me, o,|where
sad true-|love nev|er find|my grave,
　　　　to weep|there.

　　　　　　　　　　　　[*Twelfth Night*, 2.4.51ff.]

Another of these dactylics comes from Touchstone in *As you like it*,
where he is playing upon sir Oliver [3.3.99ff.: 'O sweet Oliver,/
O brave Oliver, Leave me not behind thee']. But in
truth the numbers are in all respects similar to those of the song
preceding; and (like that in its sixth line) it has one initial
redundancy, the (*I*) of the line it ends with. The song call'd
anapestic is that admirable one in the *Tempest* that graces Stephano's entrance at [2.2.46ff.: 'The master, the swabbler, the boatswain, and I']. But as an Iambus (common Iambus) begins every
line of it (the last excepted), terminates two of them (the third and
fourth), and has the forming of the whole second line, it is not seen
why we should go out of those times and call the other feet
anapests when, by admitting a foot which reason assents to, we
may have absolute consonance throughout its whole composition.
Set it down then as an Iambic, and that a pure one; having syllables
in it (a few) in quarter-time places, such as that measure admits of
whose examen will close the '*Essay*' before us, *videlicet* Dogrel, a
first-cousin at least to such songs as is Stephano's.

　　A most faint image of the measure bearing that name is found in
two or three ancient Moralities, and one of Skelton's particularly
that is titl'd '*Magnificence*,' that might set the inventive brain of our
Poet upon expanding, or (rather) new-molding it, after the manner
we see it lye at this present; principally, in three early comedies, the
Taming of the Shrew, Love's Labour's lost, and the *Comedy of Errors,*
and a little in the *Two Gentlemen of Verona*. Characters which we
may almost call buffoon ones, and the link'd in discourse with
them, are the parties the measure comes from. It has drollery in
itself, and receives a further surcharge of it from its never-failing
accompaniment, *videlicet* rime; but being wholly unfit for dialogue,
and withal of difficult management in the delivery (as that actor
would find who should make the experiment), it had in very short
time a dismission from its inventor, together with its accompaniment. The regular of this kind are Iambic tetrameters, of the semi-
breve species; and pure, as is the following distich—

　　　　　　　　　　　　269

I should kick,|being kick'd;|and, being|at that pass,
You would keep|from my heels,|and beware|of an ass.

[*Comedy of Errors*, 3.1.17f.]

with exception of one foot only, the third of its first line; whose *'being'* is made a whole time *per crasin*, and the foot a common Iambus. But such regulars tyring in repetition, and lying open to even greater objections than that of the Heroic, when regular; all the licences of the latter—its redundancies; mixture of various feet, various measure, &c.—have a place in this verse, and that in larger proportion. Upon surveying the whole of it, in all the plays above-mention'd, there appear'd to this writer no other way of facilitating a reader's conception of it but by laying before him (generally) all its irregulars; which shall be done in the following pages. . . . (II.ii. 202–8)

To this last specimen of the irregular Dogrel in this play succeed immediately a couple of distichs which are declar'd to be quotation[1] (see the words they are follow'd by). They are made to come from that speaker not as Dogrel, but in banter of a ridiculous measure which prevail'd at that time, classicks being translated, and even plays writ in it ['Poulter's measure', of alternately 12 and 14 syllables]. Costard's 'Pompey,' and Holofernes's *'Sonnet,'* had the same design probably; and in Pistol the thing is evident; his

Rouze up revenge from ebon den with fell Alecto's snake,

[*2 Henry IV*, 5.5.37]

and some other magnificencies of like sort admitting no other comment. One specimen of the measure is given by Shakespeare seriously: 'tis the epitaph of Timon at that play's end [5.4.70ff.], and was had from Plutarch's translator, whose verse it is mostly. (II.ii.214)

[Capell sums up his argument, listing the categories he has distinguished.]

Whatever syllables else—that is, not making part of some of the feet aforesaid—occur in any one verse (and there are which have many of them, and that in different parts), such are the *Redundancies* spoken of as a further invention; raising this Poet's verse to a further perfection still in the line to which it belongs, which asks

[1] *Two Gentlemen of Verona*, 2.1.165ff.: Speed: "'For often have you writ to her; and she in modesty,/Or else for want of idle time, could not again reply;/Or fearing else some messenger, that might her mind discover,/Herself hath taught her love himself to write unto her lover." All this I speak in print, for in print I found it.'

ease and variety, join'd to powers of expression, all which are promoted by this discovery. A very early perception of it and of his other invention, the feet lately spoke of, was of the highest service possible for the avoiding of frequent blemishes that disgrace his text in the moderns. And that a system the consequence of this perception, and lay'd down in these pages, is a true system can have no better vouchers, than (first) the simplicity that is immediately seen in it; and (next) the fulness that will shew itself upon trial for solution of every difficulty that has been found in our verse at large, and in that of Shakespeare particularly, in which they are more numerous, and are made by writers inexplicable. (II.ii. 216)

[Capell now adds an 'Appendix; consisting of Examples and Lists, additional', an inventory of Shakespeare's usage of the 'Semi-breve Iambus', 'Common Trochee', 'Semi-breve Trochee', 'Redundant Syllable', 'Syllable accented, short', 'Monosyllable Foot', 'Six-foot Verse'; and 'Of Words; extended, or shorten'd; unusually accented; unusually terminated': pp. 217–31. Under 'Diaeresis' he quotes from *Richard III*:]

> **O**, let | them keep | it 'till | thy sins | be ripe,
> And then | hurl down | their in | digna | tion
> On thee, | the troub | ler of | the poor | world's peace !   [1.3.218ff.]

Shakespeare deals in it largely: his *Henry IV* (both parts) and his *Merchant of Venice* are strongly mark'd with it; and as well in them as elsewhere it is made the principal causer of divers fine adaptations either to the passion that is delivering or the character of the deliverer. Of this the man of taste will see one proof in Queen Margaret's '*indignation*' above; and may read a second with pleasure in this answer of Viola's to Olivia's '*How does he love me?*' —

> With adorations, with fertil tears,
> With groans that thunder love, with sighs of fire.
> [*Twelfth Night*, 1.5.254f.] (II.ii. 226)

[In this conclusion Capell notes that many of the words found in his lists will not be found in other eighteenth-century editions, since they have been modernized or emended.]

The Lists are made as full and compleat as the memory of the compiler would serve, for this very good purpose: a great proof of such usage, in each case severally, lyes in its analogous usage in so many other cases. For that purpose, too, were the Examples that go before them encreas'd, and from both may result the benefit following, that Shakespeare will (at last) be permitted the use of his own language, and of the numbers which he thought aptest.

(II.ii. 231)

264. Henry Mackenzie, on the character of Hamlet

1780

From the *Mirror*, Edinburgh, nos 99 (17 April 1780) and 100 (22 April). Mackenzie conducted this periodical from 23 January 1779 to 27 May 1780.

Henry Mackenzie (1745–1831), who studied law at Edinburgh University and in London, achieved celebrity with his first novel, *The Man of Feeling* (1771); later novels included *The Man of the World* (1773) and *Julia de Roubigné* (1777). Mackenzie was one of the leaders of the new taste: he made the first important estimate of the poetry of Burns (*Lounger*, no. 97, 1786), and was among the first to praise Byron, in 1807. His *Account of the German Theatre*, read at the Royal Society of Edinburgh in April 1788, and praising Romantic drama, especially Schiller's *Die Räuber*, created a great interest in German literature, and influenced Walter Scott, whom he also encouraged, and who became a lifelong friend. See H. W. Thompson, *A Scottish Man of Feeling* (1931), and his edition of *The Anecdotes and Egotisms of Henry Mackenzie, 1745–1831* (1927).

. . . No author, perhaps, ever existed of whom opinion has been so various as *Shakespeare*. Endowed with all the sublimity and subject to all the irregularities of genius, his advocates have room for unbounded praise, and their opponents for frequent blame. His departure from all the common rules which criticism, somewhat arbitrarily perhaps, has imposed, leaves no legal code by which the decision can be regulated; and in the feelings of different readers the same passage may appear simple or mean, natural or preposterous, may excite admiration or create disgust.

But it is not, I apprehend, from particular passages or incidents that *Shakespeare* is to be judged. Though his admirers frequently contend for beauty in the most distorted of the former, and probability in the most unaccountable of the latter; yet it must be owned that in both there are often gross defects which criticism cannot justify, though the situation of the poet and the times in which he wrote may easily excuse. But we are to look for the superiority of *Shakespeare* in the astonishing and almost supernatural powers of his invention, his absolute command over the passions, and his wonderful knowledge of Nature. Of the structure of his stories or the probability of his incidents he is frequently careless; these he took at random from the legendary tale or the extravagant romance, but his intimate acquaintance with the human mind seldom or never forsakes him, and amidst the most fantastic and improbable situations the persons of his drama speak in the language of the heart, and in the stile of their characters.

Of all the characters of *Shakespeare* that of *Hamlet* has been generally thought the most difficult to be reduced to any fixed or settled principle. With the strongest purposes of revenge he is irresolute and inactive; amidst the gloom of the deepest melancholy he is gay and jocular; and while he is described as a passionate lover he seems indifferent about the object of his affections. It may be worth while to inquire whether any leading idea can be found upon which these apparent contradictions may be reconciled, and a character so pleasing in the closet, and so much applauded on the stage, rendered as unambiguous in the general as it is striking in detail. I will venture to lay before my readers some observations on this subject, though with the diffidence due to a question of which the public has doubted, and much abler critics have already written.

The basis of *Hamlet*'s character seems to be an extreme sensibility of mind, apt to be strongly impressed by its situation, and over-powered by the feelings which that situation excites. Naturally of the most virtuous and most amiable dispositions, the

273

circumstances in which he was placed unhinged those principles of action which, in another situation, would have delighted mankind and made himself happy. That kind of distress which he suffered was, beyond all others, calculated to produce this effect. His misfortunes were not the misfortunes of accident, which, though they may overwhelm at first the mind will soon call up reflections to alleviate, and hopes to cheer; they were such as reflection only serves to irritate, such as rankle in the soul's tenderest part, his sense of virtue and feelings of natural affection; they arose from an uncle's villany, a mother's guilt, a father's murder!—Yet, amidst the gloom of melancholy and the agitation of passion in which his calamities involve him, there are occasional breakings-out of a mind richly endowed by nature and cultivated by education. We perceive gentleness in his demeanour, wit in his conversation, taste in his amusements, and wisdom in his reflections.

That *Hamlet*'s character, thus formed by Nature, and thus modelled by situation, is often variable and uncertain I am not disposed to deny. I will content myself with the supposition that this is the very character which *Shakespeare* meant to allot him. Finding such a character in real life, of a person endowed with feelings so delicate as to border on weakness, with sensibility too exquisite to allow of determined action, he has placed it where it could be best exhibited, in scenes of wonder, of terror, and of indignation, where its varying emotions might be most strongly marked amidst the workings of imagination and the war of the passions.

This is the very management of the character by which, above all others, we could be interested in its behalf. Had *Shakespeare* made *Hamlet* pursue his vengeance with a steady determined purpose, had he led him through difficulties arising from accidental causes, and not from the doubts and hesitation of his own mind, the anxiety of the spectator might have been highly raised; but it would have been anxiety for the event, not for the person. As it is, we feel not only the virtues but the weaknesses of *Hamlet* as our own; we see a man who, in other circumstances, would have exercised all the moral and social virtues, one whom Nature had formed to be

> *Th' Expectancy and Rose of the fair State,*
> *The Glass of Fashion, and the Mold of Form,*
> *Th' observ'd of all Observers,* [3.1.152ff.]

placed in a situation in which even the amiable qualities of his mind serve but to aggravate his distress and to perplex his conduct. Our compassion for the first, and our anxiety for the latter, are excited in the strongest manner; and hence arises that indescribable charm in *Hamlet* which attracts every reader and every spectator, which the more perfect characters of other tragedies never dispose us to feel.

The *Orestes* of the Greek poet, who at his first appearance lays down a plan of vengeance which he resolutely pursues, interests us for the accomplishment of his purpose; but of him we think only as the instrument of that justice which we wish to overtake the murderers of *Agamemnon*. We feel with *Orestes* (or rather with *Sophocles*, for in such passages we always hear the poet in his hero), that 'it is fit that such gross infringements of the moral law should be punished with death, in order to render wickedness less frequent;' but when *Horatio* exclaims on the death of his friend,

> *Now crack'd a noble Heart!* [5.2.359]

we forget the murder of the King, the villainy of *Claudius*, the guilt of *Gertrude*. Our recollection dwells only on the memory of that '*sweet prince*,' the delicacy of whose feelings a milder planet should have ruled, whose gentle virtues should have bloomed through a life of felicity and of usefulness.

Hamlet, from the very opening of the piece, is delineated as one under the dominion of melancholy, whose spirits were overborn by his feelings. Grief for his father's death, and displeasure at his mother's marriage prey on his mind, and he seems, with the weakness natural to such a disposition, to yield to their controul. He does not attempt to resist or combat these impressions, but is willing to fly from the contest, though it were into the grave:

> *Oh! that this too too solid flesh would melt*, &c. [1.2.129ff.]

Even after his father's ghost has informed him of his murder, and commissioned him to avenge it, we find him complaining of that situation in which his fate had placed him.

> *The time is out of joint; oh! cursed spight,*
> *That ever I was born to set it right!* [1.5.188f.]

And afterwards, in the perplexity of his condition, meditating on the expediency of suicide,

To be, or not to be, that is the question.   [3.1.55]

The account he gives of his own feelings to *Rosencrantz* and *Guildenstern*, which is evidently spoken in earnest, though somewhat covered with the mist of his affected distraction, is exactly descriptive of a mind full of that weariness of life which is characteristic of low-spirits:

> *This goodly frame the Earth, seems to me a steril promontory*, &c.
>
> [2.2.298ff.]

And indeed, he expressly delineates his own character as of the kind above mentioned when, hesitating on the evidence of his uncle's villainy, he says

> The spirit that I have seen
> May be the Devil, and the Devil hath power
> T' assume a pleasing shape; yea, and perhaps,
> *Out of my weakness and my melancholy*
> Abuses me to damn me.   [2.2.598ff.]

This doubt of the grounds on which our purpose is founded is as often the effect as the cause of irresolution, which first hesitates, and then seeks out an excuse for its hesitation.

It may, perhaps, be doing *Shakespeare* no injustice to suppose that he sometimes began a play without having fixed in his mind, in any determined manner, the plan or conduct of his piece. The character of some principal person of the drama might strike his imagination strongly in the opening scenes; as he went on this character would continue to impress itself on the conduct as well as the discourse of that person, and, it is possible, might affect the situations and incidents, especially in those romantic or legendary subjects where history did not confine him to certain unchangeable events. In the story of *Amleth*, the son of *Horwendil*, told by *Saxo-Grammaticus*, from which the tragedy of *Hamlet* is taken, the young prince who is to revenge the death of his father, murdered by his uncle *Fengo*, counterfeits madness that he may be allowed to remain about the court in safety and without suspicion. He never forgets his purposed vengeance, and acts with much more cunning towards its accomplishment than the *Hamlet* of *Shakespeare*. But *Shakespeare*, wishing to elevate the hero of his tragedy and at the same time to interest the audience in his behalf, throws around him from the beginning the majesty of melancholy, along with that sort of weakness and irresolution which frequently attend it. The incident of the *Ghost*, which is entirely the poet's own, and not to be found in the Danish legend, not only produces the happiest stage-effect but is also of the greatest advantage in unfolding that character which is stamped on the young prince at the opening of the play. In the communications of such a visionary being there is an uncertain kind of belief, and dark unlimited honour, which are aptly suited to display the wavering purpose and varied emotions of a mind endowed with a delicacy of feeling that often shakes its fortitude, with sensibility that overpowers its strength.

The view of *Hamlet*'s character exhibited in my last number may, perhaps, serve to explain a difficulty which has always occurred both to the reader and the spectator on perceiving his madness at one time put on the appearance not of fiction, but of reality; a difficulty by which some have been induced to suppose the distraction of the Prince a strange unaccountable mixture, through-out, of real insanity and counterfeit disorder.

The distraction of *Hamlet*, however, is clearly affected through the whole play, always subject to the controul of his reason, and subservient to the accomplishment of his designs. At the grave of *Ophelia*, indeed, it exhibits some temporary marks of a real disorder. His mind, subject from Nature to all the weakness of sensibility, agitated by the incidental misfortune of *Ophelia*'s death, amidst the dark and permanent impression of his revenge, is thrown for a while off its poise, and in the paroxysm of the moment breaks forth into that extravagant rhapsody which he utters to *Laertes*.

Counterfeited madness, in a person of the character I have ascribed to *Hamlet*, could not be so uniformly kept up as not to allow the reigning impressions of his mind to shew themselves in the midst of his affected extravagance. It turned chiefly on his love to *Ophelia*, which he meant to hold forth as its greatest subject; but it frequently glanced on the wickedness of his uncle, his know-ledge of which it was certainly his business to conceal.

In two of *Shakespeare*'s tragedies are introduced at the same time instances of counterfeit madness and of real distraction. In both plays the same distinction is observed, and the false discriminated from the true by similar appearances. *Lear*'s imagination con-stantly runs on the ingratitude of his daughters and the resignation of his crown; and *Ophelia*, after she has wasted the first ebullience of her distraction in some wild and incoherent sentences, fixes on the death of her father for the subject of her song,

> *They bore him bare-fac'd on the bier* ——
> *And will he not come again,*
> *And will he not come again?* &c.   [4.5.165ff.]

But *Edgar* puts on a semblance as opposite as may be to his real situation and his ruling thoughts. He never ventures on any expression bordering on the subjects of a father's cruelty or a son's misfortune. *Hamlet*, in the same manner, were he as firm in mind as *Edgar*, would never have hinted any thing in his affected disorder that might lead to a suspicion of his having discovered the villany of his uncle; but his feeling, too powerful for his prudence, often breaks through that disguise which it seems to have been his original and ought to have continued his invariable purpose to maintain, till an opportunity should present itself of accomplishing the revenge which he meditated.

Of the reality of *Hamlet*'s love doubts also have been suggested. But if that delicacy of feeling, approaching to weakness, which I contend for be allowed him, the affected abuse, which he suffers at last to grow into scurrility of his mistress will, I think, be found not inconsistent with the truth of his affection for her. Feeling its real force, and designing to play the madman on that ground, he would naturally go as far from the reality as possible. Had he not loved her at all, or slightly loved her, he might have kept up some appearance of passion amidst his feigned insanity; but really loving her, he would have been hurt by such a resemblance in the counterfeit. We can bear a downright caricature of our friend much easier than an unfavourable likeness.

It must be allowed, however, that the momentous scenes in which he is afterwards engaged seem to have smothered, if not extinguished the feelings of his love. His total forgetfulness of *Ophelia*, so soon after her death, cannot easily be justified. It is vain, indeed, to attempt justifying *Shakespeare* in such particulars. '*Time*,' says Dr Johnson, '*toil'd after him in vain*.' He seems often to forget its rights, as well in the progress of the passions as in the business of the stage. That change of feeling and of resolution which time only can effect he brings forth within the limits of a single scene. Whether love is to be excited or resentment allayed, guilt to be made penitent or sorrow chearful, the effect is frequently produced in a space hardly sufficient for words to express it.

It has been remarked that our great poet was not so happy in the delineation of *love* as of the other passions. Were it not treason against the majesty of *Shakespeare* one might observe that, though he looked with a sort of instinctive perception into the recesses of Nature, yet it was impossible for him to possess a knowledge of the refinements of delicacy, or to catch in his pictures the nicer shades of polished manners; and without this knowledge love can seldom be introduced on the stage without a degree of coarseness which will offend an audience of good taste. This observation is not meant to extend to *Shakespeare*'s tragic scenes: in situations of deep distress or violent emotion the *manners* are lost in the *passions*; but if we examine his *lovers*, in the lighter scenes of ordinary life, we shall generally find them trespassing against the rules of decorum and the feelings of delicacy.

That gaiety and playfulness of deportment and of conversation which *Hamlet* sometimes not only assumes, but seems actually disposed to is, I apprehend, no contradiction to the general tone of melancholy in his character. That sort of melancholy which is the most genuine as well as the most amiable of any, neither arising from natural sourness of temper nor prompted by accidental chagrine, but the effect of delicate sensibility impressed with a sense of sorrow or a feeling of its own weakness, will, I believe, often be found indulging itself in a sportfulness of external behaviour amidst the pressure of a sad, or even the anguish of a broken heart. Slighter emotions affect our ordinary discourse; but deep distress, sitting in the secret gloom of the soul, casts not its regard on the common occurrences of life, but suffers them to trick themselves out in the usual garb of indifference or of gaiety, according to the fashion of the society around it or the situation in which they chance to arise. The melancholy man feels in himself (if I may be allowed the expression) a sort of double person; one that, covered with the darkness of its imagination, looks not forth into the world nor takes any concern in vulgar objects or frivolous pursuits; another, which he lends, as it were, to ordinary men, which can accommodate itself to their tempers and manners, and indulge, without feeling any degradation from the indulgence, a smile with the chearful and a laugh with the giddy.

The conversation of *Hamlet* with the *Grave-digger* seems to me to

279

be perfectly accounted for under this supposition; and instead of feeling it counteract the tragic effect of the story I never see him in that scene without receiving, from his transient jests with the clown before him, an idea of the deepest melancholy being rooted at his heart. The light point of view in which he places serious and important things marks the power of that great impression which swallows up every thing else in his mind, which makes *Caesar* and *Alexander* so indifferent to him that he can trace their remains in the plaster of a cottage or the stopper of a beer-barrel. It is from the same turn of mind which, from the elevation of its sorrows, looks down on the bustle of ambition and the pride of fame, that he breaks forth into the reflection in the 4th act on the expedition of *Fortinbras*.

It is with regret, as well as deference, that I accuse the judgement of Mr *Garrick*, or the taste of his audience; but I cannot help thinking that the exclusion of the scene of the *Grave-digger* in his alteration of the tragedy of *Hamlet* was not only a needless but an unnatural violence done to the work of his favourite poet.

Shakespeare's genius attended him in all his extravagancies. In the licence he took of departing from the regularity of the drama, or in his ignorance of those critical rules which might have restrained him within it, there is this advantage, that it gives him an opportunity of delineating the passions and affections of the human mind as they exist in reality, with all the various colourings which they receive in the mixed scenes of life; not as they are accommodated by the hands of more artificial poets to one great undivided impression, or an uninterrupted chain of congenial events. It seems, therefore, preposterous to endeavour to regularize his plays at the expence of depriving them of this peculiar excellence, especially as the alteration can only produce a very partial and limited improvement, and can never bring his pieces to the standard of criticism or the form of the *Aristotelian* drama. Within the bounds of a pleasure-garden we may be allowed to smooth our terrasses and trim our hedge-rows; but it were equally absurd and impracticable to apply the minute labours of the *roller* and the *pruning-knife* to the noble irregularity of trackless mountains and impenetrable forests. (393–400)

265. Edmond Malone and others, supplements to Shakespeare

1780

From *Supplement to the Edition of Shakespeare's Plays published in 1778 by Samuel Johnson and George Steevens. In two Volumes. Containing additional Observations by several of the former Commentators: to which are subjoined the genuine Poems of the same Author, and seven Plays that have been ascribed to him; with Notes by the Editor and others* (1780). Malone prepared a 'Second Appendix' to this supplement in 1783, No. 275.

Edmond Malone (1741–1812) was educated privately and at Trinity College, Dublin. A lawyer for ten years, he established himself in London in 1777 as a private man of letters, and became a close friend of Johnson, Boswell, Reynolds, Percy, Walpole, Burke, Farmer, and Steevens. He assisted Boswell with his biography of Johnson, and edited several reissues of that work; in addition to his Shakespearian labours he edited the works of Goldsmith (1780) and Reynolds (1791), and Dryden's prose works (1800). Malone also published an account of the origin of the plot of *The Tempest* (2 vols, 1808–9), and exposed the forgeries of Chatterton's Rowley poems, and Ireland's Shakespeare papers. He left his materials for a new edition of Shakespeare to James Boswell the younger, who issued a twenty-one volume edition in 1821. The bulk of his collection of early printed books and manuscripts is in the Bodleian. See John Nichols, *Illustrations of the Literary History of the Eighteenth Century* (London, 1817–58, 8 vols), v (1828), pp. 444–67; James Prior, *Life of Edmond Malone* (1860); D. N. Smith, 'Malone', *Huntington Library Quarterly*, 3 (1939), 23–36; Arthur Brown, *Edmond Malone and English Scholarship* (inaugural lecture, University College, London, 1963).

[1] [From Malone's 'Supplemental Observations', on theatre production methods in Shakespeare's time]

... If a bed-chamber is to be exhibited no change of scene is mentioned, but the property-man is simply ordered *to thrust forth a bed.* When the fable requires the Roman capitol to be exhibited we find two officers enter, 'to lay cushions, *as it were* in the capitol.' So, in *King Richard II.* act iv. sc. i. 'Bolingbroke, &c. enter *as* to the parliament.' [Folio.] Again, in *Sir John Oldcastle,* 1600: 'Enter Cambridge, Scroop, and Gray, *as* in a chamber.' In *Romeo and Juliet* I doubt much whether any exhibition of Juliet's monument was given on the stage. I imagine Romeo only opened with his mattock one of the stage trap-doors (which might have represented a tomb-stone), by which he descended to a vault beneath the stage where Juliet was deposited; and this idea is countenanced by a passage in the play, and by the poem on which the drama was founded*. . .

All these circumstances induce me to believe that our ancient theatres, in general, were only furnished with curtains, and a single scene composed of tapestry, which appears to have been some-times ornamented with pictures: and some passages in our old dramas incline one to think that when tragedies were performed the stage was hung with black. (I, 18–21)

[From the additional notes]
[2] [On *Much Ado About Nothing,* 5.1.16: 'Bid sorrow wag cry hem!']

With respect to the word *wag,* the using it as a verb, in the sense of *to play the wag,* is entirely in Shakespeare's manner. There is scarcely one of his plays in which we do not find substantives used as verbs. Thus we meet—to testimony, to boy, to couch, to grave, to bench, to voice, to paper, to page, to dram, to stage, to fever, to fool, to palate, to mountebank, to god, to virgin, to passion, to mystery, to fable, to wall, to period, to spaniel, to stranger, &c. &c. MALONE. (I, 109)

---

* 'Why I *descend* into this bed of death.' *Romeo and Juliet, act v.* So, in *The Tragical History of Romeus and Juliet,* 1562:

> And then our Romeus, the *vault-stone set up-right,*
> *Descended* downe, and in his hand he bore the candle light.

Juliet, however, after her recovery speaks and dies upon the stage.—If therefore, the exhibition was such as has been now supposed, Romeo must have brought her up in his arms from the vault beneath the stage, after he had killed Paris, and then addressed her—'O my love, my wife, &c.'

[3] [On *Macbeth*, 1.6.1ff.]

This castle hath a pleasant seat.] This short dialogue between Duncan and Banquo, whilst they are approaching the gates of Macbeth's castle, has always appeared to me a striking instance of what in painting is termed *repose*. Their conversation very naturally turns upon the beauty of its situation, and the pleasantness of the air; and Banquo observing the martlet's nests in every recess of the cornice, remarks that where those birds most breed and haunt the air is delicate. The subject of this quiet and easy conversation gives that repose so necessary to the mind after the tumultuous bustle of the preceding scenes, and perfectly contrasts the scene of horror that immediately succeeds. It seems as if Shakespeare asked himself, What is a prince likely to say to his attendants on such an occasion? Whereas the modern writers seem, on the contrary, to be always searching for new thoughts, such as would never occur to men in the situation which is represented. Sir J. REYNOLDS. (I, 152)

[4] [*Ibid.*, 2.2.62: 'the multitudinous seas incarnadine']

By *the multitudinous seas* the poet, I suppose, meant not the various seas, or seas of every denomination, as the Caspian &c. but the seas which swarm with myriads of inhabitants . . . It is objected by a rhetorical commentator on our author[1] that Macbeth in his present disposition of mind would hardly have adverted to a property of the sea which has so little relation to the object immediately before him; and if Macbeth had really spoken this speech in his castle of Invernesse the remark would be just. But the critick should have remembered that this speech is not the real effusion of a distempered mind but the composition of Shakespeare; of that poet who has put a circumstantial account of an apothecary's shop into the mouth of Romeo the moment after he has heard the fatal news of his beloved Juliet's death; and has made Othello, when in the anguish of his heart he determines to kill his wife, digress from the object which agitates his soul to describe minutely the course of the Pontick sea. MALONE. (I, 153–4)

[5] [On *Hamlet*, 3.4.30: Queen: 'As kill a king!']

It has been doubted whether Shakespeare intended to represent the queen as accessary to the murder of her husband.[2] The surprize she here expresses at the charge seems to tend to her exculpation.

---

[1] William Kenrick, *Introduction to the School of Shakespeare* (1774), pp. 34–6.

[2] See Steevens's reply to Voltaire, p. 199 above.

Where the variation is not particularly marked out, we may presume, I think, that the poet intended to tell his story as it had been told before. The following extract therefore from *The Hystory of Hamblet*,[1] black letter, relative to this point, will probably not be unacceptable to the reader. [Quotes passages where Gertrude is said to be guilty of incest only, and defends herself from the charge of complicity in murder.]

It is observable that in the drama neither the king or queen make so good a defence. Shakespeare wished to render them as odious as he could, and therefore has not in any part of the play furnished them with even the semblance of an excuse for their conduct. MALONE. (I, 358–9)

[6] [On the complicity of Rosencrantz and Guildenstern, in Saxo Grammaticus and *The Hystory of Hamblet*]

From this narrative it appears that the faithful ministers of Fengon were not unacquainted with the import of the letters they bore. Shakespeare, who has followed the story pretty closely, probably meant to describe their representatives, Rosencrantz and Guildenstern, as equally guilty; as confederating with the king to deprive Hamlet of his life. So that his procuring their execution, though certainly not absolutely necessary to his own safety, does not appear to have been a wanton and unprovoked cruelty, as Mr. Steevens has supposed in his very ingenious observations on the general character and conduct of the prince throughout this piece. [Cf. Vol. 5, pp. 540f.]

In the conclusion of his drama the poet has entirely deviated from the fabulous history, which in other places he has frequently followed. MALONE (I, 361–2)

[7] [On *Venus and Adonis*]

This poem is received as one of Shakespeare's undisputed performances, a circumstance which recommends it to the notice it might otherwise have escaped.

There are some excellencies which are less graceful than even their opposite defects; there are some virtues which, being merely constitutional, are entitled to very small degrees of praise. Our poet might design his Adonis to engage our esteem; and yet the

---

[1] Modern scholarship has shown this pamphlet to be later than the play.

sluggish coldness of his disposition is as offensive as the impetuous forwardness of his wanton mistress. To exhibit a young man insensible to the caresses of transcendent beauty is to describe a being too rarely seen to be acknowledged as a natural character; and when seen, of too little value to deserve such toil of representation. No elogiums are due to Shakespeare's hero on the score of mental chastity, for he does not pretend to have subdued his desires to his moral obligations. He strives indeed, with Platonick absurdity, to draw that line which was never drawn; to make that distinction which never can be made; to separate the purer from the grosser part of love; assigning limits, and ascribing bounds to each, and calling them by different names; but if we take his own word he will be found at last only to prefer one gratification to another, the sports of the field to the enjoyment of immortal charms. The reader will easily confess that no great respect is due to the judgment of such a would-be Hercules with such a choice before him.—In short, the story of Joseph and the wife of Potiphar is the more interesting of the two; for the passions of the former are repressed by conscious rectitude of mind and obedience to the highest law. The present narrative only includes the disappointment of an eager female and the death of an unsusceptible boy. The deity, from her language, should seem to have been educated in the school of Messalina; the youth, from his backwardness, might be suspected of having felt the discipline of a Turkish seraglio.

It is not indeed very clear whether Shakespeare meant on this occasion, with Le Brun, to recommend continence as a virtue, or to try his hand with Aretine on a licentious canvas. If our poet had any moral design in view, he has been unfortunate in his conduct of it. The shield which he lifts in defence of chastity is wrought with such meretricious imagery as cannot fail to counteract a moral purpose—Shakespeare, however, was no unskilful mythologist, and must have known that Adonis was the offspring of Cynaras and Myrrha. His judgment therefore would have prevented him from raising an example of continence out of the produce of an incestuous bed.—— Considering this piece only in the light of a *jeu d'esprit*, written without peculiar tendency, we shall even then be sorry that our author was unwilling to leave the character of his hero as he found it; for the common and more pleasing fable assures us that

———when bright Venus yielded up her charms,
The blest Adonis languish'd in her arms.

We should therefore have been better pleased to have seen him in the situation of Ascanius,

—cum gremio fotum dea tollit in altos
Idaliæ lucos, ubi mollis amaracus illum
Floribus et multa aspirans complectitur umbra;[1]

than in the very act of repugnance to female temptation; self-denial being rarely found in the catalouge of Pagan virtues.

If we enquire into the poetical merit of this performance it will do no honour to the reputation of its author. The great excellence of Shakespeare is to be sought in dramatick dialogue; expressing his intimate acquaintance with every passion that sooths or ravages, exalts or debases the human mind. Dialogue is a form of composition which has been known to quicken even the genius of those, who in mere uninterrupted narrative have sunk to a level with the multitude of common writers. The smaller pieces of Otway and Rowe have added nothing to their fame.

Let it be remembered too that a contemporary author, Dr. Gabriel Harvey, points out the *Venus and Adonis* as a favourite only with *the young*; while *graver* readers bestowed their attention on the *Rape of Lucrece*. Here I cannot help observing that the poetry of the Roman legend is no jot superior to that of the mythological story. A tale which Ovid has completely and affectingly told in about one hundred and forty verses, our author has coldly and imperfectly spun out into near two thousand. The attention therefore of these *graver* personages must have been engaged by the moral tendency of the piece rather than by the force of style in which it is related. STEEVENS.

This first essay of Shakespeare's Muse does not appear to me so entirely void of poetical merit as it has been represented. In what high estimation it was held in our author's life-time, may be collected from what has been already observed in the preliminary remark, and from the circumstances mentioned in a note which the reader will find at the end of *The Rape of Lucrece*. [See next item.] MALONE (I, 462–3)

---

[1] Virgil, *Aeneid*, 1.692ff.: 'Venus pours over the limbs of Ascanius the dew of gentle repose and, fondling him in her bosom, uplifts him with divine power to Idalia's high groves, where soft marjoram enwraps him in flowers and the breath of its high shade.'

[8] [On *The Rape of Lucrece*]

In examining this and the preceding poem we should do Shakespeare injustice were we to try them by a comparison with more modern and polished productions; or with our present idea of poetical excellence.

It has been observed that few authors rise much above the age in which they live. If their performances reach the standard of perfection established in their own time, or surpass somewhat the productions of their contemporaries, they seldom aim farther; for if their readers are satisfied it is not probable that they should be discontented. The poems of *Venus and Adonis* and *The Rape of Lucrece*, whatever opinion may be now entertained of them, were certainly much admired in Shakespeare's life-time. In thirteen years after their first appearance six impressions of each of them were printed; while in the same period his *Romeo and Juliet* (one of his most popular plays) passed only twice through the press. They appear to me superior to any pieces of the same kind produced by Daniel or Drayton, the most celebrated writers in this species of narrative poetry that were then known. The applause bestowed on *The Rosamond* of the former author, which was published in 1592, gave birth, I imagine, to the present poem. The stanza is the same in both.

No compositions were in that age oftner quoted, or more honourably mentioned, than these two of Shakespeare. . . .

If it should be asked, how comes it to pass that Shakespeare in his dramatick productions also, did not content himself with only doing as well as those play-wrights who had gone before him, or perhaps somewhat surpassing them; how it happened that whilst his contemporaries on the stage crept in the most groveling and contemptible prose, or stalked in ridiculous and bombastick blank verse, he has penetrated the inmost recesses of the human mind, and not contented with ranging through the wide field of nature has with equal boldness and felicity often expatiated *extra flammantia mœnia mundi*;[1] the answer, I believe, must be that his disposition was more inclined to the drama than to the other kinds of poetry; that his genius for the one appears to have been almost a gift from heaven, his abilities for the other only the same as those of other mortals.

The great defect of these two poems seems to be the wearisome

[1] Lucretius, *de Rerum Natura*, 1.72ff.: 'he passed on far beyond the fiery walls of the world'.

circumlocution with which the tale in each of them is told. When the reader thinks himself almost at his journey's end he is led through many an intricate path, and after travelling for some hours finds his inn yet at a distance: nor are his wanderings repaid, or his labour alleviated, by any extraordinary fertility in the country through which he passes; by grotesqueness of imagery, or variety of prospect. MALONE. (I, 574–5)

[9] [On Sonnet 1:]

> —*this glutton be,*
> *To eat the world's due,* by the *grave and thee.*]

The ancient editors of Shakespeare's works deserve at least the praise of impartiality. If they have occasionally corrupted his noblest sentiments, they have likewise depraved his most miserable conceits; as perhaps in this instance. I read (piteous constraint, to read such stuff at all!)

> ——this glutton be;
> To eat the world's due, *be thy* grave and thee.

i.e. be at once thyself and thy grave. The letters that form the two words were probably transposed. I did not think the late Mr. Rich had such example for the contrivance of making Harlequin jump down his own throat. STEEVENS. (I, 577–8)

[10] [On Sonnet 20: 'the master–mistress of my passions']
It is impossible to read this fulsome panegyrick, addressed to a male object, without an equal mixture of disgust and indignation. We may remark also that the same phrase employed by Shakespeare to denote the height of encomium is used by Dryden to express the extreme of reproach:

> That woman, but more daub'd; or, if a man,
> Corrupted to a woman; thy *man-mistress.*
>
> *Don Sebastian.*

Let me be just, however, to our author, who has made a proper use of the term *male varlet* in *Troilus and Cressida.* STEEVENS (I, 596)

[11] [On Sonnet 30: 'And moan the expence of many a vanish'd sight']
I cannot see any connexion between this and the foregoing or

subsequent lines; nor do I well understand what is meant by the *expence* of many a vanish'd sight. I suspect the author wrote:

> And moan the expence of many a vanish'd *sigh*,

which in his time might have been pronounced so hard as to make some kind of rhime to *night*. So, in *2 K. Henry VI*: 'blood-*consuming sighs*.' [3.2.61]
Again, in *Pericles*: 'Do not *consume* your blood with *sorrowing*.' [4.1.22f.] MALONE.

Such laboured perplexities of language, and such studied deformities of style, prevail throughout these Sonnets that the reader (after our best endeavours at explanation) will frequently find reason to exclaim with Imogen:

> I see before me, neither here, nor here,
> Nor what ensues; but have a fog in them
> That I cannot look through.   [*Cymbeline*, 3.2.78ff.]

I suppose, however, that by the *expence of many a vanish'd sight* the poet means the *loss of many an object* which, being 'gone hence, *is no more seen*.' STEEVENS. (I, 606)

[12] [On Sonnet 54:]

> *The* canker-blooms *have full as deep a dye,*
> *As the perfumed tincture of the roses,*]

The *canker* is the *canker-rose* or *dog-rose*. The rose and the canker are opposed in like manner in *Much ado about Nothing*: 'I had rather be a *canker* in a hedge than a *rose* in his grace.' MALONE.

Shakespeare had not yet begun to observe the productions of nature with accuracy, or his eyes would have convinced him that the *cynorhodon* is by no means of as deep a colour as the *rose*. But what has truth or nature to do with Sonnets? STEEVENS. (I, 624–5)

[13] [On Sonnet 73: 'Bare ruin'd choirs']
. . . *Quires* or *choirs* here means that part of cathedrals where divine service is performed, to which, when uncovered and in ruins, 'A naked subject to the weeping clouds,' the poet compares the trees at the end of autumn, stripped of that foliage which at once invited and sheltered the feathered songsters of summer. So, in *Cymbeline* [3.3.60ff.]:

> Then was I as a *tree*
> Whose boughs did bend with fruit; but in one night,
> A storm, or robbery, call it what you will,
> Shook down my mellow hangings, nay, my *leaves*,
> And left me *bare to weather*.   MALONE.

This image was probably suggested to Shakespeare by our desolated monasteries. The resemblance between the vaulting of a Gothick aisle and an avenue of trees whose upper branches meet and form an arch over-head, is too striking not to be acknowledged. When the roof of the one is shattered and the boughs of the other leafless, the comparison becomes yet more solemn and picturesque. STEEVENS. (I, 640)

[14] [On Sonnet 93:]

> *So shall I live, supposing thou art true,*
> *Like a deceived husband;*—]

Mr. Oldys observes in one of his manuscripts that this and the preceding Sonnet '*seem to have been addressed by Shakespeare to his beautiful wife on some suspicion of her infidelity.*' He must have read our author's poems with but little attention; otherwise he would have seen that these, as well as all the preceding Sonnets, and many of those that follow are not addressed to a female. I do not know whether this antiquarian had any other authority than his misapprehension concerning these lines for the epithet by which he has described out great poet's wife. He had made very large collections for a life of our author; and perhaps in the course of his researches had learned this particular. However this may have been, the other part of his conjecture (that Shakespeare was jealous of her) may perhaps be thought to derive some probability from the following circumstances. It is observable that his daughter, and not his wife, is his executor; and in his Will he bequeaths the latter only an old piece of furniture[1]; nor did he even think of her till the whole was finished, the clause relating to her being an interlineation. What provision was made for her by settlement does not appear. It may likewise be remarked that jealousy is the principal hinge of *four* of his plays; and in his great performance

---

[1] This is Malone's interpretation of the reason for Shakespeare's bequest to his wife—according to Malone's reading of the Will—of 'his brown best bed': 'our author's forgetfulness of his wife'. (I, 657) The Will in fact reads 'second best', that is, the bed that Shakespeare and his wife slept in.

(*Othello*) some of the passages are written with such exquisite feeling as might lead us to suspect that the author had himself been *perplexed* with doubts, though not perhaps *in the extreme*.—By the same mode of reasoning, it may be said, he might be proved to have stabbed his friend or to have had a *thankless* child; because he has so admirably described the horror consequent on murder, and the effects of filial ingratitude, in *K. Lear* and *Mecbeth*. He could indeed assume all shapes, and therefore it must be acknowledged that the present hypothesis is built on an uncertain foundation. All I mean to say is that he appears to me to have written more immediately *from the heart* on the subject of jealousy than on any other; and it is therefore not improbable he might have felt it. The whole is mere conjecture. MALONE.

As all that is known with any degree of certainty concerning Shakespeare is—*that he was born at Stratford upon Avon,—married and had children there,—went to London, where he commenced actor, and wrote poems and plays—returned to Stratford, made his will, died, and was buried*—I must confess my readiness to combat every unfounded supposition respecting the particular occurrences of his life. STEEVENS.

[Steevens goes on to reject the authenticity of the anecdote that Shakespeare wrote Thomas Combe's epitaph.]

That our poet was jealous of this lady is likewise an unwarrantable conjecture. Having, in times of health and prosperity, provided for her by settlement (or knowing that her father had already done so), he bequeathed to her at his death not merely *an old piece of furniture* but perhaps, as a mark of peculiar tenderness,

> The very bed that on his bridal night
> Receiv'd him to the arms of Belvidera.

His momentary forgetfulness as to this matter must be imputed to disease. . . .

That Shakespeare has written with his utmost power on the subject of jealousy is no proof that he had ever felt it. Because he has with equal vigour expressed the varied aversions of Apemantus and Timon to the world, does it follow that he himself was a Cynic, or a wretch deserted by his friends? Because he has, with proportionable strength of pencil, represented the vindictive cruelty of Shylock, are we to suppose he copied from a fiend-like original in his own bosom?

291

Let me add (respecting the four plays alluded to by Mr. Malone) that in *Cymbeline* jealousy is merely incidental. In the *Winter's Tale* and the *Merry Wives of Windsor* the folly of it is studiously exposed. *Othello* alone is wholly built on the fatal consequences of that destructive passion. Surely we cannot wonder that our author should have lavished his warmest colouring on a commotion of mind the most vehement of all others; or that he should have written with sensibility on a subject with which every man who loves is in some degree acquainted. Besides, of different pieces by the same hand one will prove the most highly wrought, though sufficient reasons cannot be assigned to account for its superiority.

No argument however, in my opinion, is more fallacious than that which imputes the success of a poet to his interest in his subject. Accuracy of description can be expected only from a mind at rest. It is the unruffled lake that is a faithful mirror. STEEVENS. (I, 653–6)

[15] [On Sonnet 127: 'In the old age black was not counted fair']
All the remaining Sonnets are addressed to a female. MALONE.

A Sonnet was surely the contrivance of some literary Procrustes. The single thought of which it is to consist, however luxuriant, must be cramped within fourteen verses, or, however scanty, must be spun out into the same number. On a chain of certain links the existence of this metrical whim depends; and its reception is secure as soon as the admirers of it have counted their expected and statutable proportion of rhimes. The gratification of head or heart is no object of the writer's ambition. That a few of these trifles deserving a better character may be found, I shall not venture to deny; for chance co-operating with art and genius will occasionally produce wonders.

Of the Sonnets before us, one hundred and twenty-six are inscribed (as Mr. Malone observes) to a friend: the remaining twenty-eight (a small proportion out of so many) are devoted to a mistress. Yet if our author's Ferdinand and Romeo had not expressed themselves in terms more familiar to human understanding, I believe few readers would have rejoiced in the happiness of the one, or sympathized with the sorrows of the other. Perhaps indeed, quaintness, obscurity, and tautology are to be regarded as the constituent parts of this exotick species of composition. But, in whatever the excellence of it may consist, I profess I am one of those who should have wished it to have expired in the country where it was born, had it not fortunately provoked the ridicule of *Lope de Vega*; which, being faintly imitated by *Voiture*, was at last transfused into English by Mr. Roderick, and exhibited as follows, in the second volume of Dodsley's Collection.

A Sonnet

Capricious Wray a sonnet needs must have;
  I ne'er was so put to't before:—a sonnet!
Why, fourteen verses must be spent upon it:
'Tis good, howe'er, to have conquer'd the first stave.

Yet I shall ne'er find rhymes enough by half,
  Said I, and found myself i' the midst o' the second.
If twice four verses were but fairly reckon'd,
I should turn back on th' hardest part, and laugh.

Thus far, with good success, I think I've scribled,
  And of the twice seven lines have clean got o'er ten.
Courage! another'll finish the first triplet.
  Thanks to thee, Muse, my work begins to shorten,
There's thirteen lines got through, driblet by driblet.
  'Tis done. Count how you will, I warr'nt there's fourteen.

[Steevens cites, as another 'unpoetical' sonnet, Milton's 'A book was writ of late call'd Tetrachordon', and refers readers further to the works of Joshua Sylvester.]

In the mean time, let inferiour writers be warned against a species of composition which has reduced the most exalted poets to a level with the meanest rhimers; has almost cut down Milton and Shakespeare to the standards of Pomfret and—but the name of Pomfret is perhaps the lowest in the scale of English versifiers. As for Mr. Malone, whose animadversions are to follow mine, 'Now is he for the numbers that Petrarch flowed in.' Let me however borrow somewhat in my own favour from the same speech of Mercutio by observing that 'Laura had a better love to be-rhyme her.' Let me adopt also the sentiment which Shakespeare himself, on his amended judgment, has put into the mouth of his favourite character in *Love's Labour's Lost* [4.3.156].

  Tut! none but minstrels like of *Sonneting*.   STEEVENS.

I do not feel any great propensity to stand forth as the champion of these compositions. However, as it appears to me that they have been somewhat under-rated, I think it incumbent on me to do them that justice to which they seem entitled.

Of Petrarch (whose works I have never read) I cannot speak; but I am slow to believe that a writer who has been warmly admired for four centuries by his own countrymen is without merit, though he has been guilty of the heinous offence of addressing his mistress in pieces of only that number of lines which by long usage has been appropriated to the sonnet.

The burlesque stanzas which have been produced to depretiate the poems before us, it must be acknowledged, are not ill executed; but they will never decide the merit of this species of composition until it shall be established that ridicule is the test of truth. The fourteen rugged lines that have been quoted from Milton for the same purpose are equally inconclusive; for it is well known that he generally failed when he attempted rhime, whether his verses assumed the shape of a sonnet or any other form. These pieces of our author therefore must at last stand or fall by themselves.

When they are described as mass of affectation, pedantry, circumlocution, and nonsense, the picture appears to me over-charged. Their great defects seem to be a want of variety, and the majority of them not being directed to a female, to whom alone such ardent expressions of esteem could with propriety be addressed. It cannot be denied too that they contain some farfetched conceits; but are our author's plays entirely free from them? Many of the thoughts that occur in his dramatick productions are found here likewise; as may appear from the numerous parallels that have been cited from his dramas, chiefly for the purpose of authenticating these poems. Had they therefore no other merit, they are entitled to our attention as often illustrating obscure passages in his plays.

I do not perceive that the versification of these pieces is less smooth and harmonious than that of Shakespeare's other compositions. Though many of them are not so simple and clear as they ought to be, yet some of them are written with perspicuity and energy. A few have been already pointed out as deserving this character; and many beautiful lines scattered through these poems will, it is supposed, strike every reader who is not determined to allow no praise to any species of poetry except blank verse or heroick couplets. MALONE.

The case of these Sonnets is certainly bad when so little can be

294

advanced in support of them. Ridicule is always successful where it is just. A burlesque on *Alexander's Feast* would do no injury to its original. Some of the rhime compositions of Milton (Sonnets excepted) are allowed to be eminently harmonious. Is it necessary on this occasion to particularize his *Allegro, Penseroso*, and *Hymn on the Nativity*? I must add, that there is more conceit in any thirty-six of Shakespeare's *Sonnets*, than in the same number of his *Plays*. When I know where that person is to be found who *allows no praise to any species of poetry, except blank verse and heroic couplets*, it will be early enough for me to undertake his defence. STEEVENS.

That ridicule is generally successful when it is just, cannot be denied; but whether it be just in the present instance is the point to be proved. It may be successful when it is not just; when neither the structure nor the thoughts of the poem ridiculed deserve to be derided.

No burlesque on *Alexander's Feast* certainly would render it ridiculous; yet undoubtedly a successful parody or burlesque piece might be formed upon it, which in itself might have intrinsick merit. The success of the burlesque therefore does not necessarily depend upon, nor ascertain, the demerit of the original. Of this Cotton's *Virgil Travestie* affords a decisive proof. The most rigid muscles must relax on the perusal of it; yet the purity and majesty of the *Eneid* will ever remain undiminished.—With respect to Milton (of whom I have only said that he *generally*, not that he *always* failed in rhyming compositions), Dryden, at a time when all rivalry and competition between them were at an end, when he had ceased to write for the stage, and when of course it was indifferent to him what metre was considered as best suited to dramatick compositions, pronounced that he composed his great poem in blank verse 'because rhime was not his talent. He had neither (adds the Laureate) the ease of doing it, nor the graces of it; which is manifest in his *Juvenilia* or Verses written in his youth; *where his rhime is always constrained, and forced, and comes hardly from him*, at an age when the soul is most pliant, and the passion of love makes almost every man a rhimer, though not a poet.' MALONE.

Cotton's work is an innocent parody, was designed as no ridicule on the Æneid, and consequently will not operate to the disadvantage of that immortal poem. The contrary is the case with Mr. Roderick's imitation of the Spaniard. He wrote it as a ridicule on the *structure*, not the *words* of a *Sonnet*; and this is a purpose

295

which it has completely answered. No one ever retired from a perusal of it with a favourable opinion of the species of composition it was meant to deride.

The decisions of Dryden are never less to be trusted than when he treats of blank verse and rhime, each of which he has extolled and depreciated in its turn. When this subject is before him his judgment is rarely secure from the seductions of convenience, interest or jealousy; and Gildon has well observed that in his prefaces he had always confidence enough to defend and support his own most glaring inconsistencies and self-contradictions. What he has said of the author of *Paradise Lost* is with a view to retaliation. Milton had invidiously asserted that Dryden was *only a rhymist*; and therefore Dryden, with as little regard to truth, has declared that Milton was *no rhymist at all*. Let my other sentiments shift for themselves. Here I shall drop the controversy. STEEVENS.

In justice to Shakespeare, whose cause I have undertaken, however unequal to the task, I cannot forbear to add that a literary Procrustes may as well be called the inventor of the couplet, the stanza, or the ode as of the Sonnet. They are all in a certain degree restraints on the writer; and all poetry, if the objection now made be carried to its utmost extent, will be reduced to blank verse. The admirers of this kind of metre have long remarked with triumph that of the couplet the first line is generally for sense, and the next for rhime; and this certainly is often the case in the compositions of mere versifiers; but is such a redundancy an essential property of a couplet, and will the works of Dryden and Pope afford none of another character?—The bondage to which Pindar and his followers have submitted in the structure of strophé, antistrophé, and epode is much greater than that which the Sonnet imposes. If the scanty thought be disgustingly dilated, or luxuriant ideas unnaturally compressed, what follows? Not surely that it is impossible to write good Odes, or good Sonnets, but that the poet was injudicious in the choice of his subject, or knew not how to adjust his metre to his thoughts. MALONE. (I, 682–7)

[16] [Malone on *Pericles*]
There is, I believe, no play of our author's, perhaps I might say in the English language, so incorrect as this. The most corrupt of Shakespeare's other dramas, compared with *Pericles*, is purity itself. The metre is seldom attended to; verse is frequently printed as prose, and the grossest errors abound in almost every page. (II, 4)

In a former disquisition concerning this play I mentioned that
the dumb shows which are found in it induced me to doubt
whether it came from the pen of Shakespeare. The sentiments that
I then expressed were suggested by a very hasty and transient
survey of the piece. I am still, however, of opinion, that this
consideration (our author having expressly ridiculed such exhibitions) might in a very doubtful question have some weight. But
weaker proofs must yield to stronger. It is idle to lay any great
stress upon such a slight circumstance when the piece itself
furnishes internal and irresistible evidence of its authenticity. The
congenial sentiments, the numerous expressions bearing a striking
similitude to passages in his undisputed plays, the incidents, the
situations of the persons, the colour of the style, at least through
the greater part of the play, all, in my apprehension, conspire to set
the seal of Shakespeare on this performance. What then shall we
say to these dumb shows? Either that the poet's practice was not
always conformable to his opinions (of which there are abundant
proofs), or (what I rather believe to be the case) that this was one of
his earliest dramas, written at a time when these exhibitions were
much admired, and before he had seen the absurdity of such
ridiculous pageants: probably in the year 1590, or 1591.

Mr. Rowe in his first edition of Shakespeare says 'it is owned
that some part of *Pericles* certainly was written by him, particularly
the last act.'[1] Dr. Farmer, whose opinion in every thing that relates
to our author has deservedly the greatest weight, thinks the hand
of Shakespeare may be sometimes seen in the latter part of the play
and there only. The scene in the last act, in which Pericles discovers
his daughter, is indeed eminently beautiful; but the whole piece
appears to me to furnish abundant proofs of the hand of
Shakespeare. The inequalities in different parts of it are not greater
than may be found in some of his other dramas. (II, 158–9)

[Malone then announces that Steevens disagrees, and prints first
Steevens's dissertation, which is in answer to his own
(pp. 160–79), giving himself the last word (pp. 179–86).]

[17] [Steevens on *Pericles*]
That this tragedy has some merit, it were vain to deny; but that it is
the entire composition of Shakespeare is more than can be hastily
granted. I shall not venture, with Dr. Farmer, to determine that the
hand of our great poet is *only* visible in the last act, for I think it
appears in several passages dispersed over each of these divisions. I

[1] Vol. 2, p. 192.

find it difficult however to persuade myself that he was the original fabricator of the plot, or the author of every dialogue, chorus, &c. and this opinion is founded on a concurrence of circumstances which I shall attempt to enumerate, that the reader may have the benefit of all the lights I am able to throw on so obscure a subject. (II, 160)

[Steevens's argument is based on the metre of the choruses; on differences in vocabulary; on Shakespeare's infrequent use of Gower; on the dumb shows.]

Next it may be remarked that the valuable parts of *Pericles* are more distinguished by their poetical turn than by variety of character, or command over the passions. Partial graces are indeed almost the only improvements that the mender of a play already written can easily introduce; for an error in the first concoction can be redeemed by no future process of chemistry. A few flowery lines may here and there be strewn on the surface of a dramatick piece; but these have little power to impregnate its general mass. Character, on the contrary, must be designed at the author's outset, and proceed with gradual congeniality through the whole. In genuine Shakespeare it insinuates itself every where, with an address like that of Virgil's snake—

> ————*fit tortile collo*
> *Aurum ingens coluber; fit longæ, tænia vittæ,*
> *Innectitque comas, et membris lubricus errat.*[1]

But the drama before us contains no discrimination of manners (except in the comick dialogues), very few traces of original thought, and is evidently destitute of that intelligence and useful knowledge that pervade even the meanest of Shakespeare's undisputed performances. To speak more plainly, it is neither enriched by the gems that sparkle through the rubbish of *Love's Labour's Lost*, nor the good sense which so often fertilizes the barren fable of the *Two Gentlemen of Verona.*—*Pericles*, in short, is little more than a string of adventures so numerous, so inartificially crowded together, and so far removed from probability, that in my private judgement I must acquit even the irregular and lawless Shakespeare of having constructed the fabrick of the drama,

---

[1] *Aeneid*, 7.352ff.: 'The huge snake becomes the collar of twisted gold about her neck, becomes the festoon of the long fillet, entwines itself into her hair, and slides smoothly over her limbs'.

though he has certainly bestowed some decoration on its parts. Yet even this decoration, like embroidery on a blanket, only serves by contrast to expose the meanness of the original materials. That the plays of Shakespeare have their inequalities likewise is sufficiently understood; but they are still the inequalities of Shakespeare. He may occasionally be absurd, but is seldom foolish; he may be censured, but can rarely be despised.

I do not recollect a single plot of Shakespeare's formation (or even adoption from preceding plays or novels), in which the majority of the characters are not so well connected, and so necessary in respect of each other, that they proceed in combination to the end of the story; unless that story (as in the cases of *Antigonus* and *Mercutio*) requires the interposition of death. In *Pericles* this continuity is wanting;

> ——*disjectas moles, avulsaque saxis*
> *Saxa vides;——* [1]

and even with the aid of *Gower* the scenes are rather loosely tacked together than closely interwoven. We see no more of *Antiochus* after his first appearance. His anonymous daughter utters but one unintelligible couplet, and then vanishes. *Simonides* likewise is lost as soon as the marriage of *Thaisa* is over; and the punishment of *Cleon* and his wife, which poetick justice demanded, makes no part of the action but is related in a kind of epilogue by *Gower*. This is at least a practice which in no instance has received the sanction of Shakespeare. From such deficiency of mutual interest and *liaison* among the personages of the drama, I am farther strengthened in my belief that our great poet had no share in constructing it. (II, 163–4)

[Steevens notes that although many names of Shakespeare's characters recur in other plays—Antonio, Helena, Balthazar, etc.—those in *Pericles* are almost unique, and several of them are derived neither from Gower nor from *Apollonius, Prince of Tyre*. He also contests Malone's argument that Shakespeare avoided repeating in *The Winter's Tale* situations which he had already used in *Pericles*, an early play.]

Mr. Malone is likewise solicitous to prove, from the wildness and irregularity of the fable, &c. that this was either our author's

[1] *Aeneid*, 2.608: 'shattered piles and rocks torn from rocks'.

first or one of his earliest dramas. It might have been so; and yet I am sorry to observe that the same qualities predominate in his more mature performances; but there these defects are instrumental in producing beauties. If we travel in *Antony and Cleopatra* from *Alexandria* to *Rome*—to *Messina*—into *Syria*—to *Athens*—to *Actium*, we are still relieved in the course of our peregrinations by variety of objects and importance of events. But are we rewarded in the same manner for our journeys from *Antioch* to *Tyre*, from *Tyre* to *Pentapolis*, from *Pentapolis* to *Tharsus*, from *Tharsus* to *Tyre*, from *Tyre* to *Mitylene*, and from *Mitylene* to *Ephesus*?—In one light, indeed, I am ready to allow *Pericles* was our poet's first attempt. Before he was satisfied with his own strength, and trusted himself to the publick, he might have tried his hand with a partner, and entered the theatre in disguise. Before he ventured to face an audience on the stage it was natural that he should peep at them through the curtain.

What Mr. Malone has called the *inequalities of the poetry*, I should rather term the *patchwork of the style*, in which the general flow of Shakespeare is not often visible. An unwearied blaze of words, like that which burns throughout *Phædra and Hippolitus*, and *Mariamne*, is never attempted by our author; for such uniformity could be maintained but by keeping nature at a distance. Inequality and wildness, therefore, cannot be received as criterions by which we are to distinguish the early pieces of Shakespeare from those which were written at a later period.

But one peculiarity relative to the complete genuineness of this play has hitherto been disregarded, though in my opinion it is absolutely decisive. I shall not hesitate to affirm that through different parts of *Pericles* there are more frequent and more aukward ellipses than occur in all the other dramas attributed to the same author; and that these figures of speech appear only in such worthless portions of the dialogue as cannot with justice be imputed to him. Were the play the work of any single hand it is natural to suppose that this clipt jargon would have been scattered over it with equality. Had it been the composition of our great poet he would be found to have availed himself of the same licence in his other tragedies; nor perhaps, would an individual writer have called the same characters and places alternately Perĭcles and Perīcles, Thaïsa and Thaīsa, Pentapŏlis and Pentapōlis. Shakespeare never varies the quantity of his proper names in the compass of one play. In *Cymbeline* we always meet with Posthūmus, not Posthŭmus; Arvirāgus, and not Arvirăgus.

It may appear singular that I have hitherto laid no stress on such parallels between the acknowledged plays of Shakespeare and *Pericles* as are produced in the course of our preceding illustrations. But perhaps any argument that could be derived from so few of these ought not to be decisive; for the same reasoning might tend to prove that every little coincidence of thought and expression is in reality one of the petty larcenies of literature; and thus we might in the end impeach the original merit of those whom we ought not to suspect of having need to borrow from their predecessors.* I can only add on this subject (like Dr. Farmer), that the world is already possessed of the *Marks of Imitation*;[1] and that there is scarce one English tragedy but bears some slight internal resemblance to another. (II, 167–8)

[Nevertheless Steevens adds a long note (pp. 168–175) on Shakespeare's supposed share in *The Two Noble Kinsmen*, in which, largely on the basis of verbal parallels with Shakespeare (of which he cites thirty-seven), he concludes 'this tragedy to have been written by Fletcher in silent *imitation* of our author's manner'. As for *Pericles*, he concludes that it 'was in all probability the composition of some friend whose interest the "gentle Shakespeare" was industrious to promote. He therefore improved his dialogue in many places; and knowing by experience that the strength of a dramatick piece should be augmented towards its catastrophe, was most liberal of his aid in the last act'. (II, 176)]

Before I close this enquiry, which has swelled into an unexpected bulk, let me ask whose opinion confers most honour on Shakespeare, my opponent's or mine? Mr. Malone is desirous that his favourite poet should be regarded as the sole author of a drama which, collectively taken, is unworthy of him. I only wish the reader to adopt a more moderate creed, that the *purpurei panni*[2] are Shakespeare's, and the rest the production of some inglorious and forgotten playwright . . . . (II, 178)

---

* Dr. Johnson once assured me that when he wrote his *Irene* he had never read *Othello*; but meeting with it soon afterwards, was surprized to find he had given one of his characters a speech very strongly resembling that in which Cassio describes the effects produced by Desdemona's beauty on such inanimate objects as the *gutter'd rocks and congregated sands*. The doctor added that on making the discovery, for fear of imputed plagiarism, he struck out this accidental coincidence from his own tragedy.

[1] By Richard Hurd: cf. Vol. 4, No. 162b.

[2] Horace, *Ars Poetica* 14: 'purple patches'.

[18] [Malone disputes many of these points, referring to what he claims to be similar usages in the authentic plays]

Is it true that Shakespeare has rigidly abstained from introducing incidents or characters similar to those which he had before brought upon the stage? Or rather, is not the contrary notorious? In *Much Ado about Nothing* the two principal persons of the drama frequently remind us of two other characters that had been exhibited in an early production, — *Love's Labour's Lost*. In *All's Well that Ends Well* and *Measure for Measure* we find the same artifice twice employed: and in many other of his plays the action is embarrassed, and the denouement effected, by contrivances that bear a striking similitude to each other.

The conduct of *Pericles* and *The Winter's Tale*, which have several events common to both, gives additional weight to the supposition that the two pieces proceeded from the same hand. In the latter our author has thrown the discovery of Perdita into narration, as if through consciousness of having already exhausted, in the business of Marina, all that could render such an incident affecting on the stage. Leontes too says but little to Hermione, when he finds her; their mutual situations having been likewise anticipated by the Prince of Tyre and Thaisa, who had before amply expressed the transports natural to unexpected meeting after long and painful separation.

All the objections which are founded on the want of *liaison* between the different parts of this piece, on the numerous characters introduced in it, not sufficiently connected with each other, on the various and distant countries in which the scene is laid, — may, I think, be answered by saying that the author pursued the story exactly as he found it either in the *Confessio Amantis* or some prose translation of the *Gesta Romanorum*; a practice which Shakespeare is known to have followed in many plays, and to which most of the faults that have been urged against his dramas may be imputed.* (II, 182)

* In the conduct of *Measure for Measure* his judgment has been arraigned[1] for certain deviations from the Italian of Cinthio; in one of whose novels the story on which the play is built may be read. But on examination it has been found that the faults of the piece are to be attributed not to Shakespeare's departing from, but too closely pursuing *his* original; which, as Dr. Farmer has observed, was not Cinthio's novel but the *Heptameron* of Whetstone.[2] In like manner the catastrophe of *Romeo and Juliet* is rendered less affecting than it might have been made by the author's having implicitly followed the poem of *Romeus and Juliet*, on which his play appears to have been formed. (II, 182–3, notes)

[1] By Mrs Lennox: see Vol. 4, pp. 110–17.
[2] See Vol. 5, p. 269.

After all, perhaps, the internal evidence which this drama itself affords of the hand of Shakespeare is of more weight than any other argument that can be adduced. (II, 184)

I am yet therefore unconvinced that this drama was not written by our author. The wildness and irregularity of the fable, the artless conduct of the piece, and the inequalities of the poetry, may, I think, be all accounted for by supposing it either his first or one of his earliest essays in dramatick composition. MALONE. (II, 186)

[19] [On *A Yorkshire Tragedy*]

I confess I have always regarded this little drama as a genuine but a hasty production of our author. Though he was seldom vigilant of reputation as a poet, he might sometimes have been attentive to gain as a manager. Laying hold therefore on the popular narrative of this 'bloody business,' it was natural enough that he should immediately adapt it to the stage. His play indeed has all the marks of an unpremeditated composition. . . .

If, on the whole, it has less *poetical* merit than some of the serious dialogues in the *Midsummer Night's Dream* or *Love's Labour's Lost*, it has surely as much of nature as will be discovered in many parts of these desultory dramas. Murder, which appears ridiculous in *Titus Andronicus*, has its proper effect in the *Yorkshire Tragedy*; and the command this little piece may claim over the passions will be found to equal any our author has vested in the tragick divisions of *Troilus and Cressida*,—I had almost said in *King Richard the Second*, which criticks may applaud, though the successive audiences of more than a century have respectfully slumbered over it as often as it has appeared on the stage. Mr. Garrick had once resolved on its revival; but his good sense at last overpowered his ambition to raise it to the dignity of the acting list. Yet our late Roscius's chief expectations from it, as he himself confessed, would have been founded on scenery displaying the magnificence of our ancient barriers.—To return to my subject, this tragedy in miniature (exhibiting at least three of the characteristicks of Shakespeare, I mean his quibbles, his facility of metre, and his struggles to introduce comick ideas into tragick situations) appears at present before the reader with every advantage that a careful comparison of copies, and attention to obscurities, could bestow on it; and yet among the slight outlines of our theatrical Raphael, and not among his finished paintings, can it expect to maintain a place. . . . STEEVENS (II, 675–8)

266. Thomas Warton, Shakespeare and the golden age of English poetry

1781

From *The History of English Poetry*, III (1781).

Thomas Warton (1728–90), younger brother of Joseph Warton, poet and critic, was educated at Trinity College, Oxford, and spent his life as a tutor there. He wrote much poetry at and about Oxford, and published learned biographies of two distinguished members of his college, Ralph Bathurst (1761) and Sir Thomas Pope (1772, 1780). As a literary historian Warton made his name with *Observations on the Faery Queen of Spenser* (1754; enlarged edition, 2 vols, 1762). He was a lifelong friend of Johnson, for whom he obtained an Oxford M. A. in 1755. He helped to find subscribers for Johnson's Shakespeare edition, and he wrote numbers 33, 93, and 96 of the *Idler* for him. The first volume of his history appeared in 1774, the second in 1778; a fragment of the fourth has been published by R. M. Baine (Los Angeles, 1953). The deficiencies of Warton's knowledge of Old English were exposed by Joseph Ritson in *Observations on the three first Volumes of the History of English Poetry* (1782), an over-violent but justly critical work (Lawrence Lipking judges that it inaugurated 'a new era of literary scholarship'), while Walpole, Mason, and Scott commented on its lack of organization. However, Warton collected much historical information, helped to revive an interest in sixteenth- and seventeenth-century literature, and performed a valuable function as a bibliographer and as an exponent of historical interpretation. See D. N. Smith, 'Warton's History of English Poetry', *Proceedings of the British Academy*, 15 (1929), and L. Lipking, *The Ordering of the Arts in Eighteenth-Century England* (Princeton, N. J., 1970).

[1] [On the dumb-show and its vogue in the sixteenth century]

Our ancestors were easily satified with this artificial supplement of one of the most important unities, which abundantly filled up the interval that was necessary to pass, while a hero was expected from the Holy Land, or a princess was imported, married, and brought to bed. [Quotes the Dumb-show to Act IV of *Gorboduc*.] Here, by the way, the visionary procession of kings and queens long since dead evidently resembles our author Sackville's original model of the MIRROUR OF MAGISTRATES; and, for the same reason, reminds us of a similar train of royal spectres in the tent-scene of Shakespeare's KING RICHARD THE THIRD.

I take this opportunity of expressing my surprise that this ostensible comment of the Dumb Shew should not regularly appear in the tragedies of Shakespeare. There are even proofs that he treated it with contempt and ridicule. Although some critics are of opinion that because it is never described in form at the close or commencement of his acts, it was therefore never introduced. Shakespeare's aim was to collect an audience, and for this purpose all the common expedients were necessary. No dramatic writer of his age has more battles or ghosts. His representations abound with the usual appendages of mechanical terror, and he adopts all the superstitions of the theatre. This problem can only be resolved into the activity or the superiority of a mind which either would not be entangled by the formality, or which saw through the futility of this unnatural and extrinsic ornament. It was not by declamation or by pantomime that Shakespeare was to fix his eternal dominion over the hearts of mankind. (III, 360–2)

[2] [On Shakespeare's knowledge of the classics]

It is remarkable that Shakespeare has borrowed nothing from the English Seneca. Perhaps a copy might not fall in his way. Shakespeare was only a reader by accident. Holinshed and translated Italian novels supplied most of his plots or stories. His storehouse of learned history was North's Plutarch. The only poetical fable of antiquity which he has worked into a play is TROILUS. But this he borrowed from the romance of Troy. Modern fiction and English history were his principal resources. These perhaps were more suitable to his taste: at least he found that they produced the most popular subjects. Shakespeare was above the bondage of the classics. (393)

[3] [On Brooke's translation of Bandello: *The Tragicall Hystory of Romeus and Juliet* (1562)]

It is evident from a coincidence of absurdities and an identity of phraseology that this was Shakespeare's original, and not the meagre outline which appears in Painter. . . . Shakespeare, misled by the English poem, missed the opportunity of introducing a most affecting scene by the natural and obvious conclusion of the story. In Luigi's novel, Juliet awakes from her trance in the tomb before the death of Romeo. . . .

The enthusiasts to Shakespeare must wish to see more of Arthur Brooke's poetry, and will be gratified with the dullest anecdotes of an author to whom perhaps we owe the existence of a tragedy at which we have all wept. (471–2)

[4] [On George Whetstone's translations of Cinthio in *Heptameron* (1582)]

Shakespeare, in MEASURE FOR MEASURE, has fallen into great improprieties by founding his plot on a history in the HEPTA-MERON, imperfectly copied or translated from Cinthio's original. Many faults in the conduct of incidents for which Shakespeare's judgement is arraigned often flowed from the casual book of the day, whose mistakes he implicitly followed without looking for a better model, and from a too hasty acquiescence in the present accommodation. But without a book of this sort Shakespeare would often have been at a loss for a subject. Yet at the same time we look with wonder at the structures which he forms, and even without labour or deliberation, of the basest materials. (483–4)

[5] [From the conclusion, a survey of Elizabethan poetry]

The age of queen Elisabeth is commonly called the golden age of English poetry. It certainly may not improperly be styled the most POETICAL age of these annals.

Among the great features which strike us in the poetry of this period are the predominancy of fable, of fiction, and fancy, and a predilection for interesting adventures and pathetic events. I will endeavour to assign and explain the cause of this characteristic distinction, which may chiefly be referred to the following principles, sometimes blended, and sometimes operating singly: the revival and vernacular versions of the classics, the importation and translation of Italian novels, the visionary reveries or refinements of false philosophy, a degree of superstition sufficient for the purposes of poetry, the adoption of the machineries of romance, and the frequency and improvements of allegoric exhibition in the popular spectacles. . . . (490–1)

This inundation of classical pedantry soon infected our poetry. Our writers, already trained in the school of fancy, were suddenly dazzled with these novel imaginations, and the divinities and heroes of pagan antiquity decorated every composition. The perpetual allusions to antient fable were often introduced without the least regard to propriety. Shakespeare's Mrs. Page, who is not intended in any degree to be a learned or an affected lady, laughing at the cumbersome courtship of her corpulent lover Falstaff, says 'I had rather be a giantess and lie under mount Pelion.'* This familiarity with the pagan story was not, however, so much owing to the prevailing study of the original authors, as to the numerous English versions of them which were consequently made. The translations of the classics which now employed every pen gave a currency and a celebrity to these fancies, and had the effect of diffusing them among the people. (494)

But the reformation had not yet destroyed every delusion, nor disinchanted all the strong holds of superstition. A few dim characters were yet legible in the mouldering creed of tradition. Every goblin of ignorance did not vanish at the first glimmerings of the morning of science. . . . Prospero had not yet *broken and buried his staff,* nor *drowned his book deeper than did ever plummet sound.* The Shakespeare of a more instructed and polished age would not have given us a magician darkening the sun at noon, the sabbath of the witches, and the cauldron of incantation. . . . (496)

It may here be added that only a few critical treatises, and but one ART OF POETRY were now written. Sentiments and images were not absolutely determined by the canons of composition: nor was genius awed by the consciousness of a future and final arraignment at the tribunal of taste. A certain dignity of inattention to niceties is now visible in our writers. Without too closely consulting a criterion of correctness every man indulged his own capriciousness of invention. The poet's appeal was chiefly to his own voluntary feelings, his own immediate and peculiar mode of conception. And this freedom of thought was often expressed in an undisguised frankness of diction. A circumstance, by the way, that

* *Merry Wives of Windsor* [2.1.79f]

greatly contributed to give the flowing modulation which now marked the measures of our poets, and which soon degenerated into the opposite extreme of dissonance and asperity. Selection and discrimination were often overlooked. Shakespeare wandered in pursuit of universal nature. The glancings of his eye are from heaven to earth, from earth to heaven. We behold him breaking the barriers of imaginary method. In the same scene he descends from his meridian of the noblest tragic sublimity to puns and quibbles, to the meanest merriments of a plebeian farce. In the midst of his dignity he resembles his own Richard the second, the *skipping king*, who sometimes discarding the state of a monarch, 'Mingled his royalty with capering fools' [*1 Henry IV*, 3.2.63]. He seems not to have seen any impropriety in the most abrupt transitions, from dukes to buffoons, from senators to sailors, from counsellors to constables, and from kings to clowns. Like Virgil's majestic oak,

—— Quantum vertice ad auras
Ætherias, tantum radice in Tartara tendit.[1] [499–500]

The importance of the female character was not yet acknowledged, nor were women admitted into the general commerce of society. The effect of that intercourse had not imparted a comic air to poetry, nor softened the severer tone of our versification with the levities of gallantry and the familiarities of compliment, sometimes perhaps operating on serious subjects, and imperceptibly spreading themselves in the general habits of style and thought. I do not mean to insinuate that our poetry has suffered from the great change of manners which this assumption of the gentler sex, or rather the improved state of female education has produced, by giving elegance and variety to life, by enlarging the sphere of conversation, and by multiplying the topics and enriching the stores of wit and humour. But I am marking the peculiarities of composition: and my meaning was to suggest that the absence of so important a circumstance from the modes and constitution of antient life must have influenced the cotemporary poetry. Of the state of manners among our ancestors respecting this point many traces remain. Their style of courtship may be collected from the love-dialogues of Hamlet, young Percy, Henry the fifth, and Master Fenton. Their tragic heroines, their

[1] *Georgics*, 2.291: 'which strikes its roots down towards the nether pit as far as it lifts its top to the airs of heaven'.

Desdemonas and Ophelias, although of so much consequence in the piece, are degraded to the back-ground. In comedy their ladies are nothing more than MERRY WIVES, plain and chearful matrons, who stand upon the *chariness of their honesty*. In the smaller poems, if a lover praises his mistress she is complimented in strains neither polite nor pathetic, without elegance and without affection: she is described, not in the address of intelligible yet artful panegyric, not in the real colours and with the genuine accomplishments of nature, but as an eccentric ideal being of another system, and as inspiring sentiments equally unmeaning, hyperbolical, and unnatural.

All or most of these circumstances contributed to give a descriptive, a picturesque, and a figurative cast to the poetical language. This effect appears even in the prose compositions of the reign of Elisabeth. In the subsequent age prose became the language of poetry.

In the mean time general knowledge was encreasing with a wide diffusion and a hasty rapidity. Books began to be multiplied, and a variety of the most useful and rational topics had been discussed in our own language. But science had not made too great advances. On the whole we were now arrived at that period, propitious to the operations of original and true poetry, when the coyness of fancy was not always proof against the approaches of reason, when genius was rather directed than governed by judgement, and when taste and learning had so far only disciplined imagination as to suffer its excesses to pass without censure or controul, for the sake of the beauties to which they were allied. (500–1)

267. James Harris, Shakespeare and the rules of criticism

1781

From *Philological Inquiries in Three Parts* (1781). Published posthumously yet, according to the *Monthly Review*, 'printed before his death': lxvi (1782), pp. 428f. Chapter 6 is called 'Dramatic speculations', and was reprinted in the *London Magazine*, 1 (1781), p. 534.

James Harris (1709–80), of independent means, was a scholar, M. P. for Christchurch, and (between 1763 and 1765) a lord of the admiralty and the treasury. He was the nephew of Shaftesbury, and a friend of Fielding, Handel, Reynolds, Gibbon, and George Grenville. An Aristotelian in the period of Locke, he wrote *Three Treatises. On Art; On Music, Painting and Poetry,* and *On Happiness* (1744); *Hermes, or a Philosophical Inquiry concerning Universal Grammar* (1751); *Philosophical Arrangements* (1775); and the present collection, which the *Monthly* described as 'perspicuous' and 'elegant', showing the 'true judgment' of an author 'highly and deservedly respected'. See R. Marsh, *Four Dialectical Theories of Poetry* (Chicago, 1965), and L. Lipking, *The Ordering of the Arts in Eighteenth-Century England* (Princeton, N. J., 1970), pp. 86–105.

[On the plot-form of tragedy]

. . . On the contrary, when the REVOLUTION, as in the *second* sort, is *from Good to Bad* (that is, *from Happy to Unhappy*, from *Prosperous to Adverse*) here we discover the *true Fable* or *Story* proper for TRAGEDY. Common sense leads us to call, even in *real* life, such Events, TRAGICAL. . . .

OTHELLO commences with a prospect of *Conjugal Felicity*; LEAR* with that of *Repose*, by *retiring from Royalty*. DIFFERENT

* This Example refers to the *real Lear* of *Shakespeare*, not the *spurious* one commonly acted under his name, where the imaginary Mender seems to have paid the same Complement to his

REVOLUTIONS (arising from Jealousy, Ingratitude, and other culpable affections) change both of these pleasing prospects into the deepest distress, and with this distress each of the Tragedies concludes. . . . (150–2)

On FABLES, COMIC as well as TRAGIC, we may alike remark that when *good*, like *many other fine things*, they are *difficult*. And hence perhaps the Cause why *in this respect* so many *Dramas* are *defective*; and why their *Story* or *Fable* is commonly no more than either *a jumble of Events* hard to comprehend, or *a Tale taken from some wretched Novel*, which has little foundation either in Nature or Probability.

Even in the Plays we most admire we shall seldom find our Admiration to arise from the FABLE: 'tis either from THE SENTIMENT, as in *Measure for Measure*; or from the purity of THE DICTION, as in *Cato*; or from the CHARACTERS and MANNERS, as in Lear, Othello, Falstaff, Benedict and Beatrice, Ben the Sailor, Sir Peter and Lady Teazle, with the other Persons of that pleasing Drama, *The School for Scandal*. . . . (160–1)

[On consistency in 'manners', or the behaviour of characters]

As soon as we have seen the violent *Love* and weak *Credulity* of OTHELLO, the *fatal Jealousy* in which they terminate is no more than what we may *conjecture*. When we have marked the *attention* paid by MACBETH to *the Witches*, to the persuasions of *his Wife*, and to the flattering dictates of *his own Ambition*, we suspect *something atrocious*; nor are we surprised that in the Event he murders *Duncan*, and then *Banquo*. Had he changed his conduct, and been only wicked by halves, his MANNERS would not have been as they now are, *poetically good*.

If the leading Person in a Drama, for example HAMLET, appear to have been *treated most injuriously* we naturally infer that he will meditate *Revenge*; and should that Revenge prove fatal to those who had injured him, 'tis no more than was *probable* when we consider the Provocation.

But should *the same Hamlet* by chance kill an *innocent old Man*, an old Man from whom he had *never received Offence*; and with whose *Daughter* he *was actually in love*;—what should we expect *then*?

audience as was paid to other audiences two thousand years ago, and *then* justly censured. [Referring to Aristotle's *Poetics*, ch. 13, where the happy ending to tragedy is denounced as a sop to the audience's taste.]

Should we not look for *Compassion*, I might add, even for *Compunction*? Should we not be shockt if instead of this he were to prove *quite insensible*—or (what is even worse) were he *to be brutally jocose*?

Here the MANNERS are *blameable* because they are *inconsistent*; we should *never conjecture from* HAMLET any thing *so unfeelingly cruel.*

Nor are *Manners* only to be blamed for being thus *inconsistent.* CONSISTENCY itself is blameable if it exhibit *Human* Beings *completely* abandoned, *completely* void of Virtue, prepared, like King *Richard [III]*, at their very *birth*, for mischief. 'Twas of such models that a jocose Critic once said they might make *good Devils* but they could never make *good Men*: not (says he) that they want *Consistency*, but 'tis of a *supernatural* sort, which *Human* Nature never knew.

Quodcumque ostendis mihi sic, incredulus odi.[1]   [166–9]

[On the necessity for rules in writing]

And yet 'tis somewhat singular in *Literary Compositions*, and perhaps *more so in Poetry* than elsewhere, that many things have been done *in the best and purest taste long before* RULES *were established, and systematized in form.* This we are certain was true with respect to HOMER, SOPHOCLES, EURIPIDES, and other GREEKS. In *modern* times it appears as true of our admired SHAKESPEARE; for who can believe that *Shakespeare* studied Rules or was ever versed in *Critical Systems?* . . .

. . . If at that *early Greek Period* Systems of *Rules* were not established, THOSE GREAT and SUBLIME AUTHORS WERE A RULE TO THEMSELVES. They may be said indeed to have excelled not by *Art* but by NATURE; yet by a *Nature* which gave birth to the perfection of ART.

The Case is nearly the same with respect to our SHAKESPEARE. There is hardly any thing we applaud among his *innumerable beauties which will not be found strictly conformable to the* RULES *of sound and antient Criticism.*

That this is true with respect to his CHARACTERS and his SENTIMENT is evident hence, that in explaining *these Rules* we have so often recurred to him for Illustrations. (225–6)

We venture to add, returning *to* RULES, that if there be any things in *Shakespeare* OBJECTIONABLE (and who is hardy enough to

[1] Horace, *Ars Poetica*, 188: 'Whatever you thus show me, I discredit and abhor'.

deny it?) THE VERY OBJECTIONS, as well as THE BEAUTIES, *are to be tried* BY THE SAME RULES, as the same Plummet alike shews both what is *out of* the Perpendicular and *in* it; the same Ruler alike proves both what is *crooked* and what is *strait*.

We cannot admit that *Geniuses*, tho' *prior to Systems*, were *prior also to Rules*, because RULES from the beginning *existed in their own Minds*, and were a part of that *immutable Truth* which is eternal and every where. *Aristotle* we know did not form *Homer, Sophocles*, and *Euripides*; 'twas *Homer, Sophocles*, and *Euripides* that formed *Aristotle*.

And this surely should teach us to pay attention to RULES, in as much as THEY and GENIUS are so *reciprocally* connected that 'tis GENIUS which discovers *Rules*; and then RULES which govern *Genius*.

'Tis by this *amicable concurrence*, and by *this alone*, that every Work of Art justly merits Admiration, and is rendered as highly perfect as by human Power it can be made. (230–2)

268. Samuel Johnson, on Shakespeare and his critics

1781

From *Lives of the Poets* (4 vols, 1781).

On Johnson see the head-notes to Vol. 3, Nos 105, 129; Vol. 4, No. 160, and Vol. 5, Nos 205, 240. If Johnson was somewhat behind current scholarship in 1765 he appears even more so now: his defence of Pope as a Shakespeare editor seems especially anachronistic after the criticisms of Roberts and Theobald in the 1720s and 1730s, and the subsequent work of Edwards, Heath, Tyrwhitt, Capell, Steevens, and Malone.

[From the *Life of Dryden*: on his *Essay of Dramatick Poesie*, 1688: cf. Vol. 1, p. 138, and Johnson's Preface, Vol. 5, pp. 99f.]

It will not be easy to find, in all the opulence of our language, a treatise so artfully variegated with successive representations of opposite probabilities, so enlivened with imagery, so brightned with illustrations. His portraits of the English dramatists are wrought with great spirit and diligence. The account of Shakespeare may stand as a perpetual model of encomiastick criticism; exact without minuteness, and lofty without exaggeration. The praise lavished by Longinus on the attestation of the heroes of Marathon by Demosthenes fades away before it. In a few lines is exhibited a character so extensive in its comprehension, and so curious in its limitations that nothing can be added, diminished, or reformed; nor can the editors and admirers of Shakespeare, in all their emulation of reverence, boast of much more than of having diffused and paraphrased this epitome of excellence, of having changed Dryden's gold for baser metal, of lower value though of greater bulk. (II, 110–11)

[On the sources of literary value]

It is not by comparing line with line that the merit of great works is to be estimated, but by their general effects and ultimate result. It is easy to note a weak line, and write one more vigorous in its place; to find a happiness of expression in the original, and transplant it by force into the version: but what is given to the parts may be subducted from the whole, and the reader may be weary, though the critick may commend. Works of imagination excel by their allurement and delight; by their power of attracting and detaining the attention. That book is good in vain which the reader throws away. He only is the master who keeps the mind in pleasing captivity; whose pages are perused with eagerness, and in hope of new pleasure are perused again; and whose conclusion is perceived with an eye of sorrow, such as the traveller casts upon departing day.

By his proportion of this predomination I will consent that Dryden should be tried; of this which, in opposition to reason, makes Ariosto the darling and the pride of Italy; of this which, in defiance of criticism, continues Shakespeare the sovereign of the drama. (II, 173–4)

[From the *Life of Pope*]

He gave the same year (1721) an edition of *Shakespeare*. . . . On this undertaking, to which Pope was induced by a reward of two hundred and seventeen pounds twelve shillings, he seems never to have reflected afterwards without vexation; for Theobald, a man of heavy diligence, with very slender powers, first in a book called *Shakespeare Restored*, and then in a formal edition,[1] detected his deficiencies with all the insolence of victory; and, as he was now high enough to be feared and hated, Theobald had from others all the help that could be supplied, by the desire of humbling a haughty character. From this time Pope became an enemy to editors, collaters, commentators, and verbal criticks; and hoped to persuade the world, that he miscarried in this undertaking only by having a mind too great for such minute employment.

Pope in his edition undoubtedly did many things wrong, and left many things undone; but let him not be defrauded of his due praise. He was the first that knew, at least the first that told, by what helps the text might be improved. If he inspected the early editions negligently, he taught others to be more accurate. In his Preface he expanded with great skill and elegance the character which had been given of Shakespeare by Dryden; and he drew the publick attention upon his works, which though often mentioned had been little read. (IV, 73–4)

[1] See Vol. 2, Nos 74, 82.

269. Unsigned essay, Hamlet defends himself

1782

From 'A Dialogue between two theatrical heroes of Shakespeare and Corneille', *London Magazine*, li (November 1782), pp. 513–15.

Theseus is the hero of Corneille's play *Oedipe* (1659).

THESEUS AND HAMLET.

Thes. What, *still* that contracted brow! still those deep traces of grief and disappointment! I expected to find in thee a savage barbarous joy—an exulting triumph, for thou at *last* killedst thy uncle with all his imperfections on his head—with all his crimes full blown.

Ham. The sneers of Theseus I never expected, nor dreaded his reproaches. The savage tamer of monsters—the betrayer of Ariadne—the licentious favourite of a gigantic amazon, would have been silent. It is the *French* Theseus, the frivolous coxcomb—the effeminate dangler, who lives only in his mistress's smiles—who dares now to insult the avenger of his father's murderer and the usurper of his throne. I once adored thee, Theseus!—thy power controlled those monsters which were the most dangerous pests of infant society—thy authority curbed for a time the licence of faction, and thy force compelled when thy eloquence could not persuade. But from the hands of thy second parent thou art the glittering butterfly of a summer's day, which every ruder blast will destroy. The name of Theseus, by recalling what thou *hast* been, is the severest satire on what thou *art*.

Thes. Thy railings and thy flattery make an equal impression—they shall not divert me from my purpose. I might in my turn soothe thy ear by courtesy, or rouse thee by upbraidings; but I would more calmly enquire into thy conduct in thy second

316

existence, and ask thee how thou would defend thy cruel and inconsistent conduct. Thou wishest to appear gentle, generous, and good, yet thy insults to Ophelia were cruel and unmanly, if you did not feign that passion for her which you constantly expressed. You upbraided your mother with the most unexampled and unjustifiable severity, since she could not know the extent of her fault, and, with the most diabolical revenge, refused to punish a crime of which you were appointed the avenger, because you could not add eternal perdition to the present penalty.

Ham. I cannot coolly reason on subjects which I feel so nearly.—A mind distracted with contending passions—torn at the same time by love and pity—by horror and revenge, cannot candidly distribute poetical justice—nor, like Theseus, while Thebes is depopulated by a devouring pestilence, dread only his mistress's frown. The author of my ideal existence copied only his own feelings. *He* was at the *time*, the Hamlet solemnly called on by a venerable being—a supernatural spirit—the spirit of his murdered father—burning with revenge against an incestuous monster—the murderer of his parent—the usurper of his throne. Was this a time for him to pipe in a mistress's chamber? To crown his brow with garlands? Or amble to the warblings of a lute? To utter his words to soft music, or to string them in rhime?—The most eager credulity shrinks at the thought.

Thes. Start not from the subject—nor think by a poetical rhapsody to oppose the dictates of cool reason. How were your cruel insults to Ophelia connected with your revenge? Your guise of madness, assumed without reason, and laid aside without its having answered any purpose, might have been conducted at a distance from your soul's fond idol, and mistress of your heart. The wildest madmen have their aversions and inclinations, and it would have been no proof of your reason, had you avoided her whom you were accustomed to seek with solicitude—and covered with an air of reserve the fondest emotions of your love. Your scheme might have been carried on any where but in the chamber of Ophelia.

Ham. You are mistaken, Theseus. I was in the court of a cruel usurper, who had already waded through blood to the throne, and might be expected to support it by the same means—continually surrounded by the basest court sycophants, ready to misinterpret, and eager to misrepresent. In this situation I could only expect to

317

live by appearing an object unworthy of jealousy, and almost beneath contempt. I am surprized that my senses were really preserved, and am not clear if much of my flighty extravagance was not owing to an imagination really disordered.

Thes. Hold, Hamlet—this is not the first time that thy incongruity has been defended in that manner by thy fond admirers, and a living commentator of thy high authority (Digges) is said to have spoken a strange speech of thine, in a scene subsequent to thy father's story, in a manner which seems to support it:

> There's not a villain in all Denmark [*gravely*,]
> But he's an arrant knave—[*flightily and wildly.*] [1.5.123f.]

Thou art not, however, the Prince of Denmark whom Saxo Grammaticus has described—thou art the ideal being of the dramatic poet. He is thy second parent, who has invested thee with new powers and properties, and he has given us no notice of thy real madness. In this way therefore you cut the knot, instead of untying it.

Ham. Your remark is just, but still my behaviour to Ophelia does not deserve these keen reproofs, these bitter sarcasms. Your own refinements leave little room for the real exertions of the heart. Our first interview was conducted with the silent respect which you yourself have dictated. It had the appearance of sorrow rather than of madness. I did not, however, harrow up her soul, by unfolding my tale. I wished to spare her feeling heart—besides, it would have been to disappoint my dearest hopes to permit the least tittle to escape. Would it be a crime even in the pages of Corneille for a lover to wish to see his mistress? It is indeed unpardonable, *there*, to sigh and bear his griefs in silence. But this calmness—this concealed distress was not the guise which in the more publick rooms it would have been safe to put on. Our meeting there was accidental, and I had only to resume my extravagance to escape detection. It was a dreadful alternative.

Thes. Indeed I pity thee. In my new character, I have felt what it is to love, and blush to reflect on the situation into which I have been betrayed by it. My soul abhors those scenes of deceit and cunning, equally repugnant to my character and situation. But, go on—

Ham. The murder of Polonius was an involuntary crime. The death of Ophelia deprived me of one of my dearest wishes, and life was little longer desireable. I did not hesitate therefore to oppose the brutal violence of Laertes, to tear off the mask, and to trust to accident or open violence for the accomplishment of my wishes.

Thes. I thank thee for thy explanation. But tell me, for I now begin to enquire from affection rather than curiosity, how you can excuse your treatment to your mother? Her situation surely required more tenderness.

Ham. How, Theseus! was it not enough that she married with an usurper—the brother of a beloved husband scarcely yet interred—that she rushed with eagerness to the marriage bed, while the funeral of her former husband was loosely and imperfectly celebrated, lest it might impede the succeeding raptures?—Need I add the murderer—

Thes. Remember, my friend—for you must now permit me to call you so, that you know not whether she was ever informed of the practices of her present husband on the life of her last. Your father forbad you to attempt any thing against her, but to leave her to the stings of her own conscience. Her hasty marriage could not be reflected on with calmness and composure. Her conduct had been neither prudent nor discreet, but it is not said to be criminal. She felt not the satire of the play, and in the subsequent conversation was not conscious that it had any relation to the circumstance in which she had been so nearly concerned. Besides, your own words acquitted her. When you observed her composure it was only remarkable from the recent death of her husband, not from the complicated guilt of having married his murderer.

Ham. I allow all—but yet to marry so *soon.*—

Thes. Yourself at the university—she perhaps in the hands of an artful faction, headed by a deep designing villain. To whom could she look for protection? Her own life and thine perhaps depended on the step—and there was probably no other alternative between open violence, or the more subtile effects of a 'drugged posset.'

Ham. Theseus, you have profited by your new existence. You *reason* when you should *feel*, you *declaim* when you should *act*. The rival of Hercules would have thought and felt very differently, but your present existence is indeed ideal.

Thes. I acknowledge it, and after all, your palliators fear that you cannot be compared to the gentle, generous scholar of Saxo Grammaticus.—But you have omitted to answer *one* of my accusations. It is usual for guilt to elude enquiry when it cannot defend its conduct.

Ham. What can I say? Consider the aggravated guilt of the culprit, and agitation of my own mind, and the common, though mistaken opinion of retaliation—will not these alleviate my guilt? Your silence confesses it. Oh Theseus, you know little of Shakespeare's fiery genius—educated in the cold correctness of Corneille—you cannot excuse his exceeding the bounds of probability. But remember, his creations are glowing, though inconsistent. He writ what he felt; and though reason cannot justify his faults, yet candour will excuse them; and where so much is excellent, forgive the little that is exceptionable.   *Farewell!*

270. John Stedman, letters on Shakespeare

1782

From *Laelius and Hortensia; or, Thoughts on the Nature and Objects of Taste and Genius, in a series of letters to Two Friends* (Edinburgh, 1782).

John Stedman, M. D. (d. 1791), published *Physiological Essays and Observations* (Edinburgh, 1769) and *The history and statutes of the Royal Infirmary of Edinburgh* (1778). He is also credited with the authorship of a translation of the *Ars Poetica*: *Horace's Epistle to the Pisos* . . . (1784), and *Moral Fables* (1784).

[From 'Letter XVI. To Hortensia'. On tragedy]
We may well distinguish between tragical subjects, as that expression is commonly understood, and subjects proper for tragedies. Histories of all ages teem with the former, and examples of them will be found in one part of the world or another, as long as irregular passions shall continue to agitate the mind of man. Shakespeare was not delicate in the choice of his subjects, which

must be ascribed not to a defect of taste in that author but to the period in which he wrote. Subjects which act forcibly upon the mind, affecting it with awe and horror, were then better received than those which touch the more delicate passions. It is not Shakespeare's fables that please, but his peculiar manner of treating them; yea, the improprieties of these fables are a certain proof of the natural powers of that author. It can be but little gratifying to a mind possessed of a delicate taste to hear plots laid for murders, and to be told afterwards that these murders have been perpetrated with the disagreeable circumstances attending them. An age of less refinement than the present might relish apparitions, enchantments, the equivocal predictions of witches, and the like machinery; nor was that author blameable for availing himself of it while it could serve his purpose. But Shakespeare, from an intimate acquaintance with nature, hath excelled all other dramatists in tracing and unfolding the feelings of the soul, particularly in touching that canker-worm which attends a consciousness of guilt, and which fastens on human minds; so that, whether asleep or awake, they are unable ever afterwards to shake themselves loose of this tormentor.

We may lay it down as an invariable rule, that the more culpable or criminal the suffering parties of a tragedy are, our solicitude for their fate will be the less. It is not enough that the hero of a tragedy be innocent; he ought, from a greatness of mind, and a consciousness of rectitude, to meet his misfortunes with intrepidity and to triumph even in death. Thus, while our sympathy and tears are drawn out, we feel a tacit satisfaction in seeing virtue and a nobleness of soul superior to every natural evil; and we are able to account for our desire to be present at the exhibition of tragedies, though their terminations be disastrous and mournful. What hath added an appearance of difficulty to the solution of this problem is the improper choice of subjects. A well disposed mind would not wish to witness the representation of *Hamlet*, of *Richard III*, or of *Macbeth*, for the sake of the fables alone. It is Shakespeare's singular and various methods of describing the workings of the human mind, and particularly its agitations after the perpetration of the worst of crimes, that attract our applause; but every dramatist is not a Shakespeare.

It is to be regretted that the admired author did not choose his subjects of the kind mentioned above, such as the fate of Regulus, of Phocion, or of Socrates. It is not doubted but these will generally be held barren subjects; and so they would prove to the greater part of dramatical authors. Were we, for the first time, to hear, perhaps in a few sentences, and in the common course of conversation, the story of Lear and his daughters, we would not readily believe that any one would attempt a tragedy from materials so unpromising. Any of the three subjects just mentioned would be found, in Shakespeare's hand, much superior to that of Lear.

The French and English authors have entertained the public with a controversy relating to the merits of Shakespeare, compared with those of Racine and Corneille. Shakespeare seems to me to differ so widely from these two French authors as hardly to admit of a comparison. Some people are delighted with a garden highly and regularly dressed; the walks smooth, with their edges cut in right lines; espaliers drawn exactly parallel to these; the trees planted in exact order, and every thing conducted with the same precision. Others are better pleased with a vast extended forest, abounding with stately and towering trees, with shrubs, wild flowers, and vegetables of all kinds; with unequal grounds, having in some places stupendous rocks, pouring down natural cataracts; in others, smooth hills or plains, with gentle rills of water, and other like objects. The garden is Racine and Corneille. The forest is Shakespeare. But why should we condemn the admirers of either for being pleased with the excellencies of the one in preference to those of the other? We see nature both in the garden and in the forest. In the former, art, applied to nature, appears every where. In the other, artless nature appears in a bold and majestic luxuriancy. (156–61)

Shakespeare, in his deepest tragedies, frequently introduces low characters, making them speak in their own vulgar and proverbial style. He hath likewise often recourse to mean objects for his figures and metaphors. These, when translated into the language of a people rigidly attached to the dignity of the Cothurnus, have an aukward, and sometimes a ludicrous appearance. But the delineations of nature by this author, however coarse, are for the most part bold, just, and striking. They may well be compared to those of Hemskirk, or Albert Durer; whereas the genius and taste of the two French dramatists correspond to those of Grignon, or the like artists, whose works are noted for minute and laboured finishing. The former dash on without reserve, regardless of such small slips as will not offend a liberal critic; while the others, sollicitous to avoid improprieties, however small, dwell with tedious and unwearied labour on high polishing. . . .

I would not have you understand me here as believing that the drama may be conducted without regard to the unities. The contrary is the truth. It must be owned, notwithstanding the preceding observations, that Shakespeare, while we give him full credit for his merit in delineating nature, hath not been so happy in conducting his fables. I am aware that many advocates have undertaken his defence in this circumstance; but it is not uncommon, when we contract a strong attachment to any particular person or author, not only to overlook his faults but even to imagine we see beauties in them. I know likewise that some modern critics have condemned the unities of the antients, considering them as fetters to a bold and enterprising genius. These have been declared as a-kin to shackles fixed to the limbs of a fine dancer. When we have recourse to figure and metaphor, in order to elucidate our ideas to others, we are sometimes apt to mislead ourselves. Why should we consider Addison to have been in fetters when he composed his *Cato*? . . .

If an author, in treating the like dramatical subjects, find himself under the necessity of flying to distant places, and of protracting his subject to a great length of time, for the sake of incidents, he must ascribe this to the sterility of his genius, and not to the subject itself; for an author is allowed to invent incidents, provided he do not exceed probability. I am far from insinuating here that Shakespeare laboured under a defect of invention. On the contrary, he every where discovers a remarkable fecundity of genius, as well as a rich, though not always regular, imagination. Yea, the applause he hath acquired from his pictures of Nature, while he was unsupported by the unities, is a proof of his merit. In Shakespeare's time the taste for theatrical representations was not delicate; nor doth it appear that the laws of the drama were well understood, perhaps not by Shakespeare himself. (163–6)

271. B. Walwyn, Shakespearian comedy

1782

From *An Essay on Comedy* (1782). According to the Advertisement (p. ix) this essay had previously appeared in one of the newspapers. 'Philo-Drama' is identified as Thomas Davies (see head-note to No. 277). It was unfavourably reviewed by both the *Monthly*, lxvi (1782), pp. 308f., and the *Critical*, liv (1782), p. 239.

Walwyn (b. 1750) also published *Chit-chat; or, The penance of polygamy* (1781), which he reworked as a verse burletta with the title *A Matrimonial Breakfast* (1787); a novel, *The errors of nature; or, The history of Charles Manley* (3 vols, 1783), and two other musical pieces, *The Water-Cross Girl* (1780), and *The ridiculous courtship* (1784).

Comedy is the mirror of human nature, which reflects our follies, defects, vices, and virtues; so that we may laugh at the first, ridicule the second, satirize the third, and enforce the latter. Thus we find it is not merely a picture but a reflector of human life. If the expression may be allowed, it is a reflecting painting—in other words, a dramatic camera.* (1-2)

The comic scene has either been filled with the cant of sentiment, the filth of obscenity, the tattle of repartee, the froth of pun, the jargon of broken language, or affectation of wit. These illegitimates of genius have usurped the prerogative of Comedy's natural offspring—design, character, humour, passion, and expression. Yet the latter is entirely banished; for when wits (or witlings, more properly) of the age find a strength of comic character beyond what they have powers either to feel or describe, they exclaim 'This is a Tragedy!' They forget, or, perhaps, never knew, the Roman Critic says, 'Comedy sometimes raises her voice.'[1] What is this, but saying that incident and character may

---

* Tragedy is a dramatic microscope that enlarges the virtues and vices of human nature, in order to make the greater impression on the heart and mind of the observers.

[1] Horace, *Ars Poetica*, 93: 'interdum tamen et vocem Comoedia tollit'.

sometimes unite to raise her strength of expression to the dignity of Tragedy? Is it not one of the superior excellencies of Shakespeare's Comedies? Do we not find most of his serious scenes equal in dignity and expression to any of his Tragedies? Why then should modern genius seek to dilute a natural strength of passion with the water of puny criticism?

In my solicitude for asserting the natural dignity of Comedy let me not lose sight of its humour, which is equally—if not more essential to its perfection. Sentiment, wit, repartee, and observation, may alternately serve her as handmaids; but humour must be our sole dependance for entertainment. Her sources of pleasing are four—whim, pecularity, vivacity, and novelty, which she blends either in an expression, character, or incident. Shakespeare is remarkable for humour in the two former; Shadwell in the latter only. (2–4)

Criticism has authoritively said, an under-plot is indespensible. Surely this law, like every other literary edict, has arisen more from example than necessity. Ancient comic writers made use of these plots—not through necessity, but a voluntary desire of giving the whole design a more pleasing variety. How then should it become an edict for every other writer to observe? Although their use should not be denied, yet their absolute necessity should not be countenanced; for that depends entirely on their utility. So that if one principal design is capable of a sufficient variety to render it interesting, an under-plot would then only tend to confuse those scenes it was meant to embellish. In reality they too frequently weaken the fabric they were meant to support. The necessity of winding up the under-plot in the *Merchant of Venice* has tacked what would have been more proper for an Interlude to one of the most interesting Comedies of the immortal Shakespeare. The compleat unity of action finishes with the trial. Hence, Shakespeare's powers cannot banish from us that unpleasing emotion which every person of taste and sensibility must experience during the fifth act. It can only be compared to the necessity of turning our attention from the ocean to a fish-pond. (6–7)

In respect to character, I must beg leave to dissent from a truly eminent critic, Du Bos, who says comic characters should be domestic. Were this true, in what light must we consider most of Shakespeare's Comedies? If the passion differed in nature, as well as in degree with the climate, neither tragic nor comic character should be foreign; for they would not be congenial with the feeling of the audience. But whilst Love, Hatred, Compassion, and Revenge, with the rest of the passions, have all the same complexion in every climate the comic scene, were it only in favour of novelty and variety, may be indulged with foreign character. (7–8)

Characters should not be drawn with temporary traits; for such grow obsolete with the fashion of the times. This is the fate of most of Jonson's characters—particularly those in *Every Man in his Humour*. While those in the play* from whence most of them seem to have been taken, will exist with human nature. Captain Bobadil is a starvling Falstaff, without either his wit or his humour. Master Stephen is a tolerable likeness of Master Slender. Kitely imitates Ford in all but his sense. Downright is the testy Shallow without his humour. Dame Kitely is the shadow of Mrs. Ford. Thus we perceive these characters of Shakespeare are disguised by Jonson, with an affected resemblance to some particular persons of that period. (8–9)

To return, the difference of temporary and eternal characters is particularly displayed between those of Shakespeare and of Jonson. I shall, therefore, consider the traits of the one, and the tints of the other. For in Jonson the passions are scarcely coloured, but in Shakespeare they are imitated by feeling.

Although it has been said—Shakespeare's Falstaff was meant to satirize a particular person of his day, every one who looks at human nature will find Falstaffs in abundance. But they will never find a Bobadil. Falstaff is a voluptuous knave, gross in sense, manners, and appearance. His pleasantry depending on his sack, and his cowardice on his selfishness. Every trait is consistent with each other. Had Shakespeare given him courage, he would have made him inconsistent with himself; the sordid and selfish may be desperate, but never courageous. They dread the loss of enjoyment in their lives, and therefore never hazard life but when emergency makes them desperate. This consistency will make Falstaff a character of entertainment whenever it may be represented. (9–20)

[Walwyn prints at the end of his essay a letter from 'Philo-Drama', raising some objections.]

* *Merry Wives of Windsor.*

I perfectly agree with the Author that characters should be drawn with temporary traits. I grant too, that the portraits of Shakespeare are made to last till Doomsday; while the lustring and fashionable shadows of the day drawn by Ben Jonson grow obsolete in the wearing of them. But he has unhappily mistaken his aim. The characters of *Every Man in his Humour* could not be taken from Shakespeare's *Merry Wives of Windsor*; for the former play was prior to the latter about three years. . . . For my own part, I can see no family likeness, either in the personage or conduct of the two plays. They are both strongly discriminated. Poor Old Ben is fallen so low in the opinion of the public, that it would be a charity to give him a lift where we possibly can. The Slender of Shakespeare is not, in my humble judgment, so proper a character for Comedy as the Master Stephen of Jonson; the latter is the Fop of Fashion, the other, the Fool of Nature; and for that reason no object of comic mirth. We may as well laugh at the lame and the blind, as the meer changling, the poor abortive escape of propagation. Though I do not entirely approve his criticism on Bobadil, I admire his masterly outline of Falstaff. (23–4)

[In reply Walwyn urges 'the acknowledged superiority of Shakespeare' to his contemporaries.]

Although he borrowed his plots from Novels, and some scenes from the Antients, yet no positive proof can be given of his either taking plots, scenes, incidents, or characters, from any of his cotemporaries. On the contrary, while he borrowed the main parts of the fable he is remarked for his wonderful facility and power in the invention of characters in nature, and the creation of characters beyond nature. He did not, like other puny writers of the scene, make nature monstrous. He made monsters natural. Is this a man to be supposed dependent on a Jonson for character? Forbid it genius, judgment, and I had almost said, conviction. (28–9)

. . . Has not Falstaff the traits of vanity, boasting, and cowardice? Are not these the only traits of Bobadil? Is not Ford jealous without cause, and passionate without revenge? For all the punishment Falstaff receives is from the hurt, pride, and indignation of Mrs. Ford, and Mrs. Page. Can it be said that Kitely has any other traits or circumstances? His observation in respect to the Fool of Nature not being a proper character for Comedy does him honour; but this greatly depends in what light that fool is placed. If placed in a ridiculous light, we must then despise the author and pity the character. Should he be placed in merely a risible light he then becomes an innocent uninjured character to enliven the scene. Ridicule is Satire seated in the vehicle of Mirth. Risibility is Innocence seated in the vehicle of Humour. Shakespeare's Slender is not a character of ridicule, but of risibility; but Jonson's Stephen, being ridiculous, blends our contempt with our laughter. (30)

272. Hugh Blair, lectures on Shakespeare

1783

From *Lectures on Rhetoric and Belles Letters*. This text is from 'the Second Edition, Corrected' (3 vols, 1785).

Hugh Blair (1718–1800) was a distinguished preacher (several volumes of his sermons being issued in many editions), and from 1760 to 1783 was professor of rhetoric and belles lettres at Edinburgh University. These lectures were given there in 1760, and he acknowledges a debt to the manuscript of a series of lectures given in that university by Adam Smith in 1748–51: these have been recently discovered, and edited by J. M. Lothian under the title *Lectures on Rhetoric and Belles Lettres* (1963). Blair was awarded a pension of £200 in 1780. He was a member of the Poker Club in Edinburgh, associating with Hume, A. Carlyle, Adam Ferguson, Adam Smith, Thomas Robertson, and Lord Kames; Johnson thought highly of him.

Instances I admit there are of some works that contain gross transgressions of the laws of Criticism, acquiring nevertheless a general and even a lasting admiration. Such are the plays of Shakespeare, which, considered as dramatic poems are irregular in the highest degree. But then we are to remark that they have gained the public admiration not by their being irregular, not by their transgressions of the rules of art, but in spite of such transgressions. They possess other beauties which are conformable to just rules; and the force of these beauties has been so great as to overpower all censure, and to give the Public a degree of satisfaction superior to the disgust arising from their blemishes. Shakespeare pleases, not by his bringing the transactions of many years into one play; not by his grotesque mixtures of Tragedy and Comedy in one piece, nor by the strained thoughts and affected witticisms which he sometimes employs. These we consider as blemishes, and impute them to the grossness of the age in which he lived. But he pleases by his animated and masterly representations of characters, by the liveliness of his descriptions, the force of his sentiments, and his possessing beyond all writers the natural language of passion: Beauties which true Criticism no less teaches us to place in the highest rank than nature teaches us to feel. (I, 50–1)

[On the correct use of metaphor]

The second rule which I give respects the choice of objects from whence Metaphors and other Figures are to be drawn. The field for Figurative Language is very wide. All nature, to speak in the style of Figures, opens its stores to us, and admits us to gather from all sensible objects whatever can illustrate intellectual or moral ideas. Not only the gay and splendid objects of sense, but the grave, the terrifying, and even the gloomy and dismal may, on different occasions, be introduced into Figures with propriety. But we must beware of ever using such allusions as raise in the mind disagreeable, mean, vulgar, or dirty ideas. Even when Metaphors are chosen in order to vilify and degrade any object, an author should study never to be nauseous in his allusions.... Shakespeare, whose imagination was rich and bold in a much greater degree than it was delicate, often fails here. The following, for example, is a gross transgression; in his *Henry V*, having mentioned a dunghill, he presently raises a Metaphor from the steam of it; and on a subject too, that naturally led to much nobler ideas. [Quotes 4.3.98ff.: the sun shall 'draw their honours reeking up to heaven'.] (I, 381–2)

... In the fifth place, to make two different Metaphors meet on one object. This is what is called Mixed Metaphor, and is indeed one of the grossest abuses of this Figure; such as Shakespeare's expression 'to take arms against a sea of troubles.' This makes a most unnatural medley, and confounds the imagination entirely. Quintilian has sufficiently guarded us against it.*... Observe, for instance, what an inconsistent groupe of objects is brought together by Shakespeare in the following passage of *The Tempest*; speaking of persons recovering their judgment after the enchantment which held them was dissolved [quotes 5.1.64ff.]. So many ill-sorted things are here joined that the mind can see nothing clearly; the morning *stealing* upon the darkness, and at the same time *melting* it; the senses of men *chasing fumes, ignorant fumes,* and *fumes* that *mantle*. So again in *Romeo and Juliet*:

> ———as glorious,
> As is a winged messenger from heaven,
> Unto the white upturned wondering eyes
> Of mortals, that fall back to gaze on him,
> When he bestrides the lazy pacing clouds,
> And sails upon the bosom of the air.   [2.2.27ff.]

Here, the Angel is represented as at one moment *bestriding* the clouds and *sailing* upon the air, and upon the *bosom* of the air too; which forms such a confused picture that it is impossible for any imagination to comprehend it. (I, 388–90)

[On tragedy]

Sophocles and Euripides are much more successful in this part of Composition. In their pathetic scenes we find no unnatural refinement, no exaggerated thoughts. They set before us the plain and direct feelings of nature in simple expressive language; and therefore, on great occasions, they seldom fail of touching the heart. This too is Shakespeare's great excellency; and to this it is principally owing that his dramatic productions, notwithstanding their many imperfections, have been so long the favourites of the Public. He is more faithful to the true language of Nature, in the midst of passion, than any Writer. He gives us this language unadulterated by art; and more instances of it can be quoted from him than from all other Tragic Poets taken together. I shall refer

* 'We must be particularly attentive to end with the same kind of Metaphor with which we have begun. Some, when they begin the figure with a Tempest, conclude it with a Conflagration; which forms a shameful inconsistency.' [*Institutes of Oratory*, VIII, vi, 50]

only to that admirable scene in *Macbeth*, where Macduff receives the account of his wife and all his children being slaughtered in his absence. The emotions, first of grief, and then of the most fierce resentment rising against Macbeth, are painted in such a manner that there is no heart but must feel them, and no fancy can conceive any thing more expressive of Nature. (III, 334–5)

It only now remains to speak of the state of Tragedy in Great Britain. . . .

The first object which presents itself to us on the English Theatre is the great Shakespeare. Great he may be justly called, as the extent and force of his natural genius, both for Tragedy and Comedy, are altogether unrivalled. But at the same time it is genius shooting wild; deficient in just taste, and altogether unassisted by knowledge or art. Long has he been idolised by the British nation; much has been said, and much has been written concerning him. Criticism has been drawn to the very dregs in commentaries upon his words and witticisms; and yet it remains to this day in doubt whether his beauties or his faults be greatest. Admirable scenes and passages, without number, there are in his Plays; passages beyond what are to be found in any other Dramatic Writer; but there is hardly any one of his Plays which can be called altogether a good one, or which can be read with uninterrupted pleasure from beginning to end. Besides extreme irregularities in conduct, and grotesque mixtures of serious and comic in one piece, we are often interrupted by unnatural thoughts, harsh expressions, a certain obscure bombast, and a play upon words which he is fond of pursuing; and these interruptions to our pleasure too frequently occur on occasions when we would least wish to meet with them. All these faults, however, Shakespeare redeems by two of the greatest excellencies which any Tragic Poet can possess; his lively and diversified paintings of character; his strong and natural expressions of passion. These are his two chief virtues; on these his merit rests. Notwithstanding his many absurdities, all the while we are reading his Plays we find ourselves in the midst of our fellows; we meet with men, vulgar perhaps in their manners, coarse or harsh in their sentiments, but still they are men. They speak with human voices, and are actuated by human passions; we are interested in what they say or do, because we feel that they are of the same nature with ourselves. It is therefore no matter of wonder that from the more polished and regular, but more cold and artificial performances of other Poets, the Public should return with pleasure to such warm and genuine representations of human nature. Shakespeare possesses likewise the merit of having created, for himself, a sort of world of præternatural beings. His witches, ghosts, fairies, and spirits of all kinds are described with such circumstances of awful and mysterious solemnity, and speak a language so peculiar to themselves as strongly to affect the imagination. His two masterpieces, and in which in my opinion the strength of his genius chiefly appears, are *Othello* and *Macbeth*. With regard to his historical plays they are, properly speaking, neither Tragedies nor Comedies; but a peculiar species of Dramatic Entertainment, calculated to describe the manners of the times of which he treats, to exhibit the principal characters, and to fix our imagination on the most interesting events and revolutions of our own country. (III, 348–51)

273. William Jackson, Shakespeare and Jonson

1783

From *Thirty Letters on Various Subjects* (2 vols, 1783); excerpts appeared in *Walker's Hibernian Magazine* for May 1783. A second edition, 'corrected and improved', appeared in 1784 (see *Monthly Review*, lxxi (1784), pp. 346ff.), and a third, 'with considerable additions', in 1795.

William Jackson (1730–1803), known as Jackson of Exeter, was a composer who wrote many songs, quartets, and stage compositions, including the music for an adaptation of *Lycidas* performed at Covent Garden in 1767, and had great success with his opera, *The Lord of the Manor* (1780: libretto by General John Burgoyne), which held the stage for fifty years. In 1792, with some friends, he founded a literary society in Exeter, the proceedings of which were published in 1796 (see No. 306). His collection was well received by both the *Monthly*, lxviii (1783), pp. 391ff. ('this pleasing Miscellany'), and the *Critical*, lv (1783), pp. 161ff.

LETTER XIV

We are got into a custom of mentioning Shakespeare and Jonson together, and many think them of equal merit, tho' in different ways. In my opinion, Jonson is one of the dullest writers I ever read; and his plays, with some few exceptions, the most unentertaining I ever saw.[1] He has some shining passages now and then, but not enough to make up for his deficiencies. Shakespeare, on the contrary, abundantly recompenses for being sometimes low and trifling. One of his commentators much admires his great art in the construction of his verses—I dare say they are very perfect; but it is as much out of my power to think upon the art of verse-making when I am reading this divine poet, as it is to consider of the best way of making fiddle-strings at a concert. I am not master of myself sufficiently to do any thing that requires deliberation: I am taken up like leaf in a whirlwind, and dropped at Thebes or Athens, as the poet pleases!

I have seldom any pleasure from the representation of Shakespeare's plays, unless it be from some scenes of conversation merely, without passion. The speeches which have any thing violent in the expression, are generally so over-acted as to cease to be the 'mirror of nature'—but this was always the case—'Oh! it offends me to the soul, to see a robustious perriwig-pated fellow tear a passion to tatters:'—'tho' this is a 'lamentable thing,' yet it appears to be without remedy . . . . (I.101–3)

Those who think that Shakespeare's personages are natural are deceived. If they were so, they would not be sufficiently marked for stage-effect. A strong proof of this is in the portrait of Lear, who is 'four-score and upward.' Were the character natural, Lear would be best acted by an old man: but every one must instantly perceive that it requires the strength, as well as the abilities of the vigour of life to perform it. (I, 105–6)

[1] The 1795 edition adds: 'His characters neither seem to be portraits, nor formed upon *general* ideas: we cannot fancy that there ever were or can be such people. Shakespeare's characters have that appearance of reality which always has the effect of actual life, or at least what passes for it on the stage.'(93)

274. Joseph Ritson, Shakespeare's editors corrected

1783

From *Remarks, Critical and Illustrative, on the Text and Notes of the last Edition of Shakespeare* (1783).

Joseph Ritson (1752–1803) worked his way up from a humble beginning as a clerk and conveyancer, was admitted to Gray's Inn in 1784, and was called to the bar in 1789. A lifelong student of early English poetry, especially the ballad, in 1782 he published a criticism of Warton's *History of English Poetry* which exposed many errors but gave offence by its violent tone. He attacked, in similar vein, the Johnson–Steevens 1778 edition in these *Remarks*, and the Reed revision of it in *The Quip Modest* (1788). His *Cursory Criticisms* (1792) were directed against Malone's edition, and in 1795 he exposed the Ireland forgeries. Despite his harshness in controversy and other eccentricities, his learning was universally recognized. In the *Monthly Review* Charles Burney commented on Ritson's 'petulance', but acknowledged his 'critical abilities': lxx (1784), pp. 334–8; the *Critical Review* (perhaps by Steevens) was less favourable: lvi (1783), pp. 81–9. Many of his Shakespeare corrections were absorbed into the 1785 edition by Reed, and (with virtually no acknowledgement) by Malone in 1790, and indeed (equally unacknowledged) by some modern editors. For the 1793 edition (see No. 303) Steevens used him as a virtual collaborator, but not always wisely. Ritson's many publications on early songs and Scottish poetry brought him to the attention of Sir Walter Scott, who planned to collaborate with him in a work on 'Border Minstrelsy'. In 1802 Ritson published *Bibliographica Poetica*, a catalogue of English poets from the twelfth to the sixteenth centuries, and *Ancient Engleish Metrical Romancëes*; shortly afterwards his nervous ailments caused a mental breakdown. For a full modern study see Bernard H. Bronson, *Joseph Ritson, Scholar-at-Arms* (2 Vols, Berkeley, Calif., 1938).

PREFACE

If a variety of editions and innumerable comments can be supposed to perfect and correct the inaccurate text of a celebrated author, sufficient, one would think, has been done to leave that of Shakespeare without a blemish. So slow however, or so in-efficacious is the progress and exertion of verbal criticism when moiling in the dust and cobwebs of antiquity, so much is to be demolished, so much to be rebuilt, that it will not, except to those who place implicit confidence in the interested and unqualified assertions of every publisher, be a matter of much surprise to learn that, after all that had been done by the labour of Shakespeare's numerous editors and commentators,—after all that has been urged or assumed in favour of the last edition,—as much more still remains to be done to bring his text back even to the state of correctness in which it was left by his first editors. . . .

The chief and fundamental business of an editor is carefully to collate the original and authentic editions of his author. It is otherwise impossible for him to be certain that he is giving the genuine text, because he does not know what that text is. There have been no less than eight professed editors of Shakespeare; and yet the old copies, of which we have heard so much, have never been collated by any one of them: no, not even either of the two first folios, books indifferently common and quoted by every body. And yet, strange as it may seem, not one of the eight but has taken the credit of, or actually asserted, his having collated them. One may be well allowed to pass by the pretensions of those prior to Dr. Johnson without particular notice; their falsehood is sufficiently apparent in the margin of the late edition. Surely, men who thus proudly expose and severely reprobate the crimes of their neighbours should effectually guard theirselves against similar accusations.

'I,' says Dr. Johnson, 'collated such copies as I could procure, and wished for more';* 'I collated . . . all [the folios] at the beginning, but afterwards used only the first'.† He must be very

---

* Preface, p. 59 [Vol. 5, p. 94].
† *Ibidem*, p. 49 [Vol. 5, p. 86].

hardy indeed that dares give a flat contradiction to such positive assertions as these from so respectable a character. But the cause of Shakespeare and truth obliges one to say that the learned writer is certainly mistaken. The text of his own edition, the notes of Mr. Steevens, and in some respect the remarks in the following sheets, will prove that he never collated any one of the folios,—no not for a single play,—or at least that of his collations he has made little or no use. That he picked out a reading here and there from the old editions, is true: all his predecessors did the same: but this is not *collation*. So much for Dr. Johnson.

With regard to the last edition, Mr. Steevens explicitly tells us that 'it has been constantly compared with the most authentic copies, whether collation was absolutely necessary to the sense, or not'.* 'Would not any one, from this declaration,' to use the ingenious critic's own words, 'suppose that he had at least *compared* the *folios* with each other'?† But he has been deceived, no doubt, by the person employed in this laborious but necessary work. What an abuse of that confidence and credit which the public naturally place in an editor of rank and character, to tell them that 'by a diligent collation of all the old copies hitherto discovered, and the judicious restoration of ancient readings, the text of this author seems now finally settled!'‡ To what better cause can we ascribe such unfounded assertions than to indolence and temerity? since, had the ingenious writer compared the old and present editions through a single play, he must necessaryly have perceived that all the old copies had NOT been diligently collated, that ancient readings had NOT been judiciously restored, and that the text is no more finally settled at present than it was in the time of Theobald, Hanmer, and Warburton: nay, that it is, at large, in the same state of inaccuracy and corruption in which it was left by Mr. Rowe.

These, it may be objected, are merely negative and unproved assertions. It is very true. And they who do not think them confirmed in the course of the following pages, and will not give theirselves the trouble to investigate their truth, are at liberty to disbelieve them. To publish the various readings of the old editions would be a busyness of some labour, and little utility.

* [1778 edition], Advertisement, p. 69.
† *Ibidem*, p. 68.
‡ Malone's preface to his *Supplement* [1780].

As to the notes and conjectures here offered to the public, very little need be said. Shakespeare is *the God of the writer's idolatry*, and should any one of these remarks be thought pertinent or useful in the opinion of a single individual who, like him, admires the effusions of this darling child of nature and fancy, whom *age cannot wither*, and whose *infinite variety custom cannot stale*, it will be a sufficient gratification to him for the pains bestowed in drawing them up. And if there should be a future edition of this favourite, this inimitable author, the writer is not without vanity to hope that the following sheets may stimulate the editor's care and attention to give his text with integrity, judgement, and correctness,——

> ——a consummation
> Devoutly to be wish'd;

and, which must of consequence follow, to reduce the number of exuberant and impertinent notes.* (i–vii)

[1] [On *The Merchant of Venice*, 3.4.72]

> *Por.* I could not *do* with all.

'For the sense of the word *do* in this place, see a note on *Measure for Measure*, act I. COLLINS.'[1]

The conversation of even the highest ranks was not, perhaps, in Shakespeare's time, over and above remarkable for its delicacy. But does the (*real*) commentator believe that a lady of Portia's good sense, high station, and elegant manners could *speak* (or even *think*) so *grossly*? It is impossible!

This observation, and others of the like nature from the same hand, are however, as the reader will perceive, strictly within the canon:

'He (*i.e.* the professed critic) may find out a bawdy, or immoral meaning in his author, where there does not appear to be any hint that way.' Canon XII.[2] (57)

---

* From a republication of the last edition nothing is to be expected. The work will continue, like the editions of Warburton and Hanmer, to dishonour criticism and to insult Shakespeare.

[1] On Steevens's practice of printing notes elucidating Shakespeare's bawdy, and signing them 'Collins', see Vol. 5, pp. 36, 548.

[2] From Thomas Edwards's exposure of Warburton, *The Canons of Criticism* (1748): cf. Vol. 3, pp. 390ff.

[2] [On *Macbeth*, 5.2.43ff.]

> *Macb*. And with some sweet oblivious antidote,
> Cleanse the *foul* bosom of that perilous stuff
> Which weighs upon the heart!

Stuff'd, Mr. Steevens tell us, is the reading of the old copy; but, for the sake of the *ear*, which must be *shocked* by the recurrence of so harsh a sound, he is *willing* to read *foul; foul* is accordingly read. And such is the method taken to preserve the author's genuine text. Alas! poor Shakespeare! (79)

[3] [On *1 Henry IV*, 1.1.5: 'the thirsty entrance of this soil']
. . . Never sure was there so much *drumbleing*, nor (except in this edition) were there ever so many wild and absurd conjectures as this simple passage has given rise to.[1] For so simple it certainly is, as that the little meaning it has may be easyly discovered by the most ignorant, however *doctors* may differ about it. The *thirsty entrance of the soil* is nothing more or less than the face of the earth, parched and cracked as it always appears in a dry summer; and Mr. Steevens came nearer the mark than he was aware of when he mentioned the *porous surface* of the ground. As to its being personifyed it is, certainly, no such unusual practice with Shakespeare. Every one talks familarly of *mother Earth*; and they who live upon her face may, without much impropriety, be called her children. Our author onely confines the image to his own country. The allusion is to the *Barons' wars*. (88)

[4] [On *1 Henry VI*, the portrait of Joan of Arc]
It is to be regretted that Shakespeare should have so far followed the absurd and lying stories of his time about this celebrated heroine, whom the French called the maid of God, as to represent her not onely a strumpet but a witch. If we may believe the most authentic historians she was no less distinguished for virtue than courage. She was burnt, indeed, by the barbarous English, whom she had so frequently driven before her, and who, to excuse their want of courage or policy, and to justify their inhumanity, pretended that she had dealt with the devil! But her memory will no doubt be long held in deserved veneration by her grateful countrymen, whom she so largely contributed to rescue from

[1] Cf. Warburton, Vol. 3, p. 237; Edwards, Vol. 3, p. 407f.

usurpation and slavery. And it is not the least praise of our elegant historian Mr. Hume that he has endeavoured to do justice to the much injured character of this amiable, brave, wise, and patriotic female. (114)

[5] [On Johnson's description of *Julius Caesar* as 'cold and unaffecting': see Vol. 5, p. 146]

This is a strange charge. If nature have denied to this great critic the ordinary feelings of humanity, is he therefor to accuse the poet? Surely, Dr. Johnson is the onely person living who would not be ashamed to declare hisself insensible to the interesting and pathetic scenes of this admirable drama. So far from Shakespeare's adherence 'to the real story and to Roman manners' having 'impeded the natural vigour of his genius,' he seems to have risen with the grandeur and importance of his subject; and if there be any one play in these volumes which affects the heart more than the rest it may be safely averred to be this of *Julius Cæsar*. And he who is not 'agitated in perusing it' may defy the powers of poetry to move him.

The characters or dogmatical criticisms subjoined by the above learned philosopher at the end of each play are generally (as in the present instance) as unjust in theirselves, as injurious to the immortal author; and in many cases could onely proceed from one who either had not read the drama reviewed, or from some natural defect was insensible of its beauty and merit. (145–6)

[6] [On *Titus Andronicus*, 2.1.82]

> *Dem.* She is a woman, therefore may be woo'd;
> She is a woman, therefore may be won.

Suffolk, in the *First part of king Henry VI* makes use of almost the same words:

> She's beautiful; and therefore to be woo'd:
> She is a woman, therefore to be won. [5.3.78f.]

How much or how little soever this may serve to prove, if facts and evidence be to determine our judgement there cannot remain a doubt that this play of *Titus Andronicus* is as much Shakespeare's as any other in this collection. It is not onely given to him by Meres, but is printed as his by the editors of the first folio, his fellow

339

comedians and intimate friends, who neither could have been deceived theirselves, nor could or would have deceived the public. (158–9)

[7] [On *Romeo and Juliet*, 4.3.1ff.]

> *Jul.* ——gentle nurse,
> I pray thee, leave me to myself to-night;
> For I have need of many orisons
> To move the heavens to smile upon my state.

Dr. Johnson, with that candour and politeness for which he is so remarkable, observes that Juliet plays most of her *pranks* under the appearance of religion. Perhaps, says he, Shakespeare meant to *punish* her *hypocrisy* [Vol. 5, p. 154]. If he had, we should, without doubt, have been, some how or other, informed of it. But Shakespeare would never have given the little innocent excuses her virtue and conjugal fidelity prompt her to make use of so harsh a name.—Sweet Juliet! little did'st thou dream, that, in addition to thy misfortunes, the unsullyed purity of thy angelic mind should, at this distance of time, be subject to the rude breath of criticism!—But rest in peace, sweet saint! thy fair untainted name shall live—live in thy Shakespeare's page—when even the critic's memory is no more. (183–4)

[8] [*Ibid.*, 5.3.229ff.]

Lau. I will be brief, *&c.*] Dr. Johnson thinks it 'much to be lamented that the poet did not conclude the dialogue with the action, and avoid a narrative of events which the audience already knew.' [Vol. 5, p. 154.] It was necessary, however, that the surviving characters should be made acquainted with the circumstances which produce the catastrophe, and we should have had more reason to condemn the poet for being *brief* than *tedious*. That our judicious author knew when to tell his story behind the curtain and when upon the stage is evident from the next play [*Hamlet*]; and it was, perhaps, to avoid a sameness between the conclusion of that and [the] present that he has made the friar reveal the transaction to the audience; which naturally introduces the reconciliation of the two families and the moral reflections at the end of the scene, which, whatever the critic may think, are too valuable to be sacrificed to his mere rule and compass abridgement of it. (189)

[9] [On *Hamlet*, 2.1.46]

> *Pol.* Good sir, *or so*; or friend or gentleman.

This is the reading of all the old copies; and there is not a more plain, simple, certain,* and intelligible line in these ten volumes; nor one that has more exercised the attention and ingenuity of the learned and sagacious commentators. Such readers as are better acquainted with Shakespeare than with the modern improvements upon him will not be displeased to see a list of their several *emendations*.

> Dr. WARBURTON: *Good sir, or* sire, *i.e.* father.
> Dr. JOHNSON: *Good, sir,* forsooth, *or friend or gentleman.*
> Mr. STEEVENS: *Good sir, or* so forth, *friend or gentleman.*
> Mr. TYRWHITT: *Good sir*, or sir, *&c.*

The second and third of these proposals are recommended by a long note; and there is, besides, a *memoir* by the reverend and learned Dr. Percy upon the word *forsooth*. Illustrious critics! how much is the spirit of Shakespeare indebted to your unparalleled generosity, and unexampled friendship! (195–6)

[10] [*Ibid.*, 3.4.74ff.: 'Now might I do it pat, now 'a is a-praying . . . ']

'This speech,' says Dr. Johnson, 'in which Hamlet, represented as a virtuous character, is not content with taking blood for blood, but contrives damnation for the man that he would punish, is too horrible to be read or to be uttered.' [Vol. 5, p. 159]

How far it detracts from the virtue of Hamlet to be represented as lying in wait for an opportunity to take an adequate and complete revenge upon the murderer of his father is a question not, with submission to the great moralist, quite so easily decided. The late King has reported hisself to have been destroyed in the most deliberate, horrid, and diabolical manner:

---

* That it is the true reading is sufficiently proved by what Reynaldo, a few lines lower, says to Polonius, who asks,

> Where did I leave?
> *Rey.* At closes in the consequence,
> At friend, *or so*, or gentleman. [51ff.]

But this last line, though certainly useful,—though printed in the folios,—is not taken the least notice of in this editorial specimen of accuracy and perfection.

Cut off ev'n in the blossom of his sin,
Unhousel'd, disappointed, unaneal'd,
No reckoning made, but sent to his account,
With all his imperfections on his head:
O horrible! O horrible! most horrible!   [1.5.76ff.]

Under such aggravated circumstances, for Hamlet to be content with having what Dr. Johnson calls blood for blood, would have been taking an inadequate and imperfect revenge, and consequently doing an act of injustice and impiety to the *manes* of his murdered parent. But indeed, the reasons Hamlet here gives for his conduct, as they are better than any other person can make for him, will fully justify both him and it against all such hypercritical opposition to the end of time. (205)

[11] [*Ibid.*, 4.7.139ff.]

> *Laer.* I will do't:
> And, for the purpose, I'll anoint my sword,
> I bought an unction of a mountebank. . . .

It is a matter of surprise that neither Dr. Johnson, nor any other of Shakespeare's numerous and able commentators has remarked with proper warmth and detestation the villainous assassin-like treachery of Laertes in this horrid plot. There is the more occasion that he should be here pointed out an object of abhorrence, as he is a character we are, in some preceding parts of the play, led to respect and admire. (210)

[12] [*Ibid.*, 5.2.351f.]

> *Hor.* Now cracks a noble heart: Good night, sweet prince;
> And flights of angels sing thee to thy rest.

Mr. Steevens's note on this passage is so interesting and extraordinary that it becomes necessary to insert it here at large, lest it might be thought to be partially or unfairly represented in the remarks which it has occasioned. [Quotes Steevens's note, which first appeared in the 1773 edition (see Vol. 5, pp. 540f.), together with the paragraph quoting Akenside, added in 1778: above, p. 199.]

There are very few, it is believed, at all acquainted with this inimitable author who would not be surprised, nay astonished at such a severe and unexpected attack upon his principal and most favourite character: a character every one has been hitherto led to admire and esteem, not more by universal and long established opinion than by the sentiments and feelings of his own mind. To find the amiable, the injured, the distracted, and unfortunate Hamlet represented as a worthless and immoral being, totally undeserving of the least pity from those almost numberless audiences whom the united force of Nature, Shakespeare, and Garrick has compelled to weep for his misfortunes; and whose compassion would not be less in the closet than in the theatre, seems the most extraordinary and irreconcilable proceeding in a writer of genius and learning that can be well imagined. However, as the heavy charges which are here brought against him will, upon the slightest examination, appear to be groundless, unwarrantable, and unjust, there is little reason to fear that the confidence and ingenuity with which they are advanced and supported will answer the purpose of the learned objector.

Hamlet, the onely child of the late king, upon whose death he became lawfully intitled to the crown, had, it seems, ever since that event been in a state of melancholy, owing to excessive grief for the suddenness with which it had taken place, and an indignant horror at his mother's speedy and incestuous marriage. The spirit of the king his father appears, and makes him acquainted with the circumstances of his untimely fate, which he excites him to *revenge*. This Hamlet engages to do: an engagement it does not appear he ever forgot. It behoved him, however, to conduct hisself with the greatest prudence. The usurper was powerful, and had Hamlet carryed his design into immediate execution it could not but have been attended with the worst consequences to his own life and fame. No one knew what the ghost had imparted to him till he afterwards made Horatio acquainted with it; and though his interview with the spirit gave him certain proof and satisfactory reason to know and detest the usurper, it would scarcely, in the eye of the people, have justifyed his killing their king. To conceal, and at a convenient time to effect, his purpose he counterfeits madness, and for his greater assurance, puts the spirit's evidence and the usurper's guilt to the test of a play, by which the truth of each is manifested. He soon after espies the usurper at prayers, but resolves, and with great justice resolves not to kill him in the very moment when he might be making his peace with heaven: inasmuch as a death so timed would have been rather a happyness than a punishment, and by no means a proper revenge for his father's murder. We next find him in the queen's apartment, endeavouring to make her sensible of the state of vice and horror into which her unnatural connection with the usurper had plunged her. At the beginning of this conference he mistakes Polonius, who was *behind the arras* and about to alarm the household, for the usurper, and under that apprehension stabs him. The spirit appears (not very necessaryly, perhaps) 'to whet his almost blunted purpose.' [3.4.110] He is immediately sent off to England: and in his passage discovers the treacherous and fatal purpose of the commission with which his companion and pretended friends were charged. These men, he knew, had eagerly solicited and even thrust theirselves upon this employment; and he had, of course, sufficient reason to conclude that they were well acquainted with the nature and purport of their fatal packet. That Shakespeare meant to charge them with this knowlege, and to represent them as *participes criminis*, is evident from the old black letter *Hystorie* which furnished him with the subject, where they are not only made privy to, but actually *devise* the scheme to take Hamlet's life. His own safety depended on their removal; and at such a time, and under such circumstances, he would have been fully justified in using any means to procure it.

That he is 'accountable for the distraction and death of Ophelia' is a most strange charge indeed. He had, to be sure, accidentally killed her father, whom he *took for his better* [3.4.32]. This causes her distraction; and her distraction causes her death. A most lamentable train of circumstances! and with which the moral character of Hamlet is as little concerned as that of the ingenious, though uncandid, commentator.

That 'he comes to interrupt the funeral designed in honour of this lady,' is an assertion which has nothing but the credit of the asserter to support it. Walking with his friend Horatio through a churchyard, he enters into conversation with a grave-digger: but presently, observing the approach of a funeral procession, he says to Horatio, to whom he was then speaking:

> Soft, soft, aside. Here comes the king,
> The queen, the courtiers: *Who is this they follow?*
> *And with such maimed rites?* This doth betoken

The corse they follow, did with desperate hand
Fordo its own life. 'Twas of some estate.
Couch we a while, and mark.   [5.1.224ff.]

Does it appear from hence that he knew, or had the least reason to
suspect this to be the funeral of Ophelia; or even that he was
apprised of her distraction or unfortunate death? The contrary is
most certain. He left the kingdom before her insanity broke out,
and does not return till after she is dead. He has seen no one except
Horatio, who was certainly unacquainted with the latter circumstance, so that it is next to an impossibility that he could have
known what had happened to her. But to proceed. Laertes asking
what ceremony else? Hamlet observes to Horatio, *That is Laertes; a
very noble youth* [5.1.224]. Laertes concluding his expostulation
about the further honours with the following beautyful lines:

————lay her i'the earth;
And from her fair and unpolluted flesh
May violets spring!———I tell thee, churlish priest,
A ministring angel shall *my sister* be,
When thou liest howling;   [238ff.]

Hamlet exclaims: *What! the fair Ophelia?* His surprise and
astonishment on hearing Laertes name his sister are manifestly
apparent, and may serve to convince the learned critic, and every
one who has been misled by his ill-founded accusations, that
Hamlet does NOT come to interrupt the funeral, and is guilty of NO
outrage whatever. He as little 'comes to insult the brother of the
dead,' or 'to boast of an affection for his sister, which before he had
[in a wild and careless manner when he was under the necessity of
counterfeiting madness] denied to her face.' Laertes bids

————Treble woe
Fall ten times treble on that cursed head,
Whose wicked deed thy most ingenious sense
Depriv'd thee of;   [246ff.]

an execration Hamlet cannot but perceive to be pointed at hisself.
Having uttered this curse, Laertes hastyly, and in direct violation
of all decorum, jumps into the grave, where he 'rants and mouths
it' like a player. This outrageous proceeding seems to infect
Hamlet; who, forgetting hisself, as he afterward with sorrow owns
to Horatio, and by the 'bravery' of the other's grief being worked

up 'into a towering passion,' leaps in after him: and he who thinks Hamlet's madness or sincerity counterfeit here does not appear to know so much of Shakespeare or of human nature as every one who reads this play ought to do.

The affection Hamlet now boasts for Ophelia was genuine and violent. We find him with the very same sentiments in the beginning of the play, and he has never once disowned it, except on a single occasion, when the sacrifice was required by his assumed character; a circumstance which cannot, at least ought not to, be imputed to him as a crime.

The behaviour and language of Laertes is more ranting and unnatural than noble and pathetic, and with his execration upon Hamlet previously to his leaping into the grave, and the violent shock which Hamlet might feel on learning the corse to be Ophelia's, might easyly work up to a higher pitch of extravagance, a stronger and more composed mind than that of which Hamlet appears to have been then master.

Hamlet's conversation with Laertes immediately before the fencing scene was at the Queen's earnest intreaty, and though Dr. Johnson be pleased to give it the harsh name of 'a dishonest fallacy,'[1] there are better, because more natural, judges who consider it as a most gentle and pathetic address, and cannot perceive it to be either dishonest or fallacious. For certainly Hamlet did not intend the death of *Polonius*; of consequence unwittingly, and by mere accident injured Laertes, who, after declaring that he was 'satisfyed in nature,' and that he onely delayed his perfect reconcilement till his honour were satisfyed by elder masters—whom at the same time (for he has the instrument of death in his hand) he never meant to consult—says

> ————Till that time,
> I do receive your offer'd LOVE LIKE LOVE,
> And WILL NOT WRONG IT. [5.2.244ff.]

On which the truely virtuous, innocent, and unsuspecting Hamlet replies

> ————I embrace it freely
> And will this BROTHERS' wager frankly play. [253f.]

Let the conduct and sentiments of Laertes in this interview, and

---

[1] Johnson in fact calls it a 'falsehood': see Vol. 5, p. 161.

in his conversation with the usurper, together with his villainous design against the life of Hamlet, be examined and tryed by any rules of gentility, honour, or humanity, natural or artificial, he must be considered as a treacherous, cowardly, diabolical wretch. Is such a character to rise on the fall of the generous Hamlet?

Things are sometimes obvious to very careless spectators or readers which are not discerned by those who pay closer attention to the scene. Hamlet, in a trial of skill with Laertes, receives an unexpected, a treacherous, and mortal wound. Immediately before the company enter he appears to be much troubled in mind, his spirits foreboding what was to happen: 'If it be now,' says he, "'tis not to come; if it be not to come, it will be now; if it be not now, yet it will come; the readyness is all.' [5.2.220ff.] He does not appear to have suspected Laertes of any unfair practice (he did not know so much of him as we do), but he had every reason to expect treachery and murder from the usurper; he might too have heared something of his secret juggling with Laertes; and doubtless intended to revenge the death of his father. Being thus wounded, and on the threshold of futurity, if he had not killed the usurper immediately the villain would have escaped unpunished. But he does not stab him for his treachery toward hisself—he upbraids him with his crimes of INCEST and MURDER—and consigns him to the infernal regions,

> With all his 'rank offences' thick upon him.

So that he sufficiently revenges his father, his mother (who, by the way, dyes if not deservedly, at least unpityed), and hisself. As to his own fall, every reader or spectator must sympathise with Horatio for the untimely loss of a youthful prince possessed of such great and amiable qualities, rendered miserable by such unparalleled misfortunes;

> ————For he was likely, had he been put on,
> To have prov'd most royally   [5.2.397f.]

and who falls a sacrifice to the most base and infernal machinations. His death, however, is not to be looked upon as a punishment; the most innocent, as Shakespeare well knew, are frequently confounded with the most guilty; and the virtues of Hamlet were to be rewarded among those angels which his friend Horatio invokes to escort him to everlasting rest.

Dr. Akenside was a very ingenious, sensible, and worthy man: but enough has been said to satisfy those who doubt, that the conduct of Hamlet is neither unnatural nor indefensible. That his intellects were really impaired by the circumstances enumerated by the above learned physician is very probable; and indeed Hamlet hisself more than once plainly insinuates it. See, in particular, the latter part of his soliloquy at the end of the second act [2.2.598ff.].

The opposing and refuting of general charges by proof and circumstance commonly requires much more time and space than the making of them. The writer is sensible that the arguments here adduced are neither arranged so judiciously, nor expressed so well, as the objections of the learned commentator; but from what has been said, and as it is said, it will appear that it has not been without strong and sufficient reasons that Hamlet has 'been hitherto regarded as a hero not undeserving the pity of the audience;' and the ingenious critic will not, perhaps, have much cause to congratulate hisself on being the onely person who has taken pains to point out the *immoral tendency* of as noble, as virtuous, and as interesting a character

As e'er 'imagination' cop'd withall.

(215–24)

275. Edmond Malone, additional notes on Shakespeare

1783

From *A Second Appendix to Mr. Malone's Supplement to the Last Edition of the Plays of Shakespeare, containing Additional Observations by the Editor of the Supplement* (1783). Only fifty copies of this appendix were printed, for private circulation.

On Malone see the head-note to No. 265.

[1] [On *Julius Caesar*, 4.3.137]

What should the wars do with these jigging *fools?*] i.e. with these silly *poets*. A *jig* signified in our author's time a metrical composition.—A modern editor (Mr. Capell) who, after having devoted the greater part of his life to the study of old books, appears to have been extremely ignorant of antient English literature, not knowing this, for *jigging* reads *jingling*. His work exhibits above *six hundred* alterations of the genuine text, equally capricious and unwarrantable.

This editor, of whom it was justly said by the late Bishop of Gloucester, that '*he had hung himself up in chains over our poet's grave,*' having boasted in his preface that 'his emendations of the text were at least equal in number to those of all the other editors and commentators put together,' I had lately the curiosity to look into his volumes with this particular view. On examination I found that of three hundred and twenty-five emendations of the antient copies which he has properly received into his text, *two hundred and eighty-five* were suggested by some former editor or commentator, and *forty* only by himself. The innovations and arbitrary alterations, either adopted from others, or first introduced by this editor from ignorance of our antient customs and phraseology, amount to no less a number than *six hundred and thirty-three!*[1] (38)

[2] [On *Hamlet*, 1.1.117f.]

Stars shone *with trains of fire; dews of blood* fell;

Disasters veil'd *the* sun;] Instead of my former I wish to substitute the following note.—The words *shone, fell,* and *veil'd,* having been introduced by Mr. Rowe without authority, may be safely rejected. Might we not come nearer to the original copy by reading—

> *Astres,* with trains of fire and dews of blood,
> *Disastrous, dimm'd* the sun.

There is, I acknowledge, no authority for the word *astre*; but our author has coined many words, and in this very speech there are two, *gibber* and *precurse,* that are used, I believe, by no other writer.

---

[1] This note was printed in the 1785 edition (VIII, p. 97). In his 1790 edition Malone expanded these unsupported allegations to 'above *Nine Hundred* alterations of the genuine text'; the number of emendations original to Capell is now reduced to fifteen; and the total of 'erroneous and arbitrary alterations' is increased to 972 (VII, p. 392).

He seems to have laboured here to make his language correspond with the preternatural appearances that he describes. *Astres* [from *astrum*] is of exactly the same formation as *antre*, which he has introduced in *Othello*, and which is not, I believe, found elsewhere. The word now proposed being uncommon, it is not surprising that the transcriber's ear should have deceived him, and that he should have written, instead of it, two words (*As stars*) of nearly the same sound. The word *star*, which occurs in the next line, is thus rendered not so offensive to the ear as it is as the text now stands. (54)

[3] [*Ibid.*, 3.1.79f.: 'The undiscover'd country . . .']
. . . This passage has been objected to by others on a ground which seems more plausible. Hamlet himself has just had ocular demonstration that travellers *do* sometimes return from this strange country. Shakespeare, however, appears to have seldom compared the different parts of his plays, and contented himself with general truths. It would have been easy to have written—*Few* travellers return.

Marlowe had, before our author, compared death to a journey to an undiscovered country:

> —————————weep not for Mortimer,
> That scorns the world, and, as a *traveller*,
> Goes to *discover* countries yet unknown.
> > *King Edward II* 1598 (written before 1593).

(56–7)

[4] [On *Othello*, 3.3.296f.]

> *I'll have the work* ta'en out,
> *And give it to Iago.*

This scheme of getting the work of this valued handkerchief copied, and restoring the original to Desdemona, was, I suppose, introduced by the poet to render Emilia less unamiable.

It is remarkable that when she perceives Othello's fury on the loss of this token, though she is represented as affectionate to her mistress, she never attempts to relieve her from her distress; which she might easily have done by demanding the handkerchief from her husband, or divulging the story, if he refused to restore it.—But this would not have served the plot. (62–3)

[5] [On *Othello*, 5.1.116f.]

> *Pr'ythee Emilia,*
> *Go know of Cassio where he supp'd to-night:*

In the last scene of the preceding act Iago informs Roderigo that Cassio was to sup with Bianca; that he would accompany Cassio to her house, and would take care to bring him away from thence between twelve and one.—Our author seldom compared the different parts of his plays. (64)

276. William Richardson, essays on Shakespeare's characters

1783

From *Essays on Shakespeare's Dramatic Characters of Richard the Third, King Lear, and Timon of Athens. To which are added, an Essay on the Faults of Shakespeare: and Additional Observations on the Character of Hamlet* (1783).

On Richardson see the head-note to No. 246. These 'Discourses were written at different times; and read before a Literary Society in the College of Glasgow' (p. v). Although some copies of the book are dated 1784, others are dated 1783; excerpts from it appeared in the *London Magazine* for October 1783 (lii, pp. 293–5), and in the *New Annual Register* for 1783, pp. 88–9. It was reviewed in the *European Magazine* and in the *English Review* for January 1784, while the *Monthly Review* notice (lxx, 1784, p. 134) dates it 1783. The additional observations on Hamlet seem to owe something to Ritson: No. 274.

'Essay I. On the Dramatic Character of King Richard the Third'

The *Life and Death of King Richard the Third* is a popular tragedy: yet the poet, in his principal character, has connected deformity of body with every vice that can pollute human nature. Nor are those vices disguised or softened. The hues and lineaments are as dark and as deeply impressed as we are capable of conceiving. Neither do they receive any considerable mitigation from the virtues of any other persons represented in the poem. The vices of Richard are not to serve as a foil or a test to *their* virtues; for the virtues and innocence of others serve no other purpose than to aggravate his hideous guilt. In reality, we are not much attached by affection, admiration, or esteem, to any character in the tragedy. The merit of Edward, Clarence, and some others, is so undecided, and has such a mixture of weakness as hinders us from entering deeply into their interests. Richmond is so little seen, his goodness is so general or unfeatured, and the difficulties he has to encounter are so remote from view, are thrown, if I may use the expression, so far into the back ground, and are so much lessened by concurring events, that he cannot with any propriety be deemed the hero of the performance. Neither does the pleasure we receive proceed entirely from the gratification of our resentment, or the due display of poetical justice. To be pleased with such a display it is necessary that we enter deeply into the interests of those that suffer. But so strange is the structure of this tragedy that we are less interested in the miseries of those that are oppressed, than we are moved with indignation against the oppressor. The sufferers, no doubt, excite some degree of compassion; but, as we have now observed, they have so little claim to esteem, are so numerous and disunited that no particular interest of this sort takes hold of us during the whole exhibition. Thus, were the pleasure we receive to depend solely on the fulfilment of poetical justice, that half of it would be lost which arises from great regard for the sufferers, and esteem for the hero who performed the exploit. We may also add that if the punishment of Richard were to constitute our chief enjoyment that event is put off for too long a period. The poet might have exhibited his cruelties in shorter space, sufficient however to excite our resentment; and so might have brought us sooner to the catastrophe, if that alone was to have yielded us pleasure. In truth, the catastrophe of a good tragedy is only the completion of our pleasure, and not the chief cause of it. The fable, and the view which the poet exhibits of human nature, conducted through a whole performance, must produce our enjoyment. But in the work now before us there is scarcely any fable; and there is no character of eminent importance but that of Richard. He is the principal agent: and the whole tragedy is an exhibition of guilt, where abhorrence for the criminal is much stronger than our interest in the sufferers, or esteem for those who, by accident rather than great exertion, promote his downfall. We are pleased, no doubt, with his punishment; but the display of his enormities, and their progress to this completion, are the chief objects of our attention. Thus Shakespeare, in order to render the shocking vices of Richard an amusing spectacle, must have recourse to other expedients than those usually practised in similar situations. Here, then, we are led to enquire into the nature of these resources and expedients: for why do we not turn from the Richard of Shakespeare, as we turn from his Titus Andronicus? Has he invested him with any charm, or secured him by some secret talisman from disgust and aversion? The subject is curious, and deserves our attention.

Here, then, we may observe in general, that the appearance is produced, not by veiling or contrasting offensive features and colours, but by so connecting them with agreeable qualities residing in the character itself that the disagreeable effect is either entirely suppressed, or by its union with coalescing qualities is converted into a pleasurable feeling*. In particular, though Richard has no sense of justice, nor indeed of any moral obligation, he has an abundant share of those qualities which are termed intellectual. Destitute of virtue, he possesses ability. He shews discernment of character; artful contrivance in forming projects; great address in the management of mankind; fertility of resource; a prudent command of temper; much versatility of deportment; and singular dexterity in concealing his intentions. He possesses along with these such perfect consciousness of the superior powers of his own understanding above those of other men, as leads him not ostentatiously to treat them with contempt, but to employ them, while he really contemns their weakness, as engines of his ambition. Now, though these properties are not the objects of moral approbation, and may be employed as the instruments of

---

* See Hume's *Essay on Tragedy*.

fraud no less than of justice, yet the native and unmingled effect which *most* of them produce on the spectator, independent of the principle that employs them, is an emotion of pleasure. The person possessing them is regarded with deference, with respect, and with admiration. Thus, then, this satisfaction we receive in contemplating the character of Richard in the various situations in which the poet has shewn him arises from a mixed feeling: a feeling compounded of horror on account of his guilt; and of admiration on account of his talents. (3–9)

In the first scene of the tragedy we have the loathsome deformity of Richard displayed, with such indications of mind as altogether suppress our aversion. Indeed the poet, in the beginning of Richard's soliloquy, keeps that deformity to which he would reconcile us, out of view; nor mentions it till he throws discredit upon its opposite: this he does indirectly. He possesses the imagination, with dislike at those employments which are the usual concomitants of grace and beauty. The means used for this purpose are suited to the artifice of the design. Richard does not inveigh with grave and with solemn declamation against the sports and pastime of a peaceful Court: they are unworthy of such serious assault. He treats them with irony: he scoffs at them; does not blame, but despise them. [Quotes 1.1.5–13.] By thus throwing discredit on the usual attendants of grace and beauty, he lessens our esteem for those qualities; and proceeds with less reluctance to mention his own hideous appearance. Here too, with great judgment on the part of the poet, the speech is ironical. To have justified or apologized for deformity with serious argument would have been no less ineffectual than a serious charge against beauty. The intention of Shakespeare is not to make us admire the monstrous deformity of Richard, but to make us endure it. [Quotes 1.1.14–29.]

His contempt of external appearance, and the easy manner in which he considers his own defects, impress us strongly with the apprehension of his superior understanding. His resolution, too, of not acquiescing tamely in the misfortune of his form, but of making it a motive for him to exert his other abilities, gives us an idea of his possessing great vigour and strength of mind. Not dispirited with his deformity, it moves him to high exertion. Add to this that our wonder and astonishment are excited at the declaration he makes of an atrocious character; of his total insensibility; and resolution to perpetrate the blackest crimes. [Quotes 1.1.30–41.]

It may be said, perhaps, that the colouring here is by far too strong, and that we cannot suppose characters to exist so full of deliberate guilt as thus to contemplate a criminal conduct without subterfuge, and without imposing upon themselves.[1] . . . Yet the view which Shakespeare has given us of Richard's sedate and deliberate guilt, knowing that his conduct was really guilty, is not inconsistent. He only gives a deeper shade to the darkness of his character. With his other enormities and defects, he represents him incapable of feeling, though he may perceive the difference between virtue and vice. Moved by unbounded ambition; vain of his intellectual and political talents; conceiving himself by reason of his deformity as of a different species from the rest of mankind; and inured from his infancy to the barbarities perpetrated during a desperate civil war; surely it is not incompatible with his character to represent him incapable of feeling those pleasant or unpleasant sensations that usually, in other men, accompany the discernment of right and of wrong. (12–17)

We shall now consider the decline of Richard's prosperity, and the effect of his conduct on the fall of his fortunes.

By dissimulation, perfidy, and bloodshed, he paves his way to the throne: by the same base and inhuman means he endeavours to secure his pre-eminence; and has added to the list of his crimes the assassination of his wife and his nephews. Meanwhile he is laying a snare for himself. Not Richmond, but his own enormous vices, proved the cause of his ruin. The cruelties he perpetrates excite in the minds of men hatred, indignation, and the desire of revenge. But such is the deluding nature of vice that of this consequence he is little aware. Men who lose the sense of virtue transfer their own depravity to the rest of mankind, and believe that others are as little shocked with their crimes as they are themselves. Richard having trampled upon every sentiment of justice, had no conception of the general abhorrence that had arisen against him. He thought resentment might belong to the sufferers, and their immediate adherents; but, having no faith in the existence of a disinterested sense of virtue, he appears to have felt no apprehension lest other persons should be offended with his injustice, or inclined to punish his inhuman guilt. Add to this that success administers to

[1] Cf. Kames, Vol. 4, p. 476.

his boldness; and that he is daily more and more inured to the practice of violent outrage. . . . Thus rendered familiar with perfidious cruelty; flushed with success; more elate with confidence in his own ability than attentive to the suggestions of his suspicion; and from his incapacity of feeling moral obligation, more ignorant of the general abhorrence he had incurred than averse to revenge; as he becomes, if possible, more inhuman, he certainly becomes more incautious. This appears in the wanton display of his real character, and of those vices which drew upon him even the curses of a parent. [Quotes 4.4.184–90.]

His incautious behaviour after he has arisen to supreme authority appears very striking in his conduct to his accomplices. Those whom he formerly seduced, or deceived, or flattered, he treats with indifference or disrespect. He conceives himself no longer in need of their aid: he has no occasion, as he apprehends, to assume disguise. Men of high rank who shall seem to give him advice or assistance, and so by their influence with the multitude reconcile them to his crimes or bear a part of his infamy, cease to be reckoned necessary; and he has employment for none but the desperate assassin or implicit menial. All this is illustrated in his treatment of Buckingham. (37–40)

The pleasure we receive from the ruin of Richard, though intimately connected with that arising from the various displays of his character, is nevertheless different. We are not amazed, as formerly, with his talents and his address, but shocked at his cruelty; our abhorrence is softened, or converted into an agreeable feeling, by the satisfaction we receive from his punishment. Besides, it is a punishment inflicted not by the agency of an external cause, but incurred by the natural progress of his vices. We are more gratified in seeing him racked with suspicion before the battle of Bosworth; listening from tent to tent lest his soldiers should meditate treason; overwhelmed on the eve of the battle with presages of calamity arising from inauspicious remembrance; and driven by the dread of danger to contemplate and be shocked at his own heinous transgressions. We are more affected, and more gratified with these, than with the death he so deservedly suffers. Richard and his conscience had long been strangers. That importunate monitor had been dismissed, at a very early period, from his service; nor had given him the least interruption in the career of his vices. Yet they were not entirely parted. Conscience was to visit him before he died, and chose for the hour of her visitation the eve of his death. She comes introduced by Danger; spreads before him, in hues of infernal impression, the picture of his enormities; shakes him with deep dismay; pierces his soul with a poisoned arrow; unnerves and forsakes him. [Quotes 5.3.179ff.] (42–4)

This tragedy, however, like every work of Shakespeare, has many faults; and in particular it seems to have been too hastily written. Some incidents are introduced without any apparent reason or without apparent necessity. We are not, for instance, sufficiently informed of the motive that prompted Richard to marry the widow of Prince Edward. In other respects, as was observed, this scene possesses very singular merit. The scene towards the close of the tragedy between the Queen and Richard, when he solicits her consent to marry her daughter Elizabeth, seems no other than a copy of that now mentioned. As such it is faulty; and still more so by being executed with less ability. Yet this incident is not liable to the objection made to the former. We see a good, prudential reason for the marriage of Richard with Elizabeth; but none for his marriage with Lady Anne. We almost wish that the first courtship had been omitted, and that the dialogue between Richard and Anne had been suited and appropriated to Richard and the Queen. Neither are we sufficiently informed of the motives that on some occasions influenced the conduct of Buckingham. We are not enough prepared for his animosity against the Queen and her kindred; nor can we pronounce, without hazarding conjecture, that it proceeded from envy of their sudden greatness, or from having his vanity flattered by the seeming deference of Richard. Yet these motives seem highly probable. The young Princes bear too great a share in the drama. It would seem the poet intended to interest us very much in their misfortunes. The representation, however, is not agreeable. The Princes have more smartness than simplicity; and we are more affected with Tyrrel's description of their death than pleased with any thing in their own conversation. Nor does the scene of the ghosts in the last act seem equal in execution to the design of Shakespeare. There is more delightful horror in the speech of Richard awakening from his dream than in any of the predictions denounced against him. There seems, indeed, some impropriety in representing those spectres as actually appearing which were only seen in a vision. Besides, Richard might have described them in the succeeding scene to Ratcliff so as to have produced, at least in the perusal of the work, a much stronger effect. The representation of ghosts in this passage is by no means so affecting, nor so awful as the dream related by Clarence. Lastly, there is in this performance too much deviation in the dialogue from the dignity of the buskin; and deviations still more blameable from the language of decent manners. Yet, with these imperfections, this tragedy is a striking monument of human genius; and the success of the poet in delineating the character of Richard has been as great as the singular boldness of the design. (50–3)

From 'Essay II. On the Dramatic Character of King Lear'

Those who are guided in their conduct by impetuous impulse, arising from sensibility and undirected by reflection, are liable to *extravagant* or *outrageous* excess. Transported by their own emotions they misapprehend the condition of others; they are prone to exaggeration; and even the good actions they perform excite amazement rather than approbation. Lear, an utter stranger to adverse fortune, and under the power of excessive affection, believed that his children were in every respect deserving. During this ardent and inconsiderate mood he ascribed to them such corresponding sentiments as justified his extravagant fondness. He saw his children as the gentlest and most affectionate of the human race. What condescension on his part could be a suitable reward for their filial piety? He divides his kingdom among them; they will relieve him from the cares of royalty; and to his old age will afford consolation. [Quotes 1.1.38ff.]

But he is not only extravagant in his love; he is no less outrageous in his displeasure.

The conduct proceeding from unguided feeling will be *capricious*. In minds where principles of regular and permanent influence have no authority every feeling has a right to command; and every impulse, how sudden soever, is regarded during the season of its power with entire approbation. (60–1)

Cordelia was the favourite daughter of Lear. Her sisters had replied to him with an extravagance suited to the extravagance of his affection. He expected much more from Cordelia. Yet her reply was better suited to the relation that subsisted between them than to the fondness of his present humour. He is disappointed, pained, and provoked. No gentle advocate resides in his bosom to mitigate the rigour of his displeasure. He follows the blind impulse of his resentment; reproaches and abandons Cordelia. (63–4)

Lear, in the representation of Shakespeare, possessing great sensibility and full of affection, seeks a kind of enjoyment suited to his temper. Ascribing the same sensibility and affection to his daughters, for they must have it no doubt by hereditary right, he forms a pleasing dream of reposing his old age under the wings of their kindly protection. He is disappointed; he feels extreme pain and resentment; he vents his resentment; but he has no power. Will he then become morose and retired? His habits and temper will not give him leave. Impetuous, and accustomed to authority, consequently of an unyielding nature, he would wreak his wrath, if he were able, in deeds of excessive violence. He would do he knows not what. He who could pronounce such imprecations against Goneril as, notwithstanding her guilt, appear shocking and horrid, would in the moment of his resentment have put her to death. If, without any ground of offence he could abandon Cordelia and cast off his favourite child, what would he not have done to the unnatural and pitiless Regan?

Here, then, we have a curious spectacle: a man accustomed to bear rule, suffering sore disappointment and grievous wrongs; high minded, impetuous, susceptible of extreme resentment, and incapable of yielding to splenetic silence or malignant retirement. What change can befal his spirit? For his condition is so altered that his spirit also must suffer change. What! but to have his understanding torn up by the hurricane of passion, to scorn consolation, to lose his reason! Shakespeare could not avoid making Lear distracted. Other poets exhibit madness because they chuse it, or for the sake of variety, or to deepen the distress: but Shakespeare has exhibited the madness of Lear as the natural effect of such suffering on such a character. It was an event in the progress of Lear's mind, driven by such feelings, desires, and passions as the poet ascribes to him, as could not be avoided.[1]

It is sometimes observed that there are three kinds of madness displayed in this performance:[2] that of Lear, that of Edgar; and that

---

[1] The collected edition of Richardson's Shakespeare essays omits the following paragraph, and substitutes: 'No circumstance in Lear's madness is more affecting than his dreadful anticipation and awful consciousness of its approach.' (Quotes 2.4.282ff.): 1798, p. 308.
[2] See Morgann above, p. 172.

of the Fool. The observation is inaccurate. The madness of Edgar is entirely pretended; and that of the Fool has also more affectation than reality. Accordingly, we find Lear for ever dwelling upon one idea, and reconciling every thing to one appearance. The storms and tempests were not his daughters. The gleams of reason that shoot athwart the darkness of his disorder render the gloom more horrid. Edgar affects to dwell upon one idea; he is haunted by fiends; but he is not uniform. The feeling he discovers, and compassion for the distresses of Lear, breaking out in spite of his counterfeit, render his speeches very often pathetic. The Fool, who has more honesty than understanding, and more understanding than he pretends, becomes an interesting character by his attachment to his unfortunate master.

Lear, thus extravagant, inconsistent, inconstant, capricious, variable, irresolute, and impetuously vindictive, is almost an object of disapprobation. But our poet, with his usual skill, blends the disagreeable qualities with such circumstances as correct this effect, and form one delightful assemblage. Lear, in his good intentions, was without deceit; his violence is not the effect of premeditated malignity; his weaknesses are not crimes but often the effects of misruled affections. This is not all: he is an old man; an old king; an aged father; and the instruments of his suffering are undutiful children. He is justly entitled to our compassion; and the incidents last mentioned, though they imply no merit, yet procure some respect. Add to all this that he becomes more and more interesting towards the close of the drama; not merely because he is more and more unhappy, but because he becomes really more deserving of our esteem. His misfortunes correct his misconduct; they rouse *reflection*, and lead him to that *reformation which we approve*. We see the commencement of this reformation after he has been dismissed by Goneril and meets with symptoms of disaffection in Regan. He who abandoned Cordelia with impetuous outrage and banished Kent for offering an apology in her behalf; seeing his servant grossly maltreated, and his own arrival unwelcomed, has already sustained some chastisement: he does not express that ungoverned violence which his preceding conduct might lead us to expect. He restrains his emotion in its first ebullition, and reasons concerning the probable causes of what seemed so inauspicious. [Quotes 2.4.101ff.]

As his misfortunes increase we find him still more inclined to reflect on his situation. He does not, indeed, express blame of himself; yet he expresses no sentiment whatever of overweening conceit. He seems rational and modest; and the application to himself is extremely pathetic:

>   —I am a man
> More sinn'd against than sinning. [Quotes 3.2.57ff.]

Soon after we find him actually pronouncing censure upon himself. Hitherto he had been the mere creature of sensibility; he now begins to reflect, and grieves that he had not done so before. [Quotes 3.4.28ff.: 'Poor naked wretches'.]

At last he is in a state of perfect contrition, and expresses less resentment against Goneril and Regan than self-condemnation for his treatment of Cordelia, and a perfect, but not extravagant sense of her affection. [Quotes 4.3.38–47.] (76–83)

From 'Essay III. On the Dramatic Character of Timon of Athens'

Shakespeare, in his *Timon of Athens*, illustrates the consequences of that inconsiderate profusion which has the appearance of liberality, and is supposed even by the inconsiderate person himself to proceed from a generous principle; but which in reality has its chief origin in the love of distinction. Though this is not the view usually entertained of this singular dramatic character, I persuade myself, if we attend to the design of the poet in all its parts, we shall find that the opinion now advanced is not without foundation. (85–6)

Real goodness is not ostentatious. Not so is the goodness of Timon. Observe him in the first scene of the tragedy: trumpets sound; Timon enters; he is surrounded with senators, poets, painters, and attendants; chooses that moment to display his beneficence; and accompanies his benefits with a comment on his own noble nature.

>   I am not of that feather, to shake off
> My friend when he must need me.   [1.1.100f.]

He is impatient of admonition. Knowing that he was formerly influenced by sentiments of humanity, he supposes that their power remains unchanged; and that as he continues to do good his principles of action are still the same. He is exposed to this self-imposition not only by the tendency which all men have to deceive themselves, but by the flatteries and praises he is fond of receiving.—Of consequence, he would suffer pain by being undeceived; he would lose the pleasure of that distinction which he so earnestly pursues; the prevailing passion would be counteracted. Thus, there is a disposition in his soul which leads him to be displeased with the truth; and who that is offended with the truth can endure admonition? [Quotes 1.2.240–50.]

The same self-deceit which renders him deaf to counsel, renders him solicitous and patient of excessive applause. He endures even the grossest adulation. Notwithstanding the covering which hides him from himself, he cannot be quite confident that his principles are just what he wishes and imagines them to be. The applauses he receives tend to obviate his uncertainty and reconcile him to himself. Yet it is not affirmed that the man of conscious merit is either insensible of fame, or careless of reputation. He feels and enjoys them both; but, having less need of external evidence to strengthen him in the belief of his own integrity, he is less voracious of praise and more acute in the discernment of flattery.

The favours bestowed by Timon are not often of such a kind as to do real service to the persons who receive them. Wishing to be celebrated for his bounty he is liberal in such a manner as shall be most likely to draw attention, and particularly to provoke the ostentation of those, on account of his munificence, whom he is inclined to benefit. He is therefore more liberal in gratifying their passions, and particularly their vanity, than in relieving their wants; and more desirous of contributing to flatter their imaginations than to promote their improvement. Though he performs some actions of real humanity, and even these he performs in a public manner, yet his munificence appears chiefly in his banquets and shewy presents.

He acts in the same manner in the choice he makes of those whom he serves, and on whom he confers his favours. He is not so solicitous of alleviating the distress of obscure affliction as of gratifying those who enjoy some degree of distinction, or have it in their power to proclaim his praises. He is not represented as visiting the cottage of the fatherless and widow; but is wonderfully generous to men of high rank and character. . . . These are such displays of beneficence as a man of genuine goodness would be apt to avoid. (95–9)

Timon is not more ostentatious, impatient of admonition,

desirous of applause, injudicious in gifts, and undistinguishing in the choice of his friends, than he is profuse. Desirous of superlative praises, he endeavours by lavish beneficence to have unbounded returns.

> ————He outgoes
> The very heart of kindness————
> ————Plutus, the god of wealth,
> Is but his steward. [1.1.274ff.]

The poet, with judicious invention, deduces the chief incident in the play, namely the reverse of Timon's fortune, from this circumstance in his conduct. The vanity of Timon renders him profuse; and profusion renders him indigent.

The character we are describing sets a greater value on the favours he confers than they really deserve. Of a mind un-disciplined by reason, and actuated solely by passion, he conceives the state of things to be exactly such as his present mood and desire represent them. Wishing to excite a high sense of favour he believes he has done so, and that the gratifications he bestows are much greater than what they are. He is the more liable to this self-imposition that many of those he is inclined to gratify are no less lavish of their adulation than he is of his fortune. He does not perceive that the raptures they express are not for the benefit they have received, but for what they expect; and imagines, while his chambers 'Blaze with lights, and bray with minstrelsy,' [2.2.159ff.] while his cellars weep 'with drunken spilth of wine,' while he is giving away horses and precious stones, entertaining the rulers and chief men of Athens, that he is kindling in their breasts a sense of friendship and obligation. He fondly fancies that in his utmost need he will receive from them every sort of assistance; and without reserve or reluctance, lays immediate claim to their bounty. [Quotes 2.2.186–99.] (101–3)

There is no one passage in the whole tragedy more happily conceived and expressed than the conduct of Timon's flatterers. Their various contrivances to avoid giving him assistance shew diversity of character; and their behaviour is well contrasted by the sincere sorrow and indignation of Timon's servants. They are held out to deserved scorn by their easy belief that the decay of their benefactor's fortunes was only pretended, and by their consequent renewal of mean assiduities.

It remains to be mentioned that such disappointment, in tempers like that of Timon, begets not only resentment at individuals but aversion at all mankind.

Timon imposes on himself; and while he is really actuated by a selfish passion, fancies himself entirely disinterested. Yet he has no select friends; and no particular attachments. He receives equally the deserving and undeserving; the stranger and the familiar acquaintance. Of consequence, those persons with whom he seems intimate have no concern in his welfare; yet, vainly believing that he merits their affections, he solicits their assistance, and sustains disappointment. He resentment is roused; and he suffers as much pain, though perhaps of a different kind, as in a similar situation a person of true affection would suffer. But its object is materially different. For against whom is his anger excited? Not against one individual, for he had no individual attachment, but against all those who occasioned his disappointment: that is, against all those who were, or whom he desired should be, the objects of his beneficence; in other words, against all mankind. (105–6)

The symptoms already mentioned are numerous, and indicate to the attentive observer that the state of Timon's mind is more distempered with a selfish passion than he believes: yet the poet, by a device suited to his own masterly invention, contrives an additional method of conveying a distinct and explicit view of the real design. Apemantus, a character well invented and well supported, has no other business in the play than to explain the principles of Timon's conduct. His cynic surliness, indeed, forms a striking contract to the smoothness of Timon's flatterers; but he is chiefly considered as unveiling the principal character. His manners are fierce; but his intentions are friendly: his invectives are bitter; but his remarks are true. (107–8)

There are few instances of a dramatic character executed with such strict regard to unity of design as that of Timon. This is not all. It is not enough to say that all the parts of his conduct are consistent, or connected with one general principle. They have an union of a more intimate nature. All the qualities in his character, and all the circumstances in his conduct, lead to one final event. They all co-operate, directly or indirectly, in the accomplishment of one general purpose. It is as if the poet had proposed to demonstrate how persons of good temper and social dispositions may become misanthropical. He assumes the social dispositions to be constitutional, and not confirmed by reason or by reflection. He then employs the love of distinction to bring about the conclusion. He shews its effects in superseding the influence of better principles, in assuming their appearance, and so in establishing self-deceit. He shews its effects in producing ostentation, injudicious profusion, and disappointment. And lastly, he shews how its effects contributed to excite and exasperate those bitter feelings which estranged Timon from all mankind. Timon at the beginning of the drama seems altogether humane and affectionate; at the end he is an absolute misanthrope. (109–10)

From 'Essay V. Additional Observations on Shakespeare's Dramatic Character of Hamlet'

The strongest feature in the mind of Hamlet, as exhibited in the tragedy, is an exquisite sense of moral conduct. He displays at the same time great sensibility of temper; and is, therefore, most 'tremblingly alive' to every incident or event that befalls him. His affections are ardent and his attachments lasting. He also displays a strong sense of character; and therefore a high regard for the opinions of others. His good sense and excellent dispositions, in the early part of his life and in the prosperous state of his fortune, rendered him amiable and beloved. No misfortune had hitherto befallen him; and though he is represented as susceptible of lively feelings, we have no evidence of his having ever shewn any symptoms of a morose or melancholy disposition. On the contrary, the melancholy which throws so much gloom upon him in the course of the play appears to his former friends and acquaintance altogether unusual and unaccountable.

> ———Something have you heard
> Of Hamlet's transformation: so I call it;
> Since nor th' exterior, nor the inward man,
> Resembles that it was.   [2.2.4ff.]

In the conduct, however, which he displays in the progress of the tragedy he appears irresolute and indecisive; he accordingly engages in enterprizes in which he fails; he discovers reluctance to perform actions which, we think, needed no hesitation; he proceeds to violent outrage where the occasion does not seem to justify violence; he appears jocular where his situation is most serious and alarming; he uses subterfuges not consistent with an ingenuous mind; and expresses sentiments not only immoral but inhuman.

This charge is heavy: yet every reader, and every audience, have hitherto taken part with Hamlet. They have not only pitied but esteemed him; and the voice of the people, in poetry as well as politics, deserves some attention. Let us enquire, therefore, whether those particulars which have given such offence may not be considered as the infirmities of a mind constituted like that of Hamlet, and placed in such trying circumstances, rather than indications of folly or proofs of inherent guilt. (148–51)

We are not therefore to expect that his conduct is to proceed according to the most infallible rules of discretion or of propriety. We must look for frailties and imperfections; but for the frailties and imperfections of Hamlet.

The injuries he has sustained, the guilt of Claudius and the perversion of Gertrude, excite his resentment and indignation. Regard for the opinions of others, who expect such resentment in the Prince of Denmark, promotes the passion. He therefore meditates, and resolves on vengeance. But the moment he forms his resolution the same virtuous sensibility, and the same regard to character that roused his indignation, suggest objections. He entertains a doubt concerning the ground of his suspicions, and the evidence upon which he proceeds.

> ————The spirit that I've seen
> May be a devil;   [Quotes 2.2.598ff.]

In this manner he becomes irresolute and indecisive. Additionally therefore, to the sorrow and melancholy which he necessarily feels for the situation of his family, and which his peculiar frame of mind renders unusually poignant, the harassment of such an inward struggle aggravates his affliction. . . .

This irresolution, which indeed blasts his designs but does not lessen our regard for his character, nor our compassion for his misfortunes and the misery with which it afflicts him, are pathetically described and expressed in the famous soliloquy consequent to the representation of the Players. [Quotes 2.2.550ff.] (152–4)

Thus agitated by external circumstances, torn by contending emotions, liable to the weaknesses nearly allied to extreme sensibility, and exhausted by the contests of violent passions, is it wonderful that he should exhibit dejection of mind, and express disrelish for every human enjoyment? This extreme is no less consistent with his character than his temporary violence. [Quotes 2.2.295ff.: 'I have of late . . . '.] In like manner the same state of internal contest leads him to a conduct directly opposite to that of violence or precipitancy; and when we expect that he will give full vent to his resentment, he hesitates and recedes. This is particularly illustrated in the very difficult scene where Hamlet, seeing Claudius kneeling and employed in devotion, utters the following soliloquy:

> Now might I do it pat, now he is praying;   [3.3.72ff.]

You ask me, why he did not kill the Usurper? And I answer, because he was at that instant irresolute. This irresolution arose from the inherent principles of his constitution, and is to be accounted natural: it arose from virtuous, or at least from amiable sensibility, and therefore cannot be blamed. His sense of justice, or his feelings of tenderness, in a moment when his violent emotions were not excited, overcame his resentment. But you will urge the inconsistency of this account with the inhuman sentiments he expresses:

> Up, sword, and know thou a more horrid hent:
> When he is drunk, asleep, or in his rage, &c.
> Then trip him, &c.   [88ff.]

In reply to this difficulty, and it is not inconsiderable, I will venture to affirm that these are not his real sentiments. There is nothing in the whole character of Hamlet that justifies such savage enormity. We are therefore bound, in justice and candour, to look for some hypothesis that shall reconcile what he now delivers with his usual maxims and general deportment. I would ask then, whether on many occasions we do not alledge those considerations as the motives of our conduct which really are not our motives? Nay, is not this sometimes done almost without our knowledge? Is it not done when we have no intention to deceive others; but when, by the influences of some present passion, we deceive ourselves? The fact is confirmed by experience, if we commune with our own hearts; and by observation, if we look around. . . . Consult Bishop Butler, your favourite and the favourite of every real enquirer into the principles of human conduct, and you will be satisfied concerning the truth of the doctrine.—Apply it, then, to the case of Hamlet: sense of supposed duty, and a regard to character, prompt him to slay his uncle; and he is with-held at that particular moment by the ascendant of a gentle disposition; by the scruples and perhaps weakness of extreme sensibility. But how can he answer to the world and to his sense of duty for missing this opportunity? The real motive cannot be urged. Instead of excusing it would expose him, he thinks, to censure; perhaps to contempt. He looks about for a motive; and one better suited to the opinions of the multitude, and better calculated to lull resentment, is immediately suggested. He indulges, and shelters himself under the subterfuge. He alledges as direct causes of his delay motives that could never influence his conduct; and thus exhibits a most exquisite picture of amiable self-deceit. The lines and colours are indeed very fine, and not very obvious to cursory observation. The beauties of Shakespeare, like genuine beauty of every kind, are often veiled; they are not forward nor obtrusive. They do not demand, though they claim attention.

I would now offer some observations concerning Hamlet's counterfeited or real madness: and as they are also intended to justify his moral conduct, let me beg of you to keep still in view the particular circumstances of his situation and the peculiar frame of his mind.

Harassed from without and distracted from within, is it wonderful if, during his endeavour to conceal his thoughts, he should betray inattention to those around him, incoherence of speech and manner, or break out inadvertently into expressions of displeasure? Is it wonderful that he should 'forego all mirth,' become pensive, melancholy, or even morose? Surely such disorder of mind in characters like that of Hamlet, though not amounting to actual madness yet exhibiting reason in extreme perplexity, and even trembling on the brink of madness, is not unusual. Meantime Hamlet was fully sensible how strange those involuntary improprieties must appear to others: he was conscious he could not suppress them; he knew he was surrounded with spies; and was justly apprehensive lest his suspicions or purposes should be discovered. But how are these consequences to be prevented? By counterfeiting an insanity which in part exists. Accordingly, to Ophelia, to Polonius, and others, he displays more extravagance than his real disorder would have occasioned. This particular aspect of the human mind is not unnatural; but is so peculiar and so exquisitely marked that he alone who delineated the commencing madness, the blended reason and distraction of Lear, has ventured to pourtray its lineaments. That Hamlet really felt some disorder, that he studied concealment and strove to hide his distraction under appearances of madness, is manifest in the following passage, among others of the same kind, where he discovers much earnestness and emotion, and at the same time an affectation of sprightliness and unconcern: [Quotes 1.5.153ff.].

If we allow that the poet actually intended to represent Hamlet as feeling some distraction of mind; and was thus led to extravagancies which he affected to render still more extravagant, why, in his apology to Laertes, need we charge him with deviation from truth? [Quotes 5.2.228ff.: 'I am punish'd with a sore distraction'.]

Hamlet no doubt put to death Polonius; but without intention, and in the frenzy of tumultuous emotion. He might therefore say, both of that action and of the consequent madness of Ophelia,

> Let my disclaiming from a purpos'd evil,
> Free me so far in your most generous thoughts,
> That I have shot my arrow o'er the house,
> And hurt my brother. [241ff.]

Neither is his conduct at the funeral of Ophelia to be construed into any design of insulting Laertes. His behaviour was the effect of violent perturbation; and he says so afterwards, not only to Laertes but to Horatio [quotes 5.2.75–80, 234–6].

The whole of his behaviour at the funeral shews a mind exceedingly disordered and thrown into very violent agitation. But his affection for Ophelia appears sincere; and his regard for Laertes genuine. On recovery from his transport—to which, however, Laertes provoked him—how pathetic is the following expostulation:

> ————Hear you, Sir,
> What is the reason that you us'd me thus?
> I lov'd you ever. [5.1.288ff.]

I have been the more minute in considering those particulars, that not only you, but Commentators of great reputation, have charged Hamlet in this part of his conduct with falsehood and inhumanity.[1] (156–67)

From these remarks, I hope you will now agree with me, that Hamlet deserves compassion. . . . The character is consistent. Hamlet is exhibited with good dispositions, and struggling with untoward circumstances. The contest is interesting. As he endeavours to act right we approve and esteem him. But his original constitution renders him unequal to the contest. He displays the weaknesses and imperfections to which his peculiar character is liable; he is unfortunate; his misfortunes are in some measure occasioned by his weakness: he thus becomes an object not of blame, but of genuine and tender regret. Such a character would have appeared to Aristotle peculiarly proper for theatrical representation. (169–70)

277. Thomas Davies, Shakespeare in the theatre

1784

From *Dramatic Miscellanies: consisting of Critical Observations on several Plays of Shakespeare: with a Review of his principal Characters, and those of various eminent Writers, as represented by Mr. Garrick, and other celebrated Comedians. With Anecdotes of Dramatic Poets, Actors, &c.* (3 Vols, 1784).

This is an extensive work, consisting of 452, 425, and 508 pages respectively. The second edition, 1785, added a long Postscript to Vol. III (pp. 514–75) in which Davies defended

---

[1] The collected edition of 1798 adds a footnote at this point (p. 138): 'With high respect and sincere esteem for one of the most enlightened critics, and most useful moral philosophers that ever appeared in England, this and some other remarks in the Essay on the character of Hamlet are intended, as the attentive reader will perceive, to remove some strong objections urged by Dr. Johnson against both the play, and the character.' [See Vol. 5, p. 161.]

himself from the criticisms of George Colman in the *Monthly Review*, lxx (1784), pp. 456–60, and disclosed more of the duplicities of George Steevens. Davies (1712?–85) was an actor between 1736 and 1762, when he returned to bookselling, opening a shop at 8 Russell Street, Covent Garden, where in 1763 he introduced Boswell to Johnson. He republished several early writers, such as William Browne (1772), Sir John Davies (1773), Eachard (1774), Lillo (1775), and Massinger (1779). In 1778 he became a bankrupt, and was much helped by Johnson, who later encouraged him to write his *Life of David Garrick* (1780), which had four editions, bringing him money and reputation.

---

[1] [On *King John*, Act III]

I do not recollect a third act in any tragedy of Shakespeare so rich in scenes where pity and terror distress the soul of man, and govern it by turns with equal influence, as this of *King John*. The interview between John and Hubert, where the king solicits Hubert, more by looks and action than by words, to murder his nephew Arthur, is, in the opinion of every man of taste, superior to all praise. [Compares it with a scene in Massinger's *Duke of Milan*.] The scene in Massinger is well conceived and highly finished; but the lightning itself is not brighter or quicker in its flash, nor more astonishing in its effects, than the sublime and penetrating strokes of Shakespeare. In Massinger, eloquent language and unbroken periods give easy assistance to the speaker, and calm and undisturbed pleasure to the hearer. In Shakespeare the abrupt hints, half-spoken meanings, hesitating pauses, passionate interruptions, and guilty looks, require the utmost skill of the actors while they alarm and terrify the spectator. (I, 50–1)

[2] *Ibid.*: the character of Constance]

No! I defie all comfort! all redress!

The grief, anguish, and despair of a mother, are nowhere so naturally conceived and so pathetically expressed as in the Constance of Shakespeare. The Clytemnestra, Hecuba, and Andromache of Euripides, though justly admired characters, have not those affecting touches, those heart-rending exclamations of

371

maternal distress, with which Constance melts the audience into tears. The modern imitations of the ancients are still more feeble. Nor can Crëusa or Merope approach the sublime pathos of our inimitable poet. . . .

I have already taken notice of Mrs. Cibber's uncommon excellence in Constance. It was indeed her most perfect character. When going off the stage, in this scene, she uttered the words 'O Lord! my boy!' with such an emphatical scream of agony, as will never be forgotten by those who heard her. (I, 54–6)

[3] [*Ibid.*, 4.1]
Notwithstanding that our author in this scene unluckily falls into his old fond habit of quibbling and playing upon words, yet the strong pleadings of Arthur, in the natural language of youthful innocence in distress, will touch the heart of every reader. (I, 61)

[4] [On *Richard II*, 4.1.162ff.]
We cannot suppose a more awful and affecting transaction than a prince brought before his subjects, compelled to deprive himself of his royalty, and to resign his crown to the popular claimant, his near relation. This is a subject worthy the genius of Shakespeare; and yet, it must be confessed, he has fallen infinitely short of his usual powers to excite that tumult of passion which the action merited. He was ever too fond of quibble and conceit; but here he has indulged himself beyond his usual predilection for them; and I cannot help thinking, from this circumstance alone, that *Richard II.* was written and acted much earlier than the date in the stationers' books of 1597. (I, 169–70)

[5] [From a note on *1 Henry IV*]
As for Falstaff, of whose character no man can say too much, and every man will be almost afraid to say anything, from an apprehension of his not being able to treat so fertile a subject as it deserves; he, in the confession of all men, is the great master-piece of our inimitable writer, and of all dramatic poetry. Shakespeare had given several sketches of humourous characters, as if to try his abilities, before he introduced to the public this theatrical prodigy, which then astonished Ben Jonson, the great poet of humour, and has bidden defiance to all succeeding attempts to rival it. What name too despicable can we give to those wretched imitations of

the fat knight, the Tucca of Jonson's *Poetaster*, and the Cacofogo of Fletcher? (I, 202–3)

[6] [On *1 Henry IV*, 2.4.258: 'By the Lord, I knew ye as well as he that made ye']

It is confessed by all the world that there is an uncommon force and versatility in the mirth of Falstaff, which is superior to all that dramatic poetry has hitherto invented. Prince Henry's conversation is not without wit, and abounds in easy pleasantry and a gay turn: but the Prince stands not in need of that ready power of repartee, that impenetrable shield of inventive audacity, and that ability to shift his ground continually to ward off the blows, to which the lies of Falstaff incessantly expose him. The jolly knight is never in a state of humiliation; he generally rises superior to attack, and gets the laugh on his side in spite of truth and conviction. It was by this kind of invincible courage in conversation, as well as the quickness of his conception and brilliancy of his fancy, that Foote,[1] without the help of Jack Falstaff's lies, was enabled to rise up and win the field when his opponents imagined he was laid flat and conquered outright. Garrick had a great share of wit, as well as fine animal spirits; but a smart blow of a repartee would silence him for the evening. If suffered to take the lead, he was highly entertaining; but he could not bear interruption. (I, 237–8)

[7] [*Ibid.*, 5.4.125: Falstaff's 'wounding' of Douglas's corpse: 'Therefore, sirrah, with a new wound in your thigh . . .']

A man of genius [Morgann] has taken pains to rescue the character of Falstaff from the charge of cowardice; not considering that if the knight is proved to be a man of courage half the mirth he raises is quite lost and misplaced. The Prince and Poins obtained, by their contrivance, such evident proofs of his dastardly spirit that the whole mirth, in the admired scene of his detected tergiversation, depends upon it. Old Jack is so fairly hunted down by the plain tale and keen reproaches of the Prince that he is reduced to the necessity of excusing his want of courage by attributing his fear to instinct. But if any proof of his timidity be yet wanting we have, in this scene, such as bids defiance to all question; for Falstaff, not satisfied with seeing the dead body of Percy before him, to make all sure, wounds the corpse in the thigh. Nobody, I believe, is angry

---

[1] Samuel Foote, a brilliant actor and mimic: see Vol. 3, No. 109.

that he afterwards swears he killed him. I cannot think the author of the *Essay on the Character of Falstaff* intended any thing more, by his argument, than to convince the public that he was very competent to support any hypothesis by brilliancy of wit and plausibility of argument. (I, 272–3)

[8] [On *2 Henry IV*, 4.3.106ff.: the betrayal of the rebels]

This masterpiece of infamous treachery and breach of compact, as related by our poet, is taken pretty exactly from Holinshed and Stow, though it is differently related by Hall, who makes the account much more honourable to the royalists. He says the apprehending the bishop and his confederates was an action of surprise. However, all later historians copy the two first Chronicles, and, what is very surprising, this perfidious breach of faith passes without censure of any writer from Holinshed to Hume. Our author is surely to blame for not marking this transaction with a proper stigma: he might have done it in very forcible terms from the mouth of the archbishop of York or Lord Mowbray, who strenuously opposed the proffered treaty. (I, 309–10)

[9] [On *Henry VIII*, 4.2.82ff.: the 'Vision of Angels' to Queen Katharine]

No dramatic author ever took such indefatigable pains to feed the eye and the ear, as well as the understanding, as Shakespeare. What effect this vision might produce on the audience originally is not now to be learned. . . . Though the author shews fancy in this little pantomime, yet it seems fitter, at present, to tempt an audience to mirth and ridicule than to serious attention. The grave congées, solemn dancings, and stately courtesies of these aërial beings put us in mind of Bayes's grand dance; and perhaps the Duke of Buckingham borrowed a hint of it from this vision.[1] (I, 418)

[10] [On Shakespeare's use of the clown to please English audiences]

So convinced was Shakespeare that his countrymen could not be satisfied with their dramatic exhibitions without some mixture of merriment that, in his most serious plays, he has thrown in characters of levity or oddity to enliven the scene. In *King John* we

[1] In *The Rehearsal*, Act III.

have the bastard Falconbridge; in *Macbeth* the witches—who, though not absolutely comic, never fail to provoke laughter. In *Julius Cæsar*, Casca and the mob; in *Hamlet*, Polonius, the grave-diggers, and Osric; nay, in *Othello*, his last and most finished tragedy, besides a happily-conceived drunken scene of Cassio, we are presented with the follies of a Roderigo. These comic characters, placed in proper situations to produce action arising from the plot, never failed to raise gaiety and diversion amidst scenes of the most affecting pathos and the most afflicting terror. What affords the most evident proofs of our author's infallible judgement and sagacity is that, notwithstanding the great alteration and improvement in the public taste respecting the amusements of the theatre, these characters and scenes never fail to produce the same effect at this day; and who, after all, is offended with the idle politics and silly pedantry of Polonius, after admiring the wonderful interview of Hamlet and the ghost? Who does not laugh at the prattling and gossipries of the nurse, when Juliet has taken a sad and mournful leave of her beloved Romeo? (II, 22–3)

[11] [On *All's Well that Ends Well*]
In all our comic writers, I know not where to meet with such an odd compound of cowardice, folly, ignorance, pertness, and effrontery, with certain semblances of courage, sense, knowledge, adroitness, and wit, as Parolles. He is, I think, inferior only to the great master of stage gaiety and mirth, Sir John Falstaff. (II, 40)

[12] [On the stage-history of *Macbeth*, and the persistence of D'Avenant's version, which, despite 'all his added deformities and sad mutilations', held the stage from 1665 to 1744]
Happily for the lovers of Shakespeare Mr. Garrick, some years before he was a patentee, broke through the fetters of foolish custom and arbitrary imposition: he restored *Macbeth* to the public almost in the same dress it was left us in by the author. A scene or two which were not conducive to the action, he threw out in representation; others that were too long he judiciously pruned; very few additions were made, except in some passages of the play necessary to the better explanation of the writer's intention. He composed, indeed, a pretty long speech for Macbeth when dying,[1] which, though suitable perhaps to the character was unlike

1 See Vol. 3, No. 100.

Shakespeare's manner, who was not prodigal of bestowing abundance of matter on characters in that situation. But Garrick excelled in the expression of convulsive throes and dying agonies, and would not lose any opportunity that offered to shew his skill in that part of his profession. (II, 116–8)

[13] [On *Macbeth*, 5.3.24ff.: 'that which should accompany old age']

Dr. Johnson thinks the courage of Macbeth preserves some esteem; but that quality he had in common with Banquo and others. I am of opinion that his extreme reluctance to murder his royal master, his uncommon affliction of mind after he had perpetrated the crime, with the perpetual revolt of his conscience upon the commission of each new act of cruelty, are the qualities which render Macbeth, though not worthy of our esteem, yet an object not entirely unmeriting our pity, in spite of his ambition and cruelty. (II, 191)

[14] [On Shakespeare's 'unhistorical' portrait of Julius Caesar]

. . . He has likewise not forgotten his contempt of dreams, omens, forebodings, and every species of superstition. But the poet has made him, what he never was, an ostentatious boaster, and a violent rejector of the petitions addressed to him. But perhaps Cæsar was to be lessened in order to aggrandize Brutus. (II, 198)

[15] [On *Julius Caesar*, 3.2.73ff.: 'Friends, Romans, countrymen']

It has not, I believe, been hitherto observed by any of the commentators that this admirable piece of oratory, so happily divided into exordium, narration, and peroration, is the sole product of our author's genius, unassisted by his conductor, Plutarch. The only hint which he has borrowed from that writer is Antony's shewing the dead body of Cæsar to the populace: it is composed of such topics as were most conducive to the desired effect. The artful pauses and interruptions serve to increase the skill and power of the speaker, and to rouse, astonish, and inflame the minds of the auditors. (II, 242)

. . . The art of Mark Antony is skillfully unfolded; his oration over the dead body of Cæsar is such a masterpiece of eloquence as is not to be matched in any play antient or modern. (II, 255–6)

[16] [On the apparent unpopularity of *King Lear* on the Restoration stage]

. . . It should seem then that even the action of a Betterton could not support a play with a catastrophe so shocking and terrible to human nature. (II, 260)

[17] [On Nahum Tate's adaptation of *King Lear*: see Vol. 1, No. 23]

. . . The passion of Edgar and Cordelia is happily imagined; it strongly connects the main plot of the play and renders it more interesting to the spectators; without this, and the consequent happy catastrophe, the alteration of *Lear* would have been of little worth. Besides, after those turbulent scenes of resentment, violence, disobedience, ingratitude, and rage between Lear and his two eldest daughters, with the king's consequent agony and distraction, the unexpected interview of Cordelia and Edgar in act III gives a pause of relief to the harassed and distressed minds of the audience. It is a gleam of sunshine and a promise of fair weather in the midst of storm and tempest. I have seen this play represented twenty or thirty times, yet I can truly affirm that the spectators always dismissed the two lovers with the most rapturous applause. (II, 262–3)

[Davies discusses the arguments against Tate's adaptation—by Addison (see Vol. 2, p. 273) and by Richardson, in *Clarissa* (see Vol. 3, pp. 324ff.)—then the opposite argument by Johnson (see Vol. 5, pp. 139f.).]

If these scenes are really so afflicting to a mind of sensibility in the closet, what would they produce in action? What exquisite grief and unutterable horror would such a painter as Garrick, in the last scene of the play, have raised in the breast of a spectator? Who can endure to look for any considerable time at the agonizing woe in the countenance of Count Ugolino, drawn by the inimitable pencil of Reynolds? But were you to produce that subject on the stage, in action, none but a heart of marble could sustain it. . . .

The cruel never shed tears, it is true, but to be continually weeping is more than humanity can bear. The slaughter of characters in the last act of the old *Lear* too much resembles the conclusion of *Tom Thumb*; for no man of any consequence is left alive except Albany and Edgar. (II, 265–6)

[18] [On *King Lear*, 2.4.155ff.: the character of Kent]

It is the peculiar privilege of Shakespeare to draw characters of the most singular form and such as, though acknowledged to come from nature's mint, had never entered into the mind of any other writer, antient or modern. This man combined in his imagination all the possibilities of human action with all the varieties of situation and passion. It is in this wonderful creative faculty that he excels all dramatic writers. He alone seems to have discerned how far the exercise of the noblest qualities of the mind could and ought to proceed. The generosity of Kent is not to be matched in any other drama, antient or modern. The man who has the courage in the face of a court to reprove his prince for an act of folly, violence, and injustice; after being condemned by him to perpetual banishment for his honest freedom, apprehensive lest some ill consequences should attend his master's rash conduct, assumes a mean disguise with no other view than to serve him in his utmost need, to wait upon him as his menial servant, and to do him all servile offices his necessities should require. No man will think so meanly of human nature as not to acknowledge that virtue so disinterested is the growth of humanity. None but a Shakespeare ever conceived so noble an example of persisting goodness and generous fidelity. (II, 288–9)

[19] [*Ibid.*, 3.7.67: the blinding of Gloucester]

. . . That the tragedy of *Lear*, as originally written, did not please the audience when acted soon after the Restoration by Betterton and his company, I have proved, as far as probability will warrant me, by Downes.[1] Nor can it be surprising that the spectators should be shocked at so horrible a sight as one man stamping upon the eyes of another, and at the same time encouraged to proceed in his barbarity by one of the softer sex! After all, Shakespeare might possibly contrive not to execute this horrible deed upon the stage, though it is so quoted in the book. He was extremely careful of offending the eyes, as well as ears, of the spectators by any thing outrageous. Gloucester's losing his eyes is so essential to the plot, that Mr. Colman found it impossible to throw it out.[2] However, at the present the sufferer is forced into some adjoining room; and the ears of the audience are more hurt by his cries than their eyes

---

[1] John Downes, author of *Roscius Anglicanus*: see Vol. 2, No. 46.
[2] See Vol. 5, No. 218.

can be when he is afterwards led on the stage. The gold-beater's skin applied to the sockets, as if to staunch the bleeding, abates something perhaps of the hideousness of the spectacle. (II, 303-4)

[20] [End-note to *King Lear*]

Amongst a number of Shakespeare's capital plays it is not easy to determine in which the genius of the writer shone out with greatest lustre. However, I believe it will be confessed that in none of his tragedies the passions have been extended with more genuine force, the incidents more numerous or more dramatically conducted, nor the moral more profitable than in *Lear*. There are three characters in this play of which I scarcely know that there are any counterparts in any other, ancient or modern. They are, indeed, all martyrs to virtue and piety. Though too much cannot be said of the generous offspring of our inimitable bard, Kent can no where be matched. Edgar and Cordelia follow next: such an example as Cordelia of filial piety, except perhaps in the Grecian stage,* is not to be found in dramatic poetry. Edgar is equal in merit to the lady. (II, 329)

[21] [On Dryden's *All for Love*, 'inspired with the warm flame of the original']

... Antony, in the first act,[1] is so great that the poet wanted power to keep pace with himself, and falls off from his first setting out. Dryden's Cleopatra has none of the various feminine artifices and shapes of passions of the original; nor, indeed, that greatness of soul which ennobles her last scenes in Shakespeare. She resembles more the artful kept-mistress than the irregular, but accomplished, Queen of Egypt. (II, 336-7)

[22] [On *Antony and Cleopatra*, 4.5.16ff.: 'Oh! my fortunes have/ Corrupted honest men!']

Admidst all the folly, profligacy, and mad flights of Mark Antony, some bright beams of a great and generous soul break forth with inimitable lustre. Instead of reproaching his officer for desertion and treachery, he lays the blame on his own adverse fortune, which had unhappily overthrown the principles of the best and

* The Antigone of Sophocles, in the *Œdipus Colonæus*, is a most perfect character of filial piety.
[1] See Vol. 1, No. 14.

worthiest men. This is one of our author's characteristical strokes, and perfectly suited to Mark Antony. (II, 355)

[23] [*Ibid.*, 5.2.281ff.: Cleopatra:]

> Methinks I hear
> Antony call; I see him rouse himself,
> To praise my noble act!

Cleopatra's preparation for death is animated to a degree of sublimity which greatly raises the character of the Egyptian princess, and makes us lament her in death whom living we could not praise, though it was impossible not to admire her. (365–6)

I cannot help thinking that Dr. Johnson has been rather precipitate in deciding upon the merit of *Antony and Cleopatra*.[1]—How can I submit to that sentence which pronounces that there is no discrimination of character in this play, except in Cleopatra, whom he considers only as conspicuous for feminine arts? Those she has in abundance, it is true; but her generous resolution to die rather than submit to embrace life upon ignoble terms is surely also worth remembering. But is not Antony highly discriminated by variety of passion, by boundless generosity as well as unexampled dotage? What does this truly great writer think of Enobarbus, the rough old warrior, shrewd in his remarks and humorous in his plain-dealing? I shall say nothing of Octavius or Lepidus, though they are certainly separated from other parts. The simplicity of the fable is necessarily destroyed by exhibiting such a croud of events happening in distant periods of time, a fault common to historical plays. But, in spite of all irregularities this tragedy remains unequalled by any that have been written on the same subject. (II, 367–8)

[24] [On *Hamlet*, 2.1: Polonius' spying on Laertes]
This scene, between Polonius and his servant, Reynaldo, has not been acted for more than a century, and is by no means essential to the play. (III, 36)

[25] [On Polonius: cf. Johnson's discussion, Vol. 5, pp. 156–7]
... But indeed there are abundant instances of the radical weakness of this character disseminated thoughout the

[1] Cf. Vol. 5, p. 148.

play. . . . Polonius is in no respect that I know of to be esteemed. He is more obsequious and officious than he ought to be; a conduct which borders on knavery. (III, 39–40)

[26] [On *Hamlet*, 3.1.56ff.: 'To be or not to be']
This celebrated soliloquy will be admired, got by rote, and constantly repeated by all persons of taste, as long as the existence of our language. (III, 73)

[27] [*Ibid.*, 3.2.140ff.: 'Be not you asham'd to show . . .']
Mr. Steevens reproves the author for putting into the mouth of Hamlet unbecoming expressions during his personated madness.[1] But it has been noticed by those who have visited the cells of lunatics that females, the most remarkable for modesty, have in their insanity thrown out very indecent and unbecoming expressions. In her madness the innocent Ophelia chants scraps of such songs as would not have entered into her mind when in her perfect senses. (III, 90)

[28] [*Ibid.*, 3.3.73ff.: 'Now might I do it pat . . .']
. . . The whole soliloquy is more reprehensible, perhaps, than any part of Shakespeare's works. The deferring the punishment of the King at his devotions, lest his soul should go to heaven, is not only shocking but highly improbable; and is, besides, a poor contrivance to delay the catastrophe till the last act. The first actor who rejected this horrid soliloquy was Mr. Garrick. (III, 101)

[29] [*Ibid.*, 3.4.30: 'As kill a king?']
I cannot, with Mr. Steevens,[2] suppose this interrogation of the Queen as a hint to the auditors that she had no concern in the murder of her husband. The words are absolutely equivocal, and may be a proof of her guilt as well as her innocence. The Ghost had charged her with being won to the lust of his brother and murderer; there he stopped, and with the most pathetic tenderness cautions Hamlet not to think of punishing his mother, but to leave her to heaven and her conscience. But there is one passage in the play acted before the King and Queen which brings the guilt of

[1] Cf. Vol. 5, p. 539.
[2] See above, pp. 199 and 283f.

murder home to Hamlet's mother. The Player-Queen says, among other professions of inviolable constancy,

> In second husband let me be accurst!
> None wed the second but who kill'd the first!   [3.2.179f.]

These lines we may suppose to be put into the old fable by Hamlet on purpose to probe the mind of the Queen; and his immediate reflection on her behaviour plainly proves that they stung her to the quick: 'That's wormwood!' (III, 103–4)

[30] [*Ibid.*, 3.4: the closet-scene]
This scene is one of the glories of the English stage; it may challenge a competition with any thing of the kind produced by *haughty Greece or insolent Rome*. (III, 111)

[31] [*Ibid.*, 4.7.140: 'And for that purpose I'll anoint my sword']
This unexpected change of disposition in Laertes must have struck every reader of the play. A young man of high breeding, with a noble sense of honour, who from the warmth of filial piety was ready to take arms against his sovereign, on a sudden becomes a confederate with a vile plotter to destroy a prince. Shakespeare is generally such a complete master of nature, and so faithful a delineator of character, that we must not hastily condemn him. I am afraid he has trusted more than he ought to the readers' or spectators' sagacity. (III, 128)

[32] [*Ibid.*, 5.2.218: Hamlet to Laertes: 'Give me your pardon, sir']
No part of this speech of Hamlet should be spoken but that which Mr. Steevens has restored,[1] beginning with——'Sir, in this audience,' [240] and so to the end. To the rest Hamlet gives the lie most shamefully. (III, 140)

[33] [*Ibid.*, 5.2.237: Laertes: 'I am satisfied in nature']
Laertes determined to act treacherously, and therefore seems puzzled to return a proper answer to Hamlet's fair address and noble apology. To that, I think, we must place his referring the matter in dispute to able judges of affronts. His offering to receive his antagonist's proffered love as love, and protesting not to

[1] Cf. Vol. 5, pp. 488, 541 for Steevens's objections to this passage.

wrong it, is as infamous as Hamlet's attributing his violent behaviour at Ophelia's grave to his madness. (III, 140–1)

[34] [*Ibid.*, 5.2.351: 'Now cracks a noble heart']
Hamlet is not a character for imitation; there are many features of it that are disagreeable. Notwithstanding his apparent blemishes, I do not think that he is so deformed as Mr. Steevens has represented him.[1] Aaron Hill had above forty years ago, in a paper called the *Prompter*,[2] observed that besides Hamlet's assumed insanity there was in him a melancholy which bordered on madness, arising from his peculiar situation. But surely Hamlet did not come, as Mr. Steevens says, to disturb the funeral of Ophelia; for till Laertes called the dead body his sister he knew not whose grave was before him. Nor did he manifest the least sign of wrath till Laertes bestowed a more than tenfold curse upon him. His jumping into the grave, when unexpectedly provoked, may be pardoned. Laertes seized him by the throat; and even then, instead of returning violence for violence, Hamlet begs him to desist. The madness of Ophelia is no farther to be charged to his account than as the unhappy consequence of a precipitant and mistaken action.[3]

It is evident that Hamlet considered Rosencrantz and Guildenstern as the King's accomplices and instruments; nor indeed can we absolve them of that guilt. They were the cabinet-counsellors of a villain and a murderer; and though they were strangers to *all* his guilt it is not improbable that they were acquainted with the secret of their commission. They were witnesses of the King's anxiety at and after the play which was acted before him; and when he told them *he liked him not*, they saw no apparent reason for his saying so except Hamlet's behaviour at the play, which, however frolicsome it might be, was not surely wicked. Upon a mature inspection of their conduct through the play they must be stigmatised with the brand of willing spies upon a prince, their quondam schoolfellow, whose undoubted title to the crown they well knew, and of whose wrongs they had not any feeling. In short, to sum up their character in a few words, they were ready to comply with any command provided they acquired by their compliance, honour and advantage.

[1] Cf. Vol. 5, pp. 540–1.
[2] Cf. Vol. 3, pp. 34–9.
[3] With this paragraph compare Ritson above, pp. 344f.

Mr. Garrick, about eight or nine years since, offered the public an amendment of Shakespeare's *Hamlet*.[1] The respect which the public owed to so eminent a genius disposed them to receive his alterations favourably. . . . [Davies summarizes Garrick's alterations.] To such material changes in this favourite tragedy the audience submitted during the life of the alterer; but they did not approve what they barely endured. The scenes and characters of Shakespeare, with all their blemishes, will not bear radical or violent alteration. The author had drawn Claudius a coward as well as a villain and usurper; and this strong check upon guilt and stigma upon wickedness ought by no means to be removed. Garrick, if I remember right, used to say that before his alteration of *Hamlet* the King used to be stuck like a pig on the stage.[2] But by giving the murderer courage this great actor did not see that he lessened the meanness of his character, which the author takes care to inculcate throughout the play. The brave villain, like Rich. III, we justly hate but we cannot despise him. Why the fate of Ophelia should be left uncertain, as well as that of the Queen, I cannot conceive. But the spectators of *Hamlet* would not part with their old friends the Grave-diggers.[3] The people soon called for *Hamlet* as it had been acted from time immemorial. (III, 143–7)

[1] Cf. Vol. 5, No. 236: it was in 1772, which suggests that Davies was writing this section in 1780–1.
[2] Cf. Steevens's letter to Garrick, Vol. 5, p. 457.
[3] They were restored in 1780.

278. Unsigned article, notes on Shakespeare

1785

From 'Remarks upon some Passages of Shakespeare', in the *Edinburgh Magazine*, i (January 1785), pp. 34–7, 104–6, and May 1785, pp. 396–8.

[1] [On *1 Henry IV*, dramatis personae]
It is singular that Shakespeare should have picked out the names of old English barons, and given them to the graceless companions of the Prince of Wales. Falstaff, Poins, Peto, and Bardolph, are all of this sort. It seems that he took them from the first book that lay at hand, from some of the English Chronicles. (34)

[2] [*Ibid.*, 3.3.24ff.]
'Do thou amend thy face,' &c. Bardolph had ventured to jest a little on Sir John's bulk. Sir John, fretted at his assuming such liberties, pours out a torrent of wit on the wretched retainer. It is wonderful to see the different lights in which he places the single circumstance of Bardolph's red nose! (35)

[3] [On *2 Henry IV*, 3.2.23f.]
'We knew where the Bonaroba's were.' Remark the simplicity of Shakespeare's times. Shallow brags that he and his wild companions knew where women of the town were to be found. (35)

[4] [*Ibid.*, 3.2]
The humour of the two justices, Shallow and Silence, is excellent, above the common excellence of Shakespeare. Shallow is exceedingly silly; but the author has so *underwritten* the part of Silence, that he appears much sillier than Shallow. This will be more particularly illustrated in the sequel. (35)

[5] [*Ibid.*, 3.2.243]
Bardolph says, 'I have *three* pounds to free Mouldy and Bullcalf.' It

385

should seem that *four* pounds had been promised, but Bardolph sinks *twenty* shillings. Excellently satirical! Falstaff and Bardolph were combined to take money against law; and at the same time Bardolph cheats his associate in iniquity. (36)

[6] [*Ibid.*, 4.3]
Falstaff and Coleville—It appears from the context that Falstaff did not come up till after the rebels were dispersed.—We are not to suppose that Coleville was armed; and Falstaff admits that he surrendered without offering to make any defence: so it was a mere play of fancy which, from the incident of Coleville, concluded Sir John to have been valiant.[1] (36)

[7] [*Ibid.*, 5.3.101ff.]
'Come, cousin.' He desires Silence to eat.—Silence, being drunk, sings, '*We shall do nothing but eat*', &c—Shallow says 'Be merry;' Silence breaks in, '*Be merry.*' Davy says, '*A cup of wine;*' Silence answers, '*A cup of wine.*' Falstaff drinks Silence's health; Silence pledges him out of a song.—On his pledging, Falstaff says, 'You have done me right:' Silence lays hold of the words, and sings, '*Do me right.*'—When Falstaff answers Pistol in heroics, Silence, perceiving that he spake about *an Assyrian knight and a King Cophetua*, adds the names of Robin Hood and his companions. Thus we see that he is a mere echo, and speaks such sounds as the words that he had just heard suggested to him. (36)

[8] [*Ibid.*, 5.5.85]
'Sir, I will be as good as my word.' This ought to be spoken very angrily, as if Sir John were offended at Shallow for doubting his honour.—He presently grows calm, and comforts his creditor with, 'This that you heard was but a colour.' Shallow is made to answer, 'A colour, I fear, that you will die in, Sir John.' This is rather in the style of Bardolph. Here Shakespeare makes Shallow more lively than suits his character. Perhaps it might be said that fretfulness at the loss of his money quickened his imagination. (36–7)

[9] [On *The Merry Wives of Windsor*, 1.4.90f.]
Hostess Quickly says, 'You should have heard him so loud and so

[1] Cf. Morgann above, No. 254.

melancholy,' pronouncing the word rightly yet misunderstanding its sense. Presently after she says, 'Anne Page is given too much to *allicholly* and musing,' [153f.] pronouncing the word erroneously yet understanding its sense. This is an oversight in Shakespeare. (104)

[10] [On *Antony and Cleopatra*, 5.2.7]
'Never palates more the *dung*:' probably 'the *dug*;' that is, the general nutriment of all human creatures. Thus *dish* means *food*, and *bottle* or *cup* means *drink*: the thing *containing* is used instead of the *contents*. (397)

[11] [*Ibid.*, 5.2.314]
'*Wild* world:' a world now, by the death of my mistress, become as a wilderness or desart to me.—Shakespeare shows how great a master he was of the pathetic by interesting us in the fate of Cleopatra. (397)

[12] [On *Troilus and Cressida*]
There are more loose expressions in this play than in any other of Shakespeare. Dryden, in his alteration of it, has added much gross obscenity, which an audience in our days would not endure.[1] (397)

[13] [On *Hamlet*, 1.5.121ff.]
It should seem that Hamlet meant at first to reveal to Marcellus and the others what the ghost had said, but that he checked himself. His broken sentences might be supplied thus: 'There is never a villain in all Denmark' *so execrable as the King*—'would heart of man think it'—'*That a brother and a wife should have conspired to murder a brother and a husband?*' Instead of finishing the sentence he puts his company off with some sorry jest. (398)

[14] [*Ibid.*, 3.2.131ff.]
The dumb shew is a curious representation of an ancient theatrical practice, but it is injudiciously brought in; for the King must have seen in it all that was afterwards set forth in the play itself, and consequently his conscience must have been caught at the very beginning. (398)

[1] See Vol. 1, No. 19.

[15] [*Ibid.*, 3.4.215]

'A foolish prating knave.' Shakespeare certainly knew what
character he meant to give to Polonius; and yet it has been
imagined[1] that Polonius was intended for a grave and judicious
person, tho' somewhat pedantic and formal: if ever he speaks
wisely it must be from Shakespeare having forgotten his own
notion of the character. But in truth all the wisdom of Polonius
consists in the repeating of trite remarks, and in the affectation of
much foresight. (398)

279. Isaac Reed and others, edition of Shakespeare

1785

From *The Plays of William Shakespeare. In Ten Volumes. With
the Corrections and Illustrations of Various Commentators; to which
are added Notes by Samuel Johnson and George Steevens. The Third
Edition. Revised and Augmented by the Editor of Dodsley's
Collection of Old Plays* (1785).

Isaac Reed (1742–1807) was, like Ritson, a lawyer who
worked his way up from humble beginnings, practising as a
conveyancer at Staple Inn. A widely read historian of
literature, he gave generous help to Johnson and John
Nichols, associated with Walpole and Percy, and was a close
friend of Farmer and Steevens. Of many works edited by him,
the most celebrated are *Biographica Dramatica* (1782), *Notitia
Dramatica* (a chronicle of English theatrical history from
1734 to 1785: uncompleted at his death, the MS is in the
British Library), and Dodsley's *Old Plays* (12 vols, 1780).
Reed, who was of a retiring disposition and would not allow

[1] By Warburton: see Vol. 3, pp. 247–9, and Johnson, Vol. 5, pp. 156–7.

his name to appear in any of his books, was asked by Steevens to take over this third edition of his and Johnson's Shakespeare. Following Malone's edition of 1790, Steevens assumed responsibility for the 1793 revision (No. 303), but after his death in 1800 he left Reed his corrected edition, which Reed brought out in 1803 in twenty-one volumes (the 'first *variorum*', as it is sometimes known), and which was reissued with minor changes in 1813. For studies of the copy-text for 1785 (a marked-up set of 1778, British Library shelf mark C. 117.e.3) see W. C. Woodson in *Studies in Bibliography*, 28 (1975), pp. 318–20, and 31 (1978), pp. 208–10, and with corrections by Arthur Sherbo, *ibid.*, 32 (1979), pp. 241–6.

---

[1] [On *Macbeth*, 1.7.2f.: 'If it were done', on which Johnson commented: 'Of this soliloquy the meaning is not very clear; I have never found the readers of Shakespeare agreeing about it', then offered a paraphrase: 1773 edition, IV, 28.]
We are told by Dryden that 'Ben Jonson in reading some bombast speeches in *Macbeth*, which *are not to be understood*, used to say that it was *horrour*.' Perhaps the present passage was one of those thus depretiated.[1] Any person but this envious detractor would have dwelt with pleasure on the transcendant beauties of this sublime tragedy, which, after *Othello*, is perhaps our author's greatest work; and would have been more apt to have been thrown 'into strong shudders' and blood-freezing 'agues' by its interesting and high wrought scenes, than to have been offended by any imaginary hardness of its language; for such it appears from the context is what he meant by *horrour*. That there are difficult passages in this tragedy cannot be denied; but that there are 'some *bombast* speeches in it, *which are not to be understood*,' as Dryden asserts, will not very readily be granted to him. From this assertion however, and the verbal alterations made by him and Sir W. D'Avenant in some of our author's plays, I think it clearly appears that Dryden and the other poets of the time of Charles II were not very deeply skilled in the language of their predecessors, and that Shakespeare was not so well understood fifty years after his death, as he is at this day. MALONE. (IV, 503–4)

---

[1] Compare Mrs Montagu, Vol. 5, p. 338.

[2] [*Ibid.*, 2.2.62: 'the multitudinous sea incarnadine'. Malone adds to his note in the 1780 *Supplement* (above, p. 283) and Steevens rejoins.]

There is a quaintness in this passage according to the modern regulation, —'Making the green, one red,'—that does not sound to my ears either like the quaintness of Shakespeare, or the language of the time. Our author, I am persuaded, would have written, 'Making the green *sea*,' red,' if he had not used that word in the preceding line, which forced him to employ another word here. So, in the *Tempest* [5.1.43f.]:

> And 'twixt the *green sea* and the azur'd vault
> Set roaring war.

MALONE

I . . . believe that Shakespeare referred to some visible quality in the ocean, rather than to its concealed inhabitants; to the waters that might admit of discoloration, and not to the fishes whose hue could suffer no change from the tinct of blood.—Waves appearing over waves are no unapt symbol of a crowd. 'A sea of heads' is a phrase employed by one of our poets, but by which of them I do not at present recollect. He who beholds an audience from the stage, or any other multitude gazing on some particular object, must perceive that their heads are raised over each other *velut unda supervenit undam*. If therefore our author by the '*multitudinous* sea' does not mean the *aggregate of seas*, he must be understood to design the *multitude of waves*, or *the waves that have the appearance of a multitude*. STEEVENS. (IV, 529´–30)

[3] [On *King Lear*, 5.3.306: 'And my poor fool is hang'd': in the 1778 edition (IX, 563) Steevens had written the first sentence of the following note. Now he expands it, in order to answer Reynolds's comment.]

This is an expression of tenderness for his dead Cordelia (not his fool, as some have thought) on whose lips he is still intent, and dies away while he is searching for life there.

Poor fool, in the age of Shakespeare, was an expression of endearment. So, in his *Antony and Cleopatra*:

> ——*poor* venomous *fool*,
> Be angry and dispatch.   [5.2.305f.]

Again, in *K. Henry VI*, pt. III: 'So many weeks ere the *poor fools* will yean.' [2.5.36] Again, in *Romeo and Juliet*: 'And, *pretty fool,* it stinted and said—ay.' [1.3.48]

I may add that *the* Fool of Lear was long ago forgotten. Having filled the space allotted him in the arrangement of the play, he appears to have been silently withdrawn in the 6th scene of the 3rd act.—That the thoughts of a father, in the bitterest of all moments, while his favourite child lay dead in his arms, should recur to the antic who had formerly diverted him, has somewhat in it that I cannot reconcile to the idea of genuine sorrow and despair.

Besides this, Cordelia was recently hanged; but we know not that the *Fool* had suffered in the same manner, nor can imagine why he should. The party adverse to Lear was little interested in the fate of his jester. The only use of him was to contrast and alleviate the sorrows of his master; and that purpose being fully answered, the poet's solicitude about him was at an end.

The term—*poor fool* might indeed have misbecome the mouth of a vassal commiserating the untimely end of a princess, but has no impropriety when used by a weak, old, distracted king, in whose mind the distinctions of nature only survive, while he is uttering his last frantic exclamations over a murdered daughter.

Should the foregoing remark, however, be thought erroneous, the reader will forgive it, as it serves to introduce some contradictory observations from a critic in whose taste and judgment too much confidence cannot easily be placed. STEEVENS.

I confess I am one of those who *have thought* that Lear means his *Fool*, and not *Cordelia*. If he means *Cordelia*, then what I have always considered as a beauty is of the same kind as the accidental stroke of the pencil that produced the foam.—Lear's affectionate remembrance of the *Fool* in this place, I used to think, was one of those strokes of genius, or of nature, which are so often found in Shakespeare, and in him only.

Lear appears to have a particular affection for this *Fool,* whose fidelity in attending him, and endeavouring to divert him in his distress, seems to deserve all his kindness.

Poor fool and knave, says he, in the midst of the thunder-storm, *I have one part in my heart that's sorry yet for thee.* [3.2.72f.]

It does not therefore appear to me to be allowing too much consequence to the *Fool* in making Lear bestow a thought on him, even when in still greater distress. Lear is represented as a good-natured, passionate, and rather weak old man; it is the old age of a cocker'd spoilt boy. There is no impropriety in giving to such a character those tender domestic affections which would ill become a more heroic character such as Othello, Macbeth, or Richard III.

The words—*No, no, no life*; I suppose to be spoken not tenderly but with passion: Let nothing now live—let there be universal destruction;—*Why should a dog, a horse, a rat have life, and thou no breath at all?* [5.3.306ff.]

It may be observed that as there was a necessity, the necessity of propriety at least, that this *Fool*, the favourite of the author, of Lear, and consequently of the audience, should not be lost or forgot, it ought to be known what became of him.—However, it must be acknowledged that we cannot infer much from thence; Shakespeare is not always attentive to finish the figures of his groups.

I have only to add that if an actor, by adopting the interpretation mentioned above of applying the words *poor fool* to Cordelia, the audience would, I should imagine, think it a strange mode of expressing the grief and affection of a father for his dead daughter, and that daughter a queen.———The words *poor fool* are undoubtedly expressive of endearment; and Shakespeare himself, in another place, speaking of a dying animal, calls it *poor dappled fool*:[1] but it never is, nor never can be used with any degree of propriety but to commiserate some very inferior object, which may be loved, without much esteem or respect. Sir JOSHUA REYNOLDS. (IX, 606–8)

[4] [On Malone's claim, p. 284 above, that Shakespeare wished to render both Claudius and Gertrude odious]

I know not in what part of this tragedy the king and queen could have been expected to enter into a vindication of their mutual conduct. The former indeed is rendered contemptible as well as guilty; but for the latter our poet seems to have felt all that tenderness which the ghost recommends to the imitation of her son. STEEVENS. (X, 421)

[5] [On *Othello*, 3.3.145]

Though I, perchance, am vicious in my guess,] That abruptness in the speech which Dr. Warburton complains of and would alter, may

[1] *As You Like It*, 2.1.22.

be easily accounted for. Iago seems desirous, by his ambiguous hint, *Though I*—to inflame the jealousy of Othello, which he knew would be more effectually done in this manner than by any expression that bore a determinate meaning. The jealous Othello would fill up the pause in the speech, which Iago turns off at last to another purpose, and find a more certain cause of discontent, and a greater degree of torture arising from the doubtful consideration how it might have concluded, than he could have experienced had the whole of what he enquired after been reported to him with every circumstance of aggravation.

We may suppose him imagining to himself that Iago mentally continued the thought thus, *Though I—know more than I choose to speak of.*

Vicious in my guess does not mean that he is an *ill guesser*, but that he is apt to put the worst construction on every thing he attempts to account for. STEEVENS. (X, 642–3)

280. William Shaw, Shakespeare's faults

1785

From *Memoirs of the Life and Writings of the Late Dr. Samuel Johnson; Containing Many Valuable Original Letters, and several Interesting Anecdotes both of his Literary and Social Connections. The Whole Authenticated By Living Evidence* (1785).

William Shaw (1749–1831), a Scottish minister who joined the Church of England on Johnson's advice, received encouragement from Johnson in compiling his *Galic and English Dictionary* (2 vols, 1780), and also published *An Enquiry into the Authenticity of the Poems Ascribed to Ossian* (1781). Shaw's acquaintance with Johnson was slight, and his biography (published anonymously) is padded out with derivative information. For a modern edition see that (together with Mrs

Piozzi's *Anecdotes of the Late Samuel Johnson*) edited by Arthur Sherbo (1974). His attack on Shakespeare's faults is a typical, if late, example of what might be called the Neo-classical schoolmaster approach.

Johnson was now in a state of independence; but his habit of literary composition was but little enervated, though no longer excited by necessity. The work which engrossed his attention was his long projected and promised edition of Shakespeare. This in 1765 was published by subscription, and especially since joined to the critical labours of Mr. Steevens, is become a valuable acquisition to literary criticism.

His notes in various parts of the work, his explanation of difficult passages, his developement of hidden beauties, his interpretations of obscurities, and his candour and ingenuity in reconciling inconsistencies, discover no superficial acquaintance with either men or books. Many think the text not deserving the commentary, few who are judges think the commentary at least not equal to the text. This is the favourite bard of Englishmen, and he owes his immortality to their discernment, as in every other nation his absurdities had probably buried him in oblivion. It was said by one of the Popes, with the usual decency of professional impostors, that a book which required so much explanation as the Bible ought not to have been written. This witticism applied to Shakespeare would be deemed blasphemy, and yet apart from a few splendid passages, what do we find in his plays to justify their excessive popularity, or to give the author that super-eminence which he has so long enjoyed on the English stage? Do they serve to correct the taste, improve the heart, enlighten the understanding, or facilitate any one purpose of public utility? His characters are in fact all monsters, his heroes madmen, his wits buffoons, and his women strumpets, viragos, or idiots. He confounds the relations of things by aiming at no moral object, and for pleasantry often substitutes the grossest obscenity. His creations are as preposterous as they are numerous, and whenever he would declaim, his thoughts are vulgar and his expressions quaint, or turgid, or obscure. He makes Achilles and other illustrious characters of antiquity hector like bullies in a brothel, and puts in the mouths of his heroines the ribaldry of Billingsgate. There is not a rule in dramatic composition which he does not habitually violate. He is called the poet of nature, and he certainly imitates her deformities with exactness, but seldom aims at that preference of art which consists in copying her excellence. The profusion of intemperate praise which accompanies his memory indicates much oftener an abject deference for the opinion of the multitude than any real sense of intrinsic merit. And many a reader fancies himself charm'd with the beauties, who is only a dupe to the name of an author. Johnson was not a critic to be misled by report, while he could have access to the truth. He even says that there is *not one of Shakespeare's plays which, were it now to be exhibited as the work of a contemporary writer, would be heard to the conclusion.*[1] And he states the excellencies and defects of his author in terms so equally pointed and strong that he has run into paradox, where he meant only to be impartial. (137–41)

281. John Pinkerton, observations on Shakespeare

1785

From *Letters of Literature* (1785). Published under the pseudonym of Robert Heron, this collection of letters by John Pinkerton (1758–1826) includes three constituting 'observations on the last edition of Shakespeare', the Johnson–Steevens of 1778: Letters XVIII (pp. 105–16), XXVI (pp. 162–78), and XXXVIII (pp. 301–15). There are scattered notes elsewhere.

Pinkerton, a Scottish antiquary and historian, published *Select Scottish Ballads* in 1783 (which Joseph Ritson exposed as modern forgeries), an *Essay on Medals* (1784), a *Dissertation on the Origin and Progress of the Scythians or Goths* (1787: arguing

[1] Cf. Vol. 5, p. 82.

that the Celtic races are the only surviving aborigines of Europe, genetically incapable of higher civilization), a *History of Scotland* (1797), and various other historical works. For a time editor of the *Critical Review*, Pinkerton became involved in several literary quarrels, and these *Letters* attracted unanimously unfavourable notices, including a hostile pamphlet (1786): yet Walpole and Gibbon were impressed by his learning.

---

[1] Shakespeare excels in the strength of his characters and in wit; but as plot must be regarded as an essential of good comedy, he must not be erected as a model in the comic academy; a loss sufficiently compensated by the reflection that it were vain to place him as a model whose beauties transcend all imitation. (44)

[2] [On *Love's Labour's Lost*, 4.1.32f.]
Upon this couplet,

> When for fame's sake, for praise, an outward part,
> We bend to that the working of the heart,

is this wonderful note, which I need not tell you is by Warburton: 'The harmony of the measure, the easiness of the expression, and the good sense in the thought, all concur to recommend these two lines to the reader's notice.' The lines will, I doubt not, strike you and every man of common sense not to say common taste, as utterly destitute of every quality this apostolical alchymist recommends; who in his dreams tried to convert the very dirt of Shakespeare into gold. The preservation of such nonsensical comments much arraigns the taste of his *variorum* editors. (108–9)

[3] [On *Twelfth Night*, 2.5.80f.: Malvolio: 'these be her very C's, her U's, and her T's . . . ']
The squabble between the two wise commentators about the meaning of Shakespeare's obscenity is truly diverting. In other editions, an N is put among the other capitals, and makes one of these jokes in which Shakespeare appears but one of the people. (163)

[4] [On *Macbeth*, 1.5.65f.]
'Look like the innocent flower, but be the serpent under it,' is one

of the most exquisite poetical figures in the world: and is a fine instance how much a trite remark, such as *The serpent lurks under the flower,* may be improved. (165)

[5] [*Ibid.,* 5.3.22f.]
'My way of life is fallen into the sere the yellow leaf.' A most foolish emendation of *May of life*[1] for *way of life* is here rashly admitted into the text. Shakespeare's metaphor here challenged is My way, my path of life, which formerly was among the green, the flourishing woods of summer, is now fallen into the fading groves of autumn. Can a juster metaphor be used? The reading in the text is quite absurd. How could May be suddenly changed into autumn? Was Macbeth in the May, in the spring of life? Or, to conclude all, is Shakespeare always correct in his metaphors? Yet observe, and laugh, when these annotators correct Shakespeare they correct him into blunders. (168)

[6] [On *1 Henry IV*, 2.4.512: Hal: 'The man I do assure you is not here.']
Falstaff was not *here*, or in the room, which saves the prince from the charge of an absolute falsity. The prince's speech contains not one lye; it hath only dissimulation, and might have been spoken by a quaker. (171)

[7] [On the authenticity of *Titus Andronicus*]
How the stupid play of *Titus Andronicus* comes always to appear among Shakespeare's, I cannot imagine. Dr. Percy, a superlative judge of these matters, tells us that it is not his but only corrected by him. Even the annotators of this edition, in their notes at the end of the play, shew by many arguments that it is not Shakespeare's. Why not then, in the name of God, throw it into the fire? Will no editor shew taste enough to deliver us from nonsense that would disgrace a bedlamite to write or to read? (302)

[8] [On *King Lear*, 2.1.59]
'My worthy arch and patron' is a Latinism, in which the component members of a word are separated, for 'my worthy and arch-patron.' Horace has such separations. (305–6)

---

[1] By Johnson: see Vol. 3, p. 181.

[9] [On *Hamlet*, 3.2.116]

'Country matters.' The commentator is so chaste that he seems not to know that both of these words are dissyllables. Tho' I should be sorry to claim the praise of Agnolo Poliziano, of finding obscenities where the meaning was possibly innocent, yet such *matters* should either not be understood, or understood aright. (312)

282. Unsigned essay, Shakespeare and modern tragedy

1785

From the *Westminster Magazine*, xiii, (July 1785), 359–62: 'Some Remarks on the Drama', by 'Reflector'.

This journal kept up a high standard of literary critical essays: see the witty and penetrating series 'On Novel-writing' or 'Every Man His Own Novelist' in the same volume, pp. 40–2, 301–5, 366–9, 401–5, 457–60.

... You have never been in London—You have never had occasion to see the state of the drama—You have read many of the best writings, and unluckily both for you and me, we have made Shakespeare too much our favourite. You have heard by transient report that the taste of the town in as far as it relates to the drama is sadly vitiated, but distanced as you are from the scene of action you cannot understand how this happens. If you credit the most common printed reports there never was a period when genius shone with greater splendour, or when our plays abounded more in sterling sense, fund of wit, elegance of language, or .when they were better decorated by the exertions of performers. ... [The truth is rather different.] I have been at pains since my arrival to mark the progress of dramatic merit; I have talked on the subject with some who helped to make an audience when Garrick made his first appearance, and who have been at pains to note several steps as well as the height they led to.

Genius and an enthusiasm for the observation of nature seem the requisites for a dramatic pen. But every man cannot possess these. Every man cannot be a poet—Every poet cannot write a good tragedy. Yet a poetical fancy is all they now possess who enter on the hazardous undertaking of stepping into the company of Shakespeare. Smooth, easy periods, mechanically contrived for stage effect—pompous language, too familiar ideas and trite sentiments, with a nice attention to the unities of time and place, compose the vices and virtues of modern tragedy. The plots are monstrously shocking, if not improbable, and affect the feelings of the hearers as the sight of a butcher slaughtering an innocent lamb—create horror—a painful sensation, but by no means productive of profitable sympathy, or that serious application to our own hearts which must be the foundation of any instruction derived from fictitious writings. The reason is very obvious: nature is deserted. We MAKE passions for the stage, instead of copying those in real life. Jealousy has given a plot to half the tragedies of this century, a passion so rare in private experience that we should not have known its existence but for the murderous deeds which we are told it occasions. You are surprized to hear me mention that jealousy is not common, but the instances are so rare that we find them only on record in the Newgate Calendar, where an unhappy wretch or two assassinates a friend on some slight suspicions. And is this entertainment for a British audience? Would not a stranger reasonably suppose that this was our national weakness—'the sin that most easily besets us?'

Errors in the subjects I reckon as one of the principal defects. If tragedies are written with a view to profit (and for a little I shall suppose they are) their subjects must be the vices and most common causes of ruin in the nation and age wherein they are to be performed. As for jealousy, I think *Othello* and the *Revenge*[1] anticipate every thing that may hereafter be said on the subject. I do not mean to place these on a footing as to merit, but as specimens of this class of subjects, and one taken from the best, the other from the worst rank of writers. In the one, I mean in

[1] A play by Edward Young (1721): see Vol. 4, pp. 360f., for the comparison with *Othello*.

Shakespeare's, there is as much attention to nature and the ways of men as, in the other, and every other since, there has been paid to correctness of measure, preservation of unities, and that insipid purity of manner which 'cribbs and confines' true genius. In this country perhaps the best subjects for tragedy would be the effects of the various kinds of dissipation that prevail. . . .

Next to the choice of an unprofitable subject, I would object to chusing only one incident. An author forms the design of a tragic piece thus: 'My hero must have left his parents when young, and when he returns and is not known to both or either parent, he occasions such jealousy as is productive of two or three deaths, or if one will serve, a marriage will be very properly appended.' The piece opens with the rising sun, and two men enter to inform the audience what the author would have them to understand, and what they are to expect; we see by the first act that one passion, one incident is the whole we have to attend to, and as we have amply foreseen the event the rest of our attention is directed to the language, and perhaps for one night kept up by curiosity. An absurd concatenation of circumstances take place in order to bring the matter to a conclusion exactly at the end of three hours, or five acts, when every thing takes place just as we foresaw at the beginning, and the marriage of those saved from carnage, together with the view of the dead bodies (if none of the deceased have tossed themselves into the sea) forms a spectacle neither serious nor comic, but from a mixture of both perfectly absurd. Were we to examine our own feelings this would appear evident on all occasions, but, Lord help us, it would be too much fatigue to judge for ourselves.

This huddled-together plot takes place in many of the best tragedies on our modern list, and seems to me to proceed from what is called an attention to the unities of time and place; which attention I do not hesitate to affirm is productive of more improbabilities and nonsense than the greatest poverty of genius or invention. In endeavouring to adhere to these unities our view was to preserve probability, but instead of that we have fallen into downright impossibilities. It is improbable that a man should sail from Venice to Cyprus while an overture is playing, but the author never means it as a probability, and when the scene is shifted our thoughts are as naturally attentive and present in Cyprus as they were in Venice. But to obtrude on us events as facts which in the common course of human things it is monstrous to suppose possible shocks our judgement, and did we give ourselves time to reflect would excite disgust. But if a G——or a B——*fall well*, as it is called, it is no great matter with many whether it was in compliance with sense, nature, or the time allotted for representation.

This was not the case with Shakespeare. He knew that the ways of Providence were equal, and that to croud the events of three years into as many hours would not only be contrary to nature, but cramp his own genius. His plots are by no means intricate or marvellous. You are not astonished, nor yet are you apprised of any event before it takes place in due succession. His plays are composed of a series of events, not to one main instructive point but to many. Each of these when taken by itself affords a lesson and matter for reflection, and when we hear it the appeal it makes to our own feelings is so forcible that we pronounce its striking resemblance to the ways of nature and of man. Most of his characters are perfectly drawn, and it has been one of the most pleasing tasks to a thinking mind to analyze and compare these with what nowadays occurs in our own observation. No better proof of their exalted merit needs be given than their success both on the stage and in the closet, both when adorned by the powers of favourite performers, and when examined with the cool judgement of a philosophical hour. Not so with our modern tragedies.—Excepting a very few (not a dozen in this century) if we read them once it is perhaps part of our duty, from peculiarity of taste or situation, but we never wish to see them again. The matter lies here: Shakespeare copied nature and nature only—Shakespeare had a most extensive, almost supernatural genius—and every writer since his time have acknowledged that he made nature his mistress. Yet Shakespeare has been so little the subject of imitation that there does not now exist in our language (written in this century) one single tragedy that bears the smallest resemblance to any of his, whether with respect to language, plots, or manner of treatment. For my part, I despair to see a tragedy written in the manner of Shakespeare—as this is the case you may think, and with truth, that I despair to see a good tragedy at all. . . .

I do not measure the pathos of tragedy from the number of tears produced now a-days. The Italian *delicatezza* is so prevalent among us that we have a tear ready whether a hero or a sparrow falls. . . .

Why is it that I find a passion attempted to be described, yet in such faint colours that I could not recognize the identity if it were not for the actor, whom the author has properly instructed in his meaning? This I call the want of genius, or rather I am inclined to call it want of sensibility. They who are the slaves of passion, it is true, seem often to suffer a speechless agony from them, yet their words, when they find utterance, are strongly expressive of what passes within them. He must be intimately acquainted with the human heart who can give becoming language to a weeping parent for a dying child—to a tyrant under the pressure of remorse and disappointment—to a son when he first discovers a mother to whom he was a stranger, and has all at once the tender feelings of duty and affection rushing on him like an overpowering torrent.—But here Shakespeare's genius appears with a degree of splendour to which we are inclined to give the epithet pre-ternatural, for we have seldom since seen any thing like.—There never was a person in any of the situations he describes that could not adopt his language, and that did not feel it in most perfect unison to what they felt.

As for these, if any such there still are, who dwell on the faults of Shakespeare with an envious pleasure, I consign them to their dullness; but in all my reading, which on this subject has been unlimited, I never yet heard an objection to Shakespeare that could not be accounted for from the whim and ignorance of the person who made it—or if the complaint was just, it was to be imputed to the age he lived in, or to his want of a classical education. It is much to be regretted that men of genius have been obliged to temporise with the bad taste of the times they lived in.—Shakespeare did so in some circumstances, and Dryden has spoiled all his tragedies by his rhimes, for in his days it was the rage to follow Corneille or Racine, amiable patterns for lovers of nature!

283. John Monck Mason, on editing Shakespeare

1785

From *Comments on the Last Edition of Shakespeare's Plays* (1785).

John Monck Mason (1726–1809) was educated at Trinity College, Dublin, and sat in the Irish House of Commons for much of the time between 1761 and 1798, holding various government offices. He published a four-volume edition of Massinger in 1779 (an undistinguished piece of editing), and had planned to produce an edition of Shakespeare, only to find that the Johnson–Steevens–Reed edition of 1785 included most of his 'amendments and explanations'. So he issued his *Comments* separately, and reissued them as *Comments on the Several Editions of Shakespeare's Plays, extended to those of Malone and Steevens* (Dublin, 1807); he also published *Comments on the Plays of Beaumont and Fletcher; with an Appendix containing some further Observations on Shakespeare* (1798).

---

[1] [On *Coriolanus*, 4.7.48ff.]
The obvious objection to Johnson's and Warburton's explanations of these passages arises from the peculiar temper of Coriolanus, which renders them totally inapplicable to him in the sense which they give them; for he was so far from boasting of his exploits himself that he could not bear to hear them extolled by others; but, as he says himself,

> Would rather have his wounds to heal again,
> Than hear say how he got them,
> And had rather have one scratch his head in the sun,
> When the alarm were struck, than idly sit
> To hear his nothings monster'd.

And we find that when his arch-enemy, Aufidius, sums up the defects of his character that of boasting is not upon the list. (259–60)

[2] [On *Julius Caesar*, 3.2.13ff.]

> Romans, countrymen, and friends.

I cannot agree with Warburton that this speech is very fine in its kind. I can see no degree of excellence in it, but think it a very paltry speech for so great a man on so great an occasion.—Yet Shakespeare has judiciously adopted in it the style of Brutus—the pointed sentences and laboured brevity which he is said to have affected. (278)

[3] [On *Titus Andronicus*, 2.3.10ff.]

> My lovely Aaron.

There is much poetical beauty in this speech of Tamora:—It appears to me to be the only one in the play that is in the style of Shakespeare. . . .

I agree with such of the commentators as think that Shakespeare had no hand in this abominable Tragedy; and consider the correctness with which it was printed as a kind of collateral proof that he had not. The genuine works of Shakespeare have been handed down to us in a more depraved state than those of any other contemporary writer, which was partly owing to the obscurity of his hand-writing, which appears from the facsimile prefixed to this edition, to have been scarcely legible, and partly to his total neglect of them when committed to the press; and it is not to be supposed that he should have taken more pains about the publication of this horrid performance than he did in that of his noblest productions. (306–7)

[4] [On the note on 'potatoes' in the 1773 and 1778 editions: cf. Vol. 5, pp. 546–8]

Mr. Collins has given us at the end of this play a very elaborate note upon the word *potatoes*; and seems to recommend it to every editor to imitate his labours; but after having clearly proved by a few instances from Shakespeare, Fletcher, or Massinger that potatoes were considered in those days as a provocative, I think he might

have spared his further researches, which resemble too much the
laborious idleness of that industrious gentleman, who tells us how
often the word *and* occurs in the Bible and Apocrypha. Human life
is too short for such minute disquisitions on trifling subjects. (320)

[5] [On *King Lear*, 4.6.11ff.]

> How fearfull
> And dizzy 'tis to cast one's eyes so low! &c.

This passage has suggested to Johnson[1] a very ingenious criticism,
enforced with that accuracy and strength of expression in which he
excells; and I have no doubt but his criticism is just with respect to
its general principles, though not strictly applicable to this
particular passage. For it is to be considered that Edgar is
describing an imaginary precipice, and is not therefore supposed to
be impressed so strongly with the dreadful prospect of inevitable
destruction as a person would be who really found himself on the
brink of one. (353)

[6] [*Ibid.*, 5.3.264f.]

> KENT.—Is this the promised end?
> EDGAR.—Or image of that horror.

Steevens's explanation of these lines cannot be right; the words,
that horror, must necessarily refer to the *promised end*, whatever that
may mean; and they certainly promised to themselves a successful
conclusion of the war, not any horrid catastrophe.

It appears to me that by the *promised end*, Kent does not mean
that conclusion which the state of their affairs seemed to promise,
but the end of the world. In St. Mark's Gospel,[2] when Christ
foretells to his disciples the end of the world, and is describing to
them the signs that were to precede and mark the approach of our
final dissolution, he says, 'For in those days *shall be affliction, such as
was not from* the beginning of the creation, which God created, unto
this time, neither shall be:' and afterwards he says, 'Now the
brother shall betray the brother to death; and the father the son;
and *children shall rise up against their parents, and shall cause them to be
put to death.*' Kent, in contemplating the unexampled scene of

---

[1] See Vol. 5, pp. 137f., and below, p. 570.
[2] 13.19ff.

exquisite affliction which was then before him, and the unnatural attempt of Goneril and Regan against their father's life, recollects these passages, and asks, 'whether that was the end of the world that had been foretold to us?' To which Edgar adds, 'or only a representation and resemblance of that horror.'

There is evidently an allusion to the same passages in scripture in a speech of Gloucester's, which he makes in the second scene of the first act: [quotes 1.2.103ff.: ' . . . there's son against father'].

If any criticks should urge it as an objection to this explanation that the persons of the Drama are Pagans, and of course unacquainted with the scriptures, they give Shakespeare credit for more accuracy than I fear he possessed.

So Macduff, when he calls upon Banquo, Malcolm, &c. to view Duncan murdered, says

> Up, up and see
> The great Doom's image   [2.3.77f.]
> (356–8)

[7] [On Shakespeare's *Sonnets*]
It was much the fashion in Shakespeare's days to study and imitate the Italian poets, and he has proved his particular admiration of them by a collection of no less than 154 very miserable sonnets, a quaint and languid kind of poem of Italian origin, in which a dozen insipid lines are to serve as an introduction to an epigram of two, which generally turns upon some forced conceit. Nothing but a violent attachment to those poets could have induced Shakespeare to deal so largely in a species of composition but ill adapted either to the English language or the taste of his country-men. . . . (385–6)

[8] [On *Othello*, 1.1.123: 'At this odd even and dull watch o' th' night']
Much pains have been taken by some of the editors, especially by Warburton, to introduce into the text a parcel of obsolete words which Shakespeare never dreamed of. For the obscurity of his style does not arise from the frequent use of antiquated terms but from his peculiar manner of applying and combining the words which he found in common use in his day; and when he deviates from the received language of the times it is rather by coining some harsh and high-sounding words of his own than by looking back for

those which had fallen into disuse. If therefore it be necessary to amend this passage I should chuse to read, 'at this *dull season*,' rather than 'this *dull steven*,' as an expression that would more naturally occur either to Shakespeare or to Roderigo. (400)

284. Thomas Whately, Richard III and Macbeth compared

1785

From *Remarks on Some of the Characters of Shakespeare* (1785); this text is from the second edition (Oxford, 1808).

Thomas Whately (d. 1772) was an M.P. from 1761 to his death, and was closely associated with George Grenville, and subsequently with Lord North, holding various political posts. In addition to several works on trade and finance, he was best known to his contemporaries as the author of *Observations on Modern Gardening* (1770). His brother, Joseph Whately, issued the Shakespeare volume, explaining that it was 'a *Fragment* only of a greater work', since Whately had 'intended to have gone through eight or ten of the principal characters of Shakespeare in the same manner', but left off (presumably in 1768–9) to work on his gardening project. In 1811 Whately's book attracted the attention of Charles Knight, and ultimately led to his edition of Shakespeare. The third edition, in 1839, was issued by his nephew Richard Whately, Archbishop of Dublin. In 1786 Horace Walpole wrote that 'the best comment on the marvellous powers of [Shakespeare's] genius in drawing and discriminating characters is contained in Mr. Whately's *Remarks*. . . . It ought to be prefixed to every edition of Shakespeare as a preface, and will tend more to give a just idea of that matchless genius than all the notes and criticisms on his works. It would teach men to study and discover new magic in his works. . . . How inadequate would Voltaire or Racine appear to their office, were the characters in their tragedies to be scrutinized and compared like those of Macbeth and Richard!' (*Notes by Horace Walpole on Several Characters of Shakespeare*, ed. W. S. Lewis (Farmington, Conn., 1940), pp. 18–19).

INTRODUCTION

The writers upon dramatic composition have, for the most part, confined their observations to the fable; and the maxims received amongst them, for the conduct of it, are therefore emphatically called *The Rules of the Drama*. It has been found easy to give and to apply them; they are obvious, they are certain, they are general: and poets without genius have by observing them pretended to fame; while critics without discernment have assumed importance from knowing them. But the regularity thereby established, though highly proper, is by no means the first requisite in a dramatic composition. Even waiving all consideration of those finer feelings which a poet's imagination or sensibility imparts, there is within the colder provinces of judgment and of knowledge a subject for criticism more worthy of attention than the common topics of discussion. I mean the distinction and preservation of *character*, without which the piece is at best a tale, not an action; for the actors in it are not produced upon the scene. They were distinguished by character; all men are; by that we know them, by that we are interested in their fortunes; by that their conduct, their sentiments, their very language is formed: and whenever, therefore, the proper marks of it are missing we immediately perceive that the person before our eyes is but suppositious. Experience has shewn that however rigidly, and however rightly, the unities of action, time, and place have been insisted on, they may be dispensed with, and the magic of the scene may make the absurdity invisible. Most of Shakespeare's Plays abound with instances of such a fascination. . . . (1–2)

Yet the generality of dramatic writers, and more especially of those who have chosen tragedy for their subject, have contented themselves with the distant resemblance which indiscriminate expressions of passion, and imperfect, because general, marks of

408

character can give. Elevated ideas become the hero; a professed contempt of all principles denotes a villain; frequent gusts of rage betray a violence, and tender sentiments shew a mildness of disposition. But a villain differs not more from a saint than he does in some particulars from another as bad as himself; and the same degrees of anger, excited by the same occasions, break forth in as many several shapes as there are various tempers. But these distinguishing peculiarities between man and man have too often escaped the observation of tragic writers. The comic writers have indeed frequently caught them; but then they are apt to fall into an excess the other way, and overcharge their imitations. . . .

Shakespeare has generally avoided both extremes; and however faulty in some respects is in this, the most essential part of the drama, considered as a representation, excellent beyond comparison. No other dramatic writer could ever pretend to so deep and so extensive a knowledge of the human heart; and he had a genius to express all that his penetration could discover. The characters, therefore, which he has drawn are masterly copies from nature; differing each from the other, and animated as the originals though correct to a scrupulous precision. The truth and force of the imitation recommend it as a subject worthy of criticism. . . . (6–8)

Every Play of Shakespeare abounds with instances of his excellence in distinguishing characters. It would be difficult to determine which is the most striking of all that he drew; but his merit will appear most conspicuously by comparing two opposite characters, who happen to be placed in similar circumstances. Not that on such occasions he marks them more strongly than on others, but because the contrast makes the distinction more apparent; and of these none seem to agree so much in situation, and to differ so much in disposition, as RICHARD THE THIRD and MACBETH. Both are soldiers, both usurpers; both attain the throne by the same means, by treason and murder; and both lose it too in the same manner, in battle against the person claiming it as lawful heir. Perfidy, violence, and tyranny are common to both; and those only, their obvious qualities, would have been attributed indiscriminately to both by an ordinary dramatic writer. But Shakespeare, in conformity to the truth of history as far as it led him, and by improving upon the fables which have been blended with it, has ascribed opposite principles and motives to the same designs and actions, and various effects to the operation of the same events upon different tempers. Richard and Macbeth, as represented by him, agree in nothing but their fortunes.

The periods of history from which the subjects are taken are such as at the best can be depended on only for some principal facts; but not for the minute detail by which characters are unravelled. That of Macbeth is too distant to be particular; that of Richard too full of discord and animosity to be true: and antiquity has not feigned more circumstances of horror in the one than party violence has given credit to in the other. Fiction has even gone so far as to introduce supernatural fables into both stories: the usurpation of Macbeth is said to have been foretold by some witches; and the tyranny of Richard by omens attending his birth. From these fables Shakespeare, unrestrained and indeed uninformed by history, seems to have taken the hint of their several characters; and he has adapted their dispositions so as to give to such fictions, in the days he wrote, a shew of probability. The first thought of acceding to the throne is suggested, and success in the attempt is promised, to Macbeth by the witches: he is therefore represented as a man whose natural temper would have deterred him from such a design if he had not been immediately tempted, and strongly impelled to it. Richard, on the other hand, brought with him into the world the signs of ambition and cruelty. His disposition, therefore, is suited to those symptoms; and he is not discouraged from indulging it by the improbability of succeeding, or by any difficulties and dangers which obstruct his way.

Agreeably to these ideas, Macbeth appears to be a man not destitute of the feelings of humanity. His lady gives him that character:

> ————I fear thy nature;
> It is too full o' the milk of human kindness,
> To catch the nearest way. [1.5.16ff.]

Which apprehension was well founded; for his reluctance to commit the murder is owing in a great measure to reflections which arise from sensibility: 'He's here in double trust. . . .' [1.7.12ff.] Immediately after he tells Lady Macbeth,

> We will proceed no further in this business;
> He hath honour'd me of late. [1.7.31f.]

And thus giving way to his natural feelings of kindred, hospitality, and gratitude, he for a while lays aside his purpose.

A man of such a disposition will esteem, as they ought to be esteemed, all gentle and amiable qualities in another: and therefore Macbeth is affected by the mild virtues of Duncan, and reveres them in his sovereign when he stifles them in himself. That

> ————This Duncan
> Hath borne his faculties so meekly; hath been
> So clear in his great office, [1.7.16ff.]

is one of his reasons against the murder: and when he is tortured with the thought of Banquo's issue succeeding him in the throne, he aggravates his misery by observing that 'For them the gracious Duncan have I murder'd' [3.1.65], which epithet of *gracious* would not have occurred to one who was not struck with the particular merit it expresses.

The frequent references to the prophecy in favour of Banquo's issue is another symptom of the same disposition. For it is not always from fear, but sometimes from envy, that she alludes to it: and being himself very susceptible of those domestic affections which raise a desire and love of posterity he repines at the succession assured to the family of his rival, and which in his estimation seems more valuable than his own actual possession. He therefore reproaches the sisters for their partiality, when

> Upon my head they plac'd a fruitless crown,
> And put a barren sceptre in my gripe. . . .
> For Banquo's issue have I 'fil'd my mind; [3.1.60ff.]
> (64)

Thus, in a variety of instances, does the tenderness in his character shew itself; and one who has these feelings, though he may have no principles, cannot easily be induced to commit a murder. The interventions of a supernatural cause accounts for his acting so contrary to his disposition. But that alone is not sufficient to prevail entirely over his nature. The instigations of his wife are also necessary to keep him to his purpose; and she, knowing his temper, not only stimulates his courage to the deed but, sensible that besides a backwardness in daring he had a degree of softness which wanted hardening, endeavours to remove all remains of humanity from his breast by the horrid comparison she makes between him and herself: [quotes 'I have given suck': 1.7.54ff.].

The argument is that the strongest and most natural affections are to be stifled upon so great an occasion, and such an argument is proper to persuade one who is liable to be swayed by them; but is no incentive either to his courage or his ambition.

Richard is in all these particulars the very reverse to Macbeth. He is totally destitute of every softer feeling: 'I that have neither pity, love, nor fear' [*3 Henry VI*, 5.6.68] is the character he gives of himself, and which he preserves throughout; insensible to his habitudes with a brother, to his connection with a wife, to the piety of the king, and the innocence of the babes whom he murders. The deformity of his body was supposed to indicate a similar depravity of mind; and Shakespeare makes great use both of that and of the current stories of the times concerning the circumstances of his birth to intimate that his actions proceeded not from the occasion, but from a savageness of nature. Henry therefore tells him,

> Teeth hadst thou in thy head when thou wast born,
> To signify thou cam'st to bite the world. . .[*Ibid.*, 5.6.49–56]

Which violent invective does not affect Richard as a reproach; it serves him only for a pretence to commit the murder he came resolved on, and his answer while he is killing Henry is

> I'll hear no more; die, prophet, in thy speech!
> For this, among the rest, was I ordain'd.   [*Ibid.*, 57–8]

Immediately afterwards he resumes the subject himself; and, priding himself that the signs given at his birth were verified in his conduct, he says,

> Then, since the heavens have shap'd my body so,
> Let hell make crook'd my mind to answer it   [*Ibid.*, 69–79]

Several other passages to the same effect imply that he has a natural propensity to evil. Crimes are his delight: but Macbeth is always in an agony when he thinks of them. He is sensible, before he proceeds, of 'the heat-oppressed brain' [2.1.39]. He feels 'the present horror of the time/Which now suits with it' [*Ibid.*, 59f.]. And immediately after he has committed the murder, he is 'afraid to think what he has done' [2.2.48]. He is pensive even while he is enjoying the effect of his crimes; but Richard is in spirits merely at the prospect of committing them, and what is effort in the one is sport to the other. An extraordinary gaiety of heart shews itself upon those occasions which to Macbeth seem most awful; and whether he forms or executes, contemplates the means, or looks back on the success of the most wicked and desperate designs, they are at all times to him subjects of merriment. Upon parting from his brother he bids him

> Go, tread the path that thou shalt ne'er return;
> Simple, plain Clarence! I do love thee so,
> That I will shortly send thy soul to heaven,
> If heaven will take the present at our hands.
>
> [*Richard III*, 1.1.117ff.]

His amusement, when he is meditating the murder of his nephews, . . . his ironical address to Tyrrel, 'Dar'st thou resolve to kill a friend of mine?' [4.2.69] is agreeable to the rest of his deportment: and his pleasantry does not forsake him when he considers some of his worst deeds, after he has committed them. For the terms in which he mentions them are that

> The sons of Edward sleep in Abraham's bosom;
> And Anne my wife hath bid the world good night. [4.3.38f.]

But he gives a still greater loose to his humour when his deformity, and the omens attending his birth, are alluded to, either by himself or by others, as symptoms of the wickedness of his nature. The ludicrous turn which he gives to the reproach of Henry has been quoted already; and his joy at gaining the consent of Lady Anne to marry him, together with his determination to get rid of her, are expressed in the same wanton vein when, amongst other sallies of exultation, he says 'Was ever woman in this humour woo'd?' [Quotes 1.3.227–57.] And yet, that nothing might be wanting to make him completely odious, Shakespeare has very artfully mixed with all this ridicule a rancorous envy of those who have greater advantages of figure.

> To shrink mine arm up like a wither'd shrub;
> To make an envious mountain on my back,
> Where sits deformity to mock my body!
>
> [*3 Henry VI*, 3.2.156ff.]

and,

> I, that am curtail'd of this fair proportion,
> Cheated of feature by dissembling nature . . .
>
> [*Richard III*, 1.1.18f.]

are starts of spleen which he determines to vent on such 'As are of better person than himself' [*3 Henry VI*, 3.2.167]. There is, besides, another subject on which he sometimes exercises his wit, which is his own hypocrisy. I shall have occasion hereafter to take more notice of that part of his character; at present it is sufficient to observe that to himself he laughs at the sanctified appearances which he assumes, and makes ridiculous applications of that very language by which he imposed upon others. His answer to his mother's blessing, 'Amen! and make me die a good old man!' [*Richard III*, 2.2.109] is an example both of his hypocrisy and his humour. His application of the story of Judas to the affection he had just before expressed for Edward's family,

> To say the truth, so Judas kiss'd his master;
> And cried, all hail! when as he meant all harm
>
> [*3 Henry VI*, 5.7.33f.]

is another instance of the same kind; and there are many more. But still all this turn to ridicule does not proceed from levity; for Macbeth, though always serious, is not so considerate and attentive in times of action and business. But Richard, when he is indulging that wickedness and malice which he is so prone to and fond of, expresses his enjoyment of it by such sallies of humour. On other occasions he is alert, on these only is he gay; and the delight he takes in them give an air to his whole demeanor, which induces Hastings to observe, that as

> His Grace looks cheerfully and well this morning:
> There's some conceit or other likes him well,
> When that he bids good-morrow with such spirit;
>
> [*Richard III*, 3.4.48ff.]

which observation is made at the moment when he was meditating, and but just before he accomplished, the destruction of the nobleman who makes it. That Macbeth, on the other hand, is constantly shocked and depressed with those circumstances which inspire Richard with extravagant mirth and spirits, is so obvious, that more quotations are unnecessary to prove it. . . . (6–24)

[Richard has murdered Henry VI] 'See how my sword weeps for the poor king's death' [*3 Henry VI*, 5.6.63] is the taunt he utters over his bloody corse: and when afterwards Lady Anne aggravates the assassination of Henry by exclaiming 'O he was gentle, mild, and virtuous' his answer is that he was therefore 'The fitter for the

King of heaven that hath him.' [*Richard III*, 1.2.104f.] Richard despises Henry for his meekness, and turns it into a jest when it is urged against himself as a matter of reproach. But Macbeth esteems Duncan for the same quality; and of himself, without being reminded, reflects upon it with contrition.

It would have been an inconsistency to have attributed to Richard any of those domestic affections which are proper in Macbeth. Nor are they only omitted; but Shakespeare has with great nicety shewn that His zeal for his family springs not from them but from his ambition, and from that party-spirit which the contention between the Houses of York and Lancaster had inspired. His animosity therefore is inveterate against all 'who wish the downfall of our House' [*3 Henry VI*, 5.6.65], and he eagerly pursues their destruction as the means of his own advancement. But his desire for the prosperity of his family goes no further: the execration he utters against his brother Edward, 'Would he were wasted, marrow, bones, and all' [*Ibid.*, 3.2.125] is to the full as bitter as any against the Lancastrians. The fear of children from Edward's marriage provokes him to this curse; yet not a wish for posterity from his own marriage ever crosses him: and though childless himself, he does not hesitate to destroy the heirs of his family. He would annihilate the House he had fought for all his life rather than be disappointed of the throne he aspired to; and after he had ascended it he forgets the interests of that House whose accession had opened the way to his usurpation. . . . The possession, not the descent of the crown is his object; . . . the circumstance of his being also a Lancaster does not occur to him; . . . all which conduct tallies with the principle he avows when he declares, 'I have no brother, I am like no brother. . . . I am myself alone' [*Ibid.*, 5.6.80f.]

But the characters of Richard and Macbeth are marked not only by opposite qualities; but even the same qualities in each differ so much in the cause, the kind, and the degree that the distinction in them is as evident as in the others. Ambition is common to both; but in Macbeth it proceeds only from vanity, which is flattered and satisfied by the splendor of a throne. In Richard it is founded upon pride; his ruling passion is the lust of power:

—this earth affords no joy to him,
But to command, to check, and to o'erbear.

[*Ibid.*, 3.2.165f.]

415

And so great is that joy that he enumerates among the delights of war 'To fright the souls of fearful adversaries' [*Richard III*, 1.1.11], which is a pleasure brave men do not very sensibly feel; they rather value 'Battles/Nobly, hardly fought.' But in Richard the sentiments natural to his high courage are lost in the greater satisfaction of trampling on mankind, and seeing even those whom he despises crouching beneath him. At the same time, to submit himself to any authority is incompatible with his eager desire of ruling over all. . . . (25–9)

But the crown is not Macbeth's pursuit through life. He had never thought of it till it was suggested to him by the witches; he receives their promise, and the subsequent earnest of the truth of it, with calmness. . . . He never carries his idea beyond the honour of the situation he aims at; and therefore he considers it as a situation which Lady Macbeth will partake of equally with him: and in his letter tells her,

> This have I thought good to deliver thee, my dearest partner of greatness, that thou mightest not lose the dues of rejoicing, by being ignorant of what greatness is promised thee. [1.5.10ff.]

But it was his rank alone, not his power, in which she could share: and that indeed is all which he afterwards seems to think he had attained by his usurpation. He styles himself, 'high-plac'd Macbeth' [4.1.98], but in no other light does he ever contemplate his advancement with satisfaction; and when he finds that it is not attended with that adulation and respect which he had promised himself, and which would have soothed his vanity, he sinks under the disappointment, and complains that

> . . . that which should accompany old age,
> As honour, love, obedience, troops of friends,
> I must not look to have. [5.2.24ff.]

These blessings, so desirable to him, are widely different from the pursuits of Richard. He wishes not to gain the affections but to secure the submission of his subjects, and is happy to see men shrink under his control. But Macbeth, on the contrary, reckons among the miseries of his condition

> ———— mouth-honour, breath,
> Which the poor heart would fain deny, but dare not
> [*Ibid.*, 27f.]

416

and pities the wretch who fears him.

The towering ambition of Richard, and the weakness of that passion in Macbeth [differentiate the two characters]. Upon the same principle, a distinction still stronger is made in the article of courage, though both are possessed of it even to an eminent degree. But in Richard it is intrepidity, and in Macbeth no more than resolution: in him it proceeds from exertion, not from nature. In enterprise he betrays a degree of fear, though he is able, when occasion requires, to stifle and subdue it. When he and his wife are concerting the murder his doubt 'If we should fail' [1.7.59] is a difficulty raised by apprehension; and as soon as that is removed by the contrivance of Lady Macbeth to make the officers drunk, and lay the crime upon them, he runs with violence into the other extreme of confidence, and cries out, with a rapture unusual to him,

> ———Bring forth men-children only!
> For thy undaunted metal should compose
> Nothing but males. Will it not be receiv'd,
> When we have mark'd with blood these sleepy two
> Of his own chamber, and us'd their very daggers,
> That they have done it? [1.7.72ff.]

Which question he puts to her, who but the moment before had suggested the thought of 'His spongy officers, who shall bear the guilt/Of our great quell' [71f.]. And his asking it again proceeds from that extravagance with which a delivery from apprehension and doubt is always accompanied. Then, summoning all his fortitude, he says

> ———I am settled, and bend up
> Each corporal agent to this terrible feat [79f.]

and proceeds to the bloody business without any further recoils. But a certain degree of restlessness and anxiety still continues, such as is constantly felt by a man not naturally very bold, worked up to a momentous achievement. His imagination dwells entirely on the circumstances of horror which surround him; the vision of the dagger; the darkness and the stillness of the night; and the terrors and the prayers of the chamberlains. Lady Macbeth, who is cool and undismayed, attends to the business only; considers of the place where she had laid the daggers ready, the impossibility of his missing them, and is afraid of nothing but a disappointment. She is earnest and eager; he is uneasy and impatient, and therefore wishes it over: 'I go, and it is done; the bell invites me.' [2.1.62] But a resolution thus forced cannot hold longer than the immediate occasion for it: the moment after that is accomplished for which it was necessary, his thoughts take the contrary turn, and he cries out in agony and despair: 'Wake, Duncan, with this knocking; would thou could'st!' [2.2.71] That courage, which had supported him while he was *settled and bent up*, forsakes him so immediately after he has performed the *terrible feat* for which it had been exerted that he forgets the favourite circumstance of laying it on the officers of the bed-chamber; and when reminded of it he refuses to return and complete his work, acknowledging that

> I am afraid to think what I have done;
> Look on't again I dare not. [2.2.47f.]

His disordered senses deceive him, and his debilitated spirits fail him; he owns that 'every noise appals him' [2.2.55]. He listens when nothing stirs; he mistakes the sounds he does hear; he is so confused as not to distinguish whence the knocking proceeds.

She, who is more calm, knows that it is at the south entry; she gives clear and direct answers to all the incoherent questions he asks her. But he returns none to that which she puts to him; and though after some time, and when necessity again urges him to recollect himself, he recovers so far as to conceal his distress, yet he still is not able to divert his thoughts from it. All his answers to the trivial questions of Lennox and Macduff are evidently given by a man thinking of something else; and by taking a tincture from the subject of his attention, they become equivocal:

> *Macd.* Is the king stirring, worthy Thane?
> *Macb.* Not yet.
> *Len.* Goes the king hence to-day?
> *Macb.* He did appoint so.
> *Len.* The night has been unruly. . .
> *Macb.* 'Twas a rough night. [2.3.45ff.]

Not yet implies that he will by and by, and is a kind of guard against any suspicion of his knowing that the king would never stir more. *He did appoint so* is the very counterpart of that which he had said to Lady Macbeth when, on his first meeting her, she asked him

> *Lady.* When goes he hence?
> *Macb.* To-morrow, as he purposes. [1.5.60f.]

In both which answers he alludes to his disappointing the king's intention. And when forced to make some reply to the long description given by Lennox, he puts off the subject which the other was so much inclined to dwell upon by a slight acquiescence in what had been said of the roughness of the night; but not like a man who had been attentive to the account, or was willing to keep up the conversation.

Nothing can be conceived more directly opposite to the agitation of Macbeth's mind than the serenity of Richard in parallel circumstances. Upon the murder of the Prince of Wales he immediately resolves on the assassination of Henry; and stays only to say to Clarence

> *Rich.* Clarence, excuse me to the king my brother;
> I'll hence to London on a serious matter:
> Ere ye come there, be sure to hear some news.
> *Cla.* What? What?
> *Rich.* The Tower, man, the Tower! I'll root them out.
> [*3 Henry VI*, 5.5.46ff.]

It is a thought of his own which just then occurs to him. He determines upon it without hesitation; it requires no consideration, and admits of no delay. He is eager to put it in execution; but his eagerness proceeds from ardour, not from anxiety; and is not hurry, but dispatch. . . . The humour which breaks from him upon this and other occasions has been taken notice of already as a mark of his depravity; it is at the same time a proof of his calmness, and of the composure he preserves when he does not indulge himself in ridicule. . . . (29–39)

The same determined spirit carries him through the bloody business of murdering his nephews: and when Buckingham shews a reluctance to be concerned in it, he immediately looks out for another; some 'iron-witted fool,/Or unrespective boy' [4.2.28f.], more apt for his purpose. Had Macbeth been thus disappointed in the person to whom he had opened himself, it would have disconcerted any design he had formed. But Richard does not suffer such an accident to delay his pursuit for a moment; he only wonders at the folly of the man, and says

419

Hath he so long held out with me untir'd,
And stops he now for breath? Well, be it so.   [4.2.44f.]

. . . It is needless to refer to other instances of the same resolute behaviour. He never deviates; but throughout the whole progress of his reiterated crimes he is not once daunted at the danger, discouraged by the difficulties, nor disconcerted by the accidents attending them; nor ever shocked either at the idea or the reflection.

Macbeth indeed commits subsequent murders with less agitation than that of Duncan: but this is no inconsistency in his character. On the contrary, it confirms the principles upon which it is formed; for besides his being hardened to the deeds of death, he is impelled to the perpetration of them by other motives than those which instigated him to assassinate his sovereign. In the one he sought to gratify his ambition; the rest are for his security: and he gets rid of fear by guilt, which, to a mind so constituted, may be the less uneasy sensation of the two. The anxiety which prompts him to the destruction of Banquo arises entirely from apprehension:

> —to be thus, is nothing;
> But to be safely thus:—our fears in Banquo
> Stick deep . . .   [3.1.47ff.]

For though one principal reason of his jealousy was the impression made on Macbeth's mind by the prophecy of the witches in favour of Banquo's issue, yet here starts forth another, quite consistent with a temper not quite free from timidity. He is afraid of him personally: that fear is founded on the superior courage of the other, and he feels himself under an awe before him; a situation which a dauntless spirit can never get into. . . . (40–43)

The same motives of personal fear, and those unmixed with any other, impel him to seek the destruction of Macduff. His answer to the apparition who warns him to beware of the Thane of Fife is

> Whate'er thou art, for thy good caution, thanks;
> Thou'st harp'd my fear aright.   [4.1.73f.]

And when, soon afterwards, he is told by another apparition that 'none of woman born should harm Macbeth,' though he then believed, and through his whole life confided in that assurance, yet his anxiety to be out of the reach of danger immediately recurs again and makes him revert to his former resolution. His reflections upon receiving the promise prove both his credulity and his timidity, for he says

> Then live, Macduff; what need I fear of thee?
> And yet I'll make assurance doubly sure,
> And take a bond of fate: thou shalt not live;
> That I may tell pale-hearted fear, it lies,
> And sleep in spite of thunder. [4.1.82ff.]
> (46–7)

But all the crimes Richard commits are for his advancement, not for his security. He is not drawn from one into another; but he premeditates several before he begins, and yet can look upon the distant prospect of a long succession of murders with steadiness and composure. . . .

The danger of losing the great object of his ambition is that which alone alarms Richard. But Macbeth dreads the danger which threatens his life; and that terror constantly damps all the joys of his crown. When he says

> ——Duncan is in his grave;
> After life's fretful fever, he sleeps well:
> Treason has done his worst; nor steel, nor poison,
> Malice domestic, foreign levy, nothing
> Can touch him further! [3.2.22ff.]

he only enumerates the mischiefs he fears; none of which are ever Richard's concern. Those which are present he opposes with spirit, and such as are imaginary never occur to him. . . . (49–50)

Upon no occasion, however tremendous, and at no moment of his life, however unguarded, does he betray the least symptom of fear; whereas Macbeth is always shaken upon great, and frequently alarmed upon trivial, occasions. Upon the first meeting with the witches he is agitated much more than Banquo; the one expresses mere curiosity, the other astonishment: [quotes 1.3.39–48]. Which parts may appear to be injudiciously distributed, Macbeth being the principal personage in the play, and most immediately concerned in this particular scene; and it being to him that the witches first address themselves. But the difference in their characters accounts for such a distribution; Banquo being perfectly calm, and Macbeth a little ruffled by the adventure.* The

* Another instance of an effect produced by a distribution of the parts is in Act ii.sc. 5 where, on Lady Macbeth's seeming to faint, while Banquo and Macduff are solicitous about her Macbeth, by his unconcern, betrays a consciousness that the fainting is feigned.

distinction is preserved through the rest of their behaviour; for Banquo treats them with contempt [1.3.60f.], which defiance seemed so bold to Macbeth that he long after mentions it as an instance of his dauntless spirit, when he recollects that he 'chid the sisters'. [3.1.56] (51–3)

. . . Upon the rising of Banquo's ghost, though that was a spectre which might well terrify him, yet he betrays a consciousness of too much natural timidity, by his peevish reproaches to Lady Macbeth because she had not been so frightened as himself, when he tells her,

> ——you make me strange
> E'en to the disposition that I owe,
> When now I think you can behold such sights,
> And keep the natural ruby of your cheek,
> When mine is blanch'd with fear. [3.4.111ff.]

These are all symptoms of timidity, which he confesses to have been natural to him when he owns that

> The time has been, my senses would have cool'd
> To hear a night-shriek, and my fell of hair
> Would at a dismal treatise rouse and stir,
> As life were in it. [5.5.10ff.]

But still he is able to suppress this natural timidity; he has an acquired, though not a constitutional courage, which is equal to all ordinary occasions; and if it fails him upon those which are extraordinary it is, however, so well formed as to be easily resumed as soon as the shock is over. But his idea never rises above manliness of character, and he continually asserts his right to that character; which he would not do if he did not take to himself a merit in supporting it.

> I dare do all that may become a man;
> Who dares do more, is none [1.7.46f.]

is his answer to the reproaches of Lady Macbeth for want of spirit in the execution of his design upon Duncan. Upon the first appearance of Banquo's ghost she endeavours to recover him from his terror by summoning this consideration to his view:

> *Lady.* Are you a man?
> *Macb.* Aye, and a bold one, that dare look on that
> Which might appall the Devil. [3.4.57ff.]

He puts in the same claim again upon the ghost's rising again, and says, 'What man dare, I dare' [3.4.98ff.], and on its disappearing finally he says, 'I am a man again' [*Ibid.*, 108]. And even at the last, when he finds that the prophecy in which he had confided has deceived him by its equivocation, he burst out into

> Accursed be that tongue which tells me so,
> For it hath cow'd my better part of man! [5.8.17f.]

In all which passages he is apparently shaken out of that character to which he had formed himself; but for which he relied only on exertion of courage, without supposing insensibility to fear.

But Richard never stands in need of any affectation to others, or exertion in himself. Equal to every occasion, coolly contemplating the approaches of distant dangers, and unmoved amidst the most pressing—

> Promptus metuenda pati, si cominus instant;
> Aut deferre potest——   LUCAN[1]

he never thinks of behaving like a man, or is proud of doing so, for he cannot behave otherwise . . . . (54–7)

But though Richard has no timidity in his nature which he wishes to conceal, yet he is conscious of other qualities, which it is necessary he should disguise. For if the wickedness of his heart had been fully known he could not have hoped for success in his views: and he therefore from the beginning covers his malice under an appearance of sanctity, which he himself thus describes:

> —I sigh, and with a piece of Scripture
> Tell them, that God bids us do good for evil:
> And thus I clothe my naked villany
> With old odd ends, stol'n forth of holy writ,
> And seem a saint, when most I play the Devil. [1.3.333ff.]

But he is too deep a hypocrite to expose himself to discovery by an affectation over-done: he does not quote, he only alludes to Scripture; and assumes a general meekness of behaviour without pretending to more religion or greater austerity than others. . . . (59)

An hypocrisy so refined is not easily seen through; and in him it is the less suspected on account of that frankness to which he is

---

[1] *Pharsalia*, 7.106f.: 'both quick to endure the ordeal, if it be close and pressing, and willing also to let it wait'.

often prompted by his high courage, and into which he is sometimes hurried by the impetuosity of his temper. He is, besides, so complete a master of dissimulation that his own account of himself is: 'I can smile, and murder while I smile' [*3 Henry VI*, 3.2.182]. With such arts it is not at all surprising that he for some time could conceal his character, and that he is never suspected of the mischief he intends till it is executed. For his barbarity towards the House of Lancaster gave no warning: the animosities were mutual: cruelty was common to both sides, and was not therefore imputed to the men, but to the times. . . . (61–2)

But Macbeth wants no disguise of his natural disposition, for it is not bad; he does not affect more piety than he has. On the contrary, a part of his distress arises from a real sense of religion; which, in the passages already quoted, makes him regret that he could not join with the chamberlains in prayer for God's blessing; and bewail that he has *given his eternal jewel to the common enemy of man* [3.1.67f.]. He continually reproaches himself for his deeds; no use can harden him; confidence cannot silence, and even despair cannot stifle the cries of his conscience. By the first murder he committed he *put rancours in the vessel of his peace* [3.1.66], and of the last he owns to Macduff, 'my soul is too much charg'd/With blood of thine already' [5.8.5f.]. How heavily it was charged with his crimes appears from his asking the physician, 'Canst thou not minister to a mind diseas'd?' [5.3.40] For though it is the disorder of Lady Macbeth that gives occasion to these questions, yet the feeling with which he describes the sensations he wishes to be removed; the longing he expresses for the means of doing it; the plaintive measure of the lines; and the rage into which he bursts when he says, 'Throw physic to the dogs, I'll none of it' [5.3.47] upon being told that 'therein the patient/Must minister unto himself' [45f.], evidently shew that in his own mind he is all the while making the application to himself . . . . (63–5)

Conscious therefore of all these feelings, he has no occasion to assume the appearance, but is obliged to conceal the force of them: and Lady Macbeth finds it necessary more than once to suggest to him the precautions proper to hide the agitations of his mind. After the murder of Duncan she bids him

> Be not lost
> So poorly in your thoughts   [2.2.68f.]

and while he is meditating the death of Banquo she says to him

> Come on;—
> Gentle my lord, sleek o'er your rugged looks;
> Be bright and jovial with your friends to-night.   [3.2.26ff.]

Which kind of disguise is all that is wanting to him; and yet when he had assumed it he in both instances betrays himself. In the first, by his too guarded conversation with Macduff and Lennox, which has been quoted already; and in the last, by an over-acted regard for Banquo, of whose absence from the feast he affects to complain, that he may not be suspected of knowing the cause of it, though at the same time he very unguardedly drops an allusion to that cause when he says,

> Here had we now our country's honour roof'd,
> Were the grac'd person of our Banquo present;
> Whom may I rather challenge for unkindness,
> Than pity for mischance!——   [3.4.39ff.]

Richard is able to put on a general character, directly the reverse of his disposition, and it is ready to him upon every occasion. But Macbeth cannot effectually conceal his sensations when it is most necessary to conceal them, nor act a part which does not belong to him with any degree of consistency; and the same weakness of mind which disqualifies him from maintaining such a force upon his nature, shews itself still further in that hesitation and dullness to dare which he feels in himself, and allows in others. His whole proceeding in his treason against Duncan is full of it; of which the references already made to his behaviour then are sufficient proofs. Against Banquo he acts with more determination, for the reasons which have been given: and yet he most unnecessarily acquaints the murderers with the reasons of his conduct; and even informs them of the behaviour he purposes to observe afterwards [quotes 3.1.117ff.], which particularity and explanation to men who did not desire it, the confidence he places in those who could only abuse it, and the very needless caution of secrecy implied in this speech, are so many symptoms of a feeble mind. His sending a third murderer to join the others, just at the moment of action and without any notice, is a further proof of the same imbecility; and that so glaring as to strike them who observe upon it that

He needs not our mistrust, since he delivers
Our offices, and what we have to do,
To the direction just.   [3.3.2ff.]

Richard, always determined, and taking his determination
himself, never waits to be incited nor ever idly accounts for his
conduct; but, fixed to his purpose, makes other men only his
instruments, not his confidents or advisers. . . . (66–70)

Shakespeare, who had such variety of phrase at command, does
not repeat the same without a design. An example has already been
given of a particular meaning conveyed by the frequent use which
Macbeth makes of the same terms in asserting his pretensions to the
character of manliness. Another instance of the like kind is the
repetition by Richard of the same words, *off with his head!* upon three
or four different occasions.[1] The readiness and the certainty of his
resolutions are expressed by them. . . . Macbeth, on the contrary,
is irresolute in his counsels, and languid in the execution; he
cannot look steadily at his principal object but dwells upon
circumstances, and always does too much or too little. Besides the
proofs which have been given of these weaknesses in his character
through the whole conduct of his designs against Duncan and
Banquo, another may be drawn from his attempt upon Macduff;
whom he first sends for without acquainting Lady Macbeth with
his intention, then betrays the secret by asking of her, after the
company are risen from the banquet,

> *Macb.* How say'st thou, that Macduff denies his person
> At our great bidding?
>   *Lady.* Did you send to him, Sir?
>   *Macb.* I hear it by the way; but I will send.   [3.4.127ff.]

The time of making this enquiry, when it has no relation to what
had just passed otherwise than as his apprehensions might
connect it; the addressing of the question to her, who, as appears
from what she says, knew nothing of the matter; and his aukward
attempt then to disguise it are strong evidence of the disorder of his
mind. He had not yet formed his resolution; he delays till he has
consulted the witches. Their enigmatical answers make him doubt
more: but his fear determines him on the death of Macduff, who,
during this procrastination, escapes into England. Macbeth no

---

[1] 'Chop off his head!' (3.1.193); 'Off with his head!' (3.4.76); 'Off with his son George's
head!' (5.3.344).

sooner hears of his flight than he is sensible of his own weakness; and, rushing into the contrary extreme, he vents his rage for the disappointment, impotently and needlessly, on the family of the fugitive, who were not at all the objects of his jealousy [quotes 4.1.144–54]. Thus agitated always by his fears or his fury, he ravages his kingdom with a boundless waste of cruelty till

> good men's lives
> Expir'd before the flowers in their caps,
> Dying or ere they sicken'd. [4.3.171ff.]

While Richard, though he has less remorse and less humanity, yet because he acts upon design not from passion, stops when his purpose is accomplished. He destroys without pity, not without occasion; and directs, but does not let loose his tyranny.

A mind so framed and so tortured as that of Macbeth, when the hour of extremity presses upon him, can find no refuge but in despair; and the expression of that despair by Shakespeare is perhaps one of the finest pictures that ever was exhibited. . . . It is presumption without hope, and confidence without courage. That confidence rests upon his superstition; he buoys himself up with it against all the dangers that threaten him, and yet sinks upon every fresh alarm [quotes 5.3.1–10]. His faith in these assurances is implicit; he really is persuaded that he may defy the forces of his enemies and the treachery of his friends. But immediately after, only on seeing a man who, not having the same support, is frightened at the numbers approaching against them, he catches his apprehensions, tells him 'those linen cheeks of thine/Are counsellors to fear' [5.3.16f.], and then, though nothing had happened to impeach the credit of those assurances on which he relied, he gives way to the depression of his spirits, and desponds in the midst of security. [Quotes 'I have lived long enough': 5.3.19ff.] (71–7)

After he has forbid those about him to bring him any more reports, he anxiously enquires for news; he dreads every danger which he supposes he scorns; at last he recurs to his superstition, as to the only relief from his agony [quotes 5.3.58ff.]. (79)

. . . When Birnam wood appeared to come towards Dunsinane, he trusts to the other assurance; and believes that he 'bears a charmed life, which must not yield/To one of woman born' [5.8.12f.]. . . . But his reliance on this charm being taken away by the explanation given by Macduff, and every hope now failing him, though he wishes not to fight, yet his sense of honour being touched by the threat to be made *the shew and gaze of the time*, and all his passions being now lost in despair, his habits recur to govern him; he disdains the thought of disgrace and dies as becomes a soldier.

If this behaviour of Macbeth required, it would receive illustration by comparing it with that of Richard in circumstances not very different. When he is to fight for his crown and for his life he prepares for the crisis with the most perfect evenness of temper; and rises, as the danger thickens, into ardour without once starting out into intemperance, or ever sinking into dejection. . . . Instead of giving way to it in himself he attends to every symptom of dejection in others, and endeavours to dispel them. . . . (81–5)

He deliberately, and after having *surveyed the vantage of the ground*, forms that disposition by himself. For which purpose he calls for ink and paper and, being informed that it is ready, directs his guard to watch, and his attendants to leave him; but before he retires he issues the necessary orders. They are not, like those of Macbeth, general and violent, but temperate and particular; delivered coolly, and distinctly given to different persons. . . .

He is attentive to every circumstance preparatory to the battle; and preserves throughout a calmness and presence of mind, which denote his intrepidity. [Quotes his speech to the army: 5.3.314–41.] (86–7)

But even in this sally of ardour he is not hurried away by a blind impetuosity, but still gives orders, and distinguishes the persons to whom he addresses them. From this moment he is all on fire; and, possessed entirely with the great objects around him, others of lesser note are below his attention. Swelling himself with courage, and inspiring his troops with confidence of victory, he rushes on the enemy. It is not a formed sense of honour, nor a cold fear of disgrace, which impels him to fight, but a natural high spirit, and bravery exulting in danger. . . . Having *enacted more wonders than a man* [5.4.2] [he] loses his life in an attempt so worthy of himself.

Thus, from the beginning of their history to their last moments are the characters of Macbeth and Richard preserved entire and distinct. And though probably Shakespeare, when he was drawing the one had no attention to the other, yet, as he conceived them to be widely different, expressed his conceptions exactly, and copied both from nature, they necessarily became contrasts to each other; and by seeing them together that contrast is more apparent, especially where the comparison is not between opposite qualities but arises from the different degrees, or from a particular display or total omission of the same quality. This last must often happen, as the character of Macbeth is much more complicated than that of Richard; and therefore, when they are set in opposition, the judgment of the poet shows itself as much in what he has left out of the latter as in what he has inserted. The picture of Macbeth is also, for the same reason, much the more highly finished of the two; for it required a greater variety, and a greater delicacy of painting, to express and to blend with consistency all the several properties which are ascribed to him. That of Richard is marked by more careless strokes, but they are, notwithstanding, perfectly just. Much bad composition may indeed be found in the part; it is a fault from which the best of Shakespeare's Plays are not exempt, and with which this Play particularly abounds; and the taste of the age in which he wrote, though it may afford some excuse, yet cannot entirely vindicate the exceptionable passages. After every reasonable allowance they must still remain blemishes ever to be lamented; but happily, for the most part, they only obscure, they do not disfigure his draughts from nature. Through whole speeches and scenes character is often wanting; but in the worst instances of this kind Shakespeare is but insipid. He is not inconsistent; and in his peculiar excellence of drawing characters, though he often neglects to exert his talents, he is very rarely guilty of perverting them. (88–91)

285. J. P. Kemble, in defence of Macbeth

1786

From *Macbeth re-considered; an Essay* (1786), 36 pp. A second and much enlarged edition (171 pp.) was published in 1817 with the title *Macbeth, and King Richard the Third: An Essay, in answer to Remarks on some of the Characters of Shakespeare*. In the advertisement Kemble notes that the passages printed in italics are quotations from Whately.

John Philip Kemble (1757–1823), whose acting career lasted from 1767 to 1817, performed first with Tate Wilkinson's company on the York circuit, then at Edinburgh and in Ireland, making his London début (as Hamlet) at Drury Lane on 30 September 1783. He acted over 120 roles in nineteen years at Drury Lane, and achieved celebrity with his sister, Mrs Siddons. As theatre manager and producer, first at Drury Lane and subsequently at Covent Garden, he laid especial emphasis on costume and stage settings. As an actor he had many successes, but his affectations of speech detracted from them. On his Shakespeare adaptations see G. C. D. Odell, *Shakespeare from Betterton to Irving* (New York, 1920, 1966); Harold Child, *The Shakespearian Productions of J. P. Kemble* (Oxford, 1936: Shakespeare Association lecture); and Herschel Baker, *John Philip Kemble. The Actor in his Theatre* (Cambridge, Mass., 1942).

Plays are designed, by the joint powers of precept and example, to have a good influence on the lives of men. Enquiries into the conduct of fable in the drama were useless to this end. The regular or irregular disposition of parts in a play is an artificial praise or blame, that can contribute nothing to the improvement or depravation of the mind; for the cause of morality is promoted only when, by a catastrophe resulting from principles natural to the agents who produce it, we are taught to love virtue and abhor vice.

Neglect of unity is the obvious fault of Shakespeare's pieces, truth of manners their unrivalled excellence.

This Essay does not profess to observe upon any inconsistency in the conduct of the tragedy of *Macbeth*, it concerns itself only with the sentiments of the hero of it, presuming they will more effectually serve ethicks if, in analysing his character, it shews that there is no distinction between him and king Richard in the quality of personal courage. If Macbeth be what Mr. Whately describes him, we must forego our virtuous satisfaction in his repugnance to guilt, for it arises from mere cowardice; and can gain no instruction from his remorse, for it is only the effect of imbecility. We despise him; we cannot feel for him; and shall never be amended by a wretch who is uniformly the object of our contempt.

The writer of these pages does not consider that his position will never be established till Mr. Whately's be overthrown, without perceiving how difficult and apparently invidious a task he undertakes; he relies, however, upon Shakespeare to clear Macbeth from the imputation laid on his nature; and can truly say, the argument is not taken up in a spirit of controversy, but out of a love for what is believed to be just criticism.

Having given many judicious proofs of the difference there certainly is in the characters of Macbeth and Richard, Mr. Whately proceeds to the article of courage, and says: *In Richard it is intrepidity, and in Macbeth no more than resolution. . . .*

The attempt to controvert this doctrine naturally resolves itself into three heads; namely, a repetition of the simple character of Macbeth as it stands before any change is effected in it by the supernatural soliciting of the weird sisters; a consideration of his conduct towards Banquo and Macduff; and a review of his deportment as opposed to Richard's in the *Remarks*. (3–5)

An appeal for judgement on the nature of Macbeth's courage lies to the tribunal of Shakespeare himself. The circumscribed nature of a drama renders it generally impracticable for the principal personages in it gradually to unfold themselves. It is, therefore, an allowed artifice with dramatic authors (and of which they commonly avail themselves) by an impressive description of their heroes to bring us in a great measure acquainted with them before they are actually engaged in scenes where, for want of such previous intelligence, their proceedings might appear at best confused, and generally, perhaps, inexplicable. We are bound, then, to receive the introductory portrait our author has drawn of Macbeth as a true resemblance; for a creature of the poet's arbitrary creation may be assimilated only to those features which he has thought fit to give him. Here is the picture. [Quotes 1.2.9–22: 'brave Macbeth' and his routing of Macdonwald.]

Could Shakespeare call a man brave, and insist upon his well deserving that appellation; could he grace a man with the title of valour's minion, and deem him, as he does in a subsequent passage, worthy to be matched even with the goddess of war;—could he do this, and not design to impress a full idea of the dignity of his courage? (5–7)

It is objected, though with some qualification, that Macbeth's courage *proceeds from exertion, not from nature*; and that in *enterprize he betrays a deal of fear*. Let us turn to the portrait once more. [Quotes 1.2.29–35, 52–9.]

Is it to betray fear in enterprize, already worn with the fatigues of a hard-fought field, to rush at disadvantage on fresh supplies and terrible numbers, unconcerned as eagles when they swoop on sparrows, and lions when they strike a hare? It cannot be the laboured effect of exertion, it is the spontaneous impulse of a dauntless nature that again hurries Bellona's bridegroom through all the horrors of a dismal conflict, to single out and hold the royal invader point against point, till his resistless arm has curbed his lavish spirit, and raised on his discomfiture the trophies of a second conquest.

Macbeth now enters in the scene, and a deputation from the sovereign meets him with these gracious acknowledgements to his triumphant valour. [Quotes 1.3.89–105.] (7–9)

Such is the character Shakespeare attributes to Macbeth while yet the pureness of his conscience is uncontaminated by guilt. The impetuosity of Glamis is the decision of intrepidity; the feats of his own hand assure to him the renown of gallantry; and the whole tenour of his conduct throughout this perilous adventure unequivocally displays a soul that, with Othello's, may

——————————————agnize
A natural and prompt alacrity
It finds in hardness.   [1.3.231ff.]
                                                              (10)

[Kemble then argues against Whately's claim that Macbeth is afraid of Banquo.] Macbeth, when he *confesses to Lady Macbeth that his mind is full of scorpions*, shews Banquo not to be the sole cause of his uneasiness by adding, 'Thou know'st that Banquo and his Fleance lives' [3.2.37]. Moreover, directing the assassins, he tells them the son's absence is 'no less material' to him than the father's [3.1.135f.]. He urges the death of Fleance on a motive distinct from cowardice; for, allowing one moment that he personally fear'd Banquo, it is impossible to conceive he could have felt the same dread of a boy. Again, had his fears been personal they must have ended with the removal of the object of them; but finding the son has not fallen with the father, he is again involv'd in all his former apprehensions:

> Fleance is 'scap'd.
> Then comes my fit again.   [3.4.19f.]

The witches, it is true, only point out Banquo's issue to Macbeth's jealousy; but actual is not possible progeny, and the loss of one child does not prevent a man from begetting others. Thus, the securing of his crown against Banquo's issue is so far from being a *secondary* that it is the tyrant's only instigation to this double murder. (15–16)

[Kemble quotes Macbeth's soliloquy, 3.1.47–71: 'Our fears in Banquo/Stick deep . . . '.]

The usurper, then, does not plunge into fresh crimes *to get rid of personal fear*. Ambition impels him to the murder of Duncan; and the same ambition urges him on the destruction of Banquo and Fleance, who seem destin'd to degrade him and his house from the splendors of monarchy to the obscurity of vassalage.

The *Remarks* find additional proofs of Macbeth's cowardice in his conduct towards Macduff: *The same motives of personal fear, and those unmix'd with any other, impel him to seek the destruction of Macduff*.

Macbeth is not wrought by *personal fear* to destroy Macduff but by the knowledge of his disaffection:

> How say'st thou, that Macduff denies his person,   [3.4.127f.]
> At our great bidding?
>   (19)

In a word, Macbeth does not meditate the deaths of Banquo and Macduff through *personal fear* of them, but because his ambition renders the former obnoxious to his envy, and the latter to his hatred. (22)

Does not Richard betray as much suspicion when he dares not

trust Stanley till he has taken the young lord Strange as a surety for his fidelity?—and is he not as anxious from a mere doubt of his followers, as Macbeth is on finding himself really deserted?

> *K. Rich.* O Ratcliff, I have dream'd a fearful dream!—
> What think'st thou?—Will our friends prove all true?—
> *Rat.* No doubt, my Lord.
> *K. Rich.* I fear, I fear.   [3.5.212ff.]
>   (24)

[Kemble answers Whately's description of Macbeth's confusion before the battle (5.3.33ff.) by pointing to Richard's similar confusion (4.4.433–9). Then he compares Macbeth's bravado in defying the ghost of Banquo: 3.4.70ff., 99ff.] Notwithstanding the firmness of this defiance, it cannot be suppos'd but Macbeth is as much terrify'd while he utters it as Richard is when, starting out of a dream in which the souls of those he had murder'd had appear'd to him, he cries:

> Have mercy, Jesu!—soft; I did but dream.—
> O coward conscience, how dost thou afflict me!
> The lights burn blue.—Is it not dead midnight?
> Cold fearful drops stand on my trembling flesh, &c.
>   [5.3.178ff.]

. . . It will be said, and it will be granted, that Richard presently stifles these emotions. It is only asserted that he feels them, like Macbeth; and that Macbeth, like him, can overcome them. (32–3)

[On Macbeth's 'lay on, Macduff': 5.8.30ff.] This conduct in Macbeth is stigmatized with the name of *despair.*—It certainly is of the same nature with Richard's determination;

> ———I have set my life upon a cast,
> And I will stand the hazard of the die.   [5.4.9f.]

The resolution of both tyrants in the battles that decided their fate is that mix'd effusion of grief, shame, and pride which cannot be denominated less than the despair of innate bravery. . . . (34)

Macbeth and Richard are each of them as intrepid as man can be. Yet it may be said of each, without any derogation from that character, that he is at times agitated with apprehensions. The Earl of Peterborough has left it upon record that intrepidity and sense of danger are by no means incompatible.

Having endeavour'd to prove that Macbeth has a just right to the reputation of intrepidity; that he feels no personal dread of Banquo and Macduff; and that he meets equal, not to say superior, trials as boldly as Richard; it may be expected this essay should attempt to shew in what the essential difference between these great bad men consists.

Ambition is the impulse that governs every action of Richard's life. He attains the crown by dissimulation, that owns no respect for virtue; and by cruelty, which entails no remorse on the valour that wou'd maintain his ill-acquir'd dignity. Ambition is the predominant vice of Macbeth's nature; but he gratifies it by hypocrisy, that reveres virtue too highly to be perfectly itself; and by murders, the recollection whereof at times renders his valour useless, by depriving him of all sense but that of his enormous wickedness. Richard's character is simple, Macbeth's mix'd. Richard is only intrepid, Macbeth intrepid, and feeling. Richard's mind not being diverted by reflection from the exigencies of his situation, he is always at full leisure to display his valour; Macbeth, distracted by remorse, loses all apprehension of danger in the contemplation of his guilt; and never recurs to his valour for support till the enemy's approach rouzes his whole soul, and conscience is repell'd by the necessity for exertion. (35–6)

286. Martin Sherlock, in praise of Shakespeare

1786

From *A Fragment on Shakespeare. Extracted from Advice to a Young Poet. By the Rev. Martin Sherlock. Translated from the French* (1786). This is an excerpt (pp. 50–85) from Sherlock's *Consiglio ad un Giovane Poeta* [Naples, 1779], which was translated into French by 'M.D.R.' as *Fragment sur Shakespeare, Tiré des Conseils à un Jeune Poète* (1780), and into English by an unknown hand.

Martin Sherlock (d. 1797) was admitted to Trinity College, Dublin, in 1763, travelled extensively on the continent from 1777 as chaplain to Frederick Hervey, fourth Earl of Bristol and Bishop of Derry, but failed to obtain a diplomatic post in 1781, and spent the last sixteen years of his life as a clergyman in Ireland. He published *Lettres d'un Voyageur Anglois* (Geneva, 1779; English and German translations, 1780); *Nouvelles Lettres* (1780; tr. 1781); and *Letters on Several Subjects* (1781), thirty short essays reworking many of his earlier ideas. He visited Voltaire, was granted an interview by Frederick the Great of Prussia, and moved in the London literary salons. Walpole described him as a man of abundant parts but no judgment, while Carlyle called his letters a 'flashy yet opaque dance of Will-o'-Wisps'.

Always therefore study Nature.

It is she who was thy book, O Shakespeare; it is she who was thy study day and night; it is she from whom thou hast drawn those beauties which are at once the glory and delight of thy nation. Thou wert the eldest son, the darling child, of Nature; and like thy mother enchanting, astonishing, sublime, graceful, thy variety is inexhaustible. Always original, always new, thou art the only prodigy which Nature has produced. Homer was the first of men, but thou art more than man. The reader who thinks this elogium extravagant is a stranger to my subject. To say that Shakespeare had the imagination of Dantè, and the depth of Machiavel, would be a weak encomium: he had them, and more. To say that he possessed the terrible graces of Michael Angelo, and the amiable graces of Correggio, would be a weak encomium: he had them, and more. To the brilliancy of Voltaire he added the strength of Demosthenes; and to the simplicity of La Fontaine, the majesty of Virgil. — But, say you, we have never seen such 'a being.' You are in the right; Nature made it, and broke the mould.

The merits of this poet are so extraordinary that the man who should speak of them with the most rigid truth would seem to the highest degree extravagant. But what signifies what I *seem*, if really I *be* true? I will therefore say, because a more certain truth was never said; *Shakespeare possessed, in the highest degree of perfection, all the most excellent talents of all the writers that I have ever known.*

'Horace,' says Bacon, 'is the most popular of all the poets of antiquity, because he contains most observations applicable to the business of human life.' Shakespeare contains more of them than Horace.

One of the chief merits of the Greek tragic poets (principally of Euripides) is that they abound with morality. Shakespeare has more morality than they.

Dramatic poetry is a picture made to be seen at a certain point of view. This point of sight is the theatre. Molière, who was an actor, had occasion when he was on the stage to observe the effects produced during the representation. This advantage is one of the reasons of Molière's being superior in theatric effect to all the comic actors of his nation. Shakespeare had the same advantage: he was also an actor; and in that perspective of poetry (if I may be allowed the expression) Shakespeare is equal to Molière.

Other poets have made men speak by means of words: Shakespeare alone has made silence speak. Othello, a man of a noble heart but violent to an extreme, deceived by a villain, thinks that his wife whom he adores is unfaithful to him, and kills her. In such a situation another poet would have made Othello say; *Good God! what a punishment! what miseries are equal to mine!*—Shakespeare petrifies his Othello; he becomes a statue motionless and dumb.

Tacitus and Machiavel together could not have painted nor supported the character of a villain better than that of Iago.

What is a poet, if he be stripped of his language and harmony? See then what Shakespeare is, deprived of these advantages. (He is speaking of two princes.) *They are soft as the Zephyrs which blow on the violet without moving its fragrant head; but, when their royal blood is kindled, they are furious as the storm which seizes by the top the mountain pine, and makes it bend down to the valley.* [*Cymbeline*, 4.2.171ff.]

With other poets a simile is a principal beauty: in Shakespeare the most beautiful similes are frequently lost in a croud of superior beauties. (13–16)

Tacitus is the writer of antiquity who has drawn characters with the greatest strength, vivacity, and truth. Shakespeare has drawn them better than Tacitus.

I have much studied mathematics: I think I have precision in my ideas, and I would not have these words, 'Shakespeare possesses all the most excellent talents of all writers, *and more*,' pass for a frantic and poetical start; they are true, literally true. In the history of the wars of the king of Prussia we may discover all the resources of Cæsar and Alexander, and an infinity of new resources created by the astonishing genius of that monarch. In the poetry of Shakespeare we find all the sources of poetical beauty that are known to all other poets, and an infinity of new sources of which they were ignorant. In this point of view, Shakespeare may be styled the Frederick of poetry.

> The enemies of Shakespeare shall say this,
> Then in a friend it is cold modesty.   *Jul. Cæsar.*

The beauties of this poet are never superficial: they include a fund of truth which augments their value in each perusal, and in that he is superior to all the world. But I will declaim no longer, I put it to the proof: I defy Greece, and let Truth triumph.

Let us find a passage in which a just parallel may be made. Homer, the father of poetry, was also the father of eloquence. (22–3)

[Sherlock compares the speeches in Book IX of the *Iliad* with Antony's speech over Caesar's body, *Julius Caesar*, 3.2.73–259.]

Such is Shakespeare in the veil of my barbarous prose:[1] but he is beautiful even veiled; naked, he is beauty itself.

I do not oppose this speech to any one of the three speeches in Homer, but to all three together. Now chuse that speech in Virgil which pleases you best: but when I mentioned the master-pieces of Homer, I meant to include all the most beautiful passages that the Greek and Latin poetry can produce.

I have said that Shakespeare equals all writers in the part in which each of them excells. Demosthenes and Cicero were orators by profession. Is there any one of their orations superior to this? (29)

I should not have said so much upon Shakespeare, if from Paris to Berlin, and from Berlin to Naples, I had not heard his name profaned. The words *monstrous farces* and *grave-diggers* have been repeated to me in every town; and for a long time I could not conceive why every one uttered precisely these two words, and not a third. One day happening to open a volume of Voltaire, the mystery disappeared; the two words in question were found in that volume, and all the critics had learned them by heart. . . .

---

[1] In the original edition Sherlock translated this scene into Italian prose.

Foreigners who are unacquainted with Shakespeare, are fond of comparing him to Racine. Racine wrote tragedies, and Shakespeare never wrote a tragedy. They cannot therefore be compared on that head. But I will not compare them in any thing, for I am a sincere admirer of Racine, and I will not injure him.

It cannot be said that I have been niggardly of my praises of the Greeks. They have invented much; but they have not invented every thing. The telescope, gun-powder, and the art of printing, are the inventions of modern times. Thespis invented one species of poetry; Æschylus made some progress in it; Euripides and Sophocles brought it to perfection. Racine followed these models at least *passibus æquis*. But Shakespeare, impatient of the curb, and disdaining imitation, opened to himself a new road, leaped over it under the wing of genius, and created a species quite new. Jonson, his contemporary, observed the unities; Shakespeare would not observe them; he said to Jonson, 'You place your scene at Rome; and the spectator, who knows that he is at London, must make an effort of imagination to believe himself at Rome. Let him make two efforts of imagination for me. Let him suppose himself at Rome when the curtain rises in the first act; and when it rises in the fifth let him suppose himself at Philippi. What will be the consequence of it? You will make a tragedy full of frigid declamations, which will contain some disgusting improbabilities, by crowding together some events which could never happen in twenty-four hours; and this tragedy, being destitute of action, will be opposite to the fundamental idea of theatrical representation, which ought to shew an action ($\Delta\rho\alpha\mu\alpha$) in dialogue. I will sacrifice the unities, to which one cannot submit but at the expence of action; and to be exact in some points, I will not be absurd in a thousand. Make then,' added he, 'tragedies; I will never make a tragedy. I will compose some dramatic pieces which will interest all classes of mankind as long as mankind shall exist.' Such was the idea of Shakespeare, and on this idea he must be judged. (33–5)

287. Henry Mackenzie, on Falstaff

1786

From the *Lounger*, Edinburgh, nos 68 (20 May 1786) and 69
(27 May). Mackenzie conducted this periodical from 5
February 1785 to 6 January 1787.

On Mackenzie see the head-note to No. 264, and H. W.
Drescher, *Themen und Formen des periodischen Essays im späten
18. Jahrhundert* (Frankfurt, 1971).

[The reader of poetry needs imagination.]

If in the perusal of any poet this is required, *Shakespeare* of all
poets seems to claim it the most. Of all poets Shakespeare appears
to have possessed a fancy the most prolific, an imagination the
most luxuriantly fertile. In this particular he has been frequently
compared to *Homer*, though those who have drawn the parallel
have done it, I know not why, with a sort of distrust of their
assertion. Did we not look at the Greek with that reverential awe
which his antiquity impresses, I think we might venture to affirm
that in this respect the other is more than his equal. In invention of
incident, in diversity of character, in assemblage of images we can
scarcely indeed conceive Homer to be surpassed; but in the mere
creation of fancy I can discover nothing in the *Iliad* that equals the
Tempest or the *Macbeth* of Shakespeare. The machinery of Homer is
indeed stupendous, but of that machinery the materials were
known; or though it should be allowed that he added something to
the mythology he found, yet still the language and the manners of
his deities are merely the language and the manners of men. Of
Shakespeare the machinery may be said to be produced as well as
combined by himself. Some of the beings of whom it is composed
neither tradition nor romance afforded him; and of those whom he
borrowed thence he invented the language and the manners;
language and manners peculiar to themselves, for which he could
draw no analogy from mankind. Though formed by fancy,

however, his personages are true to nature, and a reader of that pregnant imagination which I have mentioned above can immediately decide on the justness of his conceptions; as he who beholds the masterly expression of certain portraits pronounces with confidence on their likeness, though unacquainted with the persons from whom they were drawn.

But it is not only in those untried regions of magic or of witchery that the creative power of Shakespeare has exerted itself. By a very singular felicity of invention he has produced in the beaten field of ordinary life characters of such perfect originality that we look on them with no less wonder at his invention than on those preternatural beings, which 'are not of this earth;' and yet they speak a language so purely that of common society that we have but to step abroad into the world to hear every expression of which it is composed. Of this sort is the character of *Falstaff*. (269–70)

This leader of the gang which the wanton extravagance of the Prince was to cherish and protect, it was necessary to endow with qualities sufficient to make the young Henry, in his society, '*daff the world aside,/And bid it pass*.' [*1 Henry IV*, 4.1.96f.] Shakespeare therefore has endowed him with infinite wit and humour, as well as an admirable degree of sagacity and acuteness in observing the characters of men; but has joined those qualities with a grossness of mind which his youthful master could not but see, nor seeing but despise. With less talents Falstaff could not have attracted Henry; with profligacy less gross and less contemptible he would have attached him too much. Falstaff's was just 'that unyoked humour of idleness,' which the Prince could 'a while uphold,' and then cast off for ever [1.2.195ff.]. The audience to which this strange compound was to be exhibited were to be in the same predicament with the Prince, to laugh and to admire while they despised. To feel the power of his humour, the attraction of his wit, the justice of his reflections, while their contempt and their hatred attended the lowness of his manners, the grossness of his pleasures, and the unworthiness of his vice.

Falstaff is truly and literally 'ex Epicuri grege porcus,'[1] placed here within the pale of this world to fatten at his leisure, neither disturbed by feeling nor restrained by virtue. He is not, however, positively much a villain, though he never starts aside in the

---

[1] Horace, *Epistles*, 1.4.6: 'fat and sleek, a hog from Epicurus' herd'.

pursuit of interest or of pleasure when knavery comes in his way. We feel contempt, therefore, and not indignation at his crimes, which rather promotes than hinders our enjoying the ridicule of the situation, and the admirable wit with which he expresses himself in it. As a man of this world he is endowed with the most superior degree of good sense and discernment of character; his conceptions, equally acute and just, he delivers with the expression of a clear and vigorous understanding; and we see that he thinks like a wise man, even when he is not at the pains to talk wisely.

Perhaps, indeed, there is no quality more conspicuous throughout the writings of Shakespeare than that of good sense, that intuitive sagacity with which he looks on the manners, the characters, and the pursuits of mankind. The bursts of passion, the strokes of nature, the sublimity of his terrors, and the wonderful creation of his fancy are those excellencies which strike spectators the most, and are therefore most commonly enlarged on; but to an attentive peruser of his writings this acute perception and accurate discernment of ordinary character and conduct, that skill, if I may so express it, with which he delineates the plan of common life will, I think, appear no less striking, and perhaps rather more wonderful. . . . (270–1)

This power, when we read the works and consider the situation of Shakespeare, we shall allow him in a most extraordinary degree. The delineation of manners found in the Greek tragedians is excellent and just; but it consists chiefly of those general maxims which the wisdom of the schools might inculcate, which a borrowed experience might teach. That of Shakespeare marks the knowledge of intimacy with mankind. It reaches the elevation of the great, and penetrates the obscurity of the low; detects the cunning, and overtakes the bold; in short, presents that abstract of life in all its modes and indeed in every time, which every one without experience must believe, and every one with experience must know to be true.

With this sagacity and penetration into the characters and motives of mankind Shakespeare has invested Falstaff in a remarkable degree: he never utters it, however, out of character, or at a season where it might better be spared. Indeed, his good sense is rather in his thoughts than in his speech; for so we may call those soliloquies in which he generally utters it. He knew what coin was most current with those he dealt withal, and fashioned his discourse according to the disposition of his hearers; and he sometimes lends himself to the ridicule of his companions when he has a chance of getting any interest on the loan.

But we oftener laugh with than at him; for his humour is infinite, and his wit admirable. This quality, however, still partakes in him of that Epicurean grossness which I have remarked to be the ruling characteristic of his disposition. He has neither the vanity of a wit nor the singularity of a humorist, but indulges both talents, like any other natural propensity, without exertion of mind or warmth of enjoyment. . . . (271–2)

To a man of pleasure of such a constitution as Falstaff, temper and good humour were necessarily consequent. We find him therefore but once I think angry, and then not provoked beyond measure. He conducts himself with equal moderation towards others; his wit lightens, but does not burn; and he is not more inoffensive when the joker than offended when joked upon: 'I am not only witty myself, but the cause that wit is in other men.' [2 *Henry IV*, 1.2.9f.] In the evenness of his humour he bears himself thus (to use his own expression), and takes in the points of all assailants without being hurt. The language of contempt, of rebuke, or of conviction neither puts him out of liking with himself or with others. None of his passions rise beyond this controul of reason, of self-interest, or of indulgence. . . .(273)

Though I will not go so far as a paradoxical critic has done, and ascribe valour to Falstaff; yet if his cowardice is fairly examined it will be found to be not so much a weakness as a principle. In his very cowardice there is much of the sagacity I have remarked in him; he has the sense of danger but not the discomposure of fear. His presence of mind saves him from the sword of Douglas where the danger was real; but he shews no sort of dread of the sheriff's visit, when he knew the Prince's company would probably bear him out. When Bardolph runs in frightened, and tells that the sheriff with a monstrous watch is at the door, 'Out, you rogue! (answers he) play out the play; I have much to say in behalf of that Falstaff.' [1 *Henry IV*, 2.4.484f.] Falstaff's cowardice is only proportionate to the danger; and so would every wise man's be, did not other feelings make him valiant.

Such feelings it is the very characteristic of Falstaff to want. The dread of disgrace, the sense of honour, and the love of fame he neither feels, nor pretends to feel:

443

Like the fat weed
That roots itself at ease on Lethe's wharf, [*Hamlet*, 1.5.32f.]

he is contented to repose on that earthy corner of sensual indulgence in which his fate has placed him, and enjoys the pleasures of the moment without once regarding those finer objects of delight which the children of fancy and of feeling so warmly pursue.

The greatest refinement of morals, as well as of mind, is produced by the culture and exercise of the imagination, which derives, or is taught to derive its objects of pursuit, and its motives of action, not from the senses merely but from future considerations which fancy anticipates and realizes. Of this, either as the prompter or the restraint of conduct, Falstaff is utterly devoid; yet his imagination is wonderfully quick and creative in the pictures of humour and the associations of wit. But the 'pregnancy of his wit,' according to his own phrase, 'is made a tapster;' [*2 Henry IV*, 1.2.170] and his fancy, how vivid soever, still subjects itself to the grossness of those sensual conceptions which are familiar to his mind. We are astonished at that art by which Shakespeare leads the powers of genius, imagination, and wisdom in captivity to this son of earth; 'tis as if transported into the enchanted island in the *Tempest*, we saw the rebellion of *Caliban* successful, and the airy spirits of *Prospero* ministering to the brutality of his slave.

Hence perhaps may be derived great part of that infinite amusement which succeeding audiences have always found from the representation of Falstaff. We have not only the enjoyment of those combinations, and of that contrast to which philosophers have ascribed the pleasure we derive from wit in general, but we have that singular combination and contrast which the gross, the sensual, and the brutish mind of Falstaff exhibits when joined and compared with that admirable power of invention, of wit, and of humour which his conversation perpetually displays.

In the immortal work of *Cervantes* we find a character with a remarkable mixture of wisdom and absurdity, which in one page excites our highest ridicule and in the next is entitled to our highest respect. *Don Quixote*, like Falstaff, is endowed with excellent discernment, sagacity, and genius; but his good sense holds fief of his diseased imagination, of his over-ruling madness for the atchievements of knight-errantry, for heroic valour and heroic

444

love. The ridicule in the character of Don Quixote consists in raising low and vulgar incidents, through the medium of his disordered fancy, to a rank of importance, dignity, and solemnity to which in their nature they are the most opposite that can be imagined. With Falstaff it is nearly the reverse; the ridicule is produced by subjecting wisdom, honour, and other the most grave and dignified principles to the controul of grossness, buffoonery, and folly. 'Tis like the pastime of a family-masquerade, where laughter is equally excited by dressing clowns as gentlemen or gentlemen as clowns. In Falstaff the heroic attributes of our nature are made to wear the garb of meanness and absurdity. In Don Quixote the common and the servile are clothed in the dresses of the dignified and the majestic; while to heighten the ridicule *Sancho*, in the half deceived simplicity and half discerning shrewdness of his character, is every now and then employed to pull off the mask. (273–5)

. . . Shakespeare has drawn, in one of his immediately subsequent plays, a tragic character very much resembling the comic one of Falstaff, I mean that of *Richard III*. Both are men of the world, both possess the sagacity and understanding which is fitted for its purposes, both despise those refined feelings, those motives of delicacy, those restraints of virtue which might obstruct the course they have marked out for themselves. The hypocrisy of both costs them nothing, and they never feel that detection of it to themselves which rankles in the conscience of less determined hypocrites. Both use the weaknesses of others as skilful players at a game do the ignorance of their opponents; they enjoy the advantage not only without self-reproach but with the pride of superiority. Richard indeed aspires to the Crown of England, because Richard is wicked and ambitious: Falstaff is contented with a thousand pounds of Justice Shallow's, because he is only luxurious and dissipated. Richard courts Lady Anne and the Princess Elisabeth for his purposes: Falstaff makes love to Mrs Ford and Mrs Page for his. Richard is witty like Falstaff, and talks of his own figure with the same sarcastic indifference. Indeed, so much does Richard, in the higher walk of villany, resemble Falstaff in the lower region of roguery and dissipation, that it were not difficult to shew in the dialogue of the two characters, however dissimilar in situation, many passages and expressions in a style of remarkable resemblance.

445

Of feeling, and even of passion, both characters are very little susceptible; as Falstaff is the knave and the sensualist, so Richard is the villain of principle. Shakespeare has drawn one of passion in the person of *Macbeth*. Macbeth produces horror, fear, and sometimes pity; Richard, detestation and abhorrence only. The first he has led amidst the gloom of sublimity, has shown agitated by various and wavering emotions. He is sometimes more sanguinary than Richard, because he is not insensible of the weakness or the passion of revenge; whereas the cruelty of Richard is only proportionate to the object of his ambition, as the cowardice of Falstaff is proportionate to the object of his fear: but the bloody and revengeful Macbeth is yet susceptible of compassion and subject to remorse. In contemplating Macbeth we often regret the perversion of his nature; and even when the justice of Heaven overtakes him, we almost forget our hatred at his enormities in our pity for his misfortunes. Richard, Shakespeare has placed amidst the tangled paths of party and ambitions, has represented cunning and fierce from his birth, untouched by the sense of humanity, hardly subject to remorse and never to contrition; and his fall produces that unmixed and perfect satisfaction which we feel at the death of some savage beast that had desolated the country from instinctive fierceness and natural malignity.

The weird sisters, the gigantic deities of northern mythology, are fit agents to form Macbeth. Richard is the production of those worldly and creeping demons who slide upon the earth their instruments of mischief to embroil and plague mankind. Falstaff is the work of *Circe* and her swinish associates, who, in some favoured hour of revelry and riot, moulded this compound of gross debauchery, acute discernment, admirable invention, and nimble wit, and sent him for a consort to England's madcap Prince; to stamp currency on idleness and vice, and to wave the flag of folly and dissipation over the seats of gravity, of wisdom, and virtue. (275–6)

288. Richard Cumberland, essays on Shakespeare

1786

From *The Observer: being a Collection of Moral, Literary and Familiar Essays* (5 vols, 1785–91). Although numbered and dated like a normal serial, this periodical was issued in volume form, the five-volume edition being dated 1786 (vols i–iii), 1788 (vol. iv), and 1791 (vol. v).

Apart from smaller discussions, five whole essays are devoted to Shakespeare—Nos 55–8 on Macbeth and Richard III (which owes much to Whately's essay) and No. 86: 'Remarks upon the characters of Falstaff and his group'. No. 109 includes an extended comparison between the scenes of witchcraft in *Macbeth* and those in Ben Jonson's *Masque of the Queens*. On Cumberland see the head-note to Vol. 5, No. 232, and R. Dircks, *Richard Cumberland* (Boston, 1976).

[From No. 55, 'A delineation of Shakespeare's characters of Macbeth and Richard']

Let us contemplate them in the three following periods; viz. The premeditation of their crime; the perpetration of it; and the catastrophe of their death. . . . (II, 225–6)

[Quotes *Macbeth*, 1.3.130ff.: 'This supernatural soliciting/Cannot be ill; cannot be good.'] A soliloquy then ensues, in which the poet judiciously opens enough of his character to shew the spectator that these præternatural agents are not superfluously set to work upon a disposition prone to evil, but one that will have to combat many compunctious struggles before it can be brought to yield even to oracular influence. This alone would demonstrate (if we needed demonstration) that Shakespeare, without resorting to the antients, had the judgment of ages as it were instinctively. From this instant we are apprised

447

that Macbeth meditates an attack upon our pity as well as upon our horror, when he puts the following question to his conscience—

> *Why do I yield to that suggestion,*
> *Whose horrid image doth unfix my hair,*
> *And make my seated heart knock at my ribs,*
> *Against the use of nature?*   [1.3.134ff.]

Now let us turn to R*ichard*, in whose cruel heart no such remorse finds place; he needs no tempter. There is here no *dignus vindice nodus,* nor indeed any *knot* at all, for he is already practised in murder. Ambition is his ruling passion, and a crown is in view, and he tells you at his very first entrance on the scene '*I am determined to be a villain.*' [1.1.30]

We are now presented with a character full formed and compleat for all the savage purposes of the drama:—

> *Impiger, iracundus, inexorabilis, acer.*[1]   (II, 228–9)

It is manifest therefore that there is an essential difference in the development of these characters, and that in favour of Macbeth. In his soul cruelty seems to dawn, it breaks out with faint glimmerings, like a winter-morning, and gathers strength by slow degrees. In Richard it flames forth at once, mounting like the sun between the tropics, and enters boldly on its career without a herald. As the character of Macbeth has a moral advantage in this distinction, so has the drama of that name a much more interesting and affecting cast. The struggles of a soul naturally virtuous whilst it holds the guilty impulse of ambition at bay, affords the noblest theme for the drama, and puts the creative fancy of our poet upon a resource in which he has been rivalled only by the great father of tragedy Æschylus. . . . [Cumberland now compares Aeschylus and Shakespeare, concluding that Aeschylus] in his imaginary beings also will be found a respectable, though not an equal, rival of our poet. But in the variety of character, in all the nicer touches of nature, in all the extravagancies of caprice and humour, from the boldest feature down to the minutest foible, Shakespeare stands alone. Such persons as he delineates never came into the contemplation of Æschylus as a poet; his tragedy has no dealing with them. The simplicity of the Greek fable, and the great portion of the drama filled up by the chorus, allow of little variety of

---

[1] Horace, *Ars Poetica*, 120: 'impatient, passionate, ruthless, fierce'.

character, and the most which can be said of Æschylus in this particular is that he never offends against nature or propriety, whether his cast is in the terrible or pathetic, the elevated or the simple. His versification with the intermixture of lyric composition is more various than that of Shakespeare; both are lofty and sublime in the extreme, abundantly metaphorical and sometimes extravagant. . . . Both were subject to be hurried on by an uncontroulable impulse, nor could nature alone suffice for either. Æschylus had an apt creation of imaginary beings at command—

He could call spirits from the vasty deep,   [*1 Henry IV*, 3.1.52]

and they *would come*—Shakespeare, having no such creation in resource, boldly made one of his own. If Æschylus therefore was invincible, he owed it to his armour, and that, like the armour of Æneas, was the work of the gods; but the unassisted invention of Shakespeare seized all and more than superstition supplied to Æschylus. (II, 230–4)

[No. 56]
We are now to attend *Macbeth* to the perpetration of the murder which puts him in possession of the crown of Scotland; and this introduces a new personage on the scene, his accomplice and wife. She thus developes her own character—[quotes 'Come all you spirits', 1.5.40ff.]. Terrible invocation! Tragedy can speak no stronger language, nor could any genius less than Shakespeare's support a character of so lofty a pitch, so sublimely terrible at the very opening.

The part which Lady Macbeth fills in the drama has a relative as well as positive importance, and serves to place the repugnance of Macbeth in the strongest point of view. She is in fact the auxiliary of the witches, and the natural influence which so high and predominant a spirit asserts over the tamer qualities of her husband makes those witches but secondary agents for bringing about the main action of the drama. This is well worth a remark; for if they, which are only artificial and fantastic instruments, had been made the sole or even principal movers of the great incident of the murder, nature would have been excluded from her share in the drama, and Macbeth would have become the mere machine of an uncontroulable necessity, and his character, being robbed of its free agency, would have left no moral behind. I must take leave therefore to anticipate a remark which I shall hereafter repeat, that when Lady Macbeth is urging her Lord to the murder not a word is dropt by either of the witches or their predictions. It is in these instances of his conduct that Shakespeare is so wonderful a study for the dramatic poet. (II, 235–6)

His reflections upon this interview and the dreadful subject of it are soon after given in soliloquy, in which the poet has mixt the most touching strokes of compunction with his meditations. He reasons against the villany of the act, and honour jointly with nature assails him with an argument of double force—[quotes 'He's here in double trust', 1.7.12ff.]. This appeal to nature, hospitality and allegiance was not without its impression; he again meets his lady, and immediately declares—'*We will proceed no further in this business.*' [1.7.22] This draws, a retort upon him in which his tergiversation and cowardice are satirized with so keen an edge, and interrogatory reproaches are pressed so fast upon him, that catching hold in his retreat of one small but precious fragment in the wreck of innocence and honour, he demands a truce from her attack, and with the spirit of a combatant who has not yet yielded up his weapons, cries out—'*Pr'ythee, peace!*' [1.7.45] The words are no expletives; they do not fill up a sentence, but they form one. They stand in a most important pass; they defend the breach her ambition has made in his heart; a breach in the very citadel of humanity; they mark the last dignified struggle of virtue. . . . (II, 238–9)

[Quotes 'I dare do all that may become a man,/Who dares do more is none': 1.7.46f.] How must every feeling spectator lament that a man should fall from virtue with such an appeal upon his lips!

A man is not a coward because he fears to be unjust, is the sentiment of an old dramatic poet.

Macbeth's principle is honour; cruelty is natural to his wife; ambition is common to both. One passion favourable to her purpose has taken place in his heart; another still hangs about it, which being adverse to her plot is first to be expelled before she can instil her cruelty into his nature. The sentiment above quoted had been firmly delivered, and was ushered in with an apostrophe suitable to its importance. She feels its weight; she perceives it is not to be turned aside with contempt or laughed down by ridicule, as she had already done where weaker scruples had stood in the way. But, taking sophistry in aid, by a ready turn of argument she gives him credit for his sentiment, erects a more glittering though fallacious logic upon it, and by admitting his objection cunningly confutes it—

> *What beast was't then,*
> *That made you break this enterprize to me?*
> *When you durst do it, then you were a man,*
> *And to be more than what you were, you wou'd*
> *Be so much more than man.* [1.7.47ff.]

Having thus parried his objection by a sophistry calculated to blind his reason and enflame his ambition, she breaks forth into such a vaunting display of hardened intrepidity as presents one of the most terrific pictures that was ever imagined—[quotes 'I have given suck': 54ff.].

This is a note of horror, screwed to a pitch that bursts the very sinews of nature; she no longer combats with human weapon, but seizing the flash of the lightning extinguishes her opponent with the stroke. Here the controversy must end, for he must either adopt her spirit or take her life. He sinks under the attack, and offering nothing in delay of execution but a feeble hesitation, founded in fear—*If we should fail* [59]—he concludes with an assumed ferocity, caught from her and not springing from himself—

> *I am settled, and bend up*
> *Each corporal agent to this terrible feat.* [79f.]

The strong and sublime strokes of a master impressed upon this scene make it a model of dramatic composition, and I must in this place remind the reader of the observation I have before hinted at, that no reference whatever is had to the auguries of the witches. It would be injustice to suppose that this was other than a purposed omission by the poet; a weaker genius would have resorted back to these instruments. Shakespeare had used and laid them aside for a time; he had a stronger engine at work, and he could proudly exclaim—'*We defy auguries!*'—Nature was sufficient for that work, and to shew the mastery he had over nature he took his human agent from the weaker sex. (II, 239–42)

[No. 57]
Richard perpetrates several murders, but as the poet has not marked them with any distinguishing circumstances, they need not

451

be enumerated on this occasion. Some of these he commits in his passage to power, others after he has seated himself on the throne. Ferociousness and hypocrisy are the prevailing features of his character, and as he has no one honourable or human principle to combat, there is no opening for the poet to develope those secret workings of conscience which he has so naturally done in the case of Macbeth. (II, 245–6)

In these two stages of our comparison Macbeth appears with far more dramatic effect than Richard, whose first scenes present us with little else than traits of perfidiousness, one striking incident of successful hypocrisy practised on the Lady Anne, and an open unreserved display of remorseless cruelty. (II, 247)

[In Act III Macbeth has 'touched the goal of his ambition': quotes 'Thou hast it now. . .': 3.1.1ff.]

The auguries of the witches, to which no reference had been made in the heat of the main action, are now called to mind with many circumstances of galling aggravation, not only as to the prophecy which gave the crown to the posterity of Banquo, but also of his own safety from the gallant and noble nature of that general—

> Our fears in Banquo
> Stick deep, and in his royalty of nature
> Reigns that, which wou'd be fear'd. [3.1.48ff.]

Assassins are provided to murder Banquo and his son, but this is not decided upon without much previous meditation, and he seems prompted to the act more by desperation and dread than by any settled resolution or natural cruelty. He convenes the assassins, and in a conference of some length works round to his point by insinuations calculated to persuade them to dispatch Banquo for injuries done to them, rather than from motives which respect himself; in which scene we discover a remarkable preservation of character in Macbeth, who by this artifice strives to blind his own conscience and throw the guilt upon theirs. In this as in the former action there is nothing kingly in his cruelty. In one he acted under the controuling spirit of his wife, here he plays the sycophant with hired assassins, and confesses himself under awe of the superior genius of Banquo—

> ———Under him
> My genius is rebuk'd, as it is said
> Antony's was by Cæsar. [3.1.54–6]

452   (II, 248–9)

In a tragedy so replete with murder, and in the display of a character so tortured by *the scorpions of the mind* as this of Macbeth, it is naturally to be expected that a genius like Shakespeare's will call in the dead for their share in the horror of the scene. This he has done in two several ways; first, by the apparition of Banquo, which is invisible to all but Macbeth; secondly, by the spells and incantations of the witches, who raise spirits which in certain ænigmatical predictions shadow out his fate; and these are followed by a train of unborn revelations, drawn by the power of magic from the womb of futurity before their time.

It appears that Lady Macbeth was not a party in the assassination of Banquo, and the ghost, though twice visible to the murderer, is not seen by her. This is another incident highly worthy a particular remark; for by keeping her free from any participation in the horror of the sight the poet is enabled to make a scene aside between Macbeth and her, which contains some of the finest speakings in the play. The ghost in Hamlet, and the ghost of Darius in Æschylus are introduced by preparation and prelude, this of Banquo is an object of surprize as well as terror, and there is scarce an incident to be named of more striking and dramatic effect. It is one amongst various proofs that must convince every man who looks critically into Shakespeare, that he was as great a master in art as in nature. How it strikes me in this point of view I shall take the liberty of explaining more at length.

The murder of Duncan is the main incident of this tragedy; that of Banquo is subordinate. Duncan's blood was not only the first so shed by Macbeth, but the dignity of the person murdered, and the aggravating circumstances attending it, constitute a crime of the very first magnitude. For these reasons it might be expected that the spectre most likely to haunt his imagination, would be that of Duncan; and the rather because his terror and compunction were so much more strongly excited by this first murder, perpetrated with his own hands, than by the subsequent one of Banquo, palliated by evasion and committed to others. But when we recollect that Lady Macbeth was not only his accomplice but in fact the first mover in the murder of the king, we see good reason why Duncan's ghost could not be called up unless she, who so deeply partook of the guilt, had also shared in the horror of the appearance; and as visitations of a peculiar sort were reserved for her in a later period of the drama, it was a point of consummate art and judgment to exclude her from the affair of Banquo's murder, and make the more susceptible conscience of Macbeth figure this apparition in his mind's eye without any other witness to the vision.

I persuade myself these will appear very natural reasons why the poet did not raise the ghost of the king in preference, though it is reasonable to think it would have been a much more noble incident in his hands than this of Banquo. It now remains to examine whether this is more fully justified by the peculiar situation reserved for Lady Macbeth, to which I have before adverted.

The intrepidity of her character is so marked that we may well suppose no waking terrors could shake it, and in this light it must be acknowledged a very natural expedient to make her vent the agonies of her conscience in sleep. Dreams have been a dramatic expedient ever since there has been a drama; Æschylus recites the dream of Clytemnestra immediately before her son Orestes kills her. . . . This which is done by Æschylus has been done by hundreds after him. But to introduce upon the scene the very person walking in sleep, and giving vent to the horrid fancies that haunt her dream, in broken speeches expressive of her guilt, uttered before witnesses, and accompanied with that natural and expressive action of washing the blood from her defiled hands, was reserved for the original and bold genius of Shakespeare only. It is an incident so full of tragic horror, so daring and at the same time so truly characteristic that it stands out as a prominent feature in the most sublime drama in the world, and fully compensates for any sacrifices the poet might have made in the previous arrangement of his incidents. (II, 251–5)

[From No. 58]
Macbeth now approaches towards his catastrophe. The heir of the crown is in arms, and he must defend valiantly what he has usurped villainously. His natural valour does not suffice for this trial; he resorts to the witches; he conjures them to give answer to what he shall ask, and he again runs into all those pleonasms of speech which I before remarked. The predictions he extorts from the apparitions are so couched as to seem favourable to him, at the same time that they correspond with events which afterwards prove fatal. . . . (II, 255)

Let us now approach the tent of *Richard*. It is matter of

admiration to observe how many incidents the poet has collected in a small compass to set the military character of his chief personage in a brilliant point of view. A succession of scouts and messengers report a variety of intelligence, all which, though generally of the most alarming nature, he meets not only with his natural gallantry but sometimes with pleasantry and a certain archness and repartee, which is peculiar to him throughout the drama.

It is not only a curious but delightful task to examine by what subtle and almost imperceptible touches Shakespeare contrives to set such marks upon his characters as give them the most living likenesses that can be conceived. In this, above all other poets that ever existed, he is a study and a model of perfection. The great distinguishing passions every poet may describe; but Shakespeare gives you their humours, their minutest foibles, those little starts and caprices which nothing but the most intimate familiarity brings to light. Other authors write characters like historians; he like the bosom friend of the person he describes. (II, 259–60)

[Quotes 4.4.440–9: Richard's sending of Catesby to the Duke of Norfolk without any instructions: corrected, Richard replies, 'O true, good Catesby.'] I am persuaded I need not point out to the reader's sensibility the fine turn in this expression, *Good Catesby!* How can we be surprized if such a poet makes us in love even with his villains? (II, 261)

Stanley's whole scene ought to be investigated, for it is full of beauties, but I confess myself exhausted with the task, and language does not suffice to furnish fresh terms of admiration which a closer scrutiny would call forth. (II, 262)

It will be sufficient to observe that in the catastrophe of Richard nothing can be more glowing than the scene, nothing more brilliant than the conduct of the chief character. He exhibits the character of a perfect general, in whom however ardent courage seems the ruling feature; he performs every part of his office with minute attention, he enquires if certain alterations are made in his armour, and even orders what particular horse he intends to charge with. He is gay with his chief officers, and even gracious to some he confides in. His gallantry is of so dazzling a quality that we begin to feel the pride of Englishmen and, overlooking his crimes, glory in our courageous king. Richmond is one of those civil, conscientious gentlemen who are not very apt to captivate a spectator, and

Richard, loaded as he is with enormities, rises in the comparison, and I suspect carries the good wishes of many of his audience into action, and dies with their regret.

As soon as he retires to his tent the poet begins to put in motion his great moral machinery of the ghosts. Trifles are not made for Shakespeare; difficulties that would have plunged the spirit of any other poet, and turned his scenery into inevitable ridicule, are nothing in his way; he brings forward a long string of ghosts and puts a speech into each of their mouths without any fear of consequences. Richard starts from his couch, and before he has shaken off the terrors of his dream cries out—

> *Give me another horse!—Bind up my wounds!—*
> *Have mercy, Jesu!—Soft, I did but dream—*
> *O coward conscience—&c.*
> [5.3.177ff.]

But I may conclude my subject; every reader can go on with the soliloquy, and no words of mine can be wanted to excite their admiration. (II, 263–5)

[From No. 86, 'Remarks upon the characters of Falstaff and his group']
When it had entered into the mind of Shakespeare to form an historical play upon certain events in the reign of Henry the fourth of England, the character of the Prince of Wales recommended itself to his fancy as likely to supply him with a fund of dramatic incidents. For what could invention have more happily suggested than this character, which history presented ready to his hands? a riotous disorderly young libértine, in whose nature lay hidden those seeds of heroism and ambition which were to burst forth at once to the astonishment of the world and to atchieve the conquest of France. . . .

With these materials ready for creation the great artist sate down to his work. . . . His first concern was to give a chief or captain to this gang of rioters; this would naturally be the first outline he drew. To fill up the drawing of this personage he conceived a voluptuary, in whose figure and character there should be an assemblage of comic qualities. In his person he should be bloated and blown up to the size of a *Silenus*, lazy, luxurious, in sensuality a satyr, in intemperance a bacchanalian. As he was to stand in the post of a ringleader amongst thieves and cutpurses he made him a notorious liar, a swaggering coward, vain-glorious, arbitrary, knavish, crafty, voracious of plunder, lavish of his gains, without credit, honour or honesty, and in debt to every body about him. As he was to be the chief seducer and misleader of the heir apparent of the crown, it was incumbent on the poet to qualify him for that part in such a manner as should give probability and even a plea to the temptation. This was only to be done by the strongest touches and the highest colourings of a master; by hitting off a humour of so happy, so facetious and so alluring a cast as should tempt even royalty to forget itself, and virtue to turn reveller in his company. His lies, his vanity and his cowardice, too gross to deceive, were to be so ingenious as to give delight; his cunning evasions, his witty resources, his mock solemnity, his vapouring self-consequence, were to furnish a continual feast of laughter to his royal companion. He was not only to be witty himself, but the cause of wit in other people; a whetstone for raillery; a buffoon, whose very person was a jest. Compounded of these humours, Shakespeare produced the character of *Sir John Falstaff*; a character which neither ancient nor modern comedy has ever equalled, which was so much the favourite of its author as to be introduced in three several plays, and which is likely to be the idol of the English stage as long as it shall speak the language of Shakespeare. (III, 242–4)

The humour of Falstaff opens into full display upon his very first introduction with the prince. The incident of the robbery on the highway, the scene in Eastcheap in consequence of that ridiculous encounter, and the whole of his conduct during the action with Percy, are so exquisitely pleasant that upon the renovation of his dramatic life in the second part of *Henry the fourth* I question if the humour does not in part evaporate by continuation. At least I am persuaded that it flattens a little in the outset, and though his wit may not flow less copiously yet it comes with more labour and is farther fetcht. The poet seems to have been sensible how difficult it was to preserve the vein as rich as at first, and has therefore strengthened his comic plot in the second play with several new recruits who may take a share with Falstaff, to whom he no longer entrusts the whole burthen of the humour. In the front of these auxiliaries stands Pistol, a character so new, whimsical and extravagant that if it were not for a commentator now living, whose very extraordinary researches amongst our old authors have supplied us with passages to illuminate the strange rhapsodies which Shakespeare has put into his mouth, I should for one have thought Antient Pistol as wild and imaginary a being as Caliban. But I now perceive, by the help of these discoveries, that the character is *made up in great part of absurd and fustian passages from many plays, in which Shakespeare* was versed and perhaps *had been a performer*. Pistol's dialogue is a tissue of old tags of bombast, like the middle comedy of the Greeks, which dealt in parody. I abate of my astonishment at the invention and originality of the poet, but it does not lessen my respect for his ingenuity. Shakespeare founded his bully in parody, Jonson copied his from nature, and the palm seems due to Bobadil upon a comparison with Pistol. . . . (III, 245–6)

Shallow and Silence are two very strong auxiliaries to this second part of Falstaff's humours, and though they do not absolutely belong to his family they are nevertheless near of kin, and derivatives from his stock. Surely two pleasanter fellows never trode the stage; they not only contrast and play upon each other, but Silence sober and Silence tipsy make the most comical reverse in nature; never was drunkenness so well introduced or so happily employed in any drama. (III, 247)

Dame Quickly also in this second part resumes her rôle with great comic spirit but with some variation of character, for the purpose of introducing a new member into the troop in the person of Doll Tearsheet, the common trull of the times. Though this part is very strongly coloured, and though the scene with her and Falstaff is of a loose as well as ludicrous nature, yet if we compare Shakespeare's conduct of this incident with that of the dramatic writers of his time, and even since his time, we must confess he has managed it with more than common care, and exhibited his comic hero in a very ridiculous light without any of those gross indecencies which the poets of his age indulged themselves in without restraint.

The humour of the Prince of Wales is not so free and unconstrained as in the first part. Though he still demeans himself in the course of his revels yet it is with frequent marks of repugnance and self-consideration, as becomes the conqueror of Percy, and we see his character approaching fast towards a thorough reformation. But though we are thus prepared for the change that is to happen when this young hero throws off the reveller and assumes the king, yet we are not fortified against the weakness of pity when the disappointment and banishment of Falstaff takes place, and the poet executes justice upon his inimitable delinquent with all the rigour of an unrelenting moralist. The reader or spectator who has accompanied Falstaff through his dramatic story is in debt to him for so many pleasant moments that all his failings, which should have raised contempt, have only provoked laughter, and he begins to think they are not natural to his character but assumed for his amusement. With these impressions we see him delivered over to mortification and disgrace, and bewail his punishment with a sensibility that is only due to the sufferings of the virtuous.

As it is impossible to ascertain the limits of Shakespeare's genius, I will not presume to say he could not have supported his humour, had he chosen to have prolonged his existence thro' the succeeding drama of *Henry the Fifth*. We may conclude that no ready expedient presented itself to his fancy, and he was not apt to spend much pains in searching for such. He therefore put him to death, by which he fairly placed him out of the reach of his contemporaries, and got rid of the trouble and difficulty of keeping him up to his original pitch, if he had attempted to carry him through a third drama, after he had removed the Prince of Wales out of his company and seated him on the throne. I cannot doubt but there were resources in Shakespeare's genius, and a latitude of humour in the character of Falstaff, which might have furnished scenes of admirable comedy by exhibiting him in his disgrace, and both Shallow and Silence would have been accessaries to his pleasantry. Even the field of Agincourt, and the distress of the king's army before the action, had the poet thought proper to have produced Falstaff on the scene, might have been as fruitful in comic incidents as the battle of Shrewsbury. This we can readily believe from the humours of Fluellen and Pistol which he has woven into his drama; the former of whom is made to remind us of Falstaff in his dialogue with Captain Gower, when he tells him that—*As Alexander is kill his friend Clytus, being in his ales and his cups, so also Harry Monmouth, being in his right wits and his goot judgement, is turn away the fat Knight with the great pelly-doublet: He was full of jests and gypes and knaveries, and mocks; I am forget his name.—Sir John Falstaff.—That is he.* [*Henry V*, 4.7.44ff.]—This passage has ever given me a pleasing sensation, as it marks a regret in the poet to part with a favourite character, and is a tender farewel to his memory. It is also with particular propriety that these words are put into the mouth of Fluellen, who stands here as his substitute, and whose humour, as well as that of Nym, may be said to have arisen out of the ashes of Falstaff. (III, 247–50)

289. Andrew Becket, notes on Shakespeare's text

1787

From *A Concordance to Shakespeare : Suited to all the Editions : In which the distinguished and parallel Passages in the Plays of that justly admired Writer, are methodically arranged. To which are added, Three Hundred Notes and Illustrations, entirely New* (1787). Published anonymously.

The title of this compilation is misleading, since it is not a listing of all the words used by Shakespeare so much as an alphabetical collection of quotations on selected topics: 'Act', 'Action', 'Conscience', and so on, an *axiomatical or moral concordance'* as the reviewer in the *Monthly Review* put it (lxxviii (1788), p. 220). The author of that anonymous review was Andrew Becket, himself the author of the book he was reviewing. When Ralph Griffiths, editor of the journal, subsequently discovered this fact, he wrote in his copy (now in the Bodleian) '*Hic Niger est'*.[1] Becket (1749–1843), son of a bookseller, was a close associate with Griffiths in publishing the *Monthly* until they quarrelled in 1790. His *Dramatic and Prose Miscellanies* (2 vols) were published in 1838. The first proper concordance to Shakespeare was published by Samuel Ayscough as an appendix to the second edition of Stockdale's Shakespeare: *An Index to the Remarkable Passages and Words made*

[1] Horace, *Satires*, 1.4.85: 'that man is black of heart'.

*use of by Shakespeare; Calculated to point out the different meanings
to which the words are applied* (1790), a 700-page (Folio) index.

---

[1] [On *Hamlet*, 3.4.42ff.: 'takes off the rose/From the fair
forehead of an innocent love'. Warburton said this alluded to 'the
custom of wearing roses on the side of the face'; Steevens objected
that they must have been worn on the forehead.]
It is not a little extraordinary that the commentators should be for
considering literally expressions that are purely metaphorical.
Rose is beauty, and blister is deformity. The meaning plainly is,
renders love, which is naturally beautiful, ugly and deformed. (2)

[2] [On *Richard II*, 2.1.64: 'With inky blots, and rotten parchment
bonds'. 'I suspect that our author wrote, *inky bolts*. How can blots
bind in any thing? and do not *bolts* correspond better with
bonds?' STEEVENS.]
'Inky blots:' *i. e.* the *wording* of the rotten parchments. What are
inky bolts? or what have inky bolts to do with parchment bonds?
(103)

[3] [On *Antony and Cleopatra*, 3.10.10: 'Yon ribaudred nag of
Egypt . . . ']
Ribaudred is, I am persuaded, the true reading. *Ribaude*, in the
French language, is a *whore*, a *strumpet*. I would likewise read *hag*.
Ribaudred hag, i. e. a woman who has been the property of several
men; as was the case with Cleopatra. Had our author written
strumpeted hag, he would, I presume, have been generally understood: *ribaudred hag* is exactly the same. The affectation of
employing French words was extremely common in Shakespeare's
time. (131)

[4] [On *Henry V*, *Prol.* 1: 'O for a muse of fire']
'A muse of fire that would ascend the brightest heaven of
invention'—means, I apprehend, *vigour of fancy,—such as is capable of
bold and daring flights;* without any allusion to the peripatetic system,
or to the aspiring nature of fire.[1] (225)

[5] [On *Coriolanus*, 2.2.95ff.: 'In that day's feats,/When he might
act the woman in the scene,/He prov'd best man i 'the field'. 'It has

---

[1] These were the interpretations of Warburton and Johnson.

been more than once mentioned that the parts of women were, in Shakespeare's time, represented by the most smooth faced young men to be found among the players.' STEEVENS.]

This does not appear to me to have any allusion to plays or players. 'When he might act the woman in the scene,' seems to mean that from his extreme youth, little was expected from him in the field: yet at the time when he was only sixteen years of age, and when he would not have been censured had he shewn the fear and timidity of a woman, he proved himself an hero. Beside, it is Cominius who speaks, and not Shakespeare. (456)

290. George Steevens, on Richard III and Macbeth

1787

From the *European Magazine*, vi (April 1787), pp. 227–9. Steevens acknowledged the authorship of this essay when reprinting it in his 1793 edition (VII, 584–7), making a few additional points: this is the copy-text used here.

The late Mr. Whately's *Remarks on some of the Characters of Shakespeare* have shown with the utmost clearness of distinction and felicity of arrangement, that what in Richard III is fortitude, in Macbeth is no more than resolution. But this judicious critic having imputed the cause of Macbeth's inferiority in courage to his natural disposition, induces me to dissent in one particular from an Essay which otherwise is too comprehensive to need a supplement, and too rational to admit of confutation.

Throughout such parts of this drama as afford opportunities for a display of personal bravery, Macbeth sometimes *screws his courage to the sticking place* but never rises into constitutional heroism. Instead of meditating some decisive stroke on the enemy, his restless and self-accusing mind discharges itself in splenetic effusions and personal invectives on the attendants about his person. His genuine intrepidity had forsaken him when he ceased to be a virtuous character. He would not deceive himself into confidence, and depends on forced alacrity, and artificial valour, to extricate him from his present difficulties. Despondency too deep to be rooted out, and fury too irregular to be successful, have by turns possession of his mind. Though he has been assured of what he certainly credited, that *none of woman born shall hurt him*, he has twice given us reason to suppose he would have *fled*, but that he *cannot*, being *tied to the stake* and compelled to *fight the course*. Suicide also has once entered into his thoughts; though this idea, in a paroxysm of noisy rage, is suppressed. Yet here it must be acknowledged that his apprehensions had betrayed him into a strange inconsistency of belief. As he persisted in supposing he could be destroyed by *none of woman born*, by what means did he think to destroy himself? for he was produced in the common way of nature, and fell not within the description of the only object that could end the being of Macbeth. In short, his efforts are no longer those of courage but of despair excited by self-conviction, infuriated by the menaces of an injured father, and confirmed by a presentiment of inevitable defeat. Thus situated, he very naturally prefers a manly and violent to a shameful and lingering termination of life.

One of Shakespeare's favourite morals is that criminality reduces the brave and pusillanimous to a level. *Every puny whipster gets my sword,* exclaims Othello, *for why should honour outlive honesty?* [5.2.244f.] *Where I could not be honest,* says Albany, *I was never valiant.* [*King Lear*, 5.1.23f.] Iachimo imputes his *want of manhood* to the *heaviness and guilt within his bosom* [*Cymbeline*, 5.2.1f.]; Hamlet asserts that *conscience does make cowards of us all* [3.1.82]; and Imogen tells Pisanio *he may be valiant in a better cause, but now he seems a coward* [*Cymbeline*, 3.4.72f.]. The late Doctor Johnson, than whom no man was better acquainted with general nature, in his *Irene* has also observed of a once faithful Bassa,

How guilt, when harbour'd in the conscious breast,
Intimidates the brave, degrades the great!

Who then can suppose that Shakespeare would have exhibited his Macbeth with encreasing guilt but undiminished bravery? or wonder that our hero,

Whose pester'd senses do recoil and start,
When all that is within him does condemn
Itself for being there,   [5.2.23ff.]

should have lost the magnanimity he displayed in a righteous
cause, against Macdonwald and the Thane of Cawdor? Of this
circumstance, indeed, the murderer of Duncan was soon aware, as
appears from his asking himself the dreadful question—

How is't with me, when every noise *appals* me?   [2.2.55]

Between the courage of Richard and Macbeth, however, no
comparison in favour of the latter can be supported. Richard was
so thoroughly designed for a daring, impious, and obdurate
character that even his birth was attended by prodigies, and his
person armed with ability to do the earliest mischief of which
infancy is capable. Macbeth, on the contrary, till deceived by the
illusions of witchcraft, and depraved by the suggestions of his
wife, was a religious, temperate and blameless character. The vices
of the one were originally woven into his heart; those of the
other, were only applied to the surface of his disposition. They can
scarce be said to have penetrated quite into its substance, for while
there was shame there might have been reformation.

The precautions of Richard concerning the armour he was to
wear in the next day's battle, his preparations for the onset, and his
orders after it is begun, are equally characteristic of a calm and
intrepid soldier, who possesses the *wisdom* that appeared so
formidable to Macbeth and *guided* Banquo's *valour to act in safety*
[3.1.52f.]. But Macbeth appears in confusion from the moment his
castle is invested, issues no distinct or material directions,
prematurely calls for his armour, as irresolutely throws it off again,
and is more intent on self-crimination than the repulse of the
besiegers, or the disposition of the troops who are to defend his
fortress. But it is useless to dwell on particulars so much more
exactly enumerated by Mr. Whately.

The truth is that the mind of Richard, unimpregnated by
original morality, and uninfluenced by the laws of Heaven, is
harrassed by no subsequent remorse. *Repente fuit turpissimus.*[1] Even
the depression he feels from preternatural objects is speedily taken
off. In spite of ominous visions he sallies forth, and seeks his

---

[1] Juvenal, *Satires*, 2.83: 'No one reaches the depths of turpitude all at once'.

competitor *in the throat of death*. Macbeth, though he had long abandoned the practice of goodness, had not so far forgot its accustomed influence, but that a virtuous adversary whom he had injured is as painful to his sight as the spectre in a former scene, and equally blasts the resolution he was willing to think he had still possessed. His conscience (as Hamlet says of the poison) *overcrows his spirit*, and all his *enterprizes are sicklied over by the pale cast of thought*. The curse that attends on him is, *virtutem videre, et intabescere relicta*.[1] Had Richard once been a feeling and conscientious character, when his end drew nigh, he might also have betrayed evidences of timidity—'there sadly summing what he had, and lost;' and if Macbeth originally had been a hardened villain no terrors might have obtruded themselves on his close of life. *Qualis ab incepto processerat*.[2] In short, Macbeth is timid in spite of all his boasting, as long as he thinks timidity can afford resources; nor does he exhibit a specimen of determined intrepidity till the completion of the prophecy, and the challenge of Macduff, have taught him that life is no longer tenable. Five counterfeit Richmonds are slain by Richard, who, before his fall, has *enacted wonders* beyond the common ability of man. The prowess of Macbeth is confined to the single conquest of Siward, a novice in the art of war. Neither are the truly brave ever disgraced by unnecessary deeds of cruelty. The victims of Richard therefore are merely such as obstructed his progress to the crown, or betrayed the confidence he had reposed in their assurances of fidelity. Macbeth, with a savage wantonness that would have dishonoured a Scythian female, cuts off a whole defenceless family, though the father of it was the only reasonable object of his fear.—Can it be a question then which of these two personages would manifest the most determined valour in the field? Shall we hesitate to bestow the palm of courage on the steady unrepenting Yorkist, in whose bosom ideas of hereditary greatness, and confidence resulting from success, had fed the flame of glory, and who dies in combat for a crown which had been the early object of his ambition? and shall we allot the same wreath to the wavering self-convicted Thane, who, educated without hope of royalty, had been suggested into

[1] Persius, 3.38: 'that [cruel tyrants] may look on Virtue, and pine away because they have lost her!'
[2] Horace, *Ars Poetica*, 127: '[a character] kept to the end even as it came forth at the first'.

greatness and yet, at last, would forego it all to secure himself by flight, but that flight is become an impossibility?

To conclude, a picture of conscience encroaching on fortitude, of magnanimity once animated by virtue and afterwards extinguished by guilt, was what Shakespeare meant to display in the character and conduct of Macbeth.

291. Samuel Felton, Shakespeare and the artist

1787

From *Imperfect Hints towards a New Edition of Shakespeare, written chiefly in the year 1782* (1787). The following year 'Part II. and last' was published.

Samuel Felton (*fl.* 1780–92) also published *An Explanation of Several of Mr. Hogarth's Prints* (1785); *Testimonies to the genius and memory of Sir J. Reynolds* (1792); *On the portraits of English Authors on gardening* (1828); and *Gleanings on gardens, chiefly respecting those of the ancient style in England* (1829). For the Boydell Shakespeare see No. 296.

In so grand an edition as that announced by Messrs. Boydells and Nicoll, we may rest well assured that Shakespeare's volumes will receive every proper and graceful ornament. Would there be any impropriety then, in introducing in some part of the work (either in the introductory, or a supplemental part), *Fancy Designs*, by eminent artists, *to the memory of Shakespeare*? One Design might be a Fancy Portrait of the bard, *with a pen in his hand, seeming to have just conceived one of those sublime Ideas to which* (say the Abbé Grosley) *he owes his réputation*. The nature of the other Designs must be left to the imagination of each artist.

How pleasingly might an artist amuse himself in painting Fancy Portraits of Shakespeare (at whole length), as at the time of composing or conceiving some of those various and diversified scenes which have long delighted this nation.—Either at the sombre moment of his gloomy imagination diving into the mysteries of Witchery and Incantation in the cavern of the Weird Sisters, and there treading in that circle *in which none durst walk but he.*—Or when his breast was inflamed with the rapidity of preparation for Bosworth-field, and he was writing *(a noble wildness flashing from his eyes)* those words with which Mr. Garrick has so oft electrified not only his attentive audience but the very actors on the stage:—*off with his head! so much for Buckingham.*[1]—When fired with young Harry Percy—Or when indulging his fancy with some of the most pleasing fictions that ever poet feigned *of the light Fairies and the dapper Elves.*—When composing the Prologue to *Henry V.*—When ruminating on the murder of Duncan—or on those rising spectres which *daunt the pale Macbeth.*—On the awful magic of Prospero—Or when imagining some of those irresistable appeals to the humane heart which his own good mind dictated to him, and which none but his own genius could so well express. In Designs similar to this last his features should possess the mild animation of Zoust's metzotinto, with somewhat of that calm elevation which is so well expressed in Mr. Romney's print of Mrs. Yates in the Tragic Muse. He should have all the magic of the mouth open, which we have seen so well expressed in some *Italian* pictures; and Milton's *dim light* should be admitted into a chamber, somewhat resembling a *studious cloyster pale.* . . .

If he should be drawn as revolving in his mind more turbulent scenes, or when his active spirit is borne away with the grandeur of his ideas: let not his figure be disgraced as we have lately seen it (in a large print), but let somewhat of that energy of conception be given him, and somewhat of that noble air and peculiar grace which we see in the whole length portrait of Mrs. Stanhope in the rooms of Sir Joshua Reynolds. We are well assured that every muse adorned his mind; and from what is handed down to us (and the portrait which Mr. *Walpole* thinks an original, as well as the portrait by Zoust), we have some reasons to think that (like what is said of Rafaelle) every grace adorned his body. (xxii–xxiv)

[On 'Scene-Prints': paintings illustrating specific scenes. From *Titus Andronicus*, 2.3.93ff.: Tamora's description of the 'barren detested vale' and its 'abhorred pit']

---

[1] These lines are in fact from Cibber's adaptation of *Richard III*: see Vol. 2, p. 121.

To produce a metzotinto for this page will require the invention of a wild and terrible imagination—*savage as Salvator Rosa, fierce as Michael Angelo*. The gloomy terrors of Poussin should be aided with the imagination of such painters as Brueghel *d'enfer*, Callot, P. Testa, Albert Durer (who has given us a hell-scene, and a *man on horseback followed by a spectre, and accompanied by Death on horseback*), the painter of *Ugolino*, perhaps, and others, whose pencils have touched the *terrible graces*. Such only can represent this *detested, dark, and blood-drinking pit*. This admirable description of Shakespeare's well merits the exertions of genius. . . .

The *ragged entrails* of the pit will be seen by means of the light arising from the ring on the bloody finger of *Bassianus*, whose ghastly and murdered carcase must be drawn, with *Marcus* viewing it with startled fear. A human skeleton would not be improperly introduced in some corner of this doleful cave (with a toad crawling through the ribs); but the addition of fiends, swelling toads, &c. must be introduced, *ad libitum*, by some second Brueghel. (4–6)

[On *Coriolanus*, 2.1.166ff.]
Some beautiful lines will furnish a good picture of *Coriolanus*, and his wife *Virgilia*. It is needless to represent the other characters. The lines are these: ['My gracious silence, hail!']. They might be drawn as half-lengths; and his dress may be partly taken from Gravelot's print to Theobald. Her head may be gracefully declining; and her hand closed in his. The expression of *my gracious silence* sufficiently paints her character. (14)

[On *Romeo and Juliet*, 4.3.14–57: Juliet's speech as she drinks the potion.]
The images which are here presented, and which imprint such terror on the imagination of *Juliet*, are painted with a frightful and tragic pencil. This scene is perfectly suited to the wildness of Shakespeare's genius, and he cannot treat on those subjects without luxuriance. The terrifick Muse selected him her chosen painter.* . . . (Part II, 116–7)

---

* Many writers have testified their admiration of the power which our great poet discovered, in painting *Fear*. [Quotes references to Shakespeare in Gray's *Ode on the Progress of Poetry*, Dennis's *Letters* (see Vol. 2, p. 82), Collins's *Ode to Fear*, the Honourable Andrew Erskine's *Ode to Fear*, and Warton's *Monody written near Stratford-upon-Avon*.]

The natural terror which [Mrs] Cibber gave to this scene (which she performed with all the enthusiasm of her soul)—her start, and wild distracted aspect at exclaiming '*O, look! methinks I see my cousin's ghost*—' [4.3.55], accompanied with a shriek that really chill'd the blood, and made the audience fancy *the bloody Tybalt* and the *spirits of the night* were fleeting before her—her sudden transition from perturbed horror, to the mournful and entreating tenderness with which she cried '*Stay, Tybalt, stay!*' [57], her momentary pause of recollection, which recalled her scattered senses, and fixed her thoughts on him, for whose sake she chearfully swallowed the potion, and the affectionately mournful voice with which she pronounced this last line:

> '*Romeo I come!* THIS DO I DRINK TO THEE.'   [58]

this succession of tragick images was displayed by Cibber with a spirit that fell little short of inspiration—and the picture of frenzy which *she* exhibited (wrought up to a pitch scarce conceivable) established her in the hearts of the public as the darling and supreme actress of the Tragic Muse. Her fine conceptions of the Poet, and her display of unattainable excellence in *Juliet*, still lives in the memory of her fear-struck but delighted auditors. . . . (118–9)

292. Richard Stack, Morgann on Falstaff refuted

1788

From 'An Examination of an Essay on the Dramatic Character of Sir John Falstaff. By the Rev. Richard Stack, D.D., F.T.C.D., and M.R.I.A.', in *Transactions of the Royal Irish Academy*, ii (1788), pp. 3–37. Read on 11 February 1788.

Richard Stack (d. 1812) entered Trinity College, Dublin, in 1766, and became a fellow in 1779. He was rector of Omagh, vice-president of the Royal Irish Academy, and author of an introduction to chemistry and lectures on the Bible.

The essay which I intend to examine must be acknowledged to be one of the most ingenious pieces of criticism any where to be found. For though its design seems to be in contradiction to the general sentiment of mankind, yet has the writer managed his subject with so much ability and address that some have been gained over to his opinion, others hesitate, and all must admire. We are pleased with his dexterity in support of a paradox in the same manner as we are charmed with Falstaff's wit and humour, even when employed in defence of his vices. . . . If I can weaken the force of the ingenious writer's arguments on the other side, I shall consider my opinion as fully established; for he has omitted nothing of any moment that could support his singularity and refinement.

The author introduces his essay with a distinction between the conclusions of the understanding formed upon actions, and the impressions upon a certain sense somewhat like instinct, which immediately acquaints us with the principles of character without any consideration of actions, and sometimes determines our heart even against the conclusions of our reason. This observation he seems to apply in the present case thus: 'The character of Falstaff has indeed strong appearances of cowardice. In the first moment of our acquaintance with him he is involved in circumstances of apparent dishonour. We hear him familiarly called coward by his most intimate companions. We see him on occasion of the robbery at Gadshill in the very act of running away from the prince and Poins: on another of more honourable obligation, in battle and acting in his profession as a soldier, escaping from Douglas, even out of the world as it were; counterfeiting death and deserting his very existence; betrayed into those lies and braggadocios which are the usual concomitants of cowardice. But these appearances are only errors of the understanding; and the poet has contrived with infinite art to steal impressions upon his hearers or readers that shall keep their hold in spite of these errors; yet so latent and so purposely obscured that we only feel ourselves influenced by the effects without being able to explain the cause. Falstaff, in spite of all those strong appearances, recommends himself to the heart by a constitutional courage: and the occasions alluded to are only accidental imputations on this quality designed for sport and laughter, on account of actions of apparent cowardice and dishonour.' The matter which I have here brought together into a short view is subtle and refined. I may therefore be mistaken; but after an attentive reading I can make no other application of his distinction between the conclusions of the understanding and those mental impressions: and this I apprehend to be the true scope and substance of the author's criticism upon this part of the subject.

I am willing then for the present to admit that all men are conscious to themselves of certain feelings about character, independent of and even in opposition to the conclusions of the understanding. And upon the ground of this very distinction I think it might be shewn that Shakespeare has designed cowardice, rather than constitutional courage, to be a part of Falstaff's real character. When a character appeals to the understanding the judgment formed of it seems to me the result of all its various parts compared together. Its several actions, with their several springs and motives, so far as reason can discover them, must be taken into account before the understanding can form a just estimate. . . . But in addressing a character to the sense or instinct above-mentioned the case appears entirely different. As no exercise is here given to the understanding to compare, digest and reflect, the first impressions are of the highest moment. (3–6)

These observations I believe will be found to apply to most dramatic characters, and to Shakespeare's most eminently. But if a writer should neglect them, he would at least avoid all early impressions of an opposite nature: for these might engage and mislead the heart too far, and become the sources of incorrigible errors. Can we suppose then that Shakespeare, if he had designed to exhibit Falstaff as naturally brave, would in the first scene of our acquaintance with him have given strong intimations of his cowardice? which he has unquestionably done in the scheme laid for him by Poins, and in the observations made upon the probable conduct of Falstaff. 'The virtue of this jest,' says Poins, 'will be the incomprehensible lies this same fat rogue will tell us when we meet at supper: how thirty at least he fought with; what wards, what blows, what extremities he endured; and in reproof of this lies the jest,' [*1 Henry IV*, 1.2.186ff.] All this clearly implies that he would play the first part of a coward in action, and the second in lying and boasting. (7)

[Stack summarizes Morgann's claim that Poins is] an unamiable, if not a bad and brutish character: and to conclude, his conduct towards Falstaff to have arisen from malice and ill-will.—I must own this is a new impression of his character on me, who have been accustomed to view him as a wild and dissipated fellow like the rest of the party; and though he never failed to use Falstaff as a butt, yet doing this without the least malicious intent, and merely to draw out of him entertainment for the prince. To suppose that Poins contrived this plot with an ill-natured design would greatly impair, if not utterly destroy its humour; nor can I discover throughout the whole character any thing to justify the censure here passed upon him, with a view, as it should seem, to render his opinion suspected. (8)

[When Poins says that two of Falstaff's cronies are 'true-bred cowards. . . and for the third, if he fight longer than he sees cause, I will forswear arms' (1.2.183ff.), Morgann interprets this as laudatory of Falstaff:] And I cannot but observe here again that the construction given to this passage by the able critic considerably lessens its merit; for according to him, though spoken in the very spirit of detraction, it yet contains a reluctant admission of his courage. Whereas the passage as commonly understood is highly humorous; one of those forms of expression which slily conveys a sarcasm under the guise of commendation. (9)

[When Falstaff says 'I am not indeed John of Gaunt, your grandfather, but yet no coward, Hal' (2.2.67), Morgann interprets this as showing Falstaff's dignity:] If this be the natural impression of the answer, and not the very refinement of criticism, my sentiments I must own are very mistaken. For I have always considered it rather evading a charge, the force of which he had felt; and in this view of it there appears admirable address, as by indirectly admitting the charge to a certain extent, and flattering the prince with the remembrance of his grandfather's prowess and courage, he has contrived to disarm him of his wit and prevented him from urging matters to extremity. (10)

[Morgann claims that the Gadshill scene is essentially about Falstaff's lying, to which the cowardice is incidental.] This is a kind of abstraction which I must own myself incapable of making; neither do I well conceive how the writer has done so. For these lies could in fact have had no existence unless we imagine some foundation upon which they were raised; so that, as well in the order of our ideas as degree of importance, the cowardice of Falstaff at Gadshill is not incidental but the primary and essential impression. (12)

[On the scene (2.2.) where Falstaff is confronted by Hal and Poins.] And here I cannot help observing that the ingenious critic's over-strained defence of Falstaff's courage does not make amends for the loss of his inimitable wit and humour which have been sacrificed on this occasion. 'Falstaff's evasions,' says he, 'here fail him: he is at the end of his invention; and it seems fair, that in defect of wit the law should pass upon him, and that he should undergo the temporary censure of that cowardice which he could not pass off by any evasion whatever.' Strange, indeed, that the writer should discover a defect of wit in a scene where it seems to have triumphed with a more wonderful superiority over surrounding difficulties than in any other part of his dramatic character. Let us attend for a moment to the occasion: when Falstaff had finished his incomprehensible lies about the exploit at Gadshill, the prince suddenly puts him down with a plain tale, of which poor Jack could not deny a syllable. In this state of embarrassment we feel a peculiar interest about him, not conceiving how his wit, though variable and inexhaustible, could extricate him, when on a sudden, with a sort of charm, he sets both us and himself free. To the sarcasm of Poins: 'Come, let us hear, Jack, what trick hast thou now?' he replies, 'By the L—d, I knew you as well as he that made you,' [2.4.267] and then professes himself a coward upon instinct. Nothing can be more exquisite and delightful; it is not cutting the intricate knot, but unfolding it with a wonderful sleight and characteristic ease. His adversaries, who were taunting and bitter enough, have nothing to reply to this explanation. He seems to feel his victory complete, when he adds, 'But, lads, I am glad you have the money: hostess, clap to the doors; watch to-night, pray to-morrow, &c.' [275ff.]. The prince, it is true, replies to his proposal for having a play extempore, 'Content; and the argument shall be thy running away.' [281] From which, by the way, we may see the point of cowardice was a main object of the scene; and this is confirmed both by Falstaff's confession and manner of accounting for it, and also by his concluding reply to the prince in this scene. 'Ah, no more of that, Hal, if thou lov'st me.' [283] Upon the whole the lies do not appear to be the sole, nor even the principal object of this scene. The plot was originally contrived upon a previous conjecture from his character, that he would first act the coward and next the liar. The affair at Gadshill justified the opinion of Poins as to both, and the present occasion goes to their joint conviction: and yet thus convicted he baffles every attempt. The versality of his wit and gaiety of his humour delight and surprise us, so successfully does he play with those weapons which other hands dare not touch.

I have gone pretty largely into an examination of those first scenes of Falstaff's appearance, because I cannot help thinking that the poet designed them to be of great importance in impressing his character: and I have examined the impressions, not in the order assigned them by the ingenious critic, but that in which they arose under the hands of the poet. These first appearances, so far as they affect his courage, the critic maintains to be errors of the understanding; in spite of which, impressions of a very minute and delicate nature, adapted to the critical sense alluded to above, gain upon the heart and preserve their hold. Now in my opinion those early impressions are rather notices to that sense, and any following appearances that may seem contradictory to them I should incline to call errors of the understanding. My meaning is simply this: the early impressions of Falstaff's spirit are certainly those of cowardice; the heart I think soon reckons this among the number of his infirmities. . . . (13–16)

[Stack now considers Morgann's citation of comments by Mistress Quickly, Doll Tearsheet, and Justice Shallow as testimonies to Falstaff's courage: pp. 16–18.]

One should hardly think that the ingenious critic would attempt to draw an argument for Falstaff's courage from the mouth of the prince, who seems to take a pride in girding at his cowardice on every occasion. The prince says, 'I will procure this fat rogue a charge of foot.' [2.4.545ff.] And again, 'I will procure thee, Jack, a charge of foot; meet me to-morrow in the Temple hall.' [3.3.186, 199]. Both expressions seem to have been used with a view to harrass and teaze him, by putting him upon a service for which he was so unfit. . . . Falstaff ought to appear in the battle, and could not well assume a character below that of a commander. Besides, this very capacity furnishes matter of excellent wit and humour, which very naturally accounts for the introduction of him on this and other occasions; and I must observe that the critic seems to have overlooked this remark too much in search of those subtle and remote impressions on which he has formed his theory. (19–20)

. . . There is nothing indeed so very strange or indecent in his attending the prince in the camp at Shrewsbury; where, by the way, we may observe he gives no sort of advice, but mixes his humour with their most important councils. Can any one seriously imagine that he was called into the king's presence from a regard to his merit? If there were any reason for introducing him, it was probably to raise a laugh against the rebels; but indeed I look upon his presence as a matter of course, a part of the prince's train, who was too fond of his company to sacrifice it to every little punctilio of decorum. (23)

[Morgann had attempted to discredit Prince John's comment on Falstaff's 'tardy tricks' in arriving late at the battle (*2 Henry IV*, 4.3.28f.) as an attempt by the prince to gain credit with the 'grave and prudent' at court.] My objection to these remarks, as indeed to the general scheme and tenor of the whole criticism, is their excessive refinement. Dramatic characters are not drawn for speculative ingenious men in their closets, but for mankind at large. Now, I say, these fine-spun deductions from the temper and situation of Lancaster and the rest of the parties, even though they could be made out to our satisfaction, have not a strong and immediate influence. The part of his character which we know, however unamiable, does not, I think, excite those impressions of course: and for the most part arguments from one part of character to another, unless the connection be universally acknowledged, is too philosophical a business for the public understanding. (25)

The writer seems to have lost sight of the true intent of Falstaff's character, which surely never was to excite sentiments of jealousy and malice but to entertain the whole world, even those who were objects of his wit and humour. 'Men of all sorts,' says he, 'take a pride to gird at me. . . . I am not only witty in myself, but the cause that wit is in other men.' [*2 Henry IV*, 1.2.6ff.] Here we have his very essence: and it was with a view to this that every inimitable scene in which he appears was contrived by the wonderful poet. But to return: we may observe that Lancaster's charge has a reference to former misconduct of a like nature. His opinion had evidently been formed before this occasion; and therefore if Falstaff could even account for his tardy tricks in the present case, it would have only proved that his conduct was now less blameable than usual. As to his defence, I cannot think he meant it to be rational and sober. We find in it the same humorous extravagance as in every other narrative of his exploits. The fact, indeed, was true, that Sir John Coleville had surrendered to him. But it does not appear from any testimony, except his own and Falstaff's, that he was a man of courage; and if he even were, the circumstances of the transactions, in my opinion, give Falstaff very little to boast of personal bravery. (26–7)

[Quotes Falstaff's 'Do ye yield, sir?': 4.3.1–14.] Coleville's reply to this strange rhodomantade is, 'I think you are Sir John Falstaff, and in the thought yield me.' If Falstaff's speech determined Coleville's mind, he must have been an arrant coward; if not, his question was the mere formality of honour, requiring an assurance that he was going to surrender to a man of some rank and name. At this day the point is sometimes insisted upon, and certainly prevailed more generally in times of knight-errantry, when the dignity of knighthood was held in higher estimation than at present. (27–8)

[On Falstaff's 'I have led my ragamuffins where they are pepper'd; there's not three of my hundred and fifty left alive' (*1 Henry IV*, 5.3.35f.), which Morgann interprets as proving Falstaff's courage.] Some things prove a great deal too much, and so lose their credibility. John of Gaunt himself could not do more than this; and who can believe an account of such romantic bravery in Sir John Falstaff, in a man who the moment after counterfeits death to escape a single adversary? It cannot be. Shakespeare never could have committed so great a breach of decorum; for though not the strictest observer of it in all cases, yet no dramatic poet ever observed it more perfectly in character. I should therefore rather adopt the idea of his having *ordered* his ragamuffins upon this dangerous service: or if this be thought a straining of the words too far, that having led them, he there left them. (30)

[On Falstaff's counterfeiting death to avoid being killed by Douglas: *ibid.*, 5.4.77ff. Stack argues that if we think of this as part of Falstaff's cowardice we see that] his behaviour in this scene with

Douglas is very natural; the readiness of his wit supplies him with an expedient, and he baffles his adversary as he always does. But neither the quickness of his invention on this occasion, nor his sporting with danger on others, prove a constitutional courage. They only shew an inexhaustible vein of wit and humour predominating through every part of his character; triumphant over every thing, over calamity, danger and disgrace; and we might as well assert that he was insensible to all the miseries of poverty, infamy and disease, when we hear him sporting with those dismal subjects, as suppose him courageous for expressing his sense of danger in a witty form. At the moment we feel him a coward, we are delighted with his humour amid surrounding dangers; for we know and feel that habits of character break out upon the most unlikely occasions; and that habit above all others, I believe, which we are now considering. I have heard of instances of its fantastic sport in the extremes of violent grief, and even at the hour of death. And surely if ever there was a wit which could tinge every affection and passion of the soul with its gay colours, it was the inimitable vein of Falstaff, which converts every thing it touches to gold.

What remains behind of this scene is, in my humble opinion, a damning proof of Falstaff's cowardice, his stabbing Percy after his death. The critic calls this indecent, but says it has nothing to do with his courage. I think otherwise. . . . To run away armed from a living man, or to escape by counterfeiting death, are direct acts of cowardice. To stab a dead man is equally so, though not directly. For I ask, is it possible for such an idea to enter into the mind of a brave man? or of any man, except the basest coward? [Quotes Falstaff's 'Zounds, I am afraid of this gunpowder Percy . . . how if he should counterfeit too, and rise? By my faith, I am afraid he would prove the better counterfeit. Therefore I'll make him sure; yea, and I'll swear I kill'd him': *ibid.*, 5.4.117ff.] Hence it appears that he stabbed him partly for the full assurance of his own personal safety, although his apprehensions were in themselves so groundless and improbable that none but a coward's heart could entertain them. The writer has with delicate judgment slurred this matter over; and I wish his whimsical theory had not obliged me to unfold an action of such a nature, but there was no passing it by, for it speaks too plainly the poet's design as to the character. (32–3)

... I have only one or two observations more to offer on the subject. The first I would make has, indeed, occasionally occurred, and was pretty constantly in my view in the course of the essay, viz. in what manner each hypothesis would affect the essential qualities of Falstaff's character. I have endeavoured to shew that a great and delightful portion of his wit and humour would be lost if we were to adopt the writer's idea; and, indeed, he himself has sacrificed them to his theory in one of the most perfect scenes of the whole character. This I consider as a radical error, for which all his ingenuity cannot atone. I must next observe, that to accommodate his theory false opinions of Poins, Lancaster and others, must be resorted to, and systems of malice intermixed in the plot which certainly the poet never designed. These are not only in themselves mistakes of character, but have a powerful influence on the plot, and such an one as I think takes away a great deal from its real pleasantry and good humour. Another strong objection to the writer's criticism is that he often mistakes the true intent of those scenes where Falstaff is introduced. The occasions are contrived as productive of mirth; every incident consistent with plot which conduced best to this end is chosen by the poet; but the critic seems to have overlooked this principal view in quest of subtle impressions; and while we are enjoying the feast of wit and humour, he is refining. Had Shakespeare sometimes violated decorum a little to attain his end, we might excuse him for the entertainment he affords. But I am far from admitting this; and have attempted to maintain, through my remarks, that the new theory is more deserving of the charge. (34–5)

... That Falstaff is vicious, a rogue, a liar, and a profligate, is allowed on all hands; yet covered with all this infamy, he entertains, surprises and charms, nay he engages our hearts. What then? Shall an infusion of cowardice reduce the character to a caput mortuum, and no spirit, no salt remain? For my part, I can see no reason for this. A man may, in my opinion, be very witty and pleasant upon his own defects, and even upon such qualities as, though acknowledged vices, cannot be deemed flagitious. Now cowardice, if it can be called by a harsher name than defect, will at least be allowed to have in it nothing flagitious. It certainly gives a mean and contemptible idea of its possessor; but so do fraud and lying. But neither these, nor any other qualities bestowed upon Falstaff, are in their nature so far detestable, but that great endowments of mind, especially if they be such as universally charm, shall be able completely to discharge the disgust arising from them. Genius and wit never fail to recommend themselves to the notice and admiration of mankind; and always throw a dignity round a character even above its true merit. These principles are sufficient to explain the superior pleasure and peculiar interest we feel in Falstaff above all other characters which have not half his vices. His creative fancy, playful wit, characteristic humour, admirable judgment and nice discernment of character, are so rare and excellent endowments that we lose the exceptionable matter in contemplating them. Nor is it owing to these alone that we admire and almost love Falstaff, but to another exquisite contrivance of the poet in catching occasions of mirth from his very vices. Thus, by making them the ground into which he has wrought the most entertaining fancies and delightful humour, he has made it almost impossible to separate matters thus closely interwoven, and has seduced judgment to the side of wit. These are the strange arts by which Shakespeare has drawn our liking toward so offensive an object; or to speak with more precision, has contrived to veil the offensive parts of his character. Defence is a thing of too serious a nature for Falstaff, he laughs at all vindication; *crescit sub pondere virtus*.[1] His elastic vigour of mind repels all difficulties; his alacrity bears him above all disgust; and in the gay wit we forget the contemptible coward. (36–7)

---

[1] 'Virtue grows under a burden': the motto of the Earl of Denbigh.

293. Thomas Robertson, on Hamlet

1788

From 'An Essay on the Character of Hamlet, in Shakespeare's Tragedy of *Hamlet*. By the Reverend Mr. Thomas Robertson, F. R. S. Edin. and Minister of Dalmeny', in *Transactions of the Royal Society of Edinburgh*, ii (1788), pp. 251–67.

Thomas Robertson (d. 1799), a minister and honorary D.D. of Edinburgh University, was the author of *An Enquiry into the Fine Arts* (Edinburgh, 1784), a theoretical work on ancient and modern music (only the first volume of which was published), and a *History of Mary, Queen of Scots* (1793). The *Critical Review* called this 'a pleasing and ingenious essay; rather amusing than convincing': n.s. i (1791), pp. 130–1.

[Quotes 5.2.351: 'Now cracks a noble heart'.] SHAKESPEARE in these passages not only refers to the particular part which HAMLET had acted with respect to the usurper (which he calls HAMLET's *cause*) and which, upon being explained, would vindicate what he had done. He plainly intimates by the mouth of HORATIO his own idea of HAMLET's character in all other respects; as not only heroic and splendid but perfectly consistent, amiable and just; and further, from the danger that HAMLET himself, as well as his cause, might be exposed to the censure of the unsatisfied, he seems strongly to insinuate that the character could not be comprehended unless an enlarged view were taken of it, and of the different situations in which it had been placed.

HAMLET's conduct in having put the king to death was, in a great measure, already justified in the very hearing of the lords and other attendants upon the court who were witnesses to it. The queen, who had just expired in their sight, had said she was 'poisoned.' [5.2.310] HAMLET had called out 'villany!' [311] Even LAERTES, the treacherous opponent of HAMLET, had declared 'the king, the king's to blame—It is a poison tempered by himself.' [327] And

HAMLET, upon stabbing the king, had expressly charged him with 'murder.' All this passed in the presence of the court, who would hence be led to view the king as guilty of having poisoned the queen, and therefore as justly put to death by her son. It is true indeed, the king had intended to poison not the queen but HAMLET; but neither the court, nor HAMLET himself, knew this. None but LAERTES was privy to it; and as he immediately expired without saying more the secret was to last for ever.

HAMLET, therefore, could have but little cause to fear that he should leave a wounded name behind him for thus revenging his mother's death. What troubled him was the thought that posterity would condemn him for not having, before that time, revenged the murder of his father. This was the reproach with which he had often charged himself; for at the beginning he had resolved to act quite otherwise, and had expressly promised to his father's ghost, with the utmost speed to avenge the murder.

> Haste me to know it (said he in the first act)
> that I with wings as swift
> As meditation or the thoughts of love,
> May sweep to my revenge.   [1.5.29ff.]

His fervent desire now, therefore, was that HORATIO, who knew all, might survive him, not merely to reveal the murder of his father but to make known to all men the infinite indignation which this excited in him, and the plan of vengeance which he had laid. HORATIO, for this purpose, would describe the two great and leading features in the character of HAMLET, pointed out by the finger of SHAKESPEARE himself, that 'noble heart' and that 'sweetness' with which at once he was distinguished. Upon the latter of these two, HORATIO would particularly explain the scheme of counterfeiting madness which that sweetness had suggested; and which at the same time would save HAMLET from passing for a real madman in the opinion of posterity.

As certain critics, however, have thought, some that there is an incongruity, others that there is an immorality in the character of this personage, it becomes a duty in the charitable to justify the poet, and to revive the office of HORATIO in the defence of his hero.

To understand the character of HAMLET we had best perhaps take it at two different times, before the death of his father and after that period; for while the substance is in both the same the form is exceedingly different.

481

The former of these, and which was his radical and general character, was a compound of many particular qualities; an exceeding high elevation of soul, an exquisite sensibility to virtue and vice, and an extreme gentleness of spirit and sweetness of disposition. With these were conjoined the most brilliant and cultivated talents, an imagination transcendently vivid and strong, together with what may be called rather an *intuition* than an acquired knowledge of mankind. And there may be added still a singular gaiety of spirits, which hardly at any after period, the very gloomiest only excepted, seems to have failed him.

These being the fundamental properties of HAMLET, we have only to see what effects would be produced upon *such* a man by the villany of his uncle, the murder of his father, the incest of his mother, and the ghost of his father calling upon him for revenge. These were the dreadful springs which put HAMLET into motion; and in which state SHAKESPEARE brings him upon the stage.

I should venturè to imagine (both from the nature of a character so extensive, and from the various motives to action) that SHAKESPEARE had no particular plan laid out in his mind for HAMLET to walk by, but rather meant to *follow* him; and like an historian, with fidelity to record how a person so singularly and marvellously made up should act; or rather (to use the term employed by the king), to describe the 'transformation' which he should undergo. For this purpose he kept an attentive and an undeviating eye upon HAMLET's previous and general character (such as he had figured it to be), without any intention to add a single new feature, but only to take in such new aspects of it, such new exertions of his powers, and such new schemes of conduct as should naturally flow from his new situations.

This being supposed, the new colours under which HAMLET appears will be found entirely consistent with the old, and springing lineally from them: an indignation and sensibility irritated to extreme; the deepest anguish; at times a mortal melancholy; a counterfeited madness, in order to wait for opportunities of revenge; and a degree of real phrenzy, to which he seems more than once to have been actually driven by the strength of his feelings, through force of which he was sometimes upon the point of betraying his own secret. Still, however, there was neither violence, nor sorrow, nor melancholy, nor madness in the original and natural state of his mind.

What seems to explain the whole of HAMLET's conduct is the latitude of his character. He was at once a polished gentleman, a soldier, a scholar and a philosopher; as in the exclamation of OPHELIA:

O what a noble mind is here o'erthrown!
The courtier's, soldier's, scholar's, eye, tongue, sword. [3.1.150f.]

At one time mild, courteous and contemplative; at another animated with the keenest feelings; upon occasions, all wrath and fire; looking down, at all times, as if from a superior orb, upon whatever was little, insincere or base among men.

Now, in such an assemblage of qualities, combining to form the broad character of HAMLET, SHAKESPEARE appears to have seen that they were balanced in such an opposite manner that one class of them should counteract, and render inefficient the other. It is this that suffered nothing to be done; it is this that constantly impeded the action and kept the catastrophe back. Resentment, revenge, eternal indignation, stimulated HAMLET at one moment. At the next we have the mere unbending and recoil of these passions; and not only this, which was transient, but there followed almost at the same instant that gentleness which so seldom left him. From this he could not, at any time, act in cold blood. He could strike only in the fiercest moments of provocation; then 'could he drink hot blood!' [3.2.390] In the general tenor of his mind he could do nothing; he was like SAMSON when his strength was gone from him.

Meanwhile he is almost constantly chiding himself for *dull mettle, dull revenge, want of gall*; a self-reproach which, in some scenes, breaks vividly out; as upon the occasions where he saw a mere player weeping over HECUBA, and when he was told that the delicate prince FORTINBRAS was marching at the head of his troops to risk his life for an 'egg-shell.' HAMLET, in short, was not formed for action. Upon the fluctuation of his mind between contriving and executing, between elevation, sensibility and gentleness, hangs the whole business of the tragedy.

In such a state of HAMLET's frame the project of counterfeiting madness occurred to him with great consistency. It was a device to which his nature led: bent upon vengeance; destitute of resolution directly to gratify it; assuming therefore the cloak of insanity in order to lull suspicion, and to watch at leisure for those occurrences which time or chance might present. To secure by this fiction his personal safety, was in no degree his view; for 'he did not set his life at a pin's fee' [1.4.65]; but by means of his life being preserved, to embrace the opportunities of revenge. It was from the same softness in his nature that he afterwards strove to make himself believe that his father's ghost might be the devil trying to 'abuse him' [2.2.599ff.]; and which suggested to him the stratagem of getting a play to be performed before the king.

His anxious adherence to the project of counterfeiting madness, to which he made every thing else give way, explains his *rudeness*, as Dr JOHNSON calls it, to OPHELIA. For to deceive the beloved OPHELIA into a belief of his madness, and to insult *her* was the surest of all means to make it believed that he was really mad. And this also accounts for his making her brother LAERTES believe that the rough treatment he gave him at his sister's funeral proceeded not from love to OPHELIA, its true cause, but from distraction; and which is ridiculously called by Dr JOHNSON a 'falsehood unsuitable to the character of a good or a brave man.'[1] HAMLET was then in the very presence of the usurper, and, on that account, industriously 'proclaimed,' that what he had done proceeded from madness.

Connected with this point, it has been thought vain by some critics* to justify SHAKESPEARE in his making HAMLET forget (as they think) OPHELIA so soon after her death; instead of which he should have waited, they say, for the effect which time has upon the change of feeling. . . . (252-7)

It is the very mark and prerogative of a great soul upon great occasions to outrun time, to start at once, without sensible transition, into another period. Even a common soldier, in the heat of action, were his dearest companion to fall by his side would not (although he could) drop his arms and mourn over him. In a similar state, but infinitely more interesting, was HAMLET at this time. And if doubts should still be entertained about the existence of HAMLET's love to OPHELIA after her death, the question can be brought to the shortest issue. HAMLET himself will answer, that his love for OPHELIA was greater than ever. When LAERTES, half-delirious himself with grief for his sister's madness and death, leaped into her grave and imprecated 'ten times triple woe upon the cursed head of him (HAMLET) who had deprived her of her

---

* *Mirror*: &c. [by Mackenzie; above, p. 278.]
[1] See Vol. 5, p. 161.

most ingenious sense;' HAMLET burst upon him at once from his concealment, like thunder from a cloud; [quotes 'I loved Ophelia': 5.1.248–52, 263–5, 269–73]. His love had been only the deeper embosomed; it had become too sacred to be seen; and like fire when pent up, it had acquired greater force.

There seems also to be a mistake in the attempt which some* have made, in justification of SHAKESPEARE, to reconcile the melancholy to the jocularity of HAMLET. For his jocularity, I should rather conceive, sprung more from the elevated than from the melancholy parts of his nature. He was not, strictly speaking, a melancholy man; although it be true that at times he was plunged into a state of genuine and deep dejection. In such a state, and in certain kinds of it, we have heard of the *joy of grief*, and can understand it—something sweetly grave and pensive; but the *gaiety* and *pleasantry* of grief are things which probably never existed. It is, on the other hand, the exclusive act of a great mind to make truce with sorrow; to dismiss the deepest anguish; to put mirth in its stead; and HAMLET in such scenes was only for a little resuming his strength. Even the melancholy which is ascribed to him, and which indeed he ascribes to himself, was often not melancholy but wild contemplation and reverie. (258–9)

It is upon such principles I would venture to explain the pleasantries of HAMLET; in which he rose up at times from an abyss of anguish, to make a mere sport of human sufferings.

The causes of HAMLET's dilatory progress have been already pointed out in general; and the more narrowly we take a view of him the more we shall always find his sensibility to be, in the first moments, such as led to instant and mortal action, while his gentleness, like an equal weight on the other side, counteracted its whole force. SHAKESPEARE has described him, in the cool state of his mind, as averse and even shocked at the thought of killing. His mother said that in this state he was 'as patient as the female dove.' [5.1.286] If we take his own account of himself, he was a coward: [quotes the 'craven scruple' speech, 4.4.39–44].

There was a superstition also in HAMLET which prevented him from putting the usurper to death when in the act of prayer. For the reason he himself gave for deferring this was that if he killed the king in the midst of his devotions, he would in fact be doing him a good service, 'sending a villain to heaven.' [Quotes 3.3.79–82.]

* *Mirror* [above, p. 279].

He put up his sword, and waited till he should find him engaged in drink, rage, incest, gaming, swearing, or other act that had 'no relish of salvation in't;'

> Then trip him, that his heels may kick at Heaven,
> And that his soul may be as damn'd and black
> As hell, whereto it goes. [89–95]

The sentiments in this last passage have been considered as the most difficult to be defended in the whole character of HAMLET. Without having recourse to a defence of them upon the principle of retaliation and other pleas, there seems to be ground for an explication of a very different nature, founded upon what appears to be the real character of this personage, and altogether exculpating him from the charge of those horrid dispositions which he has been supposed here to possess.

HAMLET in these lines (if it may be allowed to offer a conjecture), was really *imposing* upon himself,* devising an excuse for his aversion at bloodshed, for his cowardice, his 'craven scruple.' In the first moments he proposes instantly to strike—'now I'll do't.' His ordinary softness immediately recurs; and he endeavours to hide it from himself by projecting a more awful death at a future period, but which he seems never to have thought of afterwards, and which was not at all consonant to his general character. Indeed, what the king himself said of him afterwards, upon basely proposing to LAERTES to use 'a sword unbated,' is a sufficient proof that there was nothing dark or malignant in his nature.

> ——He being remiss,
> Most generous, and free from *all* contriving,
> Will not peruse the foils. [4.7.134ff.]

The execution of his two school-fellows, ROSENCRANTZ and GUILDENSTERN, in consequence of an artifice which he contrived against them, has also drawn the censure of critics. But is there any evidence that HAMLET thought them unacquainted with the mandate which they carried for striking off his head in England? Whether they were in fact privy or not privy to this is not the question. Did not HAMLET believe they were privy to it, and even

---

* Since writing this Essay, I have the pleasure to find that the same idea has occurred to Mr Professor RICHARDSON in his additional observations on HAMLET; and which he has successfully enlarged upon. [See above, pp. 367f.]

were fond of it? 'Whom I will trust' (said he early) 'as I will adders fanged.' [3.4.203] And speaking afterwards to his confident, HORATIO, he added

> Why, man, they did make *love* to this employment;
> They are not near my conscience. [5.2.57f.]

That is, my conscience does not upbraid me; the cruelty lies not with me but with them. And in this conduct of HAMLET to the companions of his early days does SHAKESPEARE prove his skill in human nature; the strongest hatred succeeding, upon such occasions, to the strongest friendship. For that they were his school-fellows he would consider, and with reason, as a great aggravation of their guilt.

In all other respects the character of HAMLET stands confessedly fair and great. He moved in the highest sphere of men; possessed an elevated and comprehensive mind; penetrated through every character; knew the whole of human life; saw nothing noble but virtue, nothing mean and base but folly and vice. Speaking to HORATIO, [quotes 3.2.61–72: 'Give me that man/That is not passion's slave. . . .'] Men praise in others what they love and possess in themselves; and HAMLET was here drawing some of the outlines of his own character.

To the principles of morality and a consummate knowledge of mankind he joined the accomplishments of learning and the graces of life. His eloquence was such as great orators only have possessed, rich, tropical, daring, ardent, vehement. The directions he gives to the players are models of taste and laws for the stage. His wit and fancy seem to have belonged only to himself. Even in his character of soldier and hero, and which I all along consider as his weaker part, an intrepidity breaks forth at times beyond what is human; as appears in the ghost-scenes, where his courage grows with danger; where he is not only unterrified but sports with what appals the rest of mankind.

The HAMLET of SHAKESPEARE, taken all in all, seems thus to be the most splendid character of dramatic poetry; possessing not one or two great qualities, the ordinary compass of the heroes in tragedy, of a LEAR, an OTHELLO, a RODRIGUE, an HORACE, but comprehending almost the whole of what is beautiful and grand.

The mistakes which critics seem to have fallen into can be all traced perhaps to partial and side-views which they have taken of

HAMLET; but which can neither explain his whole character, nor sufficiently account for the interest which is excited.

Sensibility, for example, making a striking figure in this character, has been thought to be the sole basis of it, without considering that mere sensibility cannot excite a tragic interest; cannot attach; cannot overwhelm; and indeed seems unable to make any other impression but that of pain when viewed apart from the cause in which it acts, and from the other qualities with which it is conjoined. Neither can a SENSE OF VIRTUE be admitted as the only ruling principle; for even this does not sufficiently account for the interest; and both systems fail in explaining the inefficiency of the character, which results from the soft and amiable, and hence in a great degree the interesting parts of it. For in both the gentleness of HAMLET, the great impediment to the action, has been overlooked. Although, to supply its place a weakness and irresolution, sometimes deduced from excessive sensibility, sometimes from melancholy, are recurred to in the former, but which are certainly of a transient duration, while gentleness was a permanent quality; and in the latter, while the same office is allotted to irresolution, the irresolution itself is deduced from the moral faculty, suspending and abating resentment; but which surely would suppose, what cannot be admitted, that the pious and noble revenge of HAMLET had something morally blameable in its nature. Two elegant and ingenious publications are here alluded to;* but in both of them the ground taken is, I humbly think, too narrow; and this seems to have been the cause why recourse has been had to refinements in order to stretch it out. Facts certainly supply us here with two principles at least, sensibility and gentleness; and there hence seems no necessity for resolving the whole conduct of HAMLET into the former, as is done in one of these publications. Neither are we to recur sometimes to the one principle, sometimes to the other, taken separately, in order to explain HAMLET. It is the *struggle* between the two upon which his conduct hinges. This appears in the very opening of the tragedy.

> The time is out of joint; Oh cursed spight!
> That ever *I* was born to set it right. [1.5.188f.]

---

* The one anonymous, in No. 99. and 100. of the *Mirror*; the other, the *Analysis of* HAMLET, by Mr RICHARDSON.

Here sensibility and gentleness may be said to speak in one and the same breath; a proof that their operations were not successive but co-existent, and reigned nearly equal in power in HAMLET's breast.

ELEVATION seems to have been nearly as much overlooked as gentleness. Yet between these two was HAMLET almost always moving. For his sublimity of soul seems to have been the very spring which prompted and whetted his sensibility to the quick. SHAKESPEARE in one phrase, 'a noble heart,' meant to express both; as they were in fact intimately conjoined, and acted at once together.

There is an impression which great accomplishments and splendid talents, independent of every thing else, especially in a tragic cause, never fails to make upon mankind. These shine most powerfully in the character before us; and probably have contributed much to the charm which has made audiences hang upon HAMLET. The world for the first time saw a *man of genius* upon the stage; and the interest which the spectators have taken, and perhaps for ever will take, receiving an addition from this cause, arises thus upon the whole from the many different sources which the poet, by a superlative effort of talents and of skill, has combined together.

The fault (if any) of the play seems to lie in this, that there is not the usual interest excited in it for the final event. What SHAKESPEARE's purpose in this respect originally was cannot be affirmed. It is possible that, finding the character of HAMLET to grow upon him, he varied in the progress from what he had intended in the outsetting of the play, and giving to HAMLET on this account a fuller scope (but without departing from the character), he eventually threw more interest into the person than into the plot. Whatever may have been the cause we see the effect:—HAMLET, in his sole person predominating over, and almost eclipsing the whole action of the drama. It is he that draws the admiration; it is he that engrosses the concern; all eyes are turned more and more to him; HAMLET is wished for in every scene; king and queen, incest and murder, as objects of tragic attention, vanish almost away; the moment HAMLET's own fate arrives, the play is ended. The interest which the hearts of men take in the principal character of this tragedy stands thus in competition with the laws of the drama; and it becomes a problem which of the two, the means or the end, should preponderate.

489

On account of the interest being transferred from the action to the agent the moral, taking the same course, is to be drawn rather from the particular conduct of HAMLET than from the general business of the play. But what that particular moral is may be difficult to ascertain. We may say, perhaps, that from the conduct of HAMLET it appears how unfit for the work of revenge are the qualities of a soldier and hero when conjoined with those of a scholar and philosopher; yet we cannot presume to affirm that it was SHAKESPEARE's object merely to exemplify this, or even to conceive that he limited himself to any single object or moral. Those things which seem to have been uppermost in his mind, and which he has made to shine with most light, are the charms in the personal character of HAMLET. Enamoured with these himself, it seems to have been his chief purpose to raise the same passion in his audiences. That he has intimated this by his interpreter HORATIO, only in one or two lines at the close of the play, is to be ascribed to his judgment. The purpose which the dramatic poet has in view is to be found out by the best of judges, the feelings of the spectators. From a superior skill upon this point RACINE has merited the praises which have been given him, while, from a failure in it the great CORNEILLE has been deservedly blamed. (259–67)

294. William Richardson, on Falstaff

1788

From *Essays on Shakespeare's Dramatic Character of Sir John Falstaff, and on his Imitation of Female Characters. To which are added, Some General Observations on the Study of Shakespeare* (1788). Some copies of this book are dated 1789, others 1788. It was reviewed in the *European Magazine* (xiv, pp. 422–5), containing 'The London Review for December 1788', in the *New Annual Register* for 1788 (pp. 108–11), and the *Critical Review* for July–December 1788 (lxvi, pp. 542–5).

On Richardson see the head-note to No. 246.

'The desire of gratifying the grosser and lower appetites, is the ruling and strongest principle in the mind of Falstaff.' Such indulgence is the aim of his projects; upon this his conduct very uniformly hinges; and to this his other passions are not only subordinate but subservient. His gluttony and love of dainty fare are admirably delineated in many passages: but with peculiar felicity in the following, where the poet displaying Falstaff's sensuality in a method that is humorous and indirect, and placing him in a ludicrous situation reconciles us by his exquisite pleasantry to a mean object. [Quotes *1 Henry IV*, 2.4.528ff.] Who but Shakespeare could have made a tavern-bill the subject of so much mirth; and so happily instrumental in the display of character? The sensuality of the character is also held forth in the humorous and ludicrous views that are given of his person. [Quotes *ibid.*, 2.2.11ff., 31ff.]

Pursuing no other object than the gratification of bodily pleasure, it is not wonderful that in situations of danger the care of the body should be his chief concern. He avoids situations of danger: he does not wish to be valiant; and without struggle or reluctance adheres to his resolution. Thus his cowardice seems to be the result of deliberation rather than the effect of constitution:* and is a determined purpose of not exposing to injury or destruction that corporeal structure, foul and unwieldy tho' it be, on which his supreme enjoyment so completely depends. His well-known soliloquy on honor displays a mind that, having neither enthusiasm for fame, nor sense of reputation, is influenced in the hour of danger by no principle but the fear of bodily pain; and if man were a mere sentient and mortal animal, governed by no higher principle than sensual appetite, we might accede to his reasoning.—[Quotes *ibid.*, 5.1.129ff.]

Thus while the speaker, in expressing his real sentiments, affects a playful manner he affords a curious example of self-imposition, of an attempt to disguise conscious demerit and escape from conscious disapprobation. (11–15)

Falstaff is also deceitful: for the connection between vain-glorious affectation and unembarrassed, unreluctant deceit is natural and intimate. He is deceitful in every form of falsehood. He is a flatterer: he is even hypocritical; and tells the chief justice that he has 'lost his voice singing anthems.' [*2 Henry IV*, 1.2.189]

* *Essay on Shakespeare's Falstaff* [No. 254 above, by Morgann]

Shakespeare intending to display the magic of his skill by rendering a mean character highly interesting, has added to it as many bad qualities as, consistently with one another and with his main design, can be united in one assemblage. He accordingly represents him not only as a voluptuary, cowardly, vain-glorious, with all the arrogance connected with vain-glory, and deceitful in every shape of deceit; but injurious, incapable of gratitude or of friendship, and vindictive. The chief object of his life being the indulgence of low appetite, he has no regard for right or wrong; and in order to compass his unworthy design he practises fraud and injustice. His attachments are mercenary. He speaks disrespectfully of Prince Henry, to whose friendship he is indebted; and values his friendship for convenience rather than from regard. He is also vindictive: but as he expresses his revengeful intention, without any opportunity of displaying it in action, his resentment becomes ridiculous.

From the foregoing enumeration it appears abundantly manifest that our poet intended to represent Falstaff as very mean and worthless. . . . How then comes Falstaff to be a favorite? a favorite with Prince Henry? and a favorite on the English stage? For he not only makes us laugh but, it must be acknowledged, is regarded with some affection. (17–20)

Those qualities in the character of Sir John Falstaff which may be accounted estimable are of two different kinds, the social and intellectual.

His social qualities are joviality and good-humour. These dispositions, though they are generally agreeable, and may in one sense of the word be termed moral, as influencing the manners and deportment of mankind, are not on all occasions, as we shall see exemplified in the present instance, to be accounted virtuous. They may be agreeable without being objects of approbation. . . .

Falstaff's love of society needs no illustration; and that it is unconnected with friendship or affection is no less apparent. Yet the quality renders him acceptable.—It receives great additional recommendation from his good-humour. . . . Such seems to be the good-humour of Falstaff; for our poet discriminates with exquisite judgment, and delineates his conception with power. He does not attribute to Falstaff the good temper flowing from inherent goodness and genuine mildness of disposition; for in company with those about whose good opinion he has little concern, though his vacuity of mind obliges him to have recourse to their company he is often insolent and overbearing. It is chiefly with Prince Henry and those whom he wishes, from vanity or some selfish purpose, to think well of him, that he is most facetious.—The degree or real force of any quality is never so distinctly marked as when it is put to the test by such trying circumstances as tend to destroy its existence. Shakespeare seems aware of this; and in the first scene between the Prince and Falstaff, this part of the character is fully tried and displayed. The prince attacks Falstaff in a contest of banter and raillery. The Knight for some time defends himself with dexterity and success. But the Prince's jests are more severe than witty; they suggest some harsh truths, and some well founded terrors. [Quotes *1 Henry IV*, 1.2.30ff.] . . . I proceed to exemplify his intellectual endowments: and of these his talents for wit and humour are the most peculiar.

His wit is of various kinds. It is sometimes a play upon words. [Quotes 2.4.146ff.] One of the most agreeable species of wit, and which Falstaff uses with great success, is the ridiculous comparison. It consists in classing or uniting together by similitude objects that excite feelings so opposite as that some may be accounted great, and others little, some noble, and others mean: and this is done when in their structure, appearance, or effects they have circumstances of resemblance abundantly obvious when pointed out, though on account of the great difference in their general impression not usually attended to; but which being selected by the man of witty invention, as bonds of intimate union, enable him by an unexpected connection to produce surprise.

Falstaff. (speaking of Shallow). I do remember him at Clement's-inn, like a man made after supper with a cheese-paring. When he was naked, he was for all the world like a forked radish, with a head fantastically carved upon it with a knife. [*2 Henry IV*, 3.2.308ff.]

Another very exquisite species of wit consists in explaining great, serious, or important appearances by inadequate and trifling causes. This, if one may say so, is a grave and solemn species; and produces its effect by the affectation of formal and deep research. Falstaff gives the following example: [quotes the speech on sherris: 4.3.96ff.]. (27–30)

Falstaff is not unacquainted with the nature and value of his talents. He employs them not merely for the sake of merriment but to promote some design. He wishes, by his drollery in this scene, to cajole the Chief Justice. In one of the following acts he practises the same artifice with the Prince of Lancaster. He fails, however, in his attempt: and that it was a studied attempt appears from his subsequent reflections: 'Good faith, this same young sober-blooded boy doth not love me; nor a man cannot make him laugh.' [4.3.87ff.] That his pleasantry, whether witty or humorous, is often studied and premeditated appears also from other passages.

I will devise matter enough out of this Shallow to keep Prince Henry in continual laughter. O you shall see him laugh, till his face be like a wet cloak ill laid up. [5.1.78ff.]

It may also be remarked that the guise or raiment with which Falstaff invests those different species of wit and humour is universally the same. It is grave, and even solemn. He would always appear in earnest. He does not laugh himself, unless compelled by a sympathetic emotion with the laughter of others. He may sometimes indeed indulge a smile of seeming contempt or indignation: but it is perhaps on no occasion when he would be witty or humorous. Shakespeare seems to have thought this particular of importance, and has therefore put it out of all doubt by making Falstaff himself inform us: 'O it is much that a lie with a slight oath, and a jest with a *sad brow*, will do with a fellow that never had the ache in his shoulders.' [5.1.81ff.]

As the wit of Falstaff is various, and finely blended with humour, it is also easy and genuine. It displays no quaint conceits, studied antitheses, or elaborate contrasts. Excepting in two or three instances we have no far-fetched or unsuccessful puns. Neither has the poet recourse, for ludicrous situation, to frequent and disgusting displays of drunkenness. We have little or no swearing, and less obscenity than from the rudeness of the times and the condition of some of the other speakers we might have expected.—Much ridicule is excited by some of the other characters: but their wit, when they attempt to be witty, is different from that of Falstaff. Prince Henry's wit consists chiefly in banter and raillery. In his satirical allusions he is often more severe than pleasant. The wit of Pistol, if it be intended for wit, is altogether affected, and is of a kind which Falstaff never displays. It is an affectation of pompous language; an attempt at the mock-heroic: and consists in employing inflated diction on common occasions.

The speaker does not possess, but aim at wit; and, for want of other resources endeavours to procure a laugh by odd expressions, and an absurd application of learned and lofty phrases. (34–7)

The other intellectual talents attributed by our poet to Sir John Falstaff are discernment of character, versatility, and dexterity in the management of mankind. A discernment, however, and a dexterity of a peculiar and limited species; limited to the power of discerning whether or not men may be rendered fit for his purposes; and to the power of managing them as the instruments of his enjoyment.

We may remark his discernment of mankind, and his dexterity in employing them, in his conduct towards the Prince, to Shallow, and his inferior associates.—He flatters the Prince, but he uses such flattery as is intended to impose on a person of understanding. He flatters him indirectly. He seems to treat him with familiarity: he affects to be displeased with him: he rallies him; and contends with him in the field of wit.When he gives praise it is insinuated; or it seems reluctant, accidental, and extorted by the power of truth. In like manner, when he would impress him with a belief of his affectionate and firm attachment he proceeds by insinuation; he would have it appear involuntary, the effect of strong irresistible impulse; so strong as to appear preternatural. 'If the rascal hath not given me medicines to make me love him, I'll be hang'd.' [1 Henry IV, 2.2.18f.] Yet his aim is not merely to please the Prince: it is to corrupt and govern him; and to make him bend to his purposes, and become the instrument of his pleasures. (39–40)

Another kind of ability displayed by our hero is the address with which he defies detection and extricates himself out of difficulty. He is never at a loss. His presence of mind never forsakes him. Having no sense of character he is never troubled with shame. Though frequently detected, or in danger of detection, his inventive faculty never sleeps; it is never totally overwhelmed. Or, if it be surprised into a momentary intermission of its power, it forthwith recovers, and supplies him with fresh resources. He is furnished with palliatives and excuses for every emergency. Besides other effects produced by this display of ability, it tends to amuse, and to excite laughter: for we are amused by the application of inadequate and ridiculous causes. Of the talent now mentioned we have many instances. Thus, when detected by prince Henry in his boastful pretensions to courage, he tells him that he knew him.

'Was it for me,' says he, 'to kill the heir-apparent?' [*1 Henry IV*, 2.4.268] So also in another scene, when he is detected in his abuse of the Prince and overheard even by the Prince himself: 'No abuse, Ned, in the world; honest Ned, none. I dispraised him before the wicked, that the wicked might not fall in love with him.' [*2 Henry IV*, 2.4.318ff.]

In the admirable scene where he is detected in falsely and injuriously charging his hostess with having picked his pocket of some very valuable articles, whereas the theft was chiefly of the ludicrous tavern-bill formerly mentioned, his escape is singularly remarkable. He does not justify himself by any plea of innocence. He does not colour nor palliate his offence. He cares not what baseness may be imputed to himself: all that he desires is that others may not be spotless. If he can make them appear base, so much the better. For how can they blame him if they themselves are blameable? On the present occasion he has some opportunity. He sees and employs it. The Prince, in rifling his pocket, had descended to an undignified action. The trespass indeed was slight, and Falstaff could not reckon it otherwise. But Prince Henry, possessing the delicacies of honour, felt it with peculiar acuteness. Falstaff, aware of this, employs the Prince's feelings as a counterpart to his own baseness, and is successful. It is on this particular point, though not usually attended to, because managed with much address, that his present resource depends. [Quotes *1 Henry IV*, 3.3.131–68.]

Then he adds, after an emphatic pause, and no doubt with a pointed application in the manner: '*You* confess then that *you* picked my pocket?'

Prince Henry's reply is very remarkable. It is not direct: it contains no longer any raillery or reproach; it is almost a shuffling answer, and may be supposed to have been spoken after, or with some conscious confusion: 'It appears so,' says he, 'from the story' [169]. Falstaff pushes him no further; but expresses his triumph, under the shew of moderation and indifference, in his address to the hostess:

Hostess, I forgive thee; go, make ready breakfast; love thy husband; look to thy servants; and cherish thy guests: thou shalt find me tractable to any honest reason: thou seest I am pacified.   [3.3.170ff.]

(43–8)

[On the play's 'catastrophe']

Here the poet's good sense, his sense of propriety, his judgment, and invention, are indeed remarkable. It was not for a person so sensual, so cowardly, so arrogant, and so selfish as Falstaff to triumph in his deceitful arts. But his punishment must be suitable. He is not a criminal like Richard; and his recompence must be different. Detection, disappointment in his fraudulent purposes, and the downfall of assumed importance, will satisfy poetical justice: and for such retribution, even from his earliest appearance, we see due preparation. The punishment is to be the result of his conduct, and to be accomplished by a regular progress.

Falstaff, who was studious of imposing on others, imposes upon himself. He becomes the dupe of his own artifice. Confident in his versatility, command of temper, presence of mind, and unabashed invention; encouraged too by the notice of the Prince, and thus flattering himself that he shall have some sway in his counsels, he lays the foundation of his own disappointment. Though the flatterer and parasite of Prince Henry he does not deceive him. The Prince is thoroughly acquainted with his character, and is aware of his views. Yet in his wit, humour, and invention, he finds Amusement.—Parasites, in the works of other poets, are the flatterers of weak men, and impress them with a belief of their merit or attachment. But Falstaff is the parasite of a person distinguished for ability or understanding. The Prince sees him in his real colours; yet, for the sake of present pastime, he suffers himself to seem deceived; and allows the parasite to flatter himself that his arts are not unsuccessful. The real state of his sentiments and feelings is finely described when, at the battle of Shrewsbury, seeing Falstaff lying among some dead bodies, he supposes him dead.

What! old acquaintance! could not all this flesh keep in a little life? Poor Jack, farewell. I could have better spared a better man: O I should have a heavy miss of thee, if I were much in love with vanity. [*1 Henry IV*, 5.4.102ff.]

But Prince Henry is not much in love with vanity. By his accession to the throne he feels himself under new obligations, and under the necessity of relinquishing improper pursuits. As he forms his resolution considerately, he adheres to it strictly. He does not hesitate, nor tamper with inclination. He does not gradually loosen but bursts his fetters. 'He casts no longing lingering look behind.' He forsakes every mean pursuit, and discards every worthless dependent. But he discards them with humanity. It is to avoid their influence, for all wise men avoid temptation; it is not to punish, but to correct their vices. [Quotes *2 Henry IV*, 5.5.63–70.]

Thus in the self-deceit of Falstaff, and in the discernment of Henry, held out to us on all occasions, we have a natural foundation for the catastrophe. The incidents too, by which it is accomplished, are judiciously managed. None of them are foreign or external, but grow, as it were, out of the characters.

Falstaff brings Shallow to London to see and profit by his influence at court. He places himself in King Henry's way as he returns from the coronation. He addresses him with familiarity; is neglected; persists, and is repulsed with sternness. His hopes are unexpectedly baffled, his vanity blasted; he sees his importance with those whom he had deceived completely ruined. He is for a moment unmasked: he views himself as he believes he appears to them. . . he speaks to them in the tone of the sentiments which he attributes to them, and in the language which he thinks they would hold: 'Master Shallow, I owe you a thousand pounds.' [5.5.73] It is not that in his abasement he feels a transient return of virtue: it is rather that he feels himself for a moment helpless. He sees his assumed importance destroyed; and, among other consequences, that restitution of the sum he had borrowed will be required. This alarms him; and Shallow's answer gives him small consolation. He is roused from his sudden amazement: looks about for resources: and immediately finds them. His ingenuity comes instantly to his aid; and he tells Shallow, with great readiness and plausibility of invention,

Do not you grieve at this. I shall be sent for in private to him: look you, he must seem thus to the world. Fear not your advancement. I will be the man yet that shall make you great, &c. This that you heard was but a colour, &c. Go with me to dinner. Come, lieutenant Pistol: come Bardolph; I shall be sent for soon at night.   (76–90)

Thus Shakespeare, whose morality is no less sublime than his skill in the display of character is masterly and unrivalled, represents Falstaff not only as a voluptuous and base sycophant but totally incorrigible. He displays no quality or disposition which can serve as a basis for reformation. Even his abilities and agreeable qualities contribute to his depravity. Had he been less facetious, less witty, less dexterous, and less inventive he might have been urged to self-condemnation, and so inclined to amendment. But mortification leads him to no conviction of folly, nor determines him to any change of life. He turns as soon as possible from the view given him of his baseness; and rattles, as it were in triumph, the fetters of habituated and willing bondage.—Lear, violent and impetuous but yet affectionate, from his misfortunes derives improvement. Macbeth, originally a man of feeling, is capable of remorse. And the understanding of Richard, rugged and insensible though he be, betrays his heart to the assault of conscience. But the mean sensualist, incapable of honorable and worthy thoughts, is irretrievably lost; totally, and for ever depraved. An important and awful lesson!

I may be thought perhaps to have treated Falstaff with too much severity. I am aware of his being a favourite. Persons of eminent worth feel for him some attachment, and think him hardly used by the King. But if they will allow themselves to examine the character in all its parts they will perhaps agree with me that such feeling is delusive, and arises from partial views. They will not take it amiss, if I say that they are deluded in the same manner with Prince Henry. They are amused, and conceive an improper attachment to the means of their pleasure and amusement. (48–56)

295. Unsigned essay, on *Julius Caesar*

1789

From the *Lounger's Miscellany*, nos 12 (10 January 1789) and 13 (17 January).

This generous appreciation of the play follows the lead of Capell (Vol. 5, No. 220, and No. 263 above) and Badcock (No. 262 above) in stressing Shakespeare's independent reshaping of his sources.

There are no characters of our immortal Shakespeare in which dramatic excellence and historical truth are more powerfully combined than in those which constitute his play of *Julius Cæsar*. This drama is remarkable for containing a greater variety of beautiful sentiments than any composition that ever came from the pen of man; and that frigid critic will deservedly meet our indignation who, upon hearing it read or seeing it exhibited, shall be so little transported with its excellence as to remind us that it is deficient in the unities of time and place.

This play has been censured, but certainly without justice, for the conversation which takes place at its opening between Flavius, Marullus, and certain holiday-making Plebeians. This, say some delicate critics, is low humour, ill suited to the grandeur of the business which follows, and unlikely to have passed between the Commons and their Tribunes. They who make such observations must be told that the lower class of an hardy and free people (and the Romans were not then quite reduced to slavery) are distinguished by a certain degree of saucy wit and a fondness for joking with their superiors, particularly when a festival (as this was of the Lupercal) gives a kind of licence to such indulgences. The Englishman's observation must have been strangely limited who has not noticed such a tendency in the commonalty of his own country. Upon the whole, I cannot but consider this as happy an introduction of a good play as can be met with in the works of the most artful dramatist. (67–8)

So much for the introduction of this play. I shall now examine the character of Mark Antony, who, if not the hero of the piece, is certainly one of the leading persons in it. The minute exactness with which our poet has followed Plutarch in most instances leaves us little room to doubt that he had earnestly consulted that excellent biographer in order to give his characters as much of historical truth as was consistent with the plan of his drama. Mark Antony appears to me the only character in which truth is sacrificed to poetry. But Shakespeare perhaps knew that had he represented him in his true colours he must have given up his most perfect dramatic character, and have disgusted his audience by the exhibition of a mean, drunken, brutal, and I believe an ignorant soldier. Perhaps from Plutarch it would not be possible for our poet, or any other person, to have extracted a satisfactory and decisive history of that Roman who created such confusion, and so disgraced the annals of his country. Between the mildness and moderation of his biographer Plutarch, and the vehemence and rancour of his great political enemy Cicero, it is probable that an account might be furnished more thoroughly illustrating his true character than that which should be taken from the single record of either of those writers. Plutarch tells us that he addicted himself to the study of oratory at Athens; but he does not add that he made any proficiency in that science. Cicero ridicules him for his general ignorance and his particular inability to speak. Shakespeare, on the contrary, has made him a most eloquent and persuasive orator. Plutarch mentions that he spoke over the dead body of Cæsar. Cicero has alluded to his speech in terms perhaps ironical, calling it, '*præclara oratio.*'[1] And Shakespeare has given the substance of that speech, which, though most excellent in itself, is certainly not such a one as Antony was likely to have delivered. The art of this speech consists in the appearance of blunt and honest simplicity in the speaker, which Antony would not probably have assumed because he could not have carried it through. The particular style of oratory to which he had devoted his studies, we are told, was the Asiatic, or diffuse and flowery. Here, however, every thing is plain; no rhetorical flourish, no circumlocution, no unnecessary or ornamental Epithet: '*He only speaks right on.*' And while he is declaring to his hearers that '*he comes not to steal away their*

---

[1] *Philippics*, 1.2: 'The speech Marcus Antonius made that day was a noble one'.

hearts;'—that *'he is no orator, as Brutus is; but, as they knew him all, a plain, blunt man, that loves his friend;'* [3.2.216ff.] he has in fact so stolen away their hearts as to have reduced the mob entirely to his own management, and so established his own oratory superior to that of Brutus as to have reversed every inclination of the people to support the enemies of Cæsar. Had he attained to this degree of eloquence it is not probable that Plutarch would have left so shining a qualification unmentioned; or that Cicero would have stigmatized him for his stupidity, which he does frequently in his *Philippics*, particularly the second. (68–70)

The impression left upon our minds, respecting Shakespeare's representation of this character, is that he was not indeed free from vices, but endued with a sufficient number of good qualities to conciliate our favour; that he was brave and generous, *'one that loved his friend;'* polite, debauched, and eloquent. I believe it would be difficult to fix any of these qualities upon him from true history, except his debauchery, which was of the most ignominious kind. (70–1)

That Antony was polite, or as Enobarbus calls him in Shakespeare, *'our courteous Antony,'* no one will readily agree to who is acquainted with the *Philippics* of Cicero, in which, after every allowance is made for the bitterness of an enemy and the capacity of that orator to vilify or extol his subject, sufficient proof is established that he is a sordid and sottish debauchee, content with gratifying his lusts in the lowest and most ignominious manner. His dishonesty is sufficiently apparent in his forgeries of Cæsar's Will. Thus much for the excellent dramatic character Mark Antony; in the exhibition of which, perhaps, it may be said, *the farther the poet has departed from the truth of history, the nearer he has approached to the excellence of the drama.* (72)

Having devoted the foregoing Paper to an examination of the real and dramatic character of Mark Antony, I shall now endeavour to shew that the other *dramatis personæ* represent to us an history of those great commotions as complete, faithful, and accurate as can be extracted from the annals of any history. Shakespeare seems to have obtained from Plutarch, and that only through the medium of translation, a thorough knowledge of the minds and manners of those great persons whom he has brought forward; such were the vast powers of his mind. And with judgement no less discerning, he has conveyed his knowledge in such a manner as to have given every common spectator as accurate an idea of each character as if the biography of each were submitted to his particular attention. In this play is contained all that great and interesting series of events which took place from the beginning of the conspiracy against Julius Cæsar to the issue of the battle at Philippi—perhaps the most important period that the political history of the world can furnish; and our Bard has scarcely omitted any one circumstance that could give life and spirit to his piece; nor has he admitted any one of consequence in which he is not warranted by the records of antiquity. It might, indeed, afford some satisfaction in passing through this play, to point out those particular instances of the author's minute attention to history, for which it is so remarkable, as well as to note some trivial deviations from that standard of truth which, however, is never suffered to be out of sight. Such a discussion cannot tend to diminish the value of a performance which can be increased by no commendations, nor lessened by any censures. (73–4)

. . . Concerning the character of Cassius, the Poet has left us in a state of uncertainty as to the motives by which he was instigated to form a conspiracy agains Julius Cæsar. Nor is this, I believe, any where exactly ascertained in history. Plutarch seems to be in doubt whether his conduct arose from private pique or private enmity, or a general abhorrence of tyrants and a zeal for the public good. His artful mode of rousing the spirit of Brutus is well preserved and faithfully delineated. Nor has he omitted the circumstance of letters being thrown into the windows of Brutus. Cicero is frequently mentioned by Plutarch upon this occasion, only to inform us that he had no concern in the conspiracy. Accordingly, we find Shakespeare has kept him in the background, when he must have undoubtedly had great temptation to bring him forward as the constant opponent of Antony, and the great source of Roman eloquence. Herein he has sacrificed at least something which might have been ornamental to truth. This great character is presented indeed to us; but with such scrupulous reserve that we cannot help lamenting that he is not more engaged in the business of the drama. The sickness of Ligarius is mentioned, and forms another proof of the strictness with which the Poet observes the truth of history. Perhaps it might have given his audience a clearer and more just idea of this character, if he could have contrived to inform them that this Caius Ligarius is the same who owed his life to the oratory of Cicero and the clemency of Cæsar. Our Poet has not forgotten to inform us that the time which intervened between the forming and executing the plan of the conspiracy was spent by Brutus in unquiet nights, *'musing and sighing with his arms across'* [2.1.240]; that the conspirators disdained to bind each other by an oath; that prodigies and apparitions distinguished the night before their deed was perpetrated; that Brutus's wife Portia made trial of her own constancy by voluntarily inflicting a wound upon herself; and that she then remonstrated with her husband upon his withholding from her those secrets to which, as his wife, she was entitled to be privy. And all this information is conveyed to us in a manner so fully, faithfully, and beautifully that we know not which most to admire, the accuracy of the historian or the sublimity of the Poet. The circumstances of the conspiracy, and the order and arrangement in which the several persons concerned in it act their different parts in that great tragedy, are equally to be noticed for their truth and beauty. [Quotes 2.2.4ff.]

The dialogue which follows between Cæsar and Decius is natural and necessary to further the business of the play; but I doubt whether it can be met with in any authentic record. The truth is that Cæsar did go to the Capitol; and, according to Plutarch, really pretended he was sick in order to shorten his attendance there. Shakespeare's variation is so trifling as to be scarcely worthy of notice. Plutarch's account is not more exact than our Bard's of what follows. (75–6)

The sequel of this story is not less exact than the part which has gone before. That mildness of character which is generally found the companion of real spirit and firmness is highly manifest in Brutus, and indeed eventually becomes the source of his unfortunate end. In the consultation of the conspirators he had before objected to the motion of the wary Cassius, who proposed that Antony should fall together with Cæsar; in which instance the generosity of his temper got the better of his prudence. Another instance of this generous disposition occurs in his granting permission to Antony to speak in the order of Cæsar's funeral; which request of Antony's Cassius, with his usual caution and penetration, objected to. But, finding his objection too weak to overturn Brutus's notions of justice, he concludes his ineffectual remonstrance: '*I know not what may fall; I like it not.*' [3.1.243] The varying commotions of the people, and the effect wrought upon them by the speeches of the different orators, are such as every one acknowledges to be justly represented; but at the same time such as no man could paint who was not most intimately acquainted with the interests, actions, and passions of every order of mankind. (76–7)

To all this is added a circumstantial and interesting history of the war against Brutus and Cassius, which Antony seems to have undertaken for the sole purpose of smothering that spark of liberty which had just appeared to the Roman people; and also that he might erect to himself a throne of absolute power upon the downfall of those enemies to tyranny. When we consider that the only materials from which our Poet composed this excellent piece were the Lives of Plutarch, it is matter of great wonder that every incident should have been so exactly introduced in its proper place; and that the shades of character, which mark the different persons of the drama, should have been more strongly and more distinctly preserved than even by Plutarch himself. (77–8)

296. Unsigned notices, on Boydell's Shakespeare Gallery

1789

From (a) the *Gentleman's Magazine*, lviii (1788), pp. 778–9; (b) the *Universal Chronicle*, lxxxiv, 'Historical Chronicle' for May 1789; (c) *Walker's Hibernian Magazine* (January 1791), pp. 8–10.

John Boydell (1719–1804), an enormously successful print-publisher and dealer, conceived of the idea of creating a gallery to house paintings of scenes from Shakespeare in 1786, a prospectus inviting subscriptions being issued in December of that year. The gallery opened on 4 May 1789 with thirty-four paintings, and in 1790 Boydell issued a *Catalogue*. By 1802 the gallery held about 170 pictures, but due to financial difficulties Boydell was forced to sell it, by lottery, in 1803. For a full study, with many illustrations, see Winifred H. Friedman, *Boydell's Shakespeare Gallery* (New York, 1976).

---

[a] [*Gentleman's Magazine*; letter dated 11 Sep. 1788]

It may be suspected that, among the numerous subscribers to the magnificent plan of the Boydells, some few have formed their ideas of Shakespeare's characters according to their respective appearances at Drury-lane and Covent-garden. These people may consequently regard every Hamlet as an incompetent representative if he fails to be exhibited in a suit of black velvet, and with his head most fashionably powdered; or may suppose somewhat is wanting to the verisimilitude of Lear if his crutch-headed cane and gold-clocked stockings are omitted in the scene where he is placed on his throne and divides his kingdom.

To prevent such expectations from taking root in the minds of tasteless individuals, it would not have been amiss had Messrs. Boydell advertised us that their first instruction to their artists was to forget, if possible, they had ever seen the plays of Shakespeare as they are absurdly decorated in modern theatres, and by no means to adopt ideas of ornament or attitude from any living manager or performers of either sex, for the following very substantial reasons.

In a playhouse, anachronisms are so little guarded against that discordant devices, and modern arms, are frequently associated with ancient ensigns and weapons peculiar to distinct nations and ages remote from each other; as when the Roman banner, marked by the well known letters S.P.Q.R., is displayed among the trophies of Alexander, and the Macedonian himself advances with an English tilting-spear in his hand;—when Macbeth and Banquo are seen marching, with each a brace of pistols stuck in his girdle;—when cannon peep through embrasures for the defence of the Volsci assaulted by Coriolanus. . . . All these offences against propriety have occurred on the stages of Drury-lane and Covent-garden. Mr. Boydell's canvas, we trust, will not be disgraced by congenial absurdities.

As for stage attitudes, those which have pleased most have pleased only because they were not lasting enough to be critically examined. Before their propriety could be questioned, they were at an end. Had many a celebrated posture been rendered stationary till the survey of a few minutes would have enabled us to form a just opinion of it, our applause would have been changed into disgust. The faithful pencil of Zoffany has perpetuated Garrick as he stood shuddering after the murther of Duncan. But was any correct eye ever satisfied by the twisted figure that presented itself on this occasion? By no means. Our theatric stars only glitter while they shoot; when fixed, their brilliancy is gone.

Let, therefore, the uninformed subscriber to Messrs. Boydell be taught to dismiss all hope of seeing our Shakespearian heroes invested with the meretricious foppery of the modern stage, lest he should hereafter find himself disposed to quarrel with Reynolds and West, because their Richards and Richmonds are deprived of white silk stockings, and encounter without the carte and tierce of modern fencers. Let the same rank of spectators also be prepared to feel no disappointment if the start of Fuseli's Hamlet should appear unregulated by the lessons of Le Picq, and the robe of Romney's Ariel float in easy curves, uncopied from the operatical taylorism of Signor Lupino.

Mr. Fuseli has at last completed his scene in the tragedy of *Hamlet*. It is the first interview of the Prince of Denmark with the apparition of his father. Though it would not be easy to over-praise this performance it is difficult to furnish its appropriate commendation, as words, however skillfully disposed, are but weak representatives of such design and colouring as our truly animated painter has displayed on his expressive canvas. We therefore leave the task of encomium to Mr. Boydell's numerous and scientific subscribers, observing only that the venerable magnificence of the royal spectre—his armour illuminated by partial glimpses of the moon—the dreary expanse of lurid air and ruffled water behind him—Hamlet's struggle to get loose—and his eye rivetted all the while on the ghost in respectful attention, that bespeaks astonishment free from pusillanimity—are circumstances announcing the perfect judgement of the Alderman, when he allotted this sublime subject to the pencil of Fuseli.

The remaining figures, though inferiors of the scene, are

507

rendered conspicuous on account of expression judiciously varied in their attitudes and faces. The apparition was no fresh object to either of them. The scholastic and recollected Horatio is therefore so much familiarised to it that he confines his solicitudes to the security of the Prince of Denmark; but the less calm and philosophic Marcellus, who has not yet reconciled his eye to supernatural appearances, steals half a look at the phantom as he shrinks away from it, seeming to doubt his own safety if he ventures on more than a furtive glance at this aweful visitant from another world.

Some artists engaged in the princely undertaking of Messrs. Boydell may be said to receive patronage from it; but from Mr. Fuseli, whose imagination is thoroughly impregnated by Shakespeare, the work itself derives an Herculean support.

It is with pleasure we inform our readers that the next Shakespearian incident to be handled by Mr. Fuseli, is a fairy scene in the *Midsummer Night's Dream*. A representation of this tendency is fully congenial to the soft luxuriance of that fancy he has already indulged in the Vision of Queen Katharine, and, if we are rightly informed, in some drawings on kindred subjects which have been honoured by Sir Joshua Reynolds's warmest approbation.

[b] [*Universal Chronicle*, May 1789]

Mr. Alderman Boydell opened his Shakespeare gallery for public inspection, and we may add for public gratification, for it is a treasure of graphic excellence in the highest degree creditable to British genius.

The exquisite beauties of the greatest dramatic poet that ever existed are here embodied with a skill and force of expression in many instances with which he himself would certainly have been delighted.

The enterprising proprietor of these admirable works has done much for the arts, and they in return will do much for him; for by his spirit and taste an English school for historical painting will be established which will keep his name in perpetual remembrance.

The artists who contribute to this undertaking are the first in the country; but those whose labours stand pre-eminent are Sir Joshua Reynolds, Peters, Opie, West, Fuseli, Wright, Hamilton, Northcote, Wheatley, and Banks.

The gallery is intended to consist of three large rooms; only two of them are yet open. A very fine model of an alto relievo, to be placed in the front of the building by Mr. Banks, is exhibited in the first room. It represents Shakespeare seated on a rock, with Poetry on his right hand presenting him with a wreath of bays, while she celebrates his praise on her lyre. Her head is ornamented with a double mask, to shew that she has bestowed the double power of Tragedy and Comedy on her favourite son. On his left hand is Painting, represented as addressing the spectator with one hand extended toward Shakespeare's breast, pointing him out as the proper model for her pencil. The bard leans his left hand on her shoulder, as if accepting her assistance.

In this model there is much chastity of design and execution. The face of the poet is marked with spirit and genius, and the figure of Painting would have done honour to Athens.

Of the pictures in this gallery we observe that Sir Joshua's Death of cardinal Beaufort is, in point of conception, execution, and colouring a chef d'oeuvre of art. The general hue of the picture is exactly consonant to the scene, sober, grand, solemn. The hand and arm are perhaps equal to any thing which ever came from the pallette, and the face of the dying cardinal has that horrid convulsive grin described by the poet.

The 'Hamlet's Ghost,' by Fuseli, has all that evanescent impalpability which the character ought to exhibit: and it is scarcely too much of his 'Midsummer Night's Dream' to say that if Shakespeare had been a painter, and designed that scene, he would have given somewhat of a similar picture. Opie's 'Winter's Tale' is one of the most forcible paintings we ever saw; the story is wonderfully well told, and the naked infant most classically correct and beautiful. (274)

[c] [*Walker's Hibernian Magazine*, January 1791]

Remarks on the Exhibition at Shakespeare Gallery in London: With particular reference to Invention, Composition and Expression in Painting.

Although the preface to the catalogue of the Shakespeare Gallery has warily endeavoured to preclude the strictures of criticism by affixing the opprobrium of malignity to all animadversions which should not be favourable to the performances there exhibited, yet the very author himself could hardly suppose that such premature stigma would be found able to stifle the voice of truth. Careless, however, of his opinion I shall venture concisely to lay before you the general sentiments which *the late exhibition* produced in my mind as an impartial and unprejudiced spectator.

The productions of Paintings, like those of its sister Arts, and like the World of Plato, may be considered either as to the intellectual prototype or the visible work formed after it: either as to, I. the invention; or, II. the execution.

I. The invention has three great branches: I. the choice of the subject; II. the composition; III. the expression.

I. In the choice of their subjects the painters of the Gallery have been naturally led to adopt the excesses of horror, extravagance, vulgarity, and absurdity which are the characteristic defects of the author whose works were their model. These faults do not, therefore, so properly belong to them as to Shakespeare; or the blame falls rather upon the general taste of the nation which, along with his beauties, idolizes also these errors of its favourite poet, than upon that of the unfortunate individual painters who necessarily obey this taste. I am happy, nevertheless, that the work has taken place before the bigotry of Shakespeare is too far diminished among us to be able to support it; and though I am persuaded that the blindness of this bigotry has been, in many respects, prejudicial to good taste in our isle, yet I can hardly be persuaded to censure it when I see it produce so wonderful an edifice of art as the edition of Shakespeare, the noblest monument certainly that was ever raised to the memory of any author. The same characteristic costume of the poet, their model, has led the painters also to cloath all their figures: even the *Tempest* and *Midsummer Night's Dream* were not able to raise them above it, though every painter knows how much the naked is capable of superior skill and superior force to any drapery. Opie has, however, given in his figure of Timon of Athens one masterly exception to this remark.

II. Composition seems to be the part of invention in which the painters here have principally failed. Almost every Composition is confounded and overcharged with figures. The sublime and elegant simplicity of the classic painters of Italy seems to be strange and unknown to them. Even this defect, however, may perhaps justly be attributed to their author: the same want of unity and simplicity which hurts the picture is still more excessive in Shakespeare. A few of our painters, Boydell, Northcote, and Sir Joshua Reynolds, have risen superior to it. Some of their works possess a chaste simplicity of composition that Raphael or Guido might not have disowned.

III. Ever inspired by a portion, sometimes a double portion, of the spirit of their master and model, as the composition is the most defective so the expression is the part of the ideal division best executed by our painters. Few of these pieces fail in the representation of their story; many express it with energy; and some with genius, grace, and elegance. Were I to descend to particular criticisms I would point to the Puck of Sir Joshua Reynolds as a model of perfection with respect to the three parts of invention, though the general figure has been hackneyed by him, and the piece itself is carelessly executed. I could not say so much in favour of his Death of Cardinal Beaufort, wherein all that is excellent is confined to a little corner of a large picture; though that excellence belongs indeed to the highest efforts of the pencil, yet surely the king's back, and the two vulgar heads above, merit no great praise. Perhaps even the Cardinal's face, although pregnant with genius, has too much of the broad grin for characteristic expression; his hands are a model of contorsion and agony. Belzebub is of the race of Fuseli, the father of ghosts and spectres, and we leave him to his parent.

II. From the invention we proceed to the execution, which has two branches: I. the design; and II. the colouring.

I. Design has three species of models for imitation: 1. Vulgar Nature, such as we see it in the paintings of the Dutch school. 2. The best examples of common Nature selected from the rest, such as appear in general in the Flemish school, in the Venetian, and the Lombard. 3. The union of the most perfect parts of the most beautiful examples which Nature affords us, combined to produce complete and classic grace, such as we see it in the statues of the antients, and in the schools of Rome and Bologna, in Domenichino, Caracci, Julio Romano, Guido, and Raphael. This latter manner is the organ of grace and dignity, of the divine in painting, which raises the subject above the frailties of human-nature and makes it almost a god. Few attempts at this manner are to be found in the Gallery which at least merit to be so called: its true style seems to be little known among us, and still to be

511

confined to the southern side of the Alps. . . . The head of Lear, in the mad scene of Mr. West, is also a laudable example of this sort; and especially the figure of Juliet in Northcote's picture of her tomb. . . . But, finally, how is it possible that this chaste and correct manner could ever be brought to accord with the loads of gaudy drapery which oppress the greater part of the personages here painted?—It may be necessary to add that I have not seen Barry's picture from *King Lear*.

The second style of design is that generally adopted in the pictures of the Gallery; and we may perhaps add that the genius and peculiar character of the poet here, as in other cases, influenced the artists. The personages of Shakespeare's dramas are not Phrynes nor Apollos. We certainly have in the Gallery many successful examples of the representation of well selected common Nature. . . . Guercino has certainly rivals not despicable in the English school. The beauty also of many of the heads, considered separately from the figures to which they belong, seems intuitively to indicate their proceeding from a school chiefly attentive to portrait painting. One of the principal defects resulting from this style of design is its natural tendency to produce violent, aukward, and affected attitudes, in consequence of their being often copied from local or temporary taste, or what is usually called fashion. Such an effect it had on the works of Bernini; and perhaps the commendation his manner has received from one of our most distinguished artists has not been without its consequence, to the injury of the taste of the pictures in the Gallery and even of our school in general.

II. Colouring divides itself into two parts: 1. simple colouring; 2. aerial perspective and chiaro oscuro. But these are so intimately combined with each other that many even of the most theoretic, as well as the best practical, followers of the art have often confounded them with one another. Neither of them merit unlimited commendation in the works of the Gallery. The artists seem to have supposed that the union of vast masses of gaudy colours, yellows, reds, and purples, was the essence of the art. The eye which has been accustomed to the chaster works of Italy can hardly fail to be disgusted at first sight with the gaudy glare of the rooms, and is even tempted to refuse sufficient subsequent attention to discover the real beauties which are here to be found. Opie, however, generally deserves the praise of avoiding this defect; and some of the works of Northcote are free from it, especially his beautiful picture of Juliet's tomb. The unfortunate doctrine of what is technically called effect seems to have operated greatly to introduce the fault we are censuring. Such violent colours necessarily produce effect, however carelessly or injudiciously employed; and it is no wonder that the pupils of this doctrine should follow so easy a road to vulgar applause. It was not on effect, but on labour, that the first foundation of the Flemish, German, and Italian schools were laid. The love of glittering colours has proved equally injurious to the aerial perspective of many of these pictures. Nature always throws a brown hue over the most violent tints, which subdues their glare; a truth well known to artists, but which the painters of this gallery have often thought proper to neglect; and in consequence few of their works have that relief and aerial perspective which is perhaps one of the most refined proofs of technical skill, and of which at least one figure here, the Timon of Athens of Opie, is an eminent example. . . .

It were unjust, and even absurd, to conclude without acknowledging how much honour the idea of this enterprize does to its public spirited author; so much as even to reflect a great deal on his nation; nor does the execution disgrace the idea.

297. Thomas Twining, Shakespeare and Greek tragedy

1789

From *Aristotle's Treatise on Poetry, translated: with Notes on the Translation, and on the Original; and two Dissertations, on Poetical, and Musical, Imitation* (1789; second edition, 1812).

Thomas Twining (1735–1804) had a distinguished career as a classicist at Sidney Sussex College, Cambridge, his abilities being praised by such contemporary scholars as Samuel Parr. A country clergyman for most of his life, he was an outstanding musician, both as performer and scholar (he contributed to Charles Burney's *History of Music*), and he also left a large correspondence, edited in two volumes by his grandnephew Richard Twining (1882, 1887). His translation and commentary on the *Poetics* were received with respect, being judged superior to the translation (1778, 1792) and commentary (1792) by Henry James Pye.

[On the so-called 'correctness' of Greek tragedy]

When we speak of the Greek Tragedies as correct and perfect models we seem merely to conform to the established language of prejudice, and content ourselves with echoing without reflection or examination what has been said before us. Lord Shaftesbury, for example, talks of Tragedy's being *'raised to its height* by Sophocles and Euripides, *and no room left for further excellence or emulation.'* *Advice to an Author, Part II. Sect. 2.* . . . I should be sorry to be ranked in the class of those critics who prefer that Poetry which has the fewest faults to that which has the greatest beauties. I mean only to combat that conventional and *hearsay* kind of praise which has so often held out the Tragedies of the Greek Poets as elaborate and perfect models, such as had received the last polish of art and meditation. The true praise of Æschylus, Sophocles, and Euripides is (in *kind* at least, though not in *degree,*) the praise of Shakespeare; that of strong, but irregular, unequal, and hasty genius. Every thing which this genius and the feeling of the moment could produce in an early period of the art, before time, and long experience, and criticism had cultivated and refined it, these writers possess in great abundance: what medi-tation and *'the labour and delay of the file'*[1] only can effect they too often want. Of Shakespeare, however, compared with the Greek Poets it may justly, I think, be pronounced that he has *much* more, both of this *want* and of that *abundance*. (206–7)

[On the representation of suffering in the theatre: on *Poetics*, ch. 11, 52 b 12: 'deaths exhibited on the stage']

Aristotle is here only explaining the term πάθος; not laying down

---

[1] Horace, *Ars Poetica*, 291: 'limae labor et mora'.

a *rule*, nor deciding concerning the propriety or impropriety, of such exhibitions. Nothing is more evidently absurd than the attempts of Dacier and other French critics to transfer the delicacy of *their* theatre to that of the antients. The scrupulous *delicacy* of French Tragedy was, I believe, as unknown to the Athenian stage as its rigid and strutting *dignity*. A single passage, and that from the most polished of the three Greek Tragic Poets whose works are extant, may sufficiently prove this; I mean the *description* of Oedipus tearing out his own eyes in Sophocles. [Quotes verses 1248ff.] But Sophocles did not confine himself to *description*. Oedipus himself immediately appears upon the stage, and exhibits the shocking spectacle of his bloody eyes to the audience. Certainly, the French rule 'de ne pas ensanglanter le Theatre,' w.. not *much* more strictly observed here by Sophocles than it was by Shakespeare in his LEAR, where Gloucester's eyes are *trodden out*, ἐν φανερῳ, upon the stage. (289–90)

[On *Poetics*, ch. 13, 53 a 30: Euripides 'the most tragic of all poets']

More however, it has been observed, with respect to the emotion of *pity* than that of *terror*. And so, Quintilian.: 'In affectibus cum omnibus mirus, tum in iis qui MISERATIONE constant, facile *præcipuus*.' [*lib*. x. *c*. i.][1] Yet the powers of this admirable though unequal genius were by no means confined to emotions of tenderness and pity. *He*, too, as one of '*Nature's darlings*,' possessed that '*golden key*' which can not only '*ope the sacred source of sympathetic tears*' but can '*unlock*' also, and at the same time, the '*gates* of *horror*' and of '*thrilling fears*.' As proofs of this I am tempted to produce two passages of this Poet which I could never read without shuddering. [Quotes *Medea*, 869–931: Medea's feigned reconciliation with Jason, and her plan to kill her children, 'veiling in ambiguity her dreadful purpose of destroying them'.]

The other passage is in the *Electra*. In the fine scene between Orestes and Electra, immediately after the murder of their mother, Orestes asks his sister,

> Mark'd you not, how my mother, e'er I struck her,
> Withdrew her robe, and to our view expos'd
> The breast that nourish'd us!— [1206ff.]

[1] *Institutes of Oratory*, x.i.68: 'Finally, although admirable in every kind of emotional appeal, he is easily supreme in the power to excite pity.'

I know not what more can be said to the praise of Euripides than that no one, I believe, can read this scene without being reminded of the MACBETH of SHAKESPEARE. (309–11)

298. James Fennell, Shakespeare in the theatre

1789

From the *Prompter*, October–December 1789. This journal ran from 24 October to 10 December 1789 (nineteen issues).

For the ascription to Fennell see the *Catalogue of the Hope Collection of Periodicals in the Bodleian*, and C. H. Gray, *Theatrical Criticism in London to 1795* (New York, 1931, 1971), pp. 305–7. Fennell also conducted the *Theatrical Guardian* in March and April 1791 (six issues). James Fennell (1766–1816), educated at Eton and Trinity College, Cambridge, took up acting when he had mortgaged his inheritance at the age of 21 to pay his gambling debts. As an actor he was known especially for his Othello, with successes in both Edinburgh and London. He emigrated to America in 1793, acting and giving recitals in New York, Boston, and Philadelphia, and resorting to fraud or manual labour when pressed for money. See Fennell's autobiography, *An Apology for the life of James Fennell* (Philadelphia, 1814), and P. A. Hummert, '*The Prompter*: An Intimate Mirror of the Theatre in 1789', *Restoration and Eighteenth-Century Theatre Research*, 3 (1964), pp. 37–46.

[From no. 4, 28 October 1789; on *The Tempest* at Drury Lane]
The Tempest always brings a full house, but the audience were disappointed and displeased at the liberties taken by authors and

managers with one of our poet's most celebrated comedies. Some of the most interesting and humourous scenes are omitted. Stephano and the Counsellor Gonzalo in the storm were designed to shew the sailor and the landsman at sea, and that scene, the one of the most admired, is left out. That boisterous rudeness and characteristic diction which Shakespeare thought so essential to the first part of the play suffered an inhuman amputation, and was no where preserved but when Stephano and Trinculo meet with Caliban. It is a very hazardous attempt to alter Shakespeare's writing, for we at once lose connection, thought, stile and language. This is very observable in both Dryden and Cibber's new modelling of this Comedy. The characters of Hippolito and Dorinda[1] are well supported and afford great entertainment; but they are not so natural, or drawn with such judgment, nor are they so critically accurate as Shakespeare would have made them. The artlessness, innocence, life and novelty of Dorinda, however, give great pleasure, as does the surprise of Hippolito and his consequent love on seeing Dorinda for the first time. There is a playfulness of language, only suited to such an extraordinary situation, that makes the scenes where these two characters appear very interesting; but the effect of the whole is not uniform. Shakespeare painted this beautiful woman on an enchanted island with her father only. Excepting Caliban, she had never seen any man but him; and that monster the poet has thus figured that he might more naturally raise her surprise and astonishment at her seeing Ferdinand. Their love is instantaneous, nature is seen in every word, in every look that pass between them; and the love scene in the original, which is also omitted, is heightened with language the most beautiful and pathetic. Whereas in the alteration the dividing our attention betwixt two men and two women takes away from the interest and lessens curiosity. The duel, with whatever else has been added, does not compensate for such an encroachment on so great an author. The Manager has been very judicious in the dresses (that of Prospero particularly), scenery, decorations, and machinery. Here Shakespeare's invention has been done justice to. The storm, the furies, and ship on fire, had an awful effect; and the view of the Sea at the end of the Comedy, did honour to the taste of the artist. (22–3)

---

[1] In the Dryden–D'Avenant adaptation: see Vol. 1, No. 9.

[From no. 10, 11 November 1789; on *Romeo and Juliet*]

. . . Besides the original there have been no less than seven alterations of this celebrated Tragedy.

MR. HOWARD changed it into a Tragi-comedy, and preserved the lives of both Romeo and Juliet.[1]

MR. T. CIBBER was the next who unguardedly made considerable additions, that agree so ill with the remainder that they cannot be read with any degree of satisfaction.[2]

MR. GARRICK[3] made the alteration which is now universally adopted. He has taken away the perpetual jingling of rhymes that Shakespeare was so very fond of; and has heightened the distress of the catastrophe by making Juliet wake before the poison has any effect upon Romeo. In Shakespeare Romeo dies before Juliet is restored to her senses.—Garrick, in one alteration, was very injudicious; we allude to the poetical justice which exists in Shakespeare, and which he destroys. In the present work Romeo and Juliet fall victims without any fault on their side: whereas in the original Romeo deserts Rosalind for Juliet; and is therefore punished for his inconstancy to a prior attachment.

MR. SHERIDAN, of the Dublin Theatre, has given another alteration.

MR. LEE made another for the Edinburgh Theatre: but neither have appeared in print.

The alteration of Mr. Marsh is also concealed from the world.

The last is that of Otway, who under the title of CAIUS MARIUS[4] has ingrafted the best parts of the English poet on the stock of a Roman story. But the connection is unnatural, and the whole of his play does him little honour.

To return to the merits of the play: Shakespeare most undoubtedly laid himself out in this undertaking to paint the tenderest situation of the soft passion. . . . This play abounds with beautiful descriptions; but too frequently it may be said *non erat hic locus*. The main interest is carried on with vigour; but the mind is distressed and disappointed every other moment with the humble intervention of homely humour; which, instead of relieving the mind, destroys the effect the Tragedy is meant to produce.

[1] See Vol. 2, p. 189.
[2] See Vol. 3, pp. 9, 10, 162ff., 374ff.
[3] Vol. 3, No. 117.
[4] See Vol. 1, No. 20.

The characters of the two lovers are drawn with a masterly hand: perhaps they would be still more affecting, had they less to say.

Mercutio is one of the finest traits of Shakespeare's genius. Had he given us less of the Nurse and Peter, and more of Mercutio, he would better have attained his end, we mean that of relieving the minds of the audience. (58–9).

[From no. 13, 19 November 1789; on *Hamlet*]

This singular production is more of a grand novel than a strict Drama. Shakespeare, after having perused the wonderful tale as it is related by Saxo Grammaticus and Belleforet, set himself down to dramatize it in the very same order and succession of events as he had read it. Regardless of regularity, all he wished to preserve was truth of character, and all he aimed at was variety. Both these ends he most undoubtedly has attained; but the eye of a foreigner, ever in search of dramatic uniformity, and ever disappointed in Shakespeare, sees not the drift of our author, and consequently loses both the beauty of his characters and the happy succession and linking of his varied incidents.

That Shakespeare meant no more than to add the interest of dialogue and situation to the story of Hamlet we shall be convinced by running over the character of his Hero, whom he would, and might easily have painted in different colours, had it been his intention to make use of him merely for the purpose of revenging the murder of the king his father: that is, had it been his design to have written a regular play.

Hamlet, in obedience to the will of his father's ghost, is determined to revenge his death; and enters upon the business with a resolution which we afterwards find gradually sinking from its object by the pressure of unforeseen events. This continual intervention of new agents and fresh matter constitutes the novel, and wholly destroys the idea of a Drama. That Shakespeare did not wish to shew us a hero of fancy in Hamlet, he makes him make but one effort to keep his word, that is when he mistakes Polonius for the king. At another time he defers his purpose till he can sieze on a lucky moment when, the usurper being off his guard, he may make sure the damnation of his soul by the death of his body. Though he assassinated Polonius by accident, yet he deliberately procures the execution of his school-fellows Rosencrantz and Guildenstern, who

519

appear to have been unacquainted with the treachery of the message they were employed to carry. Their death, by his own declaration to Horatio, gives him no kind of concern; for he thinks that their obtrusion gave him a right to destroy them.

[Much of the following is derived from Steevens's notes in the 1773 and 1778 editions: cf. Vol. 5, pp. 540f., and above, p. 199]

All these observations on the character of Hamlet seem to make it pretty evident that Shakespeare never intended him for the hero of a regular Drama; but drew him as he found him, the principal and extraordinary agent in a still more extraordinary tale.

Viewing the performance in this light, *they* are wrong who insist upon tying down the author to the rules of strict Tragedy, not *Shakespeare*, who never gave it as such but faithfully follows the track of a story which he means to give us in the words of the agents themselves.

In this sense, feigned madness, real madness, fencing, drinking, fops, grave diggers, murders and merriments, are all in their place; and it can only be said that we sit down to a tale instead of a Tragedy. If this tale be at once amusing and instructive, I don't see why we should find fault with the great genius that gave life to such an heterogeneous mass.

There are in this one performance reflection, wit, judgment, fire and feeling enough, when wire-drawn, to fill volumes such as Voltaire has left us; and yet this weak, invidious, superficial writer has been audacious enough to call the works of our immortal bard—UN ENORME FUMIER! The answer that the judicious and elegant Mrs. Montagu made to this insulting wipe, on hearing the expression recited in one of Voltaire's letters in a circle at Paris, must not be forgot by the Prompter: C'EST UN FUMIER QUI A FERTILISE UN TERRAIN BIEN INGRAT! (69–71)

299. Edmond Malone, edition of Shakespeare

1790

From *The Plays and Poems of William Shakespeare, in ten volumes; collated* verbatim *with the most authentick copies, and revised: with the corrections and illustrations of various commentators; to which are added, An Essay on the chronological Order of his Plays; An Essay relative to Shakespeare and Jonson; A Dissertation on the Three Parts of King Henry VI; An Historical Account of the English Stage; and Notes; by Edmond Malone* (11 vols, London, 1790).

On Malone see the head-note to No. 265. For this major edition Malone retained, and expanded, most of the material he had produced in 1780 and 1783 (No. 275), and added much more. The *Prolegomena* increased to such an extent that they had to be printed in two volumes, described as 'Vol. 1, Part 1' and 'Vol. 1, Part 2', distinguished here as 'I, part 1', and 'I, part 2'. Malone had issued a duodecimo edition with select notes in 1786, and in the following year first published *A Dissertation on the Three Parts of 'Henry VI', tending to shew that those plays were not written originally by Shakespeare* (51 pp.).

[From the Preface]
In the following work, the labour of eight years, I have endeavoured with unceasing solicitude to give a faithful and correct edition of the plays and poems of Shakespeare. Whatever imperfection or errours therefore may be found in it (and what work of so great length and difficulty was ever free from errour or imperfection?) will, I trust, be imputed to any other cause than want of zeal for the due execution of the task which I ventured to undertake.

The difficulties to be encountered by an editor of the works of Shakespeare have been so frequently stated, and are so generally acknowledged that it may seem unnecessary to conciliate the

521

publick favour by this plea. But as these in my opinion have in some particulars been over-rated, and in others not sufficiently insisted on, and as the true state of the ancient copies of this poet's writings has never been laid before the publick,[1] I shall consider the subject as if it had not been already discussed by preceding editors. (I, part 1, i)

[Malone reprints Johnson's 1756 *Proposals* for an edition (Vol. 4 of this series, No. 160) on the difficulties encountered by an editor of Shakespeare.]

Though Dr. Johnson has here pointed out with his usual perspicuity and vigour the true course to be taken by an editor of Shakespeare, some of the positions which he has laid down may be controverted, and some are indubitably not true. It is not true that the plays of this authour were more incorrectly printed than those of any of his contemporaries: for in the plays of Marlowe, Marston, Fletcher, Massinger, and others as many errours may be found. It is not true that the art of printing was in no other age in so unskilful hands. Nor is it true, in the latitude in which it is stated, that 'these plays were printed from compilations made by chance or by stealth out of the separate parts written for the theatre:' two only of all his dramas, *The Merry Wives of Windsor* and *K. Henry V* appear to have been thus thrust into the world, and of the former it is yet a doubt whether it is a first sketch or an imperfect copy. I do not believe that words were then adopted at pleasure from the neighbouring languages, or that an antiquated diction was then employed by any poet but Spenser. That the obscurities of our authour, to whatever cause they may be referred, do not arise from the paucity of contemporary writers, the present edition may furnish indisputable evidence. And lastly, if it be true, that 'very few of Shakespeare's lines were difficult to his audience, and that he used such expressions as were then common,' (a position of which I have not the smallest doubt,) it cannot be true that 'his reader is embarrassed at once with dead and with foreign languages, with obsoleteness and innovation.'

When Mr. Pope first undertook the task of revising these plays every anomaly of language, and every expression that was not understood at that time, were considered as errours or corruptions, and the text was altered, or amended, as it was called, at

[1] But see Roberts (Vol. 2, No. 77), Theobald (Vol. 2, Nos 74, 82), Capell (Vol. 5, No. 220), and Steevens (Vol. 5, Nos 211, 212, 240).

pleasure. The principal writers of the early part of this century seem never to have looked behind them, and to have considered their own era and their own phraseology as the standard of perfection: hence from the time of Pope's edition, for above twenty years, to alter Shakespeare's text and to restore it were considered as synonymous terms. During the last thirty years our principal employment has been to *restore*, in the true sense of the word; to eject the arbitrary and capricious innovations made by our predecessors from ignorance of the phraseology and customs of the age in which Shakespeare lived.

As on the one hand our poet's text has been described as more corrupt than it really is, so on the other the labour required to investigate fugitive allusions, to explain and justify obsolete phraseology by parallel passages from contemporary authours, and to form a genuine text by a faithful collation of the original copies, has not perhaps had that notice to which it is entitled. For undoubtedly it is a laborious and a difficult task: and the due execution of this it is, which can alone entitle an editor of Shakespeare to the favour of the publick.

I have said that the comparative value of the various ancient copies of Shakespeare's plays has never been precisely ascertained. To prove this it will be necessary to go into a long and minute discussion, for which, however, no apology is necessary. For though to explain and illustrate the writings of our poet is a principal duty of his editor, to ascertain his genuine text, to fix what is to be explained, is his first and immediate object: and till it be established which of the ancient copies is entitled to preference we have no criterion by which the text can be ascertained.

Fifteen of Shakespeare's plays were printed in quarto antecedent to the first complete collection of his works, which was published by his fellow-comedians in 1623. These plays are, *A Midsummer-Night's Dream, Love's Labour's Lost, Romeo and Juliet, Hamlet, The Two parts of K. Henry IV, K. Richard II, K. Richard III, The Merchant of Venice, K Henry V, Much ado about Nothing, The Merry Wives of Windsor, Troilus and Cressida, King Lear,* and *Othello.*

The players, when they mention these copies, represent them all as mutilated and imperfect; but this was merely thrown out to give an additional value to their own edition, and is not strictly true of any but two of the whole number, *The Merry Wives of Windsor,* and *K. Henry V.*—With respect to the other thirteen copies, though undoubtedly they were all surreptitious, that is, stolen from the playhouse and printed without the consent of the authour or the proprietors, they *in general* are preferable to the exhibition of the same plays in the folio. For this plain reason, because, instead of printing these plays from a manuscript the editors of the folio, to save labour, or from some other motive, printed the greater part of them from the very copies[1] which they represented as maimed and imperfect, and frequently from a late, instead of the earliest, edition; in some instances with additions and alterations of their own. Thus therefore the first folio, as far as respects the plays above enumerated, labours under the disadvantage of being at least a second, and in some cases a third edition of these quartos. I do not however mean to say that many valuable corrections of passages undoubtedly corrupt in the quartos are not found in the folio copy; or that a single line of these plays should be printed by a careful editor without a minute examination and collation of both copies. But those quartos were in general the basis on which the folio editors built, and are entitled to our particular attention and examination as *first* editions.

It is well known to those who are conversant with the business of the press that (unless when the authour corrects and revises his own works), as editions of books are multiplied their errours are multiplied also; and that consequently every such edition is more or less correct as it approaches nearer to or is more distant from the first.[2] A few instances of the gradual progress of corruption will fully evince the truth of this assertion. . . . (I, part 1, x–xiii)

The various readings found in the different impressions of the quarto copies are frequently mentioned by the late editors. It is obvious from what has been already stated that the first edition of each play is alone of any authority,* and accordingly to no other have I paid any attention. All the variations in the subsequent quartos were made by accident or caprice. Where, however, there are two editions printed in the same year, or an undated copy, it is necessary to examine each of them, because which of them was first

---

[1] Cf. Capell, Vol. 5, p. 306.

[2] Cf. Capell, Vol. 5, p. 307.

* Except only in the instance of *Romeo and Juliet*, where the first copy, printed in 1597, appears to be an imperfect sketch, and therefore cannot be entirely relied on. Yet even this furnishes many valuable corrections of the more perfect copy of that tragedy in its present state, printed in 1599.

can not be ascertained; and being each printed from a manuscript they carry with them a degree of authority to which a re-impression cannot be entitled. Of the tragedy of *King Lear* there are no less than three copies, varying from each other, printed for the same bookseller and in the same year.

Of all the plays of which there are no quarto copies extant the first folio, printed in 1623, is the only authentick edition.

An opinion has been entertained by some that the second impression of that book, published in 1632, has a similar claim to authenticity. 'Whoever has any of the folios, (says Dr. Johnson,) has all, excepting those diversities which mere reiteration of editions will produce. I collated them all at the beginning, but afterwards used only the first, from which (he afterwards adds,) the subsequent folios never differ but by accident or negligence.' Mr. Steevens, however, does not subscribe to this opinion. 'The edition of 1632, (says that gentleman,) is not without value; for though it be in some places more incorrectly printed than the preceding one, it has likewise the advantage of various readings, which are not merely such as reiteration of copies will naturally produce.'

What Dr. Johnson has stated is not quite accurate. The second folio does indeed very frequently differ from the first by negligence or chance; but much more frequently by the editor's profound ignorance of our poet's phraseology and metre, in consequence of which there is scarce a page of the book which is not disfigured by the capricious alterations introduced by the person to whom the care of that impression was entrusted. This person in fact, whoever he was, and Mr. Pope, were the two great corrupters of our poet's text; and I have no doubt that if the arbitrary alterations introduced by these two editors were numbered, in the plays of which no quarto copies are extant, they would greatly exceed all the corruptions and errours of the press in the original and only authentick copy of those plays. (I, part 1, xviii–xx)

[Malone now gives examples of the Second Folio's errors, in two main categories: 'ignorance of Shakespeare's phraseology' and 'ignorance of the metre'. From the former come the following instances.]

Among the marks of love, Rosalind in *As you like it* mentions 'a beard neglected, which you have not;—but I pardon you for that; for, simply, your *having in* beard is a younger brother's revenue.'

[3.2.375f] Not understanding the meaning of the word *having*, this editor reads—'your having *no* beard,' &c.

In *A Midsummer Night's Dream* Pyramus says,

> I *see* a voice; now will I to the chink,
> To spy an' I can *hear* my Thisby's face   [5.1.192f.]

Of the humour of this passage he had not the least notion, for he has printed, instead of it

> I *hear* a voice; now will I to the chink,
> To spy an' I can *see* my Thisby's face.

(I, part 1, xxx)

[In his account of the Second Folio's 'ignorance of the metre' Malone claims that the pronunciation of numerous words in Shakespeare has been misunderstood. According to him, words of one syllable include 'neither; rather'; of two syllables: 'fires; sworn; charms; hour; fire; Charles; arms; pours; worn; hair; burn; hire'; of three syllables: 'English; Astraea; Henry; dazzled; tickled; country; doctrine'; of four syllables: 'contrary; perfections; Bassanio': I, part 1, xxv–xliii.]

[Malone describes his method of checking his text.]
Having often experienced the fallaciousness of collation by the eye I determined, after I had adjusted the text in the best manner in my power, to have every proof-sheet of my work read aloud to me while I perused the first folio, for those plays which first appeared in that edition; and for all those which had been previously printed the first quarto copy, excepting only in the instances of *The Merry Wives of Windsor* and *King Henry V*, which, being either sketches or imperfect copies could not be wholly relied on; and *King Richard III*, of the earliest edition of which tragedy I was not possessed. I had at the same time before me a table which I had formed of the variations between the quartos and the folio. By this laborious process not a single innovation made either by the editor of the second folio or any of the modern editors could escape me. . . .

If it be asked what has been the fruit of all this labour, I answer that many innovations, transpositions, &c. have been detected by this means; many hundred emendations have been made; and, I trust, a genuine text has been formed. Wherever any deviation is made from the authentick copies, except in the case of mere obvious errors of the press, the reader is apprized by a note; and every emendation that has been adopted is ascribed to its proper author. When it is considered that there are one hundred thousand lines in these plays, and that it often was necessary to consult six or seven volumes in order to ascertain by which of the preceding editors, from the time of the publication of the second folio, each emendation was made, it will easily be believed that this was not effected without much trouble. (I, part 1, xliv–li)

[On *Pericles*, 'now once more restored to our author']
The hand of Shakespeare being indubitably found in that piece it will, I doubt not, be considered as a valuable accession. . . .

It has long been thought that *Titus Andronicus* was not written originally by Shakespeare; about seventy years after his death Ravenscroft having mentioned that he had been 'told by some anciently conversant with the stage, that our poet only gave some master-touches to one or two of the principal parts or characters.' The very curious papers lately discovered in Dulwich College, from which large extracts are given at the end of the History of the Stage, prove what I long since suspected,[1] that this play, and *the First Part of K. Henry VI*, were in possession of the scene when Shakespeare began to write for the stage; and the same manuscripts shew that it was then very common for a dramatick poet to alter and amend the work of a preceding writer. The question therefore is now decisively settled; and undoubtedly some additions were made to both these pieces by Shakespeare. It is observable that the second scene of the third act of *Titus Andronicus* is not found in the quarto copy printed in 1611. It is therefore highly probable that this scene was added by our authour; and his hand may be traced in the preceding act, as well as in a few other places.* The additions which he made to *Pericles* are much more numerous, and therefore more strongly entitle it to a place among the dramatick pieces which he has adorned by his pen. (lix–lx)

[On the previous editors of Shakespeare: Rowe's text was 'disfigured' on almost every page 'by accumulated corruptions', partly inherited, partly introduced.]
In Mr. Pope's edition our authour was not less misrepresented; for though by examining the oldest copies he detected some errours,

---

[1] But see the Introduction above, p. 46.
* If ever the account-book of Mr. Heminge shall be discovered, we shall probably find in it—'*Paid to William Shakespeare for* mending *Titus Andronicus.*'

by his numerous fanciful alterations the poet was so completely modernized that I am confident, had he 're-visited the glimpses of the moon,' he would not have understood his own works. From the quartos indeed a few valuable restorations were made; but all the advantage that was thus obtained was outweighed by arbitrary changes, transpositions, and interpolations.

The readers of Shakespeare being disgusted with the liberties taken by Mr. Pope, the subsequent edition of Theobald was justly preferred; because he professed to adhere to the ancient copies more strictly than his competitor, and illustrated a few passages by extracts from the writers of our poet's age. That his work should at this day be considered of any value only shews how long impressions will remain when they are once made. For Theobald, though not so great an innovator as Pope, was yet a considerable innovator; and his edition being printed from that of his immediate predecessor, while a few arbitrary changes made by Pope were detected, innumerable sophistications were silently adopted. His knowledge of the contemporary authours was so scanty that all the illustration of that kind dispersed throughout his volumes has been exceeded by the researches which have since been made for the purpose of elucidating a single play. [Hanmer and Warburton are briefly dismissed.]

At length the task of revising these plays was undertaken by one whose extraordinary powers of mind, as they rendered him the admiration of his contemporaries, will transmit his name to posterity as the brightest ornament of the eighteenth century; and will transmit it without competition, if we except a great orator, philosopher, and statesman* now living, whose talents and virtues are an honour to human nature. In 1765 Dr. Johnson's edition, which had long been impatiently expected, was given to the publick. His admirable preface (perhaps the finest composition in our language), his happy, and in general just characters of these plays, his refutation of the false glosses of Theobald and Warburton, and his numerous explications of involved and difficult passages, are too well known to be here enlarged upon; and therefore I shall only add that his vigorous and comprehensive understanding threw more light on his authour than all his predecessors had done. (lxvi–lxix)

[Malone disagrees with Johnson on Shakespeare's early popu-

* The Right Honourable Edmund Burke.

larity, arguing that he is now more appreciated than in his own age, and that his superiority to Jonson, Beaumont and Fletcher, and other contemporaries is now finally recognized. He quotes the praise of Shakespeare over Jonson made by Edward Young in 1759: see Vol. 4, p. 407]

To this and the other encomiums on our great poet which will be found in the following pages I shall not attempt to make any addition. . . .

Let me, however, be permitted to remark that beside all his other transcendent merits he was the great refiner and polisher of our language. His compound epithets, his bold metaphors, the energy of his expressions, the harmony of his numbers, all these render the language of Shakespeare one of his principal beauties. Unfortunately none of his letters, or other prose compositions not in a dramatick form, have reached posterity; but if any of them ever shall be discovered they will, I am confident, exhibit the same perspicuity, the same cadence, the same elegance and vigour which we find in his plays. (I, part 1, lxxvii)

[1] [From *Some Account of the Life &c. of William Shakespeare*. Malone prints Rowe's Life (Vol. 2 of this series, No. 47) with copious additional notes and documents, including an account of the mulberry-tree at New Place, Stratford, supposedly planted by Shakespeare, a story which Malone regards as being 'as well authenticated as any thing of that nature can be'.]

Shakespeare was perhaps the only inhabitant of Stratford whose business called him annually to London; and probably on his return from thence in the spring of the year 1609 he planted this tree.

As a similar enthusiasm to that which with such diligence has sought after Virgil's tomb, may lead my countrymen to visit the spot where our great bard spent several years of his life, and died; it may gratify them to be told that the ground on which *The New-Place* once stood is now a Garden belonging to Mr. Charles Hunt, an eminent attorney, and town-clerk of Stratford. Every Englishman will, I am sure, concur with me in wishing that it may enjoy perpetual verdure and fertility.

> In this retreat our SHAKESPEARE's godlike mind
> With matchless skill survey'd all human kind.

Here may each sweet that blest Arabia knows,
Flowers of all hue, and without thorn the rose,
To latest time, their balmy odours fling,
And Nature here display eternal spring!

(I, part 1, 119 note)

[2] [On Shakespeare's last illness and death]
He died in the 53d year of his age,] He died on his birth-day, April 23, 1616, and had exactly completed his fifty-second year. From Du Cange's Perpetual Almanack, Gloss. in v. *Annus,* (making allowance for the different style which then prevailed in England from that on which Du Cange's calculation was formed,) it appears, that the 23d of April in that year was a Tuesday.

No account has been transmitted to us of the malady which at so early a period of life deprived England of its brightest ornament. . . .

While we lament that our incomparable poet was snatched from the world at a time when his faculties were in their full vigour, and before he was 'declined into the vale of years,' let us be thankful that 'this sweetest child of Fancy' did not perish while he yet lay in the cradle. He was born at Stratford-upon-Avon in April 1564; and I have this moment learned from the Register of that town that the plague broke out there on the 30th of the following June, and raged with such violence between that day and the last day of December, that two hundred and thirty eight persons were in that period carried to the grave, of which number probably 216 died of that malignant distemper; . . . Supposing one in thirty-five to have died annually, the total number of the inhabitants of Stratford at that period was 1470; and consequently the plague in the last six months of the year 1564 carried off more than a seventh part of them. Fortunately for mankind it did not reach the house in which the infant Shakespeare lay; for not one of that name appears in the dead list.—May we suppose, that, like Horace, he lay secure and fearless in the midst of contagion and death, protected by the Muses to whom his future life was to be devoted, and covered over

————sacra
Lauroque, collataque myrto,
Non sine Diis animosus infans.[1]

(I, part 1, 123–4 notes)

[1] *Odes*, 3.4.18ff.: 'with sacred bay and gathered myrtle, with the gods' help a fearless child'.

530

[3] [From *An Attempt to ascertain the Order in which the Plays of Shakespeare were written* (I, part 1, 261–386). This essay had first appeared in the Johnson–Steevens edition of 1778 (above pp. 190f.). Malone expands it considerably, and revises his dating for several plays, here omitting *Titus Andronicus*, *Pericles*, and all the apocryphal plays.]

1.	FIRST PART OF KING HENRY VI.	1589.
2.	SECOND PART OF KING HENRY VI.	1591.
3.	THIRD PART OF KING HENRY VI.	1591.
4.	A MIDSUMMER-NIGHT'S DREAM,	1592.
5.	COMEDY OF ERRORS,	1593.
6.	TAMING OF THE SHREW,	1594.
7.	LOVE'S LABOUR'S LOST,	1594.
8.	TWO GENTLEMEN OF VERONA,	1595.
9.	ROMEO AND JULIET,	1595.
10.	HAMLET,	1596.
11.	KING JOHN,	1596.
12.	KING RICHARD II.	1597.
13.	KING RICHARD III.	1597.
14.	FIRST PART OF KING HENRY IV.	1597.
15.	SECOND PART OF KING HENRY IV.	1598.
16.	THE MERCHANT OF VENICE,	1598.
17.	ALL'S WELL THAT ENDS WELL,	1598.
18.	KING HENRY V.	1599.
19.	MUCH ADO ABOUT NOTHING,	1600.
20.	AS YOU LIKE IT,	1600.
21.	MERRY WIVES OF WINDSOR,	1601.
22.	KING HENRY VIII.	1601.
23.	TROILUS AND CRESSIDA,	1602.
24.	MEASURE FOR MEASURE,	1603.
25.	THE WINTER'S TALE,	1604.
26.	KING LEAR,	1605.
27.	CYMBELINE,	1605.
28.	MACBETH,	1606.
29.	JULIUS CÆSAR,	1607.
30.	ANTONY AND CLEOPATRA,	1608.
31.	TIMON OF ATHENS,	1609.
32.	CORIOLANUS,	1610.
33.	OTHELLO,	1611.
34.	THE TEMPEST,	1612.
35.	TWELFTH NIGHT,	1614.

(I, part 1, 266–7)

[4] [On the date of *Hamlet*, and Shakespeare's knowledge of the law. Malone quotes Nashe's *Epistle* to Greene's *Arcadia* (1589), with its jeer against lawyers who turn writers, 'a sort of shifting companions, that runne through every art and thrive by none, to leave the trade of *Noverint*, whereto they were born, and busie themselves with the endevors of art, that could scarcely latinize their neck-verse if they should have neede; yet English *Seneca*, read by candle-light, yeelds many good sentences, as *Bloud is a beggar*, and so forth: and, if you intreat him faire in a frosty morning, he will affoord you whole *Hamlets*, I should say, Handfuls, of tragical speeches.']

Nashe seems to point at some dramatick writer of that time, who had originally been a scrivener or attorney who, instead of transcribing deeds and pleadings chose to imitate Seneca's plays, of which a translation had been published many years before. Our author, however freely he may have borrowed from Plutarch and Holinshed, does not appear to be at all indebted to Seneca; and therefore I do not believe that he was the person in Nashe's contemplation. The person alluded to being described as originally bred to the law (for the trade of *noverint* is the trade of an attorney or conveyancer),* I formerly conceived that this circumstance also was decisive to shew that Shakespeare could not have been aimed at. I do not hesitate to acknowledge that since the first edition of this essay I have found reason to believe that I was mistaken. The comprehensive mind of our poet embraced almost every object of nature, every trade, every art; the manners of every description of men, and the general language of almost every profession. But his knowledge of legal terms is not merely such as might be acquired by the casual observation of even his all-comprehending mind. It has the appearance of *technical* skill; and he is so fond of displaying it on all occasions that I suspect he was early initiated in at least the forms of law, and was employed, while he yet remained at Stratford, in the office of some country attorney who was at the same time a petty conveyancer, and perhaps also the Seneschal of some manor-court. I shall subjoin the proofs below.† (I, part 1, 306–8)

---

* Our ancient deeds were written in Latin, and frequently began with the words, *Noverint Universi*. The form is still retained. *Know all men*, &c.

†   ——for what in me was *purchas'd*,
     Falls upon thee in a much fairer sort.   *King Henry IV*, P. II. [4.5.200]

[5] [On the date of *King John*: 1596]
It is observable that our author's son, Hamnet, died in August, 1596. That a man of such sensibility, and of so amiable a disposition should have lost his only son, who had attained the age of twelve years, without being greatly affected by it will not be easily credited. The pathetick lamentations which he has written for Lady Constance on the death of Arthur may perhaps add some probability to the supposition that this tragedy was written at or soon after that period. (I, part 1, 311–2)

[6] [On the date of *Measure for Measure*: 1603]
Some part of this last argument in confirmation of the date which I had assigned some years ago to the comedy before us I owe to Mr. Capell; and while I acknowledge the obligation, it is but just to add that it is the only one that I met with, which in the smallest degree could throw any light on the present inquiry into the dates of our authour's plays, 'In the dry desert of *ten* thousand lines;' after wading through two ponderous volumes in quarto, written in a style manifestly formed on that of the Clown in the comedy under our consideration, whose narratives, we are told, were calculated to last out *a night in Russia, when nights are at the longest.* (I, part 1, 346–7)

Purchase is here used in its strict legal sense, in contradistinction to an acquisition by *descent.* . . .

[Malone lists such technical terms as 'fee-simple; fine and recovery; bill; warrant; quittance; single bond; impanelled; extent; enfeof'd; entail; pray in aid; terms; actions'.]

No writer but one who had been conversant with the technical language of leases and other conveyances would have used *determination* as synonymous to *end.* Shakespeare frequently uses the word in that sense. 'From and after the *determination* of such term,' is the regular language of conveyancers.

Humbly complaining to your highness.　　　*K. Richard III.* [1.1.76]

'Humbly complaining to your lordship, your orator,' &c. are the first words of every bill in chancery.

Are those *precepts* served? says Shallow to Davy in *K. Henry IV.* [Part 2, 5.1.13f.]
Precepts in this sense is a word only known in the office of a Justice of peace.

Tell me, what state, what dignity, what honour,
Can'st thou *demise* to any child of mine?　　　*K. Richard III* [4.4.248f.]

'—hath *demised*, granted, and to farm let,' is the constant language of leases. What *poet* but Shakespeare has used the word *demised* in this sense?

Perhaps it may be said that our authour in the same manner may be proved to have been equally conversant with the terms of divinity, or physick. Whenever as large a number of instances of his ecclesiastical or medicinal knowledge shall be produced, what has now been stated will certainly not be entitled to any weight.

[7] [From the essay on 'Shakespeare, Ford, and Jonson']
Having always thought with indignation on the tastelessness of the scholars of that age in preferring Jonson to Shakespeare after the death of the latter, I did not find myself much inclined to dispute the authenticity of a paper which, in its general tenour, was conformable to my own notions: but the love of truth ought ever to be superior to such considerations. Our poet's fame is fixed upon a basis *as broad and general as the casing air*, and stands in no need of such meretricious aids as the pen of fiction may be able to furnish. . . .

Nor let our poet's admirers be at all alarmed, or shrink from this discussion; for after this slight and temporary fabrick erected to his honour shall have been demolished, there will still remain abundant proofs of the gentleness, modesty, and humility, of Shakespeare; of the overweening arrogance of old Ben; and of the ridiculous absurdity of his partizans, who for near a century set *above* our great dramatick poet a writer whom no man is now hardy enough to mention as even his competitor. (I, part 1, 387–8)

[8] [From 'An Historical Account of the Rise and Progress of the English Stage'. Malone discusses John Aubrey's account of Shakespeare]
'He was a handsome well-shaped man, verie good company, and of a very ready, and pleasant, and smooth witt.'

I suppose none of my readers will find any difficulty in giving full credit to this part of the account. Mr. Aubrey, I believe, is the only writer who has particularly mentioned the beauty of our poet's person; and there being no contradictory testimony on the subject he may here be safely relied on. All his contemporaries who have spoken of him concur in celebrating the gentleness of his manners, and the readiness of his wit. [Malone quotes the testimonies of Heminge and Condell, and Jonson.] In a subsequent page I shall have occasion to quote another of his contemporaries, who is equally lavish in praising the uprightness of his conduct and the gentleness and civility of his demeanour. (I, part 2, 175)

[9] [From the same essay, in its survey of the history of Shakespeare productions since the Restoration]
From 1709, when Mr. Rowe published his edition of Shakespeare, the exhibition of his plays became much more frequent than

before. Between that time and 1740, our poet's *Hamlet, Julius Cæsar, K. Henry VIII, Othello, K. Richard III, King Lear,* and the two parts of *King Henry IV* were very frequently exhibited. Still, however, such was the wretched taste of the audiences of those days that in many instances the contemptible alterations of his pieces were preferred to the originals. (I, part 2, 281)

. . . But the great theatrical events of this year was the appearance of Mr. Garrick at the theatre in Goodman's Fields, Oct. 19, 1741; whose good taste led him to study the plays of Shakespeare with more assiduity than any of his predecessors. Since that time, in consequence of Mr. Garrick's admirable performance of many of his principal characters, the frequent representation of his plays in nearly their original state, and above all the various researches which have been made for the purpose of explaining and illustrating his works, our poet's reputation has been yearly increasing, and is now fixed upon a basis which neither the lapse of time nor the fluctuation of opinion will ever be able to shake. Here therefore I conclude this imperfect account of the origin and progress of the English Stage. (I, part 2, 283–4)

[From the Notes]
[10] [On *The Tempest,* 4.1.157]

—*We are such stuff*
As dreams *are made* on,] I would willingly persuade myself that this vulgarism was introduced by the transcriber, and that Shakespeare wrote—made *of.* But I fear other instances are to be found in these plays of this unjustifiable phraseology, and therefore have not disturbed the text. MALONE. (I, part 2, 80)

[11] [On *Pericles:* in the 1780 edition (above, pp. 296ff.) Malone had argued that the play was wholly Shakespeare's, Steevens that it was the work of another hand, only improved by Shakespeare. Malone now agrees with Steevens.]

. . . It was printed with Shakespeare's name in the title-page, in his life-time; but this circumstance proves nothing: because by the knavery of booksellers other pieces were also ascribed to him in his life-time of which he indubitably wrote not a line. Nor is it necessary to urge in support of its genuineness that at a subsequent period it was ascribed to him by several dramatick writers. I wish not to rely on any circumstance of that kind; because in all questions of this nature internal evidence is the best that can be produced, and to every person intimately acquainted with our poet's writings must in the present case be decisive. The congenial sentiments, the numerous expressions bearing a striking similitude to passages in his undisputed plays, some of the incidents, the situation of many of the persons, and in various places the colour of the style, all these combine to set the seal of Shakespeare on the play before us, and furnish us with internal and irresistible proofs that a considerable portion of this piece, as it now appears, was written by him. The greater part of the three last acts may, I think, on this ground be safely ascribed to him; and his hand may be traced occasionally in the other two divisions.

To alter, new-model, and improve the unsuccessful dramas of preceding writers was, I believe, much more common in the time of Shakespeare than is generally supposed. This piece having been thus new-modelled by our poet, and enriched with many happy strokes from his pen, is unquestionably entitled to that place among his works which it has now obtained. MALONE. (III, 636)

[12] [On *Twelfth Night*, 5.1.200: 'a passy-measures pavin']
From what has been stated, I think, it is manifest that Sir Toby means only by this quaint expression that the surgeon is a rogue, and a *grave solemn coxcomb*. It is one of Shakespeare's unrivalled excellencies that his characters are always consistent. Even in drunkenness they preserve the traits which distinguished them when sober. Sir Toby in the first act of this play shewed himself well acquainted with the various kinds of the dance. MALONE. (IV, 106)

[13] [On *Macbeth*, 1.7.58]
We fail!] I am by no means sure that this punctuation is the true one. — 'If we fail, we fail,' — is a colloquial phrase still in frequent use. Macbeth having casually employed the former part of this sentence his wife designedly completes it. *We fail*, and thereby know the extent of our misfortune. Yet *our success is certain, if you are resolute*.

Lady Macbeth is unwilling to afford her husband time to state any reasons for his doubt, or to expatiate on the obvious consequences of miscarriage in his undertaking. Such an interval for reflection to act in might have proved unfavourable to her purposes. She therefore cuts him short with the remaining part of a common saying, to which his own words had offered an apt though accidental introduction.

This reply, at once cool and determined, is sufficiently character-istick of the speaker. According to the old punctuation, she is represented as rejecting with contempt (of which she had already manifested enough) the very idea of failure. According to the mode of pointing now suggested she admits a possibility of miscarriage, but at the same instant shows herself not afraid of its result. Her answer therefore communicates no discouragement to her husband.—*We fail!* is the hasty interruption of scornful impatience. *We fail.*—is the calm deduction of a mind which, having weighed all circumstances, is prepared, without loss of confidence in itself, for the worst that can happen. So Hotspur:

> If we fall in, good night:—or sink, or swim.
>
> STEEVENS. (IV, 309–10),

[14] [*Ibid.*, 1.7.79]

and bend *up*—] A metaphor from the bow. So, in *K. Henry V*. '—*bend* up every spirit/To his full height.' [3.1.16]. Till this instant the mind of Macbeth has been in a state of uncertainty and fluctation. He has hitherto proved neither resolutely good nor obstinately wicked. Though a bloody idea had arisen in his mind after he had heard the prophecy in his favour, yet he contentedly leave the completion of his hopes to chance.—At the conclusion, however, of his interview with Duncan he inclines to hasten the decree of fate, and quits the stage with an apparent resolution to murder his sovereign. But no sooner is the king under his roof than, reflecting on the peculiarities of his own relative situation, he determines not to offend against the laws of hospitality, or the ties of subjection, kindred, and gratitude. His wife then assails his constancy afresh. He yields to her suggestions, and, with his integrity, his happiness is destroyed.

I have enumerated these particulars because the waverings of Macbeth have, by some criticks, been regarded as unnatural and contradictory circumstances in his character; not remembering that *nemo repente fuit turpissimus*,[1] or that (as Angelo observes)

---

[1] Juvenal, *Satires*, 2.83: 'No one reaches the depths of turpitude all at once'.

——when once our grace we have forgot,
Nothing goes right; we would, and we would not—:
[*Measure for Measure*, 4.4.33f.]

a passage which contains no unapt justification of the changes that
happen in the conduct of Macbeth. STEEVENS. (IV, 314)

[15] [*Ibid.*, 2.2.62: cf. Malone's note in 1780 (above, p. 283) and
Steevens's objections to it in 1785 (above, p. 390)]
Mr. Steevens objects in the following note to this explanation,
thinking it more probable that Shakespeare should refer 'to some
visible quality in the ocean,' than 'to its concealed inhabitants; to
the waters that might admit of discoloration,' than 'to the fishes
whose hue could suffer no change from the tinct of blood.' But in
what page of our author do we find his allusions thus curiously
rounded, and complete in all their parts? Or rather does not every
page of these volumes furnish us with images crouded on each
other, that are not naturally connected, and sometimes are even
discordant? Hamlet's proposing to take up *arms* against a *sea* of
troubles is a well known example of this kind, and twenty others
might be produced. Our author certainly alludes to the waters,
which are capable of discoloration, and not to the fishes. His
allusion to the waters is expressed by the word *seas*; to which, if he
has added an epithet that has no very close connection with the
subject immediately before him, he has only followed his usual
practice.

If however no allusion was intended to the myriads of
inhabitants with which the deep is peopled, I believe by the
multitudinous seas was meant, not the *many-waved* ocean, as is
suggested below, but *the countless masses of waters wherever dispersed on
the surface of the globe*; the *multitudes of seas,* as Heywood has it in a
passage that perhaps our author remembered: and indeed it must
be owned that his having used the plural *seas* seems to countenance
such an interpretation; for the singular *sea* is equally suited to the
epithet *multitudinous* in the sense of ἰχθύόεντα,[1] and would
certainly have corresponded better with the subsequent line.
MALONE. (IV, 331–2)

[16] [On Macbeth's behaviour after the murder, taken by Whately
as a sign of cowardice]

---

[1] 'The fish-inhabited sea': *Odyssey*, 4.381, 390, etc. ('where the fish swarm', tr. Lattimore).

After the horrour and agitation of this scene, the reader may perhaps not be displeased to pause for a few minutes. The consummate art which Shakespeare has displayed in the preparation for the murder of Duncan, and during the commission of the dreadful act, cannot but strike every intelligent reader. An ingenious writer, however, whose comparative view of Macbeth and Richard III has just reached my hands, has developed some of the more minute traits of the character of Macbeth, particularly in the present and subsequent scene, with such acuteness of observation, . . . [Malone quotes Whately, above, pp. 417–19.]

To these ingenious observations I entirely subscribe, except that I think the wavering irresolution and agitation of Macbeth after the murder ought not to be ascribed *solely* to a remission of courage, since much of it may be imputed to the remorse which would arise in a man who was of a good natural disposition, and is described as originally 'full of the milk of human kindness;—not without ambition, but without the illness should attend it.' MALONE. (IV, 334–6)

[17] [On *King John*, 3.1.69]
For grief is proud, and makes his owner stoop.] Our author has rendered this passage obscure by indulging himself in one of those conceits in which he too much delights, and by bounding rapidly, with his usual licence, from one idea to another. This obscurity induced Sir T. Hanmer for *stoop* to substitute *stout*; a reading that appears to me to have been too hastily adopted in the subsequent editions.

The confusion arises from the poet's having personified grief in the first part of the passage, and supposing the afflicted person to be *bowed* to the earth by that pride or haughtiness which Grief is said to possess; and by making the afflicted person, in the latter part of the passage, actuated by this very pride, and exacting the same kind of obeisance from others, that Grief has exacted from her.—'I will not go (says Constance) to these kings; I will teach my sorrows to be proud; for Grief is proud, and makes the afflicted *stoop*; therefore here I throw myself, and let them come to me.' Here, had she stopped, and thrown herself on the ground, and had nothing more being added, however we might have disapproved of the conceit we should have had no temptation to disturb the text. But the idea of throwing herself on the ground suggests a new image; and because her *stately* grief is so great that nothing but the huge earth can support it, she considers the ground as her *throne*; and having thus invested herself with regal dignity, she as queen in *misery*, as possessing (like Imogen) 'the supreme *crown* of grief,' calls on the princes of the world to bow down before her, as she has herself been *bowed down* by affliction.

Such, I think, was the process that passed in the poet's mind; which appears to me so clearly to explain the text that I see no reason for departing from it. MALONE. (IV, 492–3)

[18] [On *1 Henry IV*, 3.1.239f.: 'Then be still'—'Neither; 'tis a woman's fault']
The whole tenor of Hotspur's conversation in this scene shews that the stillness which he here imputes to women as a fault was something very different from silence; and that an idea was couched under these words which may be better understood than explained.—He is still in the Welsh lady's bed-chamber. WHITE.[1] (V, 202)

[19] [On *2 Henry IV*, 4.1.122f., the rebels' betrayal: cf. Heath (Vol. 4, pp. 556f.), Johnson (Vol. 5, p. 122), Mrs Montagu (*ibid.*, p. 334), Capell (*ibid.*, p. 559), and Davies, p. 374 above]
Shakespeare here, as in many other places, has merely followed the historians who related this perfidious act without animadversion, and who seem to have adopted the ungenerous sentiment of Choræbus:

—dolus an virtus, quis in hoste requirat?[2]

But this is certainly no excuse; for it the duty of a poet always to take the side of virtue. MALONE. (V, 386)

[20] [*Ibid.*, 5.3.50: Silence's part in this scene]
The words, *And we shall be merry*, have a reference to a song of which Silence has already sung a stanza. His speeches in this scene are for the most part fragments of ballads. Though his imagination did not furnish him with any thing original to say, he could repeat the verses of others. MALONE. (V, 425)

---

[1] T. Holt White (1724–97), Shakespeare commentator and philologist.
[2] Virgil, *Aeneid*, 2.390: 'whether deceit or valour, who would ask in warfare?'

[21] [End-note to *2 Henry IV*]
Dr. Johnson objects with good reason, I think, to the 'lame and impotent conclusion' of this play. Our author seems to have been as careless in the conclusion of the following plays as in that before us.

In *The Tempest* the concluding words are: '—please you draw near.'

In *Much ado about nothing*: '—Strike up pipers.'

In *Love's Labour's Lost*: '—You this way; we this way.'

In *The Winter's Tale*: '—Hastily lead away.'

In *Timon of Athens*: 'Let our drums strike.'

In *Hamlet*: 'Go, bid the soldiers shoot.'   MALONE. (V, 440)

[22] [On *Henry V*, Act V: Chorus 30, the allusion to Essex, 'the general of our gracious Empress']
Our author had the best grounds for supposing that Lord Essex on his return from Ireland would be attended with a numerous concourse of well-wishers; for, on his setting out for that country in the spring of the year in which this play was written, 'he took horse (says the continuator of Stowe's Chronicle,) in Seeding lane, and from thence being accompanied with diverse noblemen and many others, himselfe very plainly attired, roade through Grace-church street, Cornhill, Cheapside, and other high streets, in all which places and in the fields, the people pressed exceedingly to behold him, especially in the high way for more than foure miles space, crying, and saying, God blesse your Lordship, God preserve your honour, &c. and some followed him till the evening, only to behold him.' 'Such and so great (adds the same writer,) was the hearty love and deep affection of the people towards him, by reason of his bounty, liberalitie, affabilitie and mild behaviour, that as well schollars, souldiers, citizens, saylers, &c. protestants, papists, sectaries and atheists, yea, women and children which never saw him, that it was held in them a happiness to follow the worst of his fortunes.' That such a man should have fallen a sacrifice to the caprice of a fantastick woman, and the machinations of the detestable Cecil, must ever be lamented.—His return from Ireland, however, was very different from what our poet predicted. MALONE. (V, 585)

[23] [From 'Dissertation on the Three Parts of *King Henry VI*']
I have said that certain passages in *The Second and Third Part of*

King Henry VI are ascertained to be Shakespeare's by a peculiar phraseology. This peculiar phraseology, without a single exception, distinguishes such parts of these plays as are found in the folio, and not in the *elder* quarto dramas, of which the phraseology, as well as the versification, is of a different colour. This observation applies not only to the new original matter produced by Shakespeare but to his alteration of the old. Our author in his undoubted compositions has fallen into an inaccuracy of which I do not recollect a similar instance in the works of any other dramatist. When he has occasion to quote the same paper twice (not from memory, but *verbatim*), from negligence he does not always attend to the words of the paper which he has occasion to quote, but makes one of the persons of the drama recite them with variations, though he holds the very paper quoted before his eyes. [Quotes instances from *All's Well that Ends Well* and *2 Henry VI*.]

Many minute marks of Shakespeare's hand may be traced in such parts of the old plays as he has new-modelled. I at present recollect one that must strike every reader who is conversant with his writings. He very frequently uses adjectives adverbially; and this kind of phraseology, if not peculiar to him, is found more frequently in his writings than those of any of his contemporaries. Thus,—'I am myself *indifferent* honest;'—'as *dishonourable* ragged as an old faced ancient;' '—*equal* ravenous;'—'leaves them *invisible*'; &c. (VI, 416–18)

[24] [On *Coriolanus*, 2.3.115]

Why in this woolvish toge *should I stand here*,] I suppose the meaning is, Why should I stand in this gown of humility, which is little expressive of my feelings towards the people; as far from being an emblem of my real character as the sheep's cloathing on a wolf as expressive of his disposition. I believe *woolvish* was used by our author for false or deceitful, and that the phrase was suggested to him, as Mr. Steevens seems also to think, by the common expression,—'a wolf in sheep's cloathing.' Mr. Mason says that this is 'a ludicrous idea, and ought to be treated as such.' I have paid due attention to many of the ingenious commentator's remarks in the present edition, and therefore I am sure he will pardon me when I observe that speculative criticism on these plays will ever be liable to error unless we add to it an intimate acquaintance with the language and writings of the predecessors and contemporaries of Shakespeare. If Mr. Mason had read the following line in Churchyard's legend of Cardinal Wolsey, *Mirror for Magistrates*, 1587, instead of considering this as a ludicrous interpretation, he would probably have admitted it to be a natural and just explication of the epithet before us: 'O fye on *wolves*, that march in *masking clothes*.'

The *woolvish toge* is a gown of humility, in which Coriolanus thinks he shall appear in *masquerade*; not in his real and natural character.

Woolvish cannot mean *rough, hirsute*, as Dr. Johnson interprets it, because the gown Coriolanus wore has already been described as *napless*. MALONE. (VII, 210–11)

[25] [*Ibid.*, 4.7.81ff.: 'power . . ./Hath not a tomb so evident as a chair/To extol what it hath done']
If our authour meant to place Coriolanus in this *chair* he must have forgot his character, for as Mr. Mason has justly observed,[1] he has already been described as one who was so far from being a boaster, that he could not endure to hear 'his nothings monster'd.' But I rather believe, 'in the utterance' alludes not to Coriolanus himself, but to the high encomiums pronounced on him by his friends; and then the lines of Horace quoted [below][2] may serve as comment on the passage before us. MALONE. (VII, 278)

[26] [On *Antony and Cleopatra*, 4.15.32: Cleopatra: 'Here's sport, indeed.': Johnson commented in 1765 (VII, 227), 'I suppose the meaning of these strange words is, *here's* trifling, *you* do not work *in earnest*'.]
Perhaps rather, here's a curious game, the last we shall ever play with Antony! Or perhaps she is thinking of fishing with a line, a diversion of which we have been already told she was fond. Shakespeare has introduced ludicrous ideas with as much incongruity in other places. MALONE. (VII, 571)

[27] [On *Troilus and Cressida*, 1.1.55f.]
Handlest *in thy discourse, O, that her hand*, &c.] *Handlest* is here used

[1] See above pp. 403f.
[2] '*Urit enim fulgore suo, qui praegravat artes/Infra se positas*': *Epistles*, 2.1.13ff.: 'For a man scorches with his brilliance who outweighs merits lowlier than his own' (on the topic 'Envy is quelled only by death').

metaphorically, with an allusion at the same time to its literal meaning; and the jingle between *hand* and *handlest* is perfectly in our authour's manner.

The beauty of a female hand seems to have made a strong impression on his mind. Antony cannot endure that the hand of Cleopatra should be touched: [quotes 3.13.124f.; also *Romeo and Juliet*, 3.3.36f.].

In the *Winter's Tale* Florizel with equal warmth, and not less poetically, descants on the hand of his mistress [quotes 4.4.362ff.]. MALONE. (VIII, 147)

[28] [*Ibid.*, 3.2.77ff.]
—*weep seas, live in fire, eat rocks, tame tygers*;] Here we have, not a Trojan prince talking to his mistress, but Orlando Furioso vowing that he will endure every calamity that can be imagined; boasting that he will achieve more than ever *knight* performed. MALONE. (VIII, 219)

[29] [On *Cymbeline*, 2.3.22f.: 'His steeds to water at those springs/On chalic'd flow'rs that lies'. Steevens noted that 'Shakespeare frequently offends in this manner against the rules of grammar', mixing singular and plural]
There is scarcely a page of our authour's works in which similar false concords may not be found: nor is this inaccuracy peculiar to his works, being found in many other books of his time and of the preceding age. Following the example of all the former editors I have silently corrected the error, in all places except where either the metre, or rhymes, rendered correction impossible. Whether it is to be attributed to the poet or his printer, it is such a gross offence against grammar as no modern eye or ear could have endured, if from a wish to exhibit our authour's writings with strict fidelity it had been preserved. The reformation therefore, it is hoped, will be pardoned, and considered in the same light as the substitution of modern for ancient orthography. MALONE. (VIII, 357)

[30] [*Ibid.*, 3.2.17ff.: another alleged 'inconsistency' in the quotation of a letter]
The *words* here read by Pisanio from his master's letter, (which is afterwards given at length, and in *prose*,) are not found there, though the *substance* of them is contained in it. This is one of many

proofs that Shakespeare had no view to the publication of his pieces. There was little danger that such an inaccuracy should be detected by the ear of the spectator, though it could hardly escape an attentive reader. MALONE. (VIII, 379)

[31] [On *King Lear*, 1.2.136f.]
O, these eclipses do portend these divisions! fa, sol, la, mi.] The commentators, not being musicians, have regarded this passage perhaps as unintelligible nonsense, and therefore left it as they found it, without bestowing a single conjecture on its meaning and import. Shakespeare however shews by the context that he was well acquainted with the property of these syllables in solmisation, which imply a series of sounds so unnatural that ancient musicians prohibited their use. The monkish writers on musick say, *mi contra fa est diabolus*: the interval *fa mi*, including a *tritonus*, or sharp 4th, consisting of three tones without the intervention of a semi-tone, expressed in the modern scale by the letters F G A B, would form a musical phrase extremely disagreeable to the ear. Edmund, speaking of eclipses as portents and prodigies, compares the dislocation of events, the *times being out of joint*, to the unnatural and offensive sounds, *fa sol la mi*. BURNEY.[1] (VIII, 513)

[32] [*Ibid.*, 1.4.217: 'So out went the candle, and we were left darkling']
Shakespeare's fools are certainly copied from the life. The originals whom he copied were no doubt men of quick parts; lively and sarcastick. Though they were licenced to say any thing, it was still necessary to prevent giving offence, that every thing they said should have a playful air. We may suppose therefore that they had a custom of taking off the edge of too sharp a speech by covering it hastily with the end of an old song, or any glib nonsense that came into the mind. I know no other way of accounting for the incoherent words with which Shakespeare often finishes this fool's speeches. SIR JOSHUA REYNOLDS. (VIII, 527)

[33] [On *Romeo and Juliet*, 2.1.38: 'An Open—*etcætera*, thou a poperin pear!']
These two lines, which are found in the quartos of 1597, 1599, and

---

[1] Charles Burney (1726–1814), music historian.

in the folio, were rejected by Mr. Pope, who in like manner has rejected *whole scenes* of our authour; but what is more strange, his example has in this instance been followed by the succeeding editors.

However improper any lines may be for recitation on the stage, an editor in my apprehension has no right to omit any passage that is found in all the authentick copies of his author's works. I know not on what authority it has been said that these lines are a proof that 'either the poet or his friends knew sometimes how to blot.' They appear not only in the editions already mentioned but also in that copy which has no date, and in the edition of 1637.

I have adhered to the original copy. The two subsequent quartos and the folio read, with a slight variation,

> An open—*or* thou a poperin pear.

Shakespeare followed the fashion of his own time, which was, when something indecent was meant to be suppressed, to print *etcætera*, instead of the word. See Minsheu's Dictionary, p. 112, col. 2. Our poet did not consider that however such a practice might be admitted in a printed book, it is absurd where words are intended to be recited. When these lines were spoken, as undoubtedly they were to our ancestors, who do not appear to have been extremely delicate, the actor must have evaded the difficulty by an abrupt sentence.

The unseemly name of the apple here alluded to is well known. *Poperingue* is a town in French Flanders, two leagues distant from Ypres. From hence the *Poperin* pear was brought into England. What were the peculiar qualities of a *Poperin* pear, I am unable to ascertain. The word was chosen, I believe, merely for the sake of a quibble, which it is not necessary to explain. MALONE. (IX, 56)

[34] [On *Hamlet*, 3.4.30: 'As kill a king!' In 1780 Malone had stated that Shakespeare wished to render Claudius and Gertrude 'odious' (above, pp. 283f.) to which Steevens had replied in 1785 (above, p. 392). Malone adds a further paragraph to his first note, then replies to Steevens: cf. above, p. 199]

Though the inference already mentioned may be drawn from the surprize which our poet has here made the queen express at being charged with the murder of her husband, it is observable that when the player-queen in the preceding scene says,

In second husband let me be accurst!
None wed the second, *but who kill'd the first*,   [3.2.179f.]

he has made Hamlet exclaim—'*that's wormwood.*' The prince, therefore, both from that expression and the words addressed to his mother in the present scene, must be supposed to think her guilty.[1]—Perhaps after all this investigation, the truth is that Shakespeare himself meant to leave the matter in doubt.

Had Shakespeare thought fit to have introduced the topicks I have suggested, can there be a doubt concerning his ability to introduce them? The king's justification, if to justify him had been the poet's object (which it certainly was not,) might have been made in a soliloquy; the queen's, in the present interview with her son. MALONE. (IX, 331—2)

[35] [On Steevens's 1773 attack on Hamlet: Vol. 5, pp. 540—1; cf. Ritson's defence, above, pp. 342ff.]
Some of the charges here brought against Hamlet appear to me questionable at least, if not unfounded. I have already observed that in the novel on which this play is constructed, the ministers who by the king's order accompanied the young prince to England, and carried with them a packet in which his death was concerted, were apprized of its contents; and therefore we may *presume* that Shakespeare meant to describe their representatives, Rosencrantz and Guildenstern, as equally criminal, as combining with the king to deprive Hamlet of his life. His procuring their execution therefore does not with certainty appear to have been an unprovoked cruelty, and *might* have been considered by him as necessary to his *future safety*; knowing, as he must have known, that they had devoted themselves to the service of the king in whatever he should command. The principle on which he acted, is ascertained by the following lines, from which also it may be inferred that the poet meant to represent Hamlet's school-fellows as privy to the plot against his life: [quotes 3.4.202ff.: 'They bear the mandate'].

Another charge is, that '*he comes to disturb the funeral of Ophelia:*' but the fact is otherwise represented in the first scene of the fifth act: for when the funeral procession appears, (which he does not seek, but finds,) he exclaims, '*who is this they follow.*/And with such

---

[1] Cf. Davies, No. 277 above, note 29.

maimed rites?' [5.1.218f.], nor does he know it to be the funeral of Ophelia till Laertes mentions that the dead body was that of his sister.

I do not perceive that he is accountable for the madness of Ophelia. He did not mean to kill her father when concealed behind the arras, but the king; and still less did he intend to deprive her of her reason and her life. Her subsequent distraction therefore can no otherwise be laid to his charge, than as an unforeseen consequence from his too ardently pursuing the object recommended to him by his father.

He appears to have been induced to leap into Ophelia's grave not with a design to insult Laertes, but from his love to her (which then he had no reason to conceal), and from the *bravery of her brother's grief*, which excited him (not to condemn that brother, as has been stated, but) to *vie* with him in the expression of affection and sorrow:

> Why, I will fight with him upon this theme,
> Until my eyelids will no longer wag.—
> I lov'd Ophelia; forty thousand brothers
> Could not with all their quantity of love
> Make up my sum. [5.1.266ff.]

When Hamlet says, 'the bravery of his grief did put me into a *towering passion*,' I think, he means, into a lofty expression (not of *resentment*, but) of *sorrow*. So, in *King John*, 'She is *sad* and *passionate* at your highness' tent.' [2.1.544] Again, more appositely in the play before us:

> The instant burst of clamour that she made,
> (Unless things mortal move them not at all,)
> Would have made milch the burning eyes of heaven,
> And *passion* in the gods. [2.2.515ff.]

I may also add that he neither assaulted nor insulted Laertes, till that nobleman had cursed him, and seized him by the throat. MALONE. (IX, 424–5)

[36] [End-note to *Othello*]
To Dr. Johnson's admirable and nicely discriminative character of *Othello*, it may seem unnecessary to make any addition; yet I cannot forbear to conclude our commentaries on this transcendent poet

with the fine eulogy which the judicious and learned Lowth[1] has pronounced on him, with a particular reference to this tragedy, perhaps the most perfect of all his works [Lowth is referring to the Greek tragedians, who excelled in both poetry and philosophy, as all poets should]:

> Should it be objected that some have been eminent in this walk of Poetry who never studied in the schools of the Philosophers, nor enjoyed the advantages of an education above the common herd of mankind; I answer that I am not contending about the vulgar opinion, or concerning the meaning of a word. The man who, by the force of genius and observation, has arrived at a perfect knowledge of mankind, who has acquainted himself with the natural powers of the human mind, and the causes by which the passions are excited and repressed; who not only in words can explain, but can delineate to the senses every emotion of the soul; who can excite, can temper and regulate the passions; such a man, though he may not have acquired erudition by the common methods, I esteem a true Philosopher. The passion of jealousy, its causes, circumstances, its progress, and effects, I hold to be more accurately, more copiously, more satisfactorily described in one of the dramas of Shakespeare, than in all the disputations of the schools of Philosophy.
>
> MALONE. (IX, 647–8)

[37] [End-note to *Venus and Adonis*, expanding his defence of it in 1780 (above, pp. 286ff.). Malone cites further seventeenth-century testimonies to Shakespeare's excellence as a poet.]

Let us, however, view these poems uninfluenced by any authority.—To form a right judgment of any work we should always take into our consideration the means by which it was executed, and the contemporary performances of others. The smaller pieces of Otway and Rowe add nothing to the reputation which they have acquired by their dramatick works, because preceding writers had already produced happier compositions; and because there were many poets during the period in which Rowe and Otway exhibited their plays, who produced better poetry, not of the dramatick kind, than theirs. But, if we except Spenser, what poet of Shakespeare's age produced poems of equal, or nearly equal, excellence to those before us? Did Turberville? Did Golding? Did Phaer? Did Drant? Did Googe? Did Churchyard?

---

[1] Malone quotes from the Latin text *De sacra Poesie Hebraeorum* (1753). I substitute the English translation by G. Gregory of Lowth's *Lectures on the Sacred Poetry of the Hebrews* (London, 1787), pp. 14–15.

Did Fleming? Did Fraunce? Did Whetstone? Did Gascoigne? Did Sidney? Did Marlowe, Nashe, Kyd, Harrington, Lilly, Peele, Greene, Watson, Breton, Chapman, Daniel, Drayton, Middleton or Jonson? Sackville's *Induction* is the only small piece of that age that I recollect which can stand in competition with them. If Marlowe had lived to finish his *Hero and Leander*, of which he wrote little more than the first two Sestiads, he too perhaps might have contested the palm with Shakespeare.

Concerning the length of these pieces, which is I think justly objected to, I shall at present only observe that it was the fashion of the day to write a great number of verses on a very slight subject, and our poet in this as in many other instances adapted himself to the taste of his own age.

It appears to me in the highest degree improbable that Shakespeare had any *moral view* in writing this poem; Shakespeare, who, (as Dr. Johnson has justly observed,) generally 'sacrifices virtue to convenience, and is so much more careful to please than to instruct, that he seems to write without any moral purpose;'—who 'carries his persons indifferently through right and wrong, and at the close dismisses them without further care, and leaves their examples to operate by chance.'[1] As little probable is it, in my apprehension, that he departed on any settled principles from the mythological story of Venus and Adonis. As well might we suppose that in the construction of his plays he deliberately deviated from the rules of Aristotle (of which after the publication of Sir Philip Sidney's Treatise he could not be ignorant), with a view to produce a more animated and noble exhibition than Aristotle or his followers ever knew. His method of proceeding was, I apprehend, exactly similar in both cases; and he no more deviated from the classical representation on any formed and digested plan in the one case than he neglected the unities in the other. He merely (as I conceive,) in the present instance, as in many others, followed the story as he found it already treated by preceding English writers; for I am persuaded that *The Sheepheard's Song of Venus and Adonis*, by Henry Constable, preceded the poem before us. MALONE. (X, 72–3)

[38] [End-note to *The Rape of Lucrece*]
Of these two poems *Venus and Adonis* appears to me entitled to

1 See Vol. 5, p. 65.

superior praise. Their great defect is the wearisome circumlocution with which the tale in each of them is told, particularly in that before us. [Cf. 1780, above, pp. 287f.]

Let us, however, never forget the state of poetry when these pieces appeared; and after perusing the productions of the contemporary and preceding writers Shakespeare will have little to fear from the unprejudiced decision of his judges. In the foregoing notes we have seen almost every stanza of these poems fraught with images and expressions that occur also in his plays. To the liquid lapse of his numbers, in his *Venus and Adonis*, his *Lucrece*, his *Sonnets*, his *Lovers Complaint*, and in all the *songs* which are introduced in his dramas, I wish particularly to call the attention of the reader. In this respect he leaves all his contemporaries many paces behind him.—Even the length of his two principal poems will be pardoned when the practice of his age is adverted to. Like some advocates at the Bar, our elder poets seem to have thought it impossible to say too much on any subject. On the story of *Rosamond* Daniel has written above nine hundred lines. Drayton's *Legend of Rollo duke of Normandy* contains nine hundred and forty five lines; his *Matilda* six hundred and seventy two; and his *Legend of Pierce Gaveston* seven hundred and two. On the story of *Romeo and Juliet*, Arthur Brooke has left a poem of above *four thousand* lines; and that of *Troilus and Cressida* Chaucer has expanded into no less than *eight thousand* verses. MALONE. (X, 187–8)

[39] [On Sonnet 20: cf. Steevens's note in 1780, above, p. 288]

Some part of this indignation might perhaps have been abated if it had been considered that such addresses to men, however indelicate, were customary in our authour's time, and neither imported criminality, nor were esteemed indecorous. See a note on the words—'thy deceased *lover*,' in the 32d Sonnet. To regulate our judgment of Shakespeare's poems by the modes of modern times is surely as unreasonable as to try his plays by the rules of Aristotle.

Master-mistress does not perhaps mean *man*-mistress, but *sovereign* mistress. MALONE. (X, 207)

[40] [On Sonnet 29: see the first note by Steevens in the 1780 *Supplement*, above, p. 288]

When in disgrace with fortune and men's eyes, &c.] These nervous and animated lines, in which such an assemblage of thoughts, cloathed in the most glowing expressions, is compressed into the narrow compass of fourteen lines, might I think have saved the whole of this collection from the general and indiscriminate censure thrown out against them [by Steevens]. MALONE (X, 217)

[41] [On Sonnet 32: 'These poor rude lines of thy deceased lover'] The numerous expressions of this kind in these Sonnets, as well as the general tenour of the greater part of them, cannot but appear strange to a modern reader. In justice therefore to our authour it is proper to observe that such addresses to men were common in Shakespeare's time, and were not thought indecorous. That age seems to have been very indelicate and gross in many other particulars beside this, but they certainly did not think themselves so. Nothing can prove more strongly the different notions which they entertained on subjects of decorum from those which prevail at present, than the elogiums which were pronounced on Fletcher's plays for the *chastity* of their language; those very plays which are now banished from the stage for their *licentiousness* and *obscenity.*

We have many examples in our authour's plays of the expression used in the Sonnet before us, and afterwards frequently repeated. See Vol. III. p. 67, n. 7.[1] Thus, also, in *Coriolanus*:

> —I tell thee fellow,
> Thy general is my *lover*. [5.2.14f.]

Again, in *Troilus and Cressida, Ulysses* says, 'Farewell, my lord; I as your *lover* speak.' [3.3.214]

So also the Soothsayer in *Julius Cæsar* concludes his friendly admonition to the dictator with the words:—'Thy *lover*, Artemidorus.' [2.3.9]

So, in one of the Psalms: 'My *lovers* and friends hast thou put away from me, and hid mine acquaintance out of my sight.'

In like manner Ben Jonson concludes one of his letters to Dr. Donne by telling him that he is his 'ever true *lover*,' and Drayton in a letter to Mr. Drummond of Hawthornden informs him that Mr. Joseph Davies is *in love* with him.

Mr. Warton, in confirmation of what has been now advanced,

---

[1] A note on *The Merchant of Venice*, 3.4.16 (Antonio being the 'bosom lover' of Bassanio): 'In our author's time this term was applied to those of the same sex who had an esteem for each other'.

observes in his HISTORY OF ENGLISH POETRY, that 'in the reign of Queen Elizabeth whole sets of Sonnets were written with this sort of attachment.' He particularly mentions *The Affectionate Shepherd* of Richard Barnefielde, printed in 1595. MALONE. (X, 219–20)

[42] [On Sonnet 37]
So I, made lame by fortune's dearest *spite,*] *Dearest* is *most operative.* So, in *Hamlet*: ' 'Would I had met my *dearest* foe in heaven.' [1.2.182]

A late editor,[1] grounding himself on this line, and another in the 89th Sonnet, 'Speak of my *lameness,* and I straight will halt,—' conjectured that Shakespeare was literally lame: but the expression appears to have been only figurative. So again in *Coriolanus*:

> —I cannot help it now,
> Unless by using means I *lame* the foot
> Of our design.   [4.7.6ff.]

Again, in *As you Like it*:

> Which I did store to be my foster-nurse,
> When service should in my old limbs lie *lame.*   [2.3.40f.]

In the 89th Sonnet the poet speaks of his friend's imputing a fault to him of which he was not guilty, and yet, he says, he would acknowledge it: so, (he adds,) were he to be described as lame, however untruly, yet rather than his friend should appear in the wrong, he would immediately halt.

If Shakespeare was in truth lame, he had it not in his power to *halt occasionally* for this or any other purpose. The defect must have been fixed and permanent.

The context in the verses before us in like manner refutes this notion. If the words are to be understood literally, we must then suppose that our admired poet was also *poor* and *despised,* for neither of which suppositions there is the smallest ground. MALONE. (X, 225)

[43] [On Sonnet 93, and Shakespeare's relationship with his wife: cf. the exchange by Malone and Steevens in 1780 (above, pp. 290ff.)]
Every author who writes on a variety of topicks will have sometimes occasion to describe what he has himself felt. To

[1] Capell: *Notes and Various Readings,* 1774, I.i.60.

attribute to our great poet (to whose amiable manners all his contemporaries bear testimony) the moroseness of a cynick, or the depravity of a murderer, would be to form an idea of him contradicted by the whole tenour of his character, and unsupported by any kind of evidence: but to suppose him to have felt a passion which it is said 'most men who ever loved have in some degree experienced' does not appear to me a very wild or extravagant conjecture.—Let it also be remembered that he has not exhibited *four* Shylocks, nor *four* Timons, but *one* only of each of those characters.

Our authour's forgetfulness of his wife, from whatever cause it arose, cannot well be imputed to the *indisposed and sickly fit*; for, from an imperfect erasure in his will (which I have seen) it appears to have been written (though not executed) *two* months before his death; and in the first paragraph he has himself told us that he was, at the time of making it, in *perfect health*: words which no honest attorney, I believe, ever inserted in a will when the testator was notoriously in a contrary state. Any speculation on this subject is indeed unnecessary; for the various regulations and provisions of our authour's will show that at the time of making it (whatever his *health* might have been,) he had the entire use of his *faculties*. Nor, supposing the contrary to have been the case, do I see what in the two succeeding months he was to recollect or to alter. His wife had not wholly escaped his memory; he had forgot her,—he had recollected her,—but so recollected her as more strongly to mark how little he esteemed her; he had already (as it is vulgarly expressed) cut her off, not indeed with a shilling, but with an old bed.

However, I acknowledge, it does not follow that because he was inattentive to her in his will he was therefore jealous of her. He might not have loved her; and perhaps she might not have deserved his affection.

This note having already been extended to too great a length, I shall only add that I must still think that a poet's intimate knowledge of the passions and manners which he describes will generally be of use to him; and that in some *few* cases experience will give a warmth to his colouring, that mere observation may not supply. No man, I believe, who had not felt the magick power of beauty ever composed love-verses that were worth reading. Who (to use nearly our authour's words,)

> In leaden contemplation *e'er* found out
> Such fiery numbers as the prompting eyes
> Of beauteous tutors have enrich'd *men* with?
>
> [*Love's Labour's Lost*, 4.3.318ff.]

That in order to produce any successful composition the mind must be at ease is, I conceive, an incontrovertible truth. It has not been suggested that Shakespeare wrote on the subject of jealousy during the paroxysm of the fit. MALONE. (X, 268–9)

[44] [Head-note to *Titus Andronicus*]

On what principle the editors of the first complete edition of our poet's plays admitted this into their volume cannot now be ascertained. The most probable reason that can be assigned is that he wrote a few lines in it, or gave some assistance to the authour in revising it, or in some other way aided him in bringing it forward on the stage. . . .

To enter into a long disquisition to prove this piece not to have been written by Shakespeare would be an idle waste of time.[1] To those who are not conversant with his writings, if particular passages were examined, more words would be necessary than the subject is worth; those who are well acquainted with his works cannot entertain a doubt on the question.—I will however mention one mode by which it may be easily ascertained. Let the reader only peruse a few lines of *Appius and Virginia, Tancred and Gismund, the Battle of Alcazar, Jeromino, Selimus Emperor of the Turks, the Wounds of Civil War, the Wars of Cyrus, Locrine, Arden of Feversham, King Edward I, the Spanish Tragedy, Solyman and Perseda, King Leir,* the old *King John,* or any other of the pieces that were exhibited before the time of Shakespeare, and he will at once perceive that *Titus Andronicus* was coined in the same mint[2]. . . . MALONE. (X, 375–6)

---

[1] But see Malone's later note in the Preface above, p. 527.
[2] Capell, in his 1768 edition, had shown the homogeneity of *Titus Andronicus* with plays of this period and type: see Vol. 5, pp. 319f.

300. W. N., on *Othello*

From 'Critical Remarks on the *Othello* of Shakespeare', in the *Bee, or Literary Weekly Intelligencer*, vol. i: for 12 January 1791 (pp. 56–62), 19 January (pp. 87–90), 29 January (pp. 132–6), and 2 February (pp. 176–81).

The *Bee*, a miscellaneous literary journal, appeared between 1790 and 1794, and was edited by James Anderson (1739–1808), the economist and agriculturalist. It described itself as 'A work calculated to disseminate useful knowledge among all ranks of people at a small expence'.

Of those who possess that superiority of genius which enables them to shine by their own strength, the number has been few. . . .

Among those to whom mankind is most indebted the first place is perhaps due to Homer and to Shakespeare. They both flourished in the infancy of society, and the popular tales of the times were the materials upon which they exerted their genius; they were equally unassisted by the writings of others. The dramatic compositions with which Shakespeare was acquainted were as contemptible as the crude tales which served as the foundation of Homer's poem. The genius of both poets was then of undoubted originality, and varied, as the scene is with which they were conversant. It cannot perhaps be said that an idea is to be found in their works, imitated from another. To whatever subject they turned their attention a picture of nature, such as was capable of filling their minds alone, arose in full prospect before them. An idea imagined by any other would be inadequate to the grasp of their genius, and uncongenial with their usual mode of conception. Intimately acquainted with the original fountains of human knowledge, accustomed themselves to trace the operations of nature, they disdained to take notice of, or submit to the obscure and imperfect tracts which had been marked out by an inferior pencil. They walked alone, and in their own strength; and wherever they have trod have left marks which time will never efface, or perhaps which no superior splendor of genius will obscure or eclipse, but will ever continue to be the highest objects of human ambition and admiration.

... Like his rival in modern times [Homer] was conspicuous for a display of character; but these were chiefly of the warlike kind. The steady magnanimity of Agamemnon, the irresistible fury of Achilles, the prudent valour of Ulysses, and the bodily strength of Ajax, are painted in strong and striking colours: and though he be not deficient in those of a more humble and amiable kind, yet in this sphere Homer, and every other writer, ancient or modern, are left far behind by Shakespeare, whose merit in this respect is indeed astonishing. He hath described the great and the ludicrous, the good and the bad with equal facility, in all their shades of character, and in every scene of human life. Succeeding writers have seldom mentioned his name without the epithet of *Inimitable*, and with much justice. For there has not been wanting in the English language dramatic writers of merit, who were not insensible to the singular abilities of Shakespeare; but of what writer except himself can it be said that no imitation has been attempted, none of his characters have been assumed? His simplicity, his sentiments, and even his stile is altogether his own. In imitating Homer many writers have not been unsuccessful. Virgil in beauty and tenderness has exceeded him. Tasso in strength of description has often equalled him. In enraptured sublimity Milton has gone beyond him. But none has yet in any degree appropriated the spirit and the manner of Shakespeare.

In every work of this great author we discover all the marks of his genius; his diversity of character, his boundless imagination, his acute discernment, and his nervous expression; but in none of them are these qualities more conspicuous than in the tragedy of *Othello*; a work also, the freest of his irregularities, his puns, his bombast, and conceits. No where has he painted virtue with more flaming sublimity than in the character of Othello; with more amiable tenderness than in that of Desdemona; and no where are all the artifices of human nature more fully displayed than in the character of Iago. From the whole he has contrived a plot, the most moral in its tendency, which winds up to the highest pitch our sympathetic feelings in concern for unsuspicious virtue, and at the same time rouses our utmost indignation against deep-laid villainy. From a review of the conduct of the poet in producing such a noble effect we may expect much pleasure and improvement.

It may be observed of the productions of a profound mind, that like the source from whence they proceed they are not apprehended at first sight. Shakespeare often begins his deepest tragedies with the lowest buffoonery of the comic kind, with conversations among the inferior characters that do not seem to be connected with the main plot; and there is often introduced throughout the work the opinions of those engaged about the lower offices about the principal actors, and the great designs that are carrying on; and their inadequate conceptions has an excellent effect in enlivening the story, for besides the humour that is thereby produced it elucidates the subject by placing it in a variety of lights. Examples of such a conduct are frequent in all our author's works, and are not to be expected but from that extensive capacity which is capable at once to view the subject in its rise and progress, and connected with all its circumstances. (56–9)

... Were the subject of *Othello* to be managed in the French mode or by their English imitators, we might expect, in an introductory soliloquy, to see the nature of jealousy, with all its dire effects, explained with much pomp of language, perhaps by the personage who is chiefly concerned in the story, or by a female confident observing all at once the altered mind of her lord; and the same subject would be the continual theme from speech to speech till the fatal conclusion, which never fails to be caused by some long-expected and obvious discovery. (60)

The characters which make a chief figure in the tragedy of *Othello* are the Moor himself, Desdemona, and Iago. The subject is the destruction of Desdemona; and this catastrophe the author never loses sight of. It is indeed remarkable for unity of action, which of all the three unities is of principal consequence. Unity of time and place, peculiar to this species of composition, arise from the nature of dramatic representation, the action being supposed to be in view of spectators for a moderate space of time. . . . To be scrupulously attentive to the unities of time and place confines the genius of the writer, makes the work barren of incidents, and consequently less interesting. Much must be forced and improbable; and the internal merit, and beauty of the story must be sacrificed to the external and artificial nature of representation. (61)

I have made these observations, as Shakespeare is more remarkable for adhering to unity of action than to the other two; the one is the offspring of genius alone, the other of art. (62)

Shakespeare has adorned the hero of this tragedy with every virtue that can render human nature great and amiable; and he has brought him into such trying situations as give full proof of both. His love for Desdemona is of the most refined and exalted kind; and his behaviour upon the supposition of his false return is an indication of his great spirit, and such as might be expected from his keen sense of honour and warlike character. Though naturally susceptible of the tenderest passions, yet being engaged from his early youth in scenes that required the exercise of those of a higher nature, he has not learned

> Those soft parts of conversation
> That Chamberers have.   [3.3.264f.]

> Rude (says he) am I in speech,
> And little bless'd with the set phrase of peace.   [1.3.81f.]

His manners have nothing of that studied courtesy which is the consequence of polite conversation—a tincture of which is delicately spread over the behaviour of Lodovico and Gratiano; but all is the natural effusion of gentleness and magnanimity. His generous and soaring mind, always occupied with ideas natural to itself, could not brook, according to his own expression, *to study all the qualities of human dealings*; the artifices of interest, and the meanness of servile attentions. (87–8)

With so much nature and dignity does he always act that, even when distorted with angry passions, he appears amiable.

> *Emil.* I would you had never seen him.
> *Des.* So would not I; my love doth so approve him,
> That even his stubborness, his checks and frowns,
> Have grace and favour in them.   [4.3.18ff.]

A character of this kind commands respect; and in his actions we naturally interest ourselves.

Iago, who is the prime mover of the events of this tragedy, is a character of no simple kind; he possesses uncommon sagacity in judging of the actions of men, good and bad . . . . (88)

In his first interview with Othello Iago begins his deep schemes very successfully by labouring, with bold and masterly cunning, to impress him with a strong sense of his fidelity and attachment to his interests. He represents himself as sustaining a difficult conflict between two of the best principles, regard to his master and a fear of seeming to act with a malicious cruelty. He speaks like a person fired with anger that he cannot contain; he does not give a detail of Brabantio's proceedings like an unconcerned spectator, but in that confused and interrupted manner worthy of the truest passion; his reflections which, according to calm reason ought to come last, according to passion come first. (89)

[Quotes 1.2.4–17.]

Hitherto Iago seems not to have formed any determined plan of action. A bait is laid for him in the simplicity of Roderigo; and how to get possession of his treasures seems to be the only object he had at first in view. . . . However, while his orders are executing he has leisure to consider what he is about; for Iago, at his first setting out, seems to have no intention of dipping so deep in wickedness as the dreadful event. Finding no method to gratify Roderigo, he dexterously makes him a tool for promoting the interests of his own. The suit of Roderigo, and the active hand he had taken in it, had brought him to think of a scheme of which the same persons were to be the subject. To render Cassio odious to Othello by scandalous aspersions, and by these means to be preferred in his place are the objects which he now has in view; a pursuit which he did not perhaps think would be attended with such a fatal train of consequences, though his sagacious mind discerns something that strikes him with horror.

> Hell and night
> Must bring this monstrous birth to the world's light.   [1.3.40]

Shakespeare has shown great judgment in the darkness which he makes to prevail in the first counsels of Iago. To the poet himself all the succeeding events must have been clear and determined; but to bring himself again into the situation of one who sees them in embryo, to draw a mist over that which he had already cleared, must have required an exertion of genius peculiar to this author alone. In so lively a manner does he make Iago shew his perplexity about the future management of his conduct, that one is almost tempted to think that the poet had determined as little himself about some of the particulars of Iago's destruction. When with much reasoning about their propriety he is by himself digesting his schemes, he says

> 'Tis here—but yet confused;
> Knavery's plain face is never seen till used.   [2.1.311f.]

But however much at a loss he may be about the method of accomplishing his designs, yet for the present he lets slip no opportunity that will promote them. He lays his foundation sure, as knowing what a hazardous structure he had to rear upon it. He had already laboured to exhibit himself in the best light to the unsuspicious Moor, and he succeeded to the height of his wishes; for we find him congratulating himself upon the advantages that will accrue from it.

> He holds me well;
> The better shall my purpose work upon him.   [1.3.390f.]

Upon the same principles does he go on working the downfall of Cassio. His blameless and well established character must be first tarnished; he must be known capable of irregularity before the crime he is accused of obtain full belief; and this more difficult part of his undertaking the indefatigable Iago finds means to accomplish, and with such ability as to promote at the same time the opinion of his own honesty and goodness. One would have imagined that he would have remained content with all the lucky events of the tumultuous adventure on the platform, and exult for a little. But he wisely determines not to triumph before he has gained a complete victory; his thoughtful and piercing mind sees another use to which the disgrace of Cassio may be applied. Under a cover of zeal to serve him he advises the virtuous man to a scheme that will further work his ruin; and by hinting to him the great power which Desdemona had over her husband he opens a very likely method for regaining his favour through her mediation. The bait is swallowed, and an appearance of intimacy most favourable to his design is thereby produced. (132–4)

. . . He assumes the appearance of one whose mind laboured with the knowledge of some flagrant impropriety which he could not contain; and when any circumstance recals the abhorred idea an involuntary remark escapes, and immediately he affects to recover himself. He kindles the jealousy of Othello by tantalizing him with imperfect accounts and ambiguous arguments. He agitates and distracts his soul by confusedly opening one source of suspicion, and leaving him in the perplexity of doubt; immediately by displaying the matter in another point of view, gives him a farther glimmering into the affair; until at last, frantic with rage and jealousy, Othello insists upon satisfactory information; and by these means the discoveries which he makes are made to appear more the effect of necessity than inclination.

> Villain, be sure thou prove my love a whore.   [3.3.359]

Incomplete knowledge of what concerns us deeply, besides the tortures of suspense into which it throws the mind, has a natural effect to make it appear in the most hideous colours which is possible to devise. (134)

Upon the whole, in this intercourse betwixt Iago and Othello Shakespeare has shewn the most complete knowledge of the human heart. Here he has put forth all the strength of his genius; the faults which he is so prone to fall into are entirely out of sight. We find none of his quibbling, his punning, or bombast; all is seriousness, all is passion. He brings human nature into the most difficult situation that can be conceived; and with matchless skill he supports it. Who can read those admirable scenes without being touched in the most sensible manner for the high grief of Othello? Plunged into a sea of troubles which he did not deserve, we see him torn asunder in the most cruel manner. How feeling are his reflections on his own state of mind. [quotes 3.3.351ff., 4.2.48–65]

After sustaining a violent conflict betwixt love and revenge his high spirit finally resolves into the latter. (135–6)

It has been observed of Shakespeare, that he has not often exhibited the delicacy of female character; and this has been sufficiently apologized for from the uncivilized age in which he lived; and women never appearing upon the stage in his time might have made him less studious in this department of the drama. Indeed, when we consider his strength of mind, his imagination, which delighted in whatever was bold and daring, we would almost think it impossible that he could enter into all the softness and refinement of love. But in spite of all these disadvantages, he has shewn that in whatever view he choosed to behold human nature he would perform it superior to any other. For no where in the writings of Shakespeare, or any where else, have we found the female character drawn with so much tenderness and beauty as in that of Desdemona. The gentleness with which she behaves to all with whom she converses, the purity, the modesty, the warmth of her love, her resignation in the deepest distress, together with her personal accomplishments attract our highest regard. But that which chiefly distinguishes her is that exquisite sensibility of imagination which interested her so much in the dangers of Othello's youthful adventures, a passion natural enough indeed, though it is not every one who is capable of experiencing it. Othello, as we have seen, was naturally of an heroic and amiable disposition; but when by his bold undertakings he is exposed to imminent dangers, he would then shine in his brightest colours. All his magnanimity, and all his address, are brought to view; at that moment all the generous affections of the soul would be drawn towards him; admiration of his virtues, wishes for his success, and solicitude for his safety. And when the best feelings of the heart are thus lavished on a certain object it is no wonder it should settle into fixed love and esteem.

Such was the sublimated passion of Desdemona, inspired solely by internal beauty. The person of Othello had every thing to cool desire, possessing not only the black complexion and the swarthy features of the Africans; he was also declined, as he says, into the vale of years. But his mind was every thing to Desdemona; it supplied the place of youth by its ardour, and of every personal accomplishment by its strength, its elevation, and its softness. Where, in all the annals of love, do we find so pure and so disinterested a passion supported with so much dignity and nature? She loved him *for the dangers he had passed*; upon this fleeting and incorporeal idea did she rest her affections, upon abstract feelings and qualities of the mind, which must require in her all that warmth of imagination and liveliness of conception which distinguish the finest genius.

The character of this exquisite lady is always consistently supported. Her behaviour towards Cassio shews, in a particular manner, her liberal and benevolent heart; and her conversation with Emilia about the heinousness of infidelity is a striking picture of innocent purity. It is artfully introduced, and adds much to the pathos of the tragedy. The circumstances of ordering her wedding-sheets to be put on her bed, and the melancholy song of a willow, are well imagined, and awaken the mind to expect some dreadful revolution. Indeed, throughout the whole scene before her death an awful solemnity reigns. The mind of Desdemona seems to be in a most agitated condition; she starts an observation about Lodovico, and immediately falls into her gloomy thoughts, paying no attention to the answer of Emilia, though connected with an anecdote that would have at another time raised her curiosity. This absence of mind shews beyond the power of language her afflicted and tortured state. But what gives a finishing stroke to the terror of this midnight scene is the rustling of the wind, which the affrighted imagination of Desdemona supposes to be one knocking at the door. This circumstance, which would have been overlooked as trifling by an inferior writer, has a most sublime effect in the hands of Shakespeare; and till the fatal catastrophe the same horribly interesting sensations are kept up. Othello enters her bed-chamber with a sword and candle, in that perturbation and distraction of mind which marked his behaviour since the supposed discovery of her guilt; remains of tenderness still struggling with revenge in his bosom, and a conversation is protracted; during which the mind is arrested in a state of the most dreadful suspense that can well be imagined.

Had Othello been actuated by cruelty alone in this action; had he, to gratify a savage nature, put Desdemona to death the scene would have been shocking, and we would have turned from it with aversion. But instigated as he is by the noble principles of honour and justice, and weighing at the same time the reluctance with which he performs it and the great sacrifice which he makes to his finest feelings, it on these accounts produces those mournfully pleasing sensations which to attain is the highest praise of the tragic poet.

In the final unravelling of the plot there is often great difficulty; it is the grand point to which the author aims in the course of successive scenes; and upon the proper execution of it depends much of the merit of the work. Here Shakespeare has not fallen off. The same high tone of passion is preserved. Upon the discovery of Desdemona's innocence, and the intrigues of Iago, all the characters act a very consistent and natural part. Othello's distraction is painted in an inimitable manner. Unwilling to believe that he had acted upon false grounds, and confounded with contrary evidence, he knows not where to betake himself. After uttering a few incoherent speeches, which shew in the strongest

564

light a mind rent with grief and remorse, he gradually recovers himself; and resuming, as much as possible, his natural composure and firmness he looks around him a little, and deliberately views his wretched situation; but finding no peace for him on earth he terminates his existence.

Iago also stands forth in the group, a just monument of his own crimes. Seeing the proof too plain against him, he can brave it out no longer. He sees no prospect of escape from any quarter; his own arts are now of no avail, and he knows that he deserves no pity; he gives up all for lost, and resolves upon a state of dumb desperation, most expressive of the horror of his mind. In this state we have the satisfaction to see him dragged to deserved punishment.

It might now be expected that we should proceed to the ungrateful task of pointing out what a critic would blame in this tragedy. I have already observed that it is perhaps the most sublime and finished of Shakespeare's compositions; yet were I to point out all its redundancies, puns, conceits, and other faults which are commonly taken notice of in this author, I might fill some pages. Such a detail, however, would be trivial and impertinent. No person who can relish its beauties will be much offended with any thing of this kind in the course of perusing *Othello*. Its excellencies are so bold and so striking as to make the blemishes almost wholly vanish in the midst of their splendor. In a rude age, it is indeed even the mark of a rich and luxuriant mind to abound in faults, in the same manner that a strong and fertile soil produces most weeds—

> What are the lays of artful Addison,
> Coldly correct, to Shakespeare's warblings wild?

It is with much regret, however, we must observe that after Shakespeare had supported with uniform propriety one of the most difficult characters Genius ever attempted, he should at last fall off, and put a trifling conceit in the mouth of a dying man.

> *Oth.* I kissed thee e'er I killed thee—no way but this,
> Killing myself to die upon a kiss.   [5.2.358f.]

It might also be objected to the contrivance of the plot that Iago had not sufficient motives for the perpetration of so many horrid crimes; and this the sagacity of Shakespeare has foreseen, and with much address obviated. In the course of our observations we have already noticed that he does not suppose Iago, in his first setting

565

out, resolutely to plan the destruction of Desdemona and Cassio. The objects he had in view were to get possession of the wealth of Roderigo, and to be preferred in the place of Cassio; but seeing matters beginning to be embroiled around him, the firm and undaunted Iago will not stop short, whatever should be the consequence. By thus viewing his conduct it will appear natural and probable. He wishes (as human nature ever must) to view himself even for a moment in the light of an honest man——

And what's he then that says I play the villain? &c. [2.3.336f.]

But the principal fault which we observe in this performance is a want of consistency in supporting the upright and disinterested character of Emilia. We can easily suppose, in the first place, that she might procure Desdemona's napkin for her husband, without seeming to concur with him or even suspect his schemes. But when afterwards, in the tenth scene of the third act, she sees the improper use to which this napkin is applied and the great distress which the loss of it occasioned to Desdemona, without so much as wishing to explain the misunderstanding, she is no more the open and virtuous Emilia but a coadjutor with her dark and unfeeling husband.[1] This is a remarkable violation of every appearance of probability, when we contrast it with her noble and spirited conduct afterwards. We are surprised to find a slip of so much magnitude from the clear and piercing judgment of Shakespeare, especially when we consider that it could have been very easily remedied by removing her during this interview. (176–81)

---

[1] This point had been made by an anonymous contributor to *Walker's Hibernian Magazine* (February 1780), p. 72, and was also made by Malone in his 1783 'Second Appendix', above, p. 350, and in the 1785 edition (X, 655).

301. James Boswell, Johnson on Shakespeare

1791

From *The Life of Samuel Johnson, Ll.D.* . . . This text is from 'The Second Edition, Revised and Augmented' (3 vols, 1793).

Boswell's evidence for Johnson's opinions on Shakespeare cannot be taken as straightforward literary criticism, since Johnson's utterances were often coloured by the context of the discussion. If a writer, or critic, or actor had been praised too highly, in Johnson's opinion, he would often take the opposing side and deny them any excellence; or he would set out to tease his friends for their advocacy; or they would set out to provoke him. Johnson's opinions, produced in such ways, and as recorded by Boswell, are expressed more coarsely and variably than in his own written work. Mrs Piozzi, in her *Anecdotes of the Late Samuel Johnson, Ll.D.* (1786), has left the best account of this process:

It was not very easy, however, for people not quite intimate with Dr. Johnson to get exactly his opinion of a writer's merit, as he would now and then divert himself by confounding those who thought themselves obliged to say to-morrow what he had said yesterday; and even Garrick, who ought to have been better acquainted with his tricks, professed himself mortified that one time when he was extolling Dryden in a rapture that I suppose disgusted his friend, Mr. Johnson suddenly challenged him to produce twenty lines in a series that would not disgrace the poet and his admirer. Garrick produced a passage that he had once heard the Doctor commend, in which he *now* found, if I remember rightly, sixteen faults, and made Garrick look silly at his own table. When I told Mr. Johnson the story, 'Why, what a monkey was David now (says he), to tell of his own disgrace!' And in the course of that hour's chat he told me how he used to teize Garrick by commendations of the tomb scene in Congreve's *Mourning Bride*, protesting that Shakespeare had in the same line of excellence nothing as good: 'All which is strictly *true* (said he); but that is no reason for supposing Congreve is to stand in competition with Shakespeare: these fellows know not how to blame, nor how to commend.' I forced him one day, in a similar humour, to prefer Young's description of Night to the so much admired ones of Dryden and Shakespeare,[1] as more forcible, and more general. (ed. A. Sherbo, 1974, p. 79)

[From the *Life* for 1792; Aetat. 20]
... He told me that from his earliest years he loved to read poetry, but hardly ever read any poem to an end; that he read Shakespeare at a period so early that the speech of the Ghost in *Hamlet* terrified him when he was alone; ... (I, 48)

[1758: Aetat. 49]
Here he gave Mr. Burney Mrs. Williams's history, and shewed him some volumes of his Shakespeare already printed, to prove that he was in earnest. Upon Mr. Burney's opening the first volume, at the *Merchant of Venice*, he observed to him that he seemed to be more severe on Warburton than Theobald. 'O poor Tib.! (said Johnson) he was ready knocked down to my hands; Warburton stands between me and him.' 'But, Sir, (said Mr. Burney,) you'll have Warburton upon your bones, won't you?' 'No, Sir; he'll not come out: he'll only growl in his den.' 'But you think, Sir, that Warburton is a superiour critick to Theobald?' — 'O, Sir, he'd make two-and-fifty Theobalds, cut into slices! The worst of Warburton is, that he has a rage for saying something when there's nothing to be said.' (I, 299)

[1765: Aetat. 56]
In the October of this year he at length gave to the world his edition of Shakespeare, which, if it had no other merit but that of producing his Preface, in which the excellencies and defects of that immortal bard are displayed with a masterly hand, the nation would have had no reason to complain. A blind indiscriminate admiration of Shakespeare had exposed the British nation to the ridicule of foreigners. Johnson, by candidly admitting the faults of his poet, had the more credit in bestowing on him deserved and

---

[1] For Johnson's comparison of passages in Dryden's *The Indian Emperor or, the Conquest of Mexico* and *Macbeth*, see his 1745 essay, Vol. 3, pp. 173–4.

indisputable praise; and doubtless none of all his panegyrists have done him half so much honour. Their praise was, like that of a counsel, upon his own side of the cause: Johnson's was like the grave, well considered, and impartial opinion of the judge, which falls from his lips with weight, and is received with reverence. What he did as a commentator has no small share of merit, though his researches were not so ample, and his investigations so acute as they might have been, which we now certainly know from the labours of other able and ingenious cricticks who have followed him. He has enriched his edition with a concise account of each play, and of its characteristick excellence. Many of his notes have illustrated obscurities in the text, and placed passages eminent for beauty in a more conspicuous light; and he has, in general, exhibited such a mode of annotation as may be beneficial to all subsequent editors . . . .

Mr. Burney having occasion to write to Johnson for some receipts for subscriptions to his Shakespeare, which Johnson had omitted to deliver, when the money was paid he availed himself of that opportunity of thanking Johnson for the great pleasure which he had received from the perusal of his Preface to Shakespeare; which although it excited much clamour against him at first, is now justly ranked among the most excellent of his writings. To this letter Johnson returned the following answer:

> *To* CHARLES BURNEY, *Esq. in Poland-street.*
> 'SIR,
> . . . I defend my criticism in the same manner with you. We must confess the faults of our favourite, to gain credit to our praise of his excellencies. He that claims, either in himself or for another, the honours of perfection, will surely injure the reputation which he designs to assist. . . .'

(I, 460–1, 462–3)

[16 October 1769: Aetat. 60]
Johnson said, that the description of the temple, in *The Mourning Bride*, was the finest poetical passage he had ever read; he recollected none in Shakespeare equal to it. — 'But, (said Garrick, all alarmed for 'the God of his idolatry,') we know not the extent and variety of his powers. We are to suppose there are such passages in his works. Shakespeare must not suffer from the badness of our memories.' Johnson, diverted by this enthusiastick jealousy, went on with greater ardour: 'No, Sir; Congreve has

nature,' (smiling on the tragick eagerness of Garrick;) but composing himself, he added, 'Sir, this is not comparing Congreve on the whole with Shakespeare on the whole; but only maintaining that Congreve has one finer passage than any that can be found in Shakespeare. Sir, a man may have no more than ten guineas in the world, but he may have those ten guineas in one piece; and so may have a finer piece than a man who has ten thousand pounds: but then he has only one ten-guinea piece.—What I mean is, that you can shew me no passage where there is simply a description of material objects, without any intermixture of moral notions, which produces such an effect.' Mr. Murphy mentioned Shakespeare's description of the night before the battle of Agincourt; but it was observed, it had *men* in it. Mr. Davies suggested the speech of Juliet, in which she figures herself awaking in the tomb of her ancestors. Some one mentioned the description of Dover Cliff. JOHNSON. 'No, Sir; it should be all precipice,—all vacuum. The crows impede your fall. The diminished appearance of the boats, and other circumstances, are all very good description; but do not impress the mind at once with the horrible idea of immense height. The impression is divided; you pass on by computation, from one stage of the tremendous space to another.[1] Had the girl in *The Mourning Bride* said, she could not cast her shoe to the top of one of the pillars in the temple, it would not have aided the idea, but weakened it.' (I, 541–3)

Mrs. Montagu, a lady distinguished for having written an Essay on Shakespeare, being mentioned;—REYNOLDS 'I think that essay does her honour.' JOHNSON. 'Yes, Sir; it does *her* honour, but it would do nobody else honour. I have, indeed, not read it all. But when I take up the end of a web, and find it packthread, I do not expect, by looking further, to find embroidery. Sir, I will venture to say, there is not one sentence of true criticism in her book.' GARRICK. 'But, Sir, surely it shews how much Voltaire has mistaken Shakespeare, which nobody else has done.' JOHNSON. 'Sir, nobody else has thought it worth while. And what merit is there in that? You may as well praise a schoolmaster for whipping a boy who has construed ill. No, Sir, there is no real criticism in it; none shewing the beauty of thought, as formed on the workings of the human heart.' . . .

[1] Cf. Johnson's note in 1765: Vol. 5, pp. 137f., disagreeing with Addison's praise of it, and Mason's comment, above p. 405.

JOHNSON. 'We have an example of true criticism in Burke's *Essay on the Sublime and Beautiful*; and, if I recollect, there is also Du Bos; and Bouhours, who shews all beauty to depend on truth. There is no great merit in telling how many plays have ghosts in them, and how this Ghost is better than that. You must shew how terrour is impressed on the human heart.—In the description of night in *Macbeth* the beetle and the bat detract from the general idea of darkness,—inspissated gloom.' (I, 546–7)

[19 October 1769: Aetat. 60]

I complained that he had not mentioned Garrick in his Preface to Shakespeare; and asked him if he did not admire him. JOHNSON. 'Yes, as 'a poor player, who frets and struts his hour upon the stage;—as a shadow.' BOSWELL. 'But has he not brought Shakespeare into notice?' JOHNSON. 'Sir, to allow that, would be to lampoon the age. Many of Shakespeare's plays are the worse for being acted: *Macbeth*, for instance.' BOSWELL. 'What, Sir, is nothing gained by decoration and action? Indeed, I do wish that you had mentioned Garrick.' JOHNSON. 'My dear Sir, had I mentioned him, I must have mentioned many more: Mrs. Pritchard, Mrs. Cibber,—nay, and Mr. Cibber too; he too altered Shakespeare.' (I, 546–7)

[8 April 1775: Aetat. 66]

Mrs. Pritchard being mentioned, he said, 'Her playing was quite mechanical. It is wonderful how little mind she had. Sir, she had never read the tragedy of *Macbeth* all through. She no more thought of the play out of which her part was taken, than a shoemaker thinks of the skin, out of which the piece of leather, of which he is making a pair of shoes, is cut.' (II, 222)

[12 April 1776: Aetat. 67]

I observed the great defect of the tragedy of *Othello* was, that it had not a moral; for that no man could resist the circumstances of suspicion which were artfully suggested to Othello's mind. JOHNSON. 'In the first place, Sir, we learn from *Othello* this very useful moral, not to make an unequal match; in the second place, we learn not to yield too readily to suspicion. The handkerchief is merely a trick, though a very pretty trick; but there are no other circumstances of reasonable suspicion, except what is related by

Iago of Cassio's warm expressions concerning Desdemona in his sleep; and that depended entirely upon the assertion of one man. No, Sir, I think *Othello* has more moral than almost any play.' (II, 402)

[8 April 1779: Aetat. 70]
... We talked of Shakespeare's witches. JOHNSON. 'They are beings of his own creation; they are a compound of malignity and meanness, without any abilities; and are quite different from the Italian magician. King James says, in his *Dæmonology*, "Magicians command the devils; witches are their servants." The Italian magicians are elegant beings.' RAMSAY. 'Opera witches, not Drury-lane witches.' (III, 176)

[1780: Aetat 71]
Drinking tea one day at Garrick's with Mr. Langton, he was questioned if he was not some what of a heretick as to Shakespeare; said Garrick, 'I doubt he is a little of an infidel.' 'Sir, (said Johnson) I will stand by the lines I have written on Shakespeare, in my Prologue at the opening of your Theatre.' Mr. Langton suggested that in the line

And panting Time toil'd after him in vain;

Johnson might have had in his eye the passage in the *Tempest*, where Prospero says of Miranda,

> She will outstrip all praise,
> And make it halt behind her.   [4.1.10f.]

Johnson said nothing. Garrick then ventured to observe, 'I do not think that the happiest line in the praise of Shakespeare.' Johnson exclaimed (smiling), 'Prosaical rogues! next time I write, I'll make both time and space pant.' (III, 271–2)

302. Unsigned essay, a rhapsody on Shakespeare

1792

From *Farrago. Containing Essays, Moral, Philosophical, Political, and Historical* . . . (2 vols, 1792).

This collection of essays was 'Published for the Benefit of the Society for the Discharge and Relief of Persons imprisoned for Small Debts'. It is sometimes confused with *Farrago: or, Miscellanies in Verse and Prose* published by Richard Barton in 1739. Taylor, in the *Monthly Review* for 1794 (n.s. xiii, pp. 414–16), described these essays as being

> written with perspicuity and with urbanity: they glide over a variety of subjects, and, if they do not often effervesce with original ideas, they are seldom stale with very familiar opinions.

The rhapsody is largely a cento, or tissue of quotations, from Shakespeare.

Spiritus intus alit, totamque infusa per Artus
Mens agitat molem,—

VIRG. [*Aeneid*, 6.726f.]

In this choice work, the God himself we find
Mixt with the mass; HE fill'd the mighty mind.

So much has been written concerning our favorite author that if the subject were not inexhaustible, what any one may have to add might very well be dispensed with; but there will ever be cause for the exertion of the most enlightened mind, when the exalted merit of this more than mortal is in question; an irresistable fervour agitates us, the contemplation of his powers urges the mind to find a form of words adequate to the subject and to its own feelings.

If all other books and the memory of them were obliterated, his works alone would illumine the understanding of the nation, his ever-blooming irradiancy, his unexampled fame, will always be in proportion to the capability of the human mind as that expands, his

573

transcendent mode of information will always be found adequate to the filling it with admiration and delight.

We must do the justice to Garrick of acknowledging that his exhibitions of some characters, like the chiaro obscuro of a picture, brought forward many beauties which would not so readily have obtained their value in the general notice. It is now more than thirty years that the thermometer of Shakespeare's glory, which is graduated to the end of time, has been constantly rising.

Of the mind of every other author we can allot the true value of his acquirements, and apportion the *quantum meruit* of his genius by the common standard, but here we are at a loss for a comparison.

When we see him within the compass of a few years an idle libertine in the country, and then furnishing plays in the capital, and those performances so much above the cast of mind of the audience, which in general was best pleased with what we now reject, it strikes us with surprize. The giddiness of youth might naturally enough precede the most comprehensive dormant genius; but at a later period the history of his holding horses at the play-house, with his assistant blackguard boys, 'puzzles the will,' and stifles all analysis.

It is in genius, in that divine emanation, which in its nature is inexplicable, that we are to seek the means of resolving this problem.

The author fears that he may not have the good fortune to explain to others, what he himself finds no difficulty to understand. He thinks the *flatus Dei*,[1] the divinity within, might dictate those comprehensive forms of speech which passed through Shakespeare's mind unnoticed, but as relative to his subject, intirely without that great effect they communicate to others; and that they were not in any sense the result of reflection, labour, and contrivance, like the composition of other writers: from him those wonders fell as the ripe acorn unheeded by the oak. . . .

A RHAPSODY.

Dost thou love pictures?—Look here upon this picture—that has so dazzled my reason's light.—How infinite in faculties!—in apprehension how like a God!—of most excellent fancy, either for

---

[1] Genesis, 2.vii: 'God formed man of the dust of the ground, and breathed into his nostrils the breath of life'.

Tragedy or Comedy—I know not which pleases me better—He would drown the stage with tears—Then! such shaping fantasies, for jest and courtesy! the top of admiration.—

If I should anatomize him to thee as he is—his possessions are so huge—there is not chastity enough in language to utter them—of wondrous virtues! he is a good divine—a scholar and a soldier—shines brightly as a king—a judge—a counsellour—and of government, the properties to unfold, as pregnant in, as art and practice has enriched any—and gives to every power, a power, above their functions, and their offices—never school'd, yet learned—and for the liberal arts without a parallel!—Before my God I might not this believe, without the sensible and true avouch of mine own eyes.

Admiring of his virtues—let me have audience for a word or two of commendation—Heaven nature charg'd, that one body should be filled with all the graces—'Tis He! This is He!—His words are my soul's food—screw'd to my memory—of more value than stamps of gold—He's all my exercise, my mirth, my matter—He makes a July's day short as December—Cures in my thoughts, that, should chill my blood—I count myself in nothing so happy, as in a soul rememb'ring all his matchless graces.—

But, He's gone!—and my idolatrous fancy must sanctify his relicks—I do beseech you, whither is he gone?—I speak to you, Sir—you are certainly a gentleman—clerk-like experienc'd—I pray you mark me—I will prophesy—He is in heaven—ay, by my life—doubt it not—come deal justly with me—by your smiling you seem to say so—there's a kind of confession in your looks—if you think other, remove your thought.—I never shall be satisfied till I behold him—to come into his presence in the court of heaven.—

I do entreat your patience—by the world I count no fable—this is all true, as it is strange—think not I flatter—not I, for this fair island—that would dishonour him—I swear I do not—by each particular star in heaven, and all their influences—for what advancement may I hope?—no—let the candied tongue lick absurd pomp, where thrift may follow.—Far behind his worth come all the praises that I now bestow—well learned is that tongue that well can him commend—I speak not this, that you should bear a good opinion of my understanding—assure you—I am sorry that with better judgment, I had not quoted him.

575

This is not my writing, though I confess much like the character—all this I speak in print—for in print I found it.—And so, fare you well.

> Our SHAKESPEARE only, has the god-like art,
> To rouze each passion slumbring in the heart;
> Can pangs of rage, and jealousy impose,
> And then with pity every wound can close;
> Make airy nothing some strange body fill,
> Then hail it tyrant, of the human will;
> O'er earth, cross seas, through air, from pole to pole,
> Can waft in rapture, all the yielding soul;
> When e'er the master waves his magic wand,
> The sense resistless, owns his dread command.

303. George Steevens and others, edition of Shakespeare

1793

From *The Plays of William Shakespeare. In Fifteen Volumes. With the Corrections and Illustrations of Various Commentators. To which are added, Notes by Samuel Johnson and George Steevens. The Fourth Edition. Revised and Augmented (With a Glossarial Index) by the Editor of Dodsley's Collection of Old Plays* (15 vols, 1793).

Although credit is again given to Reed (as in 1785: No. 279), this edition was in fact the work of Steevens. As his obituary in the *Gentleman's Magazine* for 1800 (lxx, p. 178) recorded, Steevens devoted to this work

solely and exclusively of all other attentions a period of 18 months; and, during that time, he left his house every morning at one o'clock with the Hampstead patrole, and, proceeding without any consideration of the weather or the season, called up the compositor and woke all his devils. . . . The nocturnal toil greatly accelerated the printing of the work; as, while the printers slept, the editor was awake: and thus, in less than 20 months, he completed his last splendid edition of Shakespeare, in 15 large 8vo. volumes; an almost incredible labour, which proved the astonishing energy and persevering powers of his mind.

Steevens's dedication was partly motivated by a desire to surpass the 1790 edition of Malone, by whom he felt slighted, and he solicited contributions from Ritson, now well established as Malone's most caustic critic. Although crowning his labours in supplying contemporary glosses and parallels to Shakespeare's language and usage, in other respects this edition is a throw-back to earlier and less critical work. For Malone's comments on it see B. H. Bronson, *Joseph Ritson* (Berkeley, 1938), pp. 538–40.

[From the Preface]
. . . The play of *Pericles* has been added to this collection, by the advice of Dr. Farmer. To make room for it *Titus Andronicus* might have been omitted; but our proprietors are of opinion that some ancient prejudices in its favour may still exist, and for that reason only it is preserved.

We have not reprinted the *Sonnets*, &c. of Shakespeare, because the strongest act of Parliament that could be framed would fail to compel readers into their service; notwithstanding these miscellaneous Poems have derived every possible advantage from the literature and judgement of their only intelligent editor, Mr. Malone, whose implements of criticism, like the ivory rake and golden spade in Prudentius, are on this occasion disgraced by the objects of their culture.—Had Shakespeare produced no other works than these, his name would have reached us with as little celebrity as time has conferred on that of Thomas Watson, an older and much more elegant sonnetteer.

What remains to be added concerning this republication is, that a considerable number of fresh remarks are both adopted and supplied by the present editors. They have persisted in their former track of reading for the illustration of their author, and cannot help observing that those who receive the benefit of explanatory extracts from ancient writers little know at what expence of time and labour such atoms of intelligence have been collected.—That the foregoing information, however, may communicate no alarm, or induce the reader to suppose we have 'bestowed our whole tediousness' on him, we should add that many notes have likewise been withdrawn. A few, manifestly erroneous, are indeed retained, to show how much the tone of Shakespearian criticism is changed, or on account of the skill displayed in their confutation; for surely every editor in his turn is occasionally entitled to be seen, as he would have shown himself, with his vanquished adversary at his feet. (I, vii–ix)

Every re-impression of our great dramatick master's works must be considered in some degree as experimental; for their corruptions and obscurities are still so numerous, and the progress of fortunate conjecture so tardy and uncertain, that our remote descendants may be perplexed by passages that have perplexed us; and the readings which have hitherto disunited the opinions of the learned may continue to disunite them as long as England and Shakespeare have a name. In short, the peculiarity once ascribed to the poetick isle of Delos may be exemplified in our author's text, which on account of readings alternately received and reprobated must remain in an unsettled state, and float in obedience to every gale of contradictory criticism.—Could a perfect and decisive edition of the following scenes be produced, it were to be expected only (though we fear in vain) from the hand of Dr. Farmer, whose more serious avocations forbid him to undertake what every reader would delight to possess.

But as we are often reminded by our 'brethren of the craft' that this or that emendation, however apparently necessary, is not the *genuine text of Shakespeare*, it might be imagined that we had received this text from its fountain head, and were therefore certain of its purity. Whereas few literary occurrences are better understood than that it came down to us discoloured by 'the variation of every soil' through which it had flowed, and that it stagnated at last in the muddy reservoir of the first folio.* In plainer terms, that the

* It will perhaps be urged that to this first folio we are indebted for the only copies of sixteen or seventeen of our author's plays. True: but may not our want of yet earlier and less corrupted editions of these very dramas be solely attributed to the monopolizing vigilance of its editors, Messieurs Heminge and Condell? Finding they had been deprived of some tragedies and comedies which, when opportunity offered, they designed to publish for their own emolument, they redoubled their solicitude to withhold the rest, and were but too

vitiations of a careless theatre were seconded by those of as ignorant a press. The integrity of dramas thus prepared for the world is just on a level with the innocence of females nursed in a camp and educated in a bagnio. — As often therefore as we are told that by admitting corrections warranted by common sense and the laws of metre, we have not rigidly adhered to the text of Shakespeare, we shall entreat our opponents to exchange that phrase for another 'more germane,' and say instead of it that we have deviated from the text of the publishers of single plays in quarto, or their successors, the editors of the first folio; that we have sometimes followed the suggestions of a Warburton, a Johnson, a Farmer, or a Tyrwhitt, in preference to the decisions of a Heminge or a Condell, notwithstanding their choice of readings might have been influenced by associates whose high-sounding names cannot fail to enforce respect, viz. William Ostler, John Shanke, William Sly, and Thomas Poope.* (I, x–xiii)

[Steevens attacks what he considers to be too slavish adherence to the original texts, especially if it results in Shakespeare being credited with 'ungrammatical nonsense, and such rough and defective numbers as would disgrace a village school-boy in his first attempts at English poetry'.]

The truth is that from one extreme we have reached another. Our incautious predecessors, Rowe, Pope, Hanmer, and Warburton, were sometimes justly blamed for wanton and needless deviations from ancient copies; and we are afraid that censure will as equitably fall on some of us for a revival of irregularities which have no reasonable sanction, and few champions but such as are excited by a fruitless ambition to defend certain posts and passes that had been supposed untenable. The 'wine of collation,' indeed, had long been 'drawn,' and little beside the 'mere lees was left' for very modern editors 'to brag of.' It should therefore be remembered that as judgement, without the aid of collation, might have insufficient materials to work on, so collation, divested of judgement, will be often worse than thrown

---

successful in their precaution. 'Thank fortune (says the original putter-forth of *Troilus and Cressida*) for the scape it hath made amongst you; since by the *grand possessors'* wills, I believe, you should have pray'd for it rather than beene pray'd.'—Had quartos of *Macbeth, Antony and Cleopatra, All's well that ends well*, &c. been sent into the world, from how many corruptions might the text of all these dramas have been secured!

* See first Folio, &c, for the List of Actors in our author's Plays.

away, because it introduces obscurity instead of light. To render
Shakespeare less intelligible by a recall of corrupt phraseology is
not, in our opinion, the surest way to extend his fame and multiply
his readers; unless (like Curll the bookseller, when the Jews spoke
Hebrew to him), they happen to have most faith in what they least
understand. Respecting our author therefore, on some occasions,
we cannot join in the prayer of Cordelia:—

> ————————*Restoration* hang
> Thy medicine on his lips!   [*King Lear*, 4.7.25f.]

It is unlucky for him, perhaps, that between the interest of his
readers and his editors a material difference should subsist. The
former wish to meet with as few difficulties as possible, while the
latter are tempted to seek them out, because they afford opportunities for explanatory criticism.

Omissions in our author's works are frequently suspected, and
sometimes not without sufficient reason. Yet, in our opinion, they
have suffered a more certain injury from interpolation; for almost
as often as their measure is deranged or redundant, some words,
alike unnecessary to sense and the grammar of the age may be
discovered, and in a thousand instances might be expunged,
without loss of a single idea meant to be expressed; a liberty which
we have sometimes taken, though not (as it is hoped) without
constant notice of it to the reader. Enough of this, however, has
been already attempted to show that more, on the same plan, might
be done with safety.—So far from understanding the power of an
ellipsis, we may venture to affirm that the very name of this figure
in rhetorick never reached the ears of our ancient editors. Having
on this subject the support of Dr. Farmer's acknowledged
judgement and experience, we shall not shrink from controversy
with those who maintain a different opinion, and refuse to
acquiesce in modern suggestions if opposed to the authority of
quartos and folios, consigned to us by a set of people who were
wholly uninstructed in the common forms of style, orthography
and punctuation.—We do not therefore hesitate to affirm that a
blind fidelity to the eldest printed copies is on some occasions a
confirmed treason against the sense, spirit, and versification of
Shakespeare.

All these circumstances considered, it is time, instead of a timid
and servile adherence to ancient copies, when (offending against

sense and metre) they furnish no real help, that a future editor, well acquainted with the phraseology of our author's age, should be at liberty to restore some apparent meaning to his corrupted lines, and a decent flow to his obstructed versification. The latter (as already has been observed) may be frequently effected by the expulsion of useless and supernumerary syllables, and an occasional supply of such as might fortuitously have been omitted, notwithstanding the declaration of Heminge and Condell, whose fraudulent preface asserts that they have published our author's plays 'as absolute in their numbers as he conceived them.' (I, xiv–xvii)

[Steevens praises Malone, 'whose attention, diligence, and spirit of enquiry, have very far exceeded those of the whole united phalanx of his predecessors'.]

Of his notes on particular passages a great majority is here adopted. True it is, that on some points we fundamentally disagree; for instance, concerning his metamorphosis of monosyllables (like *burn, sworn, worn, here* and *there, arms* and *charms,*) into dissyllables; his contraction of dissyllables (like *neither, rather, reason, lover,* &c.) into monosyllables; and his sentiments respecting the worth of the variations supplied by the second folio.—On the first of these contested matters we commit ourselves to the publick ear; on the second we must awhile solicit the reader's attention. The following conjectural account of the publication of this second folio (about which no certainty can be obtained) perhaps is not very remote from truth.

When the predecessor of it appeared, some intelligent friend or admirer of Shakespeare might have observed its defects, and corrected many of them in its margin, from early manuscripts, or authentick information. . . .

That oral information concerning his works was still accessible, may with similar probablity be inferred; as some of the original and most knowing performers in his different pieces were then alive (Lowin and Taylor, for instance,); and it must be certain that on the stage they never uttered such mutilated lines and unintelligible nonsense as was afterwards incorporated with their respective parts, in both the first quarto and folio editions. The folio therefore of 1623, corrected from one or both the authorities above mentioned, we conceive to have been the basis of its successor in 1632.

At the same time, however, a fresh and abundant series of errors and omissions was created in the text of our author; the natural and certain consequence of every re-impression of a work which is not overseen by other eyes than those of its printer. Nor is it at all improbable that the person who furnished the revision of the first folio wrote a very obscure hand, and was much cramped for room, as the margin of this book is always narrow. Such being the case, he might often have been compelled to deal in abbreviations, which were sometimes imperfectly deciphered and sometimes wholly misunderstood. Mr. Malone, indeed, frequently points his artillery at a personage whom we cannot help regarding as a phantom; we mean the *Editor* of the second folio; for perhaps no such literary agent as an editor of a poetical work unaccompanied by comments was at that period to be found. This office, if any where, was vested in the printer, who transferred it to his compositors; and these worthies discharged their part of the trust with a proportionate mixture of ignorance and inattention. (I, xxi–xxiv)

The same gentleman also speaks with some confidence of having *proved* his assertions relative to the worthlessness of this book. But how are these assertions proved? By exposing its errors (some of which nevertheless are of a very questionable shape), and by observing a careful silence about its deserts. The latter surely should have been stated as well as the former. Otherwise, this proof will resemble the 'ill-roasted egg' in *As you like it*, which was done only 'on one side.' . . .

To conclude, though we are far from asserting that this republication, generally considered, is preferable to its original, we must still regard it as a valuable supplement to that work; and no stronger plea in its favour can be advanced than the frequent use made of it by Mr. Malone. The numerous corrections from it admitted by that gentleman into his text,* and pointed out in his notes, will, in our judgement, contribute to its eulogium; at least cannot fail to rescue it from his prefatory imputations of—'being of no value whatever,' and afterwards of—'not being worth—three shillings.' (I, xxvii–xxix)

[1] [From the list of early editions of Shakespeare: a note on the subsequent history of the First Folio]

* Amounting to (as we are informed by a very accurate compositor who undertook to count them) 186.

Every possible adulteration has of late years been practised in fitting up copies of this book for sale.

When leaves have been wanting, they have been reprinted with battered types, and foisted into vacancies, without notice of such defects and the remedies applied to them.

When the title has been lost, a spurious one has been fabricated, with a blank space left for the head of Shakespeare, afterwards added from the second, third, or fourth impression. To conceal these frauds thick vermillion lines have been usually drawn over the edges of the engravings, which would otherwise have betrayed themselves when let into a supplemental page, however craftily it was lined at the back, and discoloured with tobacco-water till it has assumed the true *jaune antique*.

Sometimes leaves have been inserted from the second folio, and, in a known instance, the entire play of *Cymbeline*; the genuine date at the end of it [1632] having been altered into 1623.

Since it was thought advantageous to adopt such contrivances while the book was only valued at six or seven guineas, now it has reached its present enormous price may not artifice be still more on the stretch to vamp up copies for the benefit of future catalogues and auctions?—Shakespeare might say of those who profit by him what Antony has observed of Enobarbus—

> ——————— my fortunes have
> Corrupted honest men.

Mr. Garrick, about forty years ago, paid only £1. 16s. to Mr. Payne at the Meuse Gate for a fine copy of this folio.—After the death of our Roscius it should have accompanied his collection of old plays to the British Museum; but had been taken out of his library, and has not been heard of since.

Here I might particularize above twenty other copies; but as their description would not always meet the wishes or interests of their owners, it may be as well omitted.

Perhaps the original impression of the book did not amount to more than 250; and we may suppose that different fires in London had their share of them. Before the year 1649 they were so scarce that (as Mr. Malone has observed) King Charles I. was obliged to content himself with a folio 1632, at present in my possession.

Of all volumes, those of popular entertainment are soonest injured. It would be difficult to name four folios that are oftener found in dirty and mutilated condition than this first assemblage of Shakespeare's plays—God's Revenge against Murder—The Gentleman's Recreation—and Johnson's Lives of the Highwaymen.

Though Shakespeare was not, like Fox the Martyrologist, deposited in churches to be thumbed by the congregation, he generally took post on our hall tables; and that a multitude of his pages have 'their effect of gravy,' may be imputed to the various eatables set out every morning on the same boards. It should seem that most of his readers were so chary of their time that (like Pistol, who gnaws his leek and swears all the while,) they fed and studied at the same instant. I have repeatedly met with thin flakes of piecrust between the leaves of our author. These unctuous fragments, remaining long in close confinement, communicated their grease to several pages deep on each side of them.—It is easy enough to conceive how such accidents might happen;—how aunt Bridget's mastication might be disordered at the sudden entry of the Ghost into the Queen's closet, and how the half-chewed morsel dropped out of the gaping 'Squire's mouth, when the visionary Banquo seated himself in the chair of Macbeth. Still, it is no small elogium on Shakespeare, that his claims were more forcible than those of hunger.—Most of the first folios now extant are known to have belonged to ancient families resident in the country.

Since our breakfasts have become less gross, our favourite authors have escaped with fewer injuries; not that (as a very nice friend of mine observes) those who read with a coffee-cup in their hands are to be numbered among the contributors to bibliothecal purity.

I claim the merit of being the first commentator on Shakespeare who strove, with becoming seriousness, to account for the frequent stains that disgrace the earliest folio edition of his plays, which is now become the most expensive single book in our language; for what other English volume without plates, and printed since the year 1600, is known to have sold, more than once, for thirty-five pounds, fourteen shillings? STEEVENS. (I, 455–7, notes)

[From the Notes]
[2] [On *The Tempest*, 1.2.162: on Gonzalo, '*who* being then appointed'. Steevens had suggested *he*, but Malone rejected the

emendation, 'that mode of phraseology being the idiom of Shakespeare's time'.]

I have left the passage in question, as I found it, though with slender reliance on its integrity. What Mr. Malone has styled 'the idiom of Shakespeare's time' can scarce deserve so creditable a distinction. It should be remembered that the instances adduced by him in support of his position are not from the early quartos, which he prefers on the score of accuracy, but from the folio 1623, the inaccuracy of which with equal judgment he has censured.

The genuine idiom of our language, at its different periods, can only be ascertained by reference to contemporary writers whose works were skilfully revised as they passed through the press, and are therefore unsuspected of corruption. A sufficient number of such books are before us. If they supply examples of phraseology resembling that which Mr. Malone would establish, there is an end of controversy between us. Let, however, the disputed phrases be brought to their test before they are admitted; for I utterly refuse to accept the jargon of theatres and the mistakes of printers as the idiom or grammar of the age in which Shakespeare wrote. Every gross departure from literary rules may be countenanced, if we are permitted to draw examples from vitiated pages; and our readers, as often as they meet with restorations founded on such authorities, may justly exclaim, with Othello,—'Chaos is come again.' STEEVENS. (III, 22–3)

[3] [*Ibid.*, 2.1.235f.: '(For he's a spirit of persuasion, only/*Professes to persuade*)'. Steevens rejected the italicized words as spurious.]

I cannot help regarding the words—'*professes to persuade*'—as a mere gloss or paraphrase on '—*he has a spirit of persuasion.*' This explanatory sentence, being written in the margin of an actor's part, or playhouse copy, was afterwards injudiciously incorporated with our author's text. Read the passage (as it now stands in the text,) without these words, and nothing is wanting to its sense or metre.

On the contrary, the insertion of the words I have excluded, by lengthening the parenthesis, obscures the meaning of the speaker and, at the same time, produces redundancy of measure.

Irregularity of metre ought always to excite suspicions of omission or interpolation. Where somewhat has been omitted, through chance or design, a line is occasionally formed by the junction of hemistichs previously unfitted to each other. Such a line will naturally exceed the established proportion of feet; and when marginal observations are crept into the text they will have just such aukward effects as I conceive to have been produced by one of them in the present instance. . . .

Though I once expressed a different opinion, I am now well convinced that the metre of Shakespeare's plays had originally no other irregularity than was occasioned by an accidental use of hemistichs. When we find the smoothest series of lines among our earliest dramatic writers (who could fairly boast of no other requisites for poetry) are we to expect less polished versification from Shakespeare? STEEVENS. (III, 67–8)

[4] [On *Twelfth Night*, 5.1.389ff.: 'When that I was and a little tiny boy'. Farmer had dismissed the lyric in a note beginning 'Here again we have an old song, scarcely worth correction'.]

Though we are well convinced that Shakespeare has written slight ballads for the sake of discriminating characters more strongly, or for other necessary purposes in the course of his mixed dramas, it is scarce credible that after he had cleared his stage he should exhibit his Clown afresh, and with so poor a recommendation as this song, which is utterly unconnected with the subject of the preceding comedy. I do not therefore hesitate to call the nonsensical ditty before us some buffoon actor's composition, which was accidentally tacked to the Prompter's copy of *Twelfth-Night*, having been casually subjoined to it for the diversion, or at the call, of the lowest order of spectators. In the year 1766 I saw the late Mr. Weston summoned out and obliged to sing *Johnny Pringle and his Pig* after the performance of Voltaire's *Mahomet* at the Theatre Royal in Drury-Lane. STEEVENS. (IV, 173)

[5] [On *Measure for Measure*, 4.3.89: 'To yond generation, you shall find'; Steevens emends to 'The under generation . . .']

Mr. Malone reads:

> To yond *generation, you shall find* ——

But surely it is impossible that *yond* should be the true reading; for unless ge-ne-ra-ti-on were sounded as a word of five syllables, (a practice from which every ear must revolt,) the metre would be defective. It reminds one too much of Peascod, in Gay's *What d'ye call it :*

> The Pilgrim's Progress—eighth—e-di-ti-on,
> Lon-don prin-ted for Ni-cho-las Bod-ding-ton.

By the *under generation* our poet means the *antipodes*. . . . STEEVENS (IV, 343)

[6] [*Ibid.*, 4.5.1: the Duke gives letters to Friar Peter to deliver. Johnson commented in 1765 (I, 358): 'Peter never delivers the letters, but tells his story without any credentials. The poet forgot the plot which he had formed'.]
The first clause of this remark is undoubtedly just; but, respecting the second, I wish our readers to recollect that all the plays of Shakespeare, before they reached the press, had passed through a dangerous medium, and probably experienced the injudicious curtailments to which too many dramatic pieces are still exposed from the ignorance, caprice, and presumption of transcribers, players, and managers. STEEVENS. (IV, 352)

[7] [*Ibid.*, 5.1.445ff.: Isabel's plea on behalf of Angelo. See Johnson's note attacking 'our varlet poet', Vol 5, p. 105.]
It is evident that Isabella condescends to Mariana's importunate solicitation with great reluctance. Bad as her argument might be, it is the best that the guilt of Angelo would admit. The sacrifice that she makes of her revenge to her friendship scarcely merits to be considered in so harsh a light. RITSON. (IV, 381)

[8] [On *A Midsummer Night's Dream*, 1.1.45]
Immediately provided in that case.] Shakespeare is grievously suspected of having been placed, while a boy, in an attorney's office. The line before us has an undoubted smack of legal common-place. Poetry disclaims it. STEEVENS. (V, 8)

[9] [On *All's Well that Ends Well*, 4.2.4ff.: Parolles' metaphor that he is 'muddied in Fortune's mood, and smell somewhat strong of her strong displeasure'. Warburton had criticized this 'odious fault', but defended Shakespeare for having 'scarce a metaphor that can offend the most squeamish reader'.]
Dr. Warburton's recollection must have been weak, or his zeal

587

for his author extravagant. Otherwise he could not have ventured to countenance him on the score of delicacy; his offensive metaphors and allusions being undoubtedly more frequent than those of all his dramatick predecessors or contemporaries. STEEVENS. (VI, 351)

[10] [From a head-note to *The Comedy of Errors*]
Sir William Blackstone, I observe, suspects 'this and all other plays where much rhime is used, and especially long hobbling verses, to have been among Shakespeare's more early productions.' But I much doubt whether any of these 'long hobbling verses' have the honour of proceeding from his pen; and, in fact, the superior elegance and harmony of his language is no less distinguishable in his earliest than his latest production. The truth is, if any inference can be drawn from the most striking dissimilarity of stile, a tissue as different as silk and worsted, that this comedy though boasting the embellishments of our author's genius in additional words, lines, speeches, and scenes, was not originally his, but proceeded from some inferior playwright, who was capable of reading the *Menæchmi* without the help of a translation, or at least did not make use of Warner's. And this I take to have been the case, not only with the three parts of *K. Henry VI*, as I think a late editor (*O si sic omnia!*) has satisfactorily proved, but with *The Two Gentlemen of Verona*, *Love's Labour's Lost*, and *K. Richard II*, in all which pieces Shakespeare's new work is as apparent as the brightest touches of Titian would be on the poorest performance of the veriest canvass-spoiler that ever handled a brush. The originals of these plays (except the *second* and *third parts of K. Henry VI*) were never printed, and may be thought to have been put into his hands by the manager for the purpose of alteration and improvement, which we find to have been an ordinary practice of the theatre in his time. We are therefore no longer to look upon the above 'pleasant and fine conceited comedie,' as intitled to a situation among the '*Six old plays on which Shakespeare founded his Measure for Measure*,[1] &c.' of which I should hope to see a new and improved edition. RITSON. (VII, 208–9)

[11] [End-note to *The Comedy of Errors*]
On a careful revision of the foregoing scenes I do not hesitate to pronounce them the composition of two very unequal writers.

---

[1] A collection of source-plays published, at Steevens's suggestion, in 1779.

Shakespeare had undoubtedly a share in them; but that the entire play was no work of his is an opinion which (as Benedick says) 'fire cannot melt out of me; I will die in it at the stake.'

In this comedy we find more intricacy of plot than distinction of character; and our attention is less forcibly engaged, because we can guess in great measure how the denoüement will be brought about. Yet the subject appears to have been reluctantly dismissed, even in this last and unnecessary scene, where the same mistakes are continued till their power of affording entertainment is entirely lost. STEEVENS. (VII, 316)

[12] [Head-note to *Macbeth*; for Johnson's note see Vol. 4, pp. 165–7]
In the concluding paragraph of Dr. Johnson's admirable introduction to this play he seems apprehensive that the fame of Shakespeare's magic may be endangered by modern ridicule. I shall not hesitate, however, to predict its security till our national taste is wholly corrupted, and we no longer deserve the first of all dramatic enjoyments; for such, in my opinion at least, is the tragedy of *Macbeth*. STEEVENS. (VII, 322)

[13] [On *Macbeth*, 1.5.38ff.: 'The raven himself is hoarse . . .']
The following is, in my opinion, the sense of this passage.
Give him tending; the news he brings are worth the speed that made him lose his breath. [*Exit Attendant.*] 'Tis certain now—*the raven himself is* spent, is *hoarse* by croaking this very message, *the fatal entrance of Duncan under my battlements.*

Lady Macbeth (for she was not yet *unsexed*) was likelier to be deterred from her design than encouraged in it by the supposed thought that the message and the prophecy, (though equally secrets to the messenger and the raven,) had deprived the one of speech, and added harshness to the other's note. Unless we absurdly suppose the messenger acquainted with the hidden import of his message, *speed* alone had intercepted his breath, as *repetition* the raven's voice; though the lady considered both as organs of that destiny which hurried Duncan into her meshes. FUSELI. (VII, 373)

[14] [*Ibid.*, 1.7.28]
And falls on the other.] Sir T. Hanmer has on this occasion added a word, and would read—

And falls on the other side.

Yet they who plead for the admission of this supplement should consider that the plural of it, but two lines before, had occurred.

I also, who once attempted to justify the omission of this word, ought to have understood that Shakespeare could never mean to describe the agitation of Macbeth's mind, by the assistance of a halting verse.[1]

The general image, though confusedly expressed, relates to a horse, who, overleaping himself, falls, and his rider under him. To complete the line we may therefore read—

And falls *upon* the other.

Thus, in *The Taming of a Shrew* : 'How he left her with the horse *upon* her.'

Macbeth, as I apprehend, is meant for the rider, his *intent* for his horse, and his *ambition* for his *spur*; but unluckily, as the words are arranged, the *spur* is said to *over-leap* itself. Such hazardous things are long-drawn metaphors in the hands of careless writers. STEEVENS. (VII, 391)

[15] [*Ibid.*, 2.3: the Porter's scene]
Though Shakespeare (see Sir J. Reynolds's excellent note on Act I. sc. vi)[2] might have designed this scene as another instance of what is called the *repose* in painting, I cannot help regarding it in a different light. A glimpse of comedy was expected by our author's audience in the most serious drama; and where else could the merriment which he himself was always struggling after be so happily introduced? STEEVENS. (VII, 426)

[16] [*Ibid.*, 2.3.53: 'Goes the King hence to-day?']
He does: *he did appoint so*.] The words—*he does*—are omitted by Pope, Theobald, Hanmer, and Warburton. But perhaps Shakespeare designed Macbeth to shelter himself under an immediate falshood, till a sudden recollection of guilt restrained his confidence, and unguardedly disposed him to qualify his assertion; as he well knew the King's journey was effectually prevented by his death. A similar trait had occurred in a former scene:

---

[1] Cf. Capell, No. 263, note 37.
[2] See No. 265, note 3.

L. M. And when goes hence?
M. To-morrow,—as he purposes.

STEEVENS.[1] (VII, 431)

[17] [*Ibid.*, 2.3.]
His silver *skin* lac'd *with his* golden *blood*; The allusion is to the decoration of the richest habits worn in the age of Shakespeare, when it was usual to *lace* cloth of *silver* with *gold*, and cloth of *gold* with *silver*. [Quotes *Much Ado*, 3.4.19f.: 'Cloth of gold . . . lac'd with silver'] STEEVENS. (VII, 437)

[18] [*Ibid.*, 3.1.22: Macbeth to Banquo: 'but we'll *take* tomorrow': Malone had read 'talk', as being more correct.]
I do not perceive the necessity of change. The poet's meaning could not be misunderstood. His end was answered if his language was intelligible to his audience. He little supposed a time would arrive when his words were to abide the strictest scrutiny of verbal criticism. With the ease of conversation, therefore, he copied its incorrectness. To *take* is to *use*, to *employ*. To *take* time is a common phrase; and where is the impropriety of saying 'we'll *take* to-morrow?' i. e. we will *make use of* to-morrow. Banquo, 'without a prompter,' must have understood by this familiar expression that Macbeth would employ to-morrow, as he wished to have employed to-day. . . . STEEVENS. (VII, 450)

[19] [*Ibid.*, 3.2.5]
Nought's had, all's spent,] Surely, the unnecessary words—*Nought's had*—are a tasteless interpolation; for they violate the measure without expansion of the sentiment.

> *For a few words. Madam, I will. All's spent.*

is a complete verse.

There is sufficient reason to suppose the metre of Shakespeare was originally uniform and regular. His frequent exactness in making one speaker complete the verse which another had left imperfect, is too evident to need exemplification. Sir T. Hanmer was aware of this, and occasionally struggled with such metrical difficulties as occurred; though for want of familiarity with ancient language, he often failed in the choice of words to be rejected or supplied. STEEVENS. (VII, 462–3)

---

[1] Compare Whately above, pp. 418f.

[20] [*Ibid.*, 5.1.3]

Since his majesty went into the field,] This is one of Shakespeare's oversights. He forgot that he had shut up Macbeth in Dunsinane, and surrounded him with besiegers. That he could *not go into the field* is observed by himself with splenetic impatience:

> Were they not forc'd with those that should be ours,
> *We might have met them dareful, beard to beard,*
> *And beat them backward home.*

It is clear also from other passages that Macbeth's motions had long been circumscribed by the walls of his fortress.

The truth may be that Shakespeare thought the spirit of Lady Macbeth could not be so effectually subdued, and her peace of mind so speedily unsettled by reflection on her guilt, as during the absence of her husband.

For the present change in her disposition, therefore, our poet (though in the haste of finishing his play he forgot his plan,) might mean to have provided, by allotting her such an interval of solitude as would subject her mind to perturbation, and dispose her thoughts to repentance.

It does not appear from any circumstance within the compass of this drama that she had once been separated from her husband, after his return from the victory over Macdonwald and the King of Norway. STEEVENS. (VII, 544–5)

[21] [*Ibid.*, 5.4.21: the scene ends with a couplet followed by an unrhymed line]

Towards which, advance the war.] It has been understood that local rhymes were introduced in plays to afford an actor the advantage of a more pointed exit, or to close a scene with additional force. Yet, whatever might be Shakespeare's motive for continuing such a practice, it may be observed that he often seems immediately to repent of it; and in the tragedy before us has repeatedly counteracted it by hemistichs with destroy the effect and consequently defeat the supposed purpose of the antecedent couplets. See the following instances, in addition to that which introduces the present note.

Leave all the rest to me.	—— Act I. end of scene v.
So pr'ythee go with me.	—— Act III. ——sc. ii.
We are yet but young in deed.	—— Act III. ——sc. iv.

But no more sights &c.	—— Act IV.	——sc. i.
I think, but dare not speak.	—— Act V.	——sc. i.
Make we our march towards Birnam.	—— Act V.	——sc. ii.

In *Hamlet* &c. we find such hemistichs after the rhymes at the ends of acts, as well as scenes. STEEVENS. (VII, 566)

[22] [*Ibid.*, 5.7: Macbeth defeating Young Siward]
This short scene is injudiciously omitted on the stage. The poet designed Macbeth should *appear* invincible, till he encountered the object destined for his destruction. STEEVENS. (VII, 575)

[23] [On *Richard II*, 3.2.42: 'the searching eye of heaven']
He fires the proud tops of the eastern pines,] It is not easy to point out an image more striking and beautiful than this in any poet, whether ancient or modern. STEEVENS. (VII, 272)

[24] [End-note to *2 Henry IV*. See Malone's note, above, p. 541, on the 'careless' conclusions of several plays.]
That there is no apparent full and energetic close to any of the plays enumerated by Mr. Malone is undeniable; but perhaps the epilogue spoken in the character of *Prospero*, the dance which terminates *Much Ado about Nothing*, a final and picturesque separation and procession of the personages in *Love's Labour's Lost* and the *Winter's Tale*, the symphony of warlike instruments at the end of *Timon*, and the peal of ordnance shot off while the survivers in *Hamlet* are quitting the stage, might have proved as satisfactory to our ancestors as the moral applications and polished couplets with which so many of our modern dramatick pieces conclude. STEEVENS. (IX, 251)

[25] [On *Henry V*, 4.3.104: 'Mark then *abounding* valour in our English'. Theobald's emendation of the Quarto *abundant* to *a bounding* was attacked by Malone.]
The preceding note (in my opinion at least) has not proved that, though Shakespeare talks of *abundant valour* in *King Richard III*, he might not have written *a bounding valour* in *King Henry V*. Must our author indulge himself in no varieties of phraseology, but always be tied down to the use of similar expressions? Or does it follow that because his imagery is sometimes incongruous, that it was always so? . . . STEEVENS. (IX, 436)

[26] [On *3 Henry VI*, 5.7.30]

Thanks, noble Clarence; worthy brother, thanks.] The quarto appropriates this line to the *Queen*. The first and second folio, by mistake, have given it to *Clarence*.

In my copy of the second folio, which had belonged to King Charles the First, his majesty has erased—*Cla*, and written—*King*, in its stead.—Shakespeare, therefore, in the catalogue of his restorers, may boast of a Royal name. STEEVENS. (X, 403)

[27] [On *Richard III*, 1.3.157ff.: 'Hear me you wrangling pirates . . .' . Warburton praised this 'scene of Margaret's imprecations' as 'fine and artful', comparing her to Cassandra, prophesying 'the following tragic revolutions'.]

Surely the merits of this scene are insufficient to excuse its improbability. Margaret, bullying the court of England in the royal palace, is a circumstance as absurd as the courtship of Gloucester in a publick street. STEEVENS. (X, 494)

[28] [End-note to *Richard III*, which Johnson (Vol. 5, pp. 133f.) and Malone (1790: VI, 618), said was overvalued]

I most cordially join with Dr. Johnson and Mr. Malone in their opinions; and yet perhaps they have overlooked one cause of the success of this tragedy. The part of Richard is perhaps beyond all others variegated, and consequently favourable to a judicious performer. It comprehends, indeed, a trait of almost every species of character on the stage. The hero, the lover, the statesman, the buffoon, the hypocrite, the hardened and repenting sinner &c. are to be found within its compass. No wonder therefore that the discriminating powers of a Burbage, a Garrick, and a Henderson should at different periods have given it a popularity beyond other dramas of the same author.

Yet the favour with which this tragedy is now received must also in some measure be imputed to Mr. Cibber's reformation of it, which generally considered, is judicious: for what modern audience would patiently listen to the narrative of Clarence's Dream, his subsequent expostulation with the murderers, the prattle of his children, the soliloquy of the Scrivener, the tedious dialogue of the citizens, the ravings of Margaret, the gross terms thrown out by the Duchess of York on Richard, the repeated progress to execution, the superfluous train of spectres, and other undramatick incumbrances which must have prevented the more valuable parts of the play from rising into their present effect and consequence?—The expulsion of languor therefore must atone for such remaining want of probability as is inseparable from an historical drama into which the events of fourteen years are irregularly compressed. STEEVENS. (X, 699–700)

[29] [On the Prologue to *Troilus and Cressida*]
I cannot regard this Prologue (which indeed is wanting in the quarto editions) as the work of Shakespeare; and perhaps the drama before us was not entirely of his construction. It appears to have been unknown to his associates, Heminge and Condell, till after the first folio was almost printed off. On this subject, indeed, (as I learn from Mr. Malone's *Emendations and Additions*, &c. there seems to have been a play anterior to the present one [citing Henslowe's advance of money to Chettle and Dekker for a play on this subject in 1599].

I conceive this prologue to have been written, and the dialogue in more than one place interpolated by some *Kyd* or *Marlowe* of the time; who may have been paid for *altering* and *amending* one of Shakespeare's plays: a very extraordinary instance of our author's negligence, and the managers' taste! RITSON. (XI, 214)

[30] [*Ibid.* 5.8.16ff.]
My half-supp'd sword, &c.] These four despicable verses, as well as the rhyming fit with which 'the blockish Ajax' is afterwards seized, could scarce have fallen from the pen of our author in his most unlucky moments of composition. STEEVENS.

Whatever may have been the remainder of this speech as it came out of Shakespeare's hands, we may be confident that this bombast stuff made no part of it. Our author's gold was stolen and the thief's brass left in its place. RITSON.

Perhaps this play was hastily altered by Shakespeare from an elder piece, which the reader will find mentioned [above]. Some of the scenes in it therefore he might have fertilized, and left others as barren as he found them. STEEVENS. (XI, 446)

[31] [End-note to *Troilus and Cressida*, 5.10.30ff.: the final appearance of Pandarus]

——— *with comfort go:*
Hope of revenge shall hide our inward woe.]

This couplet affords a full and natural close to the play; and though I once thought differently, I must now declare my firm belief that Shakespeare designed it should end here, and that what follows is either a subsequent and injudicious restoration from the elder drama mentioned [above], or the nonsense of some wretched buffoon who represented Pandarus. When the hero of the scene was not only alive, but on the stage, our author would scarce have trusted the conclusion of his piece to a subordinate character whom he had uniformly held up to detestation. It is still less probable that he should have wound up his story with a stupid outrage to decency, and a deliberate insult on his audience.—But in several other parts of this drama I cannot persuade myself that I have been reading Shakespeare.

As evident an interpolation is pointed out at the end of *Twelfth Night* [the Clown's song]. STEEVENS. (XI, 449–50)

[32] [On *Antony and Cleopatra*, 2.2.234–5]

Age cannot wither her, nor custom stale
Her infinite variety:]

Such is the praise bestowed by Shakespeare on his heroine; a praise that well deserves the consideration of our female readers. Cleopatra, as appears from the tetradrachms of Antony, was no Venus; and indeed the majority of ladies who most successfully enslaved the hearts of princes are known to have been less remarkable for personal than mental attractions. The reign of insipid beauty is seldom lasting; but permanent must be the rule of a woman who can diversify the sameness of life by an inexhausted variety of accomplishments. STEEVENS. (XII, 485)

[33] [*Ibid.*, 3.13.49–52: Malone suspected that this speech belonged to Cleopatra, not Enobarbus, who would not 'presume to interfere' in the negotiations between her and Caesar's messenger, Thidias.]

Enobarbus, who is the buffoon of the play, has already presumed [2.2.103ff.] to interfere between the jarring Triumvirs, and might therefore have been equally flippant on the occasion before us.—For this reason, as well as others, I conceive the speech in question to have been rightly appropriated in the old copy.—What a diminution of Shakespeare's praise would it be if four lines that exactly suit the mouth of Enobarbus could come with equal propriety from the lips of Cleopatra! STEEVENS. (XII, 576)

[34] [*Ibid.*, 4.15.32: 'Here's sport indeed;': cf. Malone's note, above, p. 543]
Cleopatra perhaps, by this affected levity, this phrase which has no determined signification, only wishes to inspire Antony with cheerfulness, and encourage those who are engaged in the melancholy task of drawing him up into the monument. STEEVENS. (XII, 639)

[35] [On *Cymbeline*, 5.3.95, stage direction]
Enter Cymbeline, &c.] This is the only instance in these plays of the business of the scene being entirely performed in dumb show. The direction must have proceeded from the players, as it is perfectly unnecessary, and our author has elsewhere (in *Hamlet*) expressed his contempt of such mummery. RITSON. (XIII, 199)

[36] [*Ibid.*, 5.4.29ff.: the dumb-show and masque, which Pope in 1725 (Vol. 2, p. 418) had dismissed as an interpolation of the players 'for mere show']
Every reader must be of the same opinion. The subsequent narratives of Posthumus, which render this masque &c. unnecessary, (or perhaps the scenical directions supplied by the poet himself) seem to have excited some manager of a theatre to disgrace the play by the present metrical interpolation. Shakespeare, who has conducted his fifth act with such matchless skill, could never have designed the vision to be twice described by Posthumus, had this contemptible nonsense been previously delivered on the stage. STEEVENS. (XIII, 202)
   One would think that, Shakespeare's style being too refined for his audiences, the managers had employed some playwright of the *old school* to regale them with a touch of 'King Cambyses' vein.' The margin would be too honourable a place for so impertinent an interpolation. RITSON. (XIII, 202–3)

[37] [On *Pericles*, Prologue to Act 1]

Being now convinced that all the irregular lines detected in *The Midsummer Night's Dream, Macbeth,* and *Pericles,* have been prolonged by interpolations which afford no additional beauties, I am become more confident in my attempt to amend the passage before us. Throughout this play it should seem to be a very frequent practice of the reciter or transcriber to supply words which, for some foolish reason or other, were supposed to be wanting. Unskill'd in the language of poetry, and more especially in that which was clouded by an affectation of antiquity, these ignorant people regarded many contractions and ellipses as indications of somewhat accidentally omitted; and while they inserted only monosyllables or unimportant words in imaginary vacancies, they conceived themselves to be doing little mischief. Liberties of this kind must have been taken with the piece under consideration. The measure of it is too regular and harmonious in many places for us to think it was utterly neglected in the rest. As this play will never be received as the entire composition of Shakespeare, and as violent disorders require medicines of proportionable violence, I have been by no means scrupulous in striving to reduce the metre to that exactness which I suppose it originally to have possessed. Of the same license I should not have availed myself had I been employed on any of the undisputed dramas of our author. Those experiments which we are forbidden to perform on living subjects may properly be attempted on dead ones, among which our *Pericles* may be reckoned; being dead, in its present form, to all purposes of the stage, and of no very promising life in the closet. STEEVENS. (XIII, 390)

[38] [*Ibid.*, 4.6.169]

As hath been belch'd on by infected lungs.] Marina, who is designed for a character of juvenile innocence, appears much too knowing in the impurities of a brothel; nor are her expressions more chastised than her ideas. STEEVENS. (XIII, 567)

[39] [*Ibid.*, 5.1.107f.]

> ———*such a one*
> *My daughter might have been:*]

So, Demones in the *Rudens* of Plautus exclaims on beholding his long-lost child:

O filia
Mea! cum ego hanc video, mearum me absens miseriarum
commones,
Trima quæ periit mihi: *jam tanta effet, si vivit, scio*.[1]

It is observable that some of the leading incidents in this play
strongly remind us of the *Rudens*. There Arcturus, like Gower,
πρoλoγιζει.—In the Latin comedy fishermen, as in *Pericles*, are
brought on the stage, one of whom drags on shore in his net the
wallet which principally produces the catastrophe; and the heroines
of Plautus and Marina fall alike into the hands of a procurer. A
circumstance on which much of the plot in both these dramatick
pieces depends. HOLT WHITE. (XIII, 584)

[40] [On *King Lear*, 1.5.51f.: 'She that's a maid now, and laughs at
my departure,/Shall not be a maid long']
unless things be cut shorter.] This idle couplet is apparently addressed
to the females present at the performance of the play; and, not
improbably, crept into the playhouse copy from the mouth of
some buffoon actor who 'spoke more than was set down for him.'

I am aware that such liberties were exercised by the authors of
Locrine, &c; but can such another offensive and extraneous address
to the audience be pointed out among all the dramas of
Shakespeare? STEEVENS. (XIV, 80)

[41] [*Ibid.*, 2.2.15ff.: Kent's cursing of Oswald]
Kent is not only boisterous in his manners but abusive in his
language. His excessive ribaldry proceeds from an over solicitude
to prevent being discovered: like St. Peter's swearing from a
similar motive. HENLEY. (XIV, 92)

[42] [*Ibid.*, 4.3.1f.]
Why the king of France is so suddenly gone back &c.] The king of France
being no longer a necessary personage, it was fit that some pretext
for getting rid of him should be formed before the play was too
near advanced towards a conclusion. Decency required that a
Monarch should not be silently shuffled into the pack of
insignificant characters; and therefore his dismission (which could

---

[1] *Rudens*, 742–4: 'Ah, daughter dear, absent though you are, you remind me of my sorrow
when I look at this girl! Three years old when I lost her, and now the size of this lass, no
doubt, if she's alive!'

be effected only by a sudden recall to his own dominions) was to be accounted for before the audience. For this purpose, among others, the present scene was introduced. It is difficult indeed to say what use could have been made of the King had he appeared at the head of his own armament, and survived the murder of his queen. His conjugal concern on the occasion might have weakened the effect of Lear's parental sorrow; and, being an object of respect as well as pity, he would naturally have divided the spectator's attention, and thereby diminished the consequence of Albany, Edgar, and Kent, whose exemplary virtues deserved to be ultimately placed in the most conspicuous point of view. STEEVENS. (XIV, 213–14)

[43] [*Ibid.*, 4.6.235ff.: Edgar's adopted dialect]
When our ancient writers have occasion to introduce a rustick they commonly allot him this Somersetshire dialect. Mercury, in the second book of Ovid's *Metamorphoses*, assumes the appearance of a clown, and our translator *Golding* has made him speak with the provinciality of Shakespeare's Edgar. STEEVENS. (XIV, 247)

[44] [*Ibid.*, 5.3.213f.: Edgar's account of Kent's meeting with himself and the dead Gloucester]
threw him *on my father*;] The quartos read,
—threw *me* on my father.
The modern editors have corrected the passage, as it is now printed, and as I suppose it to have been originally written. There is tragick propriety in Kent's throwing himself on the body of a deceased friend; but this propriety is lost in the act of clumsily tumbling a son over the lifeless remains of his father. STEEVENS. (XIV, 286)

[45] [On *Romeo and Juliet*, 5.3.87: 'Death, lie thou there, by a dead man interr'd'. Malone commented: 'Romeo being now determined to put an end to his life, considers himself as already dead'.]
Till I read the preceding note I supposed Romeo meant that he placed Paris by the side of *Tybalt* who was already dead, and buried in the same monument. The idea, however, of a man's receiving burial from a dead undertaker is but too like some of those miserable conceits with which our author too frequently counteracts his own pathos. STEEVENS. (XIV, 550)

[46] [On *Hamlet* and its various texts]
It may be worth while to observe that the title-pages of the first
quartos in 1604 and 1605 declare this play to be *enlarged to almost as
much againe as it was, according to the true and perfect copy.*

Perhaps therefore many of its absurdities as well as beauties
arose from the quantity added after it was first written. Our poet
might have been more attentive to the amplification than the
coherence of his fable.

The degree of credit due to the title-page that styles the MS.
from which the quartos, 1604 and 1605 were printed, the *true and
perfect copy* may also be disputable. I cannot help supposing this
publication to contain all Shakespeare rejected as well as all he
supplied. By restorations like the former, contending booksellers
or theatres might have gained some temporary advantage over
each other, which at this distance of time is not to be understood.
The patience of our ancestors exceeded our own, could it have out-
lasted the tragedy of *Hamlet* as it is now printed; for it must have
occupied almost five hours in representation. If, however, it was
too much dilated on the ancient stage it is as injudiciously
contracted on the modern one. STEEVENS. (XV, 15)

[47] [*Ibid.*, 1.1.139ff.]

> —*Stop it, Marcellus.*—
> Hor. *Do, if it will not stand.*]

I am unwilling to suppose that Shakespeare could appropriate
these absurd effusions to *Horatio*, who is a scholar, and has
sufficiently proved his good understanding by the propriety of his
addresses to the phantom. Such a man therefore must have known
that

> As easy might he the intrenchant air
> With his keen sword impress,

as commit any act of violence on the royal shadow. The
words—*Stop it, Marcellus,*—and *Do, if it will not stand*—better suit
the next speaker, *Bernardo*, who, in the true spirit of an unlettered
officer, *nihil non arroget armis*.[1] Perhaps the first idea that occurs to a
man of this description, is to strike at what offends him. Nicholas

---

[1] Horace, *Ars Poetica*, 122: 'let him ever make appeal to the sword'.

Poussin, in his celebrated picture of the Crucifixion, has introduced a similar occurrence. While lots are casting for the sacred vesture, the graves are giving up their dead. This prodigy is perceived by one of the soldiers, who instantly grasps his sword, as if preparing to defend himself, or resent such an invasion from the other world.

The two next speeches—*'Tis here!*—*'Tis here!*—may be allotted to *Marcellus and Bernardo*; and the third—*'Tis gone!* &c. to Horatio, whose superiority of character indeed seems to demand it.—As the text now stands Marcellus proposes to strike the Ghost with his partizan, and yet afterwards is made to descant on the indecorum and impotence of such an attempt.

The names of speakers have so often been confounded by the first publishers of our author that I suggest this change with less hesitation than I should express concerning any conjecture that could operate to the disadvantage of his words or meaning.—Had the assignment of the old copies been such, would it have been thought liable to objection? STEEVENS. (XV, 20–1)

[48] [*Ibid.*, 1.5.182]

Rest, rest, perturbed spirit!] The skill displayed in Shakespeare's management of his Ghost is too considerable to be overlooked. He has rivetted our attention to it by a succession of forcible circumstances:—by the previous report of the terrified centinels,—by the solemnity of the hour at which the phantom walks,—by its martial stride and discriminating armour, visible only *per incertam lunam*, by the glimpses of the moon,—by its long taciturnity,—by its preparation to speak when interrupted by the morning cock,—by its mysterious reserve throughout its first scene with Hamlet,—by his resolute departure with it, and the subsequent anxiety of his attendants,—by its conducting him to a solitary angle of the platform,—by its voice from beneath the earth,—and by its unexpected burst on us in the closet.

Hamlet's late interview with the spectre must in particular be regarded as a stroke of dramatick artifice. The phantom might have told his story in the presence of the officers and Horatio, and yet have rendered itself as inaudible to them, as afterwards to the Queen. But suspense was our poet's object; and never was it more effectually created than in the present instance. Six times has the royal semblance appeared, but till now has been withheld from speaking. For this event we have waited with impatient curiosity, unaccompanied by lassitude, or remitted attention.

The Ghost in this tragedy is allowed to be the genuine product of Shakespeare's strong imagination. When he afterwards avails himself of traditional phantoms, as in *Julius Cæsar* and *King Richard III*, they are but inefficacious pageants; nay, the apparition of Banquo is a mute exhibitor. Perhaps our poet despaired to equal the vigour of his early conceptions on the subject of preternatural beings, and therefore allotted them no further eminence in his dramas; or was unwilling to diminish the power of his principal shade by an injudicious repetition of congenial images. STEEVENS. (XV, 88–9)

[49] [On the guilt of Claudius and Gertrude: cf. the notes by Steevens and Malone, above pp. 283f., 392 and 546f.]
That the Queen (who may still be regarded as innocent of murder) might have offered some apology for her 'over-hasty marriage,' can easily be supported; but Mr. Malone has not suggested what defence could have been set up by the royal fratricide. My acute predecessor, as well as the novelist, must have been aware that though female weakness and an offence against the forms of the world will admit of extenuation, such guilt as that of the usurper could not have been palliated by the dramatick art of Shakespeare; even if the father of Hamlet had been represented as a wicked instead of a virtuous character. STEEVENS. (XV, 222)

[50] [On Malone's claim that Rosencrantz and Guildenstern are made accessories to Claudius's plot against Hamlet, as in the black-letter novel *Hamblet*: see above, pp. 284, 344, 547]
I apprehend that a critick and a juryman are bound to form their opinions on what they see and hear in the cause before them, and not to be influenced by extraneous particulars unsupported by legal evidence in open court. I persist in observing that from Shakespeare's drama no proofs of the guilt of Rosencrantz and Guildenstern can be collected. They may be convicted by the black letter history; but if the tragedy forbears to criminate it has no right to sentence them. This is sufficient for the commentator's purpose. It is not his office to interpret the plays of Shakespeare according to the novels on which they are founded, novels which the poet sometimes followed, but as often materially deserted.

Perhaps he never confined himself strictly to the plan of any one of his originals. His negligence of poetick justice is notorious; nor can we expect that he who was content to sacrifice the pious Ophelia should have been more scrupulous about the worthless lives of Rosencrantz and Guildenstern. Therefore I still assert that, in the tragedy before us, their deaths appear both wanton and unprovoked; and the critick, like Bayes, must have recourse to somewhat *long before the beginning of this play* to justify the conduct of its hero. STEEVENS. (XV, 322)

[51] [On *Othello*, 4.1.263: 'Goats and monkies!' Malone suggested that the words of Iago, 'as prime as goats, as hot as monkies' (3.3.403) 'still ring in the ears of Othello'.]
Though the words of Othello cited by Mr. Malone could not have escaped the deliberate reader's memory, a reference to a distant scene but ill agrees with the infuriation of Othello's mind. His fancy, haunted by still growing images of lewdness, would scarce have expressed its feelings in recollected phraseology. STEEVENS. (XV, 592)

[52] [End-note to *Othello*: commenting on Malone's end-note, above, pp. 548f.]
If by 'the most perfect' is meant the *most regular* of the foregoing plays, I subscribe to Mr. Malone's opinon; but if his words were designed to convey a more exalted praise, without a moment's hesitation I should transfer it to MACBETH.

It is true that the domestick tragedy of *Othello* affords room for a various and forcible display of character. The less familiar groundwork of *Macbeth* (as Dr. Johnson has observed) excludes the influence of peculiar dispositions. That exclusion, however, is recompensed by a loftier strain of poetry, and by events of higher rank; by supernatural agency, by the solemnities of incantation, by shades of guilt and horror deepening in their progress, and by visions of futurity solicited in aid of hope, but eventually the ministers of despair.

Were it necessary to weigh the pathetick effusions of these dramas against each other, it is generally allowed that the sorrows of Desdemona would be more than counterbalanced by those of Macduff.

Yet if our author's rival pieces (the distinct property of their subjects considered) are written with equal force, it must still be admitted that the latter has more of originality. A novel of considerable length (perhaps amplified and embellished by the English translator of it) supplied a regular and circumstantial outline for *Othello*; while a few slight hints collected from separate narratives of Holinshed were expanded into the sublime and awful tragedy of *Macbeth*.

Should readers, who are alike conversant with the appropriate excellencies of poetry and painting, pronounce on the reciprocal merits of these great productions, I must suppose they would describe them as of different pedigrees. They would add that one was of the school of Raphael, the other from that of Michael Angelo; and that if the steady Sophocles and Virgil should have decided in favour of *Othello*, the remonstrances of the daring Æschylus and Homer would have claimed the laurel for *Macbeth*.

To the sentiments of Dr. Lowth respecting the tragedy of *Othello*, a general elogium on the dramatick works of Shakespeare, imputed by a judicious and amiable critick to Milton, may be not improperly subjoined:

'There is good reason to suppose (says my late friend the Rev. Thomas Warton, in a note on *L' Allegro*,) that Milton threw many additions and corrections into the THEATRUM POETARUM, a book published by his nephew Edward Philips, in 1675.[1] It contains criticisms far above the taste of that period. Among these is the following judgement on Shakespeare, which was not then, I believe, the general opinion.'–'In tragedy, never any expressed a more lofty and tragick heighth, never any represented nature more purely to the life: and where the polishments of art are most wanting, as probably his learning was not extraordinary, he pleases with a certain WILD and NATIVE elegance.'

What greater praise can any poet have received than that of the author of *Paradise Lost*? STEEVENS. (XV, 665–6)

---

[1] See Vol. 1, p. 13. But there is no evidence that Milton contributed to Philips's collection.

304. Walter Whiter, Shakespeare's mental associations

1794

From *A Specimen of a Commentary on Shakespeare. Containing I. Notes on As You Like It. II. An Attempt to explain and illustrate Various Passages, on a New Principle of Criticism, derived from Mr. Locke's Doctrine of The Association of Ideas* (1794).

Walter Whiter (1758–1832), an undergraduate and subsequently Fellow of Clare Hall, Cambridge, from 1783 to 1797, spent the remainder of his life as rector of Hardingham, Norfolk. He was a lifelong friend of Richard Porson. Whiter also published *Etymologicon Magnum, a universal etymological dictionary on a new plan* (1800: part 1 only), *Etymologicon Universale* (3 vols, 1811, 1822, 1825), and *A Dissertation on the Disorder of Death, or that State called suspended Animation* (1819). Whiter's work on Shakespeare was not well received by contemporary reviewers, who found the associationist method old-fashioned, and held that he made too great claims for his discoveries. But it has been vindicated in our time by the work of such critics as E. E. Kellett, Caroline Spurgeon, E. A. Armstrong and Kenneth Muir. For further references see the valuable edition (which includes Whiter's later additions from a manuscript now in Cambridge University Library) by Alan Over, completed by Mary Bell (1967).

[From Part II]

The Association of Ideas is a fruitful and popular theme in the writings of metaphysicians; and they have supplied us with innumerable examples, which prove at once the extent and the activity of its influence. They have taught us that our modes of reasoning, our habits of life, and even the motions of our body are affected by its energy; and that it operates on the faculties by a kind of fascinating controul, which we sometimes cannot discover, and which generally we are unable to counteract. The consideration, however, of this doctrine (curious and extensive as it may appear) has commonly been confined to the admirers of metaphysical researches; nor has the theory, I believe, ever been systematically discussed as a point of taste or as a subject of criticism. We have seen the question totally exhausted, as it refers to the general powers of the understanding and the habitual exercise of the reasoning faculty; but we may justly be astonished that the effects of this principle should never have been investigated as it operates on the *writer in the ardor of invention*, by imposing on his mind some* remote and peculiar vein of language or of imagery. If, in the ordinary exertions of the understanding, the force of such an association has been found so powerful and extensive, it may surely be concluded that its influence would predominate with absolute authority over the vigorous workings of a wild and fertile imagination. In the pages of the poet, therefore, may we expect to be supplied with the most curious and abundant materials for the discussion of this principle; and in none can we hope to find such frequent and singular examples of its effect as may probably be discovered by the diligent reader in the writings of Shakespeare. (63–4)

In the theory of Mr. Locke, by the term *association* is *not* understood the combination of ideas *naturally* connected with each other; for these (as he observes) 'it is the office and the excellency of our reason to form and preserve in that union and correspondence, which is founded on their peculiar beings.' On the contrary, it is understood to express the combination of those ideas which have *no* natural alliance or relation to each other, but which have been united only by chance or by custom. Now it is observable that no task can be imposed on the understanding of greater difficulty than to separate ideas thus accidentally combined; as the mind is commonly passive in admitting their original formation, and often totally unconscious of the force and principle of their union. (65)

. . . I define therefore the power of this *association* over the

---

* 'Ideas, that in themselves are not at all of kin, come to be so united in some men's minds, that it is very hard to separate them; they always *keep in company*, and the one no sooner at any time comes into the understanding, but its *associate* appears with it; and if they are more than two which are thus united, *the whole gang* always inseparable shew themselves together.' (Locke's *Essay*, B. 2. C. 33. §. 5.)

genius of the poet to consist in supplying him with words and with ideas which have been suggested to the mind by a principle of union unperceived by himself, and independent of the subject to which they are applied. . . . We might thus perhaps arrange in a more ample yet inadequate manner the principal objects of the general definition; though the examples only will enable us to understand the force and propriety of the arrangement.

1. It will often happen that a certain word, expression, sentiment, circumstance, or metaphor, will lead the writer to the use of that appropriate language by which they are each of them distinguished, even on occasions where the metaphor is no longer continued, where there is no allusion intended to the circumstance, nor is there any sense conveyed under this language which bears a peculiar reference to the words or sentiments that excited it. It is merely accidental that the imagery, in whose service the language thus suggested is employed, has any affinity to the subject from which it is borrowed. Now, as it is the business of the critic to discover and establish the original language of the author, and to reject what is sometimes called the *improved* text of an *ingenious* commentator, we shall instantly perceive that from this principle may probably be derived a very important canon for the confirmation of disputed readings, which have perhaps been too hastily condemned as quaint, remote, or unintelligible. If the discerning critic should discover that the train of thought which had just occupied the attention of the writer, would naturally conduct him to the use of this controverted expression we should certainly have little difficulty in admitting the reading to be genuine, even though it had before appeared to us under a questionable shape from the singular mode in which it was applied. (68–70)

2. Certain terms containing an equivocal meaning, or sounds suggesting such a meaning, will often serve to introduce other words and expressions of a similar nature. This similarity is formed by having in some cases a coincidence in sense or an affinity arising from sound; though the signification in which they are really applied has never any reference and often no similitude to that which caused their association.

3. The remembrance of a similar phraseology, of a known metaphor, or of a circumstance *not* apparent in the text, will often lead the writer into language or imagery derived from these

608

sources; though the application may be sometimes totally different from the meaning and spirit of the original.

4. An impression on the mind of the writer, arising from something which is frequently presented to his senses or which passes within the sphere of his ordinary observation, will supply him with the union of words and sentiments which are not necessarily connected with each other, and which are combined only from the powerful influence of external impressions on the faculties of the understanding.

These objects may be general, and therefore equally apparent to the observers of every period; but the more curious examples of this nature will be derived from those impressions which are peculiar to the country, the age, and the situation of the writer. Here likewise we are still to understand that as these combinations were not formed by the invention but forced on the fancy of the poet, he is totally unconscious of the effect and principle of their union. . . . (70–1)

The first example which I shall produce is the very passage which originally led me to the present enquiry.—In *Timon of Athens*, when Timon has retired into the woods, Apemantus thus upbraids him with the contrast of his past and present condition:

> What, think'st
> That the bleak air, thy boisterous *chamberlain,*
> Will put thy *shirt* on *warm*? Will these MOIST trees,
> That have outliv'd the eagle, page thy heels,
> And skip when thou pointst out? [4.3.221ff.]

Sir Thomas Hanmer for *moist* reads very elegantly, says Dr. Johnson, *moss'd*. Mr. Steevens confirms the emendation by examples; and Mr. Malone believes it to be the true reading. I agree with our Commentators that *moss'd* is a more elegant epithet, and at the same time better calculated to express the antiquity of trees *that have outliv'd the eagle*. It is certain however that *moist* is not altogether destitute of force and propriety; as in many parts of old and rotten trees a kind of *moist* exsudation is often to be seen, though perhaps other parts may be dry and withered by age. If therefore I can shew with extreme probability, from some acknowledged principle in the mind, why this peculiar word might be suggested to our Poet, it surely ought to be considered as a valuable touchstone in the Art of Criticism, of which it is certainly the business to discover and ascertain what the author really *has* written and not what he *ought* to have done.—The reader then is to be informed that *warm* and *moist* were the appropriate terms in the days of Shakespeare for what we should now call an *air'd* and a *damp* shirt. So *John Florio* (*Second Frutes*, 1591) in a dialogue between the master *Torquato* and his servant *Ruspa*.

> *T.* Dispatch and give me a *shirt*?
> *R.* Here is one with ruffes.
> *T.* Thou dolte, seest thou not how *moyst* it is?
> *R.* Pardon me, good Sir, I was not aware of it.
> *T.* Go into the kitchen and *warme* it.

Can the reader doubt (though he may perhaps smile at the association) that the image of the *Chamberlain* putting the *shirt* on *warm* impressed the opposite word *moist* on the imagination of the Poet? Though he was himself unconscious how he came by it, and certainly never would have applied it as an epithet to trees if it had not been fixed on his mind by a kind of fascinating power, which concealed from him not only the origin but the effect likewise of so strange an association. (81–2)

. . . It will readily be understood and acknowledged that this propensity in the mind to associate subjects so remote in their meaning, and so heterogeneous in their nature, must of necessity sometimes deceive the ardour of the writer into whimsical or ridiculous combinations. As the reader however is not blinded by this fascinating principle which, while it creates the association conceals likewise its effect; he is instantly impressed with the quaintness or the absurdity of the imagery, and is inclined to charge the writer with the intention of a foolish quibble or an impertinent allusion. I shall now therefore produce some passages of Shakespeare which have fallen under suspicions of this nature, and which I think may be completely defended by the application of the present theory. Our Bard has so many grievous and undoubted quibbles of his own to answer for that it is surely unreasonable, as Mr. Steevens has somewhere observed, to censure him for those which exist only in the imagination of others.

> He had a fever when he was in Spain,
> And, when the fit was on him, I did mark
> How he did shake: 'tis true, this god did shake:

His COWARD lips did from their COLOUR FLY.
(Julius Cæsar) [1.2.119ff.]

'A plain man' (says *Warburton*) 'would have said the *colour fled from his lips*, and not his *lips from their colour*. But the false expression was for the sake of as false a piece of wit: a poor quibble, alluding to a coward flying from his colours.' The Critic has discovered the association which had escaped the Author; who indeed intended no quibble, but was himself entangled by the similitude of *colour* and *colours*. This introduced to him the appropriate terms of *coward* and *fly*; and thus, under the influence of such an embarrassment, it was scarcely possible to express the sentiment in a form less equivocal than the present. Let me add likewise another circumstance which might operate in suggesting this *military* metaphor—that the cowardice of a *soldier* is the subject of the narrative. (105–7)

. . . I shall take occasion from another passage, in the parting scene between Troilus and Cressida, to illustrate our theory with a vein of allusions which I have once marked in the preceding note. The rapid imagination of the unwary Poet, even when it is employed on sentiments the most tender and pathetic, is sometimes imperceptibly entangled in a chain of imagery which is derived from the meanest subjects and the lowest occupations.

> *Troilus.* Injurious time now, with a robber's haste,
> Crams his rich thievery up, he knows not how.
> As many farewels, as be stars in heaven,
> With distinct breath, and consign'd kisses to them,
> He fumbles up into a loose adieu;
> And *scants* us with a single *famish'd* kiss,
> *Distasted* with the *salt* of BROKEN tears.   [4.4.42ff.]

That is, says Mr. Malone, 'of *tears* to which we are not permitted to give full vent, being interrupted and suddenly torn from each other. The Poet was probably thinking of *broken sobs* or *broken slumbers*.' This word was certainly suggested to him by the *culinary* language, and the ideas annexed to it, into which he has fallen;—*Scants—famished—distasted—salt*. He was certainly thinking of *broken* MEATS—*orts* or *fragments*. In this very play we have

> *Orts* of her love,
> The *fragments, scraps,* the *bits* and greasy reliques
> Of her o'er eaten faith, are bound to Diomed.   [5.2.158ff.]

'Tis not in thee, . . . to *scant* my *sizes*.

[*King Lear*, 2.4.173f.]

Antony. Well, my good fellows, wait on me to night;
Scant not my cups.

(*Antony and Cleopatra*) [4.2.20f.]

Antony. I found you as a morsel, cold upon
Dead Cæsar's trencher: nay, you were a *fragment*
Of Cneius' Pompey's.   [3.13.116ff.]

In old English, as at present, *fragments and* BROKEN *meat* were
synonimous. In the vulgar translation of the Bible we have; 'So
they did eat and were filled: and they took up of the BROKEN meat
that was left seven baskets.' (*Mark*, viii. v. 8.) In other places we
find *fragments* used for these *broken* relics. (See *Matthew*, xiv. 20.
Mark, vi. 43. &c. viii. v. 19, 20. *John*, vi. 12, 13.)

There is a very remarkable instance in the *Lover's Complaint*
(350), where our Poet has again fallen, unconscious of his danger,
into this humble train of *culinary* or *domestick* imagery:

Oft did she heave her napkin to her eyne,
Which on it had conceited characters,
Laund'ring the silken figures in the *brine*
That *season'd* woe had *pelleted* in tears,
And often reading what contents it bears;
As often shrieking undistinguish'd woe,
In clamours of all *size*, both high and low.

'*Pelleted*,' says Mr. Steevens, 'is from the *kitchen*. *Pellet* was the
ancient culinary term for a *forced meat ball*, a well-known *seasoning*.'
Mr. Steevens is certainly right, and the reader will perceive
that the terms with which this word is surrounded are derived
from the lower objects of domestic occupation—
Laund'ring—brine—season'd—size. The familiar metaphor of
the *brine of tears* has forced on the Poet this peculiar vein of
language, though the ideas connected with it were certainly not
present to his mind. *Pelleted* is again used with another term
derived from the same source in *Antony and Cleopatra*:

By the *discandying* of this *pelleted* storm.   [3.13.165]

Discandying is the dissolving what is *candied*. So in this same play,

Their wishes, do *discandy*,* melt their *sweets*.   [4.12.22]

* The whole of this passage and the succeeding quotations are well worthy of the reader's
attention.

We have had frequent occasion of observing in the course of our enquiry that the Bard has been betrayed into these associations when some portion of the imagery is found among his favourite allusions. (135–41)

    Antony. Fortune and Antony part here; even here
Do we shake hands. All come to this?—The hearts,
That *spaniel'd me at heels*, to whom I gave
Their wishes, do *discandy*; melt their sweets
On blossoming Cæsar.   [4.12.19ff.]

Nor let the *candy*'d tongue *lick* absurd pomp;
And crook the pregnant hinges of the knee,
Where thrift may follow *fawning*.

                                     (Hamlet) [3.2.60ff.]

Will these moist trees,
That have outliv'd the eagle, *page* thy *heels*
And skip when thou point'st out? Will the cold brook,
Candied with ice, caudle thy morning taste,
To cure thy o'er night's surfeit?

                         (Timon of Athens) [4.3.223ff.]

Why what a *candy* deal of courtesy,
This *fawning greyhound* then did proffer me!

                         (Henry IV. Part I) [1.3.251f.]

These passages are very singular. The curious reader will observe that the *fawning obsequiousness* of an animal, or an attendant, is connected with the word *candy*. The cause of this strange association I am unable to discover; though the reader must know but little of the human mind—of Shakespeare—or even of the ordinary doctrine of *chances*, if he imagines that these matters were in *four* passages connected by *accident.*—When the reader shall be convinced respecting the truth of this observation his curiosity will be much gratified by the following lines from the *Tempest*, in which he will perceive that the same association still occupied the mind of the Poet, though a single *word* only is apparent, which relates to one portion of the preceding metaphor.

    Seb. But, for your conscience—
        Ant. Ay, Sir; where lies that? if it were a *kybe*,
'Twould put me to my slipper; but I feel not
This deity in my bosom: twenty consciences,
That stand 'twixt me and Milan, *candy'd* be they,
And *melt*, ere they molest.   [2.1.275ff.]

Surely the reader cannot doubt but that the introduction of the word *kybe* is to be referred to the former expressions, 'page thy *heels*,'—'Spaniel'd me at *heels*,' though it is applied to a very different metaphor. Let me add, that the quaintness of the imagery is an argument for the remoteness of the original. . . .

305. Wolstenholme Parr, on *Coriolanus* and *Othello*

1795

From *The Story of the Moor of Venice. Translated from the Italian. With two Essays on Shakespeare, and Preliminary Observations.* (1795).

Wolstenholme Parr (1752–1845) was educated at Corpus Christi College, Oxford, and held a fellowship there from 1789 to 1791. The 'Story' of *Othello* is a translation from Giraldi Cinthio's *Hecatommithi*.

[From 'On the Tragedy of *Coriolanus*']
It is the duty of the historian to record the transactions of which he undertakes to treat with such scrupulous and impartial fidelity that the imagination should never be suffered to exercise its powers to amplify or diminish them. The love of truth is the only passion which history should ever attempt to gratify; and this gratification is always impaired by any mixture of observation which lessens or destroys the simplicity of facts. (19)

If then the object of History be to inform the mind, and that of Poetry to rouse the sensibility, as the most philosophical critics have long ago determined, it is evident that these two classes of composition will require to be governed by very different laws and regulations. The page of the historian will be loaded with a minute detail of various particulars, which by the poet must be moulded into one general mass of interesting and important action. To facilitate this great and necessary operation he is not only permitted to change the real succession of events, but allowed to invent and substitute others more affecting when those which have actually happened are too mean or trivial for his purpose. (20–1)

We must suppose that the reader has already been apprized of some observations made by his commentators on the historical plays of Shakespeare. They are there considered as a new and

614

singular species of composition, which ought not to be subjected
to an examination guided by the laws which a rigorous tribunal has
established for theatrical representations in general. Did we indeed
find in them only violations of dramatic unities, and deviations
from certain formalities which custom and prejudice have ordained, we should willingly leave them to the censure of Voltaire,
and to the apologies which those have produced in their favour
who are conducted by a freer spirit in literary labours. But in
assuming the dramatic form they ought at least to have conformed
to the dramatic principle: they ought not to have been, as
Coriolanus will be found to be, a minute and exact copy of
historical detail in which the action has acquired no additional
interest or solidity from the art or combination of the poet. This is
a defect which instead of awakening our sympathy leaves us in a
cold indifference about the catastrophe which the author is
preparing for us; and becomes an inexcusable violation of a
fundamental law of nature and criticism. (22–3)

The historical plays of Shakespeare are, however, always a lively
and ingenious comment on those events which he selects for the
exercise of his observation and talents. It will be found perhaps
that he merits the highest degree of praise for the execution of this
part of his work, and for the pleasure the reader receives from it, if
we examine for a moment the character of Coriolanus himself. In
doing this we shall not be led into any long or philosophical
disquisition of his moral qualities: it is sufficient to refer them only
to that species of interest and sympathy which tragedy aims at
inspiring. If it appears that the character of the principal hero of the
drama is but ill adapted to produce the effects which the interest of
the tragic muse requires, and the composition itself is still
attractive, it will be evident he has executed with a masterly hand
his historical portraits, and assigned to each of them natural
sentiments with a just and forcible expression. This interest if
considered in general is however far too weak for tragical
exhibition; . . . (23–4)

Courage, accompanied with an extreme degree of military
ardour and activity, seems to have been the only good quality
possessed by Coriolanus.[1] This is a virtue which we easily praise
and admire; but if it be not united with the refined taste and the
polished humanity of Scipio it has certainly no claim to our love,

[1] Compare Francis Gentleman, No. 243, note 39.

615

no hold on our attachment. Valour tinctured with ferocity becomes an object of terror and disgust to the very people for whose honour or protection it has been nobly and successfully exerted. It produced in Coriolanus a rude and barbarous demeanour, which we should not be extremely sorry even in real life to see chastised, much less in the shadows of a theatrical Representation.

It is certainly possible for one individual to render very important services to another with such haughtiness and asperity of manner that he who receives the favour may reasonably consider himself as absolved from all the ties and obligations of gratitude. If this be lawful in our private and domestic capacities, it is certainly more unequivocally just with regard to the community at large; where it is the duty of every individual portion of the people to contribute as much as lies in his power to the public good. He is but a false and suspicious patriot who, when arrived at distinction, seeks only to give a freer scope to his insolence and tyranny, and thinks that when he has once given general proofs of the love of his country he may indulge without restraint his hatred and contempt for his fellow-citizens. The public will not be long held in subjection to the authority of past services; and exile is not perhaps too severe a punishment for one who considers his countrymen as vilified by his own appearance amongst them, and dishonoured by his own superior and exalted Prowess.

When we see this banished hero animated with a bloody spirit of revenge, returning to burn and pillage his native country, we almost desire his death. In that awful and tremendous moment when he has by the violence of his own conduct reduced himself to the dreadful alternative of destroying Rome or devoting himself, we feel the influence of the tragic passions; but we are not persuaded that he deserves to live till the fatal instant when he has resolved to die.

> My mother, mother, Oh!
> You've won a happy victory to Rome.
> But for your Son, believe it, Oh! believe it,
> Most dang'rously with him you have prevail'd;
> If not most mortal to him. Let it come.   [5.3.182ff.]

are perhaps the only verses in the whole piece that breathe the true and genuine spirit of the tragic muse. History affords no example;

nor is it possible for the imagination to conceive a more perfect situation, nor a more auspicious opportunity of atoning for abused authority, violated patriotism, and filial disobedience. It appears therefore that the life of Coriolanus is not a subject well adapted to tragedy; first, on account of the confusion arising from the variety and minuteness of historical detail; and secondly on account of the rough, unpleasant, and perhaps disgusting character which he discovers in his political and domestic conduct. But were the manner of his repentance and his death to be chosen by a poet of suitable feeling and capacity the theatre might derive from it one of its most moral and interesting exhibitions. Every one sees to what a beautiful and sublime series of pathetic sentiments this subject would lead; in developing the patriotism of Volumnia contrasted by her maternal affection; in unfolding the different shades of the same patriotism obstructed by the conjugal tenderness of Virgilia. The breast of Coriolanus himself would be disturbed by an obstinate and full-grown spirit of revenge, silently opposed by the spectre of dishonour that frights him from its gratification; loudly pleaded against by the friends of his youth and the protectors of his childhood, and finally overcome by filial and wedded Love. A purer sacrifice of private affections was never offered by any family at the shrine of public Virtue. (26–30)

[From 'On the Tragedy of *Othello*']

In the tragedy of the Moor of Venice the unity of action, which indeed ought never to be violated, is acknowledged even by the severer critics to be complete. The consistency of the subordinate characters, and the wonderful skill with which they are all made to contribute to the proposed catastrophe, have been fully discussed, and have received their due portion of praise. The character of Othello alone, proved by the preceding novel to have been almost wholly created by the imagination of Shakespeare, seems never to have been sufficiently considered, though it eminently deserves to be examined with a view to poetical effect. We are equally interested and surprised by every part of it; by his education, his temper, his moral and religious Principles.

So much of the conduct of men depends on the habits of early life that it was extremely necessary for the poet to describe first the original occupations of Othello, that these might serve as a ground-work to the probability of succeeding fictions. This basis of his character was to be consistent with the merit that had raised him to his distinguished rank in the Venetian army; and to explain the singular passion with which he had inspired the tender and unfortunate Desdemona, as well as to lay open the source of his opinions and his foibles. To illustrate these two leading incidents of his life it was certainly not injudicious to throw a blaze of glory round the commencement of his fortune, opposing a series of dangers to his progress that could only be surmounted by consummate Valour: 'She lov'd me for the dangers I had past.' [1.3.167]

But as if these were not sufficient to excite a general sympathy and affection, the poet has represented Desdemona as the most benevolent and compassionate of human beings; and, by a beautiful management, has effected her ruin by means of that very compassion, when excited a second time by the disgrace of Cassio. Of his military merit and capacity the mind is left to form its own ideas, assisted only by obscure indications, that extol far more than the explicit detail of history or the pomp of excessive praise. The very early period at which he began his course of warlike employments, the confused and marvellous account of his imminent perils and singular escapes, his zeal and fondness for the service, his dislike of peace and leisure, are all so many masterstrokes of Shakespeare's pencil that finish the portrait of a brave and experienced General. [Quotes 1.3.83ff.: 'For since these arms of mine had sev'n years pith. . . '.] Such a train of youthful adventures, where every thing dearest to humanity was daily hazarded, working upon a noble temper naturally destroyed all petty considerations of detriment and interest. The mind thus schooled thinks not of adopting the common measures of prudence, and scorns to make estimates and divisions of natural sentiment. It knows no medium between the extremes of a boundless confidence and an implacable hatred. When therefore his tenderness for Desdemona and his attachment to Cassio had once yielded to the surmises of jealousy, he rushed with a resistless impetuosity into the bloody and horrible projects of assassination and Murder.

His temper was hasty and violent, free and generous; neither prone to suspicion nor apt without reason to forgive; neither inclined to disturb itself with doubts nor qualified afterwards to restore its own tranquility. Dissimulation is a vice of which the practice was to him not only unintelligible but of which, without a prompter, he would not perhaps have known the existence. From the nature of his past life he was so little acquainted with the arts of conversation and the modes of society that on his elevation, probably for the first time, to a portion of civil authority, and his entrance into family affairs and domestic regulations, some confidential person became necessary for advice and instruction. Iago seemed to be formed for the perfect execution of this office. [Quotes 3.3.258ff.: 'This fellow's of exceeding honesty. . . '.]

The dark and insidious practices of this monster were so far from his thoughts that even in the last moments of his guilt and despair he expresses his astonishment at the proceeding, and his curiosity to know the Cause.

> Will you, I pray, demand that demi-devil,
> Why he hath thus ensnar'd my soul and body?   [5.2.300f.]

In his love as well as in his jealousy there are singular and original traits that belong exclusively to Othello's character. A soldier of fortune in foreign service, whose enterprizes are successful and whose merit eclipses the fame of his rivals, generally excites more envy than admiration. But the distinction between foreigner and native is infinitely weaker than between the Moors and the inhabitants of Europe. Desdemona was perhaps the first that had felt and expressed a real and unaffected sorrow for the hardships he had suffered: 'And *he* lov'd her, that she did pity them.' [1.3.168] His mind perhaps then first conceived the exquisite pleasure of social communication and attachment; and opened to him the enchanting prospect of a milder happiness than he had hitherto enjoyed. His vehement and fiery disposition grasped with avidity this unusual joy, and hinged his future hopes and affections on the object with such force that separation must produce the most tremendous and fatal Convulsions.

When Shakespeare has once established a principle of conduct that principle is not only observed, but frequently converted into a motive for succeeding revolutions of sentiment. The complexion of Othello, that had placed him at such a distance from Desdemona's love, and with other considerations had so much encreased his tenderness and gratitude for her passionate declarations in his favour, becomes afterwards a powerful weapon for the arm of jealousy.

————Haply, for I am black,
And have not those soft parts of conversation
That chamberers have; or for I am declin'd
Into the vale of years;—yet that's not much.　　[3.3.263ff.]

It was the pity that Desdemona had first felt for his early
misfortunes that had persuaded Othello of the sincerity of her
affection. The ideas then of love and compassion were from that
moment connected so closely in his mind that when she apparently
wept for the death of Cassio he instantly acquired force and cruelty
enough to execute his sanguinary Purpose.

A sensation continually present to the mind is shifted about by
all the passions, and becomes at one time the support of
confidence, and at another the slave of Suspicion. From the
blessings of love and confidence so congenial to his mind he is
hurled into all the tortures of jealousy which his nature abhorred.
The society he had gained, the sympathy he had excited, must be
now abandoned; and his misery is aggravated by all those
singularities of his fortune and situation which had before
augmented his joy. The solitude of Philoctetes is not more
wretched, nor his anguish more deplorable.

Had it pleas'd Heaven
To try me with affliction; had it rain'd
All kind of sores and shames on my bare head;
Steep'd me in poverty to the very lips;
Given to Captivity me and my hopes; [Quotes 4.2.47–64]

The moral character and opinions of Othello are more the result
of momentary feeling and the suggestions of his own private sense
of honour than the consequences of system or the just deductions
of reason. His education had precluded the general exercise of
deliberation, and his passions were gaining force while his reason
languished in the weakness which inactivity produces. A sense of
honour, which so imperfectly supplies its place, steps in on every
occasion with fragments of advice that involve him in the most
singular and surprising contradictions. When his frame is con-
vulsed and his spirit trembling at the knowledge of Desdemona's
infidelity he determines to commit a crime unworthy (as he
confesses and laments) of the military name and profession; but in
the gratification of his revenge feels not a pang of remorse for
that virtue which he abandons. [Quotes 3.3.347ff.: 'Farewell the
plum'd troops . . . Othello's occupation gone'.]

Imperfectly however as this sense supplies the place of reason in a moral view, it is certainly calculated to produce poetically a much greater beauty and variety of effect. The ardour and surprise of poetry have nothing in common with the rational and tranquil proceedings of prudence; where, without the aid of imagination, all that is to happen may be foretold by the simple force of sagacity founded on experience. Othello jealous in his chamber, and Achilles angry in his tent, are pictures that interest us more than Æneas piously bearing away his father from the flames of Troy, or patiently expostulating with the wrath of Juno and the fury of the elements. (68–79)

Happy had it been for mankind if all the mischiefs with which superstition has deformed society could have been compensated by the graces with which it has embellished poetry. So strong indeed is the alliance between those two sources of terrible and romantic fiction that an epic or a tragic character is not considered as complete without some tincture of religious ecstasy. The fancy of Shakespeare, though excessively delighted with such embellishments, did not however adopt them rashly without first being assured of their fitness and congruity. The wandering and military life of Othello must be supposed to have prevented him from conforming generally to the tenets of any particular sect; and to have left his religious faith in still more uncertainty than his moral principles. Whatever struck his imagination in the belief of either people with whom he was most conversant as applicable to his own fortune, naturally rested on his mind, and rendered it a tissue of the Christian and Mahometan persuasions. The singularity of his adventures, his numberless perils and escapes, might induce him almost reasonably to receive as true the potency of spells and the doctrines of predestination. The pleasures of love and the charms of beauty figured with so much distinction in the Mahometan scheme of happiness that whatever superstition consecrated to the benefit or protection of mankind was endued with a capacity to improve or perpetuate these enjoyments. Hence has Shakespeare judiciously taken occasion to confer a sort of preternatural importance on the handkerchief that was the last fatal confirmation of his jealousy.

> ——: That handkerchief
> Did an Ægyptian to my mother give: [Quotes 3.4.55–63]

621

The idea of an irreversible predetermined destiny returns to his mind when, conscious of the innocence of his former life and intentions, he finds himself involved in the most horrible of crimes; when, after all the dangers he had passed he sees that his courage can no longer protect him though apparently in a state of tranquility and peace: 'Who can controul his fate?' [5.2.265]

In his death the same sense of honour still prevails. In his last moments he is exhibited in all the agony of guilt without one symptom of fear; he shews a tender and anxious regard for his reputation, but none for himself; obscurely hoping that the services which he has rendered to the state may diminish the infamy attached to a foul and atrocious murder. (79–82)

306. Richard Hole, an ironical(?) defence of Iago

1796

From *Essays, by a Society of Gentlemen at Exeter* (Exeter, 1796).

This collection, the product of a literary society that was founded by William Jackson and others in 1792 (see head-note to No. 273), includes three essays on Shakespearian topics: no. XI, 'On Literary Fame and the Historical Characters of Shakespeare' (pp. 238–70); no. XVIII, 'An Apology for the Character and Conduct of Iago' (pp. 395–409); and no. XXVI, 'An Apology for the Character and Conduct of Shylock' (pp. 552–73). They were soon known as the work of Richard Hole (1746–1803), a clergyman, poet, and antiquary, who assisted Samuel Badcock in his contributions to the *Monthly Review*, and also wrote for the *London Magazine*, the *British Magazine*, and the *Gentleman's Magazine*. His 'apologies' are commonly taken as ironical, but they are pursued with some seriousness, especially that on Shylock. Francis Douce, in his copy of the book (now in the Bodleian), notes that the *British Magazine* (ii, p. 384) printed a critique on Shylock 'in direct opposition to that at the end of this volume by the Reverend learned and excellent Richard Hole'. For a modern account see E. D. Mackerness, 'Richard Hole, of the Exeter Society of Gentlemen, an Eighteenth Century Shakespearian Critic', *Reports and Transactions of the Devonshire Association for the Advancement of Science, Literature and Art*, 88 (Lynton, 1956), pp. 130–41 (but note that the top two lines on p. 138 are the first two lines of p. 137).

As I mean nothing ironical in this undertaking I am aware of incurring some suspicion of having tasted

> —— of the insane root
> That takes the reason prisoner. [*Macbeth*, 1.3.84f.]

It may be urged against me that the name of Iago is almost proverbial for a close dissembling villain; that Dr. Johnson observes, 'his character is so conducted, that he is, from the first scene to the last, hated and despised;' that 'it is so monstrous and satanical, if we are to credit Lord Kames, as not to be sufferable in a representation—not even Shakespeare's masterly hand can make the picture agreeable:' and, that old Rymer, long before them, observed, 'He was too wicked in all conscience, and had more to answer for than any tragedy or furies could inflict upon him.'[1] That, in short, he is held by the world in general no less than by Othello as the 'damned damned Iago.'

Permit me, however, first to observe that I do not absolutely undertake to vindicate him, but to shew that his conduct admits of much excuse. His character, as I apprehend, is greatly misunderstood and requires an explanation. (395–6)

[Hole contests Twining's judgment that while Richard III is presented with attractive qualities, Iago is throughout 'hated and despised'.]

Now, with all due submission to the Translator of the *Poetics*, I conceive that the crimes of Iago, when fairly compared with those

---

[1] For Johnson see Vol. 5, p. 166; for Rymer, Vol. 2, pp. 53f.

of Richard, will fade, like the new moon overpowered by meridian splendor.

To the unrelenting cruelty of a Borgia Richard added more than Pharisaic hypocrisy. The only virtue which he possessed, if an inborn faculty deserves that name, was courage; but he possessed it in common with Iago. The latter, to revenge injuries, which I shall shew were of no trivial kind, is guilty of murther: and insufficient as this plea may be to exculpate him, not one of so mitigating a nature can be urged in extenuation of the various murthers committed by Richard. The intended victims of Iago's revenge are three; Othello, Cassio and Desdemona; yet neither seems to have had the least claim to his regard. (397–8)

. . . The principal charges urged against him are his ingratitude and treachery to Othello; his perfidy to Cassio and to Desdemona.

Previous to the opening of the drama we are led to understand that Iago's character was respectable both as an officer and a man. His military services are often alluded to. He is made known to the gentlemen of Cyprus by Cassio as 'the bold Iago.' Othello reports him to the Duke of Venice as 'a man of honesty and trust.' Other speeches of a similar kind shew that Iago had often acted, by Othello's own confession, in such a manner as to deserve his favor: yet over this tried and experienced soldier, of whose prowess

> ———his eyes had seen the proof
> At Rhodes and Cyprus, and on other grounds,
> Christian and heathen, [1.1.28ff.]

He places one

> Who never set a squadron in the field,
> Nor the division of a battle knew
> More than a spinster. [1.1.22ff.]

Must not this have been a justifiable cause for resentment, if any can be so, to a brave and enterprizing soldier? Some critic styles him 'a false, dissembling, *ungrateful* rascal.' Nothing however can be more unjust than the last epithet. Othello was unkind and ungenerous; Iago not ungrateful. The strongest reason for his resentment to the Moor is yet to be told. He suspected that he had been injured by him in the most tender point; that he had seduced his wife Emilia, a suspicion which does not appear destitute of foundation. The discourse she holds with Desdemona amply demonstrates that she was very far from entertaining any rigid notions of conjugal fidelity [Quotes 4.3.68ff.] (397–401)

Whatever stress may be laid on this circumstance, it certainly required no common degree of christian charity to forgive such treatment as Iago had experienced from the Moor.

But what excuse it may be said is there for his behavior to Cassio? He never personally injured him; nor does it appear that he had at any time endeavoured to supplant Iago, tho' he was fortunately preferred before him.

I cannot however allow that he had no cause for resentment against Cassio. He suspects him no less than Othello of a criminal intercourse with Emilia: [quotes 2.1.307]. And revenge, though contrary to the precepts of the gospel, is not so strongly prohibited by the military code of honor.

Again: though it does not appear that he had attempted to supplant Iago, yet the circumstance alone of his undeserved promotion over him must have kindled in his breast, unless endowed with the apathy of a stoic or the meekness of a saint, some sparks of anger and indignation against the successful rival as well as the unjust patron. (403)

It would have been certainly much more noble in Iago to have supprest his resentment against Othello and Cassio, and wiser probably to have winked at the frailties of Emilia; but many allowances ought surely to be made for the imperfections of human nature when placed in trying situations: and why should not Iago be entitled to the benefit of this plea as well as more exalted characters? (404)

. . . Not the death of Cassio, but the depriving him of his office was Iago's original design. Had he suceeded to the command he so justly claimed we may conclude, reasoning from probabilities and the common course of events, that he would neither have betrayed Othello, defrauded Roderigo, nor acted unkindly to Cassio, but have continued 'honest, honest Iago' to the end of the chapter.

The last charge, and the severest, is his cruelty to the innocent Desdemona. This is generally considered as the very acme of villainy, and it admits indeed of less excuse than the former accusations, for she had never wronged him. Iago however does not behold her in the same point of view as a reader or a spectator of this tragedy. He is by no means convinced of her virtue and purity of heart, as appears from his observations on the first interview between her and Cassio, (Act 2. Sc. 5.) from his subsequent discourse with Roderigo, and the soliloquy which follows.

> That Cassio loves her, I do well believe it;
> That she loves him, 'tis apt and of great credit.   [2.1.286f.]

Other similar passages might be adduced: and it is not unreasonable to suppose that his suspicions of his wife had soured his temper, and excited in him a general aversion to the female sex. (406–7)

On the whole, his conduct to Roderigo, concerning which no accusation has been preferred, appears to be the least excusable. To him he was indebted for pecuniary obligations, but for none of any kind to either of the other characters. On the contrary, from the first of them he had, most decidedly and incontrovertibly, received injuries of the severest kind. He had no trivial cause for his aversion to Cassio. Desdemona, as being a woman, was not an object of his regard: as the friend of Cassio and Emilia she appeared to him in a disgusting light, and more so probably considered as the wife of Othello. In order to distress *him*, however, not to gratify any aversion towards Desdemona, he contrives her death. She is merely an instrument to effectuate his vengeance: and if vengeance can be vindicated by an accumulation of injuries, Iago's, though exorbitant, was just.

It appears therefore, notwithstanding the general opinion, that his conduct admits of much palliation.—This is all I contended for: and I trust that if you still think him a villain, you consider him as one of the lower class, 'a puny whipster' in the school of iniquity, not to be ranked with Richard the third, Aaron the moor, and others of the higher order, his usual associates. Let me add only that if I have not wholly washed the blackamoor white I trust I have taken a shade from his colour; I have offered *some* apology for his 'character and conduct.' (408–9)

307. William Richardson, further thoughts on Hamlet

1798

From *Essays on Some of Shakespeare's Dramatic Characters. To which is added, An Essay on the Faults of Shakespeare. The Fifth Edition* (1798).

This collected edition unites all thirteen of Richardson's essays previously published (Nos 246, 260, 276, and 294), having received some 'correction and improvement' (p. vi), and it was reprinted, with further material, in 1812. The passages given here are additions which show some change of mind.

[Where the 1774 and 1783 editions say that Hamlet 'resolves to conceal himself under the disguise of madness', Richardson now adds:] Conceiving designs of punishment, and sensible that he is already suspected by the king, he is thrown into violent perturbation. Afraid at the same time lest his aspect or demeanor should betray him, and aware that his project must be conducted with secrecy, his agitation is such as threatens the overthrow of his reason. He trembles as it were on the brink of madness; and is at times not altogether certain that he acts or speaks according to the dictates of a sound understanding. He partakes of such insanity as may arise in a mind of great sensibility from excessive agitation of spirit, and much labour of thought; but which naturally subsides when the perturbation ceases. Yet he must act; and not only so, he must act with prudence. He must even conceal his intentions: and his actual condition suggests a mode of concealment. Knowing that he must appear incoherent and inconsistent, he is not unwilling to have it believed that his reason is somewhat disarranged; and that the strangeness of his conduct admits of no other explanation. [Continues, as before with the 'antic disposition' speech.] (98–9)

627

[After the sentence defending 'the sincerity and ardour' of Hamlet's affection for Ophelia (above, p. 123), Richardson adds:] At any rate, Hamlet's treatment of Ophelia, who however had 'repelled his letters, and denied his access to her,' and who was employed as a spy on his conduct, has been greatly exaggerated. The spirit of that remarkable scene in particular, where he tells her, 'get thee to a nunnery,' is frequently misunderstood; and especially by the players. At least, it does not appear to me that the Poet's intention was that the air and manner of Hamlet in this scene should be perfectly grave and serious. Nor is there any thing in the dialogue to justify the tragic tone with which it is frequently spoken. Let Hamlet be represented as delivering himself in a light, airy, unconcerned, and thoughtless manner, and the rudeness so much complained of will disappear. (102)

[At the end of the original essay (above, p. 124), having concluded that despite all his 'purity of moral sentiment', rectitude, and zeal, Hamlet 'is hated, persecuted, and destroyed', Richardson adds:] Nor is this so inconsistent with poetical justice as may at first sight be apprehended. The particular temper and state of Hamlet's mind is connected with weaknesses that embarrass, or may be somewhat incompatible with bold and persevering projects. His amiable hesitations and reluctant scruples lead him at one time to indecision; and then betray him, by the self-condemning consciousness of such apparent imbecility, into acts of rash and inconsiderate violence. Meantime his adversaries, suffering no such internal conflict, persist with uniform, determined vigour in the prosecution of unlawful schemes. Thus Hamlet, and persons of his constitution contending with less virtuous opponents, can have little hope of success: and so the poet has not in the catastrophe been guilty of any departure from nature or any infringement of poetical justice. We love, we almost revere the character of Hamlet, and grieve for his sufferings. But we must at the same time confess that his weaknesses, amiable weaknesses! are the cause of his disappointments and early death. The instruction to be gathered from this delineation is that persons formed like Hamlet should retire, or keep aloof from situations of difficulty and contention; or endeavour, if they are forced to contend, to brace their minds and acquire such vigour and determination of spirit as shall arm them against malignity. (119–20)

308. Nathan Drake, Shakespeare and Elizabethan poetry

1798

From *Literary Hours, or Sketches Critical and Narrative* (Sudbury, 1798); this text is from the second edition, 'Corrected and Greatly Enlarged' (2 vols, Sudbury, 1800). In the preface Drake explains that in order to relieve 'the dryness' of criticism he has interspersed original tales and pieces of poetry. Six of the papers had been previously published in the journals.

Nathan Drake, M. D. (1766–1836), was a doctor who practised in Suffolk for over forty years, and published many collections of essays, including *The Gleaner* (1810), *Winter Nights* (1820), *Evenings in Autumn* (1822), *Noontide Leisure* (1824), and *Mornings in Spring* (1828). His two-volume collection *Shakespeare and his Times* (1817) is a valuable digest of extant knowledge, which he followed with an anthology of criticism, *Memorials of Shakespeare, or Sketches of his Character and Genius by various writers* (1828).

[From 'Number VI'. On the sonnet]

'La brevità del sonetto non comporta, che una sola parola sia vana, ed il vero subietto e materia del sonetto debbe essere qualche acuta e gentile sentenza, narrata attamente, ed in pochi versi ristretta, e fuggendo la oscurità e durezza.'[1]
Comment. di Lor. de Med. sopra i suoi Sonetti.

Lorenzo de Medici has thus, in few words, accurately defined the true character of the Sonnet, a species of composition which has lately been cultivated with considerable success in England. Italy,

[1] 'The brevity of the sonnet does not permit a single empty or superfluous word. The true subject matter of the sonnet should be some sharp and refined thought, suitably narrated, limited to a few verses, and avoiding all obscurity and harshness.'

however, may boast the honour of giving birth to this elegant and elaborate little poem, which, confined as it is to a frequent return of rhyme and limited to a certain number of lines, imposes no small difficulty on the poet. (I, 103)

The sonnets of Milton, like those of Dante, are frequently deficient in sweetness of diction and harmony of versification, yet they possess what seldom is discernable in compositions of this kind, energy and sublimity of sentiment. . . .

One of the best and earliest attempts in England to naturalize the sonnet is to be found in the pages of the gallant Surrey, whose compositions in this department, making due allowance for the imperfect state of the language in which he wrote, have a simplicity and chastity in their style and thought which merit every encomium. Our romantic Spenser, likewise, has endeavoured to transfuse the ease and amenity of the Petrarchian stanza. It is scarcely necessary to say that he has completely failed. In his long series of sonnets the critic will recognise many of the trifling conceits of the Italian, but find little to recompense the trouble of research.

These Opuscula of the gentle poet of the *Fairy Queen* are, however, far superior to the attempts of the mighty Father of the English Drama. The sonnets of Shakespeare are buried beneath a load of obscurity and quaintness; nor does there issue a single ray of light to quicken, or to warm the heavy mass. Mr. Malone has once more given them to the press, but his last Editor has, I think, acted with greater judgment in forbearing to obtrude such crude efforts upon the public eye; for where is the utility of propagating compositions which no one can endure to read? (I, 106–8)

[From 'Number XXXVIII'. On the over-valuation of earlier English literature]
Many critics more querulous than just have lately employed themselves in depreciating the efforts of the modern muses, and several of our literary and periodical publications have teemed with reflections on the sterility and want of genius apparent in the present cultivators of this enchanting art. They insist with rapture on the beauties of our ancient poets, and are willing to believe that the invention and imagery of their contemporaries are puerile and absurd. . . . These *laudatores temporis acti*, who dwell so much upon the general and superior merit of our poetry in the ages of

Elizabeth and the Charles's, would do well to reflect that in those periods the language was extremely incorrect; that beauty of arrangement, propriety of selection, and delicacy of sentiment were for the most part unknown; and it may without any hazard of contradiction be asserted that from these boasted eras no one production can be drawn possessing an uniform chastity of style and thought. Even our three great poets, Spenser, Shakespeare, and Milton are clogged with materials that press heavy on the patience of the critical reader, and certainly abound in quaintnesses, puerilities and conceits which would blast the reputation of any poet of the present day. Not to mention many cantos of Spenser which, I am afraid, must be pronounced both tedious and disgusting, the *Paradise Lost* would be greatly diminished were its metaphysic and abstruse theology, surely no proper ornaments of an epic poem, entirely expunged. The third book, its exquisite invocation, and a few other passages excepted, is more worthy the genius of Thomas Aquinas than of Milton, and of Shakespeare it may justly be affirmed that many of his plays are barely tolerated out of deference to the excellencies of his happier productions. The beauties of these writers are, however, above all praise, and I am accustomed to approach their works with an admiration almost bordering upon idolatry. (II, 155–7)

In the dramatic department occurs the mighty name of Shakespeare; but as with him all competition is hopeless, I shall only remark that his *Macbeth, Lear* and *Tempest* will perhaps to the remotest period of time, continue unrivalled. It is possible, however, to conceive that the genius of Shakespeare may be combined with the chastity and correctness of Sophocles; but the birth of such a prodigy is scarcely to be expected.

There was a period when the productions of Jonson, Beaumont and Fletcher were preferred to those of Shakespeare. We are now astonished at the miserable taste of our ancestors, for of Jonson, the celebrated but pedantic Jonson, if we except two or three of his comedies, there is little commendatory to be said. . . .

Massinger, Beaumont and Fletcher have certainly many beauties, but I question whether they possess a single piece which a correct taste could endure without very great alteration, and they are loaded with such a mass of obscenity and vulgar buffoonery that compared with them Shakespeare is chaste and decorous in the extreme. It may justly be said, I think, that their tragedies fall far, very far short indeed, of the energy and all-commanding interest of Shakespeare's, and their comedies, I suspect, are even greatly inferior to Jonson's both in plot and humour. (II, 166–7)

309. Arthur Murphy, Garrick's Shakespeare

1801

From *The Life of David Garrick, Esq.* (2 vols, London, 1801).

On Murphy see the head-note to Vol. 4, Nos 140, 161.

[Garrick's debut as Richard III]

Garrick scorned to lacky after any actor whatever; he depended on his own genius, and was completely an original performer. All was his own creation: he might truly say, '*I am myself alone!*' His first appearance on the London stage was at Goodman's Fields on the 19th of October 1741. The moment he entered the scene the character he assumed was visible in his countenance; the power of his imagination was such that he transformed himself into the very man; the passions rose in rapid succession, and before he uttered a word were legible in every feature of that various face. His look, his voice, his attitude changed with every sentiment. . . . The rage and rapidity with which he spoke

The North!—what do they in the North,
When they should serve their Sovereign in the West? [4.4.484f.]

made a most astonishing impression on the audience. His soliloquy in the tent-scene discovered the inward man. . . . When he started from his dream he was a spectacle of horror. He called out in a manly tone, 'Give me another horse;' [5.3.177]. He paused, and, with a countenance of dismay, advanced, crying out in a tone of distress, 'Bind up my wounds;' [l.77] and then, falling on his knees, said in the most piteous accent. 'Have mercy Heaven!' [178] In all this the audience saw an exact imitation of nature. His friend Hogarth has left a most excellent picture of Garrick in this scene. He was then on the eve of a battle, and in spite of all the terrors of conscience his courage mounted to a blaze. When in Bosworth field, he roared out,

A horse! a horse! my kingdom for a horse!   [5.4.13]

All was rage, fury, and almost reality. . . . It is no wonder that an actor thus accomplished made, on the very first night, a deep impression on the audience. His fame ran through the metropolis. The public went in crowds to see a young performer who came forth at once a complete master of his art. (I, 22–4)

. . . Flushed with success Garrick undertook the difficult character of *King Lear*. He was transformed into a feeble old man, still retaining an air of royalty. . . . It was in *Lear*'s madness that Garrick's genius was remarkably distinguished. He had no sudden starts, no violent gesticulation; his movements were slow and feeble; misery was depicted in his countenance; he moved his head in the most deliberate manner; his eyes were fixed, or, if they turned to any one near him he made a pause, and fixed his look on the person after much delay; his features at the same time telling what he was going to say before he uttered a word. During the whole time he presented a sight of woe and misery, and a total alienation of mind from every idea but that of his unkind daughters. He was used to tell how he acquired the hints that guided him when he began to study this great and difficult part. He was acquainted with a worthy man, who lived in Leman-street, Goodman's Fields; this friend had an only daughter, about two years old. He stood at his dining-room window, fondling the child and dangling it in his arms, when it was his misfortune to drop the infant into a flagged area, and killed it on the spot. He remained at his window screaming in agonies of grief. The neighbours flocked to the house, took up the child, and delivered it dead to the unhappy father, who wept bitterly, and filled the street with lamentations. He lost his senses, and from that moment never recovered his understanding. As he had a sufficient fortune his friends chose to let him remain in his house, under two keepers appointed by Dr. Monro. Garrick frequently went to see his distracted friend, who passed the remainder of his life in going to the window and there playing in fancy with his child. After some dalliance he dropped it, and, bursting into a flood of tears, filled the house with shrieks of grief and bitter anguish. He then sat down, in a pensive mood, his eyes fixed on one object, at times looking slowly round him as if to implore compassion. Garrick was often present at this scene of misery, and was ever after used to say that it gave him the first idea of *King Lear*'s madness. This writer has often seen him rise in company to give a representation of this unfortunate father. He leaned on the back of a chair, seeming with parental fondness to play with a child, and, after expressing the most heart-felt delight, he suddenly dropped the infant, and instantly broke out in a most violent agony of grief, so tender, so affecting and pathetic that every eye in company was moistened with a gush of tears. 'There it was,' said Garrick, '*that I learned to imitate madness*; I copied nature, and to that owed my success in *King Lear*.' (I, 27–30)

In the month of January [1744] following, Garrick resolved to adorn his brow with another laurel from the immortal Shakespeare. *Macbeth* was the object of his ambition. The character he knew was entirely different from all he had ever acted, but the various situations, the rapid succession of events, the scenes of terror, and the sudden transition of conflicting passions, form altogether such a wonderful contrast that Garrick saw it would call forth all his powers. Paragraphs in the newspapers gave notice of his intention to revive *Macbeth* as originally written by Shakespeare. The players had been long in possession of Sir William D'Avenant's alteration, and content with that they enquired no further. Even Quin, who had gained reputation by his performance of the character, cried out, with an air of surprize, 'What does he mean? don't I play *Macbeth* as written by Shakespeare?' So little was the attention of the actors to ancient literature. A paper war was immediately begun by the small wits. Garrick was easily alarmed. To blunt the edge of ill-timed and previous criticism he published an anonymous pamphlet,[1] written in a stile of irony against himself, and prefixed as a motto, '*Macbeth has murdered Garrick*.' (I, 70–2)

[On Macbeth's hesitations at killing Duncan]
His ambition is still working in his heart: in a faint tone he utters

[1] Cf. Vol. 3, No. 99, and No. 100.

his only remaining doubt, '*If we should fail?*' [1.7.69] That fear is removed by the wickedness of an ambitious woman; and he resolves to execute the deed. But Shakespeare's genius was not yet exhausted. It remained for him to give the picture of a mind going to commit a deed of horror. Conscious of his full design, *Macbeth*, with terror and dismay says, '*Is this a dagger that I see before me?*' [2.1.33] Garrick's attitude, his consternation, and his pause while his soul appeared in his countenance, and the accents that followed, astonished the spectators. The sequel was a climax of terror, till at last he finds it to be the effect of a disordered imagination, and his conscience forces him to say,

> It is the bloody business, which informs
> Thus to my eyes.   [2.1.48f.]

. . . When Garrick re-entered the scene, with the bloody dagger in his hand, he was absolutely scared out of his senses; he looked like a ghastly spectacle, and his complexion grew whiter every moment till at length, his conscience stung and pierced to quick, he said in a tone of wild despair,

> Will all great Neptune's ocean wash this blood
> Clean from my hand?   [2.2.57f.]
>
>   (I, 80–2)

[On Garrick's failure as Othello in 1745]
. . . As Garrick did not at a more advanced period retain the part, this writer is not able to offer any criticisms on the subject. He thinks proper, however, to observe that *Othello* could not be a well-chosen part for a man who performed wonders with that expressive face. The black complexion disguised his features, and the expression of the mind was wholly lost. (I, 106)

[On Garrick's adaptation of *Hamlet*,[1] 1772]
Early in December a strange phenomenon appeared on the boards of Drury-Lane. This was nothing less than the long-admired tragedy of *Hamlet*, with alterations by Garrick. The rage for re-touching and, as it was said, correcting and improving our best authors was the very error of the times. Colman, with an unhallowed hand, had defaced the tragedy of *King Lear*. Bickerstaff was another precedent, and unhappily Garrick was infected with

---

[1] Cf. Vol. 5, No. 236, and Murphy's satiric pastiche, No. 237a.

the contagion. He lopped, pruned, and cut away what he thought unnecessary branches, and instead of a flourishing tree left a withered trunk. The *Grave-Diggers* suffered amputation. Their scene, it is true, would not be admitted by Racine, Voltaire, or any of the French authors; but the genius of Shakespeare towered above the rules that excluded what he deemed a representation of nature. When a licence gave our great poet a fair opportunity of adding to the pleasure of his auditors, with him that licence was a rule. His *Grave-Diggers* are an exact imitation of nature, and their dialogue is wonderfully happy. And yet that scene, universally admired, and indeed sanctified by ages, was altogether retrenched by Mr. Garrick, though absolutely necessary for *Ophelia's* funeral. In like manner *Osrick*, the light airy courtier, is expelled from his situation. Frivolous as this personage may seem, he was still useful in the conduct of the business. Since there was to be a fencing-scene this water-fly, as *Hamlet* stiles him, was a fit fore-runner of such a scheme. But a fencing-scene is a wretched expedient. If Garrick had then used his pruning-knife, and had added from his own invention something of real importance to bring about a noble catastrophe, he would have shewn his judgment and might have spared the rest of his labours. It seems, as he never published his alterations, that he saw his error. All further remarks are therefore unnecessary. (II, 82–4)

[On the theatre managers' duty to present the classics]
It is in their power, by reviving Shakespeare and Otway, Congreve, and Vanbrugh, to shew that they are above the mere traffic, and scorn to keep a mushroom-bed for the production of trash not fit to be brought to market.

That this was not the case in Garrick's time is an honour to his memory. He suffered no invasion from German poets. They were left to amuse the Croats and Pandoors. The English stage after Booth and Cibber was reduced to the lowest ebb, but from the time when our famous Roscius appeared at Goodman's Fields dramatic poetry retrieved its honour, and *Lun* and his favourite harlequin gave way to a just representation of nature, to Shakespeare and Garrick. The first season in which he commenced manager, began in September 1747. From that time a new æra opened on mankind, and the stage was revived in all its lustre. (II, 161–2)

A true taste and manly relish for moral and instructive

composition soon prevailed, and the public ear was formed to refined pleasures, to the true sublime, to the tones of nature and harmonious numbers. Our great reformer of the stage banished rant and noise and the swell of unnatural elocution from tragedy, and buffoonery from comedy. Shakespeare rose, as it were, from his tomb, and broke out at once in all his lustre, *exortus uti ætherius sol*.[1] A subscription among ladies of quality was no longer necessary.

[Quotes Horace, *Epistles*, 2.1.210ff.[2]] According to Horace, Shakespeare may be called a great tragic rope-dancer, and the public were taught by Garrick to prefer him to the vaulting Turk. The pleasure of the eye was transferred to the ear. To accomplish this great reform was Garrick's plan through the whole course of his management. He corrected the public taste, and by incessant labour made the stage the school of virtue and useful knowledge; and this assertion is so far from being a strained panegyric that it will be found, upon due consideration, to be founded in truth. (II, 163–5)

A Select Bibliography of Shakespeare Criticism

1774–1801

Most of the relevant works have been referred to in the Preface, Introduction, and head-notes above, and in the bibliographies to previous volumes.

The *New Cambridge Bibliography of English Literature*, ed. G. G. Watson, divides the history of Shakespeare criticism awkwardly between Volumes I and II, and both volumes contain errors and

---

[1] Lucretius, *De rerum natura*, 3.1044: 'as the risen sun of heaven quenches the stars'.
[2] 'Methinks that poet is able to walk a tight rope, who with airy nothings wrings my heart, inflames, soothes, fills it with vain alarms like a magician and sets me down now at Thebes, now at Athens'.

omissions. The most useful chronological listings are in S. A. Allibone, *A Critical Dictionary of English Literature...*, Vol. II (1870), pp. 2006–54 (which begins 'Shakespeare ... the most illustrious of the sons of men'), and R. W. Babcock, *The Genesis of Shakespeare Idolatry 1766–1799* (Chapel Hill, N. C., 1931; New York, 1978), although it includes peripheral material. *The London Stage, 1660–1800 Part 5: 1776–1800*, ed. C. B. Hogan (3 vols, Carbondale, Ill., 1968), is a magnificent work of reference, but does not displace the same editor's *Shakespeare in the Theatre, 1701–1800* (2 vols, Oxford, 1952). On the adaptations see John Genest, *The English Stage from 1660–1830* (10 vols, Bath, 1832), and G. C. D. Odell, *Shakespeare from Betterton to Irving* (2 vols, New York, 1920, 1966). See also J. F. Arnott and J. W. Robinson, *English Theatrical Literature 1559–1900, A Bibliography* (1970) and C. J. Stratman, D. G. Spencer, and M. E. Devine (eds), *Restoration and Eighteenth Century Theatre Research. A Bibliographical Guide, 1900–1968* (Carbondale, Ill., 1971). The annual bibliography in *Restoration and Eighteenth Century Theatre Research* is useful.

For the background to literary theory see M. H. Abrams, *The Mirror and the Lamp: Romantic Theory and the Critical Tradition* (New York, 1953); René Wellek, *The Rise of English Literary History* (Chapel Hill, N.C., 1941; New York, 1966) and *A History of Modern Criticism, 1750–1950*, Vol. I (New Haven, Conn., and London, 1955); and Gordon McKenzie, *Critical Responsiveness: A Study of the Psychological Current in Later Eighteenth-Century Criticism* (Berkeley, Calif., 1949). Special studies include P. S. Conklin, *A History of 'Hamlet' Criticism 1601–1821* (New York, 1957, 1968); E. R. Wasserman, *Elizabethan Poetry in the Eighteenth Century* (Urbana, Ill., 1947)—on the vogue for setting and imitating Shakespeare's lyrics, pp. 166–91; R. G. Noyes, *The Thespian Mirror. Shakespeare in the Eighteenth-Century Novel* (Providence, R.I., 1953); T. M. Raysor, 'The Study of Shakespeare's Characters in the Eighteenth Century', *Modern Language Notes*, 42 (1927), pp. 495–500 (which does not find Hole's apologies for Iago and Shylock ironic: p. 500); and D. Lovett, 'Shakespeare as a Poet of Realism in the Eighteenth Century', *ELH*, 2 (1935), pp. 267–89. A useful collection of essays is *Shakespeare: Aspects of Influence*, ed. G.B. Evans (Cambridge, Mass., 1976). There is much relevant material in Samuel Schoenbaum's study of the biographical traditions, *Shakespeare's Lives* (Oxford, 1970).

Index

The Index is arranged in three parts: I. Shakespeare's works; II. Shakespearian characters; III. General index. Adaptations are indexed under the adapter's name, in III below. References to individual characters are not repeated under the relevant plays.

I SHAKESPEARE'S WORKS

639

II SHAKESPEARIAN CHARACTERS

III GENERAL INDEX

THE CRITICAL HERITAGE SERIES

GENERAL EDITOR: B. C. SOUTHAM

Volumes published and forthcoming